Place a program shortcut on the desktop to quickly start a program.

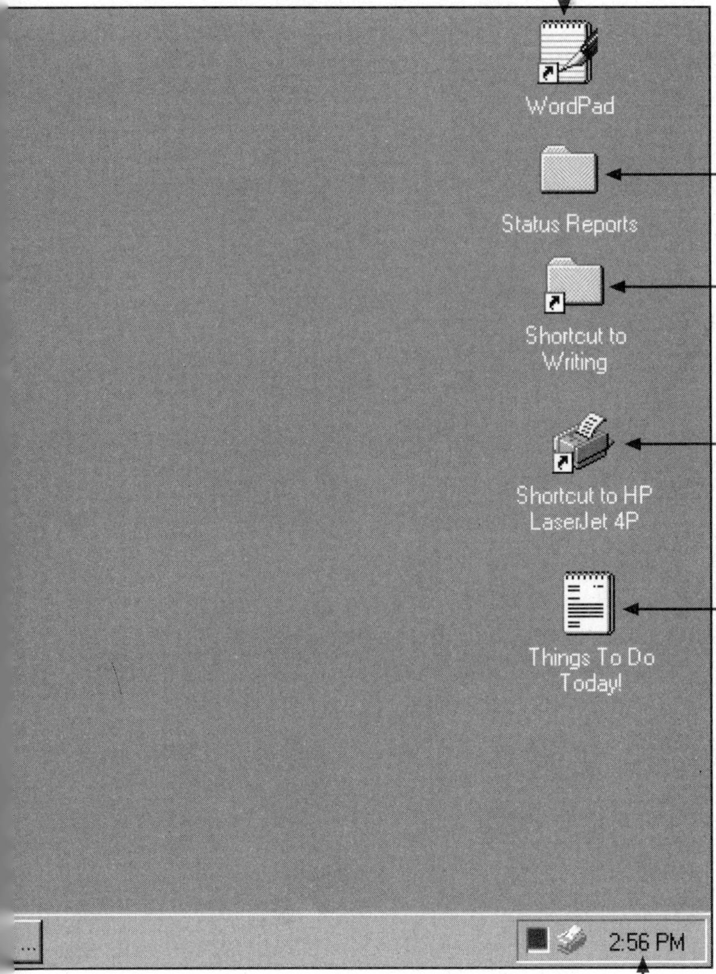

WordPad

Folders can be placed directly on the desktop.

Status Reports

You can easily open a folder with a shortcut.

Shortcut to Writing

Print documents by dragging them to a printer shortcut. Double-click the icon to check the status of the printer.

Shortcut to HP LaserJet 4P

Important documents can be placed directly on the desktop.

Things To Do Today!

2:56 PM

The notification area lets you know what's going on behind the scenes.

About the Authors

Craig Stinson An industry journalist since 1981, Craig Stinson is a contributing editor of *PC Magazine* and was formerly editor of *Softalk for the IBM Personal Computer*. Craig is the author of *Running Windows 95* and a coauthor of *Running Excel for Windows 95*, both published by Microsoft Press. In addition to his numerous computer publications, Craig has written music reviews for *Billboard*, the *Boston Globe*, the *Christian Science Monitor*, *Musical America*, and other publications. He lives with his wife and children in Colorado.

Carl Siechert began his writing career at age 8 as editor of the *Mesita Road News*, a neighborhood newsletter that reached a peak worldwide circulation of 43 during its eight-year run. Following several years as an estimator and production manager in a commercial printing business, Carl returned to writing with the formation of Siechert & Wood Professional Documentation, a Pasadena, California firm that specializes in writing and producing books and product documentation for the personal computer industry. Carl is a coauthor of *Field Guide to Microsoft Works for Windows 95* and *Field Guide to MS-DOS 6.2*, both published by Microsoft Press. Carl hiked the Pacific Crest Trail from Mexico to Canada in 1977 and would rather be hiking right now. He and his wife, Jan, live in Southern California.

RUNNING

Microsoft®

WINDOWS NT® Workstation

version 4.0

CRAIG STINSON AND
CARL SIECHERT

Microsoft®

PUBLISHED BY
Microsoft Press
A Division of Microsoft Corporation
One Microsoft Way
Redmond, Washington 98052-6399

Library of Congress Cataloging-in-Publication Data
Stinson, Craig, 1943–
Running Microsoft Windows NT workstation, version 4 / Craig Stinson, Carl Siechert.
p. cm.
Includes index.
ISBN 1-57231-226-2
1. Microsoft Windows NT. 2. Operating systems (Computers) 3. Microcomputer workstations. I. Siechert, Carl. II. Title.
QA76.76.O63S7556 1996
005.4'469--dc20 96-31590
CIP

Printed and bound in the United States of America.

3 4 5 6 7 8 9 QFQF 1 0 9 8 7

Distributed to the book trade in Canada by Macmillan of Canada, a division of Canada Publishing Corporation.

A CIP catalogue record for this book is available from the British Library.

Microsoft Press books are available through booksellers and distributors worldwide. For further information about international editions, contact your local Microsoft Corporation office. Or contact Microsoft Press International directly at fax (206) 936-7329.

Acquisitions Editor: Lucinda Rowley
Project Editor: Lucinda Rowley
Manuscript and Technical Editors: Siechert & Wood Professional Documentation

Chapters at a Glance

Table of Contents

Acknowledgments

We are much indebted to Lucinda Rowley, our multitalented, multitasking colleague at Microsoft Press who launched this project as an acquisitions editor, then became a project editor to see it through. Thanks, too, to the rest of the Microsoft Press team—Judith Bloch, Kim Eggleston, Mary DeJong, Kurt Meyer, Jim Kramer, Perry Brooks, and Wendy Zucker—for their technical and logistical assistance.

Stan DeGulis, of Siechert & Wood Professional Documentation, served as editor extraordinaire and chief error-trapper for the project, and we are grateful for his vigilance. Stan's big-picture view as well as his attention to minutiae improved this book in countless ways.

Jean Trenary and her crew at ArtSource—Katherine Erickson and Jeannie McGivern—did an incredible job of turning word processing files into real pages in short order. We said it couldn't be done, and they proved us wrong, for which we're grateful. Thanks are also due to Paula Kausch, of Siechert & Wood, for her hard work in preparing the manuscript and creating the illustrations.

Kamm Schreiner, of Sky Software, graciously provided indexing tools and assistance.

Finally, a big thank you to our own Jean and Jan, for patience, encouragement, and all manner of other vital domestic support. Thanks for the love even when it was difficult to believe that "we'll be finished soon!"

PART 1

Getting Started with Windows NT

CHAPTER 1

What's New in Windows NT 4?

Windows NT 4, known at Microsoft during its development as the "shell update release," marries the highly praised Windows 95 user interface, or shell, with the robustness, security, and scalability of Windows NT. The incorporation of the Windows 95 interface into Windows NT is by no means the only significant change in this release, but it is the most visible and consequential change, the one that will affect you every working day.

If you're moving to Windows NT 4 from Windows 95, you'll feel at home from day one. In fact, Windows NT 4 looks and feels so much like Windows 95 that, after the initial logon at the start of your day, you may forget that you've adopted a new operating system.

If you're coming to Windows NT 4 from Windows NT 3.x, you'll find the new interface makes all tasks simpler to learn and easier to carry out. Here are some highlights of what you'll find:

The Start menu. At the lower-left corner of your screen (or elsewhere, if you decide to move it), a Start button provides menu access to all the programs you regularly use, as well as to your 15 most recently opened documents. Version 3.x's division of programs into "personal" groups (those that show up only when you log on) and "common" groups (those that are visible to all users who log on at your computer) remains in version 4, but now appear as sections on the Start menu's Programs submenu—personal items in the top section, common items in the bottom section.

In addition to programs and documents, the Start menu also provides ready access to Control Panel, your printers, a powerful Find utility that helps you locate files and directories (which are now called *folders*) anywhere on your system or network, the Windows NT Help facility, a Run command, and a command for shutting down the system. The Run command is one of many ways you can execute programs that don't have entries of their own on the Start menu or its fly-out submenus. You won't need to use it much.

The taskbar. Every open application gets a button on Windows NT's new taskbar, which you can position on any edge of your screen. The taskbar makes it easier to switch between programs. But pressing Alt-Tab still works as before, and for those who want more technical details about processes that are running, Windows NT also offers a new Task Manager.

Desktop icons. Desktop icons let you get to resources on your own computer, resources on the network, your electronic mail folders, the Internet, and the new Recycle Bin (a service that lets you recover files you've accidentally deleted) with a simple double-click.

Shortcuts. You can create "shortcuts" to programs, documents, folders, Internet web sites, and other objects you use regularly. Like program items in the Windows NT 3.x Program Manager, shortcuts simply tell Windows NT where to find an object you need. They don't take up much space, and you can put them wherever they're needed.

Property sheets. Need to know how big a file is? When it was created or last accessed? Simply right-click the file and read its property sheet. Nearly everything you work with in Windows NT 4 has a property sheet. Assuming you have the proper access privileges, you can also use property sheets to change an object's attributes—to make a file read-only, for example.

Windows NT Explorer. Like Windows 95, Windows NT provides a new way of browsing and managing disk resources. A replacement for version 3.x's File Manager, Windows NT Explorer can be used in either of two modes—with or without a pane that shows an outline of your folder structure. In this book, we call the windows without outlines *folder windows* and use the term *Explorer window* for the double-paned view. Any way you look at it, use it, or describe it, it's a major improvement over File Manager.

Long filename support. From the beginning, Windows NT has allowed long filenames on disks formatted with the NT File System (NTFS). But now, long filenames are available on FAT (File Allocation Table) volumes as well. The FAT file system remains compatible with MS-DOS and earlier versions of Windows, while doing away with the archaic requirement that files be named with eight or fewer characters.

Performance Improvements

Windows NT 4 incorporates some design changes that result in faster graphical performance. Elements of the graphical subsystem have been moved from "user mode" into "kernel mode," which means that your computer has to make fewer "context switches." Graphics-intensive applications, such as CAD and games, should operate noticeably quicker as a result.

You might also notice quicker printing, thanks to Windows NT 4's use of "enhanced metafile spooling," a performance enhancement introduced first in Windows 95.

On the gaming front, meanwhile, Windows NT's architecture doesn't allow you to run MS-DOS games that write directly to your computer's video and sound hardware. But Windows NT now supports two of Microsoft's "DirectX" APIs (DirectDraw and DirectSound), which allow much faster performance from games written for the Windows environment. Most games that run effectively under Windows 95 should now perform equally well under Windows NT.

Enhanced Internet Support

Underscoring Microsoft's commitment to the Internet, Windows NT 4 supplies tools for both browsing and creating World Wide Web sites. On the browsing side, there's Internet Explorer version 3, whose advanced features include support for HTML 3.2, ActiveX Controls, and ActiveX Documents. HTML 3.2 allows you to view and design web pages with table and font tags, as well as borderless and floating frames. ActiveX Controls (which include support for Java applications) allow active web-page content, and ActiveX Documents permit you to open richly formatted documents (such as Excel spreadsheets) directly in the browser.

For web-site administrators, the Server edition of Windows NT 4 ships with Microsoft Internet Information Server version 2.0, which offers 40 percent faster performance than IIS version 1. Windows NT 4 Workstation, meanwhile, includes Peer Web Services, a tool for creating low-volume corporate intranets.

Imports from Windows 95

Like Windows 95, Windows NT 4 now includes a "universal inbox" that lets you manage multiple electronic mail systems from a single folder structure. Known as the Microsoft Exchange Inbox in Windows 95, the product has been renamed Windows Messaging in Windows NT 4, to reduce potential confusion with Microsoft's more advanced Exchange Server product (which is not part of Windows NT).

Changes that were made to the suite of accessory programs in Windows 95 have been carried over to Windows NT 4. Thus, Write and Paintbrush, the miniature word processor and paint programs included with Windows NT 3.x, have been replaced with the more versatile WordPad and Paint. And Terminal, the minimalist communication program of yore, has given way to HyperTerminal. The latter is one of a new breed of communications tools that support the Telephony Application Programming Interface (TAPI), which also makes its NT debut in version 4. TAPI's most immediate benefit is the ability to share communications ports. Your TAPI-aware fax and voicemail programs, for example, can peacefully coexist when assigned to the same COM port.

Traveling users of Windows NT, like their Windows 95 brethren, can now take advantage of a file-synchronization tool called Briefcase. Those who regularly work on both docked and undocked computing platforms will also appreciate Windows NT's new support for hardware profiles—predefined constellations of settings that make it easy to switch from one state to the other. In other respects, however,

Windows NT's support for the mobile user remains less comprehensive than that of Windows 95. Power management and Plug and Play (the industry-standard protocol that lets your computer adjust automatically to hardware changes) are slated for the next release of Windows NT ("Cairo").

The DriveSpace file compression system included with Windows 95 is not part of Windows NT 4 (and, because of architectural differences between the two operating systems, probably won't appear in any future version of Windows NT). But on drives formatted with the NT File System (NTFS), you can now use a simple procedure to compress any file or folder. Windows NT then automatically unpacks your compressed file any time you want to work with it and packs it back up when you save.

Assorted Conveniences, Services, and Bon Bons

Like Windows 95, Windows NT 4 allows you to change screen resolution without rebooting your system. A new Test button lets you see the effect of a change in display mode (and return to the current mode if the test proves unsatisfactory) before you leave the dialog box.

Several new Control Panel items and a host of "wizards" make system setup and configuration easier than before. The additions to Control Panel include Telephony (which lets you set up dialing information for any location you call from and feeds that information to TAPI-aware communications programs), SCSI Adapters (which offers one-stop configuration of SCSI devices), Tape Devices (which does the same for tape devices), and Add/Remove Programs (whose principal virtue may be the encouragement of software vendors to provide uninstall routines for their wares).

The Plus! add-in for Windows 95 is still called Plus! in Windows NT 4, but Microsoft has done the adding-in for you. A standard component of Windows NT 4, it offers smoother window dragging, font smoothing (for displays that use at least 256 colors), and a few other goodies. The desktop-themes component of Windows 95 Plus! is not part of the Windows NT counterpart, however.

If you like action games and impressive graphics, be sure to check out 3D Pinball. And don't miss the new OpenGL screen savers.

Left Behind and Not (Yet) Included

With this release, Windows NT abandons support for the 386 platform. If you use x86 computing hardware, you must have at least a 486 to run Windows NT 4. Support for 5.25-inch floppy disk drives has also been dropped.

As initially shipped, the Windows Messaging component of Windows NT 4 does not support fax or the mail component of The Microsoft Network. Fax support has been promised for the near future and may be available by the time you read this.

CHAPTER 2

Introducing Windows NT

This chapter introduces the Windows NT user interface. We'll look at the procedures for starting and ending a Windows NT session and take a brief tour of the Windows NT user interface. We'll check out the Start menu, the taskbar, the My Computer and Network Neighborhood icons, the Recycle Bin, and the Windows desktop—the features you'll be relying on every day as you use Windows NT.

Starting a Windows NT Session

To start a Windows NT session on a computer that's turned off, first be sure there's no disk in drive A, and then turn on the system. In a moment or three, you'll be in Windows NT.

If your computer has been set up to run two different operating systems—Windows NT and Windows 95, for example—you'll arrive first at the flex-boot screen. You'll see the names of the available operating systems and a countdown timer. If you do nothing, Windows NT will start when the countdown expires. To avoid the countdown delay, be sure Windows NT is highlighted (move the highlight with the arrow keys if necessary), and then press Enter.

Logging On

When Windows NT is ready, it displays a welcome message and invites you to log on by pressing Ctrl-Alt-Del.

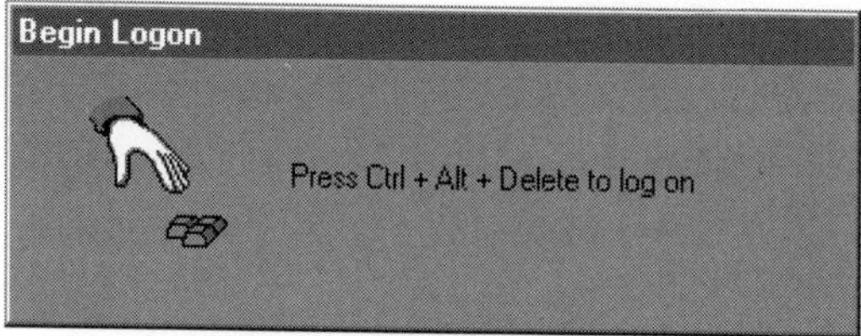

If you're accustomed to using MS-DOS, you may initially have some reservations about pressing Ctrl-Alt-Del. Not to worry—you'll never lose work in Windows NT by pressing Ctrl-Alt-Del. Rather than resetting your entire machine as it does in MS-DOS, Ctrl-Alt-Del invokes a component of Windows NT's security system, allowing you to do such things as log on or off. When you press this key combination at startup, you arrive at the Logon Information screen, where you're asked to supply your account name and password. Note that passwords in Windows NT are case-sensitive—that is, the system distinguishes capital letters from lowercase ones. If your password is gK47LnZ, for example, you must type it exactly that way every time you log on. Your account name, on the other hand, is not case-sensitive.

NOTE

> If you don't fill in the Logon Information screen within a certain amount of time, Windows NT redisplays the welcome message. Simple press Ctrl-Alt-Del again to bring back the Logon Information screen.

If your computer is part of a network, your Logon Information screen may include a third item, called *Domain*. A domain is a collection of computers that, for security purposes, "report to" a particular network server known as a *domain controller*. Depending on how your administrator has set up your system, your account name and password, as well as the information concerning your account's access privileges, may be stored on the domain server rather than on your own computer. In that case, you'll need to supply the domain name when you log on. If the correct domain name does not already appear on the Domain line of the logon screen, click the arrow at the right side of the Domain line and select the domain name from the list that unfolds.

If your computer participates in a domain but your account information is stored locally (that is, if you're not logging on to a domain account), you'll need to supply the name of your computer on the Domain line. This name, chosen by you or your administrator at the time Windows NT was set up, is the name by which your machine is identified in all its network dealings. If the name doesn't already appear on the Domain line, click the arrow at the right side of the line and select the name from the drop-down list.

Each time you log on to Windows NT, the Account Name and Domain portions of the logon screen are automatically filled out with the most recently used entries, so if you're the only one using your computer all you'll need to do is type your password. In any case, once you've supplied all the required information, simply click OK to begin your session. Windows NT completes the logon process by restoring your personal working environment, including your Start menu setup, your choice of wallpaper and screen colors, your mouse and keyboard option settings, your home directory and local path, and any network-drive connections you've established. *For more information about restoring network-drive connections at startup, see "Connecting to a Network Server," page 274.*

If a *logon script* has been associated with your user account, the commands in that script are executed. A logon script is like an Autoexec batch program in the MS-DOS world—a program that's run automatically on startup. Your system administrator might have created one for you, or you can create one yourself. *For more information, see "Specifying a Logon Script," page 566.*

Locking Your System

Locking your system protects your privacy while you're away from your machine. It also prevents other users (except ones with administrative privileges) from taking over your workstation while you're away. To lock your system, press Ctrl-Alt-Del and click the button marked Lock Workstation. Windows NT hides whatever you were working on and displays a message indicating when and by whom the system was locked.

While your system is locked, programs keep on running. Screen savers save, for example, and macros go on executing. Locking simply shuts other users out, preventing them from seeing what's going on or otherwise interacting with Windows NT.

To unlock a locked system, press Ctrl-Alt-Del again and type your password.

A Quick Tour

Figure 2-1 shows some typical Windows NT landmarks. At the bottom of the screen is the *taskbar*, your home base for interacting with Windows NT. In the upper left corner are icons labeled My Computer, Network Neighborhood, and Recycle Bin. Additional icons, with little black arrows in the lower left corners, are arrayed in columns in the lower right corner of the screen. These icons with the arrows are called *shortcuts*. The background for these objects—the visual surface on which you work in Windows—is called the *desktop*.

Mouse Terminology

To *click* an object, position the mouse pointer over that object and press the primary mouse button once. To *double-click*, position the pointer and press the primary mouse button twice in quick succession.

The *primary* mouse button is ordinarily the left button, the one that lies under the index finger of your right hand. If you're left-handed, you may want to make the right button your primary button. You can do that by choosing Settings from the Start menu, choosing Control Panel, and then double-clicking the Mouse icon. *For details, see "Setting Preferences for Your Mouse," page 113.*

In this book, as in most writing about Windows, to *right-click* means to press the secondary mouse button, whichever button that happens to be.

To *drag* an object, click it, and then while holding down the primary mouse button, move the mouse. When the object is where you want it, release the mouse button. Use the same method—except hold down the secondary mouse button—to *right-drag* an object.

To *select* a block of text with the mouse, click the beginning of the block, and hold down the mouse button while you move the mouse to the end of the block. Then release the mouse button. To *right-select*, follow the same procedure but use the secondary mouse button.

Your own screen may look quite different from the one shown in Figure 2-1. The taskbar may be positioned against a different edge of your desktop. You may have different icons in the upper left corner of your screen, or you may have the same icons with different names. You may have more or fewer shortcuts, and what shortcuts you have are undoubtedly different from the ones in the figure. But chances are your system includes most of the elements shown in Figure 2-1.

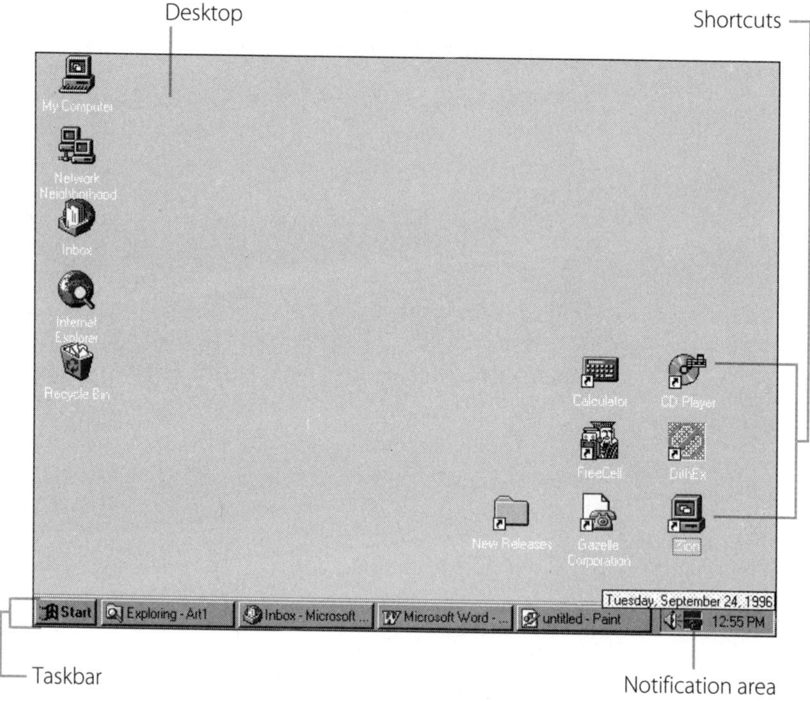

FIGURE 2-1.
A typical Windows NT desktop includes the taskbar, icons for browsing local and networked computers, and shortcuts for launching documents, folders, and programs.

The Start Menu

At the left edge of the taskbar (or at the top, if your taskbar is on the left or right edge of the desktop) is a button labeled Start. Clicking here pops up the Start menu, shown in Figure 2-2.

SEE ALSO
For information about customizing the Start menu, see "Customizing the Start Menu," page 83.

The Start menu makes most of your programs, as well as the documents you've most recently used, available with a single mouse click. It's also one of the simplest ways to accomplish several other important tasks, such as personalizing the appearance of your desktop, finding documents and programs on your own or a networked disk, and accessing basic help topics. The Start menu is

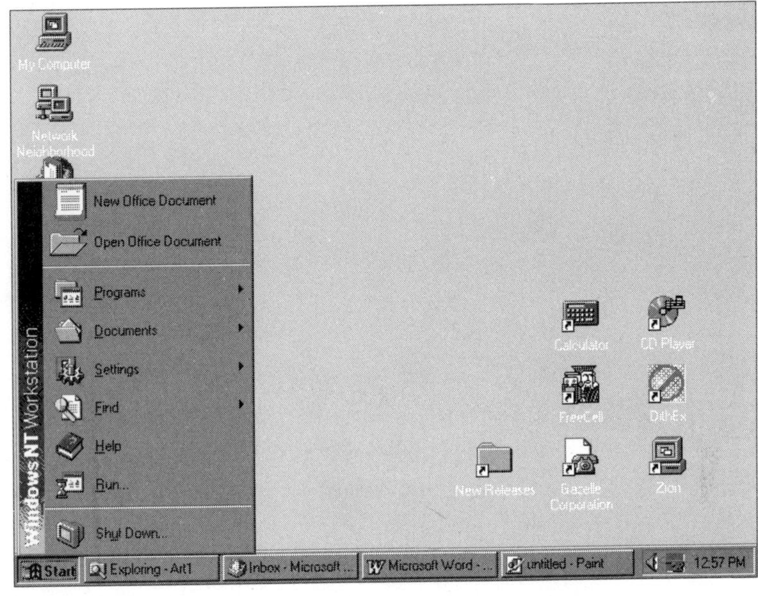

FIGURE 2-2.
The Start menu provides single-click access to the programs and documents you use most often.

also a "quit" menu; you can use its Shut Down command whenever you need to end a Windows NT session, reboot your computer, or log off to let another person use your computer.

TIP

You can open the Start menu at any time without reaching for your mouse. Simply press Ctrl-Esc.

Taskbar Buttons

SEE ALSO

For information about other ways to make the taskbar buttons more readable, see "Customizing the Taskbar," page 90.

In the center portion of the taskbar, you will see a button for each program that your system is currently running as well as for each open folder. You can click these buttons to move from one program to another.

If you have a lot of programs or folders open, Windows may truncate some of the text on the taskbar buttons. However, if you rest your mouse for a moment or two on any button whose text is not completely visible, the full text will appear in a pop-up box.

 TIP

Where's the Task List?

You can use the taskbar as a replacement for the Windows and Windows NT 3.x task list. To get to the taskbar quickly, even if it's covered, simply press Ctrl-Esc. Windows NT also includes Task Manager, a more informative version of the old task list. To run Task Manager, right-click an unoccupied segment of the taskbar and choose Task Manager. *For more information about Task Manager, see "Monitoring Performance with Task Manager," page 667.*

The Clock

 SEE ALSO

For information about changing the clock's display format, see "Specifying Regional (International) Settings," page 387.

In the right corner of the taskbar is a simple clock. You can set this clock by simply double-clicking it and filling out the ensuing dialog box. If you'd rather not know the time of day, you can banish the clock. *For details, see "Customizing the Taskbar," page 90.*

The clock also shows you the current date. Simply move the mouse pointer to the clock and leave it for a moment; the date appears in a pop-up box, as shown in Figure 2-1 on page 16.

 TIP

Setting Time Zones

If your network is spread across two or more time zones, be sure to let Windows know what time zone your own system lives in. Windows NT supports a "coordinated universal time format" that provides better tracking of time information for widely dispersed networks. To enter your time zone information, double-click the clock, and then click the Time Zone tab.

The Notification Area

In the space just to the left of the clock, Windows occasionally provides information about the status of your system. When a local printer is active, for example, a printer icon appears in this *notification area*. You can double-click the icon to inspect and manage the print queue. If you're running Windows Messaging or Microsoft Exchange, Windows displays an icon in the notification area when an e-mail message or fax arrives.

My Computer

SEE ALSO

For information about mapping network folders, see "Mapping a Network Folder to a Drive Letter," page 277.

The My Computer icon lets you browse through all the resources attached or mapped to your system. When you open My Computer, you see a *folder window* similar to the one shown in Figure 2-3. This window includes icons for each of your computer's floppy disk drives, each local hard disk, each local CD-ROM drive, and any network folders that you have mapped to your computer. It also shows *system folders* that provide access to the Windows Control Panel, your printers, and Dial-Up Networking, a program that lets you dial up network resources via your modem.

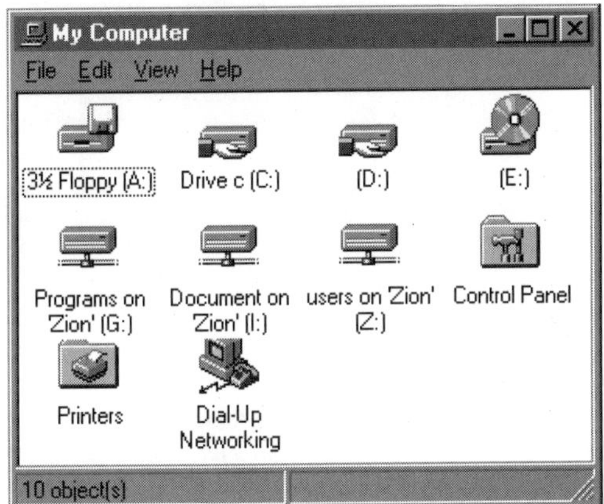

FIGURE 2-3. The My Computer icon opens into a folder window showing all resources attached or mapped to your own computer.

TIP

You can change the names of your desktop icons. If you don't fancy *My Computer*, for example, you can change it as follows: select the icon, press F2, and then type the name you prefer.

SEE ALSO
For information about browsing your own computer, see "Moving from Folder to Folder," page 120.

SEE ALSO
For information about browsing network computers, see "Using Network Neighborhood," page 272.

Double-clicking the icons in the My Computer folder window opens additional folder windows. For example, opening the icon labeled "Drive c (C:)" would show you the contents of one of your local hard disks.

Network Neighborhood

Opening the Network Neighborhood icon provides a folder window displaying the names of each computer in your own workgroup or domain. In addition, the Network Neighborhood folder includes an Entire Network icon, which you can use to access other workgroups or domains on your network. Figure 2-4 shows how the Network Neighborhood folder might appear on a system that's part of a 10-member domain.

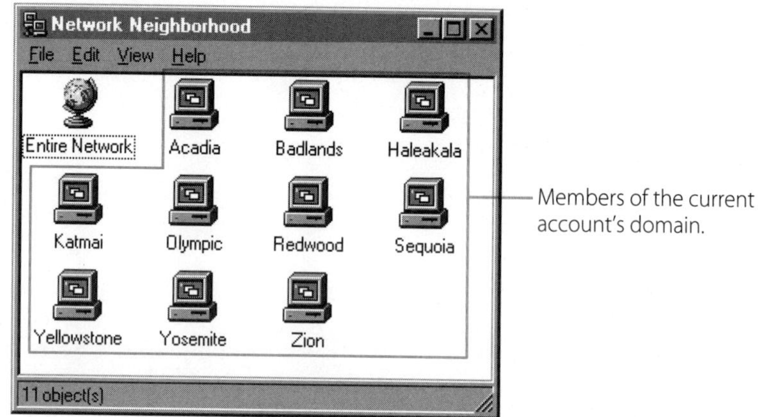

FIGURE 2-4.
The Network Neighborhood icon opens into a folder window showing all members of your own workgroup or domain.

The Recycle Bin

The Recycle Bin provides temporary storage for files that you delete. If you change your mind after deleting a file, you may be able to recover (undelete) the file by retrieving it from the Recycle Bin. *For more information, see "Restoring Deleted Items," page 149.*

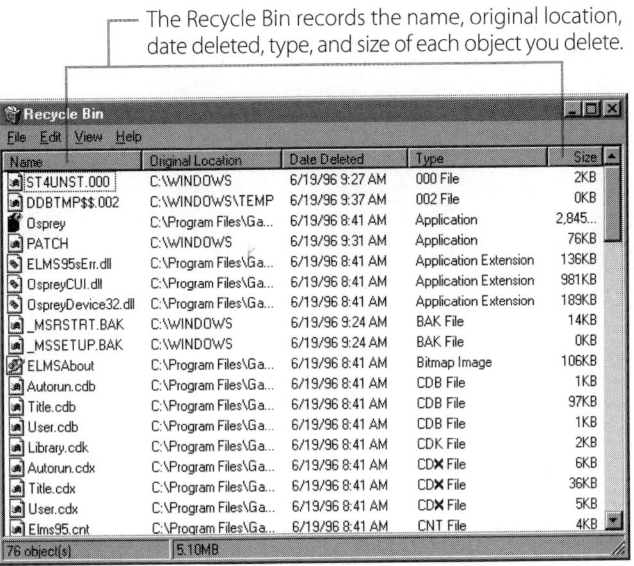

Shortcuts

SEE ALSO
For more information about shortcuts, see "Using Shortcuts to Run Programs and Open Documents," page 73.

A shortcut provides easy access to some object on your system, such as a program, a document, a printer, a local hard disk, or a network server. For example, opening the shortcut labeled New Releases in Figure 2-1 (page 16) opens a folder window containing files stored in the New Releases folder. Opening the shortcut labeled Calculator runs the Calculator program, and so on. You can create shortcuts for just about any object you use frequently.

Working with Windows

All Windows-based applications run within rectangular frames called windows. As shown in Figure 2-5 on the next page, these features are common to nearly all windows:

FIGURE 2-5.
Nearly all Windows-based applications run in windows that include these elements.

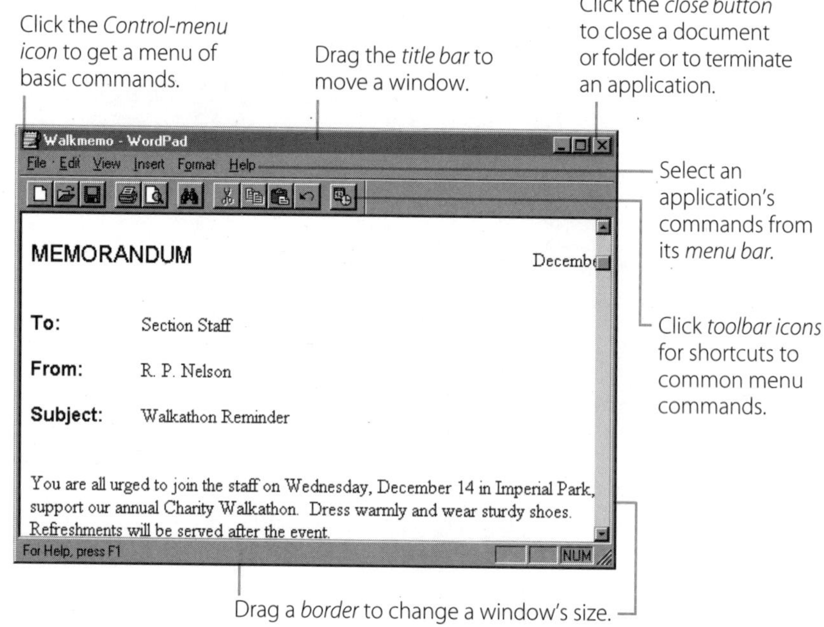

Another way to close an application window, folder window, or dialog box is to press Alt-F4.

Minimizing, Restoring, and Maximizing

To the left of the close button, you will find other buttons that look like this:

Clicking the minimize button causes a window to collapse into its taskbar button. The window is still open, and the program inside it continues to run. But the window no longer takes up space on your desktop. You can reopen a minimized window by clicking its taskbar button or by holding down the Alt key and pressing Tab.

Clicking the restore button causes a window to assume an intermediate amount of space—neither maximized nor minimized. With windows restored, you can keep two or more applications in view at the same time. You can adjust the size of a restored window by dragging its borders. (See "Sizing and Moving Windows," below.)

Clicking the maximize button causes a window to occupy all of the desktop. While you're using an application, you may want to keep its window maximized most of the time, so that you have as much screen real estate as possible to work with.

TIP

Another way to maximize a window is to double-click its title bar. If the window is already maximized, you can restore its intermediate size by double-clicking the title bar.

Sizing and Moving Windows

To change a window's size, drag its borders. For example, to make the window wider, drag either the left or right border. To make a window both wider and taller, you can drag one of the corners.

To move a window, drag its title bar.

TIP

Dialog boxes sometimes get in the way of underlying applications. To see what's under a dialog box, move it—by dragging its title bar.

Switching Between Windows

When two or more application windows are open at once, the one lying on top has what's called the *focus*. The window with the focus is the one that will respond to your next keystrokes. (The window that has the focus is sometimes also called the *foreground* or *active* window.) To switch the focus to another window, you can use any of the following techniques:

- Click anywhere on or in the window that you want to switch to.
- Click the taskbar button for the window you want to switch to.
- Press and hold the Alt key. Then press Tab to bring up the Windows task switcher. The task switcher displays an icon for each running application and draws a box around the icon whose window currently has the focus. Continue holding Alt and pressing Tab until the window you want to switch to has the focus.
- Right-click an unoccupied part of the taskbar and choose Task Manager. A window will appear, listing all programs that are currently running. Double-click the name of the program you want to switch to. *For more information about Task Manager, see "Monitoring Performance with Task Manager," page 667.*

TIP

Who's Got the Focus?

If you're ever in doubt about which window has the focus, check your windows' title bars. The active window's title bar is normally displayed in one color, while the title bars of all inactive windows are displayed in another color. In addition, the taskbar button for the active window appears to be pressed in.

Arranging Windows on the Screen

If you have a lot of windows open at once, it may be hard to see what's going on. Windows provides some handy commands for making all your windows visible. To put all the windows in a neat stack, with each window's title bar visible, do the following:

1. Right-click an unoccupied part of the taskbar. (Press Ctrl-Esc first if you can't see the taskbar.)
2. Choose the Cascade command.

With your windows in a cascade, you can easily switch focus by clicking any title bar—as well as by clicking any button on the taskbar.

If you want to see a portion of the contents of each open window, choose one of the tiling commands. Right-click an unoccupied part of the taskbar and choose either Tile Horizontally or Tile Vertically.

To minimize all open windows, right-click an unoccupied part of the taskbar and choose Minimize All Windows.

TIP

After cascading, tiling, or minimizing all windows, you can restore your windows to their previous positions by right-clicking the taskbar. The menu that appears includes a new command that reverses your previous action. For example, if you have just minimized all windows, the new command will read Undo Minimize All.

Keeping Windows on Top

Some windows are designed to stay on top, even when they don't have the focus. Windows that contain help information, for example, often behave this way, allowing you to read their helpful text even while you're working in a maximized application.

Most programs that stay on top give you the option of disabling this behavior. If a stay-on-topper becomes a visual nuisance, look in its menu system for a command such as "Always On Top" or "Stay On Top." Often you'll find it on the program's Control menu. *(For information about the Control menu, see "The Control Menu and the Menu Bar," page 30.)* These commands are usually *toggles*; you choose them once to turn the feature on and a second time to turn it off.

TIP

Hiding the Taskbar

The taskbar itself is a stay-on-top window. In its default display mode, it remains visible even when the foreground application is maximized. You can defeat this behavior by right-clicking an unoccupied part of the taskbar, choosing the Properties command, clicking the Taskbar Options tab, and deselecting the check box labeled Always On Top. (To get back to the taskbar when it's not visible, press Ctrl-Esc.)

Window Panes

Some programs use windows that are split vertically, horizontally, or even both vertically and horizontally. The resulting window divisions are called *panes*. As Figure 2-6 shows, you can use your mouse to change the distribution of space between panes.

FIGURE 2-6.
This window is divided into a left pane and a right pane.

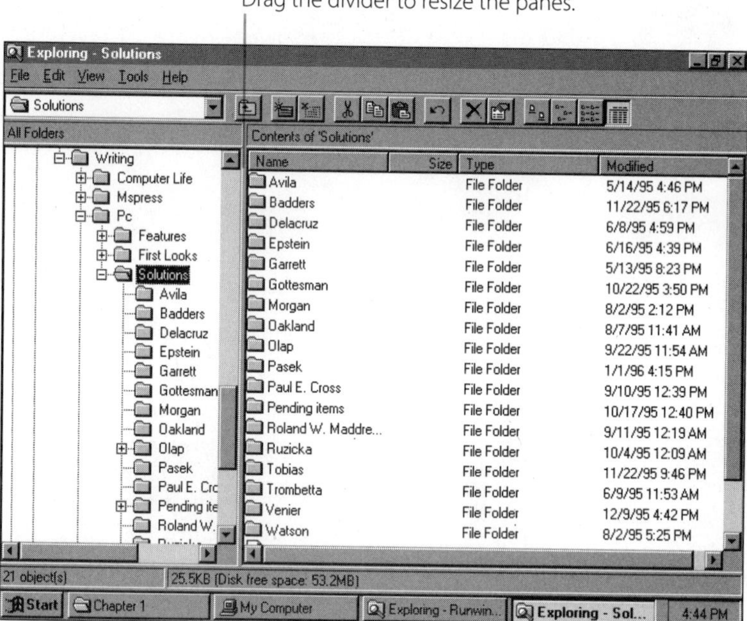

Working with Document Windows

Windows come in two varieties, called application windows and document windows. Application windows house programs or folders, can be moved freely around the desktop, and can be maximized to fill the screen or minimized to taskbar buttons. All the windows illustrated thus far in this chapter are examples of application windows.

Document windows live inside application windows. As their name implies, they are designed to hold documents, not programs. Document windows can be maximized, restored, minimized, moved, and sized, but they must remain within the confines of an application window. Figure 2-7 shows an application window containing three open and two minimized document windows.

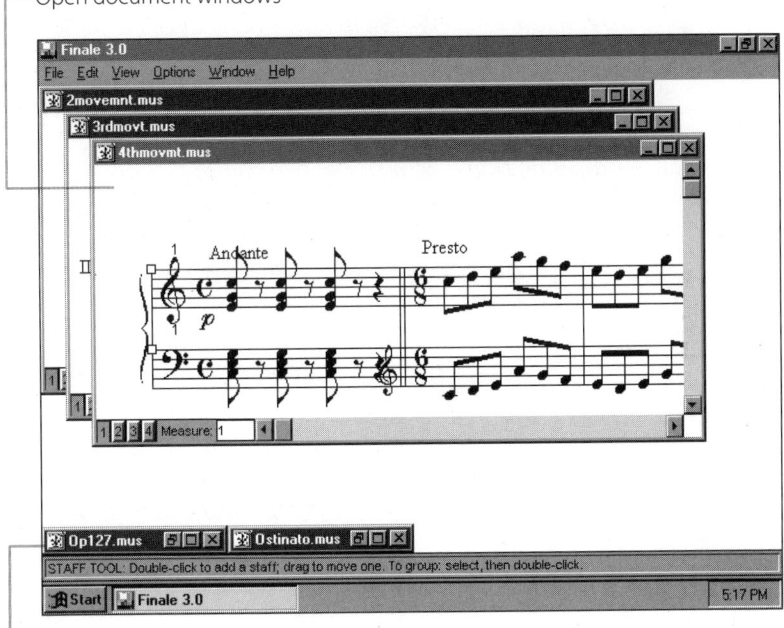

FIGURE 2-7.
This application window contains three open document windows and two minimized document windows.

Notice that the title bar for one of the document windows (the one in the front of the cascade) is the same color as the title bar for the application window. That document window currently has the focus. Also notice that document windows, when minimized, become miniature title bars.

 **TIP**

Document Window Shortcuts

You can close the current document window by pressing Ctrl-F4. In many programs, you can move from one document window to the next document window by pressing Ctrl-F6.

Working with Folders

A folder is a container for computers, disk drives, printer queues, other folders, and files. The most common kind of folder is exemplified by Figure 2-8. It's a place where programs, document files, and perhaps additional folders are kept. Such a folder is analogous to a directory in MS-DOS and earlier versions of Windows. Your computer's hard disks, as well as those of your network's servers, are organized into hierarchies of folders.

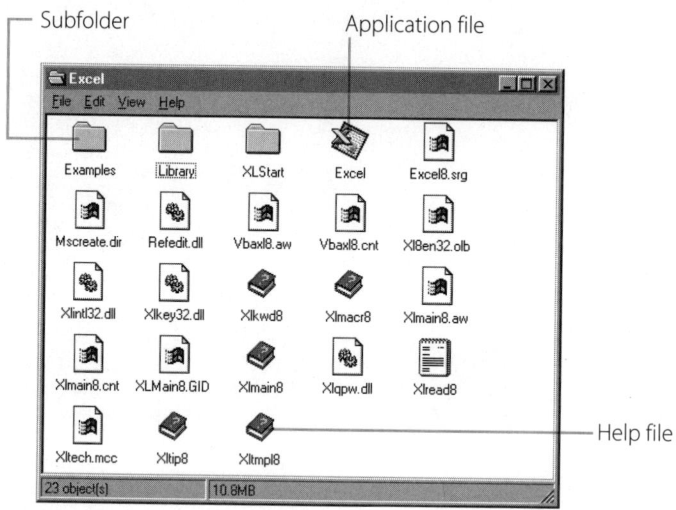

FIGURE 2-8.
This Excel folder includes three subfolders, the Excel application file, several help files, and a variety of other files.

At the top of a disk hierarchy in MS-DOS is a directory called the root directory. The Windows NT folder corresponding to the root directory goes by the volume name assigned to the disk on which it lives. If you name your C drive *George*, for example, its top level is a folder named George.

Your computer itself is a folder called My Computer. Your network workgroup is a folder called Network Neighborhood.

Windows NT uses two different types of windows to display the contents of folders. One type is shown in Figure 2-8. This book refers to windows of this type as *folder windows*. The other type, shown in

SEE ALSO

For more information about folder windows, see Chapter 5, "Working with Folders."

For more information about Windows NT Explorer windows, see Chapter 6, "Managing Folders and Files with Windows NT Explorer."

Figure 2-6 on page 26, is called a *Windows NT Explorer window.* Folder windows and Windows NT Explorer windows provide alternative ways of looking at the same information—the contents of a folder. Both are ordinary application windows.

Windows NT uses *system folders* to hold items that are related to your system. For example, you can install and configure printers by opening a system folder called *Printers*, view and install fonts in a system folder called *Fonts*, and customize Windows in a variety of ways using a system folder called *Control Panel*.

The Desktop Is Also a Folder

At the top of the Windows NT hierarchy is a folder called the desktop. This mother of all folders has some special characteristics. In particular, you don't need a folder window to see its contents. The desktop underlies all other windows and is fully visible when all your windows are minimized.

If you do want to see the desktop displayed in a folder window, don't try to get to it by opening My Computer and asking to see My Computer's parent. The desktop is the parent of My Computer, but its information is stored elsewhere. Assuming Windows NT is installed in C:\Winnt, your desktop folder will be

C:\Winnt\Profiles\Username\Desktop

where *Username* is the name you use when you log on.

Working with Menus and Dialog Boxes

In virtually all Windows applications, commands are chosen from *drop-down menus*—sets of options that emerge from a menu bar at the top of the application window. When a program needs additional information from you before it can carry out your command, it presents a *dialog box*—a smaller window with places for you to fill in blanks or choose between preset options. These devices behave in a consistent and predictable way in all Windows-based programs.

The Control Menu and the Menu Bar

The two main elements of a Windows-based application's menu system are the *Control menu* and the *menu bar*. The Control menu emerges from the icon at the left side of the title bar. The menu bar is the row of commands directly below the title bar.

The Control menu provides a set of generic commands common to all applications. With few exceptions, each program's Control menu includes the same commands.

The menu bar includes commands specific to the current application. Each word on the menu bar opens a drop-down menu of related commands. For example, a program's File menu includes commands for opening and saving files, its Edit menu has commands for changing the contents of a document, and so on.

Choosing Commands with the Mouse

SEE ALSO

For information about using the keyboard to perform mouse functions, see "Mouse Alternatives," page 40.

To get to the menu system with the mouse, simply click the desired word in the menu bar. To open the File menu, for example, click the word *File*. To open the Control menu, click the icon at the left edge of the title bar. To choose a command from a drop-down menu, simply move the mouse down until you reach the desired command, and then click.

To get out of the menu system without choosing a command, click the mouse anywhere outside the drop-down menu.

Choosing Commands with the Keyboard

To choose any command with the keyboard, begin by pressing the Alt key. (You can also access the menu system by pressing F10.) When you do that, Windows highlights the first command on the menu bar. At this point, you can use the Left arrow and Right arrow keys to move around the menu bar. To open a particular menu, move to that menu and press the Down arrow or Up arrow key.

To leave the menu system without choosing a command, press the Alt key or the Esc key.

Accelerator Keys and Other Shortcuts

A more direct way to open a particular drop-down menu is to press Alt, followed by the menu's *accelerator key*—the underlined letter in the menu's name. The accelerator key is often, but not always, the first letter of the menu name. In Microsoft Word, for example, you can open the File menu by pressing Alt-F, but to get to the Format menu, you need to press Alt-O.

Some menu commands have shortcuts assigned to them. These are single keystrokes or simple keystroke combinations that execute a command directly. In many programs, for example, pressing Ctrl-S is equivalent to choosing the File menu's Save command. When a keyboard shortcut is available, it usually appears to the right of the command name on the menu.

Context ("Right-Click") Menus

In many parts of Windows NT, as well as in many Windows-based applications, pressing the secondary mouse button brings up a small menu appropriate to the currently selected object (or the one the mouse is pointing to). For example, if you right-click the taskbar, you get a menu of commands relating only to the taskbar. If you select a block of text in Microsoft Word and then right-click, you get a menu that includes commands for formatting, moving, and copying the selected text. These right-click menus go by various names in various applications. Some programs call them "property inspectors," others call them "shortcut menus," still others identify them as "context menus." In this book, they're called *context menus.*

Whatever they're called, they often provide the quickest route to a needed menu command.

TIP

The Default Command

When you right-click certain objects in Windows NT, the context menu includes one command in boldface type. The boldface command is the one that would have been executed had you simply double-clicked the object instead of right-clicking it.

Quick Viewing and Property Inspection

Two commands that appear on many context menus are particularly important and useful. The Quick View command lets you look at the contents of a file without opening the application that created the file. For example, by right-clicking the icon for a text file, you can read the text without opening WordPad or any other text editor.

Not all files can be quick-viewed, but many can. To see if a file can be quick-viewed, open the folder in which the file is stored, and then right-click the file's icon or name. If a viewer is available for this file type, the Quick View command appears on the context menu. *For more information about the Quick View command, see "Inspecting Documents and Programs with Quick View," page 69.*

Files and folders have properties such as type, size, creation date, and location. The Properties command, which appears at the bottom of an object's context menu, lets you inspect those properties. For example, to find out when a file was last changed, you can right-click that file's icon or name in a folder window, choose Properties, and then read the "Modified" item in the property sheet that appears. To find out how much space is taken up by all the files in a folder, you can right-click the folder icon and choose Properties.

In some cases, you can not only inspect but also change an object's properties by choosing the context menu's Properties command. For example, right-clicking the taskbar and choosing Properties takes you to a dialog box in which you can customize the appearance and behavior of the taskbar and the Start menu. Right-clicking the desktop and choosing Properties lets you customize the appearance of the desktop.

Gray Commands, Check Marks, and Cascading Menus

Here are some other menu conventions observed by most Windows-based applications:

- A command that appears in gray letters on a menu is one that's not available in the current context. In Microsoft Excel, for example, the Window menu's Unhide command remains gray until at least one window has been hidden.

- A check mark beside a command indicates that a certain condition has been turned on. Choosing such a command turns the condition off and removes the check mark.
- An arrowhead to the right of a command means that choosing this command brings up a cascading submenu. The Start menu on the taskbar, for example, has four such commands: Programs, Documents, Settings, and Find. Choose any one of these commands, and another menu unfurls.

Using Dialog Boxes

An ellipsis (...) is a punctuation symbol signifying an incomplete sentence. In a Windows menu, an ellipsis following a command name indicates an incomplete command. Such a command brings up a *dialog box*, which is a device used by Windows to get more information from you.

Dialog boxes come in all sizes and shapes. Some are simple, others quite complex. But nearly all dialog boxes have the following components:

- One or more places for you to enter information or choose options
- One or more command buttons

Most dialog boxes have a command button that you click after you've filled out the dialog box to your satisfaction, and another that you click to back out of the dialog box without making an entry. In many cases, these buttons are marked OK and Cancel, respectively. Many dialog boxes also have a button labeled Help or a button with a question mark on it; you can click this kind of button if you're not sure what some of the dialog-box options mean.

TIP

> Pressing Esc or Alt-F4 in a dialog box is usually equivalent to clicking the Cancel button. It dismisses the dialog box without taking any further action. Still another way to dismiss a dialog box is to click the Close button on its title bar.

Accelerator Keys in Dialog Boxes

Like menu commands, the names of dialog box elements often have underlined letters that you can use for quick keyboard access. These accelerator keys provide a quick way to select dialog box options using the keyboard. In Figure 2-9, for example, F is the accelerator key for the Formula Bar check box; S is the accelerator for the Status Bar check box, and so on.

To use accelerator keys in a dialog box, hold down the Alt key while you press the accelerator key.

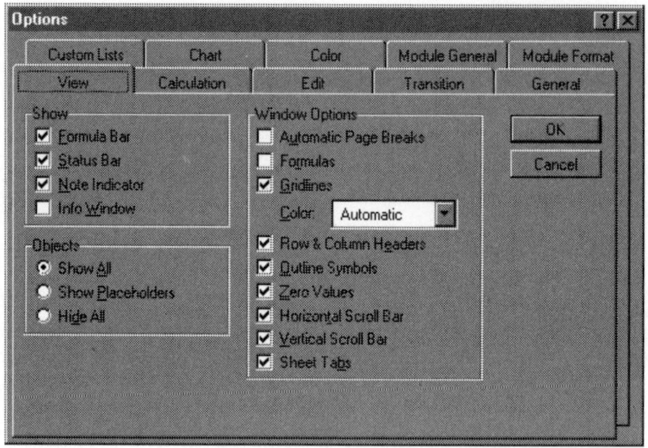

FIGURE 2-9.
The underlined letters in a dialog box, like those in a menu, provide keyboard shortcuts for selecting options. The tabs along the top of the dialog box let you shift from one page of options to another.

Dialog Box Tabs

The dialog box shown in Figure 2-9 actually includes ten "pages" of options. You select the page you're interested in by clicking its tab at the top of the dialog box. For example, the portion of the dialog box shown in the figure offers viewing options; to select editing options, click the Edit tab—and so on. Press Ctrl-Tab to flip through the pages with the keyboard.

If the current tab has a dotted marquee around it, as the View tab does in Figure 2-9, you can also move between tabs by pressing the arrow keys.

Dialog Box Elements

In the sections of a dialog box where you enter information or select options, you'll encounter the following kinds of elements:

- Text boxes
- List boxes
- Drop-down list boxes
- Option buttons
- Check boxes
- Spinners
- Sliders

A *text box*, sometimes also called an *edit box,* is a place for you to type something.

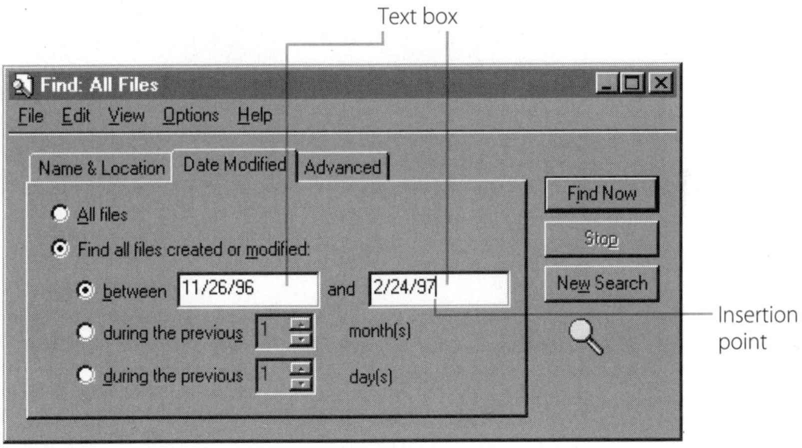

To fill out a text box, click in the box. You'll then see a flashing vertical line called an *insertion point*. If the text box is empty, the insertion point appears at the left side of the box. If the box already contains text, the insertion point appears at the spot where you clicked the mouse. In either case, the insertion point marks the place where the characters you type will appear.

A *list box* presents a set of options in the form of a list, like this:

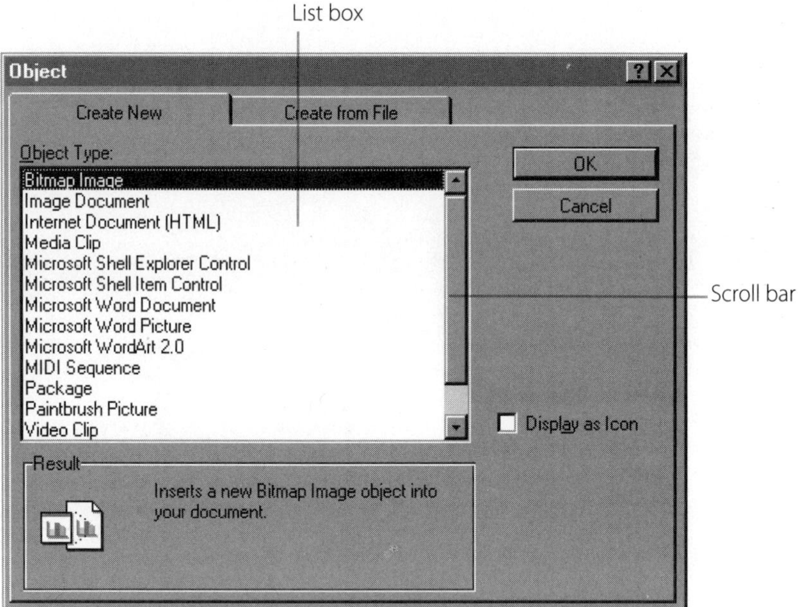

In most list boxes, you can choose only one item at a time, but in some you can choose two or more. If a list box allows you to choose more than one option at a time, hold down the Ctrl key while you click each item you want to choose.

If the list contains more items than can be displayed at once (as the list shown above does), you will find a *scroll bar* at the right side of the list box. The scroll bar helps you move quickly from one part of the list to another. *(For more information about scroll bars, see "Using Scroll Bars," page 41.)* You can also move through a list box by pressing the Up arrow or Down arrow key, PgUp, or PgDn.

TIP

Scrolling with the Keyboard

When you're scrolling through a list, the keyboard is often quicker than the mouse. In most newer applications, including the accessory programs included with Windows NT, simply type the first few letters of a list item to move the highlight to that item. (If the highlight moves as you type each letter to the next item that *begins* with that letter, the application is using an older navigation method that considers only the first letter of each list item.)

A *drop-down list box* looks like a text box with a downward-pointing arrow to the right of it. The Of Type line in the following illustration is an example.

When you click the downward-pointing arrow (or press Alt-Down arrow), an ordinary-looking list box unfolds, like this:

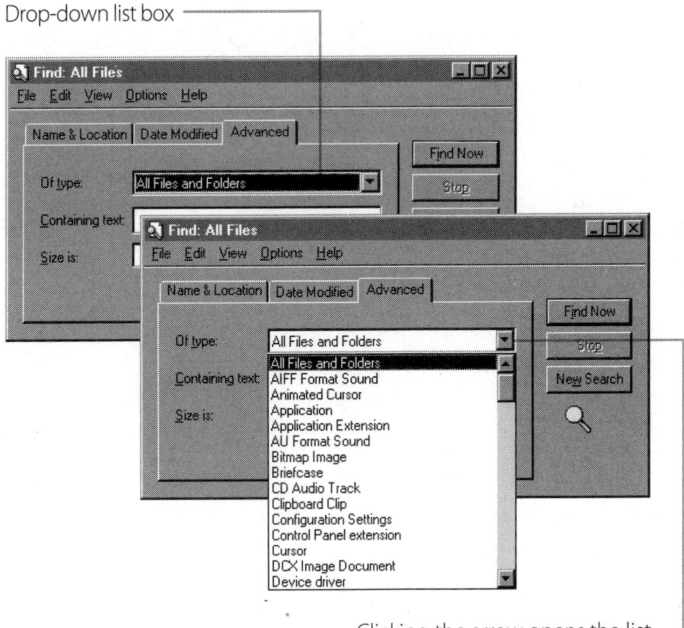

TIP

Dialog Shortcuts

You can use the arrow keys to move through a drop-down list without first opening the list box. You can type the first few letters of an item to move directly to that item. (In Windows 3.x–style applications, pressing a letter key moves to the next item that *begins* with that letter.) You can move from one item to another in a dialog box by pressing the Tab key (or Shift-Tab to go backwards).

Option buttons (sometimes called *radio buttons*) present a set of mutually exclusive options. To make your choice, click the button or anywhere in the text next to the button. Option buttons always come in groups of two or more. The buttons may be either round or diamond-shaped. Either way, they look quite different from check boxes, which are always square.

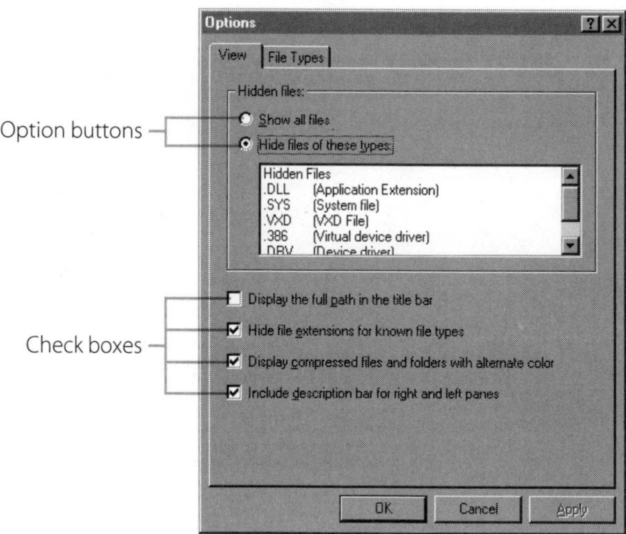

Check boxes come either in groups or one at a time. Each check box is independent of all others in the dialog box. To select an item, click the box or anywhere in the text next to the box. To deselect an item, click again.

A "yes" vote for a check box may be marked by either an *X* or a check mark.

Some check boxes have three states—checked, unchecked, and solid. Usually, a check box with a solid background means that a certain condition applies to some of a selection, but not all of it. For example, in the illustration below, some of the selected cells in a Microsoft Excel worksheet have been given the "Strikethrough" effect. The rest of the cells have not. In the Format Cells dialog box, therefore, the Strikethrough check box has a solid background.

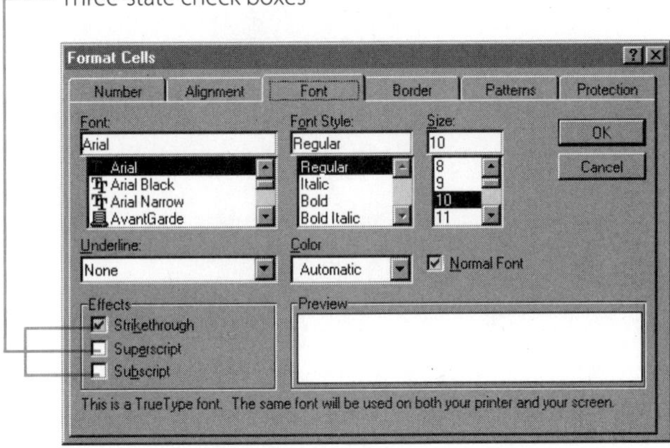

A *spinner* is a pair of arrows used to increment or decrement the value in a text box, as shown in the following illustration. To increase the value in the text box, click the up arrow; to decrease, click the down arrow.

Spinner

TIP

Just because a text box has a spinner next to it doesn't mean you can't type directly into the text box. Typing may be quicker, particularly if you want to change the value by a significant amount.

A *slider* works like the darkness setting on your toaster. The three rate and delay settings in the following illustration are examples of sliders.

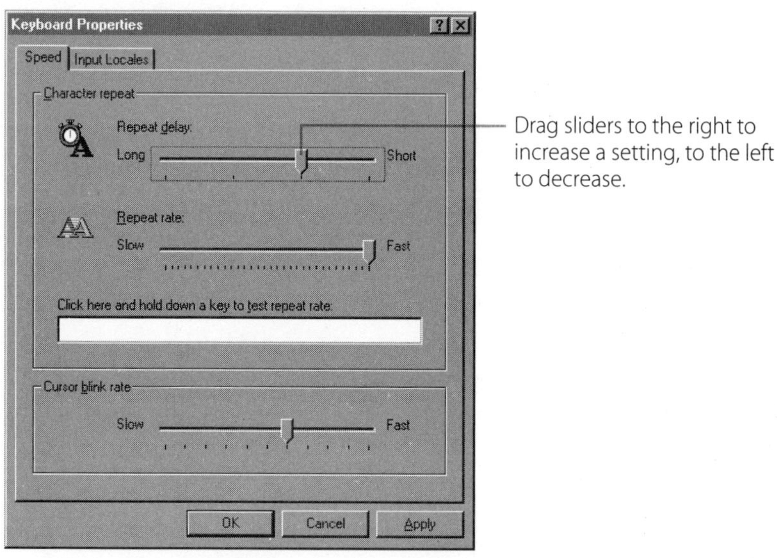

Using Scroll Bars

If a window is not long enough to display its contents completely, Windows adds a *vertical scroll bar* to the right side of the window. If the window is not wide enough, Windows adds a *horizontal scroll bar*. If it's neither long enough nor wide enough, Windows adds both kinds of scroll bars. Figure 2-10 shows a window with vertical and horizontal scroll bars.

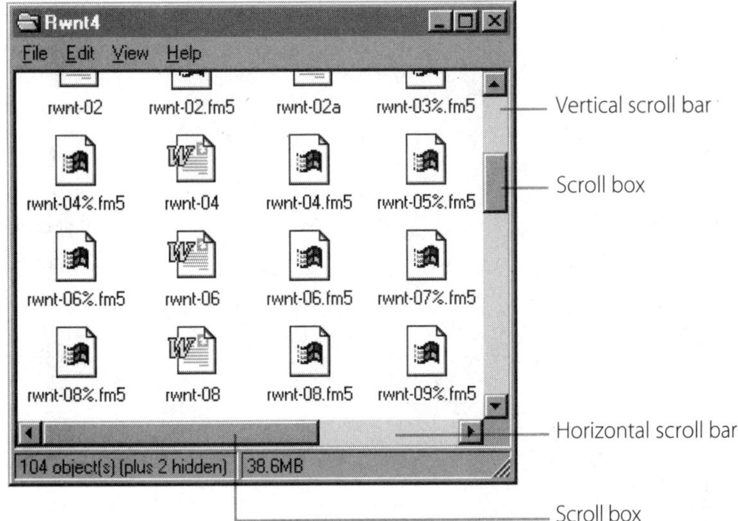

FIGURE 2-10.
Scroll bars provide information about the contents of a window and allow you to move quickly from one part of the window to another.

Scroll bars offer an easy way to navigate through a window with the mouse. They also provide useful information about the contents of the window.

In Figure 2-10, notice the rectangular *scroll box* in each scroll bar. The position of this box within the scroll bar tells you where you are in the window itself. In the vertical scroll bar, for example, the scroll box is about 20 percent of the way down the bar. That means that roughly 20 percent of the window's contents lie above your current position in the window. In the horizontal bar, the scroll box is all the way at the left edge, telling you that there's nothing more to be seen to the left of your current position.

Notice the size of the scroll boxes relative to the length of the scroll bars. The vertical box is about 20 percent of the length of the scroll bar itself. That means that about one fifth of the window's vertical extent is currently visible within the window frame. The horizontal scroll box is about two-thirds as wide as the horizontal scroll bar, which means that about two-thirds of the window's horizontal extent is now visible.

For navigation purposes, you can use scroll bars in the following ways:

- To move up or down a line at a time, simply click the arrow at either end of the vertical scroll bar. To move left or right a character at a time (or by a small increment in a noncharacter display), click the arrow at either end of the horizontal bar.
- To move by approximately one windowful, click in the scroll bar itself, on either side of the scroll box.
- To continuously scroll a line at a time, click an arrow and hold down the mouse button. To continuously scroll a windowful at a time, click in the scroll bar itself and hold down the mouse button. When you arrive where you want to be, release the button.
- To move to a specific location, drag the box. To move halfway down a long document, for example, move the vertical scroll box to about the midpoint of the vertical scroll bar.

Toolbars, Speedbars, Button Bars, and Sushi Bars

Only kidding, of course. In this version of Windows NT, there are no sushi bars. But you will find icon bars aplenty. Most major applications for Windows have adopted the convention of augmenting their menu systems with palettes of icons. The icons are shortcuts that save you the trouble of pulling down menus and submenus. These palettes go by different names in different programs. Microsoft calls them toolbars. Other vendors refer to them as button bars, SmartIcon palettes, speedbars, tool boxes, or tool kits.

The row of icons underneath the menu bar in Figure 2-11 on the next page is an example of an icon palette. In most applications, if you point your mouse at an icon a legend will appear—directly below the icon, in a pop-up balloon beside the icon, or perhaps in a status area at the bottom or top of the window. (In Microsoft programs, as in Windows itself, the icon legends appear in a small box next to the icon after you rest your mouse on an icon for about a half second.)

In many programs, the icon palettes are customizable. That is, you can set up the palette so that it includes icons for just those commands that you use most often. Customizable icon palettes can be a real convenience. If your program includes an icon palette, check its documentation to see if you can tailor the palette to suit your preferences.

Of course, icon palettes may not be your kettle of sushi. If that's the case, check your program's documentation to see if the palette can be removed. Most likely it can, and getting rid of it will give you a bigger space to work in.

Entering and Editing Text

Unless you happen to be concerned with only graphic images, you will probably spend much of your time in Windows entering and editing text—whether your primary application is word processing, financial planning, database management, project management, or communications. Even though Windows is a graphical environment and uses your computer's graphics display modes, the information you work with consists primarily of letters and numbers—in other words, text.

Fortunately, a basic set of concepts and procedures applies to text in most applications for Windows.

The Insertion Point

The flashing vertical line that you see when you work with text in a Windows-based application is called the *insertion point.* It's analogous to the cursor in a character-based program. The insertion point indicates where the next character you type will appear.

There's one difference between the insertion point and the cursor used in most character-based programs. The insertion point is always positioned *between* two characters, *before* the first character in a block, or *after* the last character in a block. It never appears directly under a character. That's because characters are always *inserted* at the insertion point.

In Figure 2-11, for example, the insertion point is located between the *i* and the *n* in the word *tiny.*

FIGURE 2-11.
The insertion point shows where characters you type will appear. You can move the insertion point by clicking the mouse at the location indicated by the I-beam pointer.

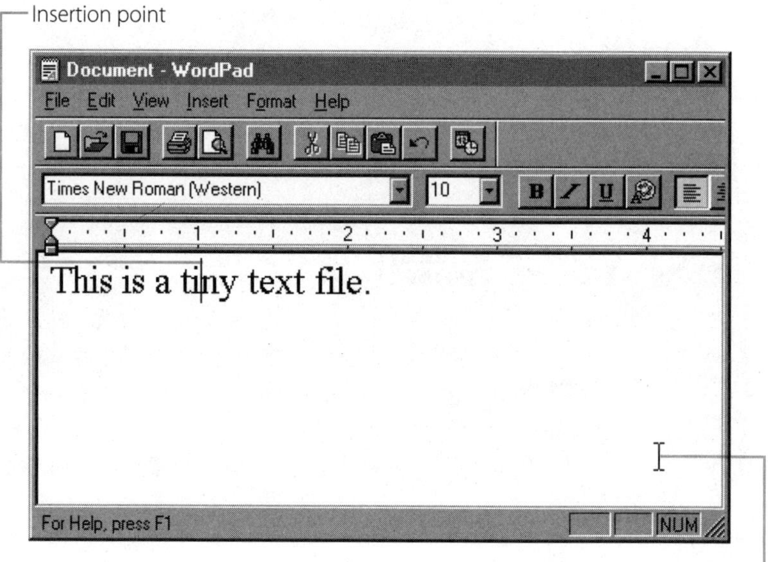

To replace existing text with new characters that you type, Windows uses a different concept, called *selection*. More about that in a moment.

The I-Beam

When you work with text, Windows changes your mouse pointer from an arrow to something that looks like a lanky capital *I*. The pointer is then usually called an *I-beam*. In Figure 2-11, you can see the I-beam in the lower right corner of the window.

The I-beam provides a way to relocate the insertion point. In the tiny text file shown in Figure 2-11, for example, if you want to move the insertion point to the beginning of the line, simply use the mouse to position the I-beam before the capital *T*, and then click. (You can also use the keyboard to move the insertion point, as we'll see in a moment.)

The Selection

To *select* something in Windows means to highlight it—with the keyboard or the mouse. In the following illustration, for example, the word *tiny* has been selected.

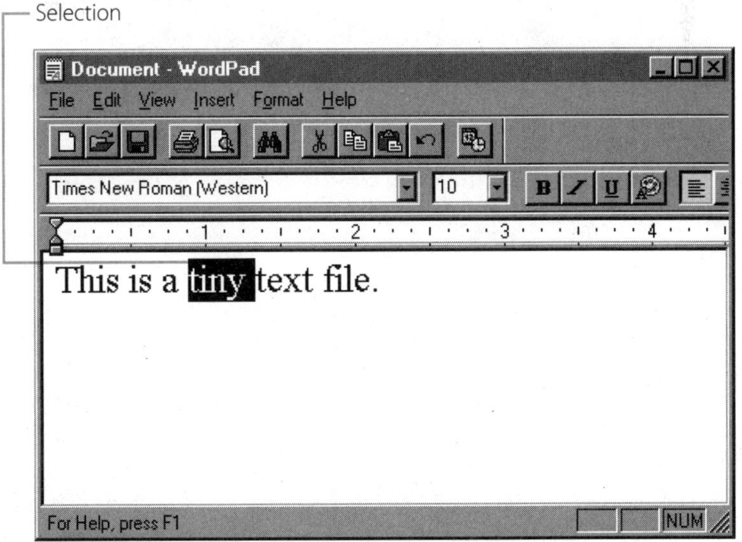

You might select a block of text for any of several reasons:

- To apply a formatting change to the entire block (In the illustration above, for example, if you click WordPad's Underline tool after selecting the word *tiny*, the entire word is underlined.)
- To *copy*, *cut*, or *delete* the entire block
- To replace the entire block

Notice that there's no insertion point in the illustration above. The insertion point disappears when you make a selection, because the next character you type *replaces* the entire selection.

Positioning the Insertion Point

The easiest way to move the insertion point is with the mouse; simply put the I-beam wherever you want the insertion point, and then click. But you can also use the keyboard. The following keystroke combinations apply to most Windows-based applications that work with text:

- The Right arrow and Left arrow keys move the insertion point forward or backward a character at a time. Ctrl-Right and Ctrl-Left move it forward or backward a word at a time.
- End moves the insertion point to the end of the line. Home moves it to the beginning of the line.
- The Up arrow and Down arrow keys move the insertion point up or down a line at a time.
- PgUp and PgDn move up or down a windowful at a time.
- Ctrl-End moves to the end of the document. Ctrl-Home moves to the beginning of the document.

Some applications use additional keystroke combinations for moving the insertion point. In Microsoft Word, for example, pressing Ctrl-Down takes you to the first word in the next paragraph, and Ctrl-Up takes you to the beginning of the previous paragraph.

Selecting Text

To select text with the mouse, put the I-beam at one end of the block you want to select. Then hold down the mouse button, move to the other end, and release the mouse button. In other words, simply drag the mouse across the text you want to select. You can select a word by double-clicking anywhere in it.

To select text with the keyboard, first put the insertion point at one end of the block you want to select. Then hold down the Shift key and *extend* the selection to the other end of the block. The same keystrokes you use to move the insertion point extend the selection.

For example, to select three characters within a word, put the insertion point before the first character, and then hold down the Shift key while pressing the Right arrow key three times. To select an entire word, position the insertion point to the left of the word, hold down the Shift key, and press Ctrl-Right. To select from the insertion point position to the end of the line, hold down the Shift key and press End—and so on.

Deleting Characters

To delete a few characters, put the insertion point where you want to make the deletion. Then use the Backspace or Del key to make your corrections. Backspace deletes characters to the left of the insertion point; Del deletes characters to the right of the insertion point.

Deleting Blocks of Text

To delete a block of text, first select the block. Then do one of the following:

- Press Del or Backspace.
- Choose the Edit menu's Delete or Clear command (if your application's menu has such a command).
- Choose the Edit menu's Cut command.

Pressing Del or Backspace deletes the selected text. Choosing Delete or Clear from the Edit menu does exactly the same thing. Choosing the Cut command, however, does something quite different. It deletes the text from your document but stores it in an area of memory called the Clipboard. After the selection has been stored on the Clipboard, you can *paste* it somewhere else—in either the same or another document (even a document created by a different application).

Undoing a Deletion

Many applications include an Undo command on their Edit menu. This command lets you change your mind about a deletion. The Undo command usually can reverse only your most recent edit, however. So, for example, if you delete a line of text, and then apply a formatting command to a different block of text, you won't be able to use the Undo command to reverse your deletion; at this point the Undo command is poised to undo the formatting change, not the deletion. (Some programs do have multiple-level Undo commands, however.)

Moving and Copying Text

For more information about using the Clipboard, see Chapter 10, "Exchanging Information: OLE and the Clipboard."

The Clipboard makes it easy to move or copy text from one place to another. Follow these steps:

1. Select the text you want to move or copy.
2. To move, choose the Edit menu's Cut command. To copy, choose the Edit menu's Copy command.
3. Move the insertion point to the place where you want to move or copy your text.
4. Choose the Edit menu's Paste command.

This simple procedure can be used to move or copy text from one place to another in the same document, from one document to another created by the same application, or from one application to an entirely different application.

Getting Help

Most Windows-based programs include a Help menu as the rightmost item on the menu bar. Any time you're unsure how a feature or command works, you can pull down the Help menu and find useful information. In many cases, the help window stays on top of all other windows by default, so you can continue reading the help text as you work. If a help window does not stay on top, or you find it inconvenient to keep it on top, you can switch back and forth between your program and the help text by pressing Alt-Tab. One Alt-Tab takes you to the help window; the next Alt-Tab returns you to your work, and so on.

Figure 2-12 on the next page shows three views of a typical Windows NT help document—in this case, the document that appears when you choose Help from the Start menu. The Help window has three tabs, labeled Contents, Index, and Find. These tabs offer three different views of the information in your program's help file.

Most of the time, you'll find what you need in either the Contents view or the Index view. These views of the help system work exactly like their analogues in a printed book. When you're looking for information about a broad topic, such as personalizing Windows, you'll want to check the Contents. When you need information about a specific topic, such as changing the clock from a 12-hour format to a 24-hour format, you'll save time by using the Index.

Like the table of contents in many books, the help system's Contents view uses an outline structure. The book icons indicate headings that can be expanded or collapsed. The question-mark icons indicate topics that can be displayed. To display a help topic, double-click it, or select it and click the Display button.

To locate an entry in the Index view, simply begin typing the first few characters of the entry in the text box at the top of the dialog box. When you see the topic you want in the list below, double-click it. Or select it and click the Display button.

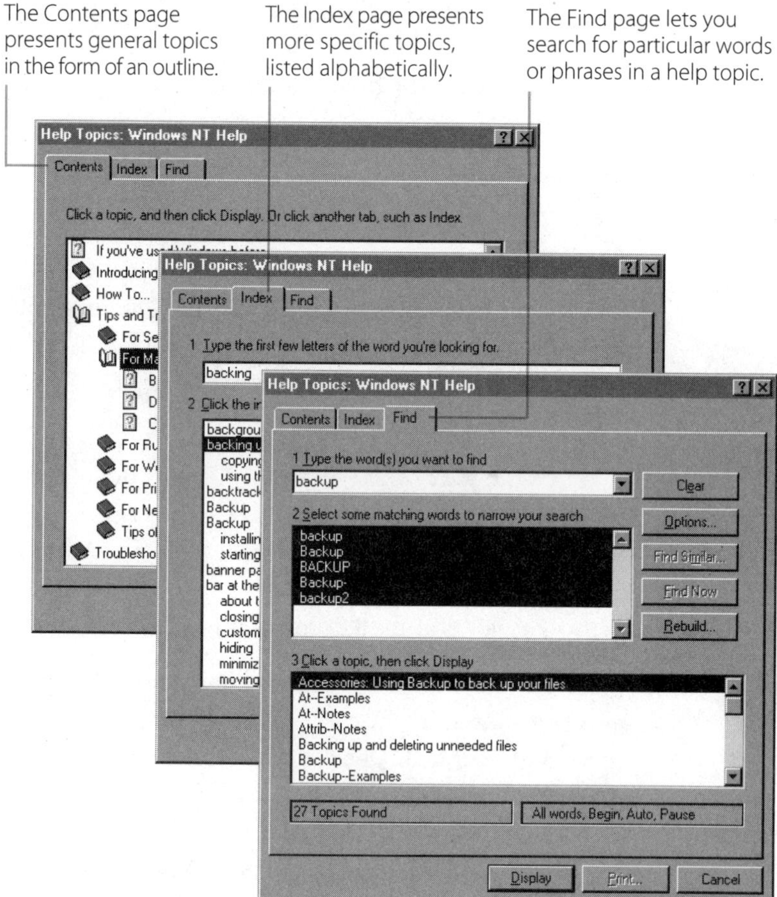

FIGURE 2-12.
The pages on a Help window provide three different ways to view Help topics.

TIP

Printing Help Topics

At any level of the Contents outline, you can print the help text in the selected topic by clicking the Print button. If you select an item marked with a book icon, your printout will include all pages under the selected heading. *For more information on printing Help topics, see "Copying and Printing Help Text," page 53.*

If you can't locate what you're looking for in either the Contents view or the Index view, try the Find page. Where the Index view lets you search through an alphabetical list of topics, Find lets you search by the actual contents of the help messages. If you want to read all the help messages that include the word *color*, for example, you can do that by specifying *color* in the Find dialog box.

Before you can use Find, you have to let the help system create a "word list" from all the messages in the current help file. When you click Find for the first time in a particular help file, the Find Setup wizard appears. (A wizard is a sequence of dialog boxes that help you complete a process, such as creating a word list for a help file.)

1 To create the word list, choose one of the three option buttons offered by the wizard.

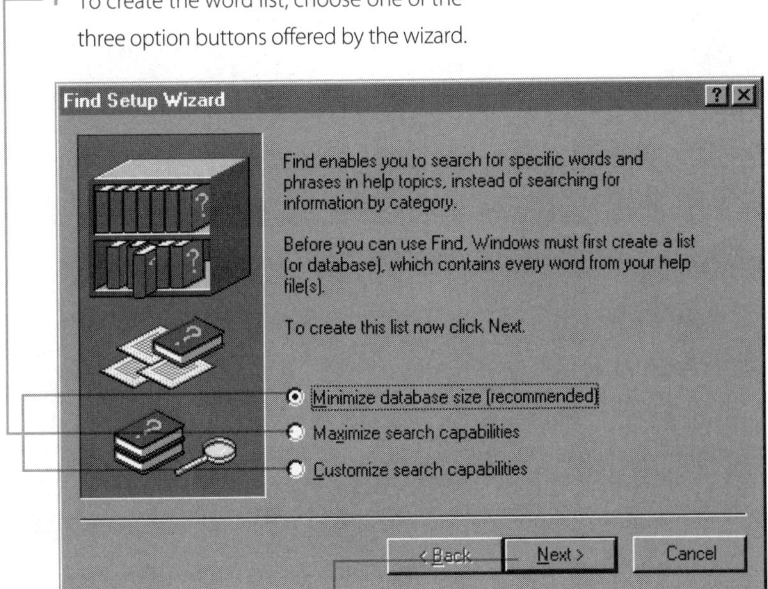

2 Click Next, and then follow the instructions in the subsequent dialog boxes.

Once you've created the word list for a particular help file, you'll be able to search for messages in that file that contain particular words or phrases. When you then click the Find tab, you'll see a dialog box similar to the one shown in Figure 2-12 on page 50. Type the word or phrase that interests you in the text box at the top of this dialog box. The help system responds by displaying the titles of messages containing your text. You can then display a message by selecting its name and clicking the Display button.

Help Text Hot Links

In the help text for some topics, you may find words or phrases underscored with dots. These are glossary terms; to see a definition, click the underscored item.

In many topics, you will find square gray buttons. When you position your mouse pointer over one of these buttons, the pointer changes shape—typically to a hand with an extended index finger. Click the button to display a related topic.

In some help topics, you may find text displayed in a contrasting color (typically green) and underscored with a solid line. Click the underscored text to display a related item.

Some help windows, such as the one shown below, include one or more shortcut buttons. A click on a shortcut button takes you directly to the area of Windows that is discussed in the help topic.

Retracing Your Path Through the Help System

The help system uses hypertext techniques to link related information. That means that you can often wander from topic to related topic just by clicking hot links in help messages. To help you find your way back to messages you've read earlier, the topic window includes a Back button that returns you to the last topic you read. Clicking Back repeatedly lets you retrace your path through the help file.

TIP

If instead of returning to a prior topic, you want to return to the index or table of contents, click the Help Topics button.

Copying and Printing Help Text

The help system provides ways to save or print its messages. You can copy a portion of any help topic, or the entire topic, to another application as follows.

SEE ALSO
For more information about copy and paste, see Chapter 10, "Exchanging Information: OLE and the Clipboard."

To copy a portion of a topic:

1. Drag your mouse across the text to select it.
2. Press Ctrl-C to copy the selected text to the Windows Clipboard.
3. Activate the application into which you want to paste the text.
4. Use the application's Paste command (or press Ctrl-V, the keyboard shortcut for Paste).

To copy all of a topic:

1. Click the Options button at the top of the topic window.
2. Choose Copy from the menu that appears.
3. Activate the application into which you want to paste the topic.
4. Use the application's Paste command (or press Ctrl-V).

For more information about printing, see Chapter 9, "Installing, Configuring, and Using Your Printers."

To print a topic, follow these steps:

1 Click the Options button.

2 Choose Print Topic from the menu that appears.

3 In the Print dialog box, make sure the printer you want to use appears on the Name line. (If it does not, choose the printer you want to use by clicking the drop-down arrow at the right side of the Name line.)

4 Click OK.

Annotating a Help Topic

You can add your own comments to any help message. Simply display the message, click the Options button, and choose Annotate from the menu that appears. An Annotate window will appear. Type your comments in the Annotate window, and then click the Save button. Windows displays a paper-clip icon beside the title of the help message. To redisplay your comments, click the paper clip.

Getting Help in Dialog Boxes

In theory, all Windows dialog boxes are entirely self-explanatory, so you'll never pause in puzzlement over what a particular button or check box does. To accommodate the divergence between theory and reality, many applications include invaluable Help buttons in their dialog boxes. If you're stumped, call for help.

In many dialog boxes, you will also see a question-mark icon right beside the close box. That's the "what's-this?" button. If you're not sure what some element of the dialog box means, click the what's-this button, and then click the element in question. An explanatory message will pop up. When you've finished reading, click inside the message box to make it go away.

Ending a Windows NT Session

CAUTION

Shutting down your computer makes all its shared resources unavailable to other users on your network. If any of your computer's resources are shared, it is usually better to "log off," rather than shut down your computer. *See "Logging Off Without Quitting," page 57.*

When it's time to quit, *never simply turn off your computer.* Instead, open the Start menu and choose Shut Down. You'll see the dialog box shown below. Choose "Shut down the computer." Windows closes any running applications, and in a moment or two, you will see another message, notifying you that it is safe to turn off your computer.

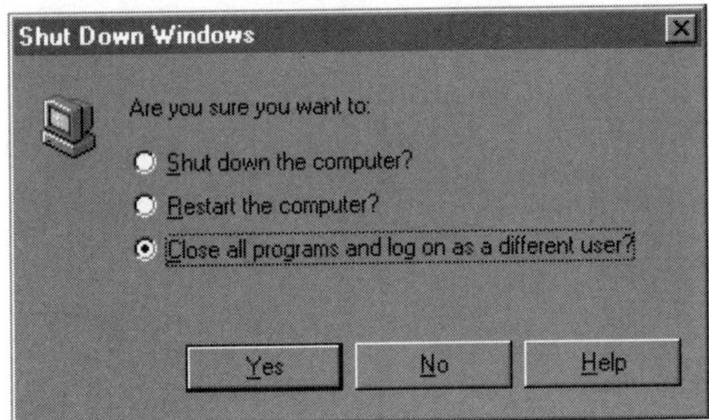

If for any reason your system is not ready to be shut down, you will be advised. For example, if you have unsaved work in an application, that program displays a prompt, giving you the opportunity to save before quitting. A program may also display a "can't quit" message if it objects to being closed for any other reason. This can happen, for example, if the program is in the middle of a communications session or if it's displaying a dialog box and waiting for you to respond.

TIP

Quick Shut Down

You can also shut the system down by pressing Ctrl-Alt-Del and clicking the Shutdown button. This sequence of steps is equivalent to choosing the Start menu's Shut Down command and selecting the first option in the Shut Down Windows dialog box.

If you respond promptly to a "can't quit" message, Windows stops trying to shut down your system. Then you can respond to your program or wait until it's no longer busy, and then use the Shut Down command again.

If you do not respond to the "can't quit" message within a certain period of time, however, Windows displays the message shown in Figure 2-13. Your choices are spelled out in the text of the message. The safest thing to do is click Cancel, return to your program, and then either respond to its needs or wait until it has finished whatever it's doing.

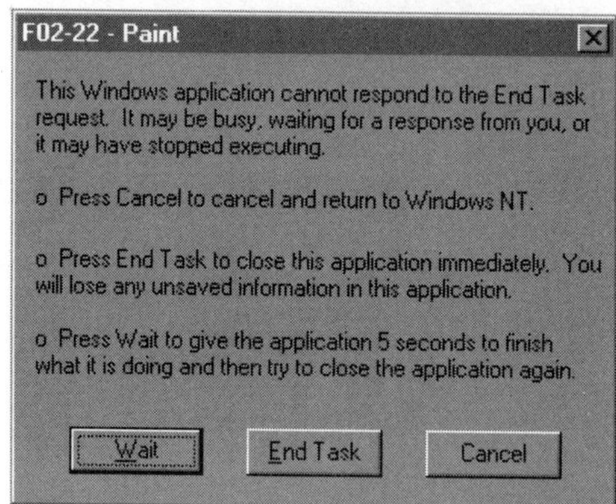

FIGURE 2-13. This message appears if you do not respond to a program's "can't quit" message or if a program is "hung."

The message shown in Figure 2-13 also appears if an application has stopped responding to the operating system. You can use the End Task button to terminate such a "hung" program. You should not use this button capriciously, however. If a program is not hung but is simply busy, terminating it against its will may have adverse consequences—such as the loss of any work you've created since the last time you used the program's Save command.

Shutting Down If You Have Shared Resources

If you have made any of your computer's local resources—folders or printers, for example—available to other users on your network, you may see an advisory message when you shut down. The message tells

SEE ALSO
For information about sharing resources, see "Sharing Folders with Other Users," page 281, and "To Share or Not to Share," page 229.

you how many users are connected to your shared resources and warns you that shutting down will disconnect those users. If you know that no one will be needing the shared resources until you return to work, it's fine to go ahead and shut down. If you're not sure, or if you want to quit without disconnecting your colleagues, you can log off without quitting Windows.

Logging Off Without Quitting

The third option in the Shut Down dialog box closes all running programs and logs you off your network, but does not shut down Windows. You may want to use this option at quitting time if someone else will be using your computer.

When you log off without quitting, any resources shared by your computer remain available to other users on the network. You might want to quit in this manner, for example, if others will be printing to a printer attached to your computer.

To log off, do either of the following:

- Click the Start menu button, and then choose Shut Down. In the dialog box that appears, click the third item—"Close all programs and log on as a different user." Then click the Yes button.
- Press Ctrl-Alt-Delete and then click the Logoff button.

  Windows NT asks you to confirm that you want to end your session. Then it closes each running application. If you have unsaved work in a running application, that application will give you the opportunity to save before it closes. If you happen to be running a program that cannot be safely terminated at that moment (for example, because it's busy writing to disk or waiting for you to respond to a dialog box), you'll see a different message, inviting you to log off later.

When you log off without quitting, Windows NT presents the same Welcome dialog box that you saw at the beginning of your current session, allowing you or another user to log back on.

CHAPTER 3

Running Programs and Opening Documents

One of the things you'll like about Windows NT is that there's usually more than one way to accomplish a given task. In many cases, there are a multitude of ways.

Take the act of running a program, for example. You can run most of the programs you need by making simple picks from the Start menu. But if you prefer using an MS-DOS–style command line, you can certainly do that as well.

One of the most useful innovations of Windows NT 4 is the *shortcut*. A shortcut is a pointer to a program, to a document, or to some other object. By creating shortcuts for programs or documents and placing them on the desktop, you can make everything you need accessible with a simple double-click.

SEE ALSO
For information about installing programs, see "Installing Applications," page 699.

In short, when it comes to running programs and opening documents, Windows NT gives you choices. You can find the working style that best suits you.

Running Programs from the Start Menu

Figure 3-1 shows the Start menu for a typical user's system. The top part of the menu contains the items that this user works with every day—a network server (Document on Zion), a local folder (Favorites), a program (Microsoft Word), and a Notepad document (Things to Do TODAY!). This area of your Start menu might include more or fewer items—or perhaps none at all. To run a program whose name appears in the top part of the Start menu, click the Start button or press Ctrl-Esc to open the Start menu. Then move the mouse until the desired program's name is highlighted, and then click.

The Windows NT Setup program does not ordinarily put anything in the top part of the Start menu. That's because this part of the menu is intended to give you access to the items you need most often, and the Setup program has no way of knowing what those items are. If your system was set up by an administrator, that person may have configured the top part of the Start menu for you. In any case, if you don't find the items you need here, you can easily add them, and you can just as easily get rid of items you don't need. (*See "Customizing the Start Menu," page 83.*)

To run a program that's not listed at the top of your Start menu, move the mouse pointer to the item labeled Programs. A submenu will appear, as shown in Figure 3-2.

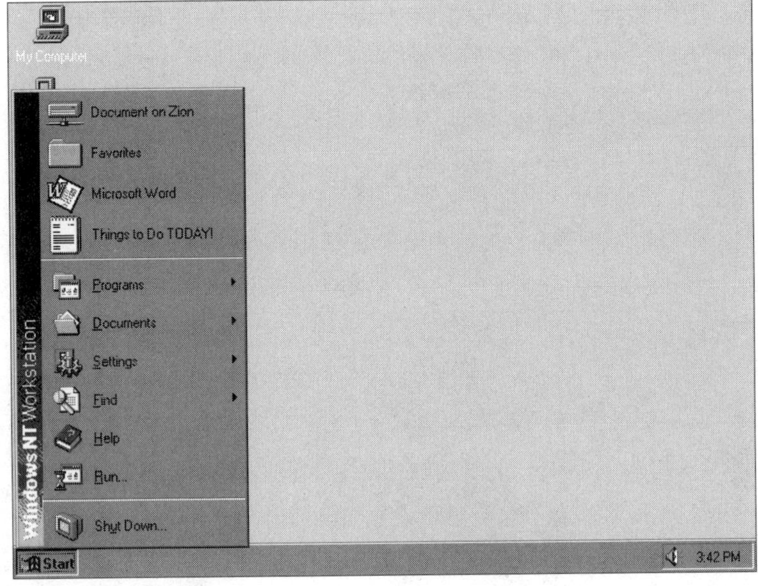

FIGURE 3-1.
The top part of the Start menu can be used for your most frequently needed programs, folders, and documents.

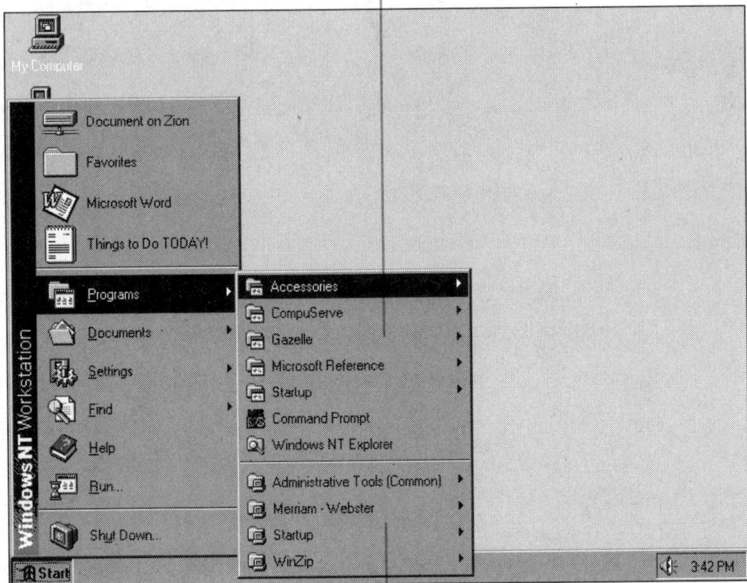

FIGURE 3-2.
The Programs submenu may include more program names, grouped by category.

For more information about personal and common entries on the Programs submenu, see "Personal and Common Groups," page 700.

Along with a few program names, your Programs submenu is likely to include several folders, each for a category of programs. The submenu in Figure 3-2, for example, includes a folder for accessories, folders for various applications, and a folder for startup programs (programs that run automatically at the beginning of each Windows session). Each of these folders opens another submenu, as Figure 3-3 shows. As you move through this tree of submenus, you eventually will come to the name of the program you want to run. When you do, give your mouse a click and your program will appear.

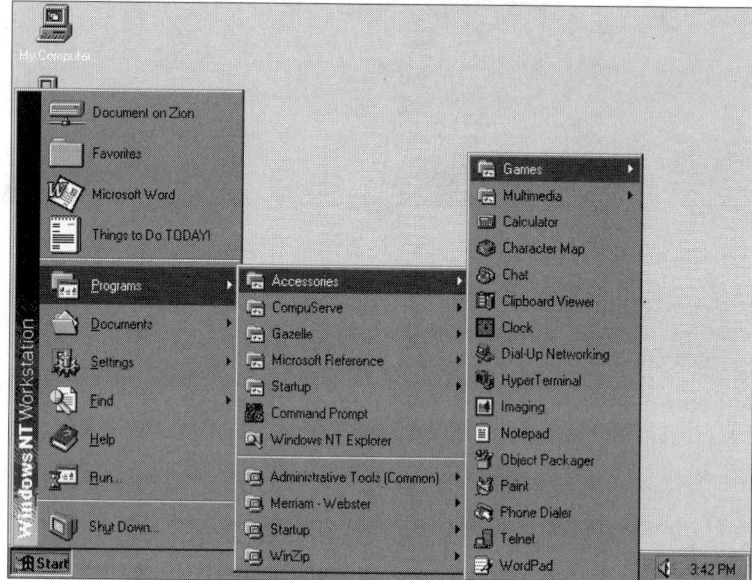

FIGURE 3-3.

A tree of submenus leads eventually to the program you want to run.

Like the top of the Start menu, the Programs submenu is customizable. If the bill of fare doesn't suit you, you can change it. *(See "Customizing the Start Menu," page 83.)*

Running MS-DOS–Based Programs

You can run MS-DOS–based programs from the Start menu, just as you can run Windows-based programs. Alternatively, if the MS-DOS–based program you want to run doesn't appear on any part of the Start menu, try running the Command Prompt item. This opens a command prompt window and presents you with a prompt similar to the familiar MS-DOS command prompt. From this prompt, you can type the name of the program you want to run (with the path if needed).

Yet another way to run an MS-DOS–based program is by using the Start menu's Run command. *(See "Running Programs and Opening Documents with the Run Command," page 71.)* Type *cmd* on the Run line to open a command prompt window, and then type your program's name at the prompt that appears.

For more information about running MS-DOS–based programs, see Chapter 17, "Using Programs for Other Operating Systems."

Opening Recently Used Documents from the Start Menu

As you work with programs and create documents, Windows keeps track of your 15 most recently used documents and makes those files available on the Documents submenu of the Start menu. You can reopen a recently used document, complete with its parent application, by clicking Start, selecting Documents, and choosing the name of the document you want to work with.

For example, suppose your Documents submenu includes an item called Letter of Introduction, and that this item is the name of a file created in Microsoft Word. When you choose Letter of Introduction on the Documents submenu, Windows NT runs Word, and Word opens your letter.

 TIP

Windows 3.x–Based Applications and the Documents Menu

Documents saved from applications written for earlier versions of Windows do not automatically appear on the Documents menu. For example, if the version of your word processor dates from the days of Windows 3.x, the files you save from that word processor will not automatically show up on the Documents menu. You can make them appear there, however. Any document that you open by double-clicking its entry in a folder or Windows NT Explorer window (or a shortcut to that entry) will appear on the Documents menu, regardless of the vintage of its parent application. *For details, see "Running Programs and Opening Documents from Folders," below.*

Once your Documents submenu contains 15 document names, newly arriving items replace least-recently-used items. If you find that most of the items on the menu are old, you might want to clear the entire menu so that you can more easily find the new arrivals. To clear the Documents submenu, choose Settings from the Start menu. From the Settings submenu, choose Taskbar. In the Taskbar Properties dialog box, click the Start Menu Programs tab. Then click the button labeled Clear.

Running Programs and Opening Documents from Folders

Another way to run a program or open a document is to double-click its icon or name in a folder or Windows NT Explorer window. The window on the next page, for example, displays the contents of a folder named Excel.

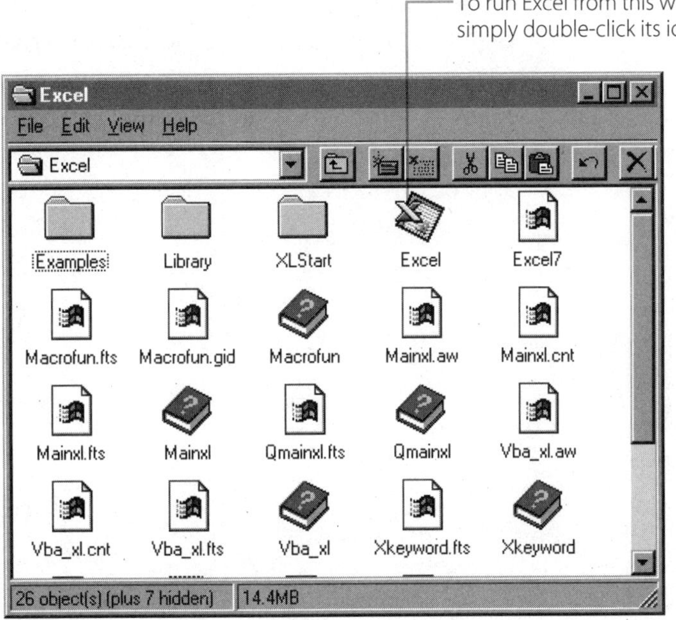

SEE ALSO
For more information about folders and folder windows, see "Working with Folders," page 28, and Chapter 5, "Working with Folders."

Alternatively, you can right-click the program's icon and choose the Open command. Or, if you prefer working with the keyboard, you can use the arrow keys to select the Excel icon, and then press Enter.

What to Do When Windows Can't Open Your Documents

Windows maintains a store of information about your system, called the *registry*. Along with many other details, the registry includes a list of applications installed on your computer, as well as information about the types of documents each application can create. It is this information that enables Windows to run the appropriate application when you select a document on the Documents submenu or double-click a document icon in a folder.

How does Windows tell one document type from another? By its filename extension. When you install an application, the application tells the registry the default extensions it uses for its documents. For example, Microsoft Excel "reserves" the extension .XLS for its workbook files, .XLA for add-in files, .XLC for chart documents created in versions of Excel prior to 5.0, and so on. (By default, folder windows and Windows NT Explorer windows do not display the extensions of document filenames that are associated with registered applications. But Windows "sees" the extensions even if it doesn't show them to you.)

Chances are, most of the documents you use are associated with some application. But now and then you might try to open a document whose application "parent" is unknown to Windows. For example, Windows NT by default recognizes many kinds of plain text files—including files with extensions .TXT, .INI, and .LOG—and opens these files with Notepad. You might have some text files with unrecognized extensions, however. If you double-click one of these, you will see the Open With dialog box, shown in Figure 3-4.

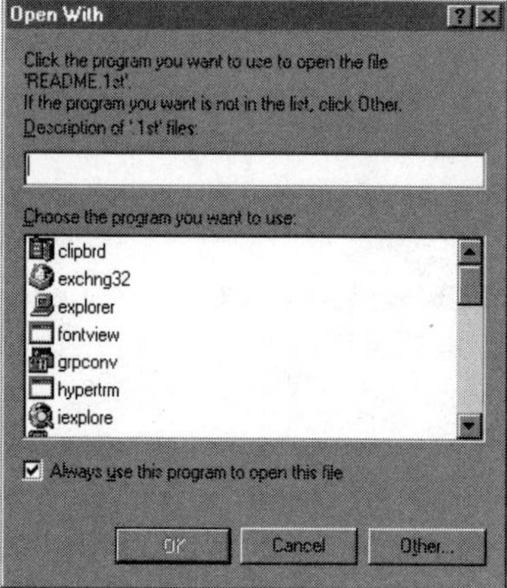

FIGURE 3-4.
If you try to open an unregistered document, Windows presents the Open With dialog box.

The Open With dialog box lets you create either a one-time or a permanent association between a document type and a program. To create a one-time association, deselect the check box at the bottom of this dialog, and then choose a program from the list in the center. To create a permanent association, enter any description you want for the document type on the line at the top, and then select the program you want from the list in the middle of the dialog box. (The description line does not appear if the document you're trying to open has no filename extension.) Note that you need to fill out the Description line only if you're making a permanent association.

TIP

The File Types List

To see a list of all document types known to the registry, and the application with which each is associated, choose the Options command on the menu bar of any folder or Windows NT Explorer window. Then click the File Types tab. *For more information about file types, see "Working with the File Types List," page 155.*

If the application list doesn't include the program you want, click the Other button. That will take you to the dialog box shown in Figure 3-5.

FIGURE 3-5.
Clicking the Other button displays the contents of the current folder. If the program you need is not shown here, you can navigate to it.

To see your folders and filenames in a different display style, right-click here and choose View.

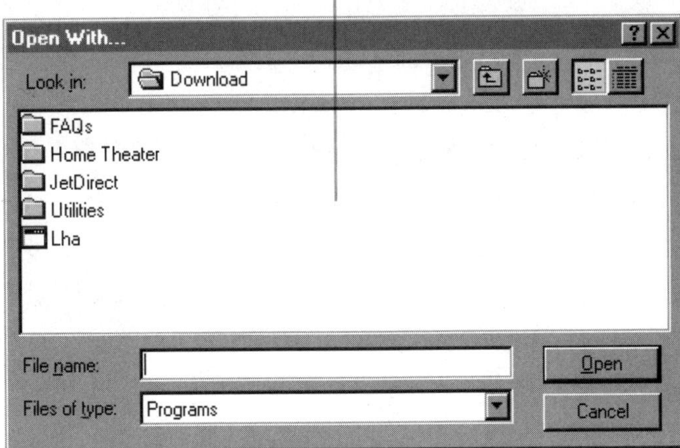

For example, the Open With dialog box in Figure 3-5 on the previous page shows that the current folder, Download, contains one program file (Lha) and four additional folders. If Lha is the program you want, you can double-click it, or click it once and then click the Open button. This will return you to the dialog box shown in Figure 3-4 on page 66, with Lha added to the program list.

TIP

Opening a File in a Different Application

You can associate a document type with only one application. If you sometimes want to open a particular kind of document with one application and sometimes with another, try using the Send To command. For example, if you usually want to open .DBF files in dBASE for Windows, but occasionally you like to import them into Excel, create a Send To shortcut for Excel. *For details, see "Customizing the Send To Menu," page 145.*

Browsing Through Folders to Find the Program You Want

The dialog box shown in Figure 3-5 on the previous page shows only the contents of the current folder. To make this window display a different folder, use the same navigation techniques that you would use in a normal folder window. *(For information about navigating in folder windows, see "Moving from Folder to Folder," page 120.)*

Running Programs and Opening Documents with the Find Command

Double-clicking an icon in a folder window is a fine way to run a program that doesn't happen to be on your Start menu—provided the folder is at hand or easy to get to. If that folder is more than a few mouse-clicks away, however, a quicker solution may be to use the Start menu's Find command. The Find command is a powerful tool for locating just about anything on your own computer or on a network server.

SEE ALSO
For more information about the Find command, see Chapter 7, "Using the Find Command."

The Find command displays its results in a window that behaves much like any folder window. That means you can run a program or open a document by simply double-clicking it within a Find window. (Alternatively, you can right-click an item and choose the Open command, or select the item with the keyboard and then press Enter.)

Inspecting Documents and Programs with Quick View

With thousands of files on your hard disk, it's not always easy to know which is the document or program you need. Wouldn't it be handy to be able to peek at a document before going to the trouble of opening it and its parent application? With Quick View, you can do just that.

To use Quick View, simply right-click a document, program, or shortcut anywhere you see it—in a folder window, in a Windows NT Explorer window, on your desktop, or in a Find window. If the item you've selected is viewable, the Quick View command appears near the top of the context menu that appears. Table 3-1 on the next page shows some of the file types that can be inspected with Quick View. In addition to these file types, others on your system may also be viewable. Figure 3-6 shows a Quick View window for a text document.

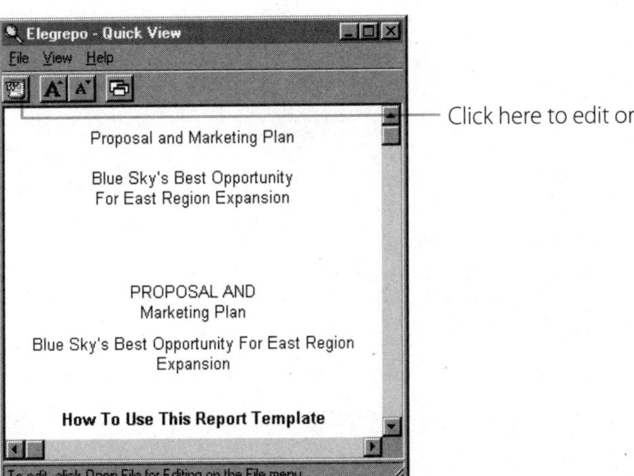

FIGURE 3-6.
Quick View displays a document without opening the document's application.

TABLE 3-1. File Types Supported by Quick View

File Type	Extension
Bitmap image	.BMP, .DIB, .RLE
CompuServe GIF image	.GIF
Configuration settings	.INI
CorelDRAW drawing	.CDR
Encapsulated PostScript file	.EPS
Lotus 1-2-3 spreadsheet or chart	.WKS, .WK1
Micrografx Draw drawing	.DRW
Microsoft Excel worksheet or chart	.XLS, .XLC
Microsoft PowerPoint presentation	.PPT
Microsoft Word document	.DOC
Microsoft Works database document	.WDB
Microsoft Works spreadsheet document	.WKS
Microsoft Works word processing document	.WPS
Multiplan spreadsheet	.MOD
Program file	.DLL, .EXE
Quattro Pro spreadsheet	.WQ1, .WQ2
Rich Text Format document	.RTF
Setup information	.INF
Text file	.TXT, .ASC
Tiff graphics image	.TIF
Windows metafile	.WMF
WordPerfect document	.DOC, .WPD
Write document	.WRI

Quick View gives you a read-only peek at your document. If you want to edit or print the document, you'll need to open it in its parent application. You can do that from within Quick View, by choosing Open File For Editing from the File menu or by clicking the first icon on the toolbar. Other menu and toolbar options let you do such things as change the font used to display your document (but not the fonts used by the document in its parent-application setting) and "zoom out" for a full-page view of your document.

TIP

Viewing Font Files
Font files cannot be inspected with Quick View. But you can display a sample of any TrueType font simply by double-clicking its icon. *For more information about inspecting fonts, see "Viewing and Printing Font Samples," page 195.*

Running Programs and Opening Documents with the Run Command

The Start menu includes a handy Run command that you can use to launch programs and open documents. Figure 3-7 illustrates the Run command.

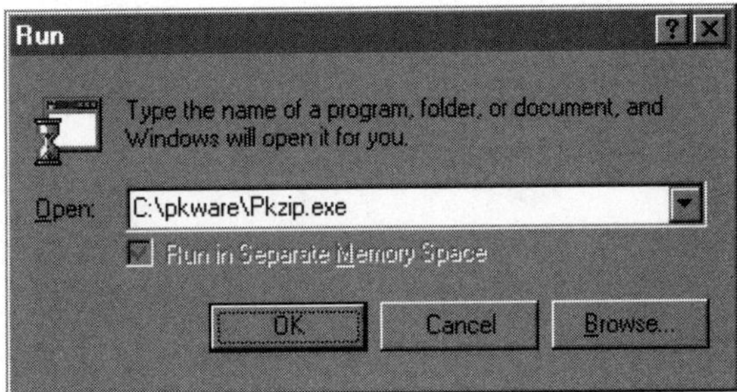

FIGURE 3-7.
The Start menu's Run command is handy for running items that aren't on your Programs menu.

You can use the Run command to launch a program, open a document, or open a folder. The Run command is particularly handy in the following situations:

- When you want to rerun or reopen a recently used program or document
- When the program you want to run needs a command-line parameter

As Figure 3-7 on the previous page shows, the Open line in the Run dialog box presents, as a default, whatever document or program name you last specified. Rerunning that item, therefore, is as simple as choosing Run on the Start menu and clicking OK. Moreover, the Open line is actually a drop-down list. Clicking the arrow at the right side of the line reveals a scrollable list of your most recently used Run commands. Thus, if you use this command regularly for a particular group of programs or documents, you will nearly always be able to pick any of those items from the list.

Windows-based programs seldom need command-line parameters, but MS-DOS–based programs sometimes do. One way to run an MS-DOS–based program that needs a parameter is to open a command prompt window. That technique takes you to an MS-DOS–like command prompt, where you can type the name of your program and any required parameters. *(For more information, see Chapter 17, "Using Programs for Other Operating Systems," and Chapter 18, "Using the Command Prompt.")* Another way you can do this is by using the Start menu's Run command.

TIP

Folders Can Run Too

You can also use the Run command to open folder windows without actually running any programs. To open a window for the folder C:\Writing\PCMag, for example, simply type that string of characters on the Run command line.

If you're not sure what to put on the command line, enter the name of the folder you're interested in, and then click the Browse button. For example, if you want to run an installation program on drive B, but you aren't sure about the name of that program, you can type *b:* on the Run line, and then click Browse. You will see a dialog box similar to the one shown in Figure 3-5 on page 67. In that dialog box, you can find or navigate to the program or document you want to use.

Using Shortcuts to Run Programs and Open Documents

Yet another way to run programs and open documents is to create shortcuts for them. A shortcut is a tiny file that's linked to a program, document, or folder. The file is represented by an icon that includes a black arrow in its lower left corner, like this:

The item to which a shortcut is linked can be anywhere—on a local hard disk or CD-ROM, on a floppy disk, or on a network server. The item to which the shortcut is linked can even *be* a local hard disk or CD-ROM drive, a floppy drive, or a network server.

TIP

Use Shortcuts for Folder Navigation

Sometimes it can be handy to store a shortcut for a folder inside another folder. For example, suppose your spreadsheet's default data directory is C:\Office97\Excel\Worksheets, but you occasionally need to open files stored in C:\Personal. Create a shortcut to C:\Personal and store that shortcut in your C:\Office97\Excel\Worksheets folder. Your shortcut to Personal will appear as a normal folder inside your Worksheets folder, and you'll save yourself a lot of folder-traversing when you need a personal worksheet. To simplify your return to the Worksheets folder, you can also create a shortcut for that folder and put it in C:\Personal.

Like any other file, a shortcut can be stored in any folder, including your desktop. If you store shortcuts for programs and documents you use often on your desktop, you can get to them easily at any time. For example, if you use a half dozen or so programs nearly every day, why not simply add shortcuts for them to your desktop? Whenever you want to run one of those programs, you can simply double-click the appropriate shortcut icon.

A shortcut is a *pointer* to an object, not the object itself. That means that you can create and delete shortcuts without in any way affecting the underlying object. It also means that you can create a shortcut to a major application without duplicating the large file that actually runs that program. Shortcuts themselves use less than 2 KB of disk storage, so a proliferation of shortcuts won't use up much of your hard disk.

If you've used Windows 3.x or an earlier version of Windows NT, you will probably recognize that a shortcut behaves like a program item in Program Manager. You can even assign a shortcut key to a shortcut, so that you can "run" the shortcut without using your mouse. *(See "Assigning a Shortcut Key to a Shortcut," page 78.)* There is one important difference between shortcuts and Program Manager program items, however: a shortcut is more versatile. You can assign it to folders, as well as to programs and documents.

Figure 3-8 shows a desktop with eight shortcuts, in addition to the standard desktop objects (My Computer, Network Neighborhood, and Recycle Bin). One shortcut on the left side points to a printer. On the right side, one points to a document (Accounts Receivable), two point to folders (Fonts and Writing), and the remaining four point to applications. In this example, the Writing folder actually resides on a network server; Windows makes no visual distinction between local and remote resources.

FIGURE 3-8.
You can identify shortcuts by the little arrow in their icon.

Creating a Shortcut

There are two easy ways to create a shortcut: with drag and drop and with the Create Shortcut wizard.

Creating a Shortcut with Drag and Drop

If the item for which you want to create a shortcut is visible in a folder or a Windows NT Explorer window, right-drag that item to wherever you want the shortcut to appear. Then, from the context menu that appears, choose Create Shortcut(s) Here.

For example, suppose you want to create a shortcut for the WordPad accessory and put that shortcut on your desktop. Start by opening the folder containing WordPad. After locating the WordPad icon, drag it with the right mouse button, and release the button when the mouse pointer is positioned somewhere on the desktop. When you release the button, Windows displays a context menu, from which you choose Create Shortcut(s) Here.

Alternatively, you can simply right-click an object and choose Create Shortcut from its context menu. Windows creates your shortcut in the same folder in which the underlying object is stored. You can then drag the new shortcut to another location.

Creating Shortcuts with the Find Command
You can use the Find command to locate the item for which you want a shortcut. From the Find window, you can then right-drag the item to create the shortcut.

Using the Create Shortcut Wizard

To use the Create Shortcut wizard, start by right-clicking in the folder where you want your shortcut to appear. (If you want the shortcut to be on your desktop, right-click the desktop.) From the context menu, choose New. Then choose Shortcut. The Create Shortcut wizard appears, as shown in Figure 3-9.

If you know the command line required to run your program or open your document, simply type it and click the Next button. (The command line is whatever you would type to run your program or open your document if you were using the Run command, described earlier in this chapter.) If you don't know the command line, or if Windows responds with an error message when you click Next, click the Browse button. This summons a dialog box similar to the one shown in Figure 3-5 on page 67. (The only difference is that the dialog box's title bar says "Browse," instead of "Open With.") Use this dialog box to locate the item for which you want to create a shortcut. Then click the Open button.

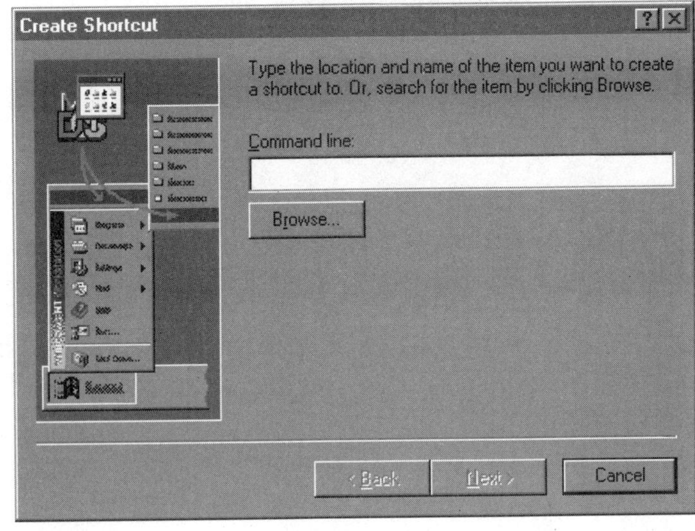

FIGURE 3-9.
The Create Shortcut wizard makes it easy to populate your desktop—or any other folder—with shortcuts.

After you click the Open button, the wizard returns you to its initial dialog box (shown in Figure 3-9), with the command line filled in. Click Next, type a name for your shortcut, click Finish, and your shortcut will appear.

TIP

Using Shortcuts as Targets for Drag and Drop

Some shortcuts can be used as targets for drag and drop. For example, if you put a shortcut for a printer on your desktop, you can print files by dragging them from folder windows to the printer shortcut. If you create a shortcut for a floppy disk drive or the top-level folder on a hard disk, you can copy files by dragging them from folder windows to the shortcut. *For more information about copying files, see "Moving or Copying Folders, Files, and Shortcuts," page ???[Ch5]. For more information about printing using drag and drop, see "How Do I Print Thee? (Let Me Count the Ways)," page 210.*

Renaming a Shortcut

When you create a shortcut, Windows gives it a default name based on the underlying object. You're not obliged to live with that name, however. To rename the shortcut, follow these steps:

1. Right-click the shortcut.
2. From the context menu, choose Rename.
3. Type the name you want to use.

 TIP

> You can also rename any object by selecting it, pressing F2, and typing the new name.

Assigning a Shortcut Key to a Shortcut

A shortcut key is a keystroke combination that runs a shortcut—that is, it runs the program or opens the dialog to which the shortcut is linked. For example, you might assign Ctrl-Alt-P as a shortcut key for a shortcut linked to Paint. Then, instead of double-clicking your Paint shortcut to start a copy of Paint, you can simply press Ctrl-Alt-P.

To assign a shortcut key to a shortcut, follow these steps:

1. Right-click the shortcut and choose Properties from the context menu, or hold down the Alt key and double-click the shortcut.
2. In the Properties dialog box, click the Shortcut tab. (If the shortcut is for an MS-DOS–based program, click the Program tab instead.)

   A dialog box similar to the one shown in Figure 3-10 appears.
3. On the Shortcut Key line, type the keystroke combination you want to use.

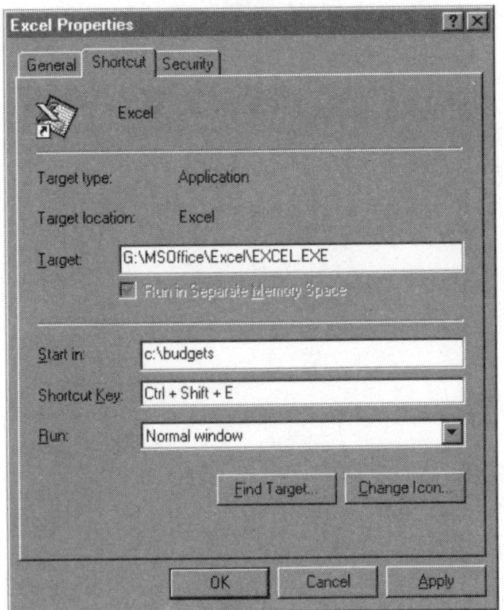

FIGURE 3-10.
With this dialog box, you can set a variety of properties for a shortcut, including its shortcut key and the type of window the shortcut should open.

> **NOTE**
>
> If you type a keystroke combination in the Shortcut Key box, and you've already assigned that combination to another shortcut, Windows runs the other shortcut! Don't be alarmed; simply return to the shortcut properties dialog box, and choose a different combination.

Using Shortcut Properties to Set a Program's Data Folder

On the Start In line of the dialog box shown in Figure 3-10, you can specify a program's default data folder. This is the folder to which the program will save new document files, unless you tell it to do otherwise. So, for example, if you want Excel to use C:\Budgets as its default data folder, do as follows:

1. Right-click the shortcut.
2. From the context menu, choose Properties.

3 Click the dialog box tab labeled Shortcut.

4 On the Start In line, type *c:\budgets*. (If you leave the Start In line blank, your default data folder will normally be the one in which your program's executable files are stored.)

NOTE

Some programs use their own menu commands to set a default data folder, overriding anything you specify on the Start In line.

TIP

Make Folder-Specific Shortcuts
If you use two or more data folders regularly with the same program, you might want to create two or more shortcuts—one for each data folder. To create a copy of a shortcut, right-click the first shortcut and choose Create Shortcut. The new shortcut will be linked, not to the first shortcut, but to the underlying object. Thus you can set properties for each shortcut independently. By repeating this process you can create as many shortcuts as you need for the same underlying object.

Specifying the Type of Window a Shortcut Opens

The Run line of the dialog box shown in Figure 3-10 on the previous page lets you indicate what kind of window you want your shortcut to open—a maximized window, a "normal" window (one that's open but not maximized), or a minimized window. If you choose minimized, your shortcut's underlying object opens as a taskbar button. To specify a window type, follow these steps:

1 Right-click the shortcut.

2 From the context menu, choose Properties.

3 Click the dialog box tab labeled Shortcut.

4 Click the drop-down arrow on the Run line. From the list that appears, select the window type you want.

Changing a Shortcut's Icon

Normally a shortcut uses the same icon as its underlying object, except that the shortcut icon includes a pointer arrow to help you recognize it as a shortcut. To choose a different icon for a shortcut, follow these steps:

1. Right-click the shortcut.
2. From the context menu, choose Properties.
3. Click the dialog box tab labeled Shortcut.
4. Click the Change Icon button. The dialog box that appears presents all the icons available in the file to which the shortcut points. With the help of the horizontal scroll bar, you can choose a different icon for your shortcut.

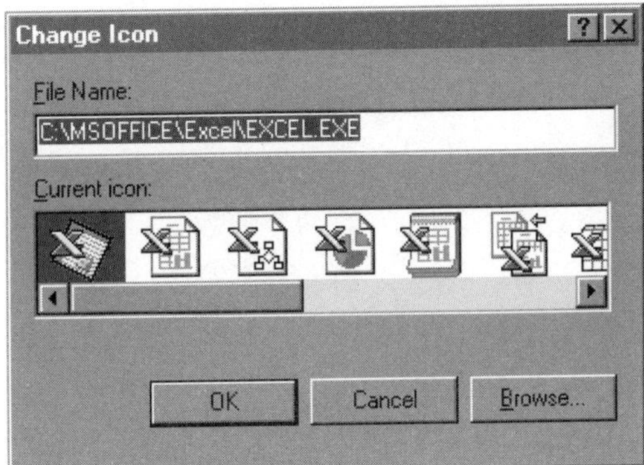

You are by no means limited to using one of the icons provided by the shortcut's underlying object. You can use any icon from any file. To search for other icons, type a different filename in the File Name text box, or click the Browse button in the Change Icon dialog box and select a different file.

TIP

With some applications, document shortcuts initially use the same icon as the application with which the document is associated. You can choose a different icon to help you recognize that the shortcut is for a document.

Repositioning Shortcuts on the Desktop

You can change the positions of your desktop shortcuts at any time. Simply drag them. You can also get Windows to help you keep your shortcuts neatly aligned. Follow these steps:

1 Use your mouse to bring your shortcut icons into approximate alignment.

2 Right-click the desktop.

3 From the context menu that appears, choose Line Up Icons.

If you want all your desktop shortcuts organized in columns starting at the left side of the desktop, right-click the desktop, choose Arrange Icons, and then choose Auto Arrange. With Auto Arrange turned on, your icons always stay neatly aligned, even if you try to drag them out of place.

Whether you choose Line Up Icons or Auto Arrange to tidy up your desktop, Windows aligns the icons to an invisible grid that evenly spaces the icons. If you want the icons to be closer together or farther apart, you can adjust the grid spacing. To do so, follow these steps:

1 Right-click the desktop.

2 From the context menu, choose Properties.

3 In the Display Properties dialog box, click the Appearance tab.

4 Open the Item drop-down list and select Icon Spacing (Horizontal) or Icon Spacing (Vertical).

5 Adjust the setting in the Size box. (A larger number increases the space between icons.)

NOTE

In addition to controlling the desktop icons, changing the icon spacing affects the spacing of icons in folders when you use Large Icon view.

Deleting a Shortcut

To remove a shortcut, simply select it and press the Del key. Or right-click it and choose Delete from the context menu. Either way, Windows asks you to confirm your intention—thereby protecting you from an accidental deletion. Note that deleting a shortcut does not delete the program or document that the shortcut points to; doing so deletes only the shortcut itself.

Customizing the Start Menu

Two sections of the Start menu—the top of the menu and the Programs submenu—are completely customizable. You can put whatever folders, programs, or documents you want in either of these places, or you can remove anything that's already there.

Adding Items to the Start Menu

Adding items to the Start menu is a matter of creating shortcuts and putting them in the proper folders. Fortunately, Windows makes this all very easy to do.

To add items to either the top of the Start Menu or the Programs submenu, follow these steps:

1. Right-click an unoccupied area of the taskbar.
2. Choose Properties from the context menu.
3. Click the Start Menu Programs tab in the dialog box that appears.
4. Click the Add button.

This sequence takes you to the Create Shortcut wizard, as shown in Figure 3-9 on page 77. Type the command line for the item you want to add to the menu, or click the Browse button to locate the item. When you have the command line filled out, click Next. You'll see a dialog box similar to the one shown in Figure 3-11 on the next page.

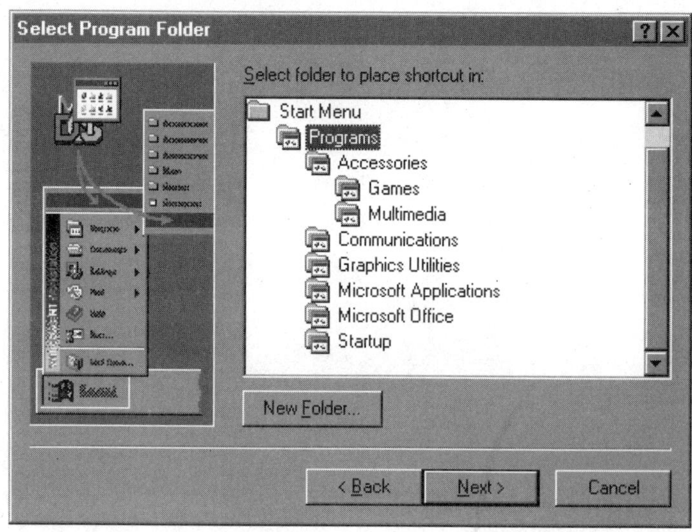

FIGURE 3-11. In this dialog box, you tell the wizard where you want your new menu item to appear.

Here the wizard presents an outline of the Programs section of your Start menu. If you want your new menu item to appear at the top of the Start menu (rather than as part of the Programs submenu), simply select Start Menu (the first folder in the outline diagram) and click Next. If you want your new item to appear somewhere within the Programs submenu, first select the heading under which you want it to appear, and then click Next.

For example, suppose you're adding a menu item for the program Microsoft Money, and you want that item to appear within the Microsoft Applications section of the Programs submenu. In the dialog box shown in Figure 3-11, you would select Microsoft Applications, and then click the Next button.

Startup Shortcuts

To make a program or document open automatically at the beginning of every Windows session, create a Start menu item for it and put that item in the Startup section of the Programs submenu.

After clicking Next, you'll be asked to name the menu item. If the document, folder, or program you're adding to the menu has a long name, you might want to choose a shortened version of that name for the menu. In any case, either accept the name proposed by the wizard or modify it, and then click the Finish button to install your new menu item.

TIP

Drag Shortcuts to the Start Menu

An alternative way to add an item to the top of the Start menu is to drag it and drop it on the Start button. For example, suppose you have a shortcut on your desktop for a document you use every day. Having this item on the top section of your Start menu might make it easier to open the document while you're working in a maximized application. To create the Start menu item, simply drag the desktop shortcut and drop it onto the Start button. Now you'll have easy access to your document from two places, the desktop *and* the Start menu.

What if you want to create a new heading on the Programs submenu and add a program, document, or folder under that heading? In that case, start by creating the shortcut for your program, document, or folder, following the procedures just described. Then, when the wizard asks where you want the new item to appear (the step shown in Figure 3-11), click the New Folder button. (If you want your new folder to be a subfolder of an existing folder, select that folder before you click New Folder.) A default-named folder entry will appear on the outline. Type the name you want to use for your menu heading, and then click Finish. Windows will create the new menu heading and put your new menu item under that heading.

Removing Items from the Start Menu

To remove an item from the Start menu, follow these steps:

1. Right-click an unoccupied area of the taskbar.
2. Choose Properties from the context menu.

3 Click the Start Menu Programs tab in the dialog box that appears.

4 Click the Remove button.

These steps summon the Remove Shortcuts/Folders dialog box, similar to the one shown in Figure 3-12.

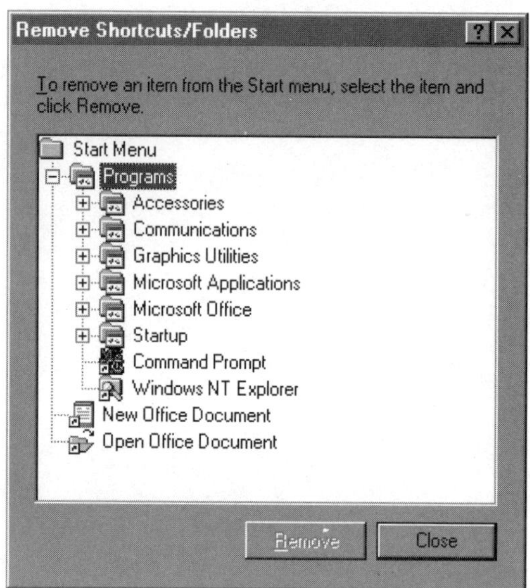

FIGURE 3-12.
You can remove items from the Start menu by navigating to them in this outline.

Navigate to the item you want to remove, and then click the Remove button. Note that items on the top of your Start menu appear at the bottom of this outline diagram, after all the items on all the branches of the Programs submenu. You might need to use the scroll bar to find those items.

Notice the plus signs in the outline shown in Figure 3-12. These indicate headings that can be expanded—that is, branches of the Programs submenu that contain further menu items or branches. To open a heading and reveal its menu items, simply click the plus sign. To remove an entire limb of the Programs submenu—that is, a heading plus all menu items within that heading, select the heading name and click Remove. The wizard prompts you to confirm your intentions.

The Start menu is designed to be extremely malleable. With these few simple mouse actions, you can keep the menu trim and efficient, so that it always contains the items you currently need—and none of the ones you don't.

CHAPTER 4

Personalizing Your Workspace

When you first install Windows NT, the Setup program provides a standard configuration for your desktop, your keyboard, and your mouse. You get a fine color arrangement, a "normal" screen resolution, appropriately sized buttons and icons, a default layout of desktop objects, and a keyboard and mouse that behave as Windows' designers think the typical user wants them to behave.

SEE ALSO

For information about more customizing options, see Chapter 14, "Customizing Windows NT."

But because one size does not fit all, Windows provides you with a great range of choices regarding the appearance and behavior of your working environment. You can control the amount of information that fits on your screen (within the limits of your display hardware), change the colors used by the various elements of the Windows user interface, change the sizes of window borders and title bars, reposition the taskbar, and decide whether or not the taskbar should remain visible while you work in maximized applications. You can add a textured background to your desktop or drape the desktop with a graphic image, increase or decrease the size of the characters Windows uses for menus and messages, or change the size of all fonts used on your system. You can speed up or slow down the movement of your mouse pointer and adjust the repeat speed of your keyboard.

Customizing the Taskbar

The default location for the taskbar is along the bottom edge of your desktop. If you're accustomed to Windows or Windows NT 3.x, which put icons for minimized applications at the bottom of the screen, you may be quite at home with this arrangement. But you're not obliged to accept it. To move the taskbar to another screen edge, simply put your mouse pointer on an unoccupied part of the taskbar, and then drag the taskbar to its new location.

Making More Room on the Taskbar

By default, the taskbar shows one row of buttons (or one column, if your taskbar is docked against the left or right side of the desktop). As you open more programs and folders, Windows squeezes more and more buttons into this limited space, truncating the buttons' captions more and more as the button population grows. At some point it may become difficult to know which button is which, and you may long for another row or two. No problem. Simply position the mouse pointer along the inner boundary of the taskbar (the edge closest to the center of the screen). When the mouse pointer becomes a two-headed arrow, drag toward the center of your screen to expand the taskbar.

You can also increase button space by removing the clock from the taskbar. If you don't need Windows to tell you the time of day, for example, you can probably squeeze at least one more button onto the bar by unloading the clock.

To remove the clock, right-click the taskbar and choose Properties from the context menu. Choose the Taskbar Options tab and then deselect the Show Clock check box.

NOTE

You can also make room for more buttons by switching to a higher-resolution display. *See "Controlling the Amount of Information That Fits On Screen," page 92.*

You can make room for more text on each taskbar button by reducing the point size of the text. You can do this by choosing a smaller size for the Inactive Title Bar item on the Appearance page of the Display Properties dialog box. To get there, right-click the desktop, choose Properties, and then click the Appearance tab. *For more information, see "Changing Colors, Fonts, and Text Sizes," page 97.*

To decode an overcrowded taskbar, rest your mouse pointer for about a half second on each button. If a button's caption is truncated, Windows displays its full text in a pop-up window. If you rest your mouse pointer on the clock, Windows displays the date in a pop-up window.

If the Taskbar Gets in Your Way

For information about stay-on-top windows, see "Keeping Windows on Top," page 25.

By default, your taskbar is a stay-on-top window. That means it remains visible even when you're working in a maximized application. If that's inconvenient, you can tell it to get out of the way. Simply right-click an unoccupied part of the taskbar, choose Properties from the context menu, and click the Taskbar Options tab. Windows displays the Taskbar Properties dialog box shown below.

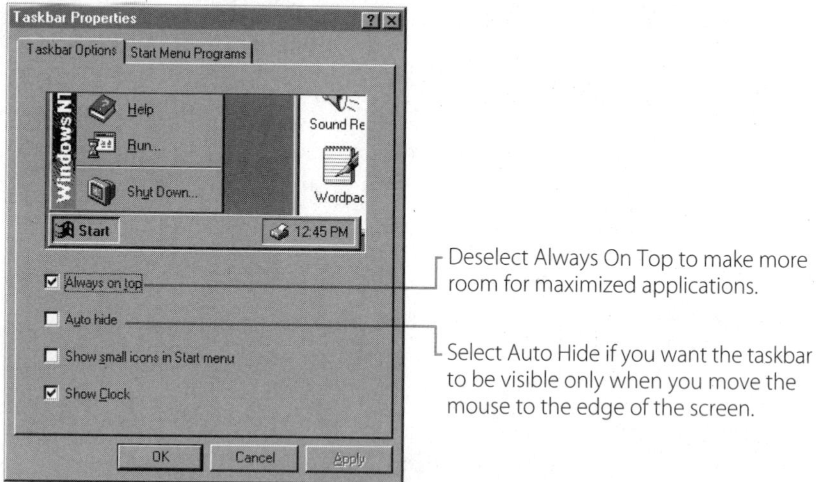

TIP

Use the Keyboard to Display the Taskbar

Regardless of how you set options in the Taskbar Properties dialog box, you can make the taskbar visible at any time by pressing Ctrl-Esc.

Controlling the Amount of Information That Fits On Screen

The default Windows NT screen resolution with most display adapters is standard VGA, which is 640 pixels horizontally by 480 pixels vertically, with a palette of 256 colors. (A *pixel* is the smallest point of light that your screen can display.) This default is the minimum resolution under which Windows NT can run.

As Figures 4-1 and 4-2 show, switching from 640×480 to a higher resolution dramatically increases the amount of information you can see on your screen. At 640×480 (Figure 4-1), a Microsoft Excel spreadsheet with standard column widths and row heights can display cells A1 through I16 (assuming the taskbar is visible). At

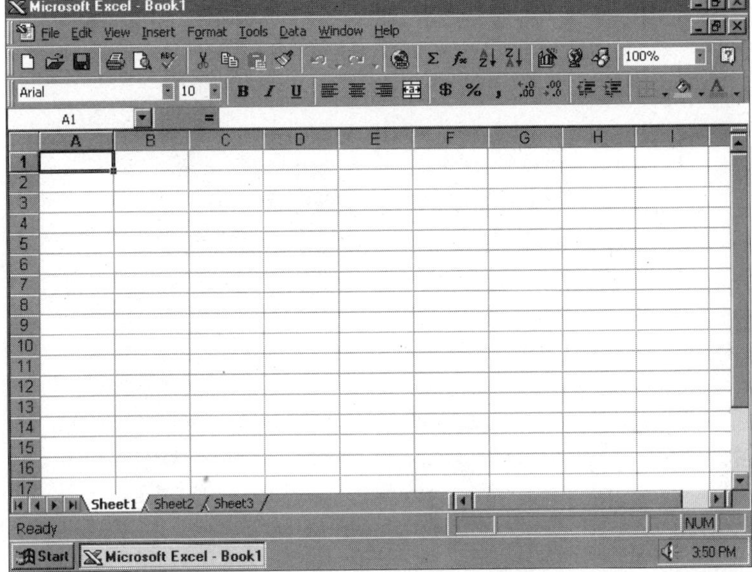

FIGURE 4-1.
At standard VGA resolution (640×480), toolbars are full and maximized applications can display a limited amount of information.

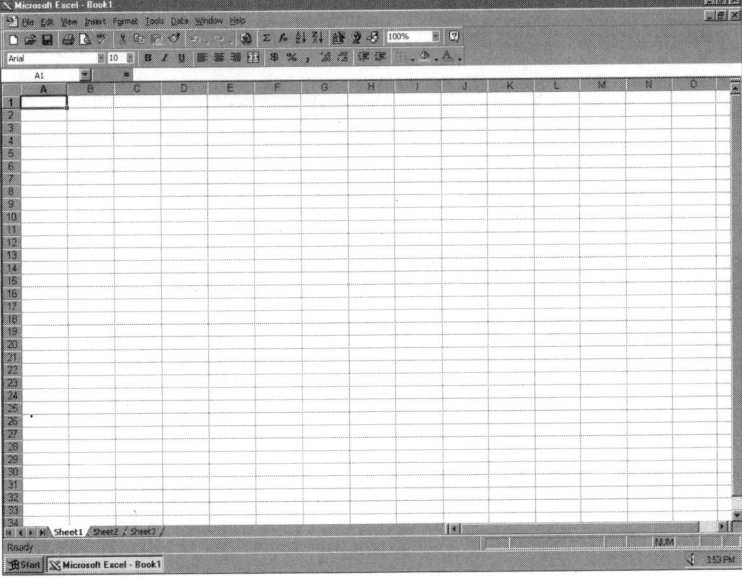

FIGURE 4-2.
Moving from standard VGA to 1024×768 lets you see almost three and a half times as many spreadsheet cells.

800×600 (not shown), your "viewport" onto this spreadsheet extends three columns and seven rows further, to cell L23. Bumping the resolution up to 1024×768 (Figure 4-2) gives you three more columns and ten more rows. Notice, too, that increasing the resolution gives you room to add new tools to customizable toolbars. At 1024×768, the standard Excel toolbars are only about two-thirds full.

Perhaps most importantly, at higher resolutions it's much easier to work with two or more open windows at once, because each window can show more information without covering its neighbors.

But higher resolutions have disadvantages as well. At higher resolutions, your computer has to work harder to manage the display, because it has more pixels to process. Therefore, you may notice some degradation in performance. (The load on your computer also varies with the number of colors you choose for your display. *See "Changing the Number of Colors," page 96.*)

Also, the more pixels you display in a given area, the smaller the pixels must be. Fortunately, when you change to a higher resolution, Windows gives you the option of increasing the relative size of your fonts. This option can help you maintain readability at high resolutions. Nevertheless, depending on the size of your monitor and the nature of the programs you use, you may find that certain display elements become vanishingly small at very high resolutions.

TIP

Use Zoom Instead of Changing Resolution

Many Windows-based applications include Zoom commands that let you magnify or reduce the size of on-screen text and graphics. With these commands, you can tailor your environment to give you the best of both worlds. For example, if you like working with graphics programs at 1024×768 but find writing impossible at this resolution, check to see if your word processor has a Zoom command. Zooming the word processor to about 150 percent makes it emulate a lower resolution, allowing you to work with text at one level and graphics at another.

SEE ALSO
For information about installing new display hardware, see "Installing a Display Adapter," page 710.

Your choice of screen resolution will probably depend on several factors—the size of your screen, the kind of work you do, the acuity of your eyesight, and the quality of your display adapter and monitor. Experiment to see what works best for you.

Changing Display Resolution

To change the resolution of your display, right-click the desktop and then choose Properties from the context menu to display the dialog box shown below.

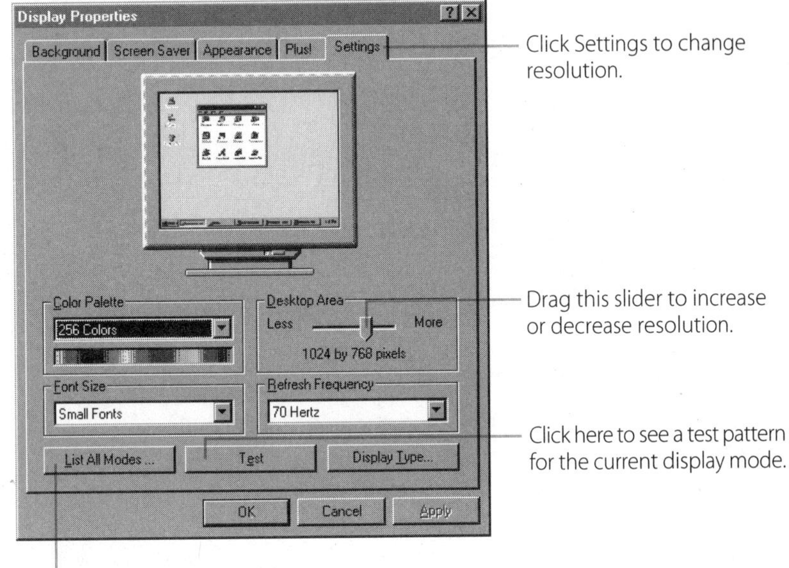

FIGURE 4-3.
The Display Properties dialog box lets you change resolution, fonts, and colors for your display.

TIP

Another Path to the Display Properties Dialog
You can also get to the Display Properties dialog box by choosing Settings on the Start menu, choosing Control Panel on the Settings menu, and then double-clicking the Display icon in Control Panel.

Changing the Font Size

If text at a particular resolution is hard to read, you might want to experiment with the Font Size on the Settings page of the Display Properties dialog box. (See Figure 4-3 on the previous page.) This drop-down list has two entries, Small Fonts (the default) and Large Fonts. If you choose Large Fonts, Windows increases the displayed size of all fonts on your system—those that Windows uses for menus, dialog boxes, and messages, as well as all fonts that you use in your documents. However, the actual point sizes of the fonts in your documents do not change. If you created a document using 10-point Times New Roman, it will still be formatted in the same font at the same point size, and it will look exactly the same on paper with either Small Fonts or Large Fonts in effect. But the letters will be larger on screen.

For text-based work, the effect of switching to Large Fonts is about the same as switching to a lower resolution. A spreadsheet at 800×600 in Large Fonts will look nearly the same as it would at 640×480 in Small Fonts. But at 800×600 in Large Fonts you will still be able to display graphic images that are 800 pixels wide by 600 pixels high. At 640×480, you would need to scroll to see all of an image that size.

TIP

Another Way to Change Font Size

You can adjust the font size used for particular types of text, such as menus or window title bars, without changing the font size for all text. *See "Changing the Size of Particular Display Elements," page 102.*

Changing the Number of Colors

As Figure 4-3 on the previous page shows, the Settings page of the Display Properties dialog box includes a drop-down list labeled Color Palette. This list includes all the color-depth options available for your display hardware in its current resolution. To choose a different number of colors, select from the list and click OK.

As with screen resolution, "color-depth" selection involves tradeoffs. A higher number of colors lets you display more realistic images but also entails more processing. The more colors your display handles, the longer it takes to draw images on the screen.

If you regularly run multimedia or other graphics applications, you will almost certainly want to use at least a 32,768-color display. If you work primarily with word processors, spreadsheets, and databases, 16 colors may be quite adequate.

> **NOTE**
>
> Windows NT supports up to 16.7 million colors, but not all display adapters support this many colors. Your available color-depth settings are determined by your display adapter.

You can switch from one color depth to another at any time, but you'll need to restart your system for the change to take effect. To switch, right-click the desktop, choose Properties from the context menu, and click the Settings tab in the Display Properties dialog box. Then select from the Color Palette drop-down list.

Changing Colors, Fonts, and Text Sizes

When you first install Windows NT, it uses a combination of colors, fonts, and sizes called Windows Standard. It's a fine arrangement, but you can also choose from a number of alternative schemes. And if you don't like any of the formatting combinations that Window NT offers, you can design your own. Once you've found a pleasing arrangement of colors, fonts, and text sizes, you can name and save the arrangement. You can design as many custom appearance schemes as you want, adding each to the menu that Windows NT supplies. As mood or necessity dictates, you can switch from one scheme to another by choosing from a simple drop-down list.

To see what the supplied appearance schemes look like, choose Properties from the context menu that appears when you right-click the desktop, and click the Appearance tab. Windows presents the following dialog box.

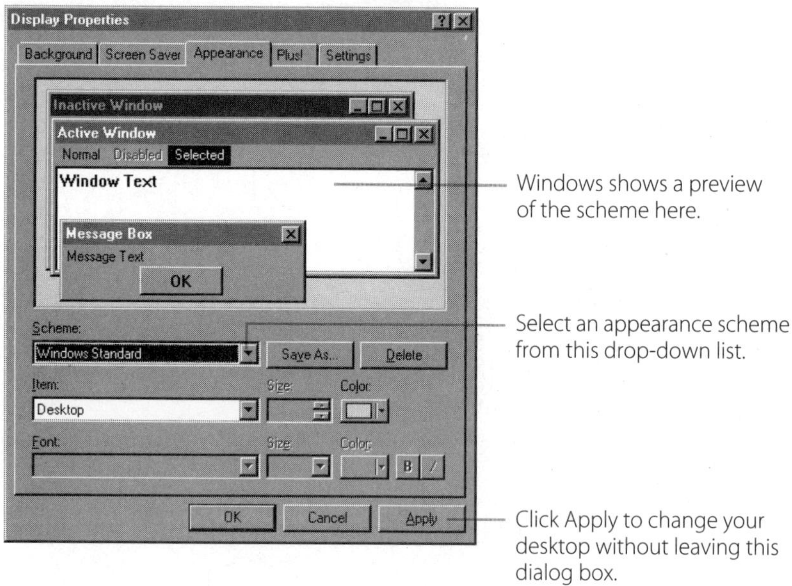

Modifying the Supplied Formatting Schemes

To modify one of the supplied appearance schemes, select its name in the Scheme drop-down list. In the preview area, click the screen element you want to change. Then use the drop-down lists and buttons at the bottom of the dialog box to make your color, font, and size selections.

For example, suppose you want to modify the Windows Standard color scheme, making the active window's title bar yellow, with black text in 12-point bold italic MS Serif. To assign this admittedly garish combination, you would do as follows:

1. Select Windows Standard in the Scheme list.
2. In the preview area of the dialog box, click the title bar labeled Active Window. (Or select Active Title Bar in the Item list.)
3. In the Font list, select MS Serif.
4. In the Size list directly to the right of the Font list, select 12.
5. Click the *I* button to the right of the font-size list.

6 Open the Color drop-down list to the right of the Item list and select yellow.

7 Open the Color drop-down list to the right of the Font list and select black.

If You Don't See the Color You Want

The drop-down lists for Item Color and Font Color offer a selection of 20 colors. If you don't see the one you're looking for, click the button labeled Other. Windows then displays a larger menu, consisting of 48 colors. Should you fail to find exactly the shade you want in this expanded offering, you can define your own custom colors.

Defining Custom Colors

To add your own colors to the ones offered by Windows, open the Color drop-down list for the screen element you want to change. (That is, if you want to customize a text element, open the Font Color drop-down list. If you want to customize a nontext element, open the Item Color drop-down list.) Then click the Other button. Windows opens the custom color selector, shown below.

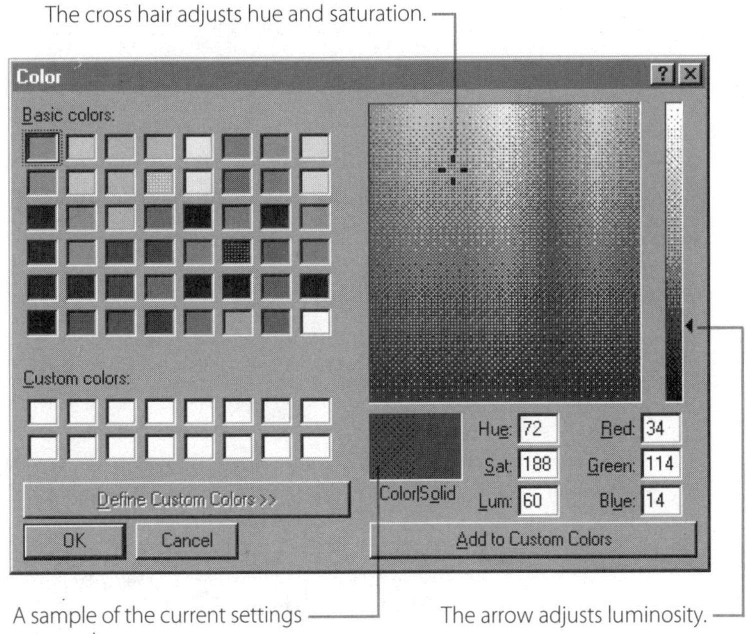

To set a custom color with the mouse, adjust the position of two pointers—the cross hair in the big square grid and the arrowhead to the right of the vertical scale. As you move these pointers, Windows displays a sample of the selected color in the box near the center of the dialog box. If you prefer using your keyboard, you can enter numbers for either or both of the two scales in the boxes at the lower right corner of the dialog box.

The sample box actually comprises two halves because your system might not be capable of displaying every possible color. For colors that your system can't display directly, Windows creates a patterned mixture of two or more colors that it can display—a process called *dithering*. The left half of the sample box (the one marked Color) displays the dithered color; the right half (marked Solid) displays a closely related color that your system can display without dithering. *For information about color parameters, see "How Colors Are Defined," on the next page.*

Experimenting with Color

In the Color dialog box, the vertical scale on the right controls luminosity (brightness). As you move its pointer higher, the color becomes lighter. Putting the pointer at the top of the scale creates pure white, no matter where the cross-hair pointer may be in the grid; putting the pointer at the bottom of the luminosity scale produces black.

The square grid controls hue and saturation. Moving the cross hair from side to side changes the hue; moving it higher increases the saturation.

To see the range of "pure" colors available, start by putting the luminosity pointer about halfway up the vertical scale. Then put the cross hair at the upper left corner of the square grid. This combination gives you a fully saturated red of medium luminosity. Now slowly drag the cross hair across the top of the grid; as you do so, you'll move from red through yellow, green, blue, violet, and back to red again. (Alternatively, you can enter values in the Hue box to step the Hue parameter from 0 to 239.)

To see the effect of luminosity on color, double-click the Solid half of the sample box or press Alt-O. This moves the cross-hair pointer to the nearest position that produces a pure color in both sample boxes. Then move the luminosity pointer up and down the scale (or change the value in the Lum box).

How Colors Are Defined

Colors in Windows are recorded as a combination of three parameters: hue, saturation, and luminosity. Roughly speaking, the basic quality of a color—its redness, blueness, or whatever—is defined by its *hue*. The purity of a color is defined by its *saturation*; a lower saturation value means more gray is mixed in. The brightness or dullness of a color is defined by its *luminosity*.

Hue, saturation, and luminosity are the parameters that Windows uses internally, but your video display hardware lives by a different set of numbers. Images on a color monitor are formed by a combination of dots, or *pixels*. To make each pixel visible, a beam of electrons is fired at three tiny spots of phosphor—one red, one green, and one blue. The result is three points of distinctly colored light so close together that they're perceived as a single light source. The apparent color of that light source is determined by the relative intensities of its red, green, and blue components.

Every combination of hue, saturation, and luminosity, therefore, is translated by Windows into varying levels of energy directed at those spots of red, green, and blue phosphor.

Thus there are two boxes in the lower right corner of the custom color dialog box—one for the parameters used by Windows, the other for the relative red, green, and blue intensities. You can define a custom color by modifying the numbers in either box—or by simply dragging the mouse pointers until you see the color you're looking for.

To see the effect of saturation, put the luminosity pointer back in the middle of the scale and drag the cross hair straight up and down in the square grid (or change the value in the Sat box).

Adding Custom Colors to Your Palette

When you find a color you like, you can add it to your Custom Colors palette by clicking Add To Custom Colors. (If you prefer to add the solid color, double-click the Solid half of the sample box or press Alt-O first.) Windows adds the color to the first available Custom Colors box. If you want to add it to a specific box in your custom palette (for example, if you want to replace a custom color), select that box with the mouse before clicking Add To Custom Colors.

When you've filled out the custom palette to your satisfaction, click OK. Now you can assign your custom colors to the screen elements exactly as you did the basic colors.

Changing the Size of Particular Display Elements

You can make certain elements of the Windows user interface—such as title bars, caption (title bar) buttons, and window borders—larger or smaller by using the Size box to the right of the Item list. If a number appears in this box, the element shown in the Item list can be sized.

Windows automatically adjusts the size of elements that contain text. For example, if you increase the font size for your active title bars, Windows adjusts the size of the title bar to accommodate the larger text. But you can override Windows' judgment by manipulating the spinners next to the Size box.

Saving an Appearance Scheme

If you hit upon a pleasing new combination of colors, fonts, and sizes, it's a good idea to name and save it before leaving the dialog box. That way, you'll be able to switch back and forth between your own custom formats and the ones supplied by Windows—or between several of your own making.

To save a scheme, simply click the Save As button and supply a name. Windows adds the name you provide to the list.

If you tire of your new scheme, you can easily remove it. Simply select its name, and then click the Delete button.

Using Patterns, Wallpaper, and Screen Savers

Windows provides several additional options for personalizing the appearance of your desktop:

- You can cover your desktop with a repeating pattern—one you create yourself or one that Windows supplies. Doing this is somewhat like throwing a tweed tablecloth over your screen; just the ticket, perhaps, if you get bored with solid colors or grays.
- For a more pictorial backdrop, you can add "wallpaper" to your desktop. The wallpaper can be a small image repeated as many times as necessary to fill the screen (like conventional wallpaper), a single image centered on the desktop, or a single image that covers the entire screen.
- To protect your screen while your computer is idle, and to hide what you were working on while you're away from your desk, you can install a screen saver.

Adding Patterns

To apply a background pattern to your desktop, right-click the desktop and choose Properties from the context menu. Then click the Background tab to get to the dialog box shown in Figure 4-4 on the next page. Select one of the patterns in the Pattern list, and click OK.

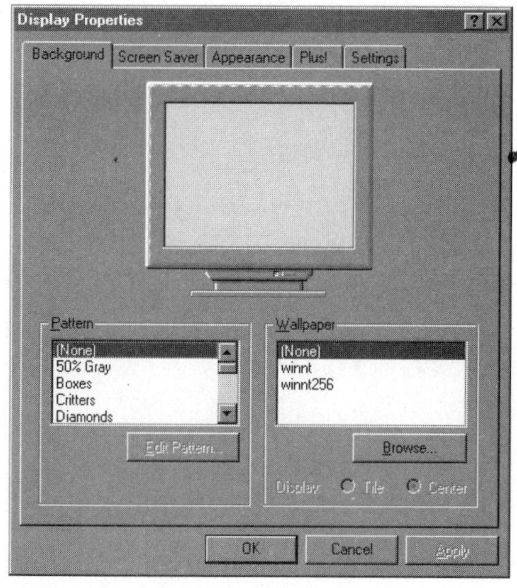

FIGURE 4-4. The Background page of the Display Properties dialog box lets you add a pattern or picture ("wallpaper") to your desktop.

Editing a Background Pattern

If you want to modify an existing pattern or create a new one, select a pattern name and then click Edit Pattern. When the Pattern Editor dialog box appears, press the Up arrow or Down arrow key to step through the list and see an enlarged sample of each pattern. Figure 4-5, for example, shows what the Thatches pattern looks like.

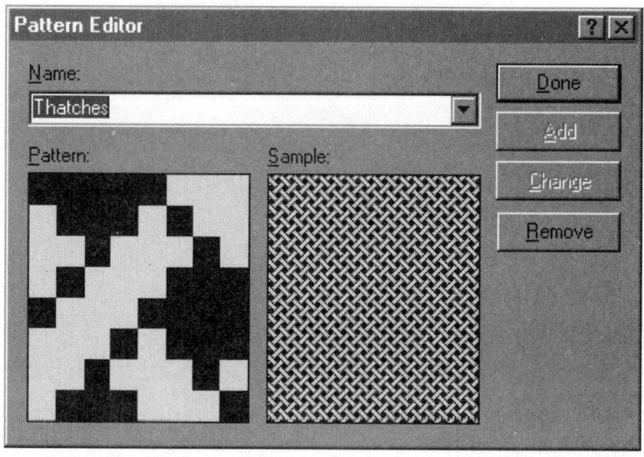

FIGURE 4-5. The Pattern Editor lets you modify or create background patterns for your desktop.

Modifying an Existing Background Pattern

The big square on the left side of the Pattern Editor dialog box represents the "cell" from which the selected background pattern is made. The cell is an eight-by-eight grid of dots; each dot is either dark or light. You can edit the background pattern by changing one or more dots from light to dark or dark to light. To do that, click the mouse on the dots you want to change. (There is no keyboard equivalent for this procedure.)

As you make changes in the dot pattern in the cell, you can see the effect of those changes in the Sample box in the center. When you're satisfied with your editing, click Change to save the revised pattern. Then click OK to select it.

Creating a New Background Pattern

The easiest way to create a background pattern is to edit an existing one, as explained above, and give it a new name by replacing the text in the Name text box in the Pattern Editor dialog box. Windows grays out the Change button and activates the Add button. Click Add, and your new pattern joins the list of existing patterns. You can then apply it to your desktop by clicking Done in the Pattern Editor dialog box and then clicking OK in the Display Properties dialog box.

Adding Wallpaper

To drape your desktop with something livelier than a simple dot pattern, try the wallpaper option. Follow these steps to display a picture as a backdrop to everything you do in Windows:

1 Right-click the desktop.

2 Choose Properties from the context menu.

3 Click the Background tab. This takes you to the dialog box shown in Figure 4-4.

4 Select an image file from the Wallpaper list. (If you don't find the file you're looking for, click the Browse button.)

When you click the Browse button in the Background dialog box, Windows displays filenames with the extension .BMP or .DIB. You can use files with either extension as wallpaper. You can also use graphics files with the extension .RLE.

Some wallpaper files produce a single image that covers your entire desktop. Others produce smaller images that can either be displayed once, in the center of the desktop, or repeated as many times as necessary to fill the screen. If you want the image to appear only once, select the Center option button; otherwise, select Tile.

Using a Screen Saver

Displays used by desktop computers create images by firing electron beams at phosphor-coated screens. If the same picture or text remains on a screen for a long period of time, the phosphor coating can be damaged, leaving a faint but permanent image on the screen. Screen savers reduce this hazard by monitoring screen activity. Whenever your screen remains unchanged for a specific length of time, the screen saver displays its own constantly varying image. As soon as you press a key or (with most savers) move the mouse, the screen saver restores the original image.

That's the ostensible purpose of a screen saver, at any rate. In truth, with current display technology, the probability that you'll damage your screen with a burned-in image is remote. But screen savers have other virtues, as well. They're fun to watch, and they're one way to prevent others in your office from prying while you're away from your machine. Many screen savers have "save now" and password options. The save-now option lets you display the saver pattern on demand, either by pressing a certain keyboard combination or by moving the mouse pointer to a particular corner of the screen. The password option ensures that only you are able to restore the original image. If your screen saver has these features, you can display the saver image any time you walk away from your computer and be reasonably confident that no one will invade your privacy.

To install one of the Windows-supplied screen savers, right-click the desktop and choose Properties from the context menu. Then click the Screen Saver tab to get to the dialog box shown in Figure 4-6.

FIGURE 4-6.
The Screen Saver page of the Display Properties dialog box offers a choice of customizable screen savers.

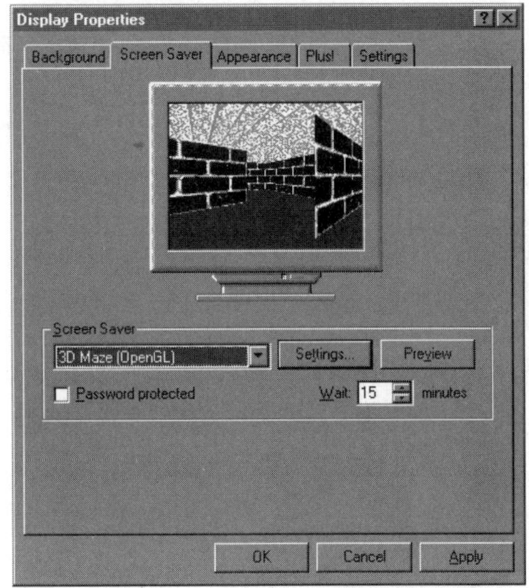

To apply a screen saver, select from the Show drop-down list. Then use the Wait spinners to specify how long a period of inactivity Windows should allow before displaying the screen saver.

All the Windows-supplied screen savers (except for Blank Screen) include options that you can set. These options let you adjust colors, speed, and other display preferences. Figure 4-7 shows the settings dialog box for the 3D Text screen saver.

FIGURE 4-7.
After choosing a screen saver, you can click the Settings button to specify display options.

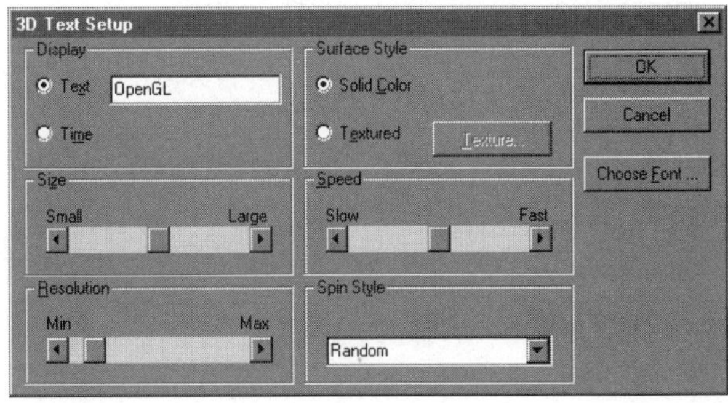

Using Plus! to Customize Your Desktop

The customizing options found on the Plus! page of the Display Properties dialog box were originally supplied as an optional add-on for users of Windows 95—hence, the name Plus! But they're a standard feature of Windows NT. As the following illustration shows, Plus! lets you make a variety of useful changes to the appearance of your desktop. To take advantage of these options, right-click the desktop and choose Properties from the context menu. Then click the Plus! tab.

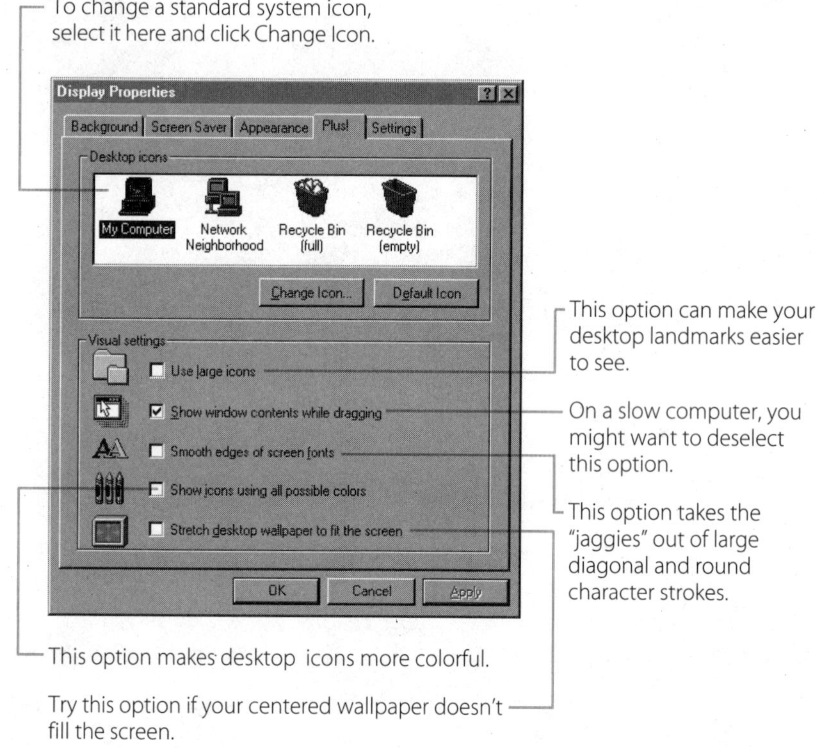

Changing Icons

Windows NT lets you change the text that appears under your My Computer, Network Neighborhood, and Recycle Bin icons by simply clicking the icon you want to change and choosing Rename from the context menu. With Plus!, you can also change the icons themselves. To select a different icon for My Computer, for example, select it in the Plus! page of the Display Properties dialog box. Then click the Change Icon button. You'll see a gallery of replacement candidates, similar to the following:

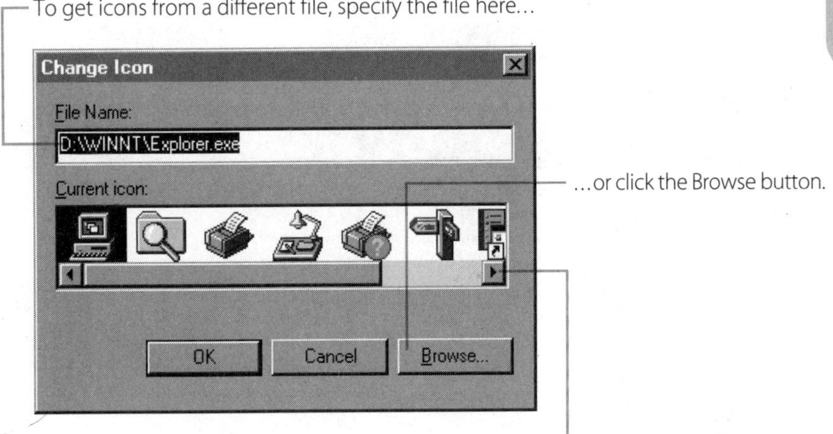

Files with the extension .ICO are icons, but files with extensions .EXE and .DLL also may contain icons—some do, some don't. For example the icons shown in this illustration are stored in the file Explorer.exe, which is located in your Winnt folder. This file contains a sizable assortment of icons, as you can see by manipulating the horizontal scroll bar. But you're not limited to the icons contained in Explorer.exe. You can supply a different file name in the edit box or click the Browse button and point to another file. You might want to take some time to explore the icon resources supplied with the applications installed on your computer.

If you change your mind and decide you want the original system icons back, simply return to the Plus! page, select the item whose icon you want to restore, and click the Default Icon button.

Using Large Icons

The Use Large Icons check box on the Plus! page does what its name suggests: it causes Windows to employ magnified versions of all its desktop icons. If you're working with a high-resolution display on a small monitor, or if your eyesight isn't quite as acute as you'd like, you might want to try this option. Note that because large icons consume more memory than small ones, the Use Large Icons option may have a slight adverse effect on your system's performance.

Using "Full-Window" Dragging

The second of the Plus! page's check boxes, labeled "Show Window Contents While Dragging," is the only one selected by default. With this option in effect, the operating system redraws an entire window as you drag it. If you deselect this check box, Windows displays a "ghost" image of the window's border while you drag but doesn't redraw the entire window until you release the mouse button.

Most users prefer to see the full window move as they drag. But on systems with a slow display adapter, this option may cause unacceptably jerky screen performance. You might want to experiment with both forms of dragging to see which works best on your system.

Smoothing Large Screen Fonts

If you choose the Smooth Edges Of Screen Fonts option, Windows uses gray tones to smooth out the jagged edges of letters that have diagonal and round character strokes—such as a capital *A* or *R*. If you regularly work with large fonts and you're bothered by the "jaggies," this option is for you.

Note that you need a display that uses at least 32,768 colors to take advantage of font smoothing.

Showing Icons with All Available Colors

Windows normally displays icons in 16 colors, regardless of how many colors your display is capable of. By selecting the Show Icons Using All Possible Colors check box, you can make all your system's colors available for icon display. Whether or not this has any effect on the appearance of your icons, of course, depends on the icons. Note that you'll need to reboot your system to make this option take effect.

Stretching Wallpaper to Fit

The last check box on the Plus! page of the Display property sheet causes Windows to stretch centered wallpaper so that it fills the screen. If you want a particular image to cover your entire desktop, you can try this option, although you may find it preferable to tile the image rather than stretch it, because stretching bitmaps generally creates unattractive distortions. Like the Show Icons With All Possible Colors option, this one requires a reboot.

Assigning Sounds to Events

If you have a sound card installed in your computer, you can customize the various beeps, squeals, squeeks, and other exclamations emitted by Windows as you go about your workday. Or you can opt for golden silence instead. You can even create named sound schemes, comparable to your named appearance schemes, for easy reuse and recall.

To change the sounds used by Windows, follow these steps:

1. Choose the Settings command from the Start menu.
2. Choose Control Panel.
3. In the Control Panel folder, double-click the Sounds icon.

You will see the Sounds property sheet, shown in Figure 4-8 on the next page.

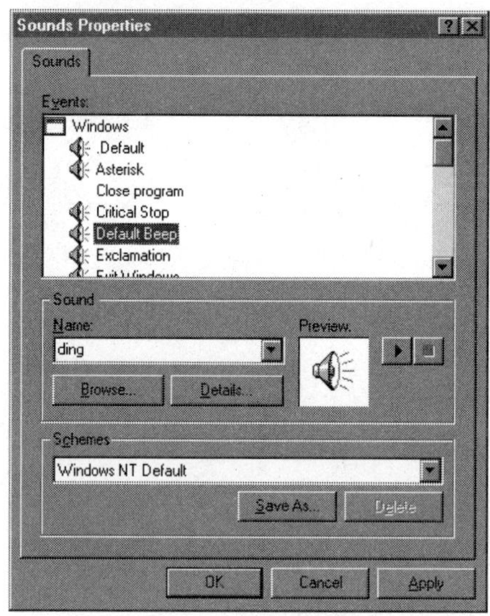

FIGURE 4-8.
The Sounds property sheet lets you assign sound files to events and create named sound schemes.

The Events list box in the Sounds property sheet lists all the different system events to which you can attach (or from which you can detach) sounds. The list is structured as a two-level hierarchy. The first top-level item is Windows itself. The events subordinate to the Windows heading include events such as opening and closing programs, maximizing and minimizing windows, starting and ending a Windows session. If you scroll downward through the Events list, you will find another top-level heading for Windows Explorer and, possibly, additional headings for other applications installed on your computer.

TIP

Adjusting the Volume

If a sound icon appears in your taskbar's notification area (next to the clock), you can click that icon to change the volume at which sounds are played. You can also temporarily disable sounds by selecting the Mute check box. *For more information about adjusting the volume, see "Setting Volume Levels," page 385.*

Directly below the Events list box is a drop-down list labeled Name. This lists all the sound files (files with the extension .WAV) that are available in the current folder.

Near the bottom of the dialog box is another drop-down list labeled Schemes. Here you will find all the named combinations of sounds and events that are currently available. You can switch from one sound scheme to another by choosing from this list.

To hear what sound is currently assigned to an event, select the event in the Events list. The name of the assigned sound appears in the Name drop-down, and an icon appears in the Preview box, to the right of the Name drop-down. Click the Play icon (the right-pointing arrow beside the Preview box) to hear the current sound.

To assign a new sound to an event, select the event, and then choose a different item from the Name drop-down list. Click the Play button to be sure you've chosen the sound you want. If the sound you're looking for isn't listed in the Name drop-down, click the Browse button. This takes you to the file-and-folder browser, where you can hunt for a different sound file.

To remove all sound from an event, select the event in the Events list. Then choose (none) in the Name drop-down.

Once you've hit upon a combination of sounds and events that pleases your ear, you can name it and add it to the Schemes drop-down. Simply click the Save As button and enter a name for your new sound scheme.

Setting Preferences for Your Mouse

Windows lets you tailor the behavior of your mouse or other pointing device to suit your personal tastes. The options available depend on what kind of device you're using, but for most pointing devices you can adjust the pointer size, as well as the pointer-movement and double-click speeds, and you can swap the functionality of the left and right mouse buttons. You might find it handy to swap mouse button functions if you're left-handed, so you can put the mouse on the left side of your keyboard and still use your index finger for most mouse commands.

To make mouse adjustments, choose Settings on the Start menu, and then choose Control Panel. In Control Panel, double-click the Mouse icon. (Or select the Mouse icon, pull down the File menu, and choose Open.) If you're using a Microsoft Mouse, you'll see a dialog box similar to the one shown in Figure 4-9.

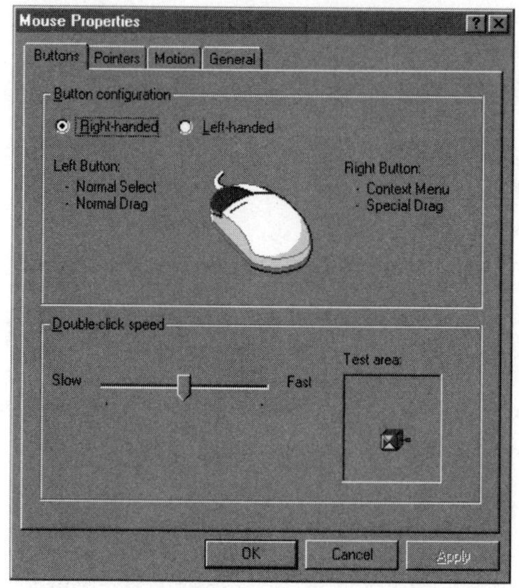

FIGURE 4-9. The Mouse Properties dialog box lets you swap mouse-button functionality, adjust double-click speed, and set other mouse preferences.

In the top part of this dialog box, you can swap mouse-button functionality. In the lower part, you can adjust the double-click speed. (The double-click speed specifies the time interval within which two mouse clicks are interpreted as a double-click.)

As you can for appearance and sound, you can select and modify a "scheme" of mouse pointers. The mouse pointer changes shape as you point to different objects and perform different actions. On the Mouse property sheet's Pointers page, you can select the pointer shapes you want.

You can select a predefined scheme from the Scheme drop-down list, or select your own pointers and save the collection as a custom scheme. Windows NT includes several alternative schemes, including some with larger pointers that are easier to find on a portable computer's display.

NOTE

If your Scheme drop-down list is empty, the optional pointers and schemes haven't been installed on your system. To install them, double-click the Add/Remove Programs icon in Control Panel, and click the Windows NT Setup tab. Highlight Accessories and then click Details. Then select Mouse Pointers and click OK two times.

SEE ALSO

For information about using the keyboard to perform mouse functions, see "Mouse Alternatives," page 400.

The Motion page of your Mouse Properties dialog box allows you to adjust the pointer speed. The pointer speed refers to the relationship between movement of the mouse on your desk and movement of the pointer on screen. If you often find your mouse pointer overshooting its target as you select commands or objects in Windows, you may find it helpful to decrease the pointer speed. On the other hand, if you find yourself "rowing"—picking up the mouse, bringing it back through the air, and then sliding it over the mouse pad again merely to get the pointer from one side of the screen to the other—try increasing the pointer speed.

Adjusting the Keyboard Repeat and Cursor Blink Rates

Unless you have disabled the "typematic" behavior of your keyboard to take advantage of Windows NT's accessibility features, Windows repeats a character after you hold its key down for a certain length of time. You can adjust both the repeat speed and the interval that Windows waits before beginning to repeat. To do this, choose Settings from the Start menu and Control Panel from the Settings submenu. In Control Panel, double-click the Keyboard icon to get to the dialog box shown in Figure 4-10 on the next page.

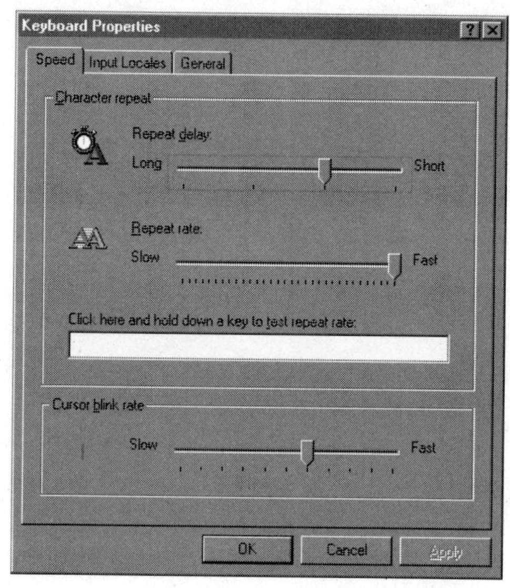

FIGURE 4-10.
The Keyboard Properties dialog box lets you adjust your keyboard's repeat speed, the speed at which the cursor blinks, and a variety of other preferences.

SEE ALSO
For more information about controlling or disabling the keyboard repeat rate, see "Keyboard Options," page 394.

SEE ALSO
For more information about international language support, see "Installing Language Support and Using Keyboard Layouts," page 389.

To shorten the delay before repeating begins, drag the Repeat Delay slider to the right. To increase the repeat speed, drag the Repeat Rate slider to the right. Putting both these sliders as far as they'll go to the right makes your keyboard as responsive as Windows will allow. If you find yourself occasionally getting unwanted repeated characters, move the Repeat Delay slider, or both sliders, to the left. You can use the text box to test your settings before clicking OK.

In the lower part of the dialog box shown in Figure 4-10, you'll find another slider for adjusting the rate at which the cursor blinks. If you're not happy with the default blink rate, experiment with moving this slider. The blinking line to the left of the slider shows your new cursor blink rate.

The Input Locales tab of the Keyboard Properties dialog box allows you to install keyboard support for a variety of languages.

CHAPTER 5

Working with Folders

A hard disk is a mansion with many wings, branches, halls, ballrooms, libraries, salons, alcoves, closets, and crannies. A typical computer system today comprises at least one such estate and often two or more. With the help of networking technology, moreover, many users are connected to virtual cities of palatial storage spaces.

Organizing one's local disks effectively and keeping track of where needed resources lie on the network used to be a daunting task, requiring mastery of arcane path syntax and networking commands. It's far simpler in Windows NT, thanks to Windows NT's unified "namespace" and comfortable browsing methods.

SEE ALSO
For information about Windows NT Explorer, see Chapter 6, "Managing Folders and Files with Windows NT Explorer."

Windows NT provides two distinct methods of navigating through local and remote resources. You can browse with folder windows, or you can use Windows NT Explorer. The choice is yours. In this chapter, we'll survey the folder method.

SEE ALSO
For information about the Find command, see Chapter 7, "Using the Find Command."

Windows NT also includes a powerful search facility to help you find folders and files anywhere on your own system or your network. Getting to a particular item "out there somewhere" is often quicker via the Find command than by any other method.

The Windows NT Namespace

The term *namespace* refers to the universe of storage entities accessible from your computer system. Figure 5-1 shows a schematic diagram of a typical workstation's namespace, and the following paragraph provides a quick review of the namespace's organization.

SEE ALSO
For information about Recycle Bin, see "Restoring Deleted Items," page 149. For information about Network Neighborhood, see "Using Network Neighborhood," page 272.

Your desktop is where all the action in Windows originates, so the top of the namespace hierarchy is called *Desktop*. At the next organizational level are three folders, called *My Computer, Network Neighborhood*, and *Recycle Bin*. My Computer is the parent folder for all disks attached to your own computer, including hard disks, floppy drives, and CD-ROM drives. Network Neighborhood is a folder comprising all network servers in your immediate workgroup or domain. Through Network Neighborhood, you can also get to network servers beyond your immediate workgroup or domain. Recycle Bin is where deleted folders, files, and shortcuts go—until you dump the trash, at which point such items are gone for good.

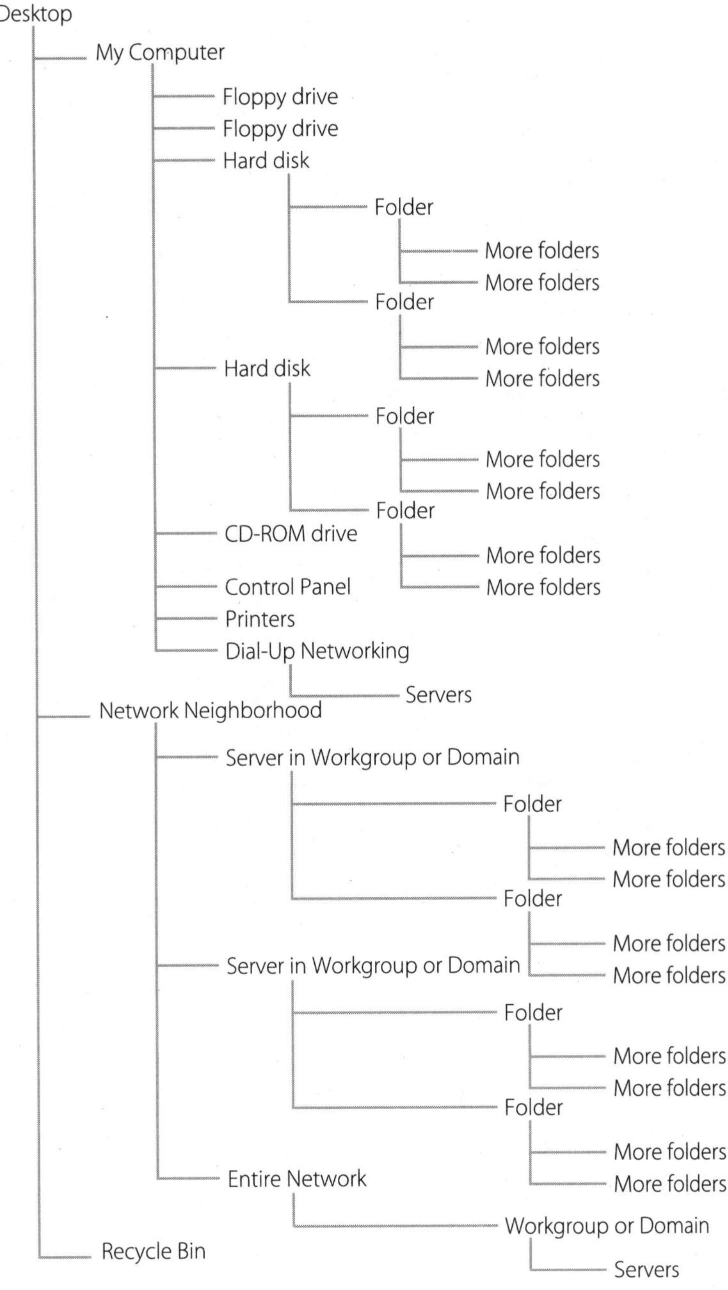

FIGURE 5-1.
The Windows NT namespace encompasses all the storage resources accessible from your system.

In this chapter, we'll concentrate on local folder operations, reserving network-specific issues for Chapter 11, "Using and Sharing Files on the Network." But bear in mind that folder navigation and housekeeping are essentially the same throughout the Windows NT namespace. Moving from folder to folder on a network server, for example, is just like moving between folders on your own hard disk.

Moving from Folder to Folder

A folder is a bin for storing files and other folders. For example, suppose that on drive C of your computer you have a folder named MSOffice, into which you have installed the various applications that make up the Microsoft Office application suite. Inside this folder, you will likely have other folders with names such as Excel, Word, PowerPoint, and perhaps Access. Within each of these subfolders, you might have additional folders. In the Excel folder, for example, you might have folders named Examples, Library, and XLStart. Inside each member of this group, you might have a collection of Excel workbook files.

Because your copy of Microsoft Office is installed on drive C, all of these folders are contained within the drive C folder. And because C is a local disk, the drive C folder is contained within My Computer, the master folder of local resources.

To move from one point to another within this structure, you can simply double-click My Computer and then double-click each subfolder in turn. Depending on how you've set Windows' browsing options, your screen might then display a proliferation of folder windows, as shown in Figure 5-2.

The Anatomy of a Folder Window

A folder window is simply a window that displays the contents of a folder. Like a miniature application, it includes a title bar, buttons for sizing and closing the window, a Control-menu icon, a menu bar, an optional toolbar, and an optional status bar. The title bar of any folder window, by default, contains exactly the same text that appears beneath the folder's icon.

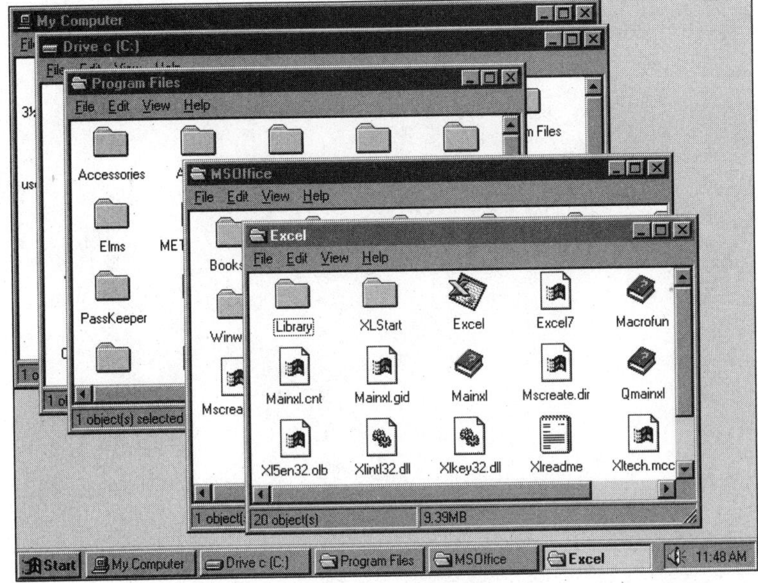

FIGURE 5-2. You can move from folder to folder by double-clicking icons or by selecting icons and choosing the File Open command.

Folder windows behave exactly like other kinds of windows. You can make them bigger or smaller by dragging the borders, you can maximize and minimize them using the buttons at the right side of the title bar, and so on. All folder windows also share a common set of menu commands.

Many Windows or One?

By default, when you double-click a folder icon in a folder window, the newly opened folder appears in a separate window, and the window for the *parent* folder (the one containing the newly opened folder) remains open. This separate-window browsing mode is shown in Figure 5-2.

The advantage of the separate-window mode is that it lets you see the parent folder and the new folder at the same time. The disadvantage of this mode is that it tends to clutter up your screen when you travel through several layers of subfolders. If the proliferation of windows becomes bothersome, you can switch to the single-window browsing mode, in which a newly opened folder window replaces its parent window.

To switch browsing modes, open any folder window's View menu and choose Options:

Your choice of browsing mode here affects all folders, not just the one you're currently viewing.

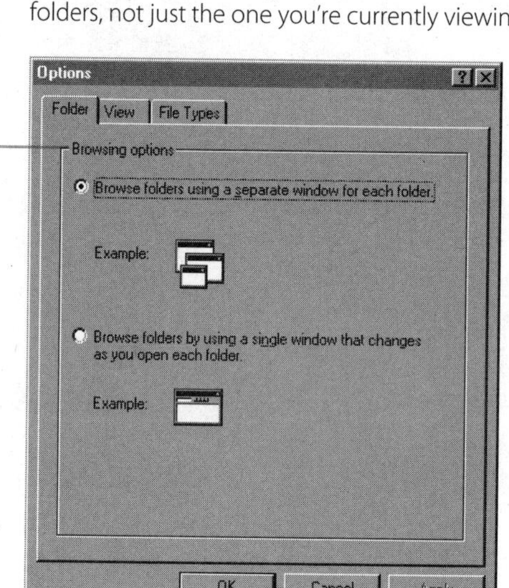

Closing a Family of Windows

If you hold down the Shift key while clicking a folder window's Close button (or while choosing its File Close command), Windows closes the current folder plus all of its "ancestor windows" (parent, grandparent, and so on). Thus, for example, you could close all five windows shown in Figure 5-2 on the previous page by holding down Shift and clicking the Excel folder's Close button.

Reselecting the Parent Folder

In the separate-window browsing mode, you can return to the parent folder by simply clicking in the parent folder window, pressing the Backspace key, or, in most cases, closing the new window. You can also reselect the parent window by pressing Alt-Tab.

In the single-window mode, you can't use these methods because the subfolder window replaces the parent window. Instead, to redisplay the parent folder window, you simply press Backspace, or click the Up One Level button on the toolbar, as shown below.

TIP

Viewing the Pathname

To see the full pathname of the current folder window, choose the View menu's Options command, select the View tab, and then select the check box labeled "Display the full path in the title bar." This option can be handy if you have many levels of subfolders and prefer the single-window approach to browsing.

Displaying and Using the Toolbar

To display the toolbar, if it's not currently visible, open the folder window's View menu and choose Toolbar. The toolbar, shown below, is the same in all folder windows that display disk directories. Table 5-1 on the next page provides a brief description of what each tool on the bar does.

TIP

The Toolbar setting is window-specific, so you will need to choose this command in each folder window in which you want the toolbar displayed.

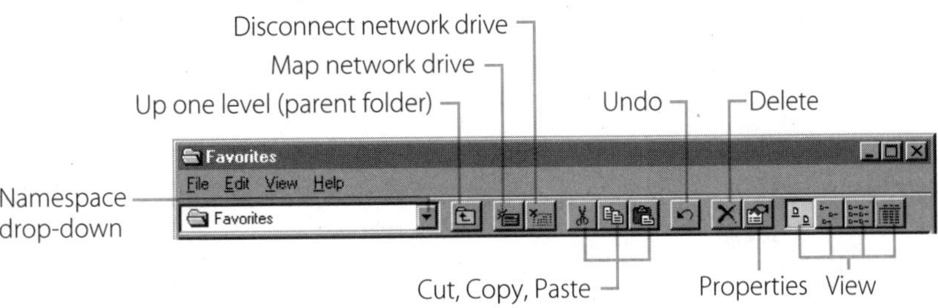

TABLE 5-1. Folder Window Toolbar

Toolbar Icon	Description	For More Information
Favorites	Allows you to move directly to a folder on a different drive or server	
	Moves to the parent of the current folder	
	Allows you to make a network folder behave as though it were a drive on your own computer—or breaks that connection	*See "Mapping a Network Folder to a Drive Letter," page 277.*
	Shortcuts for operations that move or copy files or folders	*See "Moving or Copying Objects with Menu Commands," page 143.*
	Reverses the last action you took, if possible	*See "Reversing Actions with the Undo Command," page 147.*
	Deletes the selected item(s)	*See "Deleting Folders, Files, and Shortcuts," page 148.*
	Displays the property sheet for the selected item(s)	*See "Inspecting Folder and File Properties," page 136.*
	Shortcuts for View-menu commands that provide alternative ways to display folder information	*See "Folder Viewing Options," page 127.*

Using the Status Bar to Learn About Folder Contents

At times it's helpful to have a summary of a folder's contents. You can get that by opening the View menu and choosing Status Bar. As Figure 5-3 shows, the status bar can tell you how many items a folder contains, how many hidden items it contains, and how much disk space the items use.

NOTE

Hidden items are items contained in the folder but not displayed by the folder window. Typically such items are files that your system needs in order to run, as opposed to documents or programs. The View menu's Options command, discussed later in this chapter, lets you decide whether or not to display such items in your folder windows.

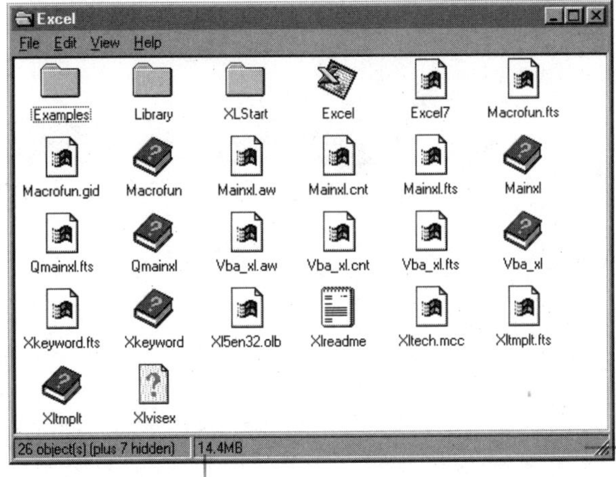

FIGURE 5-3.
The status bar can tell you how many items a folder contains and how much disk space those items use.

In Figure 5-3 on the previous page, the status bar reports the total size of the items contained in a folder. You can also use the status bar to find out how much space is used by a particular item or group of items:

- To see the space used by a particular item, simply select that item.
- To see the space used by a group of items, hold down the Ctrl key and click each member to select the group.
- To see the space used by all items in the folder, including hidden items, click anywhere in the folder window's "white space"—that is, anywhere but on an item. (The total includes all the items in the folder, but does not include the contents of its subfolders.)

You can also learn the size of a particular item by right-clicking the item and choosing Properties from the context menu. *For more information about file properties, see "Inspecting Folder and File Properties," page 136.*

Navigating in the File Open and File Save Dialogs

Many Windows-based applications use a common set of dialog boxes for their File Open, File Save, File Save As, and File Print commands. These dialog boxes are supplied by Windows and are known as the "common dialogs." Windows-based programs are not obliged to use them, but the fact that a great many programs do makes it easier for you to master new programs. Thanks to the common dialogs, the process of saving a new file is likely to be very much the same in nearly every program you use.

As the following illustration shows, the common dialogs that have to do with file management look a lot like ordinary folder windows. A drop-down list at the top of the dialog box shows the name of the current folder—the one that Windows is now prepared to save your file to or open a file from—and lets you navigate to distant folders on the same or other disks. The big window in the center of the dialog box, meanwhile, shows you all the subfolders and files contained in the current folder. You can move to a subfolder here exactly as you would in an ordinary folder window—by simply double-clicking the folder's name.

(continued)

Navigating in the File Open and File Save Dialogs *continued*

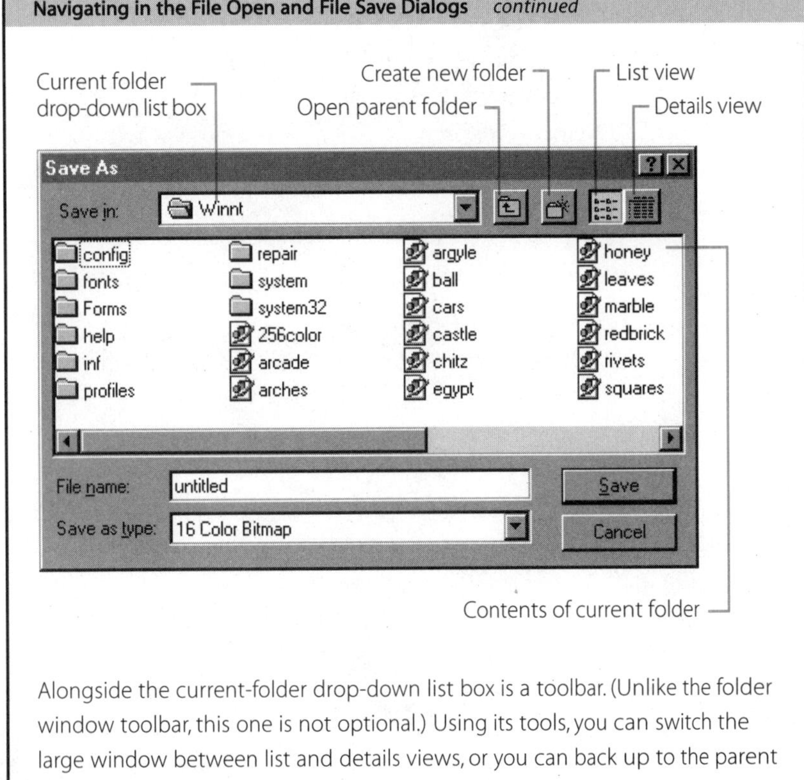

Alongside the current-folder drop-down list box is a toolbar. (Unlike the folder window toolbar, this one is not optional.) Using its tools, you can switch the large window between list and details views, or you can back up to the parent folder.

The toolbar also includes a handy tool not found on the folder window toolbar. The Create New Folder tool lets you do just that—create a new folder within the current folder. You'll find this tool invaluable when you want to save a file in a folder that you haven't created yet.

Folder Viewing Options

Windows gives you several ways to view the contents of your folders. You can choose from four display styles, sort folder entries in a number of ways, and decide whether to keep your folder entries in tidy columns or not. Each of these options can be applied separately to any of your folders.

Big Icons or Small?

By default, Windows displays a folder's contents using "large icons," but three other display styles are available. You can choose the style you prefer with commands on the View menu or tools on the toolbar. The alternatives to large-icon display are small icons, list, and details.

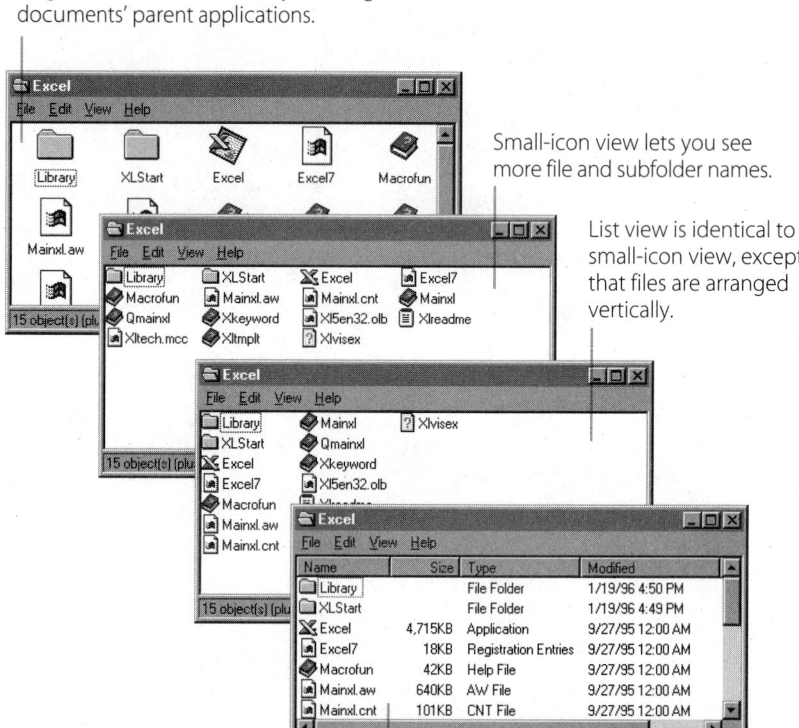

Large-icon view makes it easy to recognize documents' parent applications.

Small-icon view lets you see more file and subfolder names.

List view is identical to small-icon view, except that files are arranged vertically.

Details view lets you see size, type, most-recent-edit date, and attributes of each file.

To change the width of columns in details view, drag the column boundaries in the headings row. For example, to make the Size column wider, drag the vertical line between the Size and Type headings. To adjust a column's width automatically, so that it's just wide enough for the column's widest entry, double-click the right boundary of the column. For example, to adjust the Name column automatically, double-click the line between the Name and Size headings.

TIP

Viewing File Statistics

The details view tells you when a file was last edited. To find out when it was created and when it was last accessed, right-click the filename or icon and choose Properties from the context menu. *For more information about properties, see "Inspecting Folder and File Properties," page 136.*

Because your choice of display style applies only to the current folder, you can vary your choice depending on the contents of the folder. You might, for example, prefer the large-icon view for most folders but adopt small-icon or list view for folders containing large numbers of files.

TIP

Changing an Icon's Font

You can change the font that's used for the text that accompanies the icons in a folder window. Right-click the desktop and choose Properties from the context menu. In the Display Properties dialog box that appears, click the Appearance tab. Select Icon in the Item drop-down list, and then select a font and size.

Sorted By?

In details view, you can sort the contents of a folder by any of the column headings. In most folders, that means you can sort by name, size, file type, date of last modification, and file attributes. To sort, simply click the heading you want to sort by. Click the heading a second time to invert the order. For example, to make your ZIP files appear at the top of the folder in details view, click twice on the Type heading. The first click produces an ascending sort, with the ZIP files at or near the bottom of the list; the second click inverts the first, putting the ZIP files on top.

In large-icon, small-icon, and list view, you can sort by choosing Arrange Icons from the View menu, and then selecting a sort key (name, file type, file size, or date) from the submenu. You can also choose the Arrange Icons command from the context menu that appears when you right-click in any unoccupied area of the folder window.

Neatly Arranged or Casual?

In large-icon and small-icon views, you can have Windows automatically preserve an orderly arrangement of folder contents. To do this, open the View menu and choose Arrange Icons. If the Auto Arrange command at the bottom of the Arrange Icons submenu is not checked, select it. With Auto Arrange on, any icon you add to a folder (by creating a new file, for example) automatically falls in line with the rest of the folder's icons. If you delete an icon, the remaining icons automatically close ranks. If you drag an icon out of position, Windows snaps it back into place.

If you don't like this regimentation, you can turn it off. Simply open the View menu, choose Arrange Icons, and then deselect the Auto Arrange command. With Auto Arrange off, you can drag your icons anywhere you please. (See Figure 5-4.)

FIGURE 5-4.
Turning Auto Arrange off gives you the freedom to drag icons out of their orderly rows and columns.

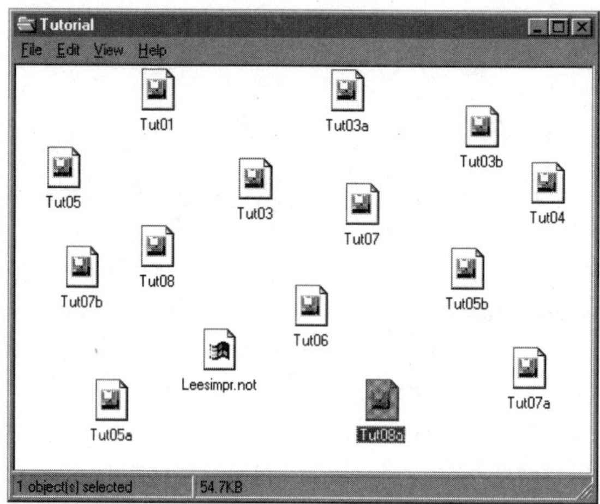

TIP

Restoring Order

When Auto Arrange is off, choosing any of the View menu's sort commands (By Name, By Type, By Size, or By Date) returns your icons to orderly rows and columns.

Turning Auto Arrange off has the advantage of letting you create ad hoc groupings. For example, you can put all the items that you're currently working with together at the top of the folder. But with this freedom comes some hazard: if you're too casual with your ad hoc arrangements, you can lose track of items. For example, if you drag an icon so far from its comrades that you have to scroll a long distance to see it, you might forget you have it.

TIP

Using Folder Space Efficiently

When Auto Arrange is off, your folder icons won't adjust their positions when you change the size of the folder window. As a result, you may get orderly columns of icons that fill only one side of the folder. The fix is simple: right-click in the folder, choose Arrange Icons, and then choose Auto Arrange.

The Auto Arrange option applies only to the current folder, so you can use it for some of your folders and not for the rest.

TIP

Auto-Arranging the Desktop

To turn Auto Arrange on or off for your desktop icons, right-click anywhere on the desktop and choose Arrange Icons.

Deciding What to Include in a Folder Window

Windows gives you some choices regarding what to include in a folder window. By default, you see all files and folders except the following:

- Hidden files
- Dynamic-link libraries (.DLL files)
- System files (.SYS files)
- Device drivers (.VXD, .386, or .DRV files)
- Setup information files (.PNF files)

SEE ALSO
For more information about hidden files, see "Setting Attributes for Folders, Files, and Shortcuts," page 153.

All these files are crucial to the operation of applications and of Windows NT itself. They're not normally included in folder windows because accidental deletion or relocation of one of them can have serious adverse consequences—possibly requiring the reinstallation of an application or of Windows NT. Therefore, unless you need to work with these types of files, it's a good idea to leave them out of sight.

To make these files (and all others) visible in your folder windows, choose the View menu's Options command, and then click the View tab. You will see the dialog box shown in Figure 5-5. Select the Show All Files option button.

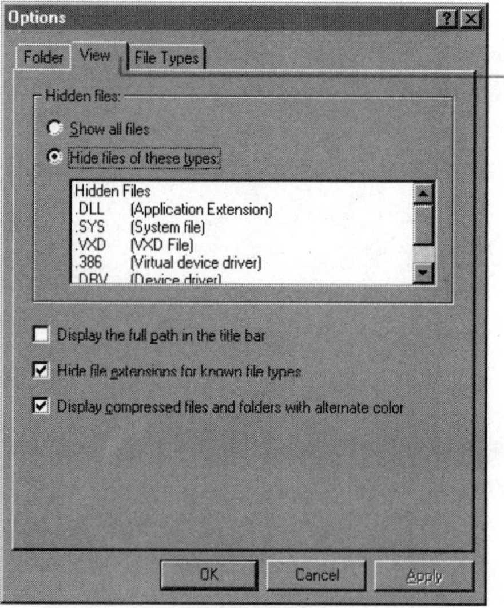

FIGURE 5-5.
The View page of the Options dialog box gives you choices about what should be included in folder windows.

TIP

Making Hidden Files Accessible to the Find Command
File types not shown in folder windows are also invisible to the Find command. If you want to be able to search for particular types of files with the Find command, be sure to make those file types visible in your folders.

Displaying Filename Extensions

A *filename extension* is any group of characters that appears after the final period in a filename. As you may know, earlier versions of Windows, as well as the versions of MS-DOS on which they were built, allowed filenames to have extensions of up to three characters. Such extensions provided a means of categorizing files. All batch files, for example, had the extension .BAT; all graphics files in the Windows bitmap format had the extension .BMP, and so on.

Windows NT, like Windows 95, has done away with this three-character extension limit—as well as the onerous eight-character limit that applied to the main part of a file's name. Windows NT filenames can consist of up to 255 characters, including as many periods as you like, and as many characters as you like after the final period.

These emancipations notwithstanding, Windows NT and Windows-based applications still use filename extensions to categorize files. Many applications, for example, automatically append an extension to any filename you supply, even though you may not see the extensions in the entries that appear in your folder windows.

Windows NT uses the registry—its central depository of information about applications, their documents, and your system—to determine what kind of icon to display next to names in folder windows. Excel

Windows NT Filename Restrictions

Names of folders and files used by programs written for Windows NT can include as many as 255 characters. Thus, there's no need to be cryptic or overly compact in your choice of a filename. Instead of naming that departmental budget worksheet EBUD97-1, you can call it Editorial Budget for 1997—First Draft.

Programs designed for earlier versions of Windows and not yet updated still adhere to the old limit of eight characters plus an optional three-character extension. If a program you're using rejects long filenames, check with the vendor to see if an updated version is available.

In any filename, long or short, certain characters are prohibited. These characters are:

* | \ < > ? / " :

Spaces and the following additional characters are prohibited in MS-DOS (short) filenames:

+ , . ; = [ ]

These characters are reserved for use by the operating system.

documents get Excel-style icons, text files get icons that look like notepads, and so on. Files for which no registry entry exists get a "miscellaneous" icon—something that looks like a Windows logo on a page with a dog-ear in its upper right corner. By default, only files of such unregistered types have their extensions displayed in folder windows. *For more information on the registry, see "Working with the Registry," page 741.*

If you'd like to see extensions for all filenames, choose the View menu's Options command and click the View tab. In the dialog box that appears (see Figure 5-5 on page 132), deselect the check box labeled "Hide file extensions for file types that are registered." You might want to make this change if you're having difficulty determining which icon represents which kind of file. You can, of course, switch back to the default display mode at any time.

To display extensions for only particular registered file types, use the File Types tab of the same dialog box. *For more information about the File Types tab, see "Specifying the Display of Extensions," page 158.*

> **Sharing Files with Systems That Don't Allow Long Filenames**
>
> To allow file sharing between Windows NT 4 and older operating systems, Windows NT stores two versions of each filename—the one you supply and another that conforms to the eight-plus-three limitation of MS-DOS. The alternative name is built from the first six characters of the long name, followed by a tilde, a numeral, a period, and the first three characters that follow the last period in your long name. So, for example, the short counterpart for the name *Accounts Receivable.xls* might be *Accoun~1.xls.*
>
> If you're going to be sharing a file with a user of Windows 3.x or MS-DOS, you might want to plan your long filenames so that the short versions don't become totally inscrutable. Try to create names in which the first characters make sense by themselves. After you've created the file, you can find out what the short name is by right-clicking the filename in a folder window and choosing the Properties command. The short name appears on the General page of the property sheet, under the heading MS-DOS Name.

Refreshing a Folder Window

The Refresh command, on a folder window's View menu, ensures that a folder window's display reflects any changes to the folder's contents that may have taken place since you opened the window. For example, if you're looking at a folder on a network server, other users may be adding, deleting, or renaming files on that folder while your window is open. To be sure that what you see matches what's out there, choose the View menu's Refresh command—or type its keyboard shortcut, F5.

Selecting Folders and Files

The first step in many operations in Windows—opening, copying, or moving a document, for example—is to select the folder or file you want to use. When a folder or file is selected, its icon and title appear highlighted in a color that's different from unselected items. You can select a folder or file in a folder window in any of the following ways:

- Click its icon or title. (Note that in details view, you must click only the icon or title to select an object—not the other parts of the description line.)
- Type the first few letters of the title.
- Use the arrow keys to move the highlight.

You'll often want to select more than one item at a time. Here are some ways to select a group of objects:

- "Lasso" them. Hold down the mouse button while you drag a rectangle around all members of the group.
- Hold down the Ctrl key while you click each item in the group.
- If the items are next to one another in the window, click the first. Then hold down the Shift key while you click the last.

TIP

Selecting All (or Almost All)

Two commands on the folder window's Edit menu can be useful when you need to select groups. If you need to select everything in a folder, choose Select All (or press Ctrl-A). If you want to select nearly all items, select those that you do *not* want to select. Then choose the Invert Selection command. This action deselects what you've already selected and selects everything else.

Inspecting Folder and File Properties

Windows NT provides you with a simple way to learn a folder or file's size, creation date, and other vital statistics. Simply right-click a folder or file and choose Properties from the context menu. (If the folder window's toolbar is visible, you can click the Properties tool to get to the property sheet directly.) Figure 5-6 and Figure 5-7 illustrate the property sheet for a folder and a file.

Notice that the folder property sheet shows how many subfolders the folder contains, as well as the number of files. The number of folders

 TIP

Finding the Folder's Property Sheet

To read the property sheet for an open folder, right-click anywhere within the folder's unoccupied space, or right-click the Control-menu icon at the left edge of the title bar. Then choose the Properties command.

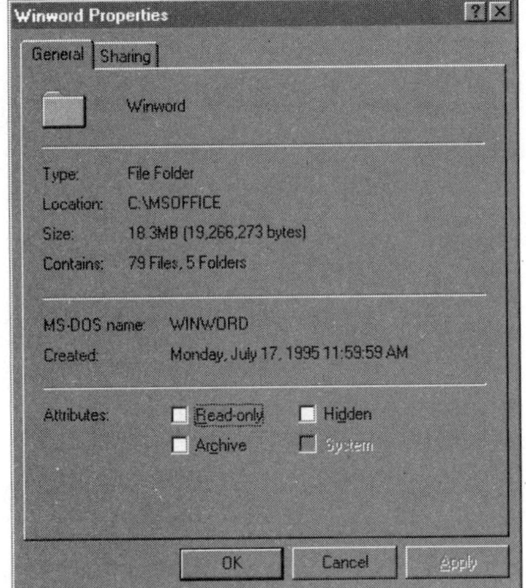

FIGURE 5-6.
This folder's property sheet shows that the folder includes 79 files and 5 subfolders, occupying a total of 18.3 MB (megabytes).

SEE ALSO
For information about sharing folders, see Chapter 11, "Using and Sharing Files on the Network."

SEE ALSO
For information about setting properties for MS-DOS–based applications, see Chapter 17, "Using Programs for Other Operating Systems." For information about the Security page, see Chapter 20, "NTFS Security," and Chapter 21, "Auditing."

and files, along with their cumulative size, includes the contents of the folder and all its subfolders. (The statistics in a folder window's status bar do not include the contents of subfolders.)

If your computer is part of a network and your system has been set up to allow file sharing, the folder property sheet includes a Sharing tab. By clicking here, you can make the folder available to others on your network (or stop making it available).

The file property sheet (see Figure 5-7 on the next page) includes three dates—the date the file was created, the date it was most recently changed, and the date it was most recently accessed. If the file is a document created by an OLE application, it may include additional information. Property sheets for Excel documents, for example, include a Summary tab and a Statistics tab (see Figure 5-7), which provide a revision number, keywords, comments, and other details. If the file is an MS-DOS–based application, the property sheet includes tabs that let you set operating parameters for the program. If the file is on an NTFS-formatted volume, the property sheet includes a Security tab, which lets you view or set permissions, auditing information, and ownership.

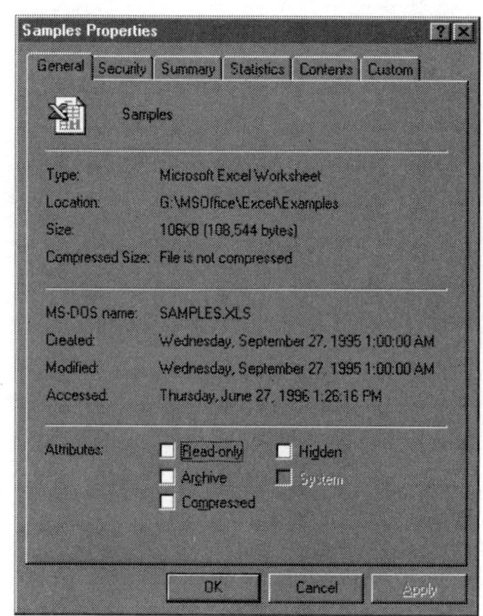

FIGURE 5-7.
Along with other details, the property sheet for this 106 KB (kilobyte) document shows when the file was created, last modified, and last accessed. Other tabs provide more details about the content of the file.

TIP

Weeding Out Old Files

The Accessed date on a file's property sheet can help you determine whether a file might be a good candidate for deletion. If it hasn't been accessed any time during the last two years, perhaps you no longer need it.

You can use the Find utility to locate all files that have not been modified within some specified period of time. Then by inspecting the properties of each such file, you can weed out the files that not only haven't been modified but also haven't even been looked at recently. You can inspect the properties of a file directly in the Find window by right-clicking the filename or icon.

For more information about the Find command, see "Finding Files and Folders," page 179.

Inspecting Properties for Groups of Objects

By selecting two or more folders or files, and then right-clicking, you can inspect properties for groups of objects. The resulting property sheet tells you the total size of the selected objects, whether they're all of the same type, and whether they're all located in the same folder. Figure 5-8 shows a property sheet for a group of files.

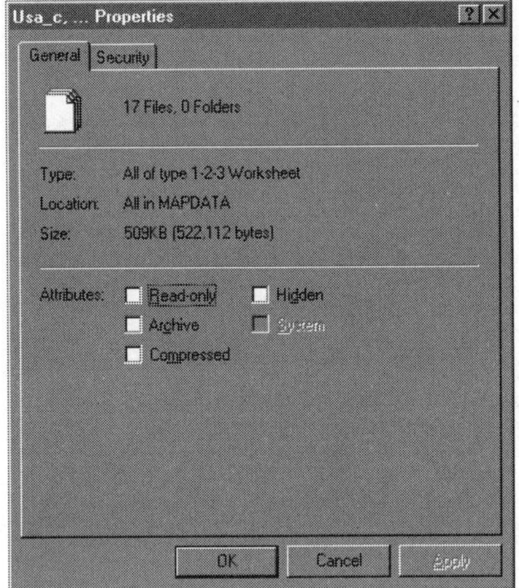

FIGURE 5-8.
This property sheet indicates that the 17 selected files are all 1-2-3 worksheets stored in the Mapdata folder, and that together they occupy 509 KB.

To select a group of folders or files, hold down the Ctrl key while clicking on each object. Or, if the objects are adjacent to one another, click the first, and then hold down the Shift key while you click the last. When you have selected the objects you're interested in, right-click to get to the property sheet.

To select a group of folders or files that are not all in the same folder, use the Find command to collect the objects in a Find window. Then hold down Ctrl while you click each object you're interested in.

Inspecting a Disk's Properties

The property sheet for a disk's top-level folder is different from all others. It uses a large pie graph to show how much of the disk is in use and how much remains available. Figure 5-9 shows an example.

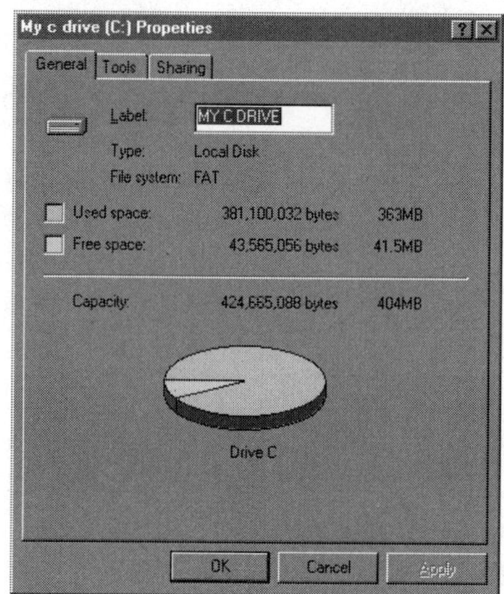

FIGURE 5-9.
The property sheet for a disk's top-level folder lets you see how much space is available.

To get to the top-level folder for a disk, begin by double-clicking My Computer. Then right-click the icon for the disk you're interested in. That icon may look like a disk instead of a folder, but the object it represents is still a folder—as you can see by double-clicking it.

Creating New Folders

Folders in Windows NT can be nested to any level. That is, you can have folders within folders within folders—to whatever degree of complexity you want.

To create a new folder, begin by displaying the folder in which you want the new folder to reside. Right-click anywhere within this parent folder's unoccupied space, and then choose New from the context menu. When the submenu appears, choose Folder. (Alternatively, you can choose New from the folder window's File menu, and then choose Folder from the submenu.)

SEE ALSO
For more information about renaming folders, see "Renaming Objects," page 146.

Your new folder will begin with a default name, such as "New Folder" or "New Folder #2." To rename it, type the name you want and press Enter.

If you click away from the new folder before renaming it, simply right-click it and choose Rename from the context menu. (Alternatively, choose Rename from the folder window's File menu.)

Moving or Copying Folders, Files, and Shortcuts

To move or copy an object in a folder window, right-drag it from its current position to its destination. When you release the mouse button, a context menu appears. From this context menu, you can choose Move Here, Copy Here, or Create Shortcut(s) Here. Make the appropriate selection, and you're done.

To move or copy an entire folder, simply display the folder's parent folder. Then right-drag the folder icon (or the folder entry, if you're working in list or details view). Be aware that this action moves or replicates not only the folder but everything within the folder as well.

If you copy an object to a new destination in the same folder, Windows gives the copy a default name, such as "Copy of Myfile." While the object is still selected, you can give it a new name by typing and pressing Enter. Alternatively, right-click it and choose Rename.

If you prefer to drag with the left mouse button, you can do so, but in this case you need to know the following:

- If you left-drag a program file from one folder to another or to the desktop, Windows leaves the program in its source folder and creates a shortcut to the program in the destination folder. (Note that Windows ignores this "rule" if more than one file is selected when you drag. The following rules remain in effect.)

- If you left-drag any other file type from one folder to another on the same disk, Windows performs a move.
- If you left-drag from a folder on one disk to a folder on a different disk, Windows performs a copy.
- If you left-drag a folder or any file other than a program file from a folder to the desktop, Windows performs a move—provided the source folder resides on the disk where you installed Windows. If the source folder is on a different disk, Windows performs a copy instead of a move.

When you drag an object from one folder to another or to the desktop, Windows displays a ghost image of the object you're dragging. If you're dragging with the left mouse button, you can look at the lower right corner of this image to see what action Windows will perform when you release the button. If Windows is going to move the object, you won't see anything in the lower right corner. If Windows is going to create a copy, you'll see a plus sign in the lower right corner. If Windows is going to create a shortcut, you'll see a shortcut arrow.

If you don't like the proposed action, click the right mouse button before you drop the object on the destination to cancel the drag operation in process.

TIP

Moving and Copying

You can force Windows to *move* the selected objects—regardless of file type and destination—by holding down the Shift key as you drag. You can force Windows to *copy* objects by holding down the Ctrl key as you drag. You can force Windows to create a shortcut by holding down Shift and Ctrl as you drag.

Moving or Copying Objects to Unopened Folders

In many cases, you can move or copy an object to a new folder without opening the destination folder. For example, suppose the file

Rough Draft is stored in the folder PMFeature and you want to move it to the folder Outtakes, which is also stored in PMFeature. Simply grab Rough Draft with your mouse, drag it to the folder icon for Outtakes, and then release the mouse button.

If the destination folder is minimized, you can move or copy an object to it by dragging the object to the folder's taskbar button. Hold the object over the button for a moment while holding down the mouse button, and the folder window will open.

TIP

Dragging to a Shortcut
If you have a shortcut for a folder on your desktop, you can move or copy items to that folder by dragging them to the shortcut.

Moving or Copying Objects with Menu Commands

If dragging and dropping is not convenient, you can move or copy objects using the Edit menu's Cut, Copy, and Paste commands (or their toolbar shortcuts).

TIP

The Keyboard Can Be Quicker
It's often quicker to use the keyboard shortcuts for Cut, Copy, and Paste than it is to visit the Edit menu. Press Ctrl-X to cut or Ctrl-C to copy, and then press Ctrl-V to paste.

- To move an object, select it and choose Cut from the source folder's Edit menu. Then choose Paste from the destination folder's Edit menu. (If the desktop is your destination, right-click the desktop and choose Paste from the context menu.)
- To copy an object, select it and choose Copy from the source folder's Edit menu. Then choose Paste from the destination folder's Edit menu. (If the desktop is your destination, right-click the desktop and choose Paste from the context menu.)

Backing Out

When you cut an item, that item is not removed from its source folder until you paste it somewhere. If you change your mind in midstream, simply press Esc.

Moving or Copying Groups of Folders and Files

To move or copy a group of folders or files, select all members of the group, and then follow the same procedure you would use to move or copy a single item. To select a group, hold down the Ctrl key while you select each member. Alternatively, if the items are located next to one another in the folder window, you can select the first, and then hold down the Shift key while you select the last. *For more information about selecting a group of folders or files, see "Selecting Folders and Files," page 135.*

Moving or Copying Objects with Send To

When you right-click a folder or file, the context menu includes a Send To command. When you select this command, Windows displays a submenu of destinations, typically including floppy drives on your system, as well as various other destinations. You can use the Send To command as a quick and easy way to move or copy a folder or file to any destination. You can also customize the Send To menu so that it includes destinations you frequently use.

When you use the Send To command with a folder destination, Windows treats the object just as if you dragged the object to the folder using the left mouse button. That is, if the destination and source folders are on the same disk, Windows performs a move; if the destination and source folders are on different disks, Windows performs a copy.

Customizing the Send To Menu

The contents of the Send To menu are determined by the contents of a folder named SendTo. Each account on your system has its own SendTo folder. In a typical Windows NT installation, the full path of an account's SendTo folder is

C:\Winnt\Profiles*Username*\SendTo

where *Username* is the name of the account. If you're not sure how to navigate to that folder, use the Find command on the Start menu. Tell Find to look for SendTo. In the list of "hits" that appears after Find has done its work, look for the one whose "In Folder" entry ends with your account name. Then double-click that entry. That should open the SendTo folder for your account.

SEE ALSO
For more information about creating short-cuts, see "Creating a Shortcut," page 75.

To add destinations to the Send To menu, simply create shortcuts for those destinations and store the shortcuts in the SendTo folder. For example, suppose you want to create a Send To menu item for a folder named Budgets, which is a subfolder of C:\Msoffice\Excel. Here is one way you can accomplish this addition:

1. Open your SendTo folder.
2. Right-click any unoccupied space in the SendTo folder, choose New from the context menu, and choose Shortcut.
3. In the Command Line text box in the Create Shortcut wizard, type *c:\msoffice\excel\budgets*. Then click Next.
4. In the wizard's next dialog box, accept or modify the wizard's proposed name for your new shortcut. Then click OK.

Of course, you can also use any other technique for creating a shortcut to your new destination folder.

Using Applications and Other Kinds of Destinations on the Send To Menu

Your Send To menu can include applications, printers, and other types of "destinations," as well as folders. If you select a document and then choose an application from the Send To menu, Windows launches the application and attempts to open the selected document. If you select a document and choose a printer, Windows tries to print your document using that printer. In all cases, Windows does what it would have done had you dragged the selected document to a shortcut for the destination object. In other words, the Send To command is a menu alternative for a drag-and-drop operation.

NOTE

If you try to drag a folder to an application on the Send To menu, you'll get an error message. You'll also get an error message (a different one) if you try to drag multiple documents to an application that can't handle multiple documents. No harm is done in either case.

TIP

Quick Viewing with Send To

Putting a shortcut for Notepad in your SendTo folder gives you a way to inspect plain text files that may not be identified in the registry as quick-viewable. For example, suppose you have a file named Read.me, and your registry knows nothing about .ME files. With Notepad on your Send To menu, you can simply right-click and send the file to Notepad for easy viewing and printing.

To add an application to the Send To menu, simply create a shortcut for that application in your SendTo folder, in the same way that you would add a folder destination to the Send To menu.

Renaming Objects

The simplest way to rename an object is to right-click it, choose Rename from the context menu, and then type a new name. But other methods are also available:

- Select the object and choose Rename from the folder window's File menu.

- Select the object. Then click the object's name. When a rectangle appears around the object's name, type a new name or edit the current name.

  When you use this method, you need to pause a moment between selecting the object and clicking the object's name. Otherwise, Windows interprets your action as a double-click and opens the selected object.

- Select the object and press F2. Then type a new name or edit the current name.

TIP

If you make a mistake while changing a name, simply press Esc to cancel the process.

Windows preserves the case (capitals and lowercase) for objects you name, with one exception: file or folder names that are eight characters or shorter and typed in all capitals. Windows displays such names with an initial capital and the rest of the name in lowercase. (This is done to "beautify" standard MS-DOS file and directory names.)

TIP

Beware the Hidden Extension

If you've chosen not to display extensions for registered files, be careful not to type the extension when you rename a file. For example, suppose you have a file named My Picture.bmp, and your folder window displays that file's name as simply My Picture. If you change the name to Your Picture, be sure to type *Your Picture*, not *Your Picture.bmp*. Otherwise, the file's name will be recorded as Your Picture.bmp.bmp.

Reversing Actions with the Undo Command

If you change your mind after moving or copying something, you can reverse your action by choosing the Undo command from any folder window's Edit menu. (If the toolbar is visible, you can simply click the Undo tool.) Be aware, however, that you must use the Undo command right away. As soon as you perform some other action, Undo will reverse that action, not your move or copy.

Deleting Folders, Files, and Shortcuts

To delete an object or a group of objects, select what you want to delete and press the Del key. If you prefer a more complicated method, try one of these:

- Right-click an object and choose Delete from the context menu.
- Select an object or group of objects, pull down the folder window's File menu, and then choose Delete.
- Select an object or a group of objects, and then drag it to the Recycle Bin icon on your desktop—or to a shortcut for the Recycle Bin.

However you do the deed, Windows presents a prompt and asks you to confirm your intent. This protects you from accidental deletions.

The Prompt Is Optional

If you don't want Windows to prompt for confirmation when you delete folders, files, or shortcuts, clear the Display Delete Confirmation Dialog check box at the bottom of the Recycle Bin's property sheet.

As further protection, items you delete from hard disk folders or the desktop are automatically transferred to the Recycle Bin. You can retrieve them from the Recycle Bin if you change your mind.

Bypassing the Bin

To delete something without moving it to the Recycle Bin, hold down the Shift key while you press Del.

TIP

Using the Undo Command

If you change your mind right away about a deletion, you can restore whatever you deleted by choosing the Undo Delete command from the folder window's Edit menu.

Restoring Deleted Items

Have you ever deleted one file when you really meant to delete a different one? Wiped out a whole directory by mistake? Or simply trashed a document you thought you were finished with, only to discover the following week that you desperately needed it back?

Windows NT provides a way to recover gracefully from accidents such as these. For a period of time after you delete an object, that object remains in the Recycle Bin. If you change your mind, a simple menu command or mouse action restores selected items to the folders from which they were deleted.

The Recycle Bin is like that large trash barrel outside your house or the dumpster in the alley behind your office. Until the big truck comes to empty that container, anything you've tossed out can still be retrieved. *For information about when the big truck arrives in Windows, see "Setting Your Recycle Bin's Capacity," page 151.*

When you double-click the Recycle Bin icon, Windows displays the names of recently deleted items in an ordinary folder window. (See Figure 5-10 on the next page.) By default, the window appears in details view and includes columns to show when each item was deleted and which folder it was deleted from. As in other folder windows, you can click column headings to change the sort order, and you can use toolbar icons or commands on the View menu to switch to list view or large- or small-icon view.

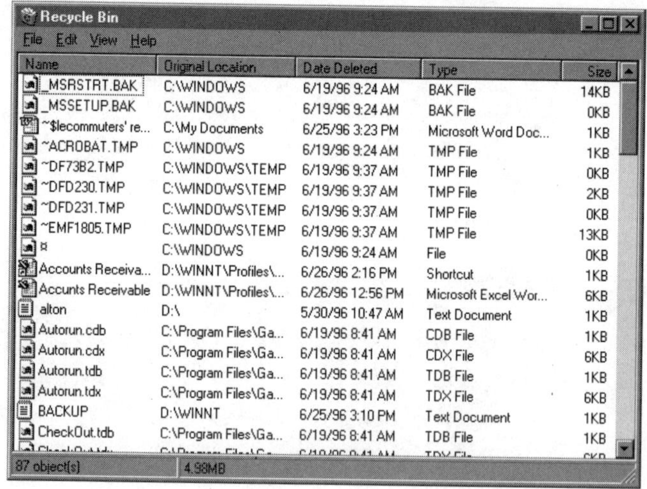

FIGURE 5-10.
Opening the Recycle Bin reveals an ordinary folder window in details view.

To restore an item from the Recycle Bin, simply select it and choose the File menu's Restore command. Or right-click the item and choose Restore from the context menu. The Restore command puts the item back in the folder from which it was deleted. If that folder doesn't currently exist, Windows asks your permission to re-create it.

TIP

Restoring a Folder

To restore all files from a folder that was accidentally deleted, sort by Original Location to group all the files from that folder. Then select those files and choose Restore from the File menu.

You also have the option of restoring a deleted item and putting it in a different folder. To do this, select the item and choose Cut from the File menu or context menu. Go to the folder in which you want the item to be restored, and then choose the Paste command on that folder window's Edit menu.

Here are three other important things to know about the Recycle Bin:

- Items deleted from floppy disks or network servers are not stored in the Recycle Bin. When you delete such an item, Windows asks you to confirm the deletion.

- Some application programs provide their own commands for deleting files. If you use an application's delete command your deleted file may not be transferred to the Recycle Bin.
- If you delete a file from the prompt in a command prompt window, that file does not go to the Recycle Bin.
- If you delete a folder, Windows stores all of the folder's files, but not the folder itself, in the Recycle Bin. When you restore an item that was deleted from a deleted folder, Windows (with your permission) re-creates the deleted folder.
- Windows NT maintains separate Recycle Bins for each hard disk on your computer, but each Recycle Bin is shared by all accounts on the computer.

TIP

Searching the Bin

The Find command cannot be used to locate items in the Recycle Bin. To search for items in the Recycle Bin, sort the Recycle Bin display on the column heading of interest. For example, to find an item when you know its name, click the Name heading so that all deleted items' names appear in alphabetical order. To find items that were deleted on a particular day, click the Date Deleted column heading.

Setting Your Recycle Bin's Capacity

Although you have only one Recycle Bin icon (plus any shortcuts to that icon that you've created), Windows actually maintains separate recycle bins for each hard disk on your system. The default size of each recycle bin is 10 percent of the capacity of the hard disk on which it's stored. When a recycle bin exceeds that limit, Windows begins removing files permanently, starting with the files that have been in the Recycle Bin the longest.

You can make your recycle bins larger or smaller by right-clicking the Recycle Bin icon and choosing Properties. (If the Recycle Bin is already open, you can get to the context menu by right-clicking the window's Control-menu icon.) You'll see a dialog box similar to the one shown in Figure 5-11, with a tab for each of your system's hard disks.

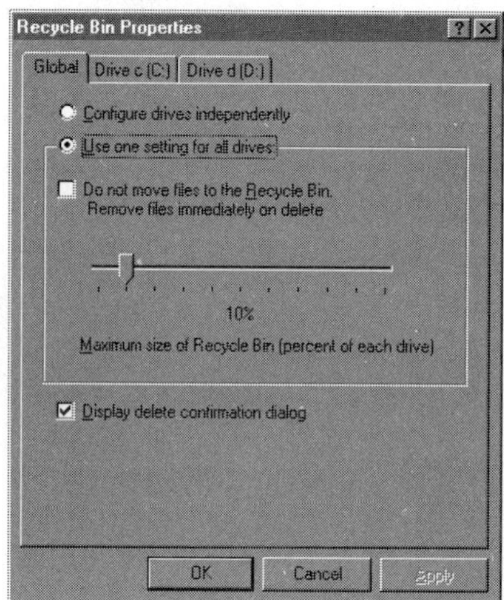

FIGURE 5-11. The Properties command lets you configure each hard disk's recycle bin.

To adjust the size of all recycle bins on your system, select the Use One Setting For All Drives option button, and then adjust the slider on the Global page. To adjust the size of recycle bins individually, select the Configure Drives Independently option button, and then adjust the sliders on each disk drive page. To turn off recycle bin functionality globally, select the check box labeled "Do not move files to the Recycle Bin; remove files immediately on delete." To do this only for a particular hard disk, select the Configure Drives Independently option button, and then select the "remove files immediately" check box on the appropriate disk page.

Purging the Recycle Bin

A deleted file sitting in your Recycle Bin takes up just as much space as it did before it was deleted. If you're deleting files in order to free up room for new programs and documents, simply transferring them from ordinary disk folders to the Recycle Bin folder won't do you much good. You need to get the old files off your system permanently. The safest way to do this, of course, is to move the files to a removable medium, such as a floppy disk. That way, you can always get your files back if you change your mind.

If you're sure you'll never need a particular file again, however, you can delete it in the normal way, and then purge it from the Recycle Bin. To delete an item from the Recycle Bin, simply display the Recycle Bin, select the item, and then press the Del key. Be aware as you answer the confirmation prompt that this deletion removes your selection permanently.

To delete a group of items from the Recycle Bin, hold down the Ctrl key while you select each one, and then press the Del key. (If the files are located next to one another in the Recycle Bin window, you can select the first member of the group, and then hold down the Shift key while you select the last member.)

TIP

Checking Properties
You can check the properties of a file before deleting it by double-clicking the file's icon in the Recycle Bin window.

To empty the Recycle Bin in one fell swoop, simply right-click the Recycle Bin icon and choose Empty Recycle Bin from the context menu. Or, if you're already in the Recycle Bin window, choose this command from the File menu.

Setting Attributes for Folders, Files, and Shortcuts

Attributes are markers that file systems employ to identify certain characteristics of files. In Windows NT, folders, files, and shortcuts can have no attributes or any combination of the following attributes: read only, archive, hidden, system, and compress. The property sheet (see Figure 5-6 on page 137 and Figure 5-7 on page 138) lets you see an item's current attributes and change them if necessary.

NOTE

The compress attribute is available only on NTFS volumes.

You can open a file with the *read-only* attribute, but you can't save it unless you first rename it. Some programs—and many users—set this attribute to prevent accidental changes to a file. To assign this attribute, right-click the file, choose Properties in the context menu, and then select the Read Only check box. Note, however, that you will need to remove this attribute (by deselecting the check box) if you want to edit the file without changing its name.

In many contexts, the read-only attribute not only prevents an item from being altered, but also keeps it from being deleted. For example, the MS-DOS Erase and Del commands refuse to delete files that are marked read-only. (You'll get the error message "Access denied" if you try.) If you select a read-only file in a folder window and press the Del key, Windows presents a confirmation prompt, reminding you that the file is read-only.

TIP

Folders Have Attributes Too
You can assign attributes to entire folders as well as to individual files. Making a folder read-only does not alter the attributes of files or folders contained within the read-only folder, but it does afford some protection against accidental deletion of the folder.

TIP

Use Permissions to Safeguard NTFS Folders
Setting permissions is a more secure way to protect folders (and the files they contain) than relying on the read-only attribute. *For details, see "Attaching Security to Folders," page 586.*

The *archive* attribute indicates that an item has been modified since it was last backed up. Each time you create a new file or change an old one, Windows assigns the archive attribute to that file. Backup programs typically remove the archive attribute when they back up a file. If you change the file after backing it up, the file again gets the archive attribute so your backup program can recognize it as needing to be backed up again.

A few programs use the *hidden* and *system* attributes (either, but usually both) to mark important files that must not be modified or deleted because they are critical components of the program or Windows.

The *compress* attribute is used to squeeze more data onto a disk that is formatted as an NTFS volume. *For details, see "Using File Compression," page 727.*

Working with the File Types List

If you choose Options on a folder window's View menu, and then click the File Types tab, Windows displays a list of all registered file types. A sample of this list is shown in Figure 5-12.

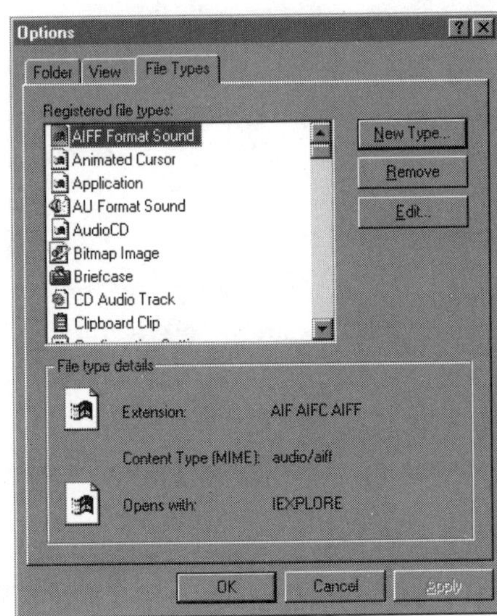

FIGURE 5-12.
The File Types page in the View menu's Options dialog box lists all file types known to the registry, provides details about how they're associated, and allows you to change document icons or add quick-view capability.

Working with this list, you can do a number of things:

- Decode the icons in your folder windows
- Change a file type's icon
- Add or remove quick-view capability for a file type
- Change the registered name of a file type
- Specify whether the file type's extension should be displayed in folder and Windows NT Explorer windows
- Remove a file type from the registry
- Change the actions carried out by commands on the file type's context menu
- Add or delete commands on the file type's context menu
- Create new file types

Decoding File Icons

As you've undoubtedly noticed, document files are marked by icons shaped like pages with a dog-ear in the upper right corner. Icons for registered documents resemble those of their parent applications, and icons for unregistered documents bear the generic Windows emblem. But if you open your Windows folder or its System subfolder, you'll probably find dozens of files with icons that may not be familiar. What do all these icons signify?

One way you can find out is by stepping through the File Types list. As you select each file type in the list, a full-size version of the file type's icon appears in the bottom of the dialog box along with the file type's extension and the icon used by its parent application (if it has one).

Changing a File Type's Icon

Just as you can change the icons used by your programs *(see "Changing a Shortcut's Icon," page 81)*, you can also reassign document icons. To do this, open a folder window's View menu, choose Options, and click the File Types tab. In the Registered File Types list, find the file type you want to modify, and then click Edit. Click the Change Icon button at the top of the ensuing dialog box, and then choose a new icon from the Change Icon gallery.

If you don't see a suitable icon in the Change Icon gallery, you can specify a different program in the File Name text box—and then "borrow" an icon from that program.

Adding or Removing Quick-View Capability

The Quick View facility lets you look at many types of files, including both text and graphics files, without invoking the applications that created them. If a file type's context menu does not include the Quick View command, you can add it as follows:

1 Select the file type in the File Types list.

2 Click the Edit button.

3 Select the Enable Quick View check box and click OK.

If Windows doesn't have a viewer specific to the selected file type, it uses the plain-text viewer. This may or may not produce an edifying display. If it doesn't, no harm is done. You can go back to the File Types list and deselect the Enable Quick View check box. *For more information about Quick View, see "Inspecting Documents and Programs with Quick View," page 69.*

Changing the Registered Name of a File Type

The names that appear in the File Types list may show up in menus used by your applications. For example, if you use the Insert Object command in WordPad (or in another program that supports OLE), you'll see a list of embeddable objects. This list is derived from the File Types list. You can change what you see on such menus by changing the names in the File Types list. There's probably no compelling reason to do this, unless you simply object to the length of some of the names.

For example, suppose you tire of seeing the name *Microsoft* before every file type created by a Microsoft application. To reduce Microsoft Access Database Application to something a bit simpler, such as Access Application, you could do as follows:

1 In the File Types list, select the Microsoft Access Database Application entry.

2 Click the Edit button.

3 In the Description Of Type box, type the short name you prefer, and then click OK.

Specifying the Display of Extensions

By default, folder and Windows NT Explorer windows do not show extensions for registered file types. You can turn on the extension display for all file types using the folder window's Options command. Using the File Types list, you can also show extensions for a particular file type, while suppressing the extensions for other registered file types. Here's how:

1 Select the file type in the File Types list.

2 Click the Edit button.

3 Select the Always Show Extension check box and click OK.

Removing a File Type from the Registry

SEE ALSO

For information about the Add/Remove Programs wizard, see "Uninstalling Applications," page 702.

If you use the Add/Remove Programs wizard to uninstall Windows-based programs that you no longer need, you should not have to "unregister" the file types used by those applications. The wizard should take care of that detail for you. But if the wizard lets you down, or if you remove a program without the wizard's assistance, you might want to visit the File Types list to clean up. You can remove a file type from the registry as follows:

1 Select the file type in the File Types list.

2 Click the Remove button and reply to the confirmation prompt. Then click OK.

Modifying a File Type's Context Menu

If you know what you're doing, you can change the contents of a file type's context menu or modify the behavior of commands on the menu. To see what commands are on the context menu, select a file type and click the Edit button. To see what a particular command does, select that command in the Actions section of the ensuing dialog box, and then click Edit in that dialog box. To make changes, modify the next dialog box that appears.

NOTE

Unless you're completely sure of your ground, this part of the File Types list is best seen but not touched. If you make mistakes here, you may need to reinstall the affected application.

Creating New File Types

SEE ALSO

For information about the Open With dialog box, see "What to Do When Windows Can't Open Your Documents," page 65.

The New Type button in the File Types list allows you to add new file types to the registry. Normally, you should have no reason to use this button. Instead, if you want to create an association between an unregistered file type and an application, simply double-click an instance of that file type in a folder window. Then fill out the Open With dialog box.

Formatting Disks

CAUTION

Formatting erases all data on a disk!

To format a disk, first insert the disk in the drive. Then right-click an icon or entry for it in a folder window and choose Format from the context menu. Windows displays the following dialog box.

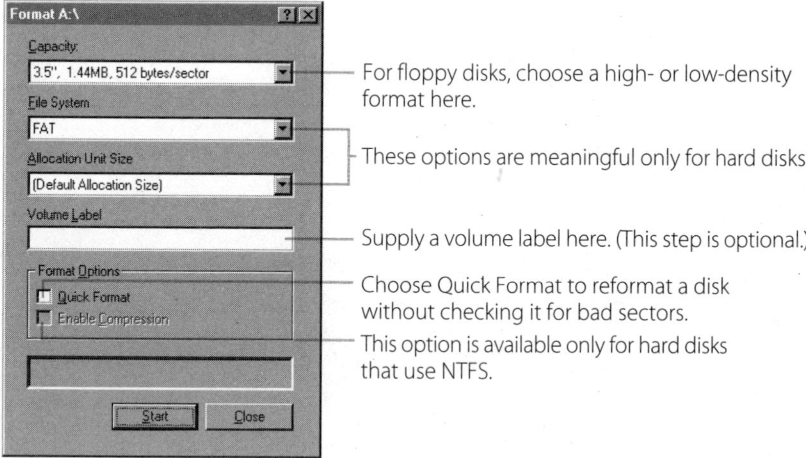

If your disk has already been formatted at least once, you can save some time by choosing the Quick Format option. Windows NT simply erases all the disk's data without checking the media for bad sectors.

You can format a hard disk, provided it's not a disk that contains your Windows NT system files. But exercise great care and make very sure this is what you want to do. Because formatting erases all data on the disk, a mistake here can really ruin your day—and wipe out several years of your computing life!

When you format a hard disk, Windows NT provides certain options not available when you format a floppy disk. (See the figure above.) You can choose between the FAT and NTFS file systems, specify the allocation-unit size, and, if you opt for NTFS, decide whether you want to apply compression to all files on the disk. *For information about these choices, see Chapter 22, "Managing Disks," and "NTFS Pros and Cons," page 580.*

Copying Floppy Disks

To copy a floppy disk, right-click its icon in a folder window and choose Copy Disk from the context menu. Make sure the Copy To and Copy From sections of the dialog box (shown below) are correctly filled out, and then click Start. When the copy is complete, the dialog box remains on screen. If you want to copy another disk, insert it and then click Start again.

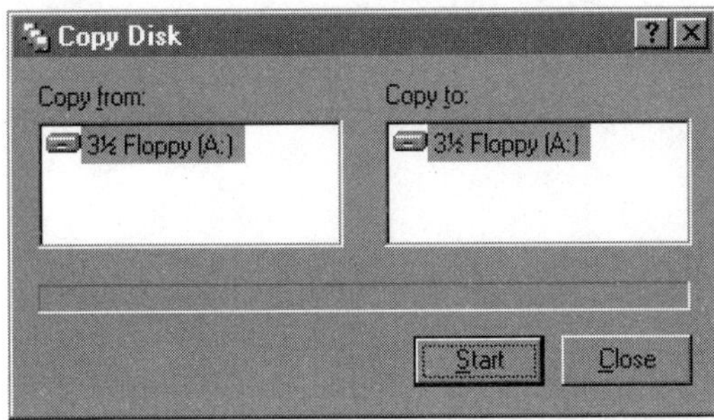

CHAPTER 6

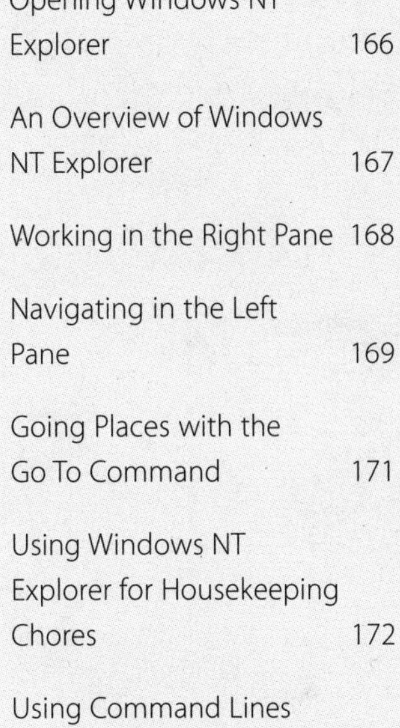

Managing Folders and Files with Windows NT Explorer

Windows Explorer was described by some early reviewers of Windows 95 as a souped-up version of the Windows 3.x File Manager—a "File Manager on steroids"—but it would be more precise to call it a folder window with an attachment. The attachment is simply an "org chart" of your computer and its network environment.

Figures 6-1 shows a folder-window view of a folder, and Figure 6-2 shows the same folder as seen through Windows NT Explorer. As you can see, the Windows NT Explorer window has a left pane and a right pane. The right pane looks just like an ordinary folder window and functions the same way. The left pane is an outline of your Windows namespace. It shows the directory structure of your local hard disks, plus any other resources attached to your computer—including floppy disks, CD-ROM drives, system folders, and network servers. The outline even provides access to printer queues, Control Panel, and the Recycle Bin.

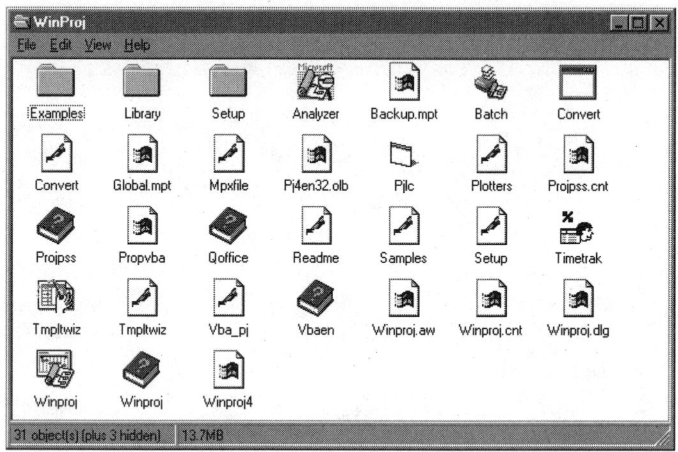

FIGURE 6-1.
A folder-window view of a Microsoft Project folder.

Like an ordinary folder window, Windows NT Explorer includes a menu bar, an optional toolbar, and an optional status bar. The menu bar is exactly like a folder window's, except that it includes an additional menu called "Tools." Also like a folder window, Windows NT Explorer's right pane offers you a choice of four viewing modes: large icons, small icons, list, and details. By default, the right pane appears in details view. We've shown it in large-icon view in Figure 6-2 to emphasize the fact that Windows NT Explorer is merely an extension of the standard folder window—not a wholly new way of interacting with Windows.

FIGURE 6-2. The same folder as seen through Windows NT Explorer.

The left pane in the Windows NT Explorer window confers three benefits: it makes it easy to move quickly between unrelated folders, it lets you see the structure of your folders at a glance, and it allows you to move and copy files by dragging them from the right pane to the left. On the other hand, the split window does make for a more complex display. If you prefer the simplicity of the standard folder window (or, should we say, if the divided window gives you a pane), you can ignore Windows NT Explorer. But if you experiment a bit with Windows NT Explorer, you may find its benefits substantial. In any case, the choice is yours. You can use Windows NT Explorer always, occasionally, or never.

TIP

If You Prefer File Manager

You can use the Windows NT 3.x File Manager as an alternative to Windows NT Explorer. To run File Manager, choose the Run command on the Start menu, type *winfile*, and press Enter. The version of File Manager that appears is the one that Microsoft shipped with Windows NT 3.x.

File Manager's chief virtue relative to Windows NT Explorer is that it offers a customizable toolbar. But if you're not already proficient with File Manager, you'll probably find it more difficult to learn and use than Windows NT Explorer.

Opening Windows NT Explorer

Windows NT Explorer normally is located on your Start menu—usually under Programs. If that's the case on your system, you can use the Start menu to get to Windows NT Explorer. Here are some additional ways to open Windows NT Explorer:

- Right-click My Computer or Network Neighborhood, and then choose Explore from the context menu.
- Right-click any folder icon, or any shortcut icon that points to a folder, and then choose Explore from the context menu.
- In a folder window, select any folder icon and then choose Explore from the File menu.
- In a folder window, select any folder icon and then hold down the Shift key while double-clicking.
- In a folder window, select any folder icon and then hold down the Shift key while pressing Enter.
- In a folder window, right-click the Control-menu icon (at the left edge of the title bar), and then choose Explore.

TIP

Making Windows NT Explorer Your Default Browser

You can make Windows NT Explorer your default browsing tool. To do so, open any folder in a folder window or in Windows NT Explorer. Choose Options from the View menu and click the File Types tab. Select Folder (*not* File Folder) in the Registered File Types list and then click the Edit button. In the Actions list, select Explore and then click the Set Default button. (This should make Explore appear in boldface type.) Click Close twice. Now whenever you double-click My Computer or any other folder, Windows NT Explorer will appear.

An Overview of Windows NT Explorer

Figure 6-3 shows a Windows NT Explorer window in its default display mode, with toolbar and status bar visible and the right pane in details view. Directly below the toolbar are legends for the two panes, which read "All Folders" for the left pane and "Contents of 'My c drive (C:)'" for the right pane. To make the legends appear in your own Windows NT Explorer (if they don't already), choose Options from the View menu, click the View tab, and select the check box labeled "Include description bar for right and left panes."

FIGURE 6-3.
By default, Windows NT Explorer's right pane appears in details view.

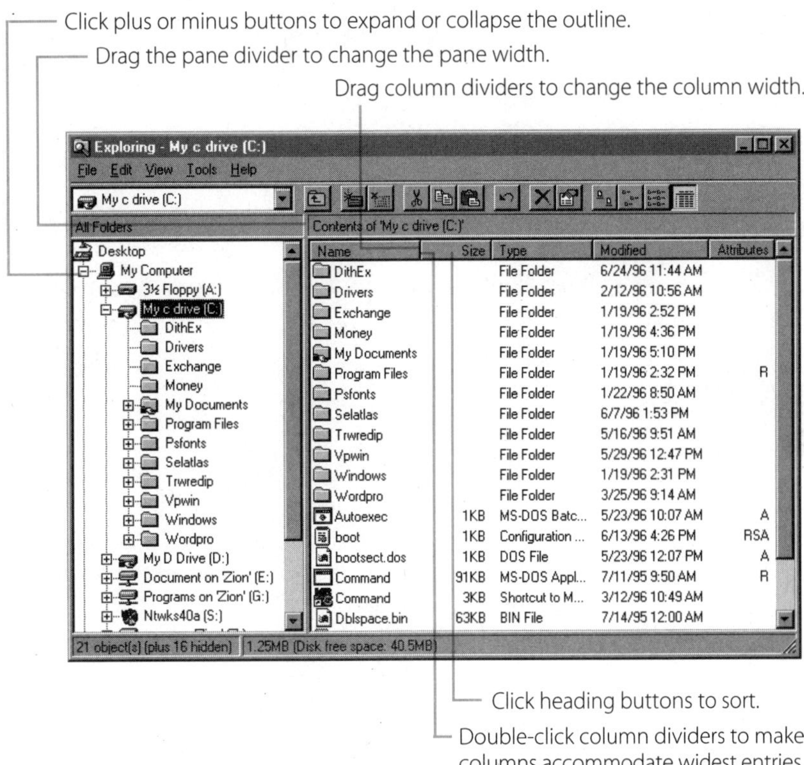

Notice that the right pane includes column headings—Name, Size, Type, Modified, and Attributes. Besides telling you what each column is for, these headings are live buttons; you can sort the pane on any column by clicking its heading.

Inverting the Sort

To reverse the sorting order of a column, click the heading a second time.

Hiding Columns

To hide a right-pane column, drag its divider line to the left until the column disappears. To restore a hidden column, position the mouse pointer on the divider line for the column heading to the left of the hidden column. When the mouse pointer changes to a split two-headed arrow (as opposed to a solid two-headed arrow), drag to the right, and the hidden column will reappear.

The headings in the right pane change, depending on the contents of the Windows NT Explorer window. When Windows NT Explorer is showing the contents of a disk folder, the headings appear as shown in Figure 6-3 on page 167. However, if you use Windows NT Explorer to examine My Computer, Network Neighborhood, Recycle Bin, or a system folder, you will see different column headings.

Checking Your Hard Disk Space

For a quick overview of the total space available on each of your hard disks, right-click My Computer and choose Explore. The third and fourth columns in the right pane will tell you the total capacity of and available space on each local hard disk. (If you don't see this information, pull down the View menu and choose Details.)

Working in the Right Pane

For more information about using Windows NT Explorer's right pane, see Chapter 5, "Working with Folders."

Working in the right pane of a Windows NT Explorer window is exactly like working in an ordinary folder window. You can run programs or launch documents in the right pane, move from folder to folder, copy and move files between folders, and do anything else that you might do in a folder window.

TIP

To open a folder window for any folder shown in the right pane, right-click the folder and choose Open from the context menu.

Navigating in the Left Pane

Moving from one folder to another using Windows NT Explorer's left pane is easy, provided you remember three things:

- To move to another folder, click the folder's name—not the plus or minus sign next to the name, but the name itself. The folder you click becomes the current folder, and its contents appear in the right pane.
- To expand or collapse an outline entry in the left pane, click the plus or minus sign to the left of the folder name. The contents of the right pane do not change when you do this, but the level of detail shown in the left pane does.
- To move to another folder and at the same time expand or collapse its outline entry, double-click the folder name—not the plus or minus sign next to the folder, but the name itself. The folder you click becomes the current folder, and its contents appear in the right pane. At the same time, the level of detail shown in the outline changes.

That's all there is to it. Here are some examples.

In Figure 6-3 on page 167, the current folder is "My c drive (C:)." To switch to drive D, click once on the entry "My D Drive (D:)" in the left pane. Figure 6-4 on the next page shows how Windows NT Explorer would appear after this action.

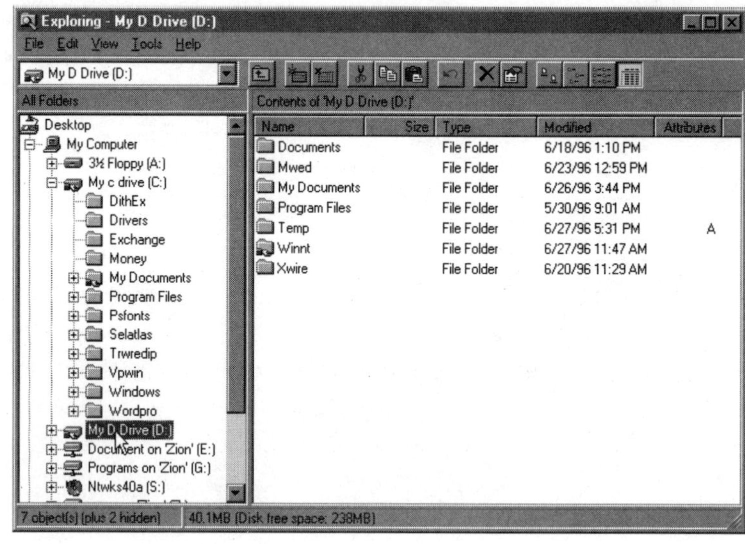

FIGURE 6-4.
Clicking the "My D Drive (D:)" entry in the left pane displays the contents of My D Drive (D:) in the right pane.

The plus sign next to the entry "My D Drive (D:)" in the left pane of Figure 6-4 indicates that this folder contains subfolders. (Of course, you can also tell that by looking at all the folder icons in the right pane.) To display the subfolders in the left pane, click the plus sign next to the entry "My D Drive (D:)." Figure 6-5 shows the result.

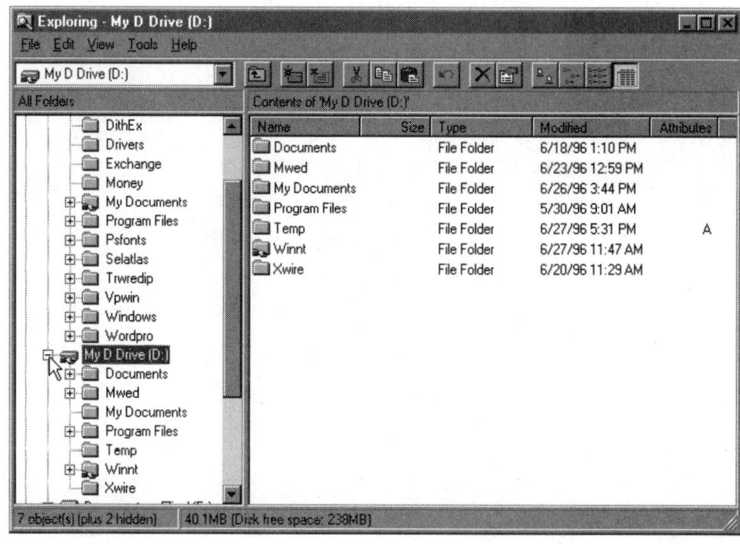

FIGURE 6-5.
Clicking the plus sign to the left of the "My D Drive (D:)" entry expands the entry in the left pane but leaves the right pane unchanged.

Notice that when you expand the entry "My D Drive (D:)," its plus sign changes to a minus sign. When you're ready to collapse that entry, click the minus sign.

Now suppose that you want to move to the Program Files folder, one of the subfolders of "My D Drive (D:)." Because there's a plus sign beside the Program Files entry, you can expand the Program Files entry at the same time that you switch to that folder. Double-clicking Program Files does the trick, and Figure 6-6 shows the result.

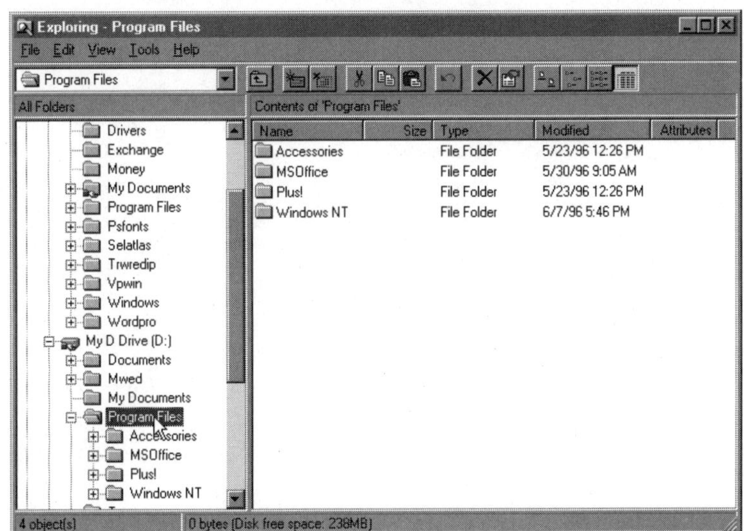

FIGURE 6-6.
Double-clicking the Program Files entry in the left pane switches to the Program Files folder and at the same time expands the Program Files outline entry.

Going Places with the Go To Command

The Tools menu includes a handy Go To command, whose dialog box is shown in Figure 6-7 on the next page. As its name implies, the Go To command is a navigational instrument. You can hop directly from one folder to another by typing the folder's name and path in the Go To Folder dialog box. For example, to get directly from C:\Money to D:\Program Files\MSOffice, without fussing with either window pane, you can simply pull down the Tools menu, choose Go To, and type *"d:\program files\msoffice"*. (When a folder name includes a space, you must enclose it in quotation marks, as shown here.)

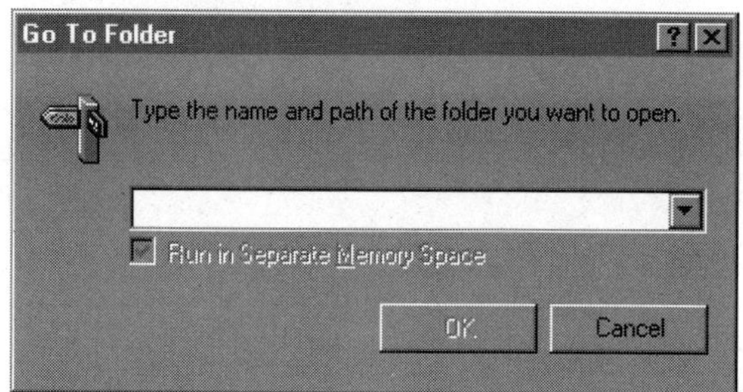

FIGURE 6-7. Windows NT Explorer's Go To command can quickly take you to a folder.

Redisplaying the Parent Folder

Whether you're working in a folder window or any part of Windows NT Explorer, pressing Backspace always takes you to the parent of the current folder.

For information about the Run command, see "Running Programs and Opening Documents with the Run Command," page 71.

The Go To command can be used for files as well as folders. If you specify a file, the command opens the folder containing that file and (if necessary) scrolls the folder's contents so that the specified filename is visible. Like the Start menu's Run command and the Task Manager's New Task command, Go To maintains a list of the folders and filenames you've most recently specified. To reuse an item, simply open the drop-down list and select it.

Using Windows NT Explorer for Housekeeping Chores

All the housekeeping operations described in Chapter 5—copying, moving, deleting, creating, and renaming objects, and working with file types—are available in Windows NT Explorer as well. Windows

NT Explorer simply provides an extra convenience—the ability to use outline entries in drag-and-drop maneuvers.

For example, suppose that after studying the folder outline shown in Figure 6-6 on page 171, you decide that the Mwed folder really should be a subfolder of Program Files. You could carry out this reorganization as follows:

1. Right-drag the Mwed entry in the left pane and drop it on the Program Files entry in the left pane.
2. From the context menu, choose Move Here.

You can drag objects from either pane to the other, as well as from one location to another in the same pane. As in folder windows, it's best to drag with the right mouse button, and then choose the action you want from the context menu. That way, you'll never inadvertently ask Windows to copy an object when you meant to move it, or vice versa.

Using Command Lines with Windows NT Explorer

If you are comfortable entering commands in "MS-DOS fashion"—that is, by typing command-line expressions—you might want to take the trouble to learn Windows NT Explorer's formal syntax. Using this syntax, you can do such things as make Windows NT Explorer display a particular folder, display a folder and select a particular object in that folder, or limit Windows NT Explorer's display to a subset of your namespace.

The syntax is as follows:

explorer [/n][/e][,/root,*object*][[,/select],*subobject*]

/n	always opens a new window, even if the specified folder is already open.
/e	opens the folder in Windows NT Explorer. If you omit /e, a folder window is opened.
/root,*object*	restricts Windows NT Explorer to *object* and all folders contained within *object*.
/select,*subobject*	gives initial focus to the parent folder of *subobject* and selects *subobject*. If /select is omitted, *subobject* specifies the folder that gets the initial focus.

Here are some examples:

explorer /e,/root,c:\winnt

opens a Windows NT Explorer view restricted to C:\Winnt (and all folders contained in C:\Winnt).

explorer /e,/select,c:\winnt\win.ini

opens a Windows NT Explorer view of C:\Winnt, with the Win.ini file selected.

explorer c:\winnt

opens a folder-window view of C:\Winnt.

explorer

opens a Windows NT Explorer view of C:\ (or the disk on which your Windows NT files are stored). Note that when no arguments are given, you don't need to include /e to get a Windows NT Explorer view.

SEE ALSO

For more information about using command lines, see Chapter 18, "Using the Command Prompt."

You can enter a Windows NT Explorer command line by choosing Run from the Start menu or by choosing New Task from Task Manager's File menu. Alternatively, you can encapsulate a Windows NT Explorer command-line string in a shortcut. For example, suppose you want to create a desktop shortcut that restricts a Windows NT Explorer view to a folder called \\MyServer\Personal. You could do that as follows:

1. Use Network Neighborhood to display \\MyServer.
2. With the right mouse button, drag the Personal folder to the desktop.
3. Choose Create Shortcut(s) Here from the context menu.
4. Right-click the new shortcut and choose Properties from the context menu.
5. Click the Shortcut tab.
6. On the Target line, type the command-line string:

```
explorer /e,/root,\\MyServer\Personal
```

CHAPTER 7

Using the Find Command

Scooting around your hard disk or network with folder windows and Windows NT Explorer is dandy when you know where you're going. But it's less dandy when all you know about the item you need is that it's "out there somewhere." In that all-too-common circumstance, you'll want to use Windows NT's versatile Find command.

The Find command can quickly locate documents, programs, folders, and even entire computers, anywhere on your own computer or amongst the shared resources of your network. You can find what you're looking for by name, creation date, size, file type, content, or any combination of these. For example, you can ask the Find command to locate all Lotus 1-2-3 for Windows documents created within the last month that are at least 30 megabytes in size and contain the word "xenon." Or you can use it to generate a list of all applications on a particular server. Or to find all files that are larger than 100 kilobytes and haven't been modified during the last six months. And so on.

After you've found an item or group of items that you're looking for, you can work with the search results directly in the Find window, just as if it was an ordinary folder window. Alternatively, you can select any item in the Find window and use a File-menu command to go directly to the item's containing folder.

If you plan to reuse a set of search criteria, you can use a simple menu command to save the criteria on your desktop. When you do this, you can either save or discard the current search results (the files and folders that currently meet the search criteria), as you choose.

Finding the Find Command

The Find command is a permanent fixture of the Start menu, so you can always invoke it there. Alternatively, you can get to the Find command by right-clicking any folder icon or folder shortcut and choosing Find on the context menu, or simply press F3 in any folder window.

When you press F3 or choose Find from a folder's context menu, Find proposes to conduct its search beginning at the current folder. Thus, if you know that the items you're looking for are in a particular folder (or one of its subfolders), and if that folder is at hand, it's more efficient to choose Find from the folder's context menu, saving you

1 Getting Started

the effort of specifying a starting point for the search. Otherwise, it's probably simpler to open the Start menu.

Finding Files and Folders

To find a file or folder, choose Find from the Start menu, and then choose Files Or Folders. You'll arrive at the following dialog box:

Type a file or folder specification here, or choose an entry from the drop-down list.

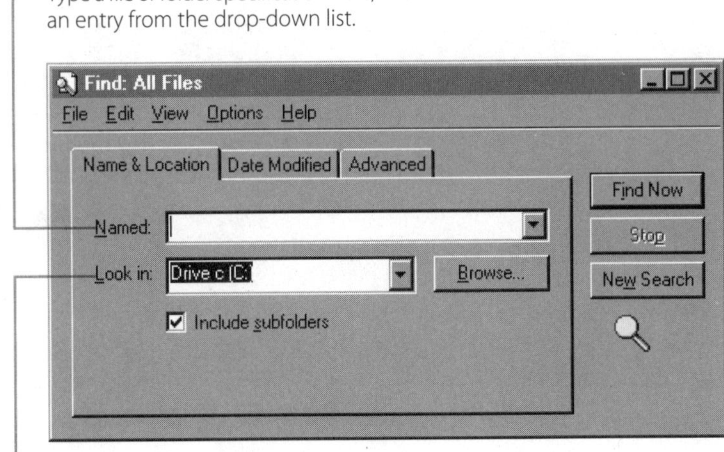

Using this drop-down list, tell Find where to search.

SEE ALSO
For information about mapping network drives, see "Mapping a Network Folder to a Drive Letter," page 277.

By default, the Look In line specifies the hard disk on which your Windows NT files are stored. Alternative search locations include local hard drives and floppy disks, local CD-ROM drives, and network drives that you have mapped to local drive letters.

If you want to search an unmapped network server or restrict the search to a particular folder, click the Browse button instead of the Look In drop-down arrow. Find then displays an outline of your entire namespace, exactly as you might see in the left pane of a Windows NT Explorer window. Select the folder where you want to begin the search, and then click OK. *For information about the namespace, see "The Windows NT Namespace," page 118.*

TIP

My Computer Versus Local Hard Drives

If you search My Computer, Find examines your local hard disks *plus* any mapped network drives, *plus* whatever happens to be in your CD-ROM drive. That may be more searching than you need. If you think the item you're looking for is on one of your local hard disks, it's quicker to choose Local Hard Drives from the Look In drop-down list.

Note that by clicking the Browse button and choosing Network Neighborhood, you can search a particular network server. In that case, Find searches all shared folders on the selected server to which you have access. Unshared folders and folders to which your account does not have access are not searched. You cannot, however, ask Find to search an entire domain or workgroup. The largest component of your network you can search is an individual server.

By default, Find searches the disk or folder specified on the Look In line, plus all the subfolders of that disk or folder. If you don't want to search the subfolders, deselect the Include Subfolders check box.

Telling Find What to Search For

You can use any of the following criteria, singly or in combination, when searching for files and folders:

- Name
- Most recent modification date
- File type
- File size
- File content

If you use a combination of criteria, Find ferrets out only those items that meet *all* criteria.

 TIP

When you finish a search, Find retains your search criteria in case you want to perform another search based on similar criteria. If you want to start a brand new search, it's a good idea to click the New Search button. That way you won't inadvertently reuse a criterion from your previous search.

Interrupting a Search

Once the item or items you're looking for appear in the Find window, there's no need to sit on your hands while Find continues searching. You can halt the search at any time by clicking the Stop button.

Alternatively, you can begin working with an item in the Find window while the search goes on. Simply select any item in the window and use it any way you like. You can right-click the item to get its context menu, double-click it to open it (if it's a document) or run it (if it's a program), drag it somewhere if you want to copy it or make a shortcut from it, and so on.

Searching by Name

To specify a search by name, click the Name & Location tab (if this tab isn't already selected) and enter the appropriate text on the Named line. If the name you're looking for is one you've recently used in a search, you can save yourself some typing by clicking the drop-down arrow at the right side of the Named line and selecting the text from the ensuing list.

You can search by name without knowing exactly how the item you want is spelled. If you know any part of it, enter that part on the Named line. Find locates all items whose names include the letters you type. For example, if you simply type *Sales* on the Named line, Find locates items with names such as Quarter 1 Sales, Quarter 2 Sales, Sales Forecast, Salespersons, and Sales Tax.

Using Wildcards

A *wildcard* is a character used as a proxy for one or more other characters. If you're an MS-DOS veteran, you may be accustomed to using wildcards in directory searches. You'll be glad to know the same wildcards also work with filename searches conducted by the Find command. The two wildcards recognized by Find are ? and *.

The question mark represents any single character. For example, specifying

199?

will get you any file or folder that includes any year from 1990 to 1999 in its name, as well as files and folders that includes 199 followed by any other character. You can use as many question-mark wildcards in a specification as you want.

The asterisk represents any single character or combination of characters—or no characters at all. For example, searching for

1*4

might turn up 123r4, 1994, 1024, 14, and so on. The most common use for the asterisk wildcard is to find all files with a common extension. For example, to find all files with the extension .XLS, you can enter

*.xls

SEE ALSO
For information about the search-by-file-type option, see "Searching by File Type," page 183. For information about the registry, see "Working with the File Types List," page 155.

on the Named line. If you simply entered *xls* without the wildcard and period, you would get, in addition to all the files with the extension .XLS, all files with "xls" anywhere else in their names. An alternative way to find all files with a certain extension is to use the search-by-file-type option. But the search-by-file-type option is useful only for file types that are recorded in your Windows registry. For extensions that are not in the registry, the wildcard approach is ideal.

Searching by Most Recent Modification Date

To use the most recent modification date as a search criterion, click the Find dialog's Date Modified tab. That takes you to the dialog box shown in Figure 7-1. Note that all the options here apply both to files and folders that were *created* within a particular time interval and to files and folders that were last *modified* during that interval. Find does not have the ability to locate files and folders that were most recently accessed (but not modified) within a certain time frame.

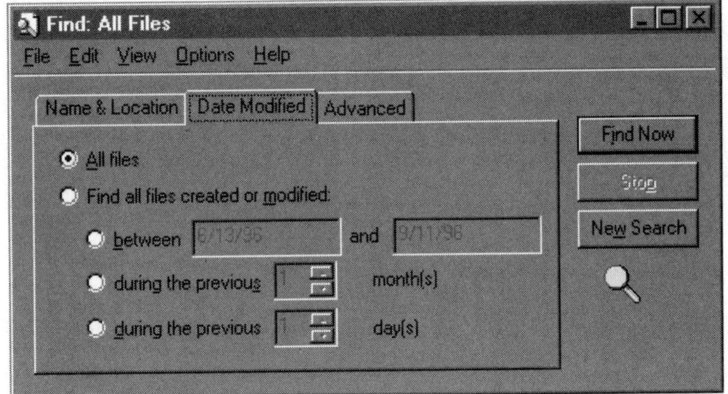

FIGURE 7-1.
You can search for files or folders last modified during a particular time interval.

The modification-date options are commonly used in conjunction with other specifications. For example, if you want to locate all Microsoft Word documents that were created or modified within the last seven days, you can select Microsoft Word Document in the Advanced tab *(see "Searching by File Type," below)* and also select "during the previous 7 days" on the Date Modified page. To set the latter criterion, click the "during the previous day(s)" option button (the one with the underlined *d*), and then use the day spinner to enter the number 7.

Note that when you tell Find to locate all objects last modified during the previous *n* days, that means the previous *n* days plus all of today. For example, if you ask Find to locate all files modified during the previous 1 day, it finds everything that was changed yesterday plus everything that was changed today.

Searching by File Type

To search for a particular kind of file, or to restrict the search to folders only, click the Advanced tab. That brings up the dialog box shown in Figure 7-2 on the next page.

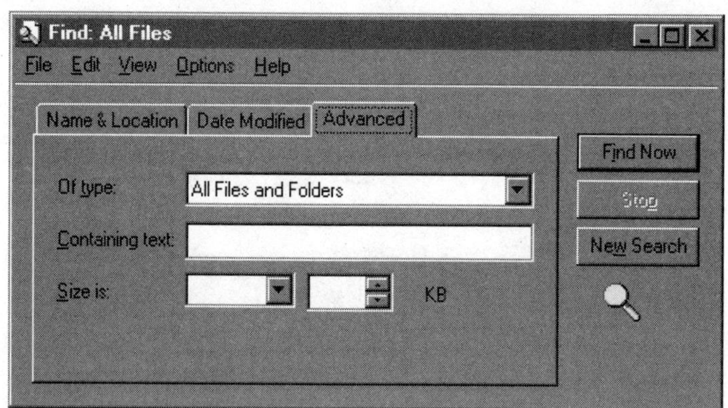

FIGURE 7-2.
Using the Advanced tab, you can search for a particular type of file, for folders only, for files containing particular text, or for files of a minimum or maximum size.

The default type specification, shown in Figure 7-2, is All Files And Folders. To narrow the search to a particular type, click the drop-down arrow on the Of Type line, and select from the ensuing list. Note that the drop-down list includes some general categories, as well as the various document types known to your registry. For example, to search for programs, choose Application. To search for folders, excluding documents and programs, choose Folder, and so on.

Searching by File Content

To search for files containing some particular text, click the Advanced tab. Then type the text you're looking for on the Containing Text line. Note that the text you type is treated literally—that is, you cannot use wildcards on the Containing Text line. Also be aware that searching for files by their content takes much longer than searching by name, modification date, type, or size. To avoid unnecessarily lengthy searches, restrict the search as much as is practical. For example, if you're looking for a Microsoft Excel spreadsheet with a particular number or phrase in it, restrict the file type to Excel documents and, if all the likely possibilities are stored in a certain folder, enter that folder name on the Look In line.

Making a Search Case Sensitive

Content searches ignore case by default. If you're sure how the text you're looking for is capitalized, you might want to make the search case sensitive. To do that, simply pull down the Options menu and

CAUTION

If you turn on the case-sensitive option, all your searches will be case sensitive until you turn the option off again. You can turn this option on or off while Find is searching, but your change doesn't take effect until the next search.

choose Case Sensitive. A check will appear beside the command name, indicating that the next search will be case sensitive.

Searching by File Size

To search for files and folders that are larger than or smaller than a particular size, click the Advanced tab. Then, in the dialog box shown in Figure 7-2, click the drop-down arrow on the Size Is line. A two-item list unfolds, giving a choice of At Least and At Most. If you're looking for files smaller than some threshold amount, choose At Most. Otherwise, choose At Least. Finally, type the size threshold in the KB text box, or manipulate its spinner to indicate the size you're interested in.

Finding a Network Server

The Network Neighborhood icon on your desktop makes it easy to locate network servers within your own domain. Locating a server outside your domain can be a challenge, however, particularly if your network includes hundreds of servers. To simplify the task, choose Find from the Start menu, then choose Computer. You'll see the dialog box shown in Figure 7-3.

FIGURE 7-3.
The Find command can help you locate a server in the vast expanse of your network.

Specify all or part of the name of the computer you want to locate. (To find a computer that's not in your domain or workgroup, you must type the computer's full name.) Find will present a list of all computers matching your search specification. When you find the computer you're looking for, you can double-click its entry to display the computer's contents in a folder window.

Note that the Find Computer dialog box does not include a Look In line. That's because Find assumes that when you're looking for a computer, you want to scan your entire network.

Working with Search Results

SEE ALSO
For more information about working with items in a folder window, see "Running Programs and Opening Documents from Folders," page 64, and Chapter 5, "Working with Folders."

As the Find command searches, it presents its findings in the bottom half of an expanded window, as shown in Figure 7-4. Here you can work with found items exactly as though they were in an ordinary folder window. For example, you can click the column headings (Name, In Folder, Size, and so on) to change the sorting order of the found items, or use commands on the View menu to switch from the default details view to an icon or list view. You can also right-click any item and choose Properties to inspect the item's property sheet or choose Quick View to take a peek at the item without opening its parent application (if a quick viewer is available for that file type). You can double-click an item to open it, or right-drag an item to the desktop or to another folder to copy, move, or create a shortcut for the selected item.

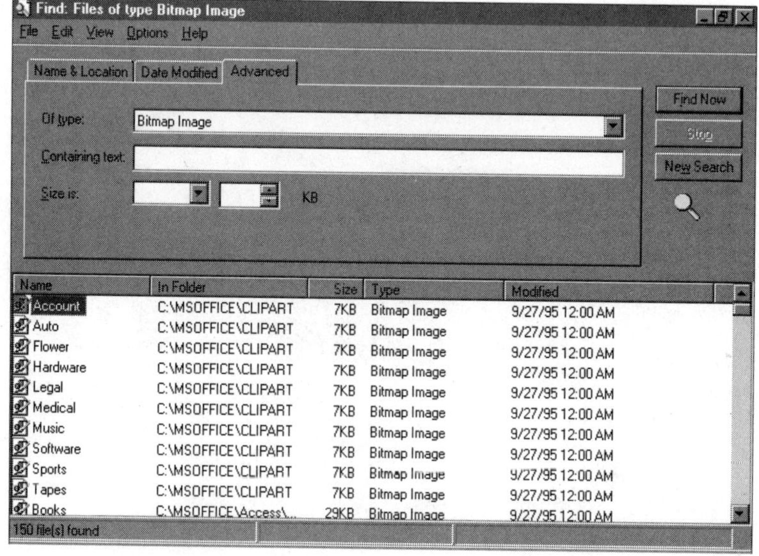

FIGURE 7-4.
The Find command presents its findings in the lower part of an expanded Find window.

In addition, the Find command's File menu includes one handy command not found in folder windows: Open Containing Folder. By selecting an item and choosing this command, Windows opens the selected item's folder window, allowing you to navigate immediately to the folder in which the item is stored.

Saving Search Results

To preserve the criteria used in a Find operation for reuse after you close the Find dialog box, pull down the File menu and choose Save Search. To preserve the current search results as well as the criteria, first choose Save Results from the Options menu. Then choose Save Search from the File menu. With results or without, Find creates an icon on your desktop and assigns that icon a default name. For example, if you ask Find to locate all folders whose names include the word *personal*, and then save the results of that search, your new desktop icon will be called something like *Files of type Folder named personal.* Because the default name is long and not always completely descriptive (it will not, for example, include modification-date specifications), you'll probably want to assign your own name to the new icon. You can do that by right-clicking it and choosing Rename.

The Save Search command puts an icon on your desktop, regardless of whether you invoked the Find command from the Start menu or from the context menu of a folder. The icon represents an ordinary document file, and you can copy it, move it, or create a shortcut to it, just as you can any other document file.

To reuse a saved set of search criteria, simply double-click the desktop icon and click Find Now.

CHAPTER 8

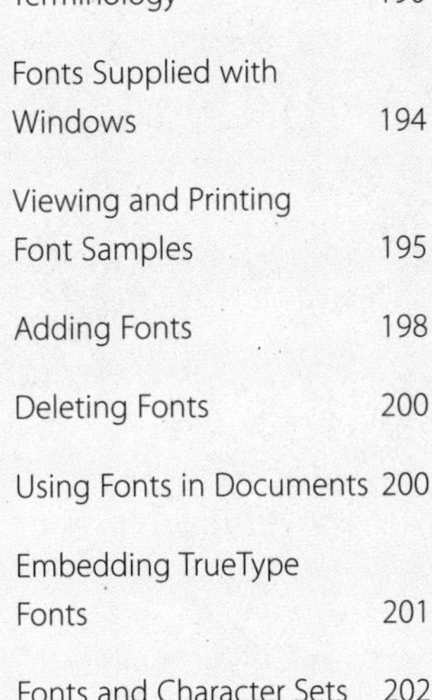

Installing and Using Fonts

One of the great advantages of creating text documents in a graphical operating environment such as Windows NT is that you can employ a variety of fonts and typographical styles and judge their impact before committing your work to paper. Within limits, and with some exceptions, what you see on screen is what you'll get from any output device, whether it be a dot-matrix printer, a laser printer, a plotter, or a fax machine.

Windows puts typography at your disposal. Using it well, however, can be a challenge. To help you meet this challenge, this chapter begins with an overview of basic terminology. Then we'll look at the procedures for adding and deleting fonts, getting better acquainted with the fonts you have, using them in your documents, and using some of the special characters—accented letters, commercial symbols, and so on—that are included with most fonts but can't be accessed with normal typewriter keystrokes.

Terminology

A *font* is a complete set of characters in one size and one typeface. For example, all the letters, numbers, punctuation marks, and other symbols available in 12-point Courier New bold italic constitute one font. The same set of characters in another size constitutes another font.

Fonts are identified by their size, typeface family, weight, and style. In the name "12-point Courier New bold italic," for example, 12-point is the size, Courier New is the typeface family, bold is the weight, and italic is the style. When the weight is "normal" and the style is "roman," these terms are usually omitted.

Font Size

A font's size is usually measured in points and expressed as a "point size." A *point* is a printer's measurement, equal to 1⁄12 of a *pica*. (A pica, in turn, is approximately 1⁄6 of an inch, so there are about 72 points in an inch.) A font's point size is approximately the distance in points from the top of its highest character to the bottom of its lowest character, as shown in Figure 8-1. (This definition applies to a font's printed size only. On screen, point size has no absolute significance at all because of the differences in screen size and resolution. For example, a 10-point font on a 16-inch screen at 640×480 resolution will probably be larger than a 12-point font on a 14-inch screen at 800×600 resolution.)

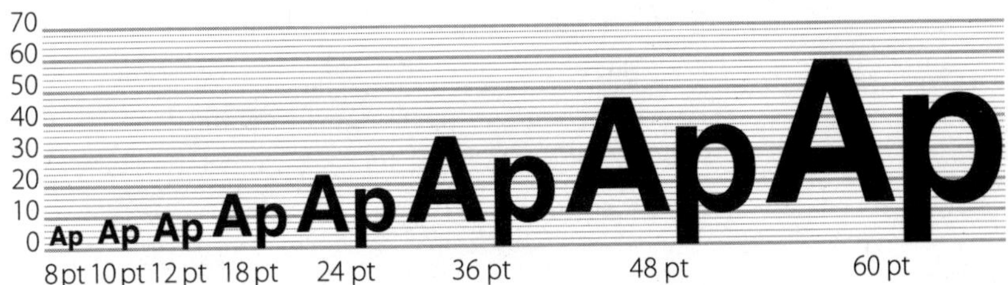

FIGURE 8-1. A font's point size is a measure of its height—from the top of its highest character to the bottom of its lowest.

Point size is a rough measure of a font's height but says nothing about its width. Many font families come in *compressed* and *expanded* variants, as well as normal width. Some programs, such as desktop publishing programs and sophisticated word processors, allow you to squeeze characters closer together without changing their individual widths. This process, called *kerning*, can change the apparent width of a font, creating a denser look and allowing you to put more words on a line. Some programs also allow you to add extra increments of space between characters, a process called *letterspacing*.

Style and Weight

The most common *style* variants for fonts are roman and italic. Roman characters are the "normal" kind, with vertical strokes predominating. Italic characters, which are forward slanting and often more rounded, are used for emphasis, for book titles, and so on.

The term *weight* refers to the thickness of a font's strokes. The most common weights are normal (also called regular) and bold, but some font families also include other weights, such as thin, light, heavy, ultra, and black.

Serif and Sans Serif Fonts

Most fonts fall into one of two categories—*serif* or *sans serif*. Serif fonts have fine lines that finish off the main strokes—for example, at the bottom of a capital *T* and at the ends of the *T*'s crossbar. These "finishing strokes," called serifs, are absent in sans serif fonts, such as the font used for the headings in this book. Serif fonts, such as Times

New Roman, are generally considered more suitable for conventional text, such as that in a newspaper or book. Sans serif fonts, such as Helvetica and Arial, have a more modern appearance and are often used in headlines, tabular material (such as spreadsheet reports), and advertising.

Monospaced and Proportionally Spaced Fonts

Fonts in which every character takes up the same amount of space are called *monospaced.* Fonts in which some characters (such as *m* and *w*) are wider than others (*i* and *t*, for example) are called *proportionally spaced.* (See Figure 8-2.) Proportionally spaced fonts produce a more typeset appearance and are generally considered easier to read. Monospaced fonts are often preferred for such things as legal documents, which have traditionally been produced on typewriters.

FIGURE 8-2.

In proportionally spaced fonts, characters have different widths. In monospaced fonts, all characters have the same width.

Microsoft Windows NT	**Microsoft Windows NT**
Proportionally spaced	Monospaced

Arial and Times New Roman are examples of proportionally spaced fonts. The most commonly used monospaced font is Courier.

Keep in mind that although the widths of letters in a proportionally spaced font vary, the widths of numerals are usually all the same so that numbers can be aligned in tables.

Scalable and Nonscalable Fonts

Fonts can also be described as *scalable* or *nonscalable.* Scalable fonts are those for which a single master can produce any point size. Nonscalable fonts are designed for use at particular sizes; enlarging or reducing them generally produces unattractive distortions, such as serrated diagonal lines and jagged curves.

Nonscalable fonts are also sometimes called *bitmap fonts* because the form in which they're stored on your hard disk (or in a printer's read-only memory) records the relative position of each dot comprising each character. For example, a capital *I* might be stored as a column of 12 dots plus two 6-dot crossbars. To generate a character from a bitmap font, your screen or printer simply reproduces the bitmap at the desired location.

Scalable fonts are sometimes called *outline* fonts because they are stored as a collection of outlines; an outline is a mathematical description of each character. To generate a character from an outline font, font-management software uses a process called *scan conversion* to convert the outlines to bitmaps, which are then reproduced on your screen or printer. To avoid jagged lines and other distortions in the final rendering, particularly at smaller point sizes, the font-management software employs *hints*—algorithms that modify the scan-conversion process to produce optimal-looking characters.

Because outline fonts are stored as mathematical descriptions, they can be scaled to a wide range of point sizes. They can also be slanted, rotated, compressed, extended, inverted, and otherwise manipulated—if you have a program that allows you to do these things. Their *metrics* (character-width specifications) can also be modified to produce kerned or letterspaced typography. The one small disadvantage of outline fonts is that the scan-conversion process takes a modest amount of processing time. The first time you use an outline font at a given point size, therefore, you might encounter a slight delay while your system performs the calculation required to convert the font's outline into the appropriate set of bitmaps. After the bitmaps have been rendered, however, they're stored in an area of memory called a *cache*. When you need to reuse the font, Windows simply grabs the bitmaps out of the cache, thereby avoiding the original calculation delay.

Fonts Supplied with Windows

Incorporated into Windows NT is a scalable font technology called TrueType. Along with this font-management technology, Windows NT includes several TrueType typeface families—Arial, Lucida, Times New Roman, Courier New, Symbol, and Wingdings—which are shown below.

Arial	No one should drive a hard bargain with an
Lucida Sans	No one should drive a hard bargain with
Lucida Console	No one should drive a hard
Times New Roman	No one should drive a hard bargain with an artist
Courier New	No one should drive a hard
Symbol	No ονε σηουλδ δριϖε α ηαρδ βαργαιν ωιτη
Wingdings	☠□ □■♏ ⬧♒□◆●♎ ♎❒♓❖♏ ♋

In addition to these TrueType families, Windows also includes three sets of bitmap fonts—MS Serif, MS Sans Serif, and Courier—to provide compatibility with earlier versions of Windows. (MS Serif was previously known as Helv, and MS Serif is the former TmsRmn.) They're available only in certain point sizes, and you can't use them with laser printers.

Along with this assortment of font resources, you might find additional fonts on your system, courtesy of particular applications that you have installed. Microsoft Word, for example, includes dozens of fonts in a variety of designs. Any font installed by an application is available not only in that program but also in any other Windows-based program you run.

Your Printer's Own Font Resources

In addition to the fonts that Windows supplies and any additional fonts that you install in Windows, you can use your printer's internal fonts. Your printer driver tells Windows which fonts the printer

SEE ALSO
For information about printer drivers, see "Adding a Printer," page 222.

provides, and those fonts appear in the Font dialog boxes used by your applications.

When you use your printer's internal fonts, Windows doesn't have to download font information or turn each page of your document into a bitmap (a time-consuming process), so printing is likely to be quicker. In exchange for this speed increase, however, you might have to sacrifice some degree of correspondence between the appearance of your document on screen and its appearance on paper.

When you format a document with an internal printer font, Windows displays the same font on screen if it can. If Windows does not have a screen font to match the printer font you select, it gives you the closest match that it can. For example, if you choose the Courier font that's built into your printer, Windows formats your text on screen using its own TrueType Courier font (Courier New). If you select your PostScript printer's Avant Garde font (and you have not installed the Avant Garde screen font), Windows uses Arial, the nearest TrueType equivalent, on screen.

Even when the screen font used by Windows doesn't exactly match the printer font you select, Windows-based applications attempt to show you where your lines will break on the printed page. The correspondence of line endings on screen to line endings on paper might not always be perfect, however, and some applications do a better job of this than others. If precise text positioning is critical, it's always best to avoid printer fonts that don't have equivalent screen fonts.

Viewing and Printing Font Samples

To see samples of the fonts installed in your system, start by opening the Fonts folder, which is stored in your Winnt folder. The easiest way to open the folder is to double-click its shortcut in Control Panel. To open Control Panel, choose Settings from the Start menu, and then choose Control Panel. Figure 8-3 on the following page shows an example of a Fonts folder.

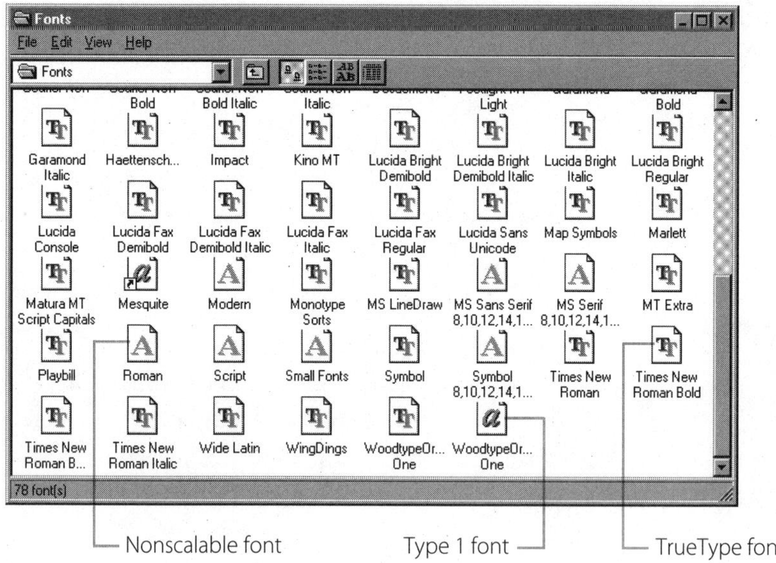

FIGURE 8-3.
To see samples of your fonts, install new fonts, or delete fonts, open your Fonts folder.

> **NOTE**
>
> PostScript fonts rendered by Adobe Type Manager do not appear in your Fonts folder. To see samples of these fonts, use Adobe Type Manager.

The icons with two *T*s represent TrueType fonts; those with an *A* represent nonscalable fonts. The point sizes for which these nonscalable fonts were designed are usually included with the font name. An icon with a lowercase *a* represents a Type 1 font. Type 1 is a font format designed for PostScript printers.

To see a sample of any TrueType or nonscalable font, simply double-click its icon—or right-click the icon and choose Open from the context menu. As Figure 8-4 shows, the ensuing window displays the font at various point sizes.

To print the font sample, click the Print button.

Viewing Options in the Fonts Folder

Like an ordinary file folder window, the Fonts folder offers icon, list, and details views of your font library. You can choose these options from the toolbar or the View menu. In addition, the Fonts folder offers another viewing option: List Fonts By Similarity. This option is also available on the View menu.

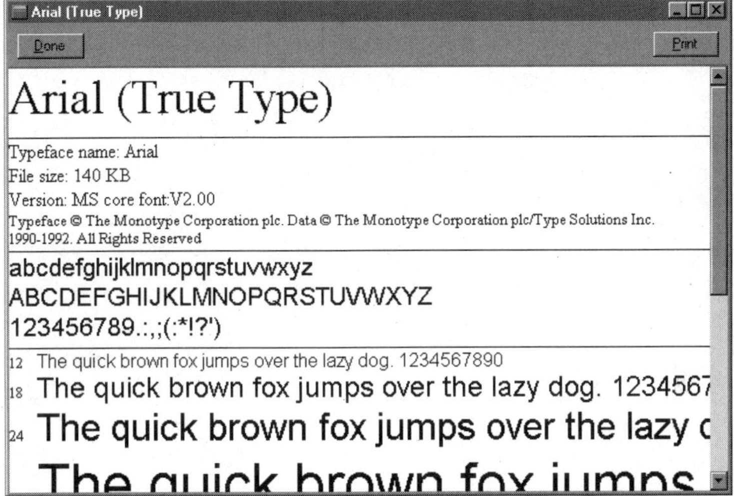

FIGURE 8-4. Double-clicking a font icon produces a printable sample of the font at various point sizes.

The List Fonts By Similarity option lets you find all the fonts in your library that are similar to some other font. As Figure 8-5 shows, when you choose this option, a drop-down list of your fonts appears below the toolbar. Your font library appears in the window listed in order of decreasing similarity to the font selected in the drop-down list.

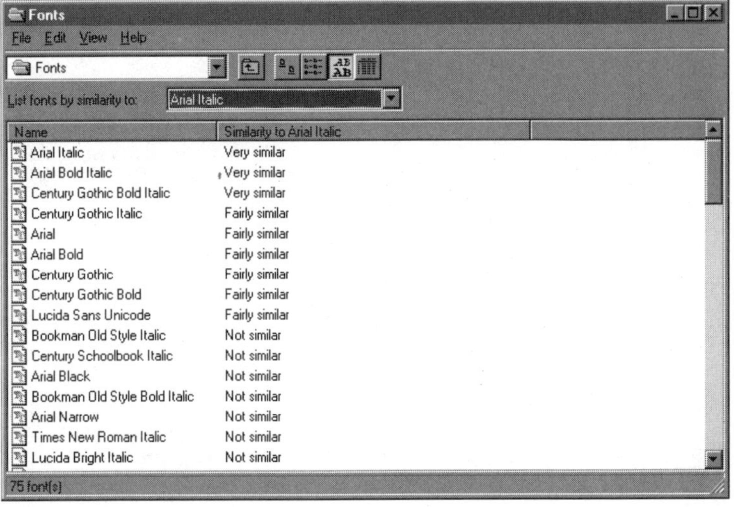

FIGURE 8-5. In this similarity view, fonts are listed in order of decreasing similarity to Arial Italic.

Adding Fonts

Scalable TrueType fonts, in addition to the ones supplied with Windows, are available from Microsoft and numerous other vendors. You can also download fonts from electronic bulletin boards, the Internet, and information services such as America Online and CompuServe. When you acquire an additional font, you need to install it so that Windows knows it's available.

To install a new TrueType font, simply open the Fonts folder and choose Install New Font from the File menu. You'll be greeted by the Add Fonts dialog box, shown below.

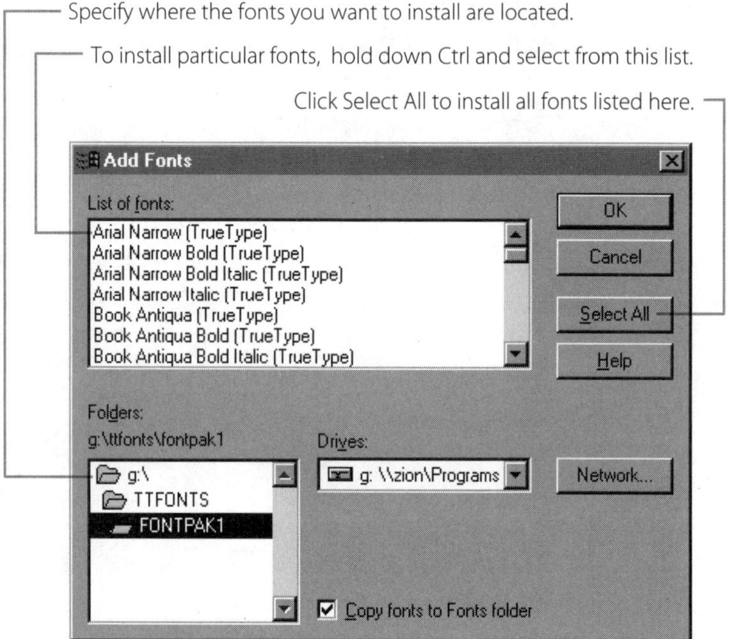

When you're finished selecting fonts, click OK. In a moment, your new fonts will appear in your Fonts folder and will be available for use in your applications.

TIP

Drag and Drop to Install

You can also use drag and drop to add fonts to your system. For example, if you have a new font stored in a folder named Download, you can install that font as follows: Display both the Download folder and the Fonts folder. Then drag the font icon from the Download folder to the Fonts folder.

To install a new Type 1 (PostScript) font, you use drag and drop. Drag the Type 1 font file (files with a .PFM extension are identified as Type 1 Font Files in a folder's details view) to the Fonts folder. You can select how you want the font to be installed in the dialog box that appears.

To Copy or Not to Copy?

If you're installing fonts from a floppy disk, be sure to select the Copy Fonts To Fonts Folder check box in the Add Fonts dialog box. Windows then copies your font files to the Fonts folder, a subfolder of your Winnt folder. If the fonts you're installing are already stored in another folder on your hard disk, Windows will duplicate your font files in the Fonts folder.

If you prefer to keep your fonts in other folders (for example, in a folder that you use for downloading files from an information service), you can do so. Simply deselect the Copy Fonts To Fonts Folder check box. Windows will remember which folder you installed your fonts from, and, provided you don't rename or move that folder, your fonts will still be available to your applications.

TIP

Safety First

It's always a good idea to select the Copy Fonts To Fonts Folder check box. That way, you're unlikely to delete font files inadvertently.

NOTE

In the Install Type 1 Font dialog box, the Copy Type 1 Font Files To Fonts Folder check box serves the same purpose as the Copy Fonts To Fonts Folder check box described above.

Deleting Fonts

To "deinstall" a font, simply remove it from your Fonts folder. You can do that by deleting the font icon or by moving the icon to another folder. If you delete a font icon, Windows stores the font in your Recycle Bin, so you can restore it if you change your mind.

Using Fonts in Documents

To use fonts in your documents, simply follow standard Windows editing procedures: select the text you want to format, and then choose your application's Font command. (You'll find it on the Format menu in most applications.) In many programs you can also select fonts by right-clicking the selected text and choosing Font from the context menu that appears, or by clicking icons on a toolbar.

In many programs, choosing the Font command brings you to a dialog box similar to the one shown in Figure 8-6. This dialog box, shown here in the form used by WordPad, is one of the Windows "common dialogs," so you can expect to see close approximations of it in many of the newer applications for Windows. Notice that you can use it to choose color and two special effects, strikeout and underlining, in addition to typeface, style, and point size.

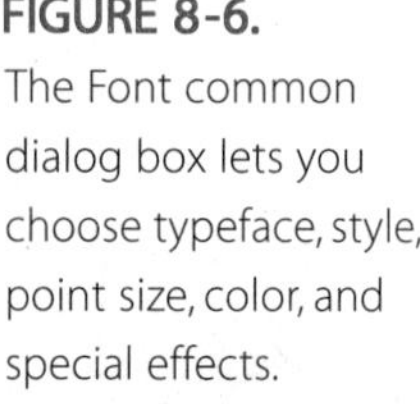

FIGURE 8-6.
The Font common dialog box lets you choose typeface, style, point size, color, and special effects.

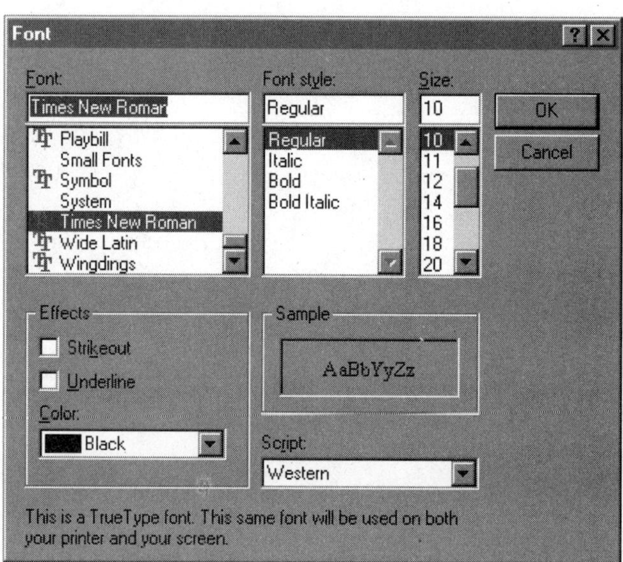

Embedding TrueType Fonts

If you create documents that will be read on other computers, it's a good idea to stick with fonts that all your readers are likely to have. The safest ones to use are Arial, Courier New, and Times New Roman—the sans serif, monospaced, and serif faces shipped with all versions of Windows.

What happens if a reader's system does not have one of the fonts used by your document? For example, suppose you've formatted your entire report in Bozo Bold, but you're the only one in your company who's installed the Bozo family? In that case, Windows substitutes a closely related font on your reader's system. For example, assuming Bozo is a serif face, your reader will probably see Times New Roman on his or her computer. (You can get an idea what fonts Windows considers "similar" by opening your Fonts folder and using the View menu's List Fonts By Similarity command.)

If it's crucial that all readers see your document in the exact fonts you've used, check to see if the application you used to create the document supports TrueType font embedding. If the program can embed the TrueType fonts your document uses, your document will include a copy of the font file for each TrueType font you use. Your readers will then see your document with its original fonts. And, unless the document has read-only status, they'll be able to edit with those fonts as well.

Note that embedding TrueType fonts adds greatly to the size of your document. A 5-KB report, for example, might easily grow to 50 KB with only one font embedded. If you use italics and boldface, along with regular roman, your document could swell another 100 KB or so. Although most TrueType fonts can be embedded, font manufacturers can disable that capability. Therefore, always check to make sure a font is embeddable before you do any work that depends on this capability. (You can tell if your font is being embedded by comparing the size of the same document saved with and without embedding.)

TIP

Embedding Fonts in Microsoft Word Documents

If you're using Microsoft Word 6.0 or later, you can turn embedding on by choosing the Options command from the Tools menu, clicking the Save tab, and selecting the Embed TrueType Fonts check box. Note that this setting is file-specific—that is, changing it for one document does not affect other documents.

Embedding Fonts in Other Programs

To see if a program offers TrueType embedding, use the Index or Find page in the program's Help facility to search for "TrueType."

Note that TrueType embedding has nothing to do with OLE. A program that supports OLE may or may not offer TrueType embedding, and one that offers TrueType embedding may or may not support OLE.

Fonts and Character Sets

Windows NT uses a character-encoding system called Unicode, in which characters are represented by numeric values from 0 to 65535. Unicode is an expansion of the American National Standards Institute (ANSI) coding system designed to accommodate non-Latin alphabets and non-alphabetic symbols. (The ANSI system, which is used by Windows 95 and earlier versions of Windows, is, in turn, an expansion of ASCII, the coding system that was used by most computer systems prior to the 1990s.)

Most Windows fonts use only the first 256 Unicode character positions (and actually not quite all of those). So unless you rely on multiple alphabets for your work, the change from ANSI to Unicode will most likely have no discernible impact on you. If you're accustomed to MS-DOS–based programs, however, you should be aware that the character sets of your Windows fonts are not identical to the "extended-ASCII" character sets used by most MS-DOS–based applications. The letters *A* through *Z* in uppercase and lowercase, the numerals 0 through 9, and the common punctuation symbols are mapped to the same values in both Unicode and extended ASCII. But the two systems diverge widely for accented letters and other special symbols. As a result of this divergence, MS-DOS procedures that use the Alt key to enter "high-bit" characters do not work in Windows.

Fortunately, Windows NT is very adept at handling conversions between extended-ASCII and Unicode. When you copy text to the Clipboard from most Windows-based programs, the text is stored on the Clipboard in several formats, including one called *OEM Text*, which is designed to facilitate pasting into MS-DOS–based programs. So, for example, if you copy the letter *a* with a circumflex accent from Word for Windows, and then paste this character into an MS-DOS–based program, you will still get an *â* in your MS-DOS–based program. Windows takes care of the translation between character sets for you. A similar conversion process takes place automatically when you copy and paste in the other direction, from MS-DOS into Windows.

Entering Special Characters with Character Map

Windows NT includes an accessory called Character Map that shows you the complete character set for each font on your system, and allows you to easily paste special characters and symbols into your documents. To open Character Map, click the Start button and then choose Programs, Accessories, Character Map. Character Map's display is shown in the following illustration.

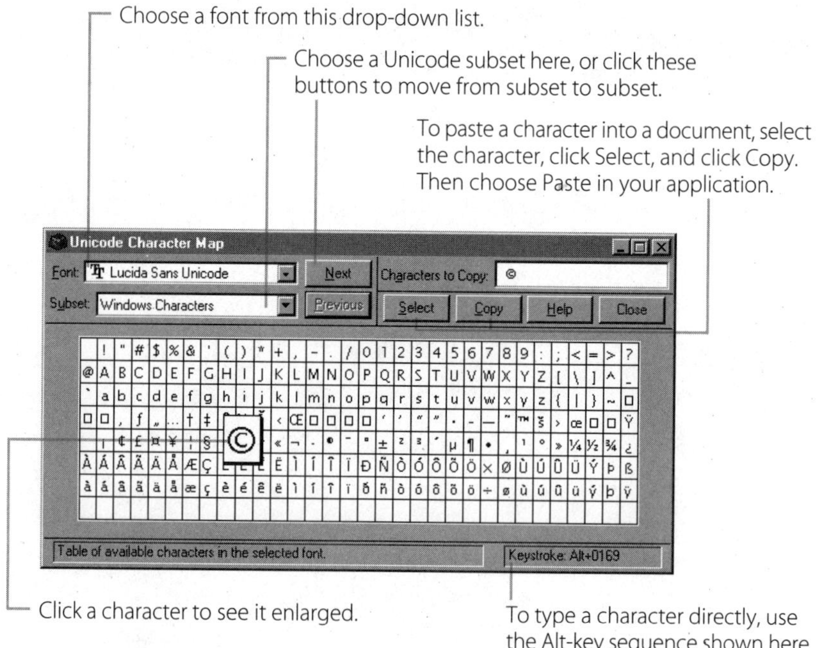

> **NOTE**
>
> If Character Map has not been set up on your computer, double-click the Add/Remove Programs item in Control Panel, click the Windows NT Setup tab, select Accessories, and click the Details button. Select Character Map and click OK two times.

In many Windows-based applications, you can type characters in the Unicode range of 0128 to 0255 directly, without pasting them from the Clipboard. First, select the character you want in Character Map and note the value that appears in the panel in Character Map's lower right corner, such as "Alt+0169" in the illustration above. Then return to your application and do the following:

1 Hold down the Alt key.

2 Using the numeric keypad (not the row of numbers at the top of your keyboard), type the value you found in Character Map, such as *0169* in the illustration.

3 Release the Alt key.

CHAPTER 9

Installing, Configuring, and Using Your Printers

When it comes to translating your work from the computer screen to the printed page, Windows NT provides a wealth of support. The operating system's printing features let you (or your system administrator) do the following things, among others:

- Print in the background to any local or shared network printer
- Print in the background from MS-DOS–based applications as well as from Windows-based applications
- Examine the print queues for any local or shared network printer
- Control the position of documents in print queues, or remove documents from queues
- Create multiple logical printers with different settings for any physical output device

In this chapter, we'll explore these and other features.

Goodbye Print Manager, Hello Printers Folder

Unlike earlier versions of Windows and Windows NT, Windows NT 4 does not include a Print Manager. In its place is a system folder called *Printers*. All the functionality that was provided by Print Manager is now available via the Printers folder.

To get to the Printers folder, choose Settings from the Start menu. Then choose Printers. (Alternatively, open the My Computer folder and double-click the folder icon labeled Printers.) The figure below shows a typical Printers folder.

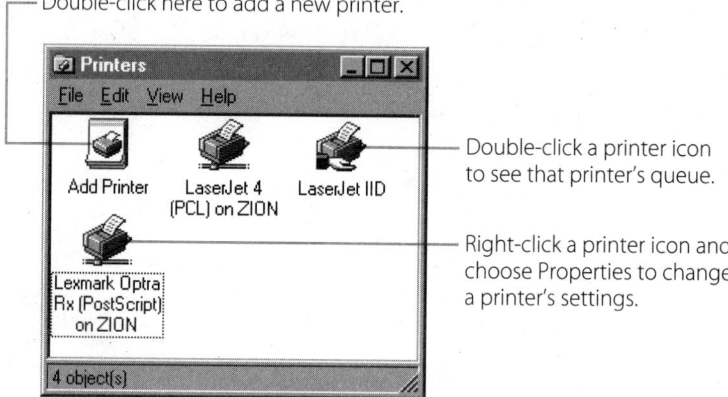

TIP

Create a Target for Drag and Drop

Drag a printer icon to the desktop and choose Create Shortcut(s) Here to create an icon for printing via drag and drop.

The Printers folder looks and acts like any other folder window. You can choose to display or not display the toolbar and status bar, display printers as icons or list entries, select browsing and viewing options from the View menu, and use standard navigation techniques to move from this folder to any other folder on your system.

Within the Printers folder, you'll find entries for each printer you've installed, including local printers and printers attached to network servers. You'll also find an icon labeled Add Printer, which you use to install new printers.

Windows uses the following icons to distinguish various kinds of printers from one another:

 A printer attached to your own computer

 A printer attached to a network server

 A printer attached to your computer but made available to other network users

 A printer attached to your computer but set up to redirect output to a disk file

SEE ALSO
For information about printer properties, see "Inspecting and Setting Printer Properties," page 231. For information about print queues, see "Inspecting and Managing a Print Queue," page 219.

To view or change the properties of any printer, right-click its icon and choose Properties.

To inspect or modify the contents of a printer's queue, double-click the printer's icon, or right-click it and choose Open.

Changing the Default Printer

The *default printer* is the printer that your applications use unless you tell them to do otherwise. This setting is account-specific. That is, if two or more accounts use the same computer, each account can have a different default printer.

You don't need special administrative privileges to change the default printer. To make a printer the default, simply right-click it in your Printers folder and choose Set As Default.

Unfortunately, you can't tell by looking at a printer icon whether that printer is currently the default. To see if it is, right-click the icon. If it's the default printer, a check mark will appear next to the Set As Default command:

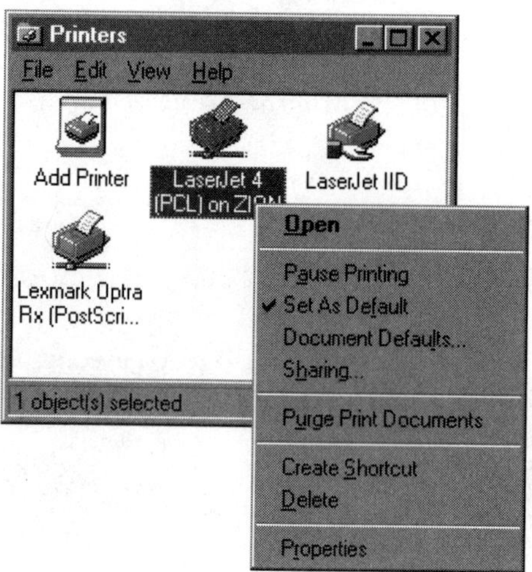

How Do I Print Thee? (Let Me Count the Ways)

In Windows, there is nearly always more than one way to accomplish a task. Printing is no exception. Here are three ways to transport information from an application to your printer:

- Use your application's Print command.
- Drag a file icon and drop it on a printer icon.
- Right-click a file icon and use the Send To command.

Printing from an Application

If the document you want to print is already open, the simplest way to print it is to pull down the File menu and choose Print. Or simply click the Print icon on the application's toolbar—if it has a toolbar with a Print icon. The toolbar approach typically bypasses all dialog boxes and sends your entire document to the current default printer.

What if you want to print to a different printer? In that case, you have a couple of choices. You can change the default printer as described on page 209, or you can use a menu command to select a printer.

Selecting a Printer

Figure 9-1 shows the Print dialog box used by most Windows-based applications. It is one of the "common dialogs" that are part of Windows, and is what you are most likely to see when you choose Print from the File menu in a Windows-based application. The Name drop-down list near the top indicates the name of the printer that will be used when you click OK. Opening the drop-down reveals a list of all installed printers. To select a printer, simply choose its name from this list. The Status line below the drop-down list tells you if the selected printer is ready to print or if it has jobs in its queue.

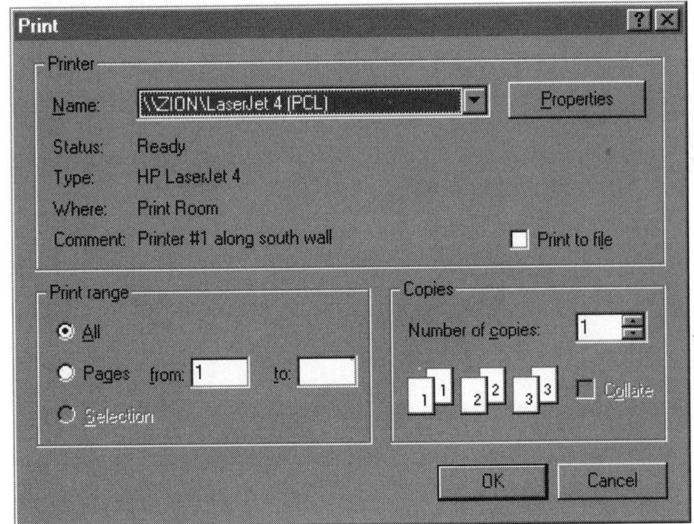

FIGURE 9-1. The common Print dialog box lets you select a printer and set options without changing system defaults.

TIP

Check the Status of Your Printers

The Status line in the common Print dialog box provides useful information about the printer selected in the Name list. In Figure 9-1 on the previous page, for example, the Status line reports that the printer named \\ZION\LaserJet 4 (PCL) is ready. If the printer is paused, the Status line so informs you. And the Status line tells you how many jobs are currently in its queue. By scrolling through the Name list and checking the status of each printer, you can determine which one has the shortest queue.

In some programs, you might find the list of printers in a dialog box labeled Choose Printer, Printer Setup, or something similar. Sometimes this dialog box is accessible via a button in the Print dialog box; in other cases, you get to it via a separate File-menu command. In any event, most Windows programs provide some mechanism for selecting a printer other than the default printer.

A few programs, particularly simple applications that handle unformatted text only, do not allow you to select a printer. To print to a different device from an application such as this, you'll need to visit the Printers folder and change the default. *See "Changing the Default Printer," page 209.*

How Much to Print?

In addition to letting you select a printer, the Print dialog box lets you set options for that printer. For example, you can specify whether you want to print all of your document, a range of pages, or only the portion of your document that's currently selected.

TIP

Changing the Default Number of Copies

If you commonly print more than one copy of each document on a particular printer, you can change the default number of copies. Right-click the printer icon and choose Document Defaults. *For more information, see "Document Defaults," page 237.*

Printing Multiple Copies

The Print dialog box also lets you choose the number of copies you want and whether you want the copies collated. If you don't collate, Windows prints all copies of your first page, followed by all copies of your second, and so on. If you collate, you'll get all pages of your first copy, followed by all pages of your next copy, and so on.

 TIP

To Collate or Not to Collate

In earlier versions of Windows and Windows NT, it was considerably quicker to print multiple copies uncollated than collated. In Windows NT 4, uncollated printing is still quicker but often insignificantly so. In any case, the difference in printing time is trivial compared to the amount of time it takes to collate copies by hand. Therefore, it's usually best to select the Collate check box when printing multiple copies.

 NOTE

Some applications and printer drivers do not support multiple copies and collating.

Switching Between Portrait and Landscape Orientation

The Print dialog box does not include an orientation option. In many applications you can switch between portrait orientation (where the printed sheet is taller than it is wide) and landscape orientation (the opposite) by choosing a Page Setup or similar command from the File menu. This command also typically allows you to set margins and choose paper size and source.

You can also change orientation by modifying the printer's document property sheet. You can view the document property sheet by clicking the Properties button in the common Print dialog box. When you change the document property sheet via the Print dialog box, your

 SEE ALSO

For more information about document property sheets, see "Document Defaults," page 237.

change affects only the current document. If you want to change the default orientation setting for all documents printed on a particular printer, visit the Printers folder, right-click the printer, and choose Document Defaults.

Changing Resolution

Resolution is a measure of the density at which a printer puts dots on paper. Higher resolutions, such as 600 or 1200 dots per inch (dpi), produce smooth, high-quality output but require longer printing times. Lower-resolutions, such as 75 dpi, produce only draft-quality output, but print quickly.

Generally speaking, resolution is associated with graphics printing; therefore, you probably won't find an option for setting resolution anywhere within your word processor's printing and page-layout dialog boxes. Your graphics programs may offer such an option, however.

You can also change resolution by modifying the printer's document property sheet, which you can view by clicking the Properties button in the common Print dialog box. When you change the document property sheet via the Print dialog box, your change affects only the current document. To change the default resolution setting for all documents printed on a particular printer, visit the Printers folder, right-click the printer, and choose Document Defaults.

Printing with Drag and Drop

If the document you want to print is not open, you can double-click its icon in a folder or Windows NT Explorer window, and then use the Print command in its parent application. But you don't need to do this. Another way to print a document is to grab its icon and drag it to a printer icon.

NOTE

You can print via drag and drop only with documents that are associated with their parent application in your Windows registry. If you try it with an unregistered document type, you'll get an error message. *For information about associating documents with applications, see "Working with the File Types List," page 155.*

TIP

Double-Click to Check the Queue

When you print, Windows NT displays a printer icon in the notification area of your taskbar. You can see what's in the queue by double-clicking that icon. When all jobs are finished printing, the icon disappears.

To print a document using drag and drop, drag the document's icon to the printer icon using either mouse button. When you reach the drop zone, the printer icon becomes highlighted and your document icon sprouts a plus sign to indicate that you are copying data to the printer (as opposed to moving it there permanently). Release the button when you reach the printer icon to begin printing.

When you drop a document onto a printer icon, Windows loads the parent application and executes its print command. Depending on the application, you may or may not have to respond to a dialog box before printing begins. As soon as the information has been transferred to the print queue, the application closes.

TIP

Create a Desktop Printer Shortcut

Although you can print by dragging a document icon to a printer icon in your Printers folder, you'll probably find it more convenient to create a desktop shortcut for each printer you plan to use this way. To create a desktop printer shortcut, open your Printers folder, right-drag the printer's icon, and release the mouse button on your desktop. From the context menu, choose Create Shortcut(s) Here.

For more information about the Send To command, see "Moving or Copying Objects with Send To," page 144.

Printing with the Send To Command

If you don't like cluttering your desktop with printer icons, or if you find it inconvenient to make those icons visible when you want to print, try using the Send To command. Simply right-click the icon for the document you want to print, choose Send To from the context menu, and then choose the name of the printer you want from the Send To menu. If the printer's name isn't on the Send To menu, you can put it there as follows:

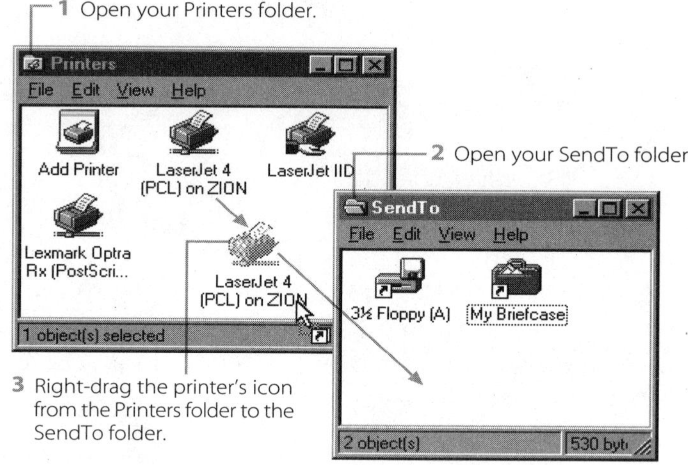

4 Choose Create Shortcut(s) Here from the context menu.

5 Right-click the new icon in the SendTo folder and choose Rename. Delete "Shortcut to" and then press Enter.

When you print with Send To, Windows first opens your document's parent application, just as it does when you drag the document to a printer icon.

SEE ALSO

For information about MS-DOS–based programs, see "Running MS-DOS–Based Applications," page 478.

Printing from MS-DOS–Based Applications

Windows NT makes printing from MS-DOS–based applications as much like printing from Windows-based applications as it can without interfering with the expectations of your MS-DOS–based programs. If you send output to a printer port that is busy with Windows print jobs, for example, your MS-DOS output gets in line and prints when its turn arrives. However, MS-DOS–based print jobs go wherever the program is configured to send them—which may or may not be the default Windows printer—because MS-DOS–based programs do not "know" anything about Windows' printing procedures.

To print from an MS-DOS–based application to a network printer, you must first map the printer name to a local port. You do this with the Net Use command, as follows:

1. Click the Start button, point to Programs, and choose Command Prompt to open a command prompt window.
2. At the command prompt, enter this command line:

   net use lpt1 *computername**printername* /persistent:yes

   Replace *computername* with the name of the computer to which the printer is attached (the print server), and replace *printername* with the share name of the printer. If you have a local printer attached to your computer's LPT1 port, use a different port (such as LPT2 or LPT3) in the Net Use command line.
3. Close the command prompt window.

Then set up your MS-DOS–based applications to print to the port you specified in the Net Use command. The /Persistent switch ensures that the mapping occurs automatically each time you log on to Windows NT.

Printing to a Network Printer

Printing to a network printer is just like printing to a local printer, provided:

- The network printer has been shared (your network administrator should do that for you)

- You have been given access to it (also a task for your network administrator)
- A copy of the printer's driver has been installed on your own computer (something you may need to do yourself)

SEE ALSO

For information about installing a network printer, see "Adding a Network Printer," page 230.

Once these provisos are taken care of, you can print an open document to a network printer using your application's Print command, just as you would for a local printer.

Getting Notification of Completed Print Jobs

Windows NT uses the Messenger service to provide notification to users when network printing jobs are complete. If you have the Messenger service running on your system and you send a job to a network printer, a message will pop up to let you know when you can fetch your printout.

If the notifications become an annoyance (and your account has the requisite privileges), you can stop them in either of two ways:

- Stop the Messenger service on your workstation, as follows: Double-click the Services icon in Control Panel. Select Messenger in the Service list, and then click Stop. (By default, the Messenger service starts automatically when you log on to Windows NT. To prevent the Messenger service from starting when you log on, select Messenger in the Services dialog box and click Startup. Select Manual and then click OK.)
- If the printer that generates the messages is attached to a server that you administer, go to that server and open its Printers folder. Right-click an unoccupied area of the folder and choose Server Properties. Click the Advanced tab, and then deselect the check box labeled "Notify when remote documents are printed."

You can also change notification settings for a particular document. *For details, see "Telling Windows NT Whom to Notify," page 222.*

Inspecting and Managing a Print Queue

When you print a document, Windows creates a temporary file, called a spool file—on your hard disk if the printer is local, or on the hard disk of the computer to which the printer is attached if it is a network printer. While this file is being created, your application is temporarily busy and unavailable. After the spool file is created, the print job enters a print queue and you can resume working in your application while printing continues in the background. If no other jobs are in the queue, your document's spool file is "despooled" to the printer. Otherwise, it waits its turn.

You can check the status of a printer's queue by double-clicking the printer's icon in your Printers folder or by double-clicking the printer icon that appears in the notification area of your taskbar. Windows NT displays the print queue in a folder window similar to the one shown below.

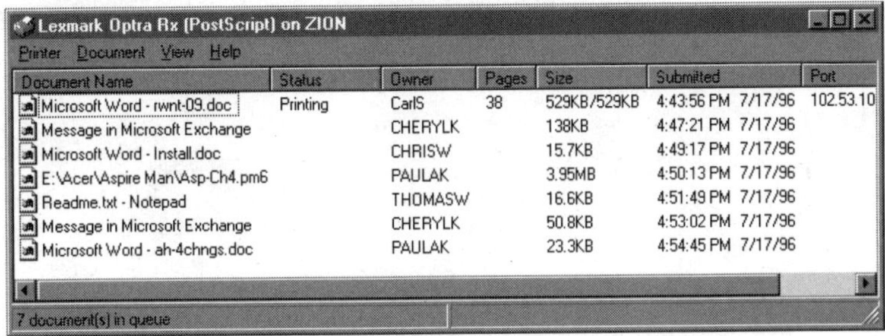

Lexmark Optra Rx (PostScript) on ZION

Printer Document View Help

Document Name	Status	Owner	Pages	Size	Submitted	Port
Microsoft Word - rwnt-09.doc	Printing	CarlS	38	529KB/529KB	4:43:56 PM 7/17/96	102.53.10
Message in Microsoft Exchange		CHERYLK		138KB	4:47:21 PM 7/17/96	
Microsoft Word - Install.doc		CHRISW		15.7KB	4:49:17 PM 7/17/96	
E:\Acer\Aspire Man\Asp-Ch4.pm6		PAULAK		3.95MB	4:50:13 PM 7/17/96	
Readme.txt - Notepad		THOMASW		16.6KB	4:51:49 PM 7/17/96	
Message in Microsoft Exchange		CHERYLK		50.8KB	4:53:02 PM 7/17/96	
Microsoft Word - ah-4chngs.doc		PAULAK		23.3KB	4:54:45 PM 7/17/96	

7 document(s) in queue

From the print queue window, you can perform the following tasks:

- To remove a document that you own from the queue, select it and press Delete.

- To pause or resume printing of a document that you own, select it and use commands on the Document menu.

- To pause the entire queue, choose Pause Printing from the Printer menu (requires Manage Documents or Full Control permission).
- To delete all jobs in the queue, choose Purge Print Documents from the Printer menu (requires Manage Documents or Full Control permission).

Printer Permissions

SEE ALSO

For more information about permissions, see Chapter 19, "Windows NT Security."

Usually, all users on a network are allowed access to shared printers and can manage their own documents in the print queue. Users who have been granted additional permissions by the system administrator can manage all documents in a queue as well as change a printer's properties. Table 9-1 shows the permissions that Windows NT provides for printers and their associated privileges.

TABLE 9-1. Printer Permissions and Privileges

Permission	Privileges
No Access	Cannot connect to printer or manipulate its queue
Print	■ Print documents ■ Control properties of owned documents ■ Pause, restart, and remove owned documents
Manage Documents	Everything allowed by Print permission, plus: ■ Pause, restart, move, and remove queued documents
Full Control	Everything allowed by Manage Documents, plus ■ Share printer ■ Change printer properties ■ Remove printer ■ Change printer permissions

By default, all users have Print permission for documents they create, and members of the Administrators and Power Users groups have Full Control permission. (On a Windows NT Server system, Administrators, Print Operators, and Server Operators have Full Control by default.)

If you have Full Control permission for a printer, you can change other users' permissions for that printer. To do so, right-click the printer in your Printers folder, choose Properties from the context menu, click the Security tab, and then click the Permissions button.

Rearranging the Queue

If you have Manage Documents or Full Control permission, you can change the order of items in a print queue. You can do this in either of two ways: by adjusting the priority assigned to selected documents, or by specifying that selected documents can be printed only during a certain time period. To use either method, right-click the document you want to modify in its queue window. Then choose Properties from the context menu to arrive at the following dialog box:

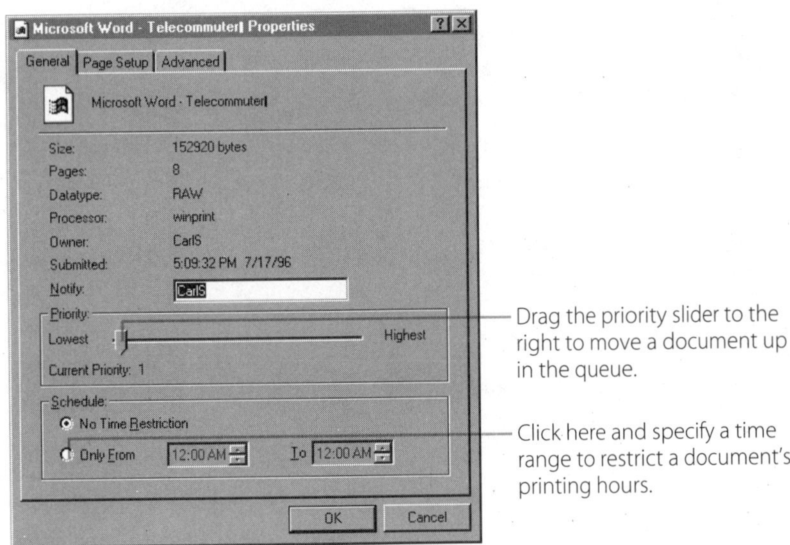

Telling Windows NT Whom to Notify

Windows NT normally notifies the owner of a print job when the job is completed by popping up a window over the foreground application. For documents that you own, you can turn off the notification or specify another person to notify by selecting the document and choosing the Document menu's Details command. Type the name of the person to notify in the Notify box.

To change the Notify setting for a document you don't own, you must have Manage Documents or Full Control permission for the printer.

Adding a Printer

> Adding a local printer (one connected to your own computer) requires administrator privileges. Adding a printer that's connected to a network server also requires administrator privileges if adding the printer requires the system to copy a driver file to your local computer.

What Windows NT calls a *printer* is more precisely a constellation of settings applied to an output device. That device may actually be a traditional printer, a fax modem, a disk file, or perhaps something else altogether. Each combination of settings and output device constitutes a *logical printer* to Windows NT. It is treated as a separate device, and displayed as a separate icon or list entry in your Printers folder. You can add as many logical printers as you like, and you can set up multiple logical printers for the same physical output device.

The items that make up a logical printer include the following:

- The name of the printer
- The local or network port to which the printer is connected
- A share name, if you want the printer to be available to other network users
- For shared printers, a description that network users will see when they browse Network Neighborhood in search of a printer

- The printer driver
- Printer properties such as the amount of memory in the printer, any font cartridges or soft fonts in use, and so on
- Default document properties such as the paper tray and paper size, orientation, and resolution
- A priority setting and, if desired, a time range during which the printer will operate
- The name of a separator-page file, if one is to be used
- The length of time Windows NT should wait before notification of an error

Adding a Local Printer

To add a *local printer*—one that's physically attached to your computer—begin by double-clicking the Add Printer icon in your Printers folder. This action summons the Add Printer wizard, whose opening screen looks like this:

Choose My Computer for a printer that's connected to your own computer.

Add Printer Wizard

This wizard helps you install your printer or make printer connections. This printer will be managed by:

My Computer

All settings will be managed and configured on this computer.

Network printer server

Connect to a printer on another machine. All settings for this printer are managed by a print server that has been set up by an administrator.

< Back | Next > | Cancel

Choose Network Printer Server for a printer that's attached to another computer on your network.

Specifying Printer Ports

Clicking Next in the Wizard's opening dialog box takes you to the following screen, where you select one or more printer ports:

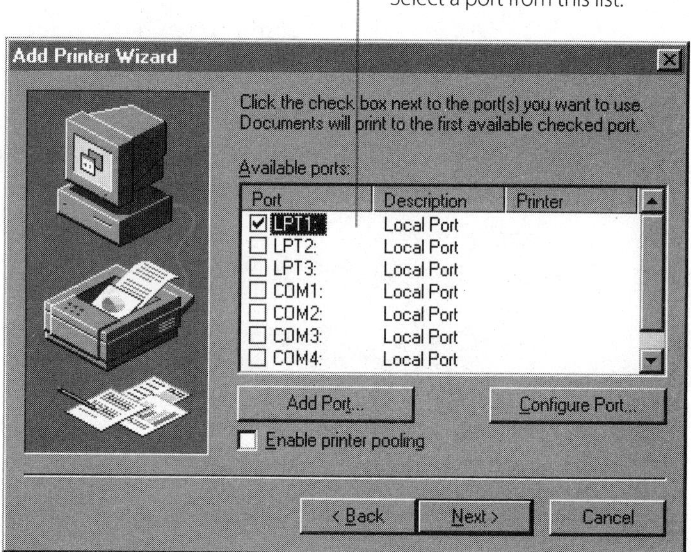

Printing to a Disk File

To send your output to a disk file, choose FILE: as your printer port. Windows NT will prompt for a filename when you print. You can copy the resulting disk file to a physical printer at a later time.

Setting Up a Printer Pool

If you have more than one printer of the same make and model attached to your computer, you can join them in a *printer pool*.

Output is then directed to the first selected port that has an available printer. To set up a printer pool:

1. Select the Enable Printer Pooling check box.
2. Select each port that is connected to a printer of the type you're installing.

Adding a Port

In certain instances, you'll need to connect a printer to a port that doesn't yet appear in the wizard's list box. For example, some printers have ports that allow them to be connected directly to the network instead of connecting them to a computer. These are called network-interface printers. Even printers that don't have a built-in network interface can be connected to an external device, such as a Hewlett-Packard JetDirect network interface, that allows a printer to be placed anywhere on the network without being tethered to a computer.

If you're going to use your computer to manage such a printer, you must add a driver that lets your computer communicate with the printer. Doing so adds an entry to the list of available ports on your computer.

If another computer manages the network-interface printer, you don't need to add a port. Instead, click Back and then, in the Add Printer wizard's first dialog box, select Network Printer Server.

The first step in adding a port, naturally, is to click the Add Port button. Beyond that, the details depend on the type of network-interface printer you have. You'll need to refer to the documentation for the printer or the network-interface device.

There's another situation in which you need to add a port: some fax drivers require that you "print" to a particular file when you want to fax a document. To do so, follow these steps:

1 Click Add Port.

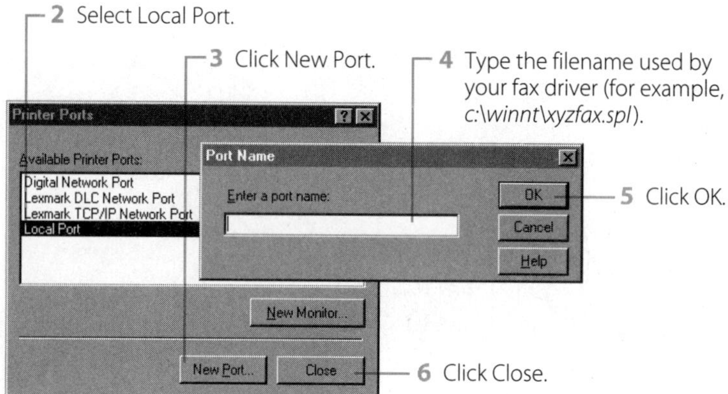

Configuring a Port

To configure one of the ports listed in the wizard's second dialog box, select it and click Configure Port. For parallel ports, the only setting you can modify is the Transmission Retry timeout. This setting tells Windows NT how long to continue trying to send output to a printer that does not respond. The default setting is 90 seconds. For serial (COM) ports, you can specify baud rate, data bits, stop bits, parity, and flow control, as well as the port address and interrupt-request (IRQ) number.

Choosing Make and Model

After you've selected one or more ports for your printer, click Next to get to the wizard's "make and model" screen, shown in the following illustration.

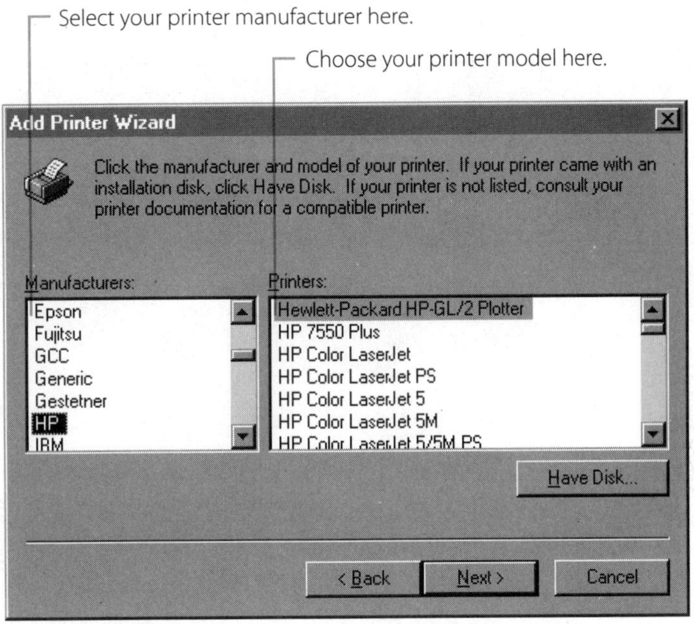

Choosing the printer manufacturer and model from this screen allows Windows NT to install the appropriate driver for your printer. After you've made your selection, you might be prompted to insert the Windows NT CD-ROM. If the required driver is already present on your hard disk, the wizard asks your permission to use it. (Knowing that your intention may be to install an updated version of the driver, the wizard does not assume it should use the existing version.)

What to Do If Your Printer Isn't on the List

If your printer isn't on the list of supported printers, you might want to contact the printer vendor to see if a driver for Windows NT is available. If you can obtain a driver, repeat the steps described above. Then click Have Disk and follow the prompts to direct the Add Printer wizard to your driver file.

If no driver is available, check your printer documentation to see if your printer emulates another printer make and model, one for which a Windows NT driver is available. If your printer can emulate a supported printer, use the emulation mode and select the supported printer.

Naming the Printer

After you select your printer and supply the driver source media if necessary, click Next to get to the following screen:

The name you type here appears under the printer's icon in your Printers folder.

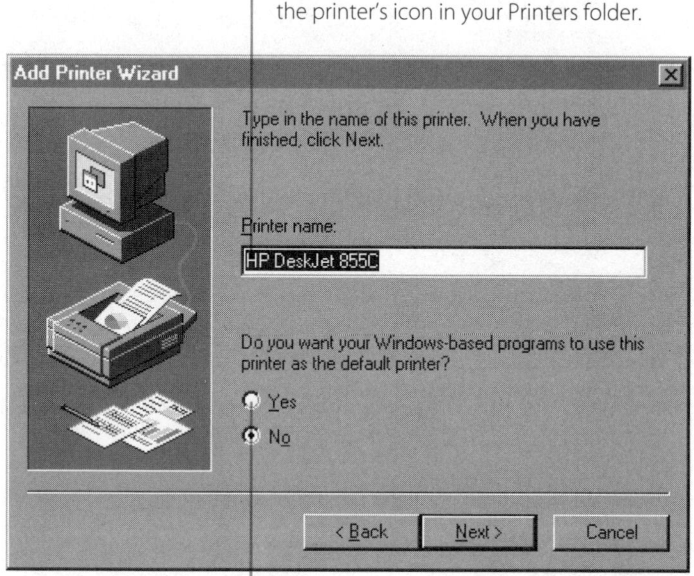

Click here if you want this printer to be the default.

You can easily revise the choices you make in this dialog box at any time. To rename a printer, simply right-click it in the Printers folder and choose Rename. To make a printer the default, right-click it and choose Set As Default.

To Share or Not to Share

After naming your new printer and clicking Next, you arrive at the wizard's sharing screen:

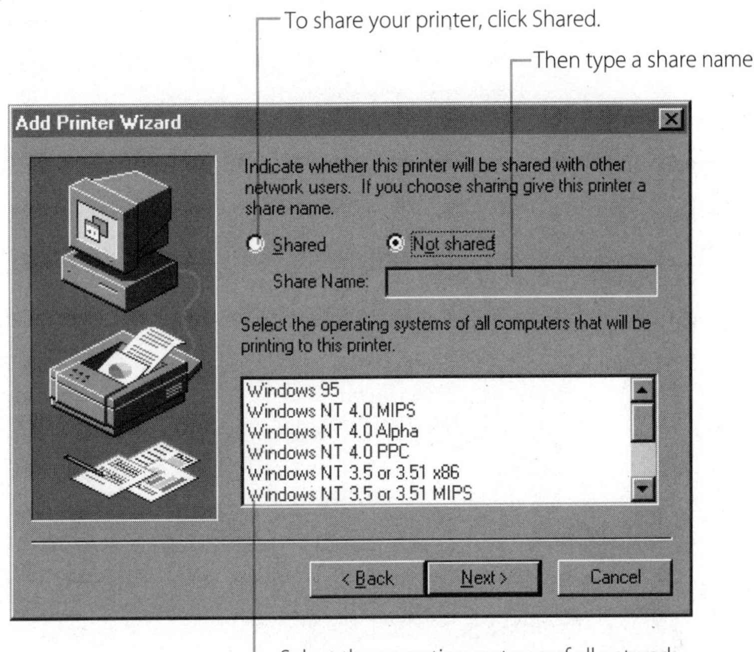

The share name is the name that other users will see when they connect to your printer. In the property sheet for your printer, described later in this chapter, you can also supply a descriptive comment and identify the location of the printer. Users can read the comment and location information by inspecting the printer property sheet on their systems.

If anyone using your shared printer is working with an operating system other than Windows NT 4 (or with Windows NT 4 on a different type of computer), select that operating system in the list at the bottom of the dialog box. Hold down Ctrl while clicking to select multiple operating systems. Doing so makes the necessary drivers available to these users when they connect to your printer.

Final Steps: The Test Page and Property Settings

The wizard's final two steps allow you to print a test page (a good idea) and supply initial property settings. We'll look at a typical property sheet later in this chapter.

Adding a Network Printer

When you "add" a network printer, you actually establish a connection to a printer that's attached to and shared by a server on your network. The steps required to accomplish this are few. Windows NT asks you to identify the printer's share name, supply an additional name (it can be the same as the share name) for the system to display below the icon in your Printers folder, and (possibly) specify certain default settings such as which paper tray to use. In some cases, the system also copies a driver file from the server to your own computer.

> If the computer to which the network printer is connected is not running Windows NT 4 on the same type of computer as yours, you may be prompted to insert the Windows NT 4 CD-ROM, or a floppy disk containing the necessary driver file.

Start by clicking the Add Printer icon in your Printers folder. At the wizard's first screen, choose the Network Printer Server option button and click Next. Windows displays a network browser dialog box, similar to the following:

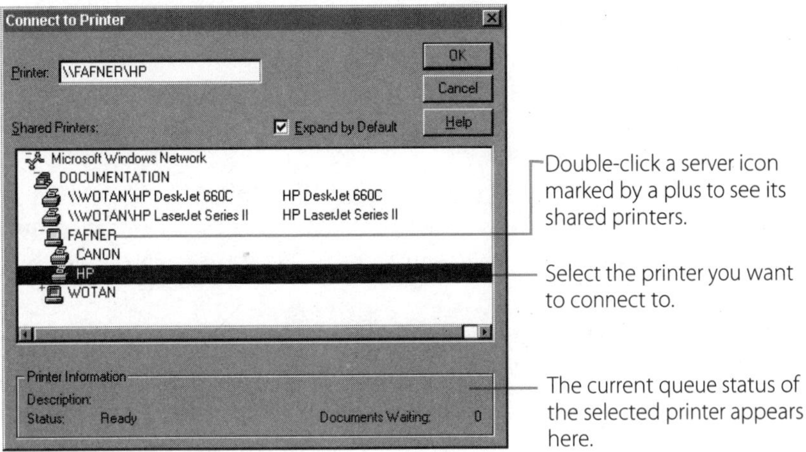

If the wizard prompts you to supply initial settings for the network printer, it will display the Settings pane of the printer's property sheet. That component of the property sheet is described later in this chapter.

 TIP

Installing a Network Printer via Drag and Drop

You can also install a network printer using drag and drop. First, find the printer's icon in your Network Neighborhood folder. Then drag that icon to your own Printers folder. Windows NT copies the necessary driver files to your computer (prompting you to insert the Windows NT CD-ROM if the files aren't available on the print server) and adds an icon to your Printers folder.

Inspecting and Setting Printer Properties

 SEE ALSO

For information about printer permissions, see "Printer Permissions," page 220.

To inspect the property settings for a printer, simply right-click the printer's icon in your Printers folder and choose Properties from the context menu. Windows will present a six-tabbed dialog box detailing everything the system knows about the printer. You can inspect all of the printer's properties, whether or not you have permission to change them. If you do not have permission to change a property setting, that setting will be displayed in gray.

The first five pages of the property dialog box cover items that pertain to all printers. The last page, called Device Settings, has to do with options that may be specific for the printer's make and model.

General Settings

The General page of the property sheet, shown below, records, among other details, an optional description of the printer and information about where the printer is located. With appropriate permissions, you can also use this page to specify a separator sheet that will be printed before each new print job.

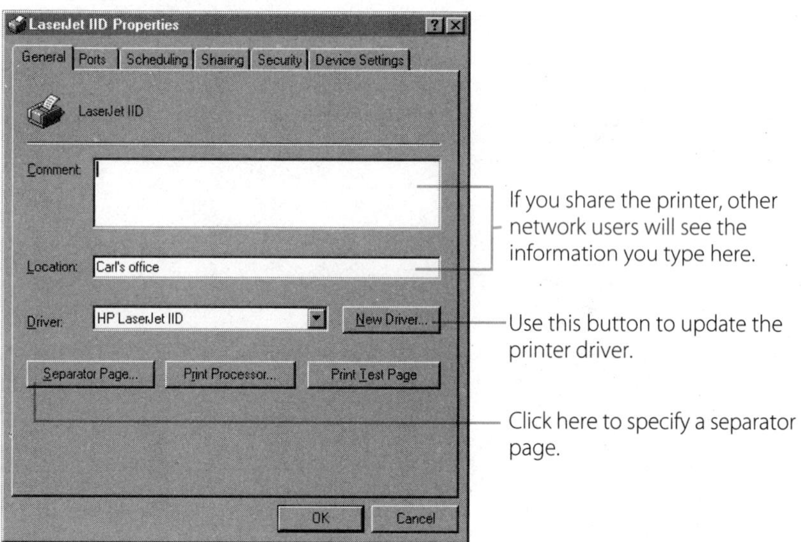

Updating the Printer Driver

Printer drivers are just like any other kind of software—subject to revision by their vendors. If a newer version of the driver becomes available after you first set up a printer, you can install that driver by clicking the New Driver button in the General page of the printer's property sheet. In the ensuing dialog box, click Have Disk and point Windows to the location of the updated driver file.

Using a Separator Page

Like a fax cover sheet, a separator page separates one print job from the next and can be used to identify the person who sent the job, the time it was sent, and other details. Separator pages can also include codes to do such things as switch a printer from the PCL page-description language to PostScript, or vice versa.

Windows NT includes three separator-page files, which you can use ready-made or customize. The supplied files are described in Table 9-2.

TABLE 9-2. Separator Page Files

Filename	Description
SYSPRINT.SEP	Prints a separator page that includes the account name and date and time of printing (for use with PostScript printers only)
PCL.SEP	Switches the printer to PCL and then prints a separator page that includes the account name (for use with PCL printers only)
PSCRIPT.SEP	Switches the printer to PostScript, but does not print a separator page

Separator page files are normally stored in your \Winnt\System32 folder. To specify a separator page, click the Separator Page button in the General page of the printer's property sheet.

Customizing and Creating Separator Pages

Separator page files are plain text files with the extension .SEP. You can create your own separator pages either by modifying the files supplied with Windows NT or by typing codes into a new plain-text document and saving that document in your \Winnt\System32 folder. Be sure to save the document as a plain-text file.

The codes you can use for your separator pages are listed in Table 9-3. Each separator file must start with a single character on a line by itself; that character becomes the *command delimiter*, which identifies commands elsewhere in the file. You can use any character as a command delimiter. In Table 9-3, the @ character is used as the command delimiter. For these commands to work, the first line of your file must contain only a single @ character.

TABLE 9-3. Separator Page Codes

Code	Description
@N	Prints the user name of the person who submitted the print job.
@I	Prints the job number.
@D	Prints the date, in the date format specified by Control Panel's Regional Settings applet.
@T	Prints the time, in the time format specified by Control Panel's Regional Settings applet.
@L	Prints all characters following @L up to the next @ code or until the page width specified by @W is reached.
@F*pathname*	Prints the contents of the file specified by *pathname*.
@H*nn*	Sends a printer-specific control code, where *nn* is a hexadecimal value. For example, use @H1B to send an escape code, which has a hexadecimal value of 1B (27 decimal).
@W*nnn*	Sets the maximum width of the separator page to the decimal value specified by *nnn*. Any characters beyond this width are truncated. (The default width is 80; the maximum is 256.)
@B@S	Prints in single-width block characters.
@B@M	Prints in double-width block characters.
@U	Turns off block-character printing.
@*n*	Skips *n* lines. (*n* can be 0 through 9.)
@E	Ejects the current page from the printer.

Changing Port Assignments and Port Properties

The Ports page of the printer property sheet shows what port(s) a printer is connected to. With appropriate permissions, you can also use this page to change port assignments and configure ports. *For more information, see "Specifying Printer Ports," page 224, and "Configuring a Port," page 226.*

Scheduling and Spooling Properties

The Scheduling page of the printer property sheet, shown in the next illustration, displays the printer's hours of operation, the priority level of the printer, and the printer's spooling characteristics.

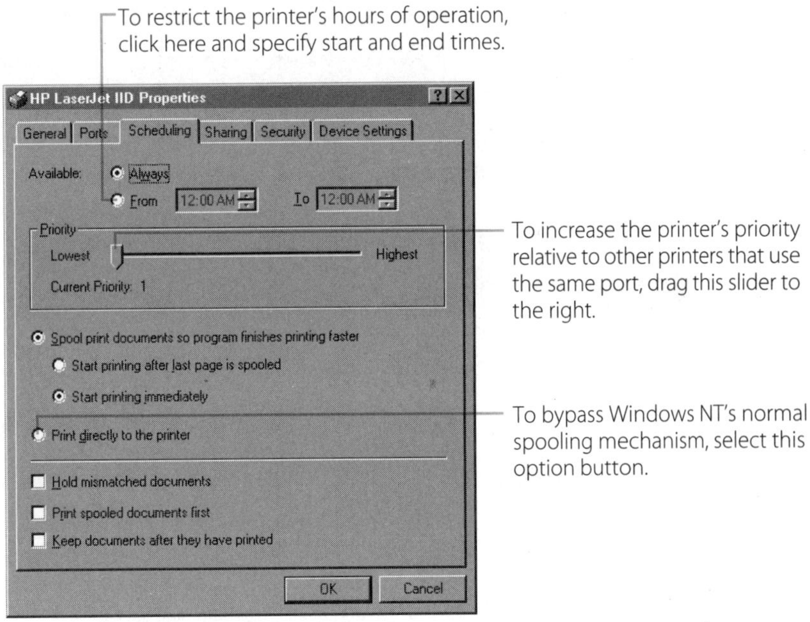

To restrict the printer's hours of operation, click here and specify start and end times.

To increase the printer's priority relative to other printers that use the same port, drag this slider to the right.

To bypass Windows NT's normal spooling mechanism, select this option button.

Note that the hours of operation and priority settings shown in this property sheet apply to all jobs sent to this printer. With appropriate permissions, you can also modify these settings for individual print jobs. To do this, right-click a print job in the queue window and choose Properties.

 NOTE

Let the Night Crew Handle It

You might want to set up a printer that is available only while you're not working—and then use it to print long jobs that would otherwise tie up your printer for long periods of time. Even when a printer's hours are restricted, your applications can still "print"—but print jobs are held in the queue until the "available" time is reached.

Printing Directly to the Printer

By default, Windows NT creates a spool file for your print job, and then feeds the spool file to the printer in the background while you go on with other tasks. That's usually a benefit, because it lets you get back to work before the job is printed. It also lets you control the priority of your print jobs.

At times, however, you might want to bypass the spooler and send a job directly to the printer. You can do this by selecting the Print Directly To The Printer option button. This option is not available when a printer is shared.

Sharing Status

SEE ALSO

For more information about sharing a printer, see "To Share or Not to Share," page 229.

The Sharing page of the printer property sheet records whether or not the printer is available to other network users. With appropriate permissions, you can change the sharing status, as well as the share name, by means of this property sheet.

Security Settings

To inspect or modify the printer permissions for individual users or groups of users, click the Security tab in the printer's property sheet, and then click the Permissions button. *For more information about permissions, see "Printer Permissions," page 220.*

Device-Specific Settings

Property settings that are specific to the printer driver—such as the presence or absence of an envelope feeder, the amount of memory installed, and the presence of font cartridges—are recorded on the Device Settings page of the printer's property sheet. The following illustration shows a sample, although your own printer's property sheet will probably differ somewhat from this one:

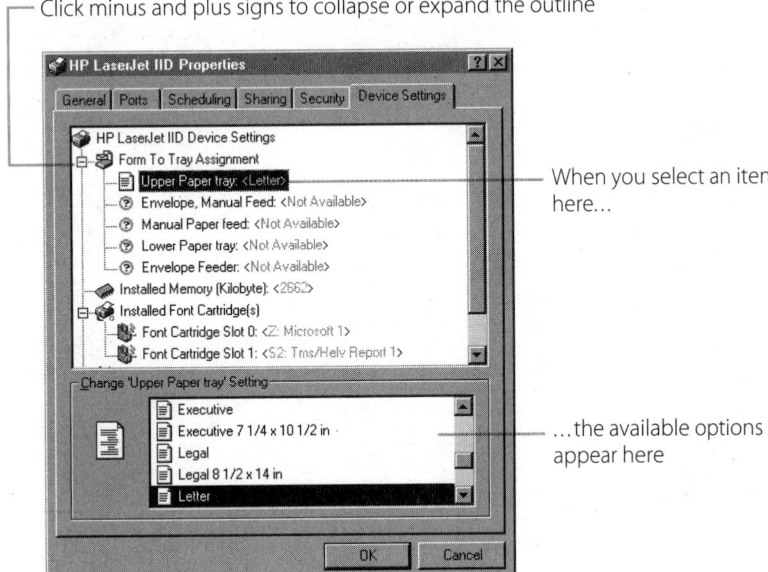

To find out what any of the options presented in this part of the property sheet mean, click the question-mark icon near the upper right corner of the dialog box. Then click the option in question.

Document Defaults

Default settings for such things as document page size and orientation appear on a separate property sheet, not on a page of the printer's property sheet. To see the current document defaults for a printer, right-click the printer icon in your Printers folder, and then choose Document Defaults. The following illustration shows a sample of what you see:

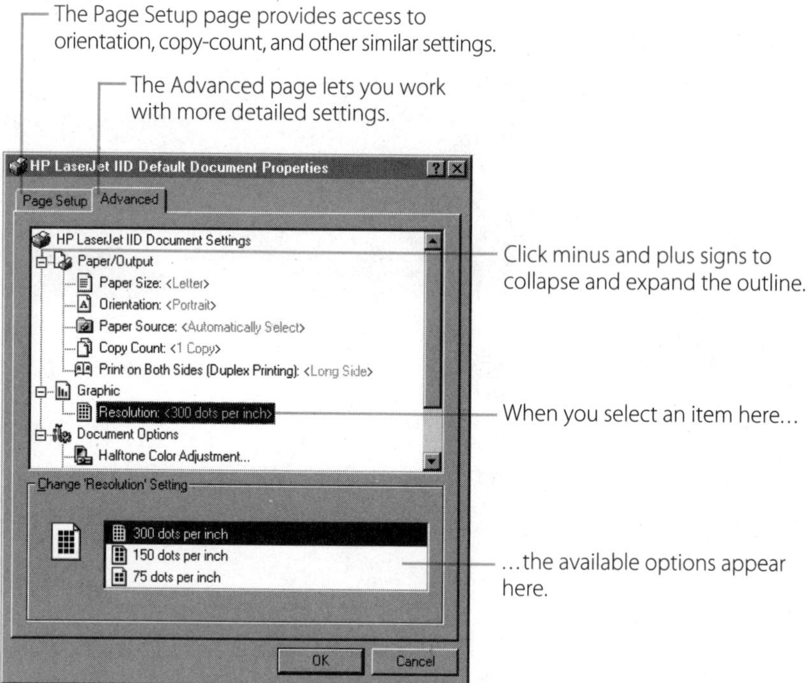

This property sheet has two tabs. The Page Setup page includes such things as default orientation (portrait or landscape), the default copy count (if your printer supports this), and the default paper size and source. The Advanced tab, shown above, includes these settings as well as options to set resolution and other graphics-related settings.

PART 2

Sharing Information and Communicating

CHAPTER 10

Exchanging Information: OLE and the Clipboard

In the bad old early days of desktop computing, transferring information from one application to another was a process beset with difficulties. In that time before Windows, if you wanted to build "compound documents"—documents with elements derived from two or more applications—you often had to rely on clumsy TSR (terminate-and-stay-resident) utilities to act as data-moving intermediaries between applications. The dearth of file-format standards and the absence of treaties governing relations among programs that shared memory made the exchange of information frustrating and perilous. Single-application documents were the norm, and a compound document was usually something assembled by a pasteup artist.

Nowadays, compound documents have become so usual that the term itself has fallen into disuse. Windows users expect to be able to move text, graphics, sound, and video freely within and between documents and are seldom disappointed. In Windows NT 4, the process of generating what used to be called a compound document is easier than ever, thanks both to improvements in the Windows user interface and the growing prevalence of a standard called OLE (pronounced *olay*, with the stress on the second syllable) object technology.

In this chapter, we'll examine the methods and mechanisms for moving information between and within applications.

Data Exchange: A Symphony with Three Movements

Three forms of data exchange are common in Windows:

- Static moves and copies
- Embedding
- Linking

A *static move* or *static copy* is a one-time transaction with a no-return policy. If you cut or copy a range of numbers from your spreadsheet and paste them statically into your word processor document, your word processor handles those numbers exactly as though you had typed them directly at the keyboard. You can format them, edit them, delete them, or stand them on their heads (if your word processor does that sort of thing), but they have no further relationship to the document and application in which they originated.

Servers, Clients, Sources, Destinations, Objects, Containers (and All That Jazz)

There are two parties to any OLE transaction. One party supplies the goods, the other receives them. For example, if you take a range from an Excel spreadsheet and embed it in a PowerPoint presentation, you have a supplying document (the Excel spreadsheet) and a receiving document (the PowerPoint presentation).

In OLE parlance, the supplying document is called the *source*, or *server*. The receiving document is known as the *destination*, the *client*, or the *container*. The goods, whatever they may be, are known simply as the *object*.

The terms *server* and *client*, of course, are also used in the context of networking. A server is a shared resource, typically a hard disk on a computer dedicated to storing files needed by many different users. A client is a computer that connects to a server. To minimize confusion in this book, we'll stick with *source* and *destination* when the subject is OLE, reserving *server* and *client* for their more traditional networking meanings.

SEE ALSO
For more information about embedding, see "How to Embed," page 250.

When you *embed* one document's data in a second document, the data remembers where it came from. If you want to edit that data, Windows lets you work in the data's original context. For example, suppose you copy a block of numbers from a spreadsheet and embed them in a word processing document. When you want to edit those numbers, the original spreadsheet application reappears, allowing you to use its commands, instead of your word processor's, to do your editing.

SEE ALSO
For more information about linking, see "How to Link," page 253.

When you *link* one document's data to a second document, the data you link is not actually stored in the receiving document. Instead, the receiving application stores only the information about where the data came from. Continuing with our spreadsheet–word processor example, if you use a linking command to paste the spreadsheet numbers into your word processor document, the numbers look exactly as if you typed them in at the keyboard. But when you save that document to a disk file, the file does not include the numbers. Instead, it includes everything Windows needs to know in order to find those numbers again the next time you open the file. If you change the numbers in the spreadsheet, your changes also appear in your word processor document.

Embedding and linking also have one other important virtue: they allow you to incorporate material into your documents that your documents cannot render directly. For example, you can embed or link a sound annotation or a video clip into documents created by most word processors, database managers, and spreadsheet programs. Those programs display an icon to indicate where the sound or video has been embedded or linked. When you want to hear the sound or see the video, you simply double-click the icon. Windows then renders the object, using the sound or video application in which the object originated.

TIP

Embedding an Icon

Many programs give you the option of displaying embedded or linked data as an icon, even if the program *can* render the data. For example, your word processor might permit you to embed a block of text but display it as an icon. The readers of your document can then skip over the embedded material if they're not interested in it. If they are interested, they can double-click the icon and read the embedded text.

The linking component of OLE is an extension of an earlier data-exchange technology called DDE (the letters stand for *dynamic data exchange*). In some applications, you might still encounter the term DDE, but unless you are a programmer, you will probably never need to concern yourself with the details about how DDE works. You can simply use your programs' Paste Link commands (as described later in this chapter) to create links and let Windows worry about what's going on under the hood.

What the Cut, Copy, Paste, and Paste Special Commands Do

As you probably know, the universal method for moving or copying an item from one place to another is as follows:

SEE ALSO

For information about selecting part of a document, see Selecting Text," page 47.

SEE ALSO

For information about selecting files and folders, see "Selecting Folders and Files," page 135.

1. Select whatever it is you want to move or copy—a block of text, a region in a graphical image, a range of spreadsheet cells, a file in a folder window, or whatever.
2. Choose the Cut command if you want to move the selected object. Choose the Copy command if you want to copy it. In virtually all Windows-based applications, these commands can be found on the Edit menu. In many applications, you can right-click and choose these commands from a context menu.
3. Move to the place where you want the data transferred and choose Paste or Paste Special. Like Cut and Copy, these commands can be found on programs' Edit menus. If you're pasting something onto the desktop or into a folder window, right-click and choose Paste from the context menu.

TIP

The Keyboard Can Be Quicker

You can save a lot of time by using keyboard shortcuts for Cut, Copy, and Paste. Use Ctrl-X for Cut, Ctrl-C for Copy, and Ctrl-V for Paste.

Now that many programs support moving and copying via drag and drop, this cut-and-paste (or copy-and-paste) sequence is no longer the only way to relocate data in Windows documents. But it's probably still the most commonly used method, so let's take a look at what happens when you use these commands.

TIP

MS-DOS and the Clipboard

You can use Copy and Paste with MS-DOS–based applications as well as Windows-based applications. *For more information, see "Using Copy and Paste," page 486.*

 CAUTION

Some applications clear the Clipboard "behind the scenes." Microsoft Excel, for example, often erases the Clipboard on its own initiative. This is uncommon behavior, however, and you're not likely to see it in most of the programs you use.

The Clipboard: Windows' Invisible Transfer Agent

When you select data and use an application's Cut or Copy command, the selected data is stored on the *Clipboard*, an area of memory used to hold data in transit. When you use an application's Paste command, the Clipboard's data is copied into the application.

Data on the Clipboard usually remains there until new data arrives to replace it. That means that you can cut or copy something to the Clipboard, and then paste it as many times in as many places as you please. But as soon as you use another Cut or Copy command, the data you were previously pasting disappears from the Clipboard.

TIP

Bypass the Clipboard

To move information without disturbing the current Clipboard contents, drag it with the mouse. (Or hold down the Ctrl key as you drag to copy information.) Many Windows-based programs offer some level of "drag and drop" support (within a document, between documents, or even between applications), and this form of data movement bypasses the Clipboard.

Be careful with the Cut command. In most programs, the data you cut disappears from its source document as soon as you use this command. If you get distracted between cutting and pasting and happen to put another item on the Clipboard before pasting the first, you may lose the first item. If you change your mind between cutting something and pasting it, simply paste it back where you cut it. (If the cut item is one or more files or folders in a folder window, the selected files or folders remain in place until you paste them in another folder.)

Controlling the Outcome with Paste Special

When you cut or copy information from an application, the application supplies the information to the Clipboard in as many formats as it can. If you cut a paragraph in a Microsoft Word document, for example, Word transfers that paragraph to the Clipboard in both text and graphics formats. If you copy a spreadsheet range from Microsoft Excel, the Clipboard receives your selection in a large assortment of formats, including some that allow the data to be exported to other spreadsheet programs.

This multiple-format arrangement allows an application to receive Clipboard data in whichever format best suits it. For example, the fact that a Microsoft Word paragraph is stored on the Clipboard in both graphics and text formats means that you can paste it into Notepad, a program that accepts only text, as well as into other programs that accept only graphics.

The multiple-format arrangement also means that you often have choices about how to paste your data. When you simply use an application's Paste command, you get whatever format the program thinks you're most likely to want. But in many programs, you can use a Paste Special command and choose an alternative format. Figure 10-1 shows an example of a Paste Special dialog box. In this example, the source data is a range of spreadsheet cells. If you want to paste a picture of those cells, rather than the text contained in the cells, you can choose either Picture or Bitmap, both of which are graphics formats.

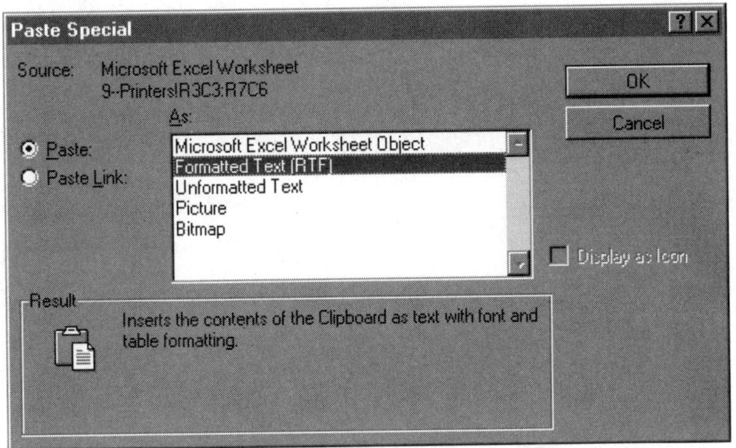

FIGURE 10-1.
The Paste Special command lets you choose what format to paste, as well as whether to embed, link, or paste statically.

Table 10-1 describes some of the data formats you might encounter in your programs' Paste Special dialog boxes.

TABLE 10-1. Common Clipboard Data Formats

Data Format	Description
Unformatted Text	Unformatted character information (without style attributes, such as boldface and italics), using the ANSI standard character set used by all Windows-based programs.
Formatted Text (RTF)	A text format that uses embedded codes to store style information, such as boldface and italics.
Unicode Text	A 16-bit text-encoding format that allows for both Latin and non-Latin alphanumeric characters, plus an assortment of commercial, mathematical, and scientific symbols.
Bitmap	A graphic format in which each pixel in an image is represented by one or more data bits. Unlike a picture or metafile, bitmap data is device specific. If you display a bitmap on a device with resolution or color capability different from the one on which it was created, you're not likely to be pleased with the result. Also, although bitmap images can be resized or reshaped, this process generally introduces gross distortions.
Picture	A graphic format in which image elements are stored as a sequence of commands. An image in picture format can be reproduced without gross distortion in different sizes or shapes, as well as on different kinds of output devices. But a bitmap image might display more quickly because it doesn't have to be re-created from programmatic instructions. An image in picture format is also sometimes called a metafile (although the terms are not precisely equivalent).
DIB	A device-independent bitmap. This format eliminates some, but not all, of the device specificity of the standard bitmap format by including information about the color palette and resolution of the originating device.
Link, OwnerLink, ObjectLink	Formats used to establish OLE links between documents.

As we'll see, Paste Special also can be used to control whether Clipboard data is embedded, linked, or pasted statically.

To Embed, to Link, or Merely to Paste?

Should you embed, should you link, or should you do neither? Here are a few guidelines:

Embedding's advantages are permanence and portability. Because the embedded data actually resides in the receiving application, you don't have to worry about what will happen if the source document becomes unavailable. So, for example, you'll want to choose embedding, not linking, if you plan to move the receiving document somewhere where it won't have access to the source document.

Linking's advantages over embedding are two. First, the resulting compound document is smaller because it stores "pointers" only, not the actual source data. Second, changes in the source data can be reflected automatically in the receiving document. You should use linking when you want your compound document to stay current with its component sources over time.

What about plain old-fashioned static pasting? If the documents involved do not support OLE, of course, that is your only choice. For example, if you paste a paragraph from a Notepad document into your word processor, that paragraph arrives as static text because Notepad is a simple program that does not support OLE. Even with OLE applications, though, there may be occasions when a straightforward static paste is more suitable than a fancy embedded object. Offsetting the convenience of editing an object in its source application, for example, is the time required for Windows to launch that application—or the component of it needed to provide in-place editing. If that delay is vexing, don't embed. OLE is a service, not an obligation.

How to Embed

In most cases you can embed an object simply by copying it in its source document and pasting it into its destination document. That's because, when multiple formats are available on the Clipboard, the format that produces an embedded object is usually the default. It is not *always* the default, however. So if you want to be certain that you're embedding something and not simply pasting it statically, it's a good idea to use the Paste Special command. In the list of available formats presented by the Paste Special dialog box, the one that does the embedding will typically have the word *object* somewhere in its name. When you select that option, the explanatory text at the bottom of the dialog box will probably include words such as "so that you can edit it using," followed by the name of the source application.

Embedding a New Object

The previous paragraph assumes that the object you want to embed already exists somewhere in its source document. But what if it doesn't? Suppose, for example, that you're working in a WordPad document and you want to embed a graphic that doesn't exist yet. In that case, you can go to the Start menu, launch your graphics application, create the object, copy it to the Clipboard, and so on. Alternatively, you can simply use the Object command on WordPad's Insert menu. Figure 10-2 shows the dialog box you will see. (In Microsoft's applications, the Object command is located on the Insert menu. In applications from other vendors, the menu on which this command is located may have a different name. In Lotus WordPro, for example, you'll find Object on the Create menu. Regardless of the menu name, the command itself is usually called Object.)

The Object Type list in this dialog box enumerates all the embeddable data types known to the Windows registry. Choose the type of object you want to embed, select the Display As Icon check box if you want the embedded object to appear as an icon, and click OK. Windows then either starts the application that's appropriate for the object type

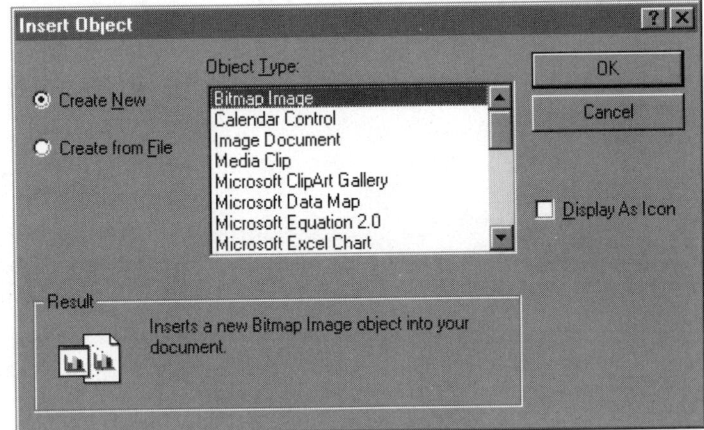

FIGURE 10-2. To embed an object that doesn't exist yet, you can use the Insert Object command.

you selected or simply displays that application's menus and toolbars. At that point, you can create the object you want to embed. For example, if you are working in WordPad and choose Bitmap Image as the object type, Windows replaces WordPad's menus with those of Paint, the application with which the Bitmap Image object type is associated. Figure 10-3 shows what you would see.

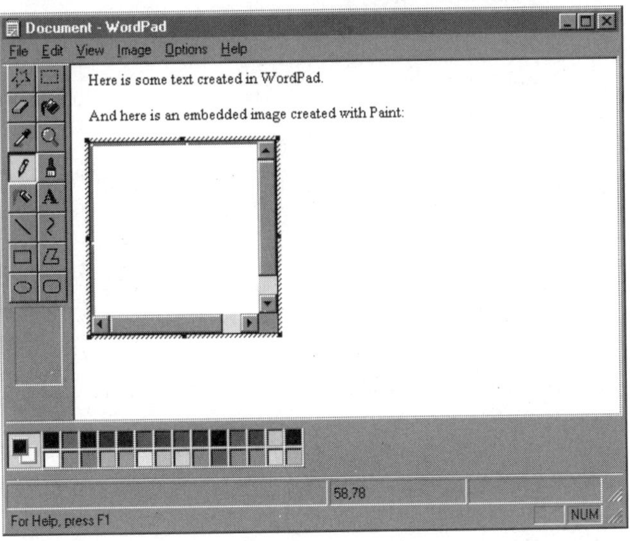

FIGURE 10-3. If you use the Object command on WordPad's Insert menu, and then choose the Bitmap Image object type, Windows replaces WordPad's menus and toolbars with those of Paint, allowing you to create a new object.

The menus and tools shown are those of Paint. The frame below the text is a Paint frame, embedded within a WordPad document. As long as the frame is selected, you can use Paint's menus and tools to create a bitmap image. When you finish, you can return to WordPad by simply selecting any part of the document outside the Paint frame.

If you choose to have the embedded object displayed as an icon, or if the program you're working with does not support in-place editing, clicking OK in the Insert Object dialog box causes Windows to launch the application that creates the object, rather than simply displaying that program's menus and toolbars within the containing document. In that case, when you finish creating the object, you can embed it by choosing the Exit & Return To Document command at the bottom of the File menu. Figure 10-4 shows what you see if you choose WordPad's Insert Object command, select Bitmap Image as the object type, and also select the Display As Icon check box.

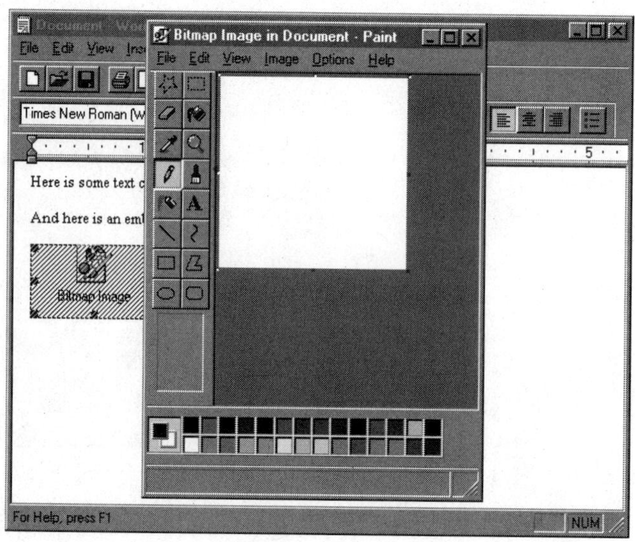

FIGURE 10-4. If you choose to display a new embedded object as an icon, or if your program does not support in-place editing, Windows launches a full copy of the program with which the object type is associated.

The copy of Paint shown in Figure 10-4 is exactly like what you get by running Paint directly from your Start menu, except for its title bar and File menu. The title bar reveals the fact that this instance of Paint was launched for the purpose of creating (or editing) an embedded object, and the File menu includes two new commands—one to quit Paint and update the containing document and one to update the containing document without leaving Paint.

How to Link

To link an object, follow these steps:

1. Select the object in its source document and copy it to the Clipboard.
2. Activate the destination document and place the insertion point where you want the linked object to go.
3. Choose the Edit menu's Paste Link command.

This creates a link to the source document and displays the source object in the default format. If you prefer a different format, choose Paste Special instead of Paste Link. In the Paste Special dialog box, select the format you want and then choose Paste Link.

Two Linking Hazards to Avoid

When you create a link, a visible change occurs in the destination document: new data arrives. At the same time, Windows makes a change in the source document, but this change is not visible. The reason for the change in the source document is that the source document now has a new "responsibility": it must notify the destination document whenever the linked object changes.

If you close the source document immediately after performing a paste link, you will be prompted to save your changes—even though you may not have done any editing in that document since your most recent save. Windows wants you to save your changes because the document has assumed the responsibility of supplying a link. If you ignore the prompt, the data in the destination document will be correct (for the time being), but the link may be broken. To avoid this mishap, be sure to save the source document after paste-linking an object into a destination document.

Another hazard arises when the source document is a spreadsheet. In a typical spreadsheet link, the source data is identified in the destination document by its cell coordinates. However, what happens to the link if someone working with the source document decides to add a few new rows or columns? Any such worksheet rearrangement can change the cell coordinates of the linked object and thereby invalidate the link—or worse, the link can remain valid as far as Windows is concerned, but it no longer contains the data you're interested in.

To avoid this trap, do the following:

1. In the source document, name the cell or range you want to link.

2. After you paste-link the object into your destination document, use the destination application's Edit Links command to verify that the link is recorded by your worksheet range name, not by cell coordinates.

3. If the link is not identified by the range name, edit the link, replacing the cell coordinates with the range name.

The exact procedure for editing the link depends on the destination application. In WordPad, for example, the Edit Links dialog box includes a Change Source command button. Clicking this button brings up a "browser" dialog box, in which you can change the name of the source file or the description of the source object. As Figure 10-5 shows, the source object is described on a line marked Item Name. To replace cell coordinates with a range name, simply edit the Item Name line.

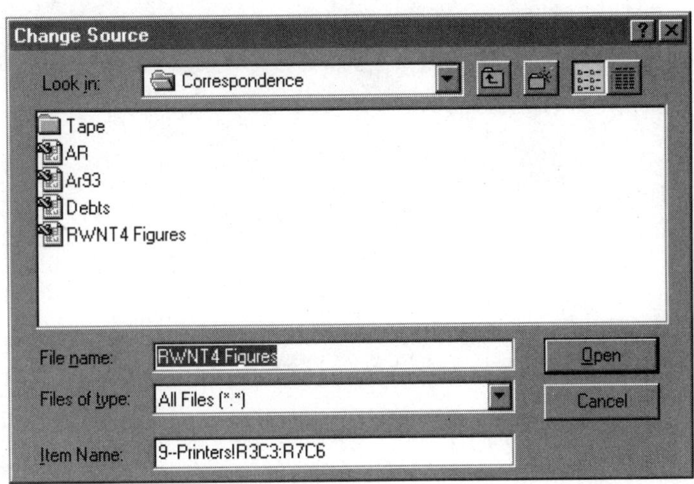

FIGURE 10-5. In WordPad, by choosing Links from the Edit menu and then clicking the Change Source button, you can change the description of the linked object. In other applications, the procedure may be slightly different.

Embedding or Linking a File

In all our examples so far, the source object to be embedded or linked has been a part of a file—for example, a range of spreadsheet cells, a paragraph in a word processing document, or a selection from a graphic image. You can also embed or link entire files. Depending on the type of file and your preferences, the destination document either displays the contents of the file or an icon representing the file.

To embed or link a file, choose the Object command, then select Create From File. The object type list in the center of the dialog box is replaced by a File text box and a Browse button, as shown in Figure 10-6 on the next page.

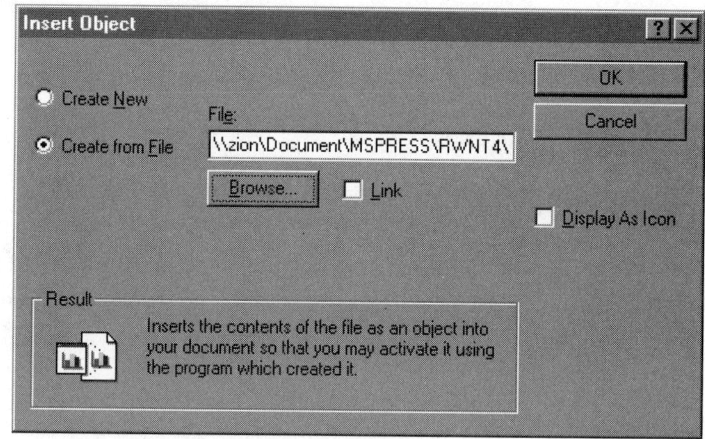

FIGURE 10-6.
If you choose the Create From File option button in the dialog box shown in Figure 10-2 on page 251, the dialog box changes to let you type a filename or browse through your folders to find the file you want to embed or link.

Working with Embedded Objects

The simplest way to edit an embedded object is to double-click it. Depending on whether the object is fully visible or shown as an icon, and depending on the level of OLE support provided by your applications, either you are transported to a copy of the object's source application or the source application's menus and toolbars appear at the top of your document. In either case, you edit the object using the facilities of the object's source application.

If you're editing in a copy of the source application, choose the last command in that application's File menu when you are finished editing. This command closes the source application and returns you to the document in which the object is embedded.

If the menus and toolbars of the object's source application have replaced those of the destination program (that is, you are editing in place), simply select another part of the destination document when you are finished editing the object. The original menus and toolbars then reappear.

Alternatively, you can edit an embedded object by selecting it and looking for an editing command at or near the bottom of the Edit menu. Figure 10-7 shows what you see on WordPad's Edit menu when you select an embedded bitmap image.

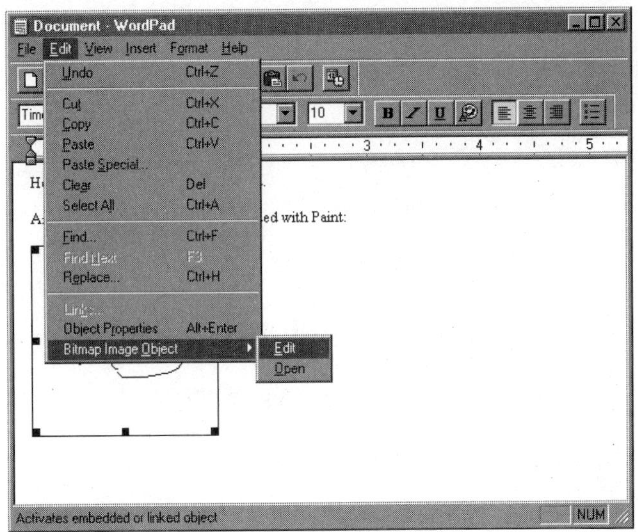

FIGURE 10-7.
To edit an embedded object, simply double-click it. Or select it and look for an editing command on the Edit menu.

Playing an Embedded Sound or Video Object

To play an embedded sound or video object, select the embedded object and choose the "Object" command on your application's Edit menu. The actual name of the command on the menu identifies the type of object you selected. If you select a sound clip created in Sound Recorder, for example, the command says *Sound Recorder Document Object*. When you choose this command, a submenu appears. Choose Play on the submenu to play the embedded object.

Modifying the Properties of an Embedded Object

Like just about everything else in Windows NT, embedded objects have properties that can be inspected and modified. To get to the property sheet for an embedded object, you can do any of the following:

- Right-click the object and choose Object Properties from the context menu.
- Select the object and press Alt-Enter.
- Select the object and choose Object Properties from the Edit menu (if you're working in a context where there is an Edit menu).

On the property sheet, you might be able to do such things as switch between a rendered and an iconic display of the object or change the object's display size. If the selected object is displayed as an icon, you can use the object's property sheet to change the icon, the icon's caption, or both. Even if you're content with the default icon, you might want to replace the default caption with something descriptive. "Picture of Mom," for example, might serve your needs better than "Bitmap Image." To do so, click the Change Icon button in the property sheet, and then modify the Label text.

Working with Links

When a data object is linked to a document, changes to the object are reflected in the destination document. Whether the object is updated automatically or only on demand is up to you. Most (but not all) programs create automatic links by default. In any case, you can switch between automatic and manual updating by opening the property sheet for the link in question. To open the property sheet, select the linked object and choose the Object Properties command on the containing application's Edit menu.

To switch between automatic and manual updating, go to the Link page of the property sheet and choose the appropriate option button in the Update group.

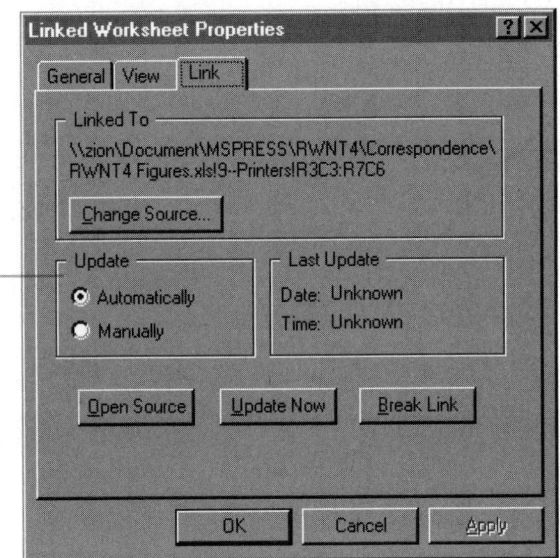

If you choose automatic updating, the containing document is refreshed any time the source document changes. If you choose manual updating, you must return to the property sheet and click the Update Now button to refresh the containing document.

TIP

No Properties? Look for Links

If your destination program does not include an Object Properties command, look for a Links command on the Edit menu. That command displays a list of all links in the current document. By selecting an item in the list and choosing command buttons in the Links dialog box, you can switch between automatic and manual updating, open the source document for editing, break the link, or respecify the source document.

Another Linking Hazard

Under certain circumstances, it is possible for an automatic link not to reflect the current state of the source document. Here's how it can happen:

1. You double-click the linked object to edit it in the source document.
2. You change the object in the source document, and the link is updated appropriately in the destination document.
3. You close the source document without saving changes.

After this sequence, the source document reverts to its original state (because you didn't save your changes), but the destination document does not revert to its former state. The two documents are now out of step with one another.

To be absolutely sure that all automatic and manual links in a destination document are up-to-date, follow these steps:

1. In the destination document, choose the Edit menu's Links command.
2. In the Links dialog box, select the first link listed. Then scroll to the bottom of the list and hold down the Shift key while selecting the last link listed. This selects all links in the list.
3. Click the Update Now button.

Breaking a Link

If you no longer want a linked object to reflect changes in the object's source, visit the Link tab of the object's property sheet, and click the Break Link button. If it can, Windows converts the item to an embedded object.

What to Do If the Source Document Is Moved or Renamed

If the source document for a link is renamed or relocated, the link becomes invalid. When you open a destination document containing such an invalid link, you might or might not receive a warning from the destination application. (It depends on the application.) If you know the link has become invalid, choose Links on the Edit menu. Then click the Change Source (or equivalent) button and follow your application's procedures for editing the link.

If you're not sure whether or not the link is valid, choose the Edit menu's Links command. Select the link in question (or all links) and click the Update Now (or equivalent) button. The destination application should then tell you if any source object is unavailable. If you have invalid links, you can click the Change Source (or equivalent) button to edit them.

Using Scrap Files to Save and Share OLE Objects

Windows NT Explorer is an OLE program. That means you can embed data objects in folders or on your desktop. So, for example, if there's a particular image you want to use repeatedly, you can drag it out of a Paint window and drop it onto your desktop. To reuse it in your word processor, simply drag it again and drop it into the receiving document.

OLE objects in folders or on the desktop are called *scrap files*. When you create such an object, Windows gives it a default name based on its contents or source, such as "WordPad Document Scrap 'Now is the time...'" You can assign your own name by pressing F2 and typing.

A scrap file must originate in a program that supports OLE as a source. If the program also supports OLE drag and drop, you can create the scrap by simply dragging the object. If not, select the object in its source program, choose the Copy command, and then move to your folder or to the desktop and choose Paste.

SEE ALSO
For information about using shared folders, see Chapter 11, "Using and Sharing Files on the Network."

By storing scrap files in a shared folder, you can make OLE objects on your system available to other network users. Similarly, by opening a shared folder on a server, you can access OLE objects stored on that server. To embed a server-based scrap file, for example, simply open the network folder in which the scrap resides, using Network Neighborhood or a mapped folder. Then drag the object to wherever you want it to go. Alternatively, select the object in the network folder, and then paste it into an application or local folder.

To activate a network scrap object's parent application, either for editing purposes or to render an object that's embedded as an icon, you must have a local copy of the parent application.

Saving and Sharing Clipboard Data with ClipBook Viewer

Windows NT includes an accessory called ClipBook Viewer that allows you to do the following:

- See the current contents of the Clipboard, as well as a list of the formats in which the current Clipboard contents are stored
- Save the Clipboard's contents for easy reuse
- Share Clipboard data with other network users
- Connect to Clipboard objects saved by other network users

Unless you've moved it, you'll find an entry for ClipBook Viewer in the Accessories section of your Start menu. When you launch ClipBook Viewer, you'll see something like the window shown in Figure 10-8.

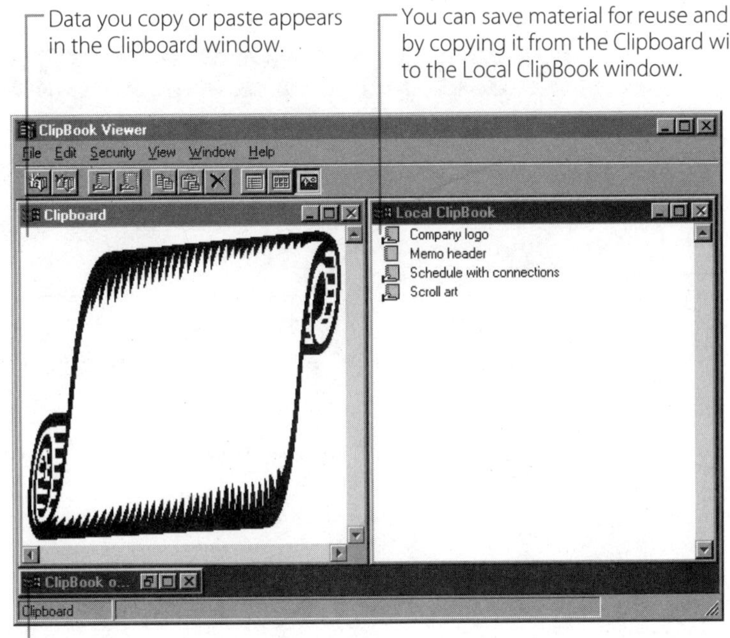

FIGURE 10-8.
ClipBook Viewer lets you view, save, and reuse Clipboard contents.

ClipBook Viewer's toolbar provides quick access to many features, as shown in Table 10-2 on the next page.

Seeing What Formats Are Available

To see what formats the current Clipboard data is stored in, activate the Clipboard window and open the View menu. The names of available formats appear in the bottom segment of this menu. Names in dark type represent formats that the Clipboard window can display. Names in gray type are formats that are available for pasting into other applications but that the Clipboard window itself cannot display. You can see what various displayable formats look like by choosing dark-type items from the View menu. To return the viewer to its initial display, choose Default Format.

TABLE 10-2. ClipBook Viewer Toolbar

Toolbar Icon	Description
	Connects to the clipbook on another computer
	Disconnects from a remote clipbook
	Shares the selected clipbook page
	Stops sharing the selected clipbook page
	Copies the selected clipbook page to the Clipboard
	Pastes the Clipboard contents to the local clipbook
	Deletes the Clipboard contents or selected clipbook page
	Displays the clipbook in Table of Contents view
	Displays the clipbook in Thumbnail view
	Displays the clipbook in Full Page view

It's important to recognize that changing the format displayed in ClipBook Viewer's window has no bearing on the format that will be pasted into a receiving application. If you use the receiving program's Paste command, the program requests a particular format from the Clipboard, regardless of what happens to be displayed in the viewer. Some applications include a Paste Special command, however, in addition to the ordinary Paste command. This command lets you choose which of several formats to paste. ClipBook Viewer's View menu, in this case, can help you make the choice by showing you which formats are there and what they look like.

Saving Clipboard Objects in Your Local Clipbook

To save the current Clipboard contents as a page in your local clipbook, switch to the Local ClipBook window and then use the Edit menu's Paste command, press Ctrl-V, or click the Paste icon on the toolbar.

The dialog box that appears prompts you for a page name and asks if you want to share the item with other users. If you choose to share the item, you'll see a new dialog box with some additional options. *For information about sharing options, see "Sharing Clipboard Data," page 266.*

Items pasted into your local clipbook are called pages and are listed alphabetically by the names you give them. On disk, they're stored in separate files, each beginning with the letters *Cbk*, followed by a random number and the extension .CLP.

TIP

Watch Out for Bulky .CLP Files

The .CLP files created by local clipbook pages preserve all of the information currently on the Clipboard. Because the Clipboard often stores the data in multiple formats, .CLP files tend to be rather large—particularly if the information they contain is graphic. If disk space is at a premium, use clipbook pages judiciously, and delete pages when you no longer need them. To delete a clipbook page, select it and press the Del key.

NOTE

The Save As command on ClipBook Viewer's File menu also preserves the current Clipboard contents as a .CLP file but does not create a new clipbook page. This command is provided for compatibility with earlier versions of Windows. Unless your local clipbook is so crowded that you're having trouble finding pages, there's no reason to use this command instead of creating a clipbook page.

Viewing the Contents of Your Local Clipbook

ClipBook Viewer can display the contents of your local clipbook (and any remote clipbooks to which you are connected) in three ways: as an alphabetical listing by page title, as a set of thumbnail sketches, or as a fully rendered presentation. An example of the alphabetical listing, called Table of Contents view, is shown in Figure 10-8 on page 263. To switch to a different view, use the commands at the bottom of the View menu or the three rightmost tools on the toolbar.

TIP

Double-Click to See the Page

You can switch to the fully rendered display (Full Page view) of a clipbook page by double-clicking the page.

Reusing Pages from Your Local Clipbook

To reuse data that you've pasted into a local clipbook page, select the page you want and choose the Edit menu's Copy command or click the Copy tool. The selected page remains in your clipbook, but a copy of it appears in the Clipboard window. You can then paste it into your spreadsheet, word processor, or other application.

Sharing Clipboard Data

To make your Clipboard data available to other users on your network, you must first Paste the data into your local clipbook, and then choose the Share command from the File menu. If you know you're going to be sharing the Clipboard information, you can accomplish both of these steps at the same time. When you choose the Edit menu's Paste command (or click the Paste tool) to transfer the data to the local clipbook, you can simply select the Share Item Now check box. Alternatively, if you have already created the clipbook page and didn't choose to share it at the time you created it, you can select the page and then choose the File menu's Share command (or click the Share tool on ClipBook Viewer's toolbar).

When you choose the Share command, ClipBook Viewer presents the dialog box shown in Figure 10-9.

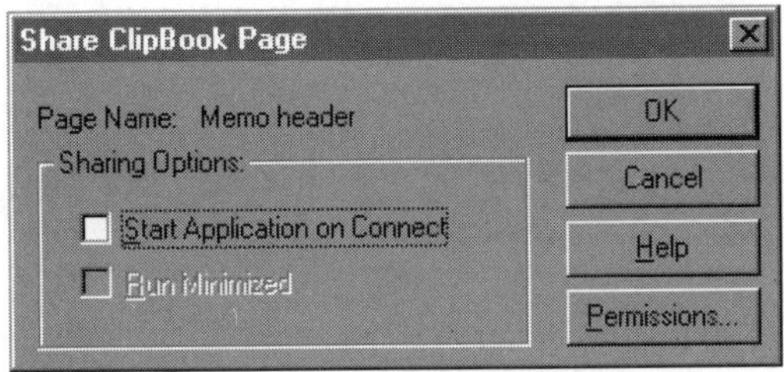

FIGURE 10-9. This dialog box lets you share an existing clipbook page.

Setting Permissions

The person who shares a clipbook page is called the page's "owner" and can set *permissions* that determine just what other users can and cannot do with the page. Table 10-3 shows the different permissions available and what privileges each bestows.

TABLE 10-3. Clipbook Page Permissions

Permission	Privileges
No Access	Clipbook data is unavailable
Read	■ View the page in ClipBook Viewer ■ Paste (embed) the contents of the page into another application
Read and Link	Everything allowed by Read permission, plus: ■ Establish a link to the page from another application
Change	Everything allowed by Read and Link permission, plus: ■ Update the source document of a linked object (unless the source document is on another computer) ■ Update the link to the source document ■ Delete the page from the clipbook
Full Control	Everything allowed by Change permission, plus: ■ Set permissions for the page ■ Take ownership of the page

By default, the owner of a clipbook page has Full Control permission. If you're the owner of a page, you can modify it, stop sharing it, or delete it. Everyone else, by default, has "Read and Link" privileges. That means that others can paste or paste-link the data, but they can't change it or delete it from the pool of shared clipbook pages.

To alter the permission for a particular user or group of users, do either of the following:

- In the Share ClipBook Page dialog box (shown in Figure 10-9 on the previous page), click the Permissions button.
- Select a page in your local clipbook and choose the Permissions command on the Security menu.

Either way, you'll see a dialog box similar to the one shown below. In the Name list box, select the name of the user or group for whom you want to change permission. Then open the Type Of Access drop-down list and select the permission you want. The privileges associated with each permission are shown in Table 10-3 on the previous page. In addition to the predefined permissions, a "Special" option allows you to create a custom set of permissions.

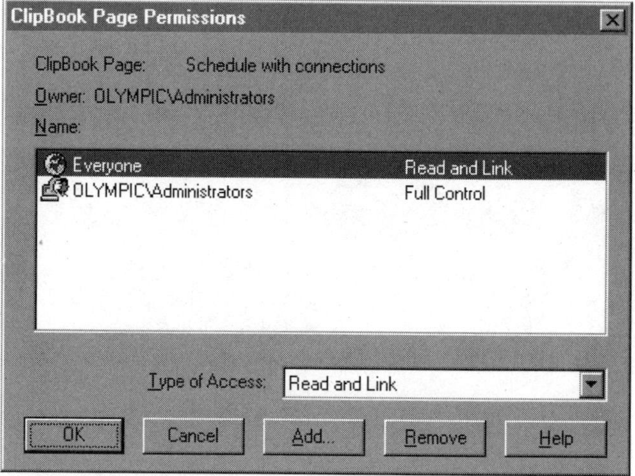

If you want to set permissions for a user or group not listed in the top of the dialog box, click the Add button. You will then arrive at the Add Users And Groups dialog box. *For information about using this dialog box, see "Adding a User or Group," page 591.*

Connecting to Other Users' Clipbook Pages

To connect to another user's local clipbook, click the leftmost icon on ClipBook Viewer's toolbar, or pull down the File menu and choose Connect. In the dialog box that appears, select the name of the computer whose local clipbook you want to use and click OK. ClipBook Viewer rewards you with another ClipBook window, identified by the network path of the remote workstation, containing all clipbook pages shared by the remote user. To paste a remote clipbook page into one of your applications, copy the page from the remote clipbook onto your Clipboard, and then paste it into the application.

CHAPTER 11

Using and Sharing Files on the Network

Windows NT was designed from the start as a network operating system. In many other networking environments, the networking functionality is superimposed on a single-user-oriented operating system. In Windows NT, networking features are fully integrated into every aspect of the system.

Windows NT provides support for networks from a number of vendors, including Microsoft, Novell, Artisoft, Banyan, Digital Equipment Corporation, and IBM. In addition, the system supports the simultaneous use of multiple networking protocols. This means that, assuming your network administrator has set up your system properly, you should be able to work successfully in a heterogeneous network environment, making use of computers that run Windows NT, Windows 95, Windows for Workgroups, Novell NetWare, and other operating systems.

For information about using network printers, see "Printing to a Network Printer," page 217. For information about remote access, see "Using Dial-Up Networking," page 415.

Best of all, using network resources and sharing your own resources with other network users is almost as simple and straightforward as using your own local resources. Browsing a network folder is just like browsing a folder on your own hard disk. Sending a document to a network printer is just like printing at your own machine. The procedures for interacting with one kind of server (say, a Windows NT server) are identical to the procedures for working with another kind (for example, a NetWare server). You don't have to learn network commands to use your network's resources.

In this chapter, we'll look at the steps involved in working with programs and documents stored on network servers, as well as at what you need to do to share your own folders and files. Other networking topics may be found in other parts of this book.

Using Network Neighborhood

Network Neighborhood is your gateway to available network resources, just as My Computer is the gateway to resources stored on your own system. Double-clicking the Network Neighborhood icon opens a folder window containing icons for all computers in your immediate domain or workgroup (as defined and configured by your network administrator). Figure 11-1 shows the Network Neighborhood folder for a typical small local-area network.

FIGURE 11-1.
The icons in the Network Neighborhood folder represent computers in your domain or workgroup.

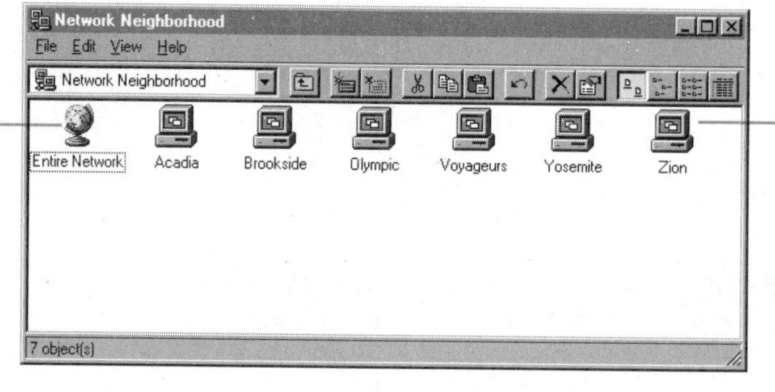

 **TIP**

Check the Comment

If you're not sure what kind of files are contained on a computer, right-click its icon and choose Properties from the context menu. On the property sheet, you may find a comment (entered by the person who uses the computer) that describes the contents of the computer.

In addition to entries in your domain or workgroup, the Network Neighborhood folder includes an entry labeled Entire Network. Double-clicking Entire Network opens a folder that displays a top-level view of your entire network. If your network is particularly complex, you might find it helpful to view its structure in a Windows NT Explorer window. To do that, right-click the Entire Network icon and choose Explore. Figure 11-2 on the next page uses Windows NT Explorer to show the "entire-network" view of the network shown in Figure 11-1.

Domains and Workgroups

All computers in a Windows NT network belong to one of two functional groupings, called *domains* and *workgroups.*

A *domain* is a set of computers that share a common security database and that can be administered as a group. If you enter a domain name when you log on to Windows NT, your account participates in that domain. All security information regarding your account is stored on one of the computers in the domain, known as the *domain controller,* and you have the freedom to log on at any computer in the domain.

A *workgroup* is a named set of computers running Windows NT, Windows 95, or Windows for Workgroups that are grouped for browsing purposes. If your account does not participate in a domain, it belongs to a workgroup.

If your account is part of a domain, the Network Neighborhood folder displays the members of your domain. If not, it displays the members of your workgroup. In either case, Network Neighborhood also includes an entry named Entire Network, which provides access to computers beyond your domain or workgroup.

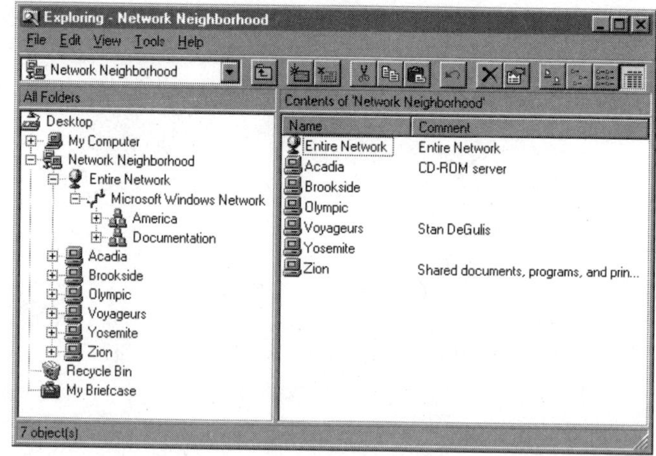

FIGURE 11-2.
The America icon in this window represents the workgroup shown in Figure 11-1 on page 272.

Network Shortcuts
If you frequently need access to a network computer that isn't included in your Network Neighborhood, create a shortcut for it and put the shortcut in your Network Neighborhood folder. To do this, simply open Entire Network, find the computer you need, right-drag its icon to the Network Neighborhood icon, and then choose Create Shortcut(s) Here from the context menu.

Connecting to a Network Server

A *server* is a remote source of shared files. It can be a computer that acts solely as a repository for shared files (a "dedicated" server), or it can simply be a shared folder on a computer used by one of your colleagues.

In either case, to interact with a server, simply double-click the icon for that server in your Network Neighborhood folder or Windows NT Explorer window. This opens a folder window such as the one shown on the next page, in which you can see all the folders and printers on the selected server to which you have been granted access. Double-clicking a folder icon reveals all folders and files stored in that folder, and so on.

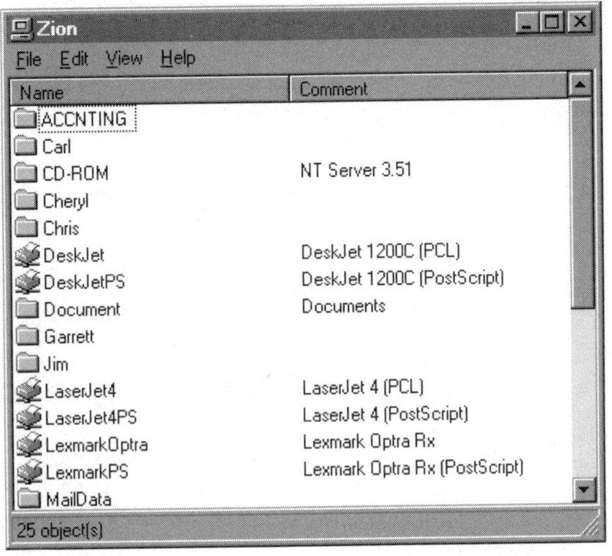

TIP

Viewing Your Own Shared Resources

Your Network Neighborhood folder also includes an icon for your own computer. By double-clicking this icon, you can see the names of all folders and printers on your own system that have been made available to other network users.

When you double-click a server-based folder, you may be asked to supply your name and a password. If so, you will see a dialog box similar to the one below.

Enter Network Password
Incorrect password or unknown username for:
\\Fatner\DATA
Connect As:
Password:
OK
Cancel
Help

This occurs when the user account you log on with doesn't have permission to use the selected folder. To gain access, you must provide the name of an account (and its password) that has permission.

Shortcuts to Network Folders

Create desktop shortcuts for the network folders you use regularly. That way, you won't have to travel through the Network Neighborhood each time you want to read or save a server-based file. To create a desktop shortcut for a network folder, simply right-drag its icon to the desktop, and then choose Create Shortcut(s) Here.

If you don't want to clutter your desktop, but you still want to avoid traveling down the Network Neighborhood path to find a folder, you can drag its icon to the Network Neighborhood folder (or any other convenient folder) instead of to the desktop.

Navigating with Find

Use the Find command to locate network servers, server-based folders, and individual server-based files. For details, see Chapter 7, "Using the Find Command."

Connecting to a Server from the Common Dialog Boxes

SEE ALSO

For more information about common dialog boxes, see the sidebar "Navigating in the File Open and File Save Dialogs," page 126.

If the program you're working with uses the Windows NT common dialog boxes, such as File Open, File Save, and File Save As, you can retrieve or save files on servers without going through your Network Neighborhood icon. Simply open the Look In or Save In drop-down list at the top of the dialog box and then choose Network Neighborhood. The big window in the center of the dialog box then displays the names of your servers, allowing you to navigate to the folder of your choice.

Mapping a Network Folder to a Drive Letter

"Mapping" a network folder makes it appear to Windows as though the folder is part of your own computer. Windows assigns the mapped folder a drive letter, just as if it were an additional local hard disk. You can still access a mapped folder in the conventional manner, by navigating to it through folder windows or Windows NT Explorer. But mapping gives the folder an alias—the assigned drive letter—that provides an alternative means of access.

Folder mapping offers the following benefits:

- It makes the network folder available to programs that don't use the Windows NT common dialog boxes.

  With programs that use the Windows NT common dialog boxes, you can navigate to network folders just as you would with Network Neighborhood. But to read a document from or save a document to a network folder using other programs, you will probably need to map the folder to a drive letter.

- It makes the network folder accessible from the My Computer icon.

  Because a mapped folder becomes a "virtual disk" on your local computer, an icon for the folder appears in the My Computer folder, right alongside your real local disks. If you do most of your work with files stored locally but occasionally need access to particular servers, you might find it convenient to map them. That way, you won't have to bother opening the Network Neighborhood icon to find the servers you need.

- Windows can automatically reconnect to your mapped network folders at startup.

  When you navigate to a server using Network Neighborhood, you might experience momentary delays while Windows locates and connects to the selected server. If you map the folder and choose the Reconnect At Logon option, any connection delays will occur at the beginning of your work session, and you'll be less likely to find them intrusive.

- Mapped folders become part of My Computer for file-search purposes.

  When you use the Find command to search for files stored on My Computer, the search encompasses not only your real local disks but also any mapped network folders. If you sometimes need to search for items that may be stored either locally or in a particular network folder, you can save yourself a search step by mapping the network folder.

To map a network folder, follow these steps:

1. Navigate to the folder in Network Neighborhood.
2. Right-click the folder icon and choose Map Network Drive from the context menu.

   The following dialog box appears.

3. Choose a drive letter in the Drive drop-down.

   Windows proposes the first available drive letter, but you can choose any letter that's not already in use. You might want to pick one that's mnemonically related to the content of the folder—for example, R for Reports.
4. Leave the Connect As line blank unless you want to log on to the server under a different account name.

5 Select the Reconnect At Logon check box if you want to connect to this server automatically at the start of each session.

By default, Windows NT uses your account name—the name under which you logged onto the operating system—to connect you to the shared folder. Your access privileges on the shared folder are those assigned by your network administrator to your account. If you want to connect to the server under a different account name, you can specify that name on the Connect As line. You will then be asked to supply a password to authenticate your use of another account name. Assuming your password is accepted, your use of the server will be governed by the access privileges assigned to that new account name.

When filling out the Connect As line, type the domain where the account name is registered, followed by a single backslash character, followed by the account name—for example, America\ChrisW.

Unmapping a Mapped Network Folder

If you change your mind about mapping a network folder, simply right-click the folder's icon in your My Computer folder. As Figure 11-3 shows, you'll see a Disconnect command in the resulting context menu. Choose this command, and the tie will be severed.

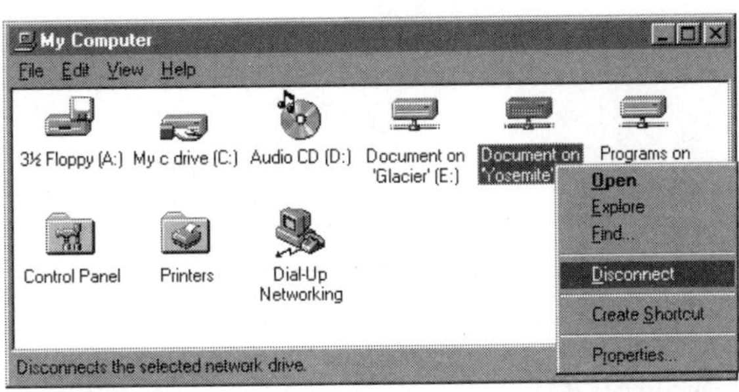

FIGURE 11-3.
To unmap a network folder, right-click the folder's icon in My Computer and choose Disconnect from the context menu.

Opening Network Folders with the Run Command

In Windows NT 4, you do not have to memorize path specifications to use network folders. Instead, you can simply navigate to the folders you need, using either folder windows or Windows NT Explorer. But every network folder does, in fact, have a path specification, and you're welcome to use those path specifications wherever you find it convenient. The network path is sometimes called a *UNC path*, because it follows the Universal Naming Convention for pathnames.

SEE ALSO

For more information about share names, see "Sharing Folders with Other Users," page 281.

A network folder's path consists of two backslash characters, followed by a server name, another backslash, and a share name. The share name is the name assigned to the folder by the person who made the folder available on the network. So, for example, the network path for the folder selected in Figure 11-3 on the previous page is

\\Yosemite\Document

because this folder's share name is Document and it's stored on a server named Yosemite.

If the server in question is part of a Windows NT domain, you may need to include the domain name in the path. For example, a folder named Fafner, stored on the Budgets server in the Marketing domain, would have the following path:

\\Marketing\Budgets\Fafner

Additionally, a network path may include subfolder names. To get to the December folder on Fafner, for example, you could specify

\\Marketing\Budgets\Fafner\December

The most likely use for network path specifications is in conjunction with the Run command. When you want to get to a network folder quickly, without traversing a sequence of folder or Windows NT Explorer windows, you can simply pop up the Start menu, choose Run, and type the path for the folder you need.

Note that you can also use this technique to open a folder window for the server itself, from which you can then choose any available subfolder. For example, to display all the shared folders on the server named Wotan, you can choose the Run command and simply type *wotan*.

Remember, too, that the Run command keeps a list of your most recently used commands. Thus, if you often need to use a particular server or network folder, you can type its path once on the Run command line, and then choose its path from the drop-down list the next time you need it.

Sharing Folders with Other Users

Provided your account has administrative privileges, you can share folders on your own system with other users on your network. To share a folder, begin by displaying the folder's icon in its parent's folder window. Right-click the icon, and then choose Sharing from the context menu. This takes you to the Sharing page of the folder's property sheet, as shown in Figure 11-4.

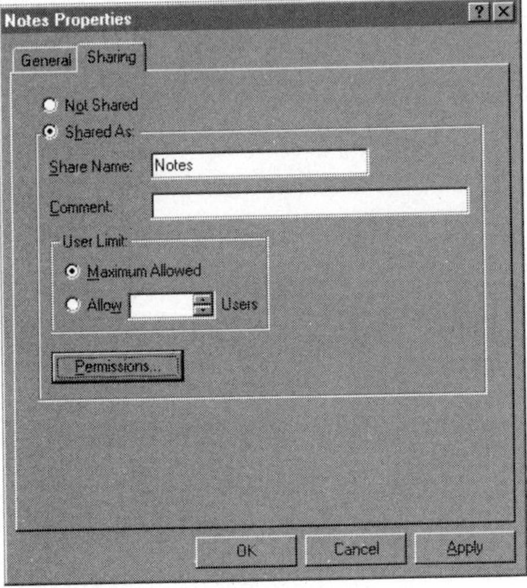

FIGURE 11-4.
To share one of your own folders, choose the Sharing command on the folder's context menu.

Choose the Shared As option button, and then either accept or change the proposed share name. The share name is the name that other users will see in their own Network Neighborhood folders. It's also the name that will be used in the shared folder's network path specification. For example, if the share name is Notes and the folder resides on a computer named Wotan, the shared folder's network path will be \\Wotan\Notes. In the dialog box shown in Figure 11-4 on the previous page, Windows NT proposes to use the folder's name as its share name. That's usually a good choice, but you're not obligated to accept it. If you already have a shared folder with that name, you'll want to pick a different name.

TIP

Hiding a Shared Folder from Casual Browsers

If you append a dollar sign to the share name (for example, *Notes$*), the folder is not visible to users who browse the network with Network Neighborhood or Windows NT Explorer. Users whom you've entrusted with the name of your shared folder can still connect to it by typing its name—including the dollar sign—in the Map Network Drive or Run dialog box.

In the Comment line, you can type a description of the folder's contents. Other users will see this description when they inspect the folder's property sheet in their Network Neighborhood folders.

In the User Limit section of the dialog box shown in Figure 11-4 on the previous page, you can restrict the number of users who will be able to log onto your shared folder concurrently. If network traffic seriously impacts the responsiveness of your system, you might want to take advantage of this option. If you accept the default choice, Maximum Allowed, the number of concurrent users is likely to be unlimited. (Your system administrator may have set a limit on the combined number of concurrent users of all shared folders on your computer. If your administrator has not done this, however, the default User Limit setting allows all comers.)

SEE ALSO
For more information about permissions on NTFS volumes, see Chapter 20, "NTFS Security."

The default permission associated with a new shared resource is Full Control to Everyone. That means that anyone on your network can do whatever they want to your files, including delete them. (If the shared folder resides on an NTFS volume, individual files may have their own access restrictions, however.) You can place limits on what particular users or groups of users can do with your shared files by clicking the Permissions button in the dialog box shown in Figure 11-4 on page 281. You will see the dialog box shown in Figure 11-5.

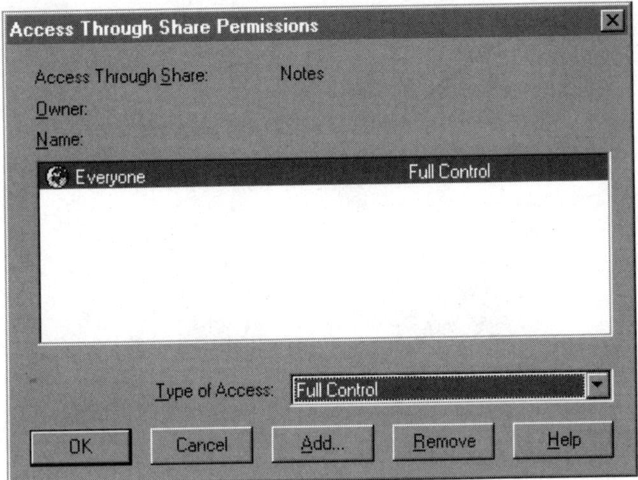

FIGURE 11-5.
By default, all users have full control over files in a new shared folder—unless access has been restricted to files individually via NTFS. You can use this dialog box to set restrictions on the entire shared folder.

The Type Of Access drop-down list in the lower right corner of this dialog box presents the following access options:

- No Access
- Read
- Change
- Full Control

No Access is self-explanatory. Read access allows users to read files but not write to them or delete them. Change access permits users to read and write, as well as rename or delete. Full Control provides all the aforementioned privileges plus the ability to take ownership of NTFS files.

You can assign these access levels to individual users or named groups of users. Begin by clicking the Add button. That takes you to the dialog box shown in Figure 11-6.

FIGURE 11-6.
The Add Users And Groups dialog box lets you assign different levels of access to individual users and groups of users.

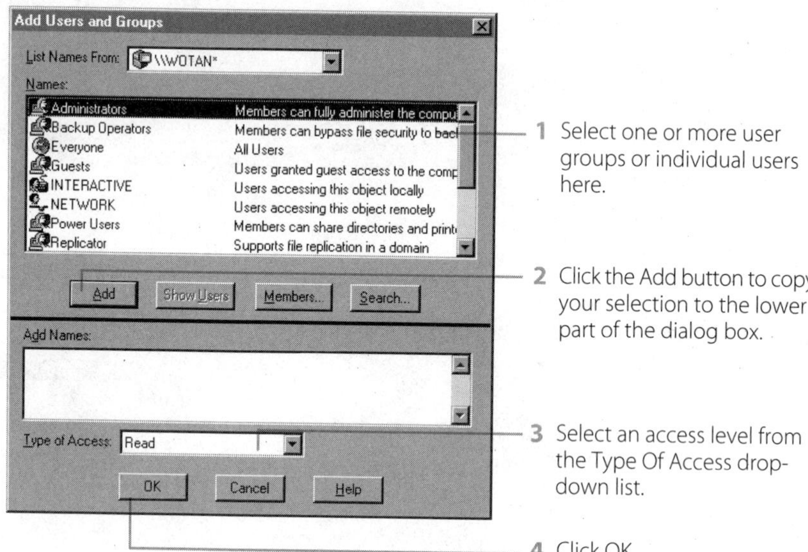

Monitoring Use of Shared Resources

One potential disadvantage of networking under Windows NT is that your own computer might have to do double duty—as a workstation for you and as a server for your workgroup-mates. If many users happen to access files on your system at the same time, you might experience significant performance degradation. At such times, you might find it helpful to know who's doing what with your shared resources. Control Panel's Server applet, shown below, can provide this information.

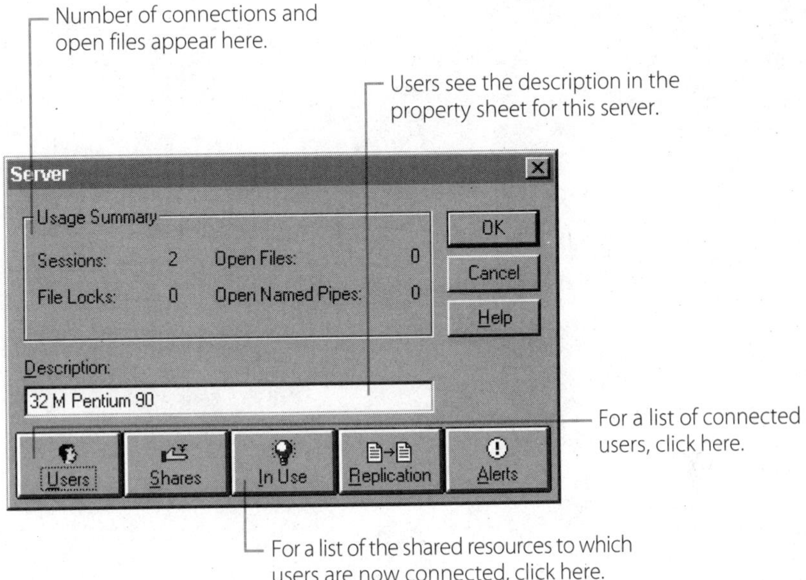

The Server applet's initial screen, depicted here, tells you how many users (sessions) are currently accessing your system and how many files they have open. The buttons along the bottom of the window provide additional details. *For more information about monitoring shared resources, see "Monitoring System Use with Server," page 662.*

CHAPTER 12

Using Windows Messaging

If you're like many computer users, you probably rely on a variety of forms of electronic communication to stay in touch with your business contacts and friends. Perhaps you use a network-based electronic mail system to exchange memos and files with office-mates, one or more public information services for sending messages to associates outside the office, and fax for communicating with people and businesses who aren't accessible via e-mail.

Electronic communication is indispensable, but managing it can be a headache, particularly when you need to use several different programs and services to stay in touch with everyone. To relieve that headache, Windows NT includes the Windows Messaging client, a program that handles most—and perhaps all—of your electronic messaging from a single universal inbox. With Windows Messaging, you can use a single address book and message editor to communicate with people using Microsoft Mail as well as your Internet mail account. "Snap-in" components serving facsimile communication or other mail systems may become available in the future. If so, you'll be able to add those to your Windows Messaging setup and manage mail for those systems using the same inbox and folder structure that you use for Microsoft Mail and your Internet mail.

Windows Messaging includes a sophisticated viewer and editor for reading and composing messages. Like a miniature word processor, the editor offers "rich text" formatting. That means you can use a variety of fonts, styles, point sizes, and colors in your messages. Because the editor supports OLE, your messages can also include linked or embedded data objects. Attaching a spreadsheet to an e-mail note, for example, is as simple as dragging an icon from a folder window and dropping it into the editor.

The chapter assumes that you have already established accounts for whatever mail services you are planning to use. Issues involving the setup and administration of a Microsoft Mail post office lie beyond the scope of this chapter (and this book).

Installing and Running Windows Messaging

If you've installed Windows Messaging, you probably have a desktop icon named Inbox. If you don't find it, but you think you have installed Windows Messaging, use the Find command to locate a file named Exchng32.exe, the executable file for Windows Messaging. You might want to right-drag it to your desktop to create a shortcut.

If you haven't yet installed Windows Messaging, you can do so as follows:

1 Choose Settings from the Start menu, and then choose Control Panel.

2 In Control Panel, double-click Add/Remove Programs, and then click the Windows NT Setup tab.

3 Select Microsoft Exchange, and then click the Details button.

4 Select the check box for Microsoft Exchange, as well as the check boxes for any mail services that you plan to use. For example, if you expect to be using both Microsoft Mail and Internet Mail, select the check boxes labeled Microsoft Exchange, Internet Mail, and Microsoft Mail. Then click OK.

5 Click OK to begin the installation.

NOTE

Windows Messaging is an updated version of a program called Microsoft Exchange that is included with Windows 95. Minor oversights allowed the old name to remain in a few places, including the Add/Remove Programs dialog box. If you don't find Microsoft Exchange on your Windows NT Setup page, the error was corrected in your version of Windows NT, and you'll likely find an entry for Windows Messaging instead.

TIP

Running Windows Messaging at Startup

If you use a LAN-based e-mail system, such as Microsoft Mail, you might want to consider putting Windows Messaging in the Startup section of your Start menu. *For instructions, see "Adding Items to the Start Menu," page 83.*

 TIP

Importing Mail
If you're upgrading from a previous installation of Microsoft Mail or another LAN-based mail system, you might be able to import messages you sent and received under the previous system. To do this, choose Import from the Windows Messaging File menu.

Working with Profiles

Before you can use Windows Messaging, you must have a *profile.* A profile is a named collection of settings, encompassing the following details:

- The name and location of at least one *personal folders file*
- The name and location of a *personal address book*
- Configuration details for each mail service you plan to use

Immediately after you install Windows Messaging, a wizard appears to guide you through the creation of a profile. If you have already installed Windows Messaging, therefore, your profile is probably already set up and your mail system is probably ready for use. If, for any reason, you don't have a working profile or you need to create a new one, you can do that by double-clicking the Mail item in Control Panel. *See "Creating a New Profile," on the next page.*

Although most users find that one profile is enough, you can set up as many as you want. If you do have multiple profiles, those profiles can use the same personal address book and personal folders file.

The Personal Folders File

SEE ALSO
For information about creating personal folder files, see "Adding a Personal Folders File," page 294.

A personal folders file is a repository for incoming and outgoing messages. Within the file, messages are kept in folders. Messages that you're about to send, for example, are stored in a folder called Outbox. Incoming messages arrive in a folder called Inbox. Messages that you have sent are (optionally) stored in a folder called Sent Items.

You can create additional folders, including folders within folders, to help you organize your mail. You can also include more than one personal folders file in your profile. You could, for example, keep separate personal folders files for current and archived messages.

All messages in a personal folders file are kept in a single disk file with the extension .PST. This file is comparable to the .MMF file used by some earlier versions of Microsoft Mail, except that the messages in a .PST file may have been sent to or originated in a variety of different mail systems, not just Microsoft Mail.

To protect your privacy, you can assign a password to your personal folders file. *See "Assigning or Changing Your Personal Folders File's Password," page 295.*

The Personal Address Book

A personal address book stores the names, e-mail addresses, and other details about the people you contact most often. In some situations, you might have separate address books for particular mail services. For example, if you use Microsoft Mail, your mail administrator may maintain a global address book of Mail users on your network. You can add names to your personal address book at any time by copying them from service-specific address books.

Your profile can have only one active personal address book, but you can create multiple personal address books and switch between them at any time. *See "Changing Your Personal Address Book," page 296.*

Creating a New Profile

To create a new profile, follow these steps:

1. Choose Settings from the Start menu, and then choose Control Panel.
2. Double-click the Mail item in Control Panel. This takes you to the property sheet for the default profile.

3 Click the Show Profiles button.

4 Click the Add button. The Microsoft Exchange Setup Wizard appears.

5 Select the check box for each mail service you plan to use.

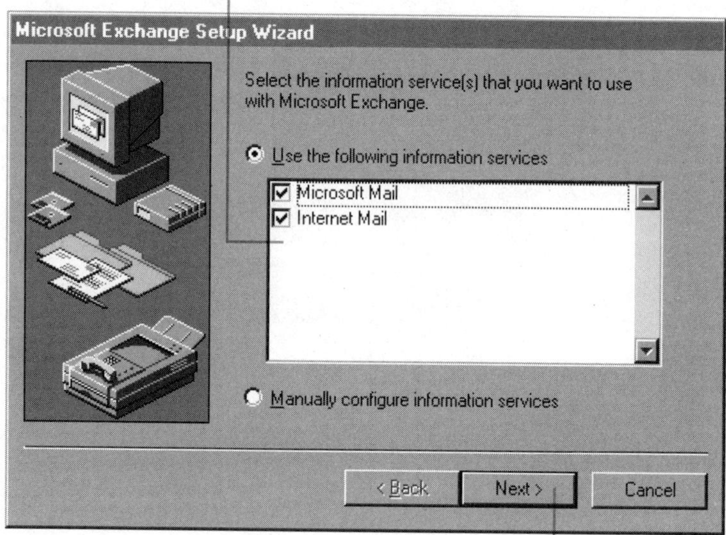

6 Click Next and let the wizard guide you through the remaining steps of creating a profile.

Modifying an Existing Profile

To modify an existing profile, follow these steps:

1 Choose Settings from the Start menu, and then choose Control Panel.

2 Double-click the Mail item in Control Panel.

3 Click the Show Profiles button.

4 Select the name of the profile you want to modify, and then click the Properties button.

Figure 12-1 shows the property sheet for a profile named Craig Stinson. The sheet includes three tabs, named Services, Delivery, and Addressing. The Services page lists two mail services (Internet Mail and Microsoft Mail), a personal address book (Personal Address Book), and a personal folders file (My current messages). Note that, while a personal folders file, an address book, and a mail service may seem like distinct fauna to you, they are all "services" to Windows Messaging, so it lumps them together in this dialog box.

FIGURE 12-1.
In a profile's property sheet, you can add or remove mail services, change the order in which Windows Messaging polls your mail services, and tailor the display of your address books.

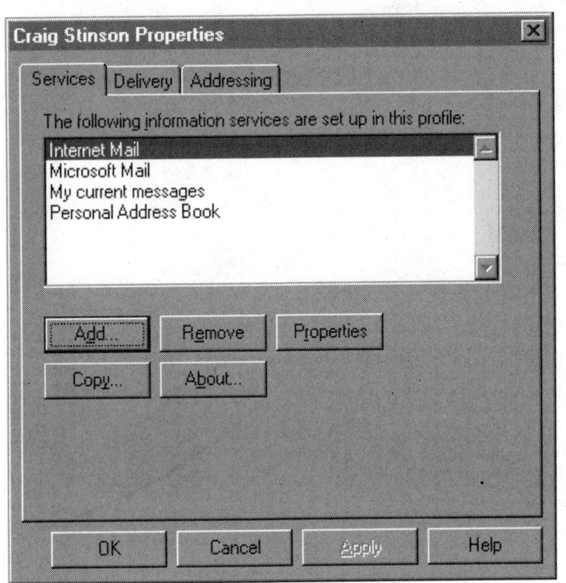

Adding or Removing a Mail Service

To add a new mail service, simply click the Add button in the Services page of your profile's property sheet. Then choose the service you want in the ensuing list. After you've done this, Windows Messaging will prompt you for whatever information it needs to set up the new service.

To remove a mail service, select its name in the Services page of your profile's property sheet. Then click the Remove button.

Modifying a Mail Service's Properties

If you need to change any details about the way you interact with a mail service—such as your logon name, account number, password, or the number you use to connect to the service—you can do so using the property sheet for the mail service. In the Services page of your profile's property sheet, select the service you're interested in. Then click the Properties button. The available choices depend on the service in question. The property sheet shown in Figure 12-2 is for the Microsoft Mail service.

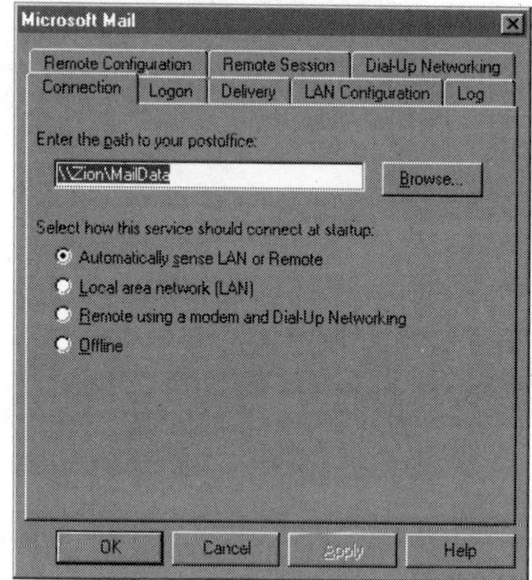

FIGURE 12-2.
You can change your logon name, account number, and other details associated with a mail service by displaying the service's property sheet.

TIP

Another Path to the Property Sheet

You can also change service-specific properties from within Windows Messaging. Choose Services from the Tools menu, and then select the name of a service to get to that service's property sheet.

Adding a Personal Folders File

You might find it useful to have more than one personal folders file associated with your profile. To add a personal folders file to a profile, follow these steps:

1 Display the property sheet for your profile and then click Add.

2 In the Add Service To Profile dialog box, select Personal Folders and then click OK.

The Create/Open Personal Folders File dialog box, a variant of the File Open common dialog box, appears.

3 To add an existing personal folders file to your profile, select its name. To create a new personal folders file, type a filename in the File Name box.

4 Click Open. If you're creating a new personal folders file, the Create Microsoft Personal Folders dialog box appears.

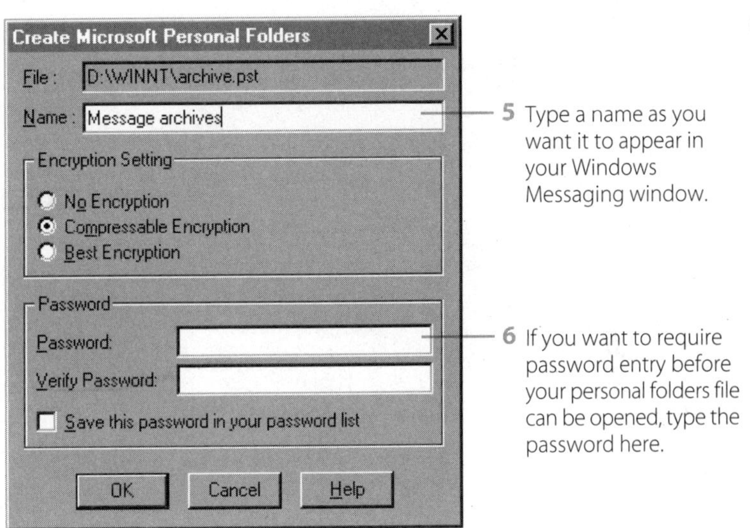

5 Type a name as you want it to appear in your Windows Messaging window.

6 If you want to require password entry before your personal folders file can be opened, type the password here.

Assigning or Changing Your Personal Folders File's Password

To assign a password to your personal folders file, or to change its existing password, display the property sheet for your profile and select your personal folders file. Then click the Properties button. In the property sheet that appears, click the Change Password button, and then fill out the ensuing dialog box.

TIP

To change the password you use for a specific mail system, visit the property sheet for that mail system. You can do that by choosing Services from the Windows Messaging Tools menu, or by double-clicking the Mail item in Control Panel, selecting the mail service, and clicking the Properties button.

Changing Your Personal Address Book

A profile can have only one personal address book active at a time. But you can create several personal address books—for example, one for business contacts and one for personal contacts—and then switch between them.

To change personal address books, first display the property sheet for your profile and select Personal Address Book. Then click the Properties button. Figure 12-3 shows the property sheet for a personal address book.

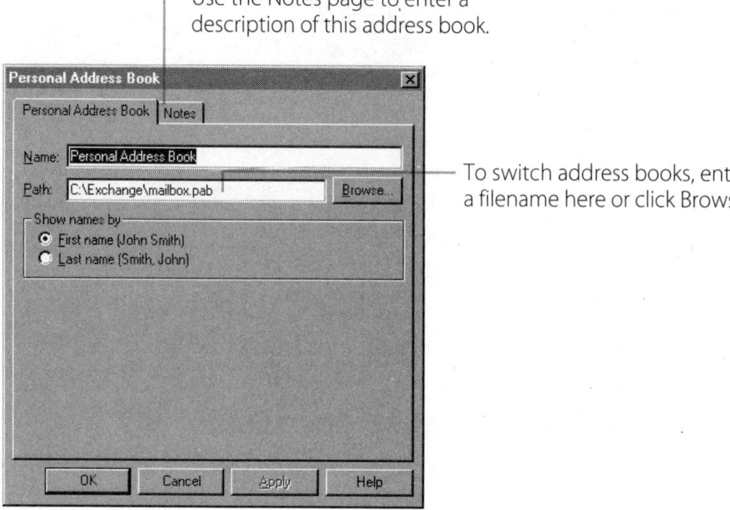

FIGURE 12-3. You can maintain separate personal address books and switch between them. To switch, display this property sheet and enter a new filename on the Path line.

 **SEE ALSO**

For more information about address books, see "Working with Address Books," page 320.

To switch to a different personal address book, enter a new filename on the Path line (or click the Browse button and point to a new filename). Then click OK. If you specify a file that doesn't exist, Windows Messaging creates a new, empty, personal address book. You can then populate this new book with entries stored in your other address books. If you specify an existing personal address book, Windows Messaging makes that the active personal address book.

Sending and Receiving Mail

Most electronic messaging systems are based on the store-and-forward principle. The mail you send goes to a "post office" on some other computer—a server on your network, for example, or an Internet mail server—and waits there until your recipients come to collect it. When Windows Messaging delivers your outgoing mail to a mail service's post office, it retrieves any messages waiting for you at that post office and deposits them in the inbox of your personal folders file. This process is called *polling*.

Exactly when polling occurs depends on the mail service. You might be able to schedule regular delivery/pickup times by visiting the property sheet for the service(s) you use.

For example, if you use Microsoft Mail, your system polls every ten minutes by default. You can change this interval by going to the Delivery page of the Microsoft Mail property sheet. (To get to the property sheet, double-click the Mail item in Control Panel, select Microsoft Mail, and click the Properties button. Or, from within Windows Messaging, choose Services from the Tools menu, and then select Microsoft Mail.)

When Windows Messaging retrieves new mail for you, a letter icon appears in the taskbar's notification area. You can double-click this icon to display your inbox. Once you've opened all new messages, the letter icon disappears.

Sending and Receiving on Demand

If your mail service doesn't offer scheduled polling times, or if you want to transfer mail immediately, choose the Deliver Now Using command on the Windows Messaging Tools menu. A submenu appears, listing each of your mail services. Choose the one you want to poll.

NOTE

> If your profile includes only one mail service, the Tools-menu command you want is called Deliver Now—not Deliver Now Using—and it doesn't have a submenu. Choosing this command immediately polls your mail service.

The submenu also includes an All Services command. If you choose this, Windows Messaging polls each service in turn, in the order specified in your profile's property sheet. To change this order, double-click the Mail item in Control Panel. Then click the Show Profiles button, select the name of your profile, and click Properties. In the property sheet, click the Delivery tab.

TIP

> **A Keyboard Shortcut**
> Ctrl-M is the keyboard shortcut for the Deliver Now Using All Services command.

The Delivery page of a profile's property sheet, shown below, lists all the mail services and shows the order in which the system polls them when you choose the Deliver Now Using All Services command.

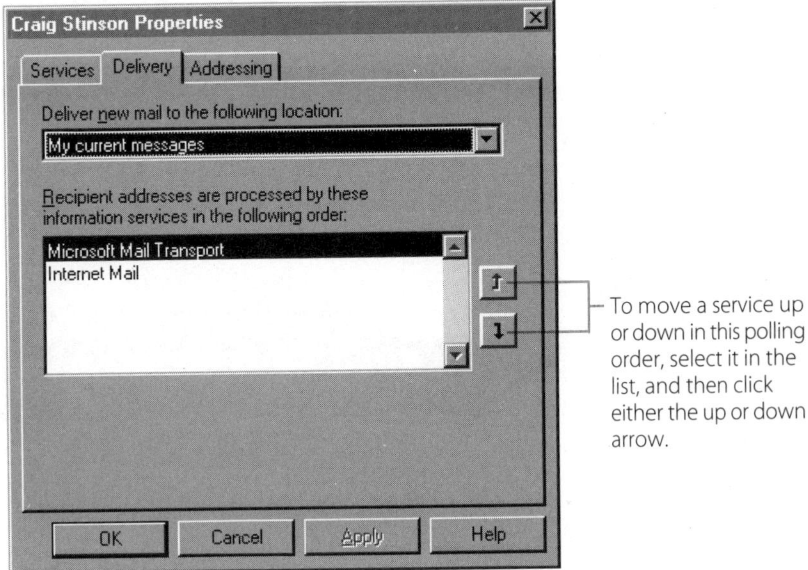

To move a service up or down in this polling order, select it in the list, and then click either the up or down arrow.

Working with Mail-Enabled Applications

A mail-enabled application is one that lets you send messages directly to others on your LAN-based mail system, without requiring you to activate Windows Messaging. Most of today's major desktop productivity applications fall into this category. If your program has a Send, Send File, Routing Slip, or other comparable command, it's mail-enabled. Any program that's enabled for MAPI mail systems (*MAPI* is Microsoft's Mail Application Programming Interface) should work fine with Windows Messaging.

Typically, when you use the Send or comparable command in a mail-enabled program, the program creates a new mail message (possibly using a custom form instead of the default Windows Messaging message form) with the current file as an attachment. In some programs you may be able to mail a selection of the current file this way, as an alternative to mailing the entire file. In some programs, you also have the option of sending the current file sequentially to a distribution list.

Note that you do not have to have Windows Messaging running to use an application's mail features. The application will open those components of Windows Messaging that it needs when you choose Send or another mail command.

Creating Messages

To create a new message, choose New Message from the Compose menu, click the New Message tool, or press Ctrl-N in the Windows Messaging main window. (The tools in the main window's default toolbar are shown in Table 12-1.) However you do it, you will see the new message window shown in Figure 12-4.

TABLE 12-1. Windows Messaging Toolbar

Toolbar Icon	Description
	Moves up one level to parent of currently displayed folder
	Displays (or hides) the folder-list pane
	Creates a new message
	Prints the selected message
	Moves the selected message to another folder
	Deletes the selected message
	Replies to the sender of the selected message
	Replies to the sender and all recipients of the selected message
	Forwards the selected message
	Opens the address book
	Opens the Inbox folder
	Displays the help pointer, which causes Windows Messaging to display help about the next item you click

FIGURE 12-4.

To create a message, fill in the blanks. You can enter addresses by clicking the To and Cc buttons and selecting names from your address books.

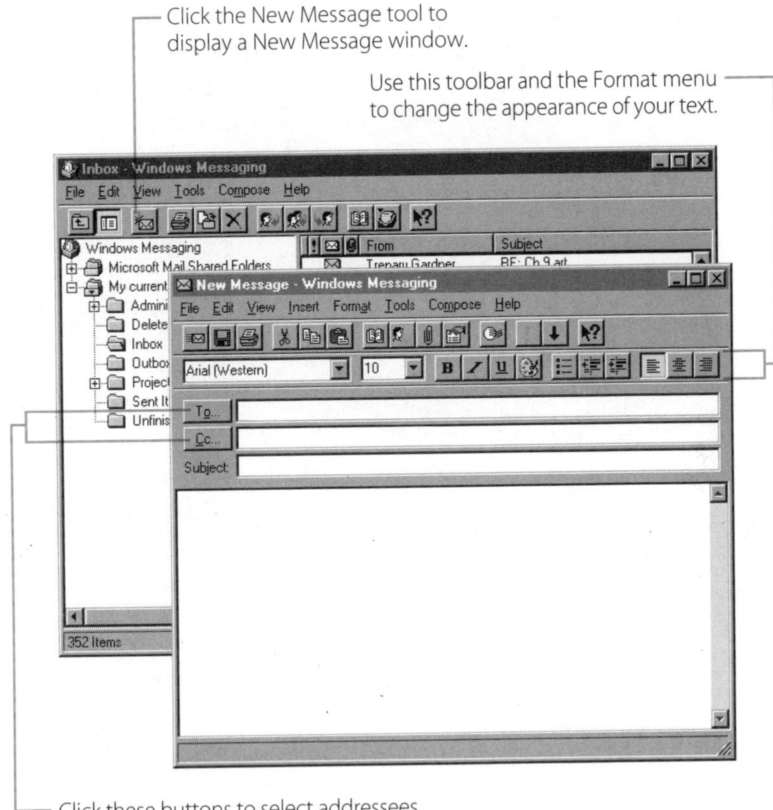

In the top portion of the window, enter the names or e-mail addresses of the recipients, the names or e-mail addresses of anyone you want to send a copy to, and a subject heading for your message. Then type your message in the large space at the bottom of the window.

 TIP

Start with Your Address Book

An alternative way to create a message is to start by displaying your address book. (Click the Address Book tool, press Ctrl-Shift-B, or choose Address Book from the Tools menu.) In the address book, select one or more names (hold down Ctrl while clicking to select multiple names), and then click the New Message tool (or press Ctrl-N). You will arrive at the new message window with your selected names already on the To line ready to compose your message.

Using WordMail

If Microsoft Word is installed on your system, you have the option of using Word as your message editor instead of the Windows Messaging editor. Word offers a number of benefits, including table and formula editors, additional formatting options, templates for creating standardized messages, and on-the-fly spelling correction.

Your system may already be set up to use Word instead of the standard Windows Messaging editor. If it isn't, and you have Word installed, choose WordMail Options from the Windows Messaging Compose menu. In the WordMail Options dialog box, select the Enable Word As Email Editor check box.

Editing commands described in this chapter are those of the standard editor, not WordMail. For more details about Word's editing features, consult your Microsoft Word documentation or the Word Help menu.

Addressing Messages

You can include as many names as you please on both the To and Cc lines. The easiest way to supply this information is by picking names from one or more of your address books. And the easiest way to get to your address books is by simply clicking the To or Cc button. Clicking either button gets you an Address Book window similar to the one shown below.

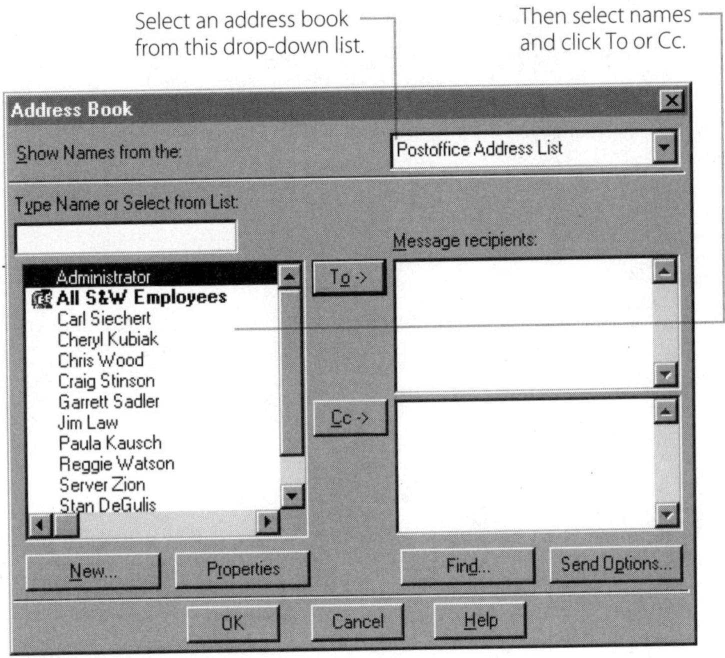

If the names you need are in a different address book, select that address book from the drop-down list in the upper right corner of the window.

TIP

Forget the Scroll Bar—Just Type
To speed up the selection of an addressee's name, simply begin typing the name in the Type Name text box, near the upper left corner of the Address Book window. Windows Messaging will scroll the list to the entry that most closely matches what you've typed.

Addressing "by Hand"

If using an address book is not convenient, you can address a message by typing the names of your recipients on the To and Cc lines, using semicolons to separate multiple recipients. If you're not sure how an addressee's name is spelled, simply type a portion of the name. When you send your message, Windows Messaging checks your address lines against all available address books. If what you've typed is sufficient to identify your addressees uniquely, Windows Messaging finishes the typing for you. If not, Windows Messaging presents a list of candidates and lets you choose. For example, if you type only the letter *C* on the To line, Windows Messaging presents a list of everyone in your primary address book whose name starts with *C*. (The primary address book is the one listed first on the Addressing page of your profile's property sheet. To view or change this setting, choose options from the Tools menu and then click the Addressing tab.)

Sending to a Distribution List

If you find yourself regularly sending messages to the same group of recipients, you might want to assemble those recipients into a distribution list. You can then simply specify the name of the list on your To or Cc line. *For information on distribution lists, see "Creating Personal Distribution Lists," page 324.*

Sending Blind Copies

In addition to the To and Cc lines, the message window also includes an optional Bcc line. Each recipient you specify on the Bcc line receives a copy of your message, but other recipients (those on the To and Cc lines) do not see their names.

To display the Bcc line in your message window, choose Bcc Box from the View menu.

Composing Messages

To compose your message, simply type in the big box at the bottom of the message window. This part of the window acts like a reasonably sophisticated word processor, with plenty of formatting options.

Applying Formatting

The default font for messages is 10-point Arial, in black. To choose a different default font, color, or style, choose Options from the

Windows Messaging Tools menu. In the ensuing dialog box, click the Send tab, and then click the Font button.

While you type your message, you can take advantage of the tools on the message window's formatting toolbar, shown in Table 12-2. Or, you can apply these formatting options by choosing commands on the Windows Messaging Format menu.

TABLE 12-2. Windows Messaging Formatting Toolbar

Toolbar Icon	Description
Arial (Western)	Changes the font (typeface) of the selection
10	Changes the font size of the selection
B	Changes the selection to boldface (or, if the selection is already boldface, changes it back to normal)
I	Changes the selection to italic (or, if the selection is already italic, changes it back to normal)
U	Underlines the selection (or, if the selection is already underlined, removes the underline)
	Changes the color of the selection
	Changes the selected paragraphs to an indented, bulleted list (or, if the selection is already bulleted, removes the bullets and indents)
	Decreases the indent from the left margin
	Increases the indent from the left margin
	Left aligns the selected paragraphs
	Center aligns the selected paragraphs
	Right aligns the selected paragraphs

 TIP

Striking Out

The Format menu's Font command also includes a strikeout option, which does not have a toolbar equivalent.

Rearranging Text with Drag and Drop

You can rearrange text in a message using the traditional cut and paste procedures. Alternatively, if a block of text is out of place, you can simply select it and drag it to wherever it's supposed to go.

To copy a block of text instead of moving it, hold down the Ctrl key while you drag.

Using Find and Replace

The Windows Messaging editor includes Find and Replace commands, comparable to those found in most word processing programs. You'll find these commands on the Edit menu. The shortcuts are Ctrl-Shift-F for Find and Ctrl-H for Replace.

Inserting Text from a File

If you plan to mail a body of text that already exists in another application, you can copy it to the Clipboard and paste it into your message. If the text is stored on disk, however, you'll find it easier to choose the File command from the message window's Insert menu. This brings up a variant of the File Open common dialog box. In the top part of this dialog box, choose the name of the file you want to insert. In the bottom part of the dialog box, choose the Text Only option button. Click OK, and your text will appear in the message window.

Attaching Documents and Files

An *attachment* is a document or other file embedded in or linked to an e-mail message. Attachments allow you to send non-text data via electronic mail. Your recipient sees the attachment as an icon and can render the attached data by double-clicking the icon.

For more information on embedding and linking, see "Embedding or Linking a File," page 255.

If the attachment is *embedded*, your recipient must have an application capable of rendering the embedded data. Typically, that application is the program that created the original document, but it doesn't have to be. If you're attaching a Microsoft Excel worksheet, for example, your recipient may be able to read it in another spreadsheet program as well as in Excel. Alternatively, your recipient can save the attachment as a file, extracting a copy of it from your message, and then use the Windows NT Quick View feature to make the data visible (assuming Quick View capability is available for the type of data you're attaching).

If the attachment is *linked* to your message, your recipient must have access to the original data. Typically you might link, rather than embed, when your recipient is another user on your own local-area network and has no need for a separate copy of the file. Linking may also be preferable to embedding when you're sending the same data to a large number of recipients. Embedding a copy of the attachment for each recipient would consume a lot of disk space on the post office computer for your network mail system.

To attach a file to a message, do the following:

1. In the message window, choose File from the Insert menu.
2. In the top part of the dialog box that appears, choose the file you want to attach.
3. In the bottom part of the dialog box, select an option button in the Insert As group.
   - To insert the text of the file into your message (as opposed to attaching the entire file), select Text Only.
   - To embed the file, select An Attachment.
   - To link the file, select Link Attachment To Original File
4. Click OK to return to the message window.

TIP

Embedding Attachments with Drag and Drop

You can also embed a file by dragging the file from a folder or Windows NT Explorer window and dropping it into your message window.

Attaching Messages

Windows Messaging includes a Forward command that lets you forward copies of messages you've received, with optional comments from you, to other recipients. *For information, see "Forwarding Messages," page 319.*

Another way to forward a message is to create a new message, and then insert the message you want to forward. To do that, choose the Message command from the message window's Insert menu. In the dialog box that appears, you'll see an outline structure representing the folders you've set up in your personal folders file, as shown below.

1 Select the folder containing the message you want to attach.

2 Select the message in this list.

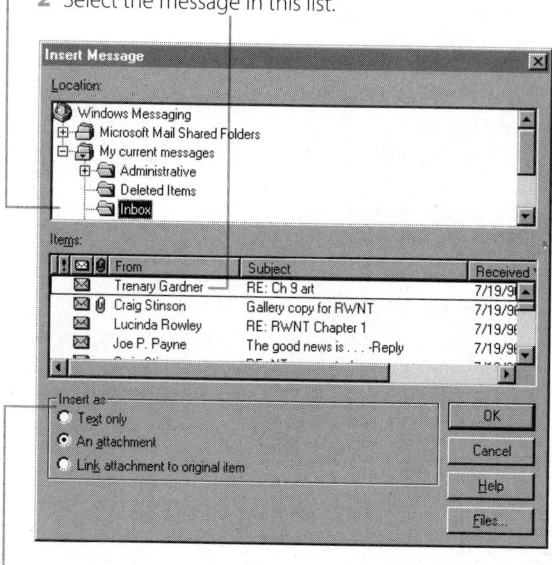

3 Use these option buttons to indicate how you want the message inserted.

Use this outline to navigate to the folder containing the message you want to insert. Then use the option buttons at the bottom of the dialog box to indicate whether you want to insert the message's text, attach the entire message, or create a link to the message. If you attach, the message will appear as an icon within your recipient's message. Your recipient can double-click the icon to read the message.

Embedding or Linking Objects

Attachments embed or link entire files. You can also embed or link a portion of a file (an *object*), provided the file originates in a program that supports OLE. To embed or link an object, copy it from its source application to the Clipboard. Then choose the Paste Special command from the message window's Edit menu. *For more information, see Chapter 10, "Exchanging Information: OLE and the Clipboard."*

Sending Messages

When you finish composing your message, you can send it using any of the following methods:

- Click the Send tool on the toolbar. (See Table 12-3 on the next page.)
- Choose the Send command from the message window's File menu.
- Press Ctrl-Enter, the keyboard shortcut for the Send command.

When you send a message using these methods, Windows Messaging stores it temporarily in your Outbox folder. It stays in that folder until Windows Messaging finishes polling the mail systems where your message's recipients are located. At that point, the message moves to your Sent Items folder—unless you have asked Windows Messaging not to retain copies of your sent mail. *See "Retaining Copies of Sent Messages," page 314.*

TABLE 12-3. New Message Toolbar

Toolbar Icon	Description
	Sends the message
	Saves the message in the Inbox folder
	Prints the message
	Uses the Clipboard to cut, copy, or paste
	Opens the address book
	Checks recipients' names against the address book
	Inserts a file in the message
	Displays the message's property sheet
	Requests a read receipt
	Sets importance to high
	Sets importance to low
	Displays the help pointer, which causes Windows Messaging to display help about the next item you click

Undeliverable Messages

Occasionally, one of your outgoing messages may prove undeliverable. This can happen, for example, if a recipient is no longer at the e-mail address you've used, if some component of the delivery sequence—such as a gateway between two e-mail systems—is not working, or if you yourself abort the transmission of a long message.

If one of your messages cannot be delivered, you will be notified in a message from the "System Administrator"—which is actually Windows Messaging itself, not a person in your organization.

Using and Customizing Windows Messaging Toolbars

All of the toolbars in Windows Messaging include Tool Tips. If you're not sure what a tool does, rest your mouse on it for a moment and read the description that emerges.

Two of the toolbars—the ones directly below the menu bar in the main window and in the message window—are customizable. You can tailor either toolbar to your liking by choosing Customize Toolbar from the Tools menu. You'll see a display like the following:

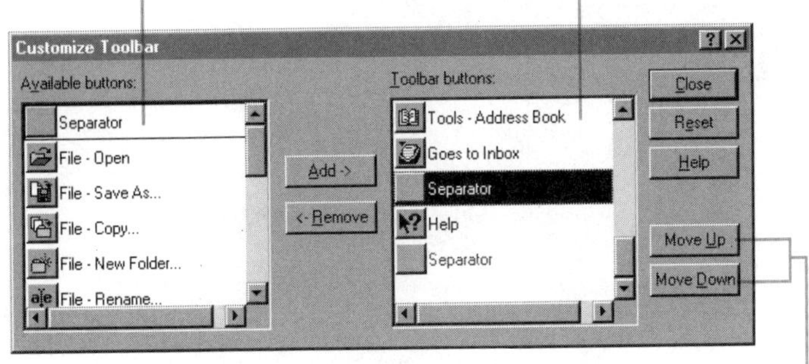

The window on the right shows the toolbar's current layout, including the separators between groups of tools. The window on the left shows tools that you can add to the toolbar.

To add a tool, select it in the left window and click the Add button. To remove a tool, select it in the right window and click the Remove button. To move a tool to the left in the current layout, select it in the right window and click the Move Up button. To move a tool to the right, select it and click Move Down. To restore the default toolbar arrangement, click Reset.

Importance Options

Windows Messaging can send mail using three importance levels—high, normal, and low. Messages that you send with high importance are flagged with a red exclamation point in your recipients' inboxes. Messages with low importance are flagged with downward-pointing black arrows. Messages with normal importance are not flagged with any symbol.

You'll find tools with these symbols on the default message window toolbar. You can mark an outgoing message as a high-importance or low-importance item by clicking the exclamation point or downward arrow before you send it. Alternatively, you can choose Properties from the message window's File menu. In the property sheet (see Figure 12-5), choose one of the buttons in the Importance option-button group.

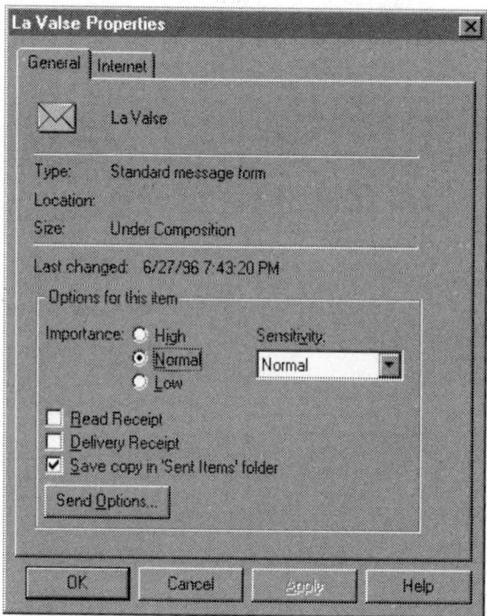

FIGURE 12-5.
The property sheet for a message lets you set importance and sensitivity options for that message.

The default importance is normal, and it's unlikely you'll want to change it to high or low. If you do, however, Windows Messaging will accommodate you. Choose Options from the Tools menu, and then click the Send tab. In the Send page of the property sheet, shown in Figure 12-6, choose one of the option buttons in the Set Importance group.

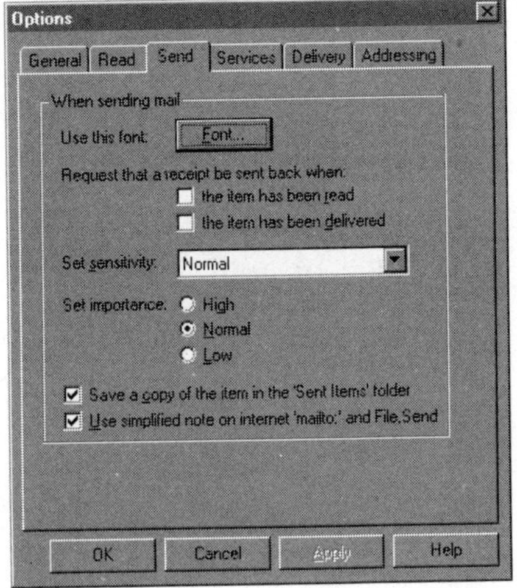

FIGURE 12-6.
By choosing Options from the Tools menu and clicking the Send tab, you can change the defaults for all outgoing messages.

NOTE

Certain mail systems may offer their own importance or priority options. If the options provided by the service you're using differ from those of Windows Messaging, you should ignore the Windows Messaging options. Instead, before sending a message, click Send Options in the message's property sheet, and then choose options from the dialog box that appears.

Sensitivity Options

SEE ALSO

For information about displaying particular columns, see "Customizing Folder Columns," page 333.

In addition to the importance options, Windows Messaging offers four mutually exclusive sensitivity options: Normal, Personal, Private, and Confidential. Messages marked Personal, Private, or Confidential are flagged as such in the Sensitivity column of your recipients' personal folders files—provided your recipients choose to display the Sensitivity column. Your recipients will also see a description of your messages as personal, private, or confidential in the status bar of their message window—assuming they have chosen to display the status bar.

In addition, messages sent with the Private sensitivity option will arrive in read-only mode. That is, your recipients will not be able to edit these messages.

To send a message with a particular sensitivity setting, choose Properties from the message window's File menu or click the Properties tool. In the message's property sheet (see Figure 12-5 on page 312), choose one of the options in the Sensitivity drop-down list.

The default sensitivity setting is Normal. To change the default setting, choose Options from the Tools menu, and then click the Send tab. In the Send page of the property sheet, shown in Figure 12-6, choose the sensitivity you want from the Set Sensitivity drop-down list.

Receipt Options

You can request two types of receipts for messages that you send: delivery receipts and read receipts. A delivery receipt is returned to your inbox as soon as your message is delivered to the recipient's inbox. A read receipt is returned when the recipient opens your message. You can request either or both of these receipts for particular messages or for all messages.

To request either type of receipt for a particular message, choose the Properties command from the message window's File menu or click the Properties tool. Then select either or both of the receipt check boxes near the bottom of the property sheet, as shown in Figure 12-5 on page 312.

To request receipts of either type for all your messages, choose Options from the Tools menu, and then click the Send tab. In the Send page of the property sheet, shown in Figure 12-6 on the previous page, select either or both of the receipt check boxes.

Retaining Copies of Sent Messages

By default, copies of outgoing messages are retained in your Sent Items folder after the messages are delivered so that you have a record of everything you send. If you want to further organize your correspondence, you can copy or move sent messages from the Sent Items folder to any other folders.

If you prefer not to retain copies of sent messages, you can turn this default off. Choose Options from the Tools menu, and then click the Send tab. In the Send page of the property sheet, shown in Figure 12-6 on page 313, deselect the check box at the bottom of the page.

If you decide not to retain copies of sent messages by default, you can still retain a copy of a particular message. Before you send a message that you want to retain, choose Properties from the message window's File menu or click the Properties tool. At the bottom of the property sheet, shown in Figure 12-5 on page 312, select the check box labeled Save Copy In Sent Items Folder.

Reading and Replying to Messages

By default, Windows Messaging signals the arrival of new mail by displaying an envelope in the notification area of your taskbar. Double-clicking the envelope opens your inbox, where you'll find new messages listed in boldface type. To read a message, double-click its entry or select it and press Enter. To close a message, press Esc or click the message window's close button.

Notification Options

Having an icon appear in your notification area might not be an adequate way to herald the arrival of important mail, particularly if you don't keep your taskbar visible at all times. If you want to be sure you know about new messages the moment they arrive, you can have Windows Messaging beep or play a tune, change the mouse pointer momentarily, or display a message in the center of your screen. To amplify the notification in any or all of these ways, choose Options from the Tools menu. In the top section of the General page of the Options dialog box (see Figure 12-7 on the next page), choose the notification methods you want.

FIGURE 12-7.
If you want to be aware of new mail the instant it arrives, choose any or all of the three options in the top section of this dialog box.

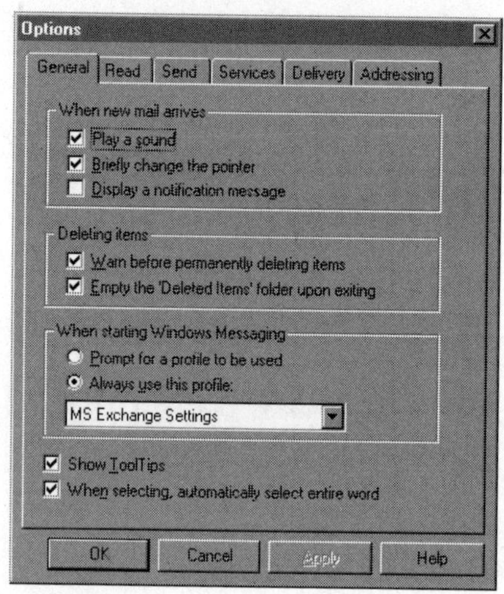

If you select the Play A Sound check box, Windows Messaging will play whatever .WAV file you've assigned to the New Mail Notification event in the Sounds section of Control Panel. (If you don't have a sound card in your computer, you'll hear a simple beep when new mail arrives.)

If you select the Briefly Change The Pointer check box, Windows Messaging will turn your customary mouse pointer into an envelope for a second or so. This is a subtle form of notification, to say the least.

For an announcement that you can scarcely miss, select Display A Notification Message. When new mail arrives, you'll be informed by means of a dialog box, which will invite you to go directly to the first new message with a single click. This option may be useful at times when responding to new mail is your top priority. At other times, you may find it an irritant.

Moving from Message to Message

While you're reading messages, you can move to the next message in the current folder by pressing Ctrl-Shift-N, pressing Ctrl->, or clicking the Next tool on the message window's toolbar. To move to the previous message, press Ctrl-Shift-P, press Ctrl-<, or click the Previous tool.

TIP

How to Know If a Sender Has Requested a Receipt

Windows Messaging does not flag received messages for which a sender has requested a read or delivery receipt. However, you can see whether a receipt has been requested by checking the message's properties. Press Alt-Enter in the message window or select the item in the main Windows Messaging window and click the Properties tool.

Reply Options

To reply to a message, simply click the Reply To Sender or Reply To All tool on the message window's toolbar. (If you prefer, choose these commands from the Compose menu or use their keyboard shortcuts—Ctrl-R and Ctrl-Shift-R, respectively.) Windows Messaging will open a new message window, with the address lines already filled out.

Including the Original Message with Your Reply

By default, Windows Messaging includes the text of the original message at the end of your reply. A rule separates your reply from the original message, and the original text is indented. Including the original with your reply can help both you and those with whom you're corresponding follow the thread of a discussion, but it does make for verbose communication. If you prefer not to include the original, choose Options from the Tools menu. Click the Read tab to get to the dialog box shown in Figure 12-8 on the next page, and deselect the Include The Original Text When Replying check box.

FIGURE 12-8.
Windows Messaging normally includes the original message text when you use the Reply To Sender or Reply To All command.

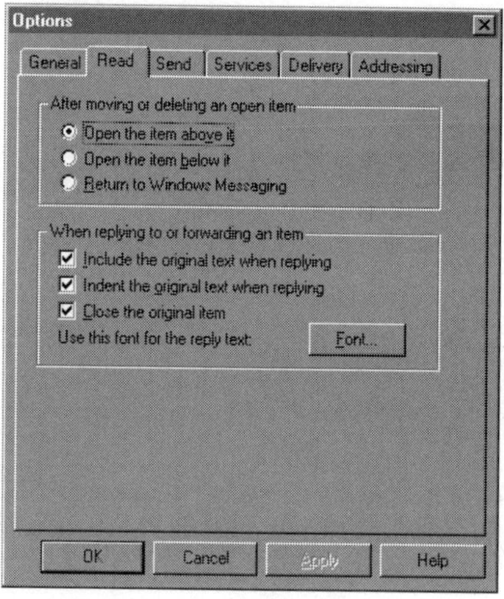

 TIP

Cascading Indents

If you sometimes maintain long chains of replies and counter-replies in your messages, you might want to turn off the automatic indenting of original text. Otherwise, the earliest entries in the chain may be crammed into a narrow space at the right side of your message window. To turn off indenting, deselect the Indent The Original Text When Replying check box in the dialog box shown in Figure 12-8.

Choosing a Default Reply Font

The dialog box shown in Figure 12-8 also lets you choose a default font for your replies. Windows Messaging normally gives you a bright blue font to help your reply stand out from the original message. With this sharply contrasting font, you can also easily interpolate comments into original text when you send back a reply.

You might want to choose a default reply font that's different in color, typeface, or size from fonts used by others in your workgroup. That way, if you create messages with lengthy chains of replies to replies, readers will more easily recognize which comments are yours. To specify a default reply font, click the Font button in the dialog box shown in Figure 12-8. (Be aware, though, that if you choose a font that recipients don't have on their systems, they will see a substituted font. For example, if you send Odd Ball Serif, your recipient will probably see Times New Roman.)

Forwarding Messages

To forward a message, do any of the following:

- Click the Forward tool in either the message window or the main Windows Messaging window.
- Choose Forward from the Compose menu.
- Press Ctrl-F.

Windows Messaging opens a new message window, with the text of the original message displayed below a separator line. Fill out the address portion of the window, add your comments (if any) above the separator line, and click the Send tool (or press Ctrl-Enter).

Editing Messages

Unless a message has been sent with the Private sensitivity option, you're free to edit it. When you close the message window, Windows Messaging will ask whether you want to preserve or discard your changes.

Saving Attachments

If a message has an attached (embedded) file, you can view the file by double-clicking its icon. You might find it convenient, however, to save the attachment as a separate file—to "detach" it from your message. You can do that as follows:

1. Choose Save As from the File menu.
2. Select the Save These Attachments Only option button, near the bottom of the Save As dialog box.
3. If your message has more than one attachment, select the one(s) you want to save in the list that appears below the Save These Attachments Only option button.

Printing Messages

To print a message, press Ctrl-P, choose Print from the File menu, or click the Print tool. You can do this either in a message window or in any Windows Messaging folder. From a Windows Messaging folder, you can select multiple messages (hold down the Ctrl key while you select) before issuing the Print command.

TIP

Moving or Copying Messages

After you finish reading a message, you might want to move or copy it from your Inbox folder to another folder. You can do this without leaving the message window by choosing the Move or Copy command from the File menu. (The keyboard shortcuts for these commands are Ctrl-Shift-M and Ctrl-Shift-C, respectively.) Windows Messaging then displays an outline diagram of your folder structure, allowing you to point to the folder where you want to move or copy the message(s). *For more information, see "Moving or Copying Messages," page 330.*

Deleting Messages

If after reading a message you never want to see it again, click the Delete tool on the toolbar, press Ctrl-D, or choose Delete from the File menu. Your message will be relocated to the Deleted Items folder. When the deleted message departs for good is up to you.

If you want the Deleted Items folder to be purged each time you quit Windows Messaging, choose Options from the Tools menu. In the General page of the Options dialog box (see Figure 12-7 on page 316), select the check box labeled Empty The 'Deleted Items' Folder Upon Exiting. If you do not select this check box, your deleted mail will remain in the Deleted Items folder until you purge that folder yourself—by selecting items there and deleting them once more.

Working with Address Books

Exactly what address books you have available to you in Windows Messaging depends on what mail services you're using, and how you're connected to those services. If you use Microsoft Mail and are on line with your network's post office, for example, you will normally have access to the Postoffice Address List. This is an address book maintained by your Mail administrator, containing entries for everyone with an account at your Microsoft Mail post office. If you use Microsoft Mail but you work off line, that address book will not be available to you.

Displaying Your Address Books

To display any available address books, click the Address Book tool on the Windows Messaging toolbar, type Ctrl-Shift-B, or choose Address Book from the Tools menu. You'll see a window similar to that shown below. Like the other Windows Messaging windows, this one includes a toolbar, and its tools are described in Table 12-4 on the next page.

By typing part of an addressee's name here, you can scroll quickly to that addressee's full name.

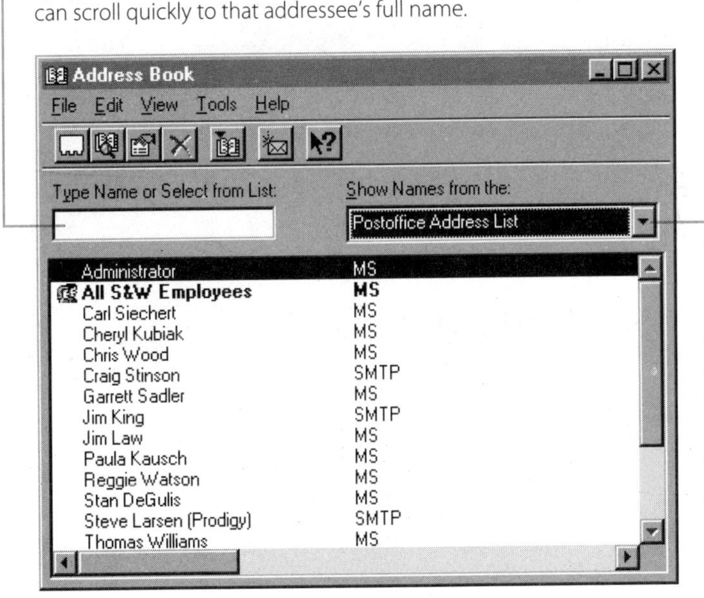

The drop-down list tells you which address book you're looking at and lets you switch to a different one, if you have more than one available.

TABLE 12-4. Address Book Toolbar

Toolbar Icon	Description
	Creates a new address book entry
	Finds a name
	Displays properties for the selected entry
	Deletes the selected entry
	Adds the selected entry to your Personal Address Book
	Creates a new message addressed to the selected entries
	Displays the help pointer, which causes Windows Messaging to display help about the next item you click

 **TIP**

Create a New Message from the Address Book

You can begin a new message from within an address book. Simply select the names of one or more recipients, and then click the New Message tool or press Ctrl-N. Windows Messaging will open a new message window, with the selected names on the To line.

Using the Personal Address Book

The Personal Address Book is designed to give you quick and dependable access to people you send mail to regularly. It's quick, because the list is (presumably) a subset of your company's complete address book with only the names you need. It's dependable because it's stored on your own hard disk instead of a remote server, which gives you access to it even when you're working off line.

To copy an entry into your Personal Address Book from any other address book, select the name you want to copy. Then click the Add To Personal Address Book tool or choose Add To Personal Address Book from the File menu.

TIP

Duplicates Are No Problem

Don't worry about creating duplicate entries in your Personal Address Book. If you copy a name that already exists in the Personal Address Book, Windows Messaging simply disregards your action.

You can also copy an address into your Personal Address Book from the addressee's property sheet, or by "capturing" the address from the To or Cc line of a message you receive. *See "Using Address Book Entry Property Sheets," page 326, and "Capturing Addresses from Received Messages," page 326.*

Using Address Book Property Sheets

To display the property sheet for an address book, first display that address book. Then right-click the entry in the drop-down list at the upper-right corner of the Address Book window and choose Properties from the context menu that appears.

Figure 12-3 on page 296 shows the property sheet for a Personal Address Book, where you can change the address book's name and specify whether you want names shown (and alphabetized) by first name or last name. Other types of address books might offer different options.

Creating New Addresses

To create a new entry in an address book, first display any address book. Then click the New Entry tool or choose New Entry from the File menu. In the New Entry dialog box, choose the type of address you want to create and the address book in which you want to create it. Windows Messaging will then display a property sheet for your new addressee, allowing you to enter the new address as well as other pertinent details.

Creating Personal Distribution Lists

A distribution list is a named collection of addressees. Entering the name of a distribution list on the To or Cc line of a message is equivalent to entering the name of each member of the list separately. To create a new personal distribution list, follow these steps:

1 Display any address book.

2 Choose New Entry from the File menu or click the New Entry tool.

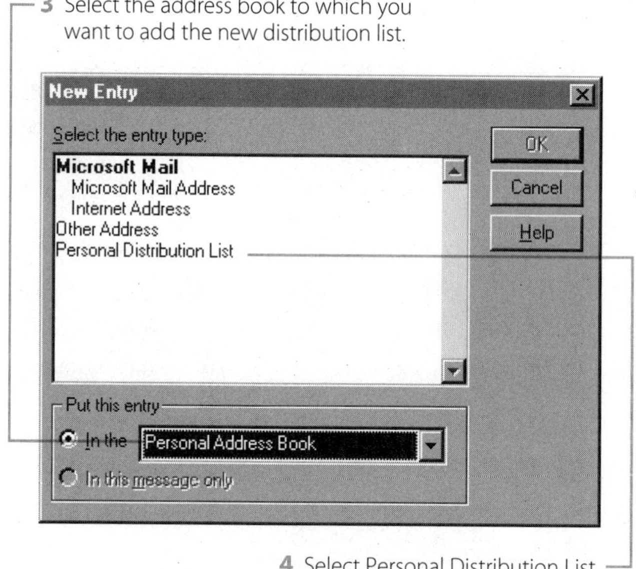

Windows Messaging then displays a property sheet for your new distribution list.

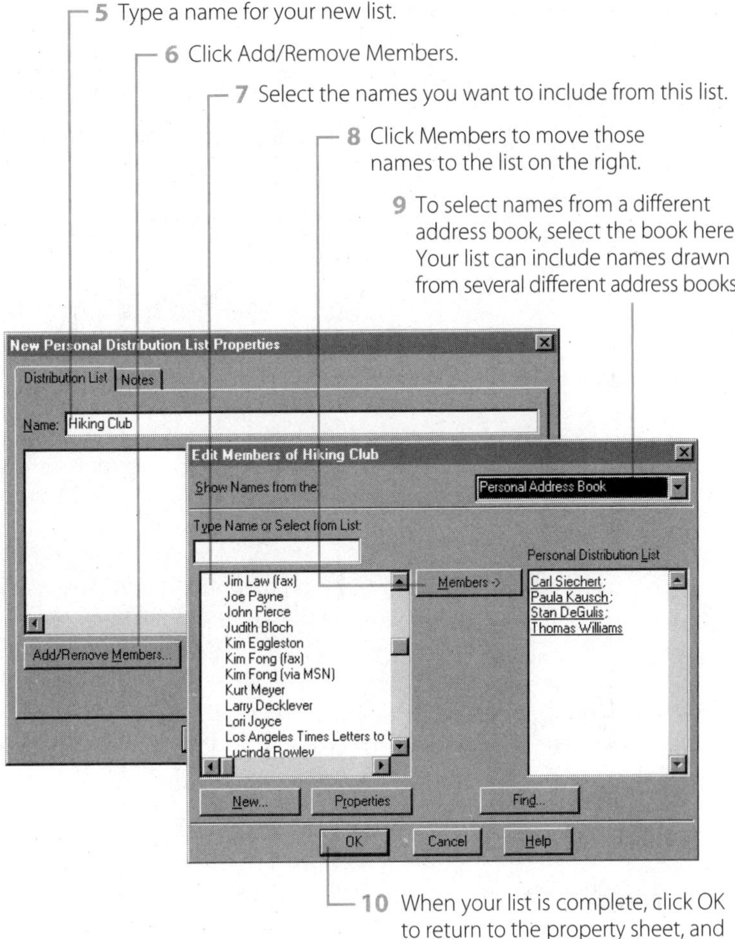

The name of your new distribution list will appear in boldface type in the address book.

Capturing Addresses from Received Messages

When you receive a message from a new correspondent, you might want to add the sender's address to your Personal Address Book. You can do so as follows:

1. Select the name in the From line of the message. (You can also select names in the To or Cc lines to add those names.)
2. Right-click and choose Add To Personal Address Book.

Using Address Book Entry Property Sheets

Like just about everything in Windows NT, address book entries have properties and property sheets. The property sheet for an address book entry includes information vital to Windows Messaging, such as the addressee's name, e-mail address, and mail service. But it also includes places where you can enter information that Windows Messaging cares nothing about—for example, the addressee's physical (Postal Service) address, home and business telephone numbers, and any miscellaneous annotations you care to supply.

To display an addressee's property sheet, select the addressee's name in an address book. Then click the Properties tool, press Alt-Enter, or choose Properties from the File menu. (Alternatively, right-click the addressee's name in an address book or on the To or Cc line of a message and choose Properties from the context menu.)

TIP

Use the Property Sheet as a Phone Dialer

If an addressee's property sheet includes telephone numbers, you can use the property sheet as a phone dialer. Simply click the Dial button beside any telephone number.

Using Message Folders

Whenever you create a new personal folders file (or when you first install Windows Messaging), Windows Messaging supplies you with a set of personal folders named Inbox, Outbox, Sent Items, and Deleted Items. New mail arrives in the Inbox folder, outgoing mail lives in the Outbox folder until it's delivered to the appropriate mail systems, copies of messages you send are (optionally) retained in the Sent Items folder, and items you delete move to the Deleted Items folder.

You don't have to live with just this default set of folders, however. You can create as many folders as you need, and you can nest folders within folders to any level of complexity. You can organize your folders by correspondent, by topic, by date range, or any other way you please. Figure 12-9 shows an example of a personal folders file that has been organized by a combination of message topics and correspondents.

NOTE

Windows Messaging is an extensible messaging system. You might have applications that create their own folder structure in Windows Messaging, in addition to the basic folder structure described in this chapter.

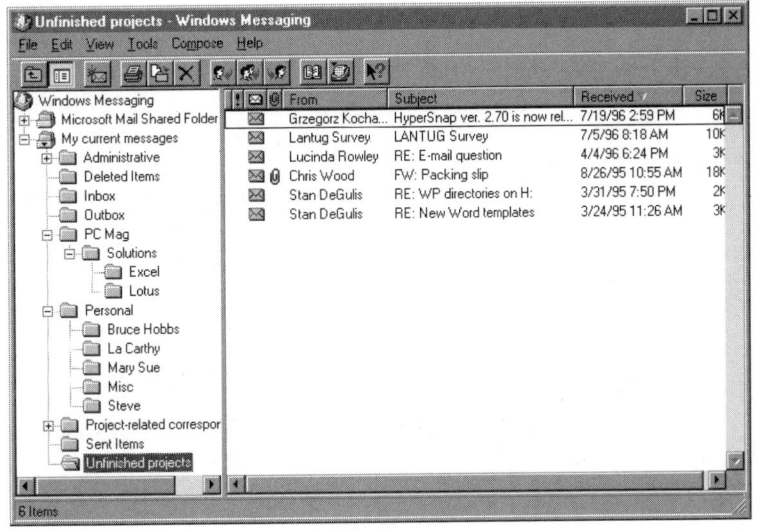

FIGURE 12-9.
To organize your messages, you can create as many folders as you need and nest them to any level of complexity.

If you've spent any time working with Windows NT Explorer, you will probably feel comfortable right away with the Windows Messaging folder system. The basic things you need to know are as follows:

- The Windows Messaging window can be divided into two panes. The left pane displays an outline of your folder structure. The contents of the folder that's selected in the left pane are displayed in the right pane. (If you don't see the left pane, choose Folders from the View menu.)
- Folders containing unread messages are identified in the left pane by boldface type.
- You can adjust the distribution of space between the two panes by dragging the vertical bar (the "split" bar) that divides the window.
- To adjust the width of any right-pane column, drag the vertical bar at the right side of the column heading. (To adjust a column's width with the keyboard, choose the Columns command from the View menu. In the right side of the dialog box, select the column you want to adjust. Then type a number in the Width box.)
- A plus sign in the left pane indicates an entry that can be expanded. To see the subentries, click the plus sign.
- A minus sign in the left pane indicates an entry that can be collapsed. Click the minus sign to collapse the entry.
- To expand an entry with the keyboard, select it and press the Right arrow key. To collapse an entry, select it and press the Left arrow key.

- To create a new folder, select the new folder's parent, and then choose New Folder from the File menu. For example, to create a folder within your Inbox folder, start by selecting Inbox in the left pane. Then choose the New Folder command.
- To rename a folder, right-click it and choose Rename from the context menu. Or select it and choose Rename from the File menu.
- While the right pane has the focus, the folder you're working in is marked by an open-folder icon in the left pane. You can also tell what folder you're working in by looking at the Windows Messaging title bar.

Using Shared Folders

Shared folders, unlike personal folders, are visible to all mail accounts at your electronic post office. You can think of them as the virtual counterpart to the posters on the Postal Service wall. What you put there is there for all to see (unless you use the Permissions property to deny read access).

If you use Microsoft Mail with Windows Messaging, you'll find the heading Microsoft Mail Shared Folders at the top level of your folder outline, in the left pane of the Windows Messaging window. You can use the File menu's New Folder command to create shared folders under this heading, just as you would create new personal folders. Once you've created your shared folders, you can use drag and drop or the File menu's Move and Copy commands to transfer messages from personal folders to shared folders.

Setting Permissions for Shared Folders

To set permissions for a shared folder, right-click the folder, choose Properties from the context menu, and then click the Permissions tab. You'll see a dialog box similar to the one shown on the next page.

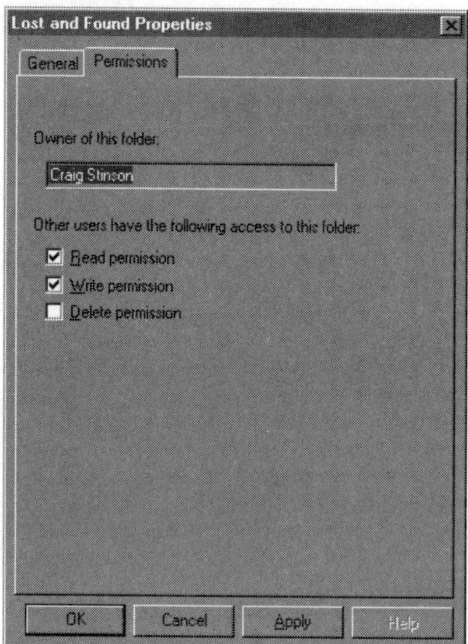

The person who creates the shared folder is the owner, and that person has control over three permission attributes. No one else, except for the post-office administrator (the person who set up your Microsoft Mail post office) can change these settings. The three permission attributes are independent of one another. That is, you can arrange them in any combination. The default permission setup, shown in the figure, allows users to read shared messages folders and add messages to the shared folder, but not to delete the shared folder.

NOTE

> If your post office is set up under Microsoft Exchange Server, you can also create message threads in shared folders. This capability is not available in the Windows Messaging client software included with Windows NT 4.

Moving or Copying Messages

To move an item to a different folder, drag the item from the right pane and drop it on the destination folder in the left pane. To copy an item to a new folder, hold down the Ctrl key while you drag it to its destination.

To move or copy an item without using drag and drop, select the item and then choose Move or Copy from the File menu. (Or right-click and choose Move or Copy from the context menu.) Windows Messaging will display your folder hierarchy in a new window (see Figure 12-10), allowing you to point to (or navigate with the keyboard to) your destination folder.

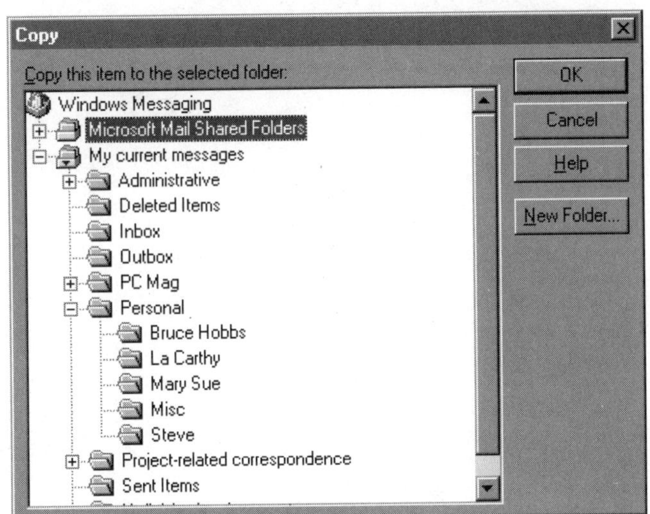

FIGURE 12-10.
You can move or copy by dragging with your mouse or by choosing commands from the File menu. If you take the latter route, Windows Messaging uses this window to let you specify a destination folder.

To move or copy multiple messages in the same folder, hold down the Ctrl key while you select each message. Then drag and drop, or choose commands from the File or context menu.

You can move or copy a folder by dragging it from either pane and dropping it on its new parent folder. For example, in Figure 12-9 on page 327, you could move the Unfinished Projects folder from its current location into the Administrative folder by dragging it in the left pane and dropping it on Administrative. (If you copy a folder to a new destination within the same folder, Windows Messaging supplies a new name based on the original name.)

Note that the Windows Messaging window displays all personal folders files in your profile. You can use the same techniques to move or copy items between personal folders files.

Deleting Messages

To delete a message, a group of messages, or an entire folder, select what you want to delete. Then click the Delete tool, press the Del key, or right-click and choose Delete from the context menu.

TIP

Restoring Deleted Items

Windows Messaging does not prompt for confirmation when you delete messages or folders. Nor does it provide an Undo command. But all deleted items (including entire folders) go to the Deleted Items folder. You can restore a deleted item by moving or copying it out of the Deleted Items folder.

Sorting Messages in a Folder

To sort the items in a folder based on the contents of any column, click the column heading. For example, to sort by subject, click the Subject heading. Alternatively, choose Sort from the View menu. In the dialog box that appears, select a column name from the drop-down list and choose either the Ascending or Descending option button.

When you sort by clicking a column heading, Windows Messaging uses the default sorting order—ascending or descending—for that column. When you sort by the Received column, for example, Windows Messaging sorts in descending order, putting the most recently received messages at the top. When you click Subject or From, Windows Messaging sorts in ascending order—that is, in "normal" alphabetical order. To reverse the sort on any heading, hold down the Ctrl key while you click.

Fortunately, you don't need to memorize the default sort orders for each column. Windows Messaging displays a gray triangle next to the heading on which you last sorted. An upward-pointing triangle denotes an ascending sort. A downward arrow means the column has been sorted in descending order.

(When you sort by Subject, Windows Messaging ignores any "RE:" and "FW:" in the Subject field of replies and forwarded messages.)

> **NOTE**
>
> In shared folders, you can't change the default sort order, which is ascending date order.

Customizing Folder Columns

New message folders, by default, display seven columns of information. From left to right, those columns are: Importance, Item Type, Attachment, From, Subject, Received, and Size. You can change the column order, delete columns, or add new columns, by choosing the Columns command from the View menu. A dialog box like the one shown below appears.

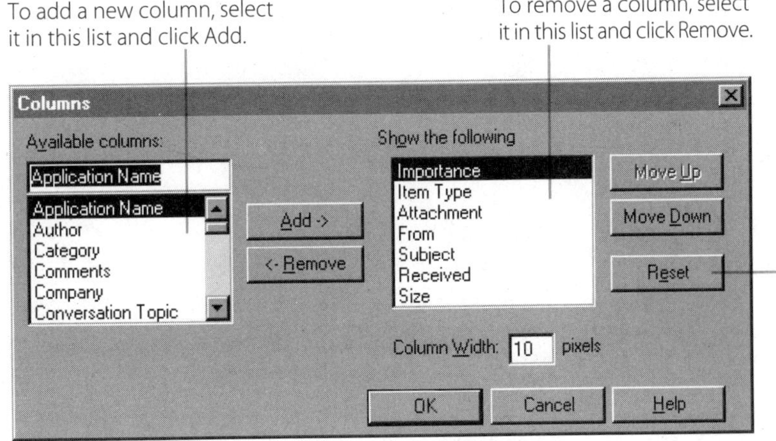

By selecting items in the right side of this dialog box, and then clicking Move Up or Move Down, you can change the order in which columns are displayed. In the figure above, for example, you could move the Item Type column to the left (making it appear before the Importance column) by selecting it and clicking the Move Up button.

Settings you make in the Columns dialog box affect only the currently displayed folder, so you can customize the appearance of each folder. If you change column settings in a shared folder, it affects only your view of the folder. Other users who view the same folder are free to customize it in their own way.

Using the Find Command

Windows Messaging includes a handy Find command that works much like the Find command on the Start menu, except that it searches Windows Messaging folders instead of disk folders. Once Find has located a message or group of messages, you can work with those items directly in the Find window. You can read messages, reply to or forward messages, move messages into folders, and so on. You can also customize the display of items in the Find window using the same techniques you use to customize any Windows Messaging folder.

You can open as many Find windows as you need. If you ask Find to look for messages from a particular sender, the sender's name will appear on Find's title bar as well as on your taskbar.

TIP

Using Find to Catch Incoming Messages

If you leave a Find window open, Find will add any new qualifying messages to the window as they arrive, identifying the new arrivals with boldface type. If you select the Only Unread Items check box (on the Advanced section of the Find dialog box), Find will remove items from its window as soon as you read them. Thus, Find is convenient for trapping particular types of new messages—high priority items, for example, or items from a particular sender—allowing you to postpone the reading of nonqualifying items.

To use the Find command, choose Find from the Tools menu, press Ctrl-Shift-F, or right-click a folder and choose Find from the context menu. Figure 12-11 shows the dialog box that appears. Click the Folder button, near the top of the dialog box, and tell Find where you want it to look. Then supply your search criteria in the remainder of the dialog box (using the Advanced section if appropriate), and click the Find Now button.

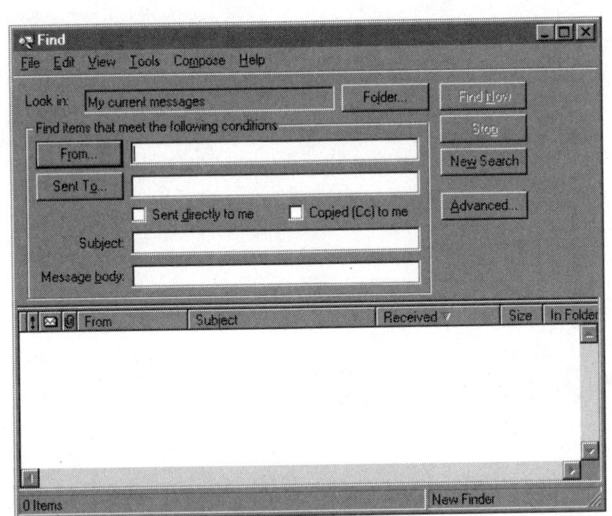

FIGURE 12-11.
You can use the Find command to locate existing messages that meet search criteria, as well as to capture newly arriving messages that meet those criteria.

TIP

Find as a Substitute for Organization

When you click the Folder button in the Find dialog box, Windows Messaging presents an outline diagram of your entire Windows Messaging hierarchy, including all personal folders files and all folders within each file. By choosing a personal folders file and selecting the Include All Subfolders check box, you can gather together messages from many different folders that have some property in common. So, for example, even if you don't take the trouble to move messages in your Sent Items folder into more particular folders, you can still use Find to collect sent and received mail on a common topic into a single window.

Archiving Messages and Folders

Windows Messaging does not include an Archive command, but you can effectively winnow aging messages from your personal folders file as follows:

1 Create a separate personal folders file for your archive. *(For details, see "Adding a Personal Folders File," page 294.)*

2 Periodically use the Find command to display items of a certain age. (To find items that you received prior to a specified date, click the Advanced button in the Find dialog box.)

3 In the Find window choose the Select All command from the Edit menu.

4 Choose the Move command from the File menu, and then double-click your archival personal folders file.

Accessing Mail with Dial-Up Networking

For more information on Dial-Up Networking, see "Using Dial-Up Networking," page 415.

If you use a mail system based on a local-area network, such as Microsoft Mail, and you sometimes need to get your mail from outside the office, check your system's property sheet to see how it handles offline work and dial-up connections. Choose Services from the Windows Messaging Tools menu, select the name of the mail system you're using, and then click Properties. If you're working with Microsoft Mail, you'll find dial-up options on the Connection page. (See Figure 12-2 on page 294.)

To use a dial-up connection to your LAN-based mail system, you must have Dial-Up Networking installed, and you must have access to a remote access server.

There are three ways to use Microsoft Mail from outside the local-area network:

- If you select Remote Using A Modem And Dial-Up Networking, Windows Messaging will always invoke Dial-Up Networking to establish a connection with Mail.
- If you select Automatically Sense LAN Or Remote, Windows Messaging will use Dial-Up Networking any time the network is unavailable.
- If you select Offline, Windows Messaging will let you post messages to your Outbox, but it won't try to send those messages until you revisit the property sheet and choose one of the other connection options.

CHAPTER 13

Surfing with Internet Explorer

Internet Explorer is an application that allows you to explore the part of the Internet known as the World Wide Web. Internet Explorer includes many features that make accessing information on the Internet as simple as pointing and clicking on items that interest you. Windows NT 4 includes Internet Explorer version 3.

SEE ALSO
For information about Dial-Up Networking, see "Using Dial-Up Networking," page 415.

This chapter assumes that you already have access to the Internet. This means that you either have a modem and an account with an Internet service provider, or a local-area network (LAN) connection to the Internet. This chapter also assumes that you (or an administrator) have already set up a Dial-Up Networking connection to your Internet service provider.

The features and commands in Internet Explorer allow you to work directly with material on the World Wide Web. Before you start using these features, however, it is important to know a few things about the Web itself. *If you are already familiar with the Internet and the World Wide Web, you can skip ahead to "Introducing Internet Explorer," page 342.*

Introducing the World Wide Web

The World Wide Web is the graphical portion of the Internet. Internet Explorer makes using the World Wide Web fairly simple. However, it's helpful to know some terms and concepts. You can refer to this short list of terms when they are used elsewhere in this chapter.

Internet. The Internet is a worldwide network of computers. If you have access to the Internet, you can view information from any public computer on the Internet.

World Wide Web. The World Wide Web, sometimes called simply "the Web," is the graphical portion of the Internet.

Web page. The World Wide Web is organized as a system of interconnected graphical documents, called *pages*. Most pages have hyperlinks, or pointers, to other Web pages. Web pages are also sometimes called *Web sites*.

Hyperlink. A hyperlink is any area on a Web page that takes you to another page when you click it. Hyperlinks can be portions of text, icons, pictures, or other graphic objects. They are often, but not always, highlighted or underlined. You can tell if an item is a hyperlink by putting the mouse pointer over it. If the pointer changes to a "hand" pointer, then the item under it is a hyperlink.

Surfing. To explore the World Wide Web, you simply start at one page, and then use hyperlinks on that page to jump to other pages that interest you. The process of jumping from page to page is known as *surfing the Web.*

Web browser. A browser is an application that allows you to view pages on the World Wide Web. Internet Explorer is an example of such an application.

Home page. The first screen that you see at any Web site is usually called the home page for that site. Home page can also refer to the first Web page you see when you start your browser, although Internet Explorer uses the term *start page* to describe that page.

URL. URL stands for Uniform Resource Locator. It is an address that uniquely identifies a World Wide Web page or other resource on the Internet. For example, the URL for Microsoft Corporation's Web site is *http://www.microsoft.com.*

HTML. HTML stands for Hypertext Markup Language. It is the system of formatting codes that most World Wide Web documents are created with.

HTTP. HTTP, which stands for Hypertext Transfer Protocol, is the protocol that is used to send HTML documents across the Internet.

FTP. FTP, which stands for File Transfer Protocol, is the protocol used to transfer files of all kinds across the Internet. FTP sites are usually repositories of files available for downloading. Unlike graphical Web pages, FTP sites consist of simple text-based lists of files.

Gopher. Gopher is another system for organizing information on the Internet. Unlike Web pages with hyperlinks, gopher sites provide simple text menus to help you find your way.

Starting and Ending an Internet Session

To begin a session on the Internet, double-click the Internet Explorer icon on your desktop. If you have set up Internet Explorer to connect automatically, this action activates the appropriate Dial-Up Networking connection, and in a moment or two you'll be ready to surf.

To set up Internet Explorer to connect automatically, right-click the Internet Explorer icon, choose Properties, click the Connection tab, and select the check box labeled "Connect to the Internet as Needed."

For information about Dial-Up Networking, see "Using Dial-Up Networking," page 415. For information about Dial-Up Networking Monitor, see "Using Dial-Up Networking Monitor," page 426.

Alternatively, you can begin a session by running Dial-Up Networking. When a message appears indicating that your connection has been made, start Internet Explorer by double-clicking its desktop icon.

To end an Internet session, right-click the Dial-Up Networking Monitor icon in the taskbar's notification area and choose Hang Up Connection from the context menu.

Introducing Internet Explorer

Before you start exploring the World Wide Web, it is important to understand the components of the Internet Explorer window. Once you know what the different items do, using Internet Explorer is pretty simple. Figure 13-1 points out the various components of the window.

The *toolbar* allows quick access to commands you use most often. The second line of the toolbar can show the URL of the current page, a set of useful "quick links," or both. The toolbar can be reduced to one line to allow a larger document area. *See "Customizing the Toolbar," page 344.*

FIGURE 13-1.
The Internet Explorer main window has a small set of tools and controls surrounding the document viewing area.

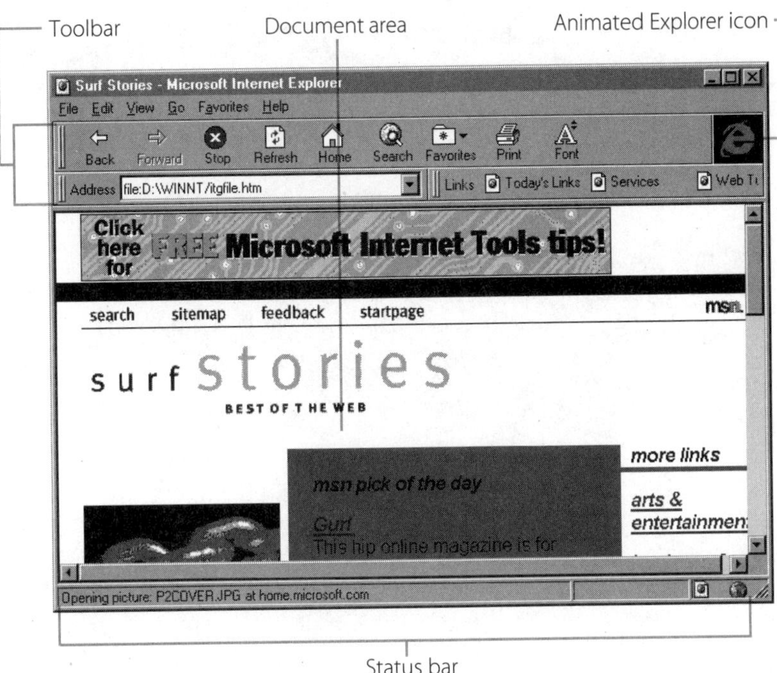

The *animated Explorer icon* indicates when Internet Explorer is waiting to receive information from a remote computer on the Internet. While the browser waits, the Internet Explorer icon appears to rotate.

The *status bar* gives you information about what Internet Explorer is currently doing. While Internet Explorer retrieves data from the Internet, detailed information appears at the status bar's left end, and graphics at the right end indicate progress.

The *document area* displays the Web page you're currently viewing. Any items that are highlighted (usually by underlining) are hyperlinks, and clicking them takes you to the page they point to.

Customizing the Toolbar

Figure 13-1 on the previous page shows a two-line toolbar with descriptive text below the icons, and with the second line divided between an Address area and a Links area. Because the toolbar is customizable, this may not be exactly what you see on your system. You can tailor the appearance of the toolbar in the following ways:

SEE ALSO

For information about other ways to customize the toolbar, see "Selecting Toolbars," page 359.

- To expand the toolbar, which can be displayed on one, two, or three lines, drag the lower boundary of the toolbar down. To collapse a multiline toolbar, drag the lower boundary of the toolbar up.
- To eliminate icon text, collapse the toolbar to a single line, and then drag a little farther upward.
- To change the distribution of space between the Address and Links areas, click on or drag the word *Address* or the word *Links*. You can do this in both the one-line and two-line versions of the toolbar.

Viewing the Document Area

The document area of Internet Explorer is where Web pages are displayed. When Internet Explorer is started, it automatically loads a document called the *start page* into the document area. Internet Explorer is initially set with a Microsoft-designed page stored on your computer as its start page. You can change the start page to something else if you want. *See "Changing the Start Page, Search Page, and Quick Links," page 357.*

Use the scroll bars to view parts of the page not currently displayed in the window. Within the window, you can click a hyperlink to jump to another page or right-click any area to display a context menu. A different context menu appears depending on whether you right-click a hyperlink, a graphic, or the document's background area.

Understanding the Status Bar

When you access pages on the World Wide Web, getting information from a site on the Internet to your computer can sometimes take a fair amount of time. In situations like this, it can be helpful to have more information about what Internet Explorer is actually doing.

The status bar provides several pieces of additional information, including the Internet address that a hyperlink points to, progress information about downloading the current page, and detailed information about what action Internet Explorer is trying to complete.

Navigating on the World Wide Web

Internet Explorer offers several routes for navigating the World Wide Web. You can:

- Click a hyperlink to go to a page
- Enter an Internet address (URL) to go to a specific page
- Use the Forward and Back commands to revisit previously viewed pages
- Go further back in your Web-browsing history with commands on the Go menu
- Return to your favorite pages by saving shortcuts to them

SEE ALSO
For information on managing the cache, see "Controlling the Cache," page 360.

As you surf the Internet, Internet Explorer stores the Web pages you visit in subfolders of a folder named Temporary Internet Files. When you click a hyperlink or shortcut, the program first checks this *cache* to see if it has the page you're looking for. If it does, Internet Explorer loads the page from the cache instead of connecting to the page's Web site.

If Internet Explorer cannot find the page in the cache, it downloads the page from the Internet.

Keyboard Shortcuts

You can use the following keyboard shortcuts as you work with Web pages in Internet Explorer:

Enter	Activates the selected hyperlink
Shift-F10	Displays the context menu for the current hyperlink
Ctrl-Tab	Cycles between frames (independently scrolling areas)
Tab	Cycles forward through links
Shift-Tab	Cycles backward through links
Alt-Left arrow or Backspace	Returns to previous page
Alt-Right arrow or Shift-Backspace	Moves to next page
Ctrl-R or F5	Refreshes display of current page
Esc	Stops display of current page
Ctrl-O	Opens a document
Ctrl-N	Opens a new window
Ctrl-S	Saves the current page as a file
Ctrl-P	Prints the current page

Using Hyperlinks to Get to Other Pages

The World Wide Web works in a fashion similar to the Help feature in most Windows-based software products. In Help, you can click any highlighted or underlined word to get more information. On the Web, these items are called hyperlinks.

Each page on the World Wide Web can have an unlimited number of hyperlinks to other pages. You can identify a hyperlink by moving the mouse pointer over a text or graphic item on a page. If the pointer icon changes to a hand when you pass over that item, as shown below, then the item is a hyperlink. Notice also that the status bar displays information about the hyperlink.

The mouse pointer assumes this shape when it points to a hyperlink.

The status bar displays information about the hyperlink that the mouse pointer is on.

2 Sharing and Communicating

To use a hyperlink, all you have to do is click it. When you do this, Internet Explorer takes you to the Web page that the hyperlink points to.

SEE ALSO

For information about setting the colors for hyperlinks, see "Selecting Colors," page 359.

Once you click a hyperlink and go to its linked page, Internet Explorer remembers that you used that hyperlink. To let you know that you've already used a hyperlink, Internet Explorer changes the color of the text for that hyperlink.

Viewing Multiple Documents Simultaneously

Internet Explorer allows you to specify whether you want to open a Web page in a new window or in the current window. This feature allows you to view one page while you are waiting to connect to another. You might find this capability useful for example, when viewing graphics-laden pages, which can take a long time to display.

If you choose the New Window command from the File menu (or press Ctrl-N), Internet Explorer opens a second window and displays the same information in both windows. You can then operate the two windows independently. Alternatively, to open a hyperlink in a new window, you can either right-click the hyperlink and choose Open In New Window or simply hold down the Shift key while you click the hyperlink.

Getting to a Specific Web Page

If you know the address of the Web page you want, Internet Explorer provides two easy ways to get there. You can use the address edit box on the toolbar or the File Open command.

The address edit box always displays the URL of the current Web page. However, you can also type the URL of the Web page you want and press Enter, and Internet Explorer will take you there. Follow these steps to enter an address:

1 Click the Address text entry box to highlight the text currently in the box.

2 Type the URL or World Wide Web address for the page you want to go to. The address should look something like this:

   http://www.microsoft.com

3 Press Enter.

   Internet Explorer finds the page that you want. (It may take a few seconds for the Web page to respond to Internet Explorer's request for information.)

To use the Open command, follow these steps:

1 Choose Open from the File menu and fill out the following dialog box:

Type a URL here, or select one from the drop-down list.

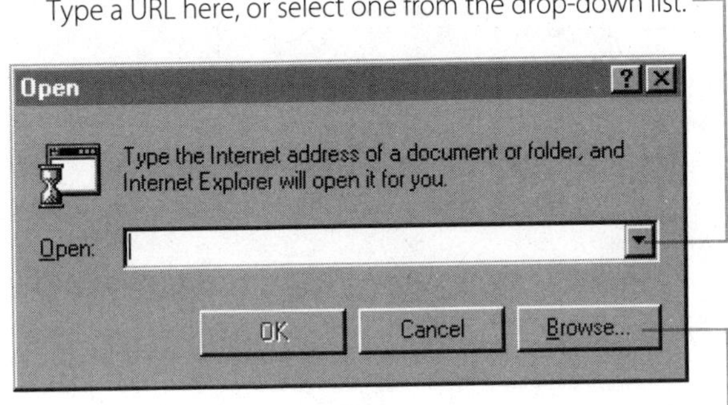

Use the Browse button to select an Internet page or shortcut that's already on your local disk or network server.

2 Type the URL or World Wide Web address for the page you want to go to. The address should look something like this:

http://www.microsoft.com

3 Click OK.

Internet Explorer finds the page that you want. It may take a few seconds for the World Wide Web page to respond to Internet Explorer's request for information.

TIP

For many Internet addresses, Internet Explorer can identify the correct protocol automatically. Therefore, you can shorten your typing for these addresses by omitting the protocol—the part of the address up to and including the two slashes, such as http:// or ftp://. So, for example, to enter the sample address in step 2 above, you could type just *www.microsoft.com*.

Surfing the Intranet?

Internet Explorer can browse HTML documents stored on your hard disk or elsewhere on your local-area network, just as it can browse documents on the Internet. This is one form of an "intranet"—an Internet-like setup that operates entirely within a corporation's walls. Corporate intranets are an increasingly popular method for making information available throughout the company.

To view a locally stored document, type its path in the toolbar's address edit box or in the File Open dialog box. Separate folder names in the path with a backslash (\). (A key difference: Internet addresses use a forward slash as a separator.)

More sophisticated intranets use a Web server that creates an environment that looks and acts exactly like the public Internet. Internet Explorer can browse such intranets with ease.

Using the Forward and Back Commands

Internet Explorer keeps a list of the pages you've already viewed. The Forward and Back commands provide a simple way to move through that list so that you can easily return to places you have already seen. Try out the commands with this simple example:

1. On the start page, click any hyperlink to move to a new Web page. (To identify a hyperlink, move the mouse pointer over various text and graphic items; when the pointer changes to a hand, you've found a hyperlink.)

2. When the new Web page appears, click the Back button on the toolbar or choose the Back command from the Go menu to move back to the start page. (Notice that the Forward toolbar button is now active.)

3. Now click the Forward button or use the Forward command on the Go menu. You will move forward to the page you visited in step 1.

 TIP

Retrace Your Steps

The Back command is particularly handy when you've gotten lost on the Web. Simply use the Back command repeatedly to retrace your steps until you find a familiar page.

Working with History

The Forward and Back commands are pretty simple to use. However, the more Web pages you visit, the harder it is to keep track of exactly how many steps back a specific page is. Internet Explorer provides an additional feature called history, which gives you an easy way to move several steps back at a time.

Near the bottom of the Go menu, Internet Explorer presents a list of the Web pages you've visited most recently. To return to one of these pages, simply select it from the Go menu:

Choose a page title in this list to return to a recently visited site.

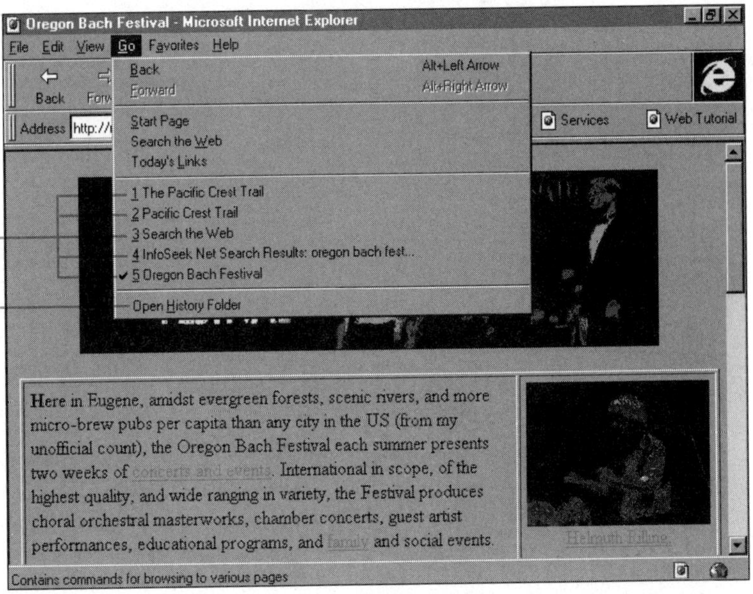

Choose Open History Folder to select an item from your History folder.

Going Further Back in History

 SEE ALSO

For information about folder windows, see Chapter 5, "Working with Folders."

The Go menu shows the last several pages you've viewed during the current session. Internet Explorer can also show you a list of the sites you've visited over the last several days. Whenever you go to a Web page, Internet Explorer creates a shortcut for that page in a folder called History. You can access the entire contents of the History folder by choosing the Open History Folder command from the Go menu. As the following illustration shows, the History folder is an ordinary folder window, and you can arrange its icons alphabetically or by date. If necessary, scroll horizontally to see all of it.

Double-click an item in this alphabetic list to return to a Web page.

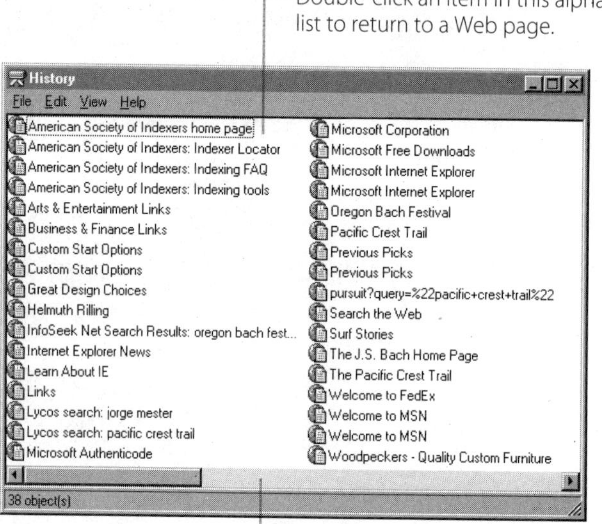

Because many page titles are long, you will likely need to scroll to see the entire list.

SEE ALSO

For more information about the Internet Explorer cache, see "Controlling the Cache," page 360. For more information about shortcuts, see "Using Shortcuts to Run Programs and Open Documents," page 73.

The items in the History folder are shortcuts to World Wide Web pages that merely tell Internet Explorer where to find the content of a particular page. When you double-click a history item, Internet Explorer first tries to find the page in the cache it maintains. If the page is not in the cache, Internet Explorer connects you to the Internet (if you are not currently connected) and retrieves the page that you want.

Keeping Track of Your Favorite Places

As you surf the Web and discover pages that you like, you will probably want a way to get back to those places easily. Internet Explorer provides a series of Favorites commands for exactly this purpose. Using Favorites commands, you can create a list of your favorite pages and organize them into folders. Then, to go to a favorite place, you can simply select the page you want from the Favorites menu.

Using the Add To Favorites Command

The Add To Favorites command allows you to create a favorite-place listing for the page you're currently viewing. You can have as many favorite pages as you like. To add the Web page you are currently viewing to your Favorites list, follow these steps:

1 Choose Add To Favorites from the Favorites menu, or right-click the page and choose Add To Favorites from the context menu. This opens the Add To Favorites dialog box, shown in Figure 13-2.

2 In the Name text box, make any changes you want to the name of the page.

3 Click the OK button. This creates a favorite-place listing for the current page.

FIGURE 13-2.
The Add To Favorites dialog box creates a favorite-place listing for the current page.

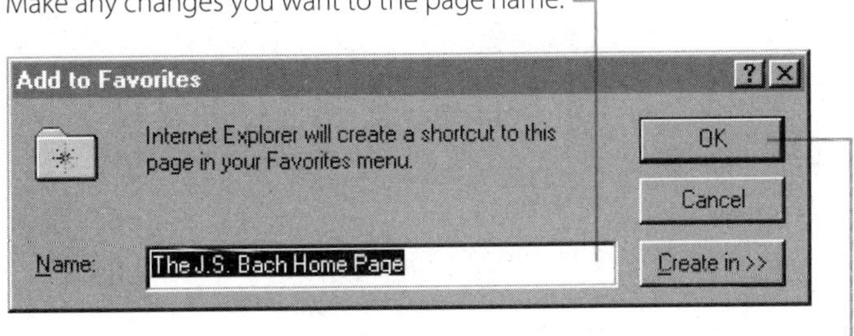

Organizing Your Favorite Places with Folders

After you've created a number of favorite places, you might have difficulty finding the particular favorite page you're looking for. To help you organize your favorite places, Internet Explorer allows you to create subfolders within your favorite places folder.

To create a subfolder, follow these steps:

1. Choose the Add To Favorites command by clicking its toolbar button or by selecting it from the Favorites menu. This brings up the Add To Favorites dialog box shown in Figure 13-2.
2. Click the Create In button. The dialog box expands to display a folder hierarchy, as shown below.

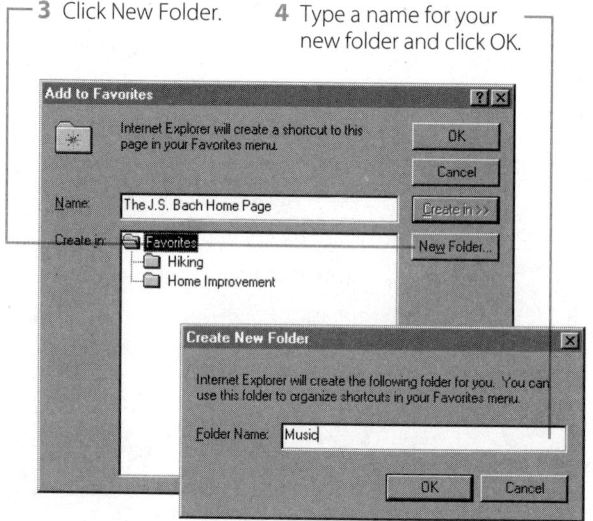

5. In the Add To Favorites dialog box, click OK to add the current page to your new folder.

The Favorites menu now includes a cascading item with a folder icon that has the name of the folder you created. Creating such a menu structure lets you group your favorite places logically.

After you create a new folder, you can add favorites to it by double-clicking the folder you want in the expanded Add To Favorites dialog box and then clicking the OK button.

Using the Organize Favorites Command

The Organize Favorites command allows you to view, organize, and return to your favorite places. When you click the Organize Favorites toolbar button or choose the Organize Favorites command from the Favorites menu, you will be presented with a dialog box displaying the contents of the Favorites folder, as shown below.

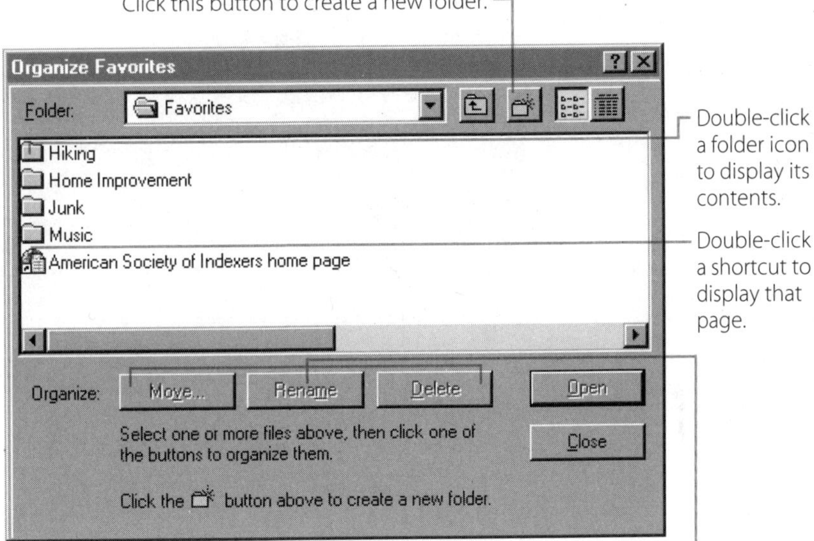

This dialog box functions much like Windows NT folder windows. You can drag files or folders to a folder icon to move them to that folder, and you can right-click files or folders to see the usual context menus. In addition, the dialog box's buttons provide a quick way to create new folders, rename items, and organize things as you see fit.

Customizing Internet Explorer

Internet Explorer presents an attractive face and offers easy access to some popular Web pages. But if the current setup is not to your liking, you can set a variety of options. For example, you can:

- Specify a different start page, the page that appears when you start Internet Explorer
- Specify a different search page, the page that appears when you click the Search tool
- Specify quick link pages, the pages that appear when you click an icon on the Links toolbar
- Increase browsing speed by disabling features you don't need
- Select colors for text, the window background, and hyperlinks
- Select a font for unformatted text
- Select toolbars to display
- Control how much hard disk space Internet Explorer uses
- Specify when pages that you've already viewed should be updated
- Prevent users on your computer from viewing offensive Web pages

To change these options, you use Internet Explorer's Options property sheet. To display the Options property sheet, use one of the following methods:

- Choose Options from Internet Explorer's View menu.
- Right-click the Internet Explorer icon on your desktop and choose the Properties command.
- Double-click the Internet icon in Control Panel.

Changing the Start Page, Search Page, and Quick Links

Several Web pages are particularly easy to get to using Internet Explorer: the *start page*, the *search page*, and the *quick links*. The start page is the one that appears automatically when you open Internet Explorer (unless you begin by launching a Web-page shortcut). The search page is the one that appears when you click the Search button on the toolbar or choose Search The Web from the Go menu. Quick links are the pages that appear when you click an icon on the Links toolbar. You don't have to use the start page, search page, and quick links that Microsoft gives you; you can substitute any pages you prefer.

To specify a different start page or search page, or different quick links, follow these steps:

1. Display the page that you want to use as the new start page, search page, or quick link.
2. Display the Options property sheet, and click the Navigation tab.

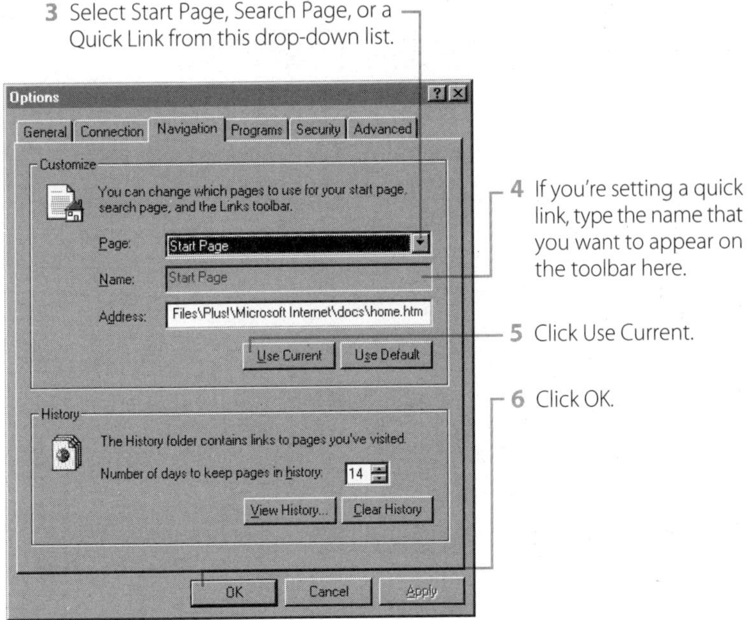

TIP

Instead of displaying the page you want to use, you can type its URL in the Address text box. If you use this method, do not click Use Current.

To restore one of Internet Explorer's original pages, return to this dialog box, select the page from the drop-down list, and then click the Use Default button.

Increasing Browsing Speed

Web pages with pictures, sound, and video can provide some impressive imagery, but they often take a long time to display. You can speed up the display of such pages by suppressing the pictures, sound, or video. To do this, display the Options property sheet and click the General tab. The dialog box shown in Figure 13-3 appears.

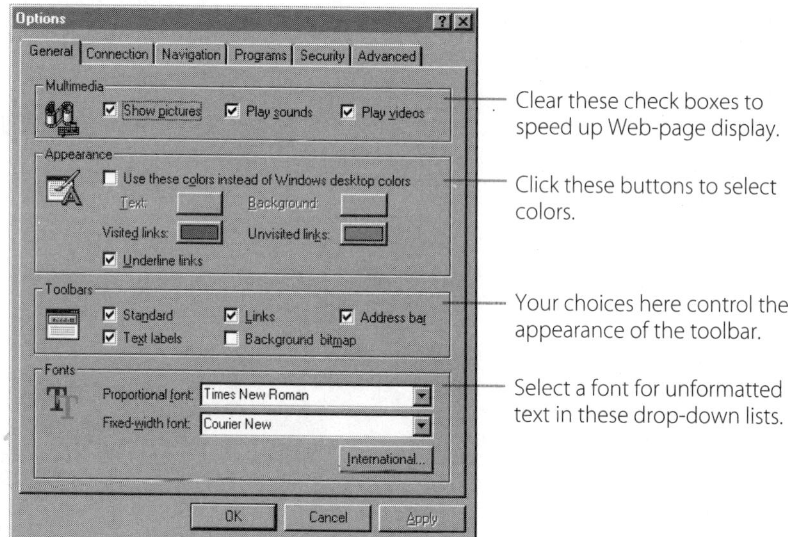

FIGURE 13-3.
The General page includes options for increasing browsing speed and selecting colors, toolbars, and fonts for the Internet Explorer window.

Selecting Colors

You can select the color used for ordinary text, hyperlinks that you've already visited, hyperlinks that you haven't visited, and the document area background. To change any of these color settings, display the Options property sheet and click the General tab to see the dialog box shown in Figure 13-3.

SEE ALSO
For information about Windows desktop colors, see "Changing Colors, Fonts, and Text Sizes," page 97.

By default, Internet Explorer uses the colors you specify in Control Panel's Display property sheet for ordinary text and for the window background. To override these defaults, select the check box labeled "Use these colors instead of Windows desktop colors."

Then, to specify the color for any of the four elements, click its button and select a color in the palette that appears.

NOTE

The colors you select here affect only documents that do not specify their own color settings, which override these settings.

Selecting Toolbars

SEE ALSO
For information about controlling the size of various toolbar elements, see "Customizing the Toolbar," page 344.

Internet Explorer has three toolbars: Standard, Links, and Address. The Standard toolbar includes Back, Forward, and Stop buttons, among others. The Links toolbar has buttons for quick access to a handful of favorite sites. The Address toolbar displays the address of the current page.

You can display these toolbars in any combination. Simply select its check box on the General page of the Options property sheet (see Figure 13-3) to display a toolbar, or clear its check box to hide a toolbar.

 TIP

To hide the toolbar altogether, choose Toolbar from the View menu.

You can dress up the toolbars by selecting the Background Bitmap check box. And you can reduce the space occupied by the Standard toolbar by deselecting the Text Labels check box.

Selecting Fonts

For information about fonts, see Chapter 8, "Installing and Using Fonts."

Many Web pages now include formatting codes that specify which fonts to use. Pages that do not include such codes display their text in one of two typefaces that you can specify on the General page of the Options property sheet, shown in Figure 13-3 on page 358.

You cannot specify a particular font size for text display—but you can select among five predefined sizes. To change the size of unformatted text in the Internet Explorer document area, choose the Fonts command from the View menu. A cascading submenu offers choices from Smallest to Largest.

Controlling the Cache

Internet Explorer stores pages that you visit in folders contained within the folder named Temporary Internet Files. These stored pages are called a *cache*, and Internet Explorer uses them to speed the display of pages you've already visited. By default, these cache folders use as much as 10 percent of the capacity of the drive on which they reside. If that's too much space (or not enough), you can change the cache size by displaying the Options property sheet and clicking the Advanced tab to display the dialog box shown on the next page.

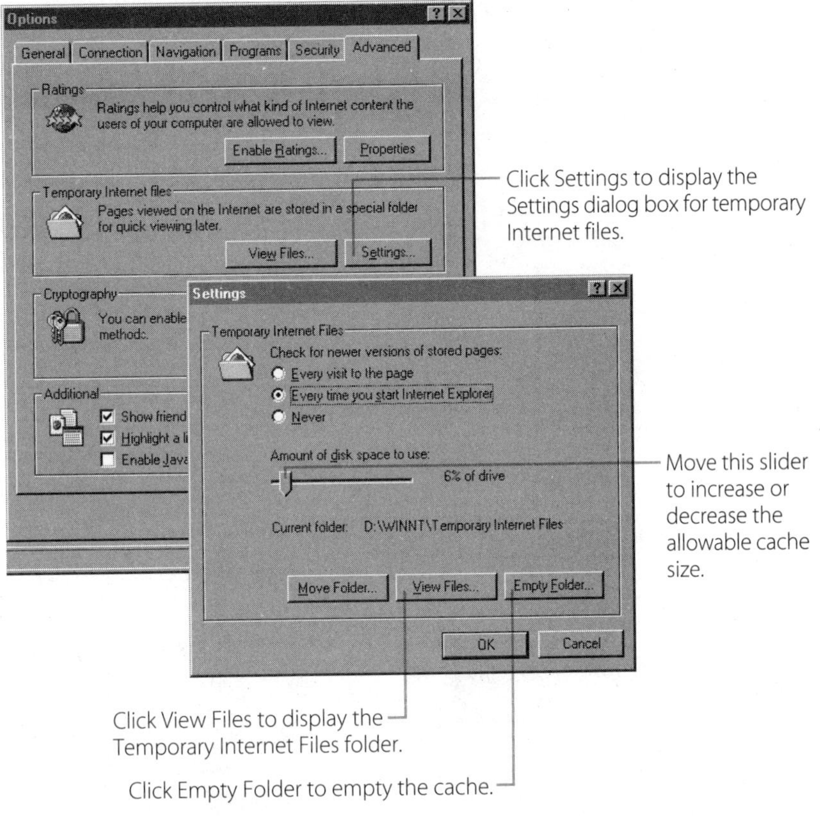

By default, if Internet Explorer finds a copy of the page you want in its cache, it uses the cached page instead of requesting another copy from the Web. Because Web pages change frequently, however, Internet Explorer checks once per session to see if the page on the Web is newer than the cached page. If the pages you're interested in never change (or you don't care if you see the latest version), you might want to override this behavior by selecting the Never option button.

Blocking Offensive Material

You can use Internet Explorer to block the display of Web pages that have been rated offensive on various scales using the Recreational Software Advisory Council (RSAC) rating system. To take advantage of this capability, you supply Internet Explorer with a supervisory password and then specify the types of Web-page content you want to block. Users will then be unable to see the blocked material unless they can supply the supervisory password.

To block the display of offensive Web pages, begin by displaying the Options property sheet and clicking the Advanced tab. In the Ratings section of the Advanced page, click Properties. You'll be asked to supply and confirm your supervisory password. After you've done that, you'll arrive at the Content Advisor dialog box, shown below.

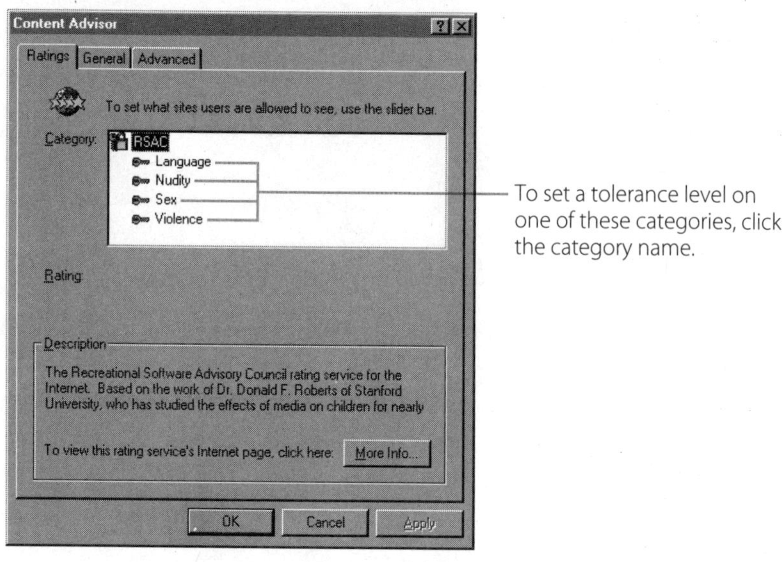

To set a tolerance level on one of these categories, click the category name.

After clicking a category name, you can use a slider to indicate how permissive or restrictive you want to be. Here, for example, is what you'll see if you select the Language scale:

Drag the slider to indicate what kind of material you want to block. Moving the slider to the right makes you more permissive. Moving it to the left has the opposite effect.

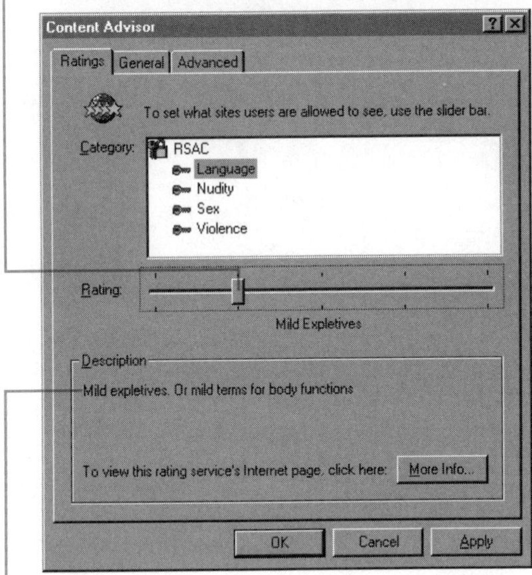

A description of the current setting appears here.

Blocking Unrated Sites

By default, Internet Explorer blocks only those sites that are rated offensive. Sites that are unrated are passed through to the user, as are sites that are rated inoffensive. If you want to block everything except sites that are rated inoffensive, display the Content Advisor dialog box and click the General tab. The dialog box shown in Figure 13-4 on the next page appears.

FIGURE 13-4.
The General page lets you block unrated sites, bypass blocking, and change the supervisory password.

Deselect this check box to block all sites except those rated inoffensive.

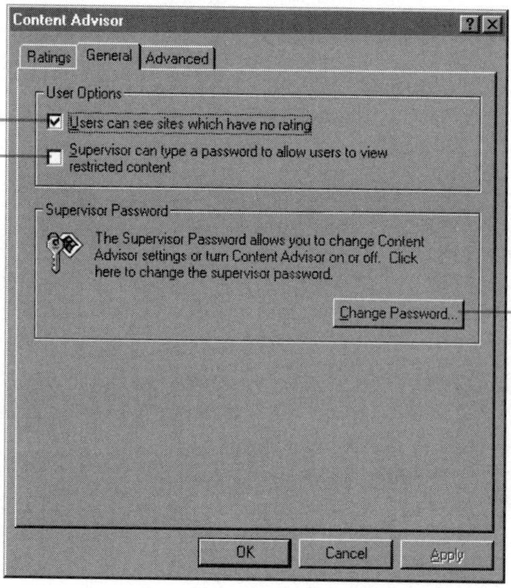

Select this check box if you want users who know the password to be able to bypass blocking.

Click Change Password to change your supervisory password.

Allowing a User to Bypass Blocking

Normally, your supervisory password is used only to turn the entire blocking mechanism on or off. If you want, however, you can allow a user to see a blocked page by supplying the password when he or she attempts to access the blocked Web page. To do this, display the Content Advisor property sheet and click the General tab. On the General page, shown in Figure 13-4, select the check box labeled "Supervisor can type a password to allow users to view restricted content."

Changing Your Supervisory Password

To change your supervisory password, display the Content Advisor property sheet and click the General tab. You will see the dialog box shown in Figure 13-4. Click the Change Password button.

Turning Off Blocking

If you change your mind about blocking offensive material, simply display the Options property sheet and click the Advanced tab. On the Advanced page, click the Disable Ratings button and enter your supervisory password.

Working with Web Pages

Surfing the Web with Internet Explorer is fine, but what can you do with the information you find? This section describes how to do the following:

- Print a Web page
- Save a Web page as a document on your computer
- Create a shortcut to a page that you can reuse or share with others
- Use a displayed image as your desktop wallpaper
- Search for text within a page

Printing a Web Page

SEE ALSO

For more information about printing, see "Printing from an Application," page 211.

Internet Explorer allows you to print any Web page; simply go to the File menu and choose Print. This brings up the common Print dialog box. This capability can be very useful when viewing long pages, or if you want to read some information while you are away from the computer.

 **TIP**

Printing Hyperlink Addresses

You might want to print the URLs of a page's hyperlinks for future reference. To do so, in the Print dialog box select the check box labeled "Print shortcuts in a table at the end of a document."

Saving a Web Page to Disk

With Internet Explorer you can save any Web page to a disk file on your computer. However, because most World Wide Web documents are created using HTML, you will have to consider what format to save them in. When you choose the Save As File command from the File menu, you can choose to save the Web page in either of two formats: HTML or Plain Text.

If you save the page in HTML format, all of the special HTML formatting codes remain intact, but you need a Web browser, such as Internet Explorer, to view it properly. If you save the page in Plain Text format, you lose all of the HTML formatting commands, but you can load the text in almost any application.

Creating Shortcuts to Web Pages

SEE ALSO

For more information about shortcuts, see "Using Shortcuts to Run Programs and Open Documents," page 73.

Internet Explorer allows you to use shortcuts to Web pages anywhere on the Internet. Once you create an Internet shortcut, you can keep it on the desktop, send it in an e-mail message to your friends, or embed it within a document in another application.

To create a shortcut for the Web page currently displayed in Internet Explorer, simply go to the File menu and choose the Create Shortcut command. (The shortcut you create, in fact, is identical to those stored in the History folder and in the Favorites folder. The Create Shortcut command simply provides an easy way to create a shortcut on your desktop.)

Once the shortcut is created, you can move it, copy it, or rename it as you see fit. To use the shortcut, simply double-click its icon, and Internet Explorer will take you to that Web page. You can use the shortcut even when Internet Explorer is not running; like other document shortcuts, shortcuts to Internet destinations launch their associated application—in this case, Internet Explorer—if it's not already running.

Using Drag and Drop on Web Pages

You can drag and drop images and text from the Internet Explorer document area to other applications or to the desktop. For example, suppose you are viewing the Microsoft home page, and decide that you would like a copy of one of the page's graphic images to place in a file on your desktop. You can do this by following these steps:

1. Make sure that Internet Explorer is not maximized, and that a portion of the desktop is visible.
2. Click the image you want and, while holding down the mouse button, drag it to the desktop. You will see the mouse pointer change as you start to drag.
3. Release the mouse button when the pointer is on the desktop. You will see an icon appear representing the image you just copied.

You can also drag and drop images to areas other than the desktop. Any application that can accept an image file can receive a Web-page image by drag and drop.

You can drag and drop text by selecting the text you want, and then using the same procedure described above. Of course, you can also move information via the Clipboard. Standard Cut, Copy, and Paste commands are available on Internet Explorer's Edit menu.

Turning a Web Image into Wallpaper

SEE ALSO
For more information about wallpaper, see "Using Patterns, Wallpaper, and Screen Savers," page 103.

If you see an image that you like on a Web page, Internet Explorer can save that image and install it as your desktop wallpaper. To do this, simply right-click any image in Internet Explorer. In the context menu that appears, select Set As Wallpaper to use the image as your Windows wallpaper.

Finding Text on a Web Page

Many Web pages have large amounts of text. To find a specific phrase or word in a large Web page, you can use Internet Explorer's Find command. Follow these steps to use this command:

1. Display the Web page on which you want to find a specific word or phrase. (The Find command works only on a single page at a time.)
2. Choose the Find (On This Page) command from the Edit menu.
3. Type the text you are looking for. You can type part of a word or the entire word.
4. Click the Find Next button, and Internet Explorer takes you to the next occurrence of your search text in the document.

Downloading Files from the Internet

On some World Wide Web sites, files are available for you to download to your computer. These files are usually shown in Internet Explorer as hyperlinks. To download a file, simply click the hyperlink that represents the file. You will then see a dialog box like this:

Select Open It to launch the file without saving it.

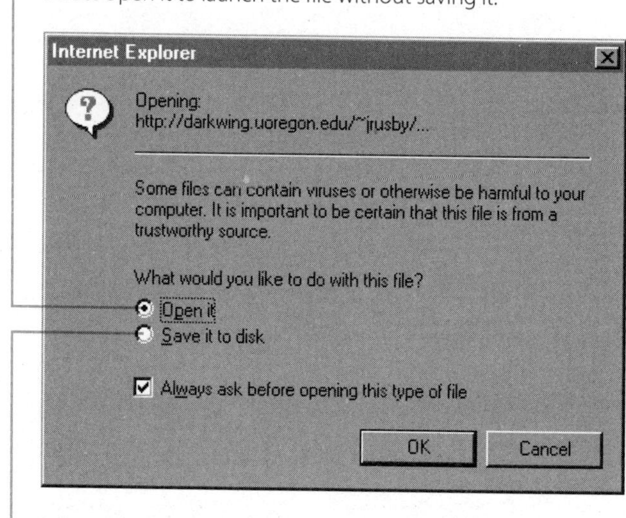

Select Save It To Disk to save the file without launching it.

If the file you're downloading is a sound file or video clip that you want to play, a program that you want to run, or a document that you want to display immediately in a word processor or other application, choose the Open It option. Otherwise, choose Save It To Disk. If you choose Open It, Windows NT will render the data, just as it would if you double-clicked an entry in a folder or Windows NT Explorer window. If you choose Save It To Disk, Internet Explorer presents a Save As dialog box after it finishes downloading the data.

TIP

Use the Stop Tool to Abort
If you start downloading a file and then change your mind, click the Stop button on the toolbar to stop the download.

Connecting to FTP and Gopher Sites

Some parts of the Internet are set up differently than the World Wide Web. Two such parts of the Internet are FTP (file transfer protocol) sites and gopher sites. These types of Internet sites usually consist of lists of documents and files for downloading. Internet Explorer provides the same interface for these Internet sites as it does for the World Wide Web, so you don't need to learn anything new to access information on Internet FTP or gopher sites.

TIP

Check the URL
One way to determine what type of site you are viewing is by checking the address: Internet addresses usually have the name of the service at the beginning. For example, the URL for Microsoft's FTP server is ftp://ftp.microsoft.com; the URL for the WELL gopher site is gopher://gopher.well.com.

To connect to an FTP or gopher site, simply enter the URL for the site you want to connect to in the same way you would for a World Wide Web page. Just as with World Wide Web addresses, you can do this with the address bar or with the File Open command.

For example, an anonymous connection (one that doesn't require a password) to the Microsoft Corporation FTP site looks like this:

> ftp://ftp.microsoft.com

To connect to an FTP server that requires you to provide your username and password, use this format:

> ftp://*name:password*@ftp.microsoft.com

(Replace *name* and *password* with the logon information assigned by the server administrator.)

PART 3

Using the Power of Windows NT

CHAPTER 14

Customizing Windows NT

In Chapter 4, we looked at some of the ways in which you can tailor your working environment to meet your preferences. Specifically, that chapter explored options for personalizing the appearance of your desktop, the responsiveness of your mouse and keyboard, and the various utterances offered up by your computer's speakers. In this chapter we'll address a few more ways in which you can customize Windows NT. Here we'll look into procedures for doing the following:

- Adjusting the date and time
- Changing modem settings
- Changing dialing settings
- Setting the volume levels for your speakers, microphone, and headphones
- Setting the window size for video playback
- Specifying "regional" settings, such as date and time formats, the default symbol for currency, and the symbol for a decimal point
- Setting up different keyboard layouts, such as the Dvorak layout or a layout for a different language
- Using Windows' support for multiple languages
- Choosing options to improve accessibility for users with special needs

Introducing Control Panel

Your key to nearly all customizing options in Windows NT—everything except options relating to your taskbar and Start menu—is a system folder called Control Panel. The easiest way to get to this folder is to choose Settings from the Start menu, and then choose Control Panel from the submenu that unfolds. Figure 14-1 shows what the Control Panel folder looks like on one of the systems used to create this book.

Your own Control Panel might not look exactly like Figure 14-1. You might have additional icons not shown in the figure, and you might lack certain icons that are shown. When Windows NT was installed, the setup program populated Control Panel with items appropriate for your hardware, and possibly also for the access privileges accorded to you by your system administrator.

Some Control Panel functions are available only when you're logged in as a member of the Administrators (or some other high-powered)

FIGURE 14-1.
The Control Panel folder contains property sheets and wizards that help you customize Windows.

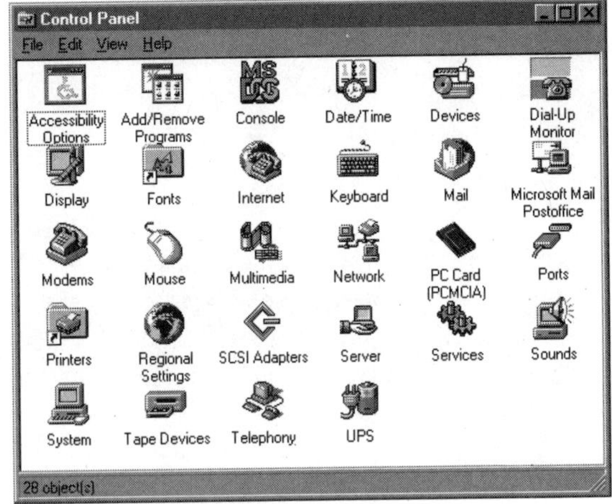

TIP

Quick Control Panel Access

Here's a nifty trick that adds a cascading Control Panel menu to your Start menu, which gives you quicker access to the Control Panel applets:

1. Right-click the Start button and choose Open.
2. In the Start Menu window that appears, right-click and choose New and then Folder.
3. Replace the folder's name (New Folder) with this mouthful: *Control Panel.{21EC2020-3AEA-1069-A2DD-08002B30309D}*

(Be sure to type everything exactly as shown, including the curly brackets.)

group. If you try to use one of these functions without the proper authority, you'll be politely, but firmly, rebuffed with an "access denied" message.

SEE ALSO
One way you can make changes for several users is with a logon script. For information about logon scripts, see "Specifying a Logon Script," page 556.

Many changes you make in Control Panel affect only the user who is currently logged in. This allows you to customize your workspace without imposing your tastes on others who share your workstation. But it also means that global changes you want to make must be made individually for each user.

In this chapter, we'll investigate the following items, which are common to most Windows NT systems: Date/Time, Modems, Telephony, Multimedia, Regional Settings, Keyboard, and Accessibility Options. Table 14-1 shows the Control Panel items that are discussed elsewhere in this book.

TABLE 14-1. Control Panel Items Described in Other Chapters

Icon	For Information, See
Add/Remove Programs	"Adding or Removing Parts of Windows NT," page 696, and "Installing Applications," page 699
Console	"Customizing Command Prompt Windows," page 506
Devices	"Customizing a Hardware Profile," page 437, and "Starting and Stopping Device Drivers," page 718
Dial-Up Monitor	"Using Dial-Up Networking Monitor," page 426
Display	"Controlling the Amount of Information That Fits on Screen," page 92, "Changing Colors, Fonts, and Text Sizes," page 97, "Using Patterns, Wallpaper, and Screen Savers," page 103, and "Installing a Display Adapter," page 710
Fonts	Chapter 8, "Installing and Using Fonts"
Internet	"Customizing Internet Explorer," page 356
Keyboard	"Adjusting the Keyboard Repeat and Cursor Blink Rates," page 115, and "Installing a Keyboard," page 711
Mail	Chapter 12, "Using Windows Messaging"

(continued)

TABLE 14-1. *continued*

Icon	For Information, See
Mouse	"Setting Preferences for Your Mouse," page 113, and "Installing a Mouse," page 712
Network	"Setting Up the Remote Access Service," page 416, and "Installing a Network Adapter," page 712
PC Card (PCMCIA)	"Installing PC Card Adapters," page 716
Printers	Chapter 9, "Installing, Configuring, and Using Your Printers"
SCSI Adapters	"Installing a SCSI Adapter," page 715
Server	"Monitoring System Use with Server," page 662
Services	"Starting the Remote Access Server Service," page 422, and "Customizing a Hardware Profile," page 437
Sounds	"Assigning Sounds to Events," page 111
System	"Using Hardware Profiles," page 434, "Initializing Environment Variables," page 538, and "Adjusting Virtual Memory Settings," page 722
Tape Devices	"Installing a Tape Drive," page 716
UPS	"Installing an Uninterruptible Power Supply," page 717

TIP

Creating Shortcuts to Control Panel

You can create shortcuts for any item in Control Panel or for the Control Panel folder itself. Follow the same procedures you would use to create any other kind of shortcut. For example, to create a desktop shortcut for Control Panel's Accessibility Options icon, simply right-drag the icon to your desktop, and then choose Create Shortcut(s) Here from the context menu.

Adjusting the Date and Time

Your computer uses its system date and time to time-stamp files when they are created or changed, to schedule events, and, naturally, to show you the current date and time.

The time normally appears in the taskbar. (If it's not there, right-click an unoccupied are of the taskbar, choose Properties, and then select Show Clock.) To display the date, let your mouse pointer hover for a moment on the taskbar's clock.

TIP

Making the Big Time

If you have to squint to see the taskbar clock, don't get new glasses. Instead, try the Clock application, which resides in the Accessories folder. Clock displays the time (and, optionally, date) in a resizable window that you can place anywhere on your screen.

Control Panel provides a simple way to adjust your system date and time settings. You'll find this feature handy if you transport your computer into a new time zone. Double-click the Date/Time icon in Control Panel, and the Date/Time property sheet appears.

NOTE

You must be logged on as a member of the Administrators or Power Users group to set the date and time. Changes you make here affect all users on your workstation.

Use the Date & Time tab to adjust your system's clock or calendar.

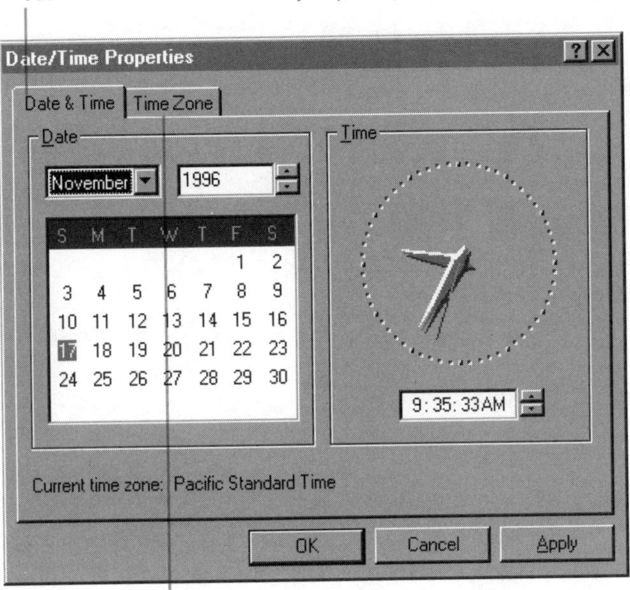

Use the Time Zone tab if you're moving to a different time zone, or to enable or disable Windows' automatic adjustment for daylight saving time.

TIP

You can also get to the Date/Time property sheet by double-clicking the time on your taskbar.

On the Date & Time tab, you can adjust the day of the month by clicking on the calendar. To choose a different month or year, select from the drop-down list and spinner above the calendar. To change the time of day, click the appropriate portion of the time edit box, and then use the spinners to the right of the edit box. For example, if the clock says 2:36 P.M., but it's really only 2:31, select the 36 and then click the downward spinner arrow five times. (Unfortunately, you can't adjust the time by dragging the hands on the clock.) If the clock says A.M., but it's actually P.M., click on or beside the "AM" and then click either spinner arrow once. After you've set the time, click Apply or OK to start the clock running again.

> **TIP**
>
> To change the display format used by the clock—for example, to change AM and PM to am and pm—use the Time tab of the Regional Settings property sheet. *For more information, see "Specifying Regional (International) Settings," page 387.*

On the Time Zone tab, select your time zone from the drop-down list at the top of the dialog box. Windows uses this information to track time information for files saved on a network that operates across multiple time zones.

Windows can automatically adjust your system's clock when daylight saving time begins or ends. If you want to use this feature, select the Automatically Adjust Clock For Daylight Saving Changes check box, on the Time Zone tab of the Date/Time property sheet.

> **TIP**
>
> **Synchronizing Your Computer's Clock with Another**
>
> If your computer is connected to a Windows NT, Windows 95, or Windows for Workgroups network, you can set your computer's clock to match the time on another computer in your network. To do so, choose the Run command from the Start menu, and type *net time \\computer /set /yes*, where *computer* is the name of the computer you want to synchronize with. (If your computer is a member of a domain, you can simply type *net time /domain /set /yes* to set your clock to match the domain controller's clock.) To synchronize your clock automatically each time you start Windows, create a shortcut with this command and place it in your Startup folder.

Changing Modem Settings

You might want to adjust some of your modem's settings from time to time. For example, you might decide that you don't need to hear the modem's speaker every time it dials, or that you'd rather hear it at a lower volume level. You can make these and other adjustments via the Modems item in Control Panel.

NOTE

You must be logged on as a member of the Administrators or Power Users group to change modem properties. Changes you make here affect all users on your workstation.

SEE ALSO

For information about dialing properties, see "Changing Dialing Settings," page 383.

You can also use the Modems item in Control Panel to let automatic dialing programs know the area code of the location in which you work. With this information, your programs can distinguish between local and long-distance calls, and dial appropriately. You can also set up multiple dialing locations, which are useful if you travel with your computer.

To change your modem or dialing settings, start by double-clicking the Modems icon in Control Panel. You will arrive at the Modems property sheet, shown below. To inspect or change the settings for a modem:

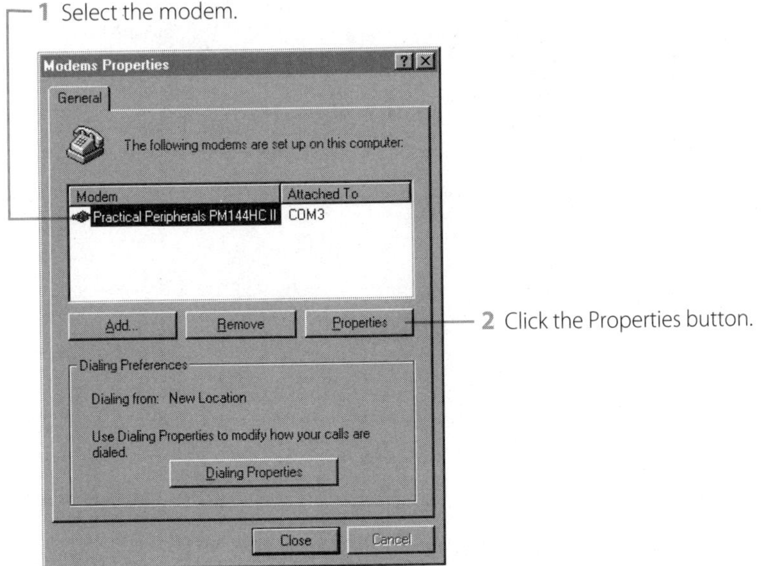

In the center of the property sheet, Windows lists all the modems currently attached to your system. When you click the Properties button, you'll see a property sheet for the selected modem. The options available on that sheet depend on the modem you're using. Figure 14-2 shows the choices for a Practical Peripherals modem.

SEE ALSO

For information about adding or removing a modem, see "Installing a Modem," page 713.

For this modem, the available options include the communications port, speaker volume, and maximum speed. Additional options on the Connection tab allow for adjustments to communications parameters—including data bits, parity, and stop bits. You might want to investigate all the tabs of your modem's property sheet to see what choices are available.

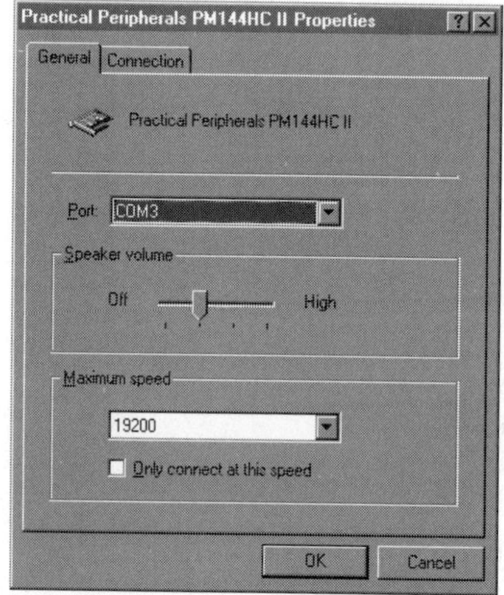

FIGURE 14-2.
The property sheet for your modem might let you adjust the communications port, the default speaker volume, maximum speed, and default communications settings (on the Connection tab, in this example).

NOTE

Settings on the modem property sheet are merely defaults. Communications programs can override these defaults.

Changing Dialing Settings

To facilitate dialing, Windows NT keeps track of several settings: your telephone area code, special codes you must dial to access an outside line, whether you use a calling card, and so on. This way, you don't have to enter all this information in every program that uses your modem; you just enter the number you want the program to dial.

If your computer travels with you, you might need different dialing settings for each location. By selecting a different location, all your programs are ready to dial without any additional changes.

To change the settings for your dialing location, or to add new dialing locations, double-click the Telephony icon in Control Panel. This brings you to the Dialing property sheet, shown in Figure 14-3.

TIP

If you already have the Modems property sheet open, you can open the Dialing property sheet by clicking the Dialing Properties button.

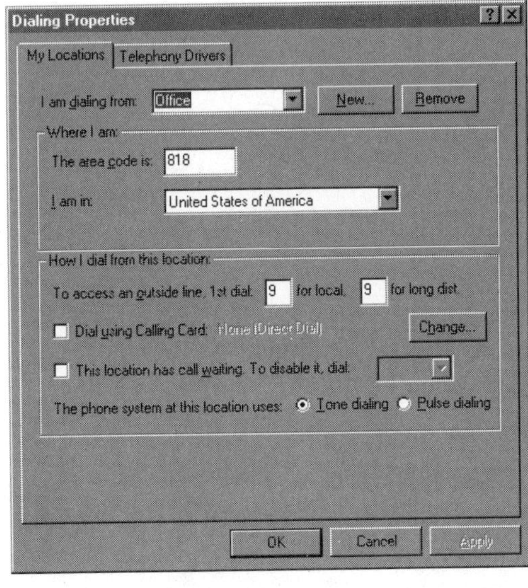

FIGURE 14-3.
The Dialing property sheet lets you specify the area code and country, as well as any access numbers required for local and long-distance calls.

NOTE

Settings on the Dialing property sheet are used only by "TAPI-aware" applications—that is, programs that take advantage of Microsoft's telephony applications programming interface (TAPI). All of the communications programs included with Windows NT—Windows Messaging, Dial-Up Networking, Phone Dialer, and HyperTerminal—are TAPI-aware. Most other communications programs written expressly for Windows NT version 4 or Windows 95 are also TAPI-aware.

This property sheet should already have settings in place for at least one location, identified as New Location. If you have set up additional locations, you can see the settings for those locations by choosing from the I Am Dialing From drop-down list. Make sure the settings are appropriate for the location from which you call.

TIP

If the phone line used by your modem has call waiting, be sure to indicate that on the Dialing property sheet, and also specify what code is used to disable the call-waiting feature. Otherwise, if an incoming call arrives while your modem is active, the call-waiting signal can disconnect the modem.

To add a new dialing location, click the New button and provide a name for the new location. After you do that and click OK, you'll be returned to the Dialing property sheet, where you can supply the area code and other settings for the new location.

NOTE

Make entries in the "local" and "long distance" text boxes only if you need to dial a number to get an outside line at this dialing location. Do not enter a long-distance dialing prefix, such as a "1," in the "long distance" box.

The Telephony Drivers tab lets you add or remove drivers that control your modem and other communications features. You shouldn't need to change the settings here. (Clicking the Configure button when the standard modem driver is selected merely provides a circuitous path to the Modems property sheet.)

Setting Volume Levels

If your computer has a sound card, you can adjust the volume of sound sent from the sound card to your speakers, the volume level for the microphone jack, and the volume of sound sent out through the headphone jack of your CD-ROM drive. To do any of these things, start by double-clicking the Multimedia icon in Control Panel. This action summons the Multimedia property sheet.

To change the speaker or microphone volume, click the Audio tab of the Multimedia property sheet.

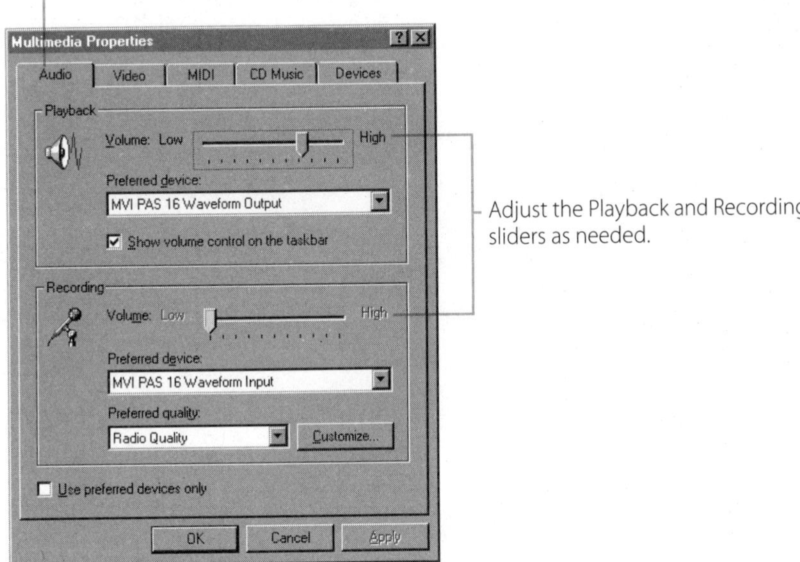

If your computer has more than one playback and recording device, you can specify the one that Windows will use by choosing from the drop-down lists in the Playback and Recording sections of the dialog box. And if your system is capable of recording at more than one quality level, choose the level you prefer from the Preferred Quality drop-down list in the Recording section of the dialog box. Be aware that higher-quality recording generates larger sound (.WAV) files.

If you select the Show Volume Control On The Taskbar check box, you can change the speaker volume level by clicking the volume icon in your taskbar's notification area. If you want to adjust the volume for a particular sound source (instead of the master speaker volume control), *double-click* the taskbar volume icon, which opens the Volume Control application.

To set the volume level used by your CD-ROM when it's playing music CDs through the headphone jack, click the CD Music tab. In the ensuing dialog box you'll find another volume slider along with a drop-down list from which you can select the drive you want to adjust (in case your computer has more than one CD-ROM drive).

Setting the Video Playback Size

The Video tab of Control Panel's Multimedia property sheet lets you specify the size at which video (.AVI) files are played back. With the default setting in effect, .AVI files are played at the same size at which they were recorded. This provides the smoothest playback and minimum graininess. But you might want to enlarge the playback size to see more detail. You can do that by double-clicking the Multimedia icon in Control Panel and then clicking the Video tab. You'll see a dialog box similar to the one shown below.

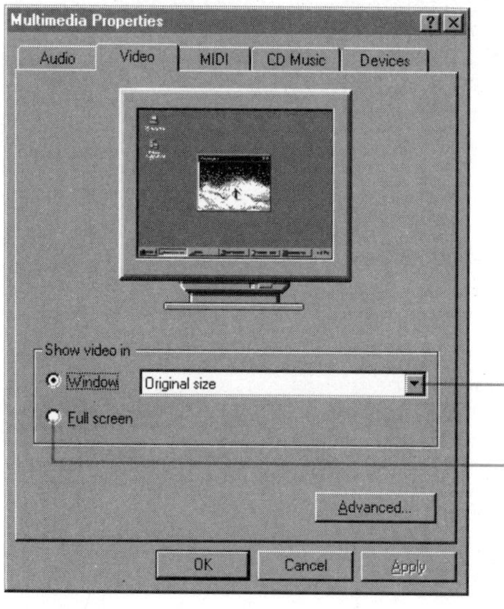

To choose a windowed playback size, open the Window drop-down list.

To play your video clips in a full screen, rather than in a window, select the Full Screen option button.

TIP

You will probably get smoother playback in full-screen mode than you will in a maximized window.

Specifying Regional (International) Settings

The Regional Settings icon in Control Panel allows you to adjust the way Windows displays dates, times, currency amounts, large numbers, and numbers with decimal fractions, as well as whether Windows should employ the U.S. or the metric system of measurement. This section of Control Panel corresponds to what was called International in earlier versions of Windows.

To modify any of Windows' regional settings, start by double-clicking the Regional Settings icon in Control Panel. You will see the six-tabbed property sheet shown below.

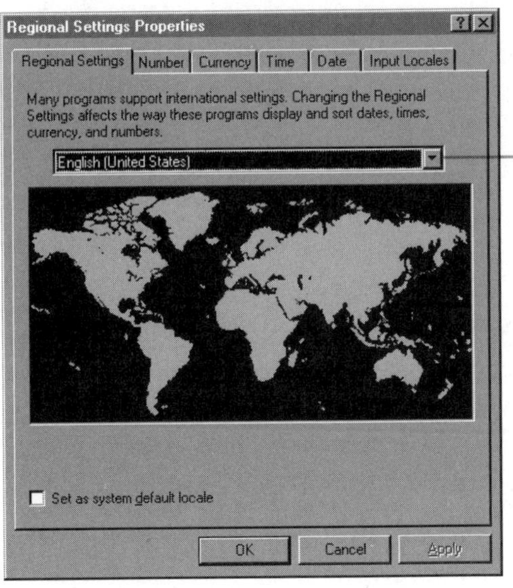

Select a country from the drop-down list to change many regional settings in one fell swoop.

On the first page of the Regional Settings property sheet, you'll find a map of the world. If you're adjusting your system for a new country—for example, if you've just taken your portable computer overseas—start by selecting the new country. In response, Windows applies the default settings for all adjustable items—numbers, currency, times, dates, and language—all at once. In most cases, you won't need to make any further changes.

When you select a country on the Regional Settings page, you're also selecting that country's language, which is used for the display of dates and selection of spell-checking dictionaries. But selecting a country does not change the keyboard layout, on the assumption that just because you're crossing a border you're not going to leave your keyboard behind. To specify a different keyboard layout or to restore your mother tongue as the display language, use the Input Locales page. *For details, see "Installing Language Support and Using Keyboard Layouts," page 389.*

To override one or more default settings for a country, click the appropriate tab of the Regional Settings property sheet and fill out the dialog box that appears. Figure 14-4 shows the dialog box you'll see if you click the Number tab. Note that the Measurement System drop-down, near the bottom of this dialog box, lets you switch between the U.S. and metric measurement systems.

TIP

To display the time in 24-hour format, click the Time tab. In the Time Style drop-down list, select a format that begins with a capital *H*. And if your marching orders require you to use military time, which includes a leading zero and no punctuation, type *HHmm* in the Time Style box.

All the settings in the Regional Settings property sheet are merely defaults. Windows makes your choices available to applications, but the applications are not required to use them. Some programs ignore the Windows default settings and instead maintain their own

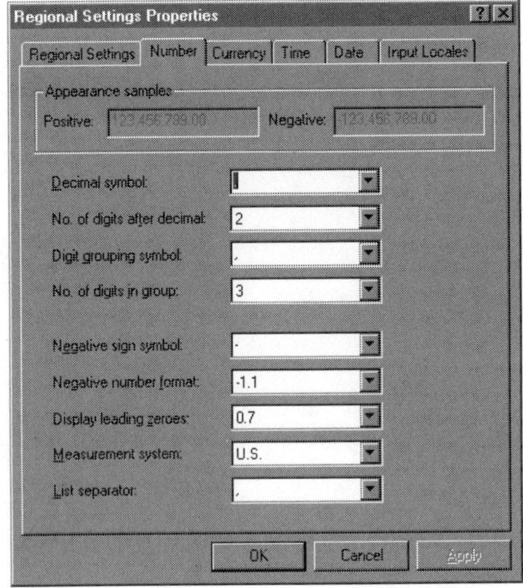

FIGURE 14-4.
On the Number tab, you can choose display formats for decimals and large numbers, and a default measurement system.

formatting defaults. If you ask for a particular display format style via Control Panel, but your application uses a different style, consult the documentation or help file for your application.

Installing Language Support and Using Keyboard Layouts

Windows NT comes with support for a multitude of languages and keyboard layouts. If you work in more than one language or communicate with speakers of other languages, you might find it convenient to have two or more languages installed simultaneously. You can then use simple mouse and keyboard procedures to switch from one language to another.

Languages and layouts are separate but related issues. When you activate another language, applications that were written with language support in mind can provide appropriate services, such as using a different spelling checker or using special characters in TrueType fonts.

Each language has an associated default keyboard layout, but you can choose alternative layouts. Even if you work only in English, you might want to check out alternative layouts. Typing letters with accents, for example, might be simpler if you use the US–International layout. And if the standard QWERTY system of typing isn't your preference, you can opt for the US–Dvorak layout.

Installing a New Language

You can install support for a new language as follows:

1. In Control Panel, double-click the Keyboard icon or the Regional Settings icon; you can install language support from either.
2. Click the Input Locales tab.

   These steps take you to the Input Locales page of the Keyboard (or Regional Settings) property sheet, as shown in Figure 14-5.
3. Click the Add button and select the language you want from the drop-down list.
4. If you want to use the language's default keyboard layout, select the Use Default Properties For This Input Locale check box. Deselect it to use your current layout.

NOTE

> Windows might prompt you to insert the Windows NT CD-ROM.

Before leaving the Keyboard or Regional Settings property sheet, select one of the option buttons for switching locales. By default, you can switch from one locale to another by holding down the Alt key on the left side of your keyboard and pressing either Shift key. If you prefer, you can opt for the combination of Ctrl and Shift instead. Or you can turn off switching-by-keystroke altogether.

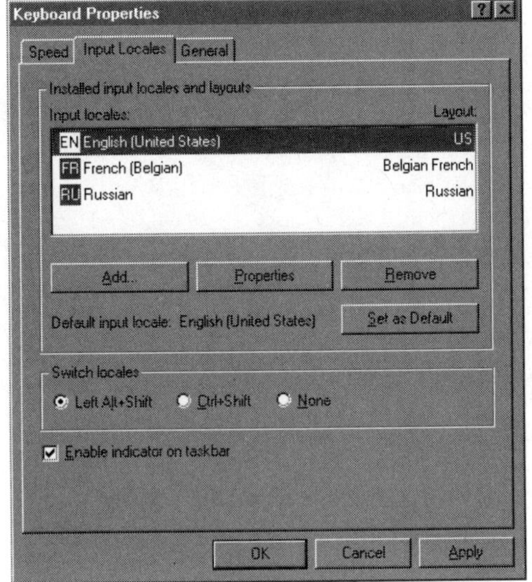

FIGURE 14-5.
In the Keyboard property sheet, you can add support for other languages or switch keyboard layouts.

By default, Windows displays a two-letter symbol in the notification area of your taskbar whenever you have more than one language installed. You can use this symbol both as a reminder and as a switching mechanism. To switch languages, click the language symbol and then choose from the list that pops up. If, for some reason, you don't want this convenience, deselect the Enable Indicator On Taskbar check box at the bottom of the Keyboard or Regional Settings property sheet.

TIP

You can go directly to the Keyboard property sheet without running Control Panel by right-clicking the language symbol in the notification area of your taskbar and choosing Properties from the context menu.

Switching Keyboard Layouts

To switch keyboard layouts, first go to the Input Locales page of the Keyboard or Regional Settings property sheet in Control Panel, following steps 1 and 2 in the previous section. Select the language for which you want to switch layouts, and then click the Properties button. Then select the layout you want from the drop-down list that appears.

Choosing Accessibility Options

Windows offers a wide range of options to make your computer easier to use in special situations or if you have special needs. Whether you work in a noisy environment, have impaired sight or hearing, find using a mouse inconvenient, or cannot use both hands for typing, the Accessibility Options icon in Control Panel provides a solution. For example, you can choose accessibility options to:

- Use Ctrl, Alt, and Shift key combinations without holding down more than one key at a time
- Use visual cues instead of sounds to alert you to system events
- Use the keyboard instead of the mouse to click, double-click, and drag
- Use an alternate input device attached to your serial port

If people with different needs use your computer, set up a different account for each user. *For information about user accounts, see "Creating an Account," page 536.*

If your Control Panel does not include an Accessibility Options icon, double-click the Add/Remove Programs icon. Then click the Windows NT Setup tab and select Accessibility Options in the Components list. Click OK to begin installation. You'll then need to close and reopen Control Panel for the Accessibility Options icon to appear.

To see the available accessibility options and choose the ones you need, begin by double-clicking the Accessibility Options icon in Control Panel. You will see the tabbed property sheet shown below.

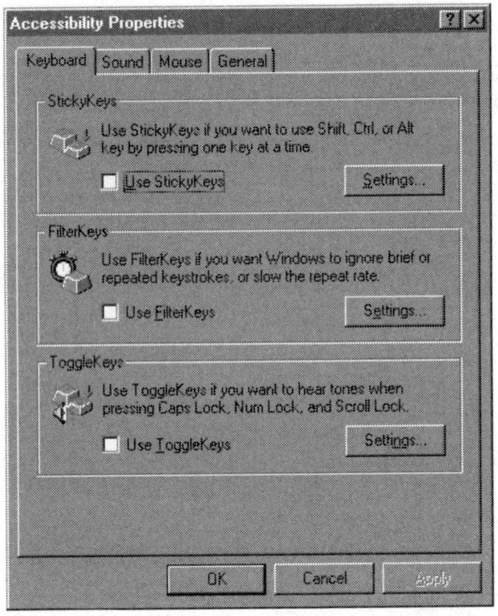

Changing Accessibility Options for the Logon Prompt

After you make the settings you want in the Accessibility property sheet, click OK. Windows NT then displays this message box:

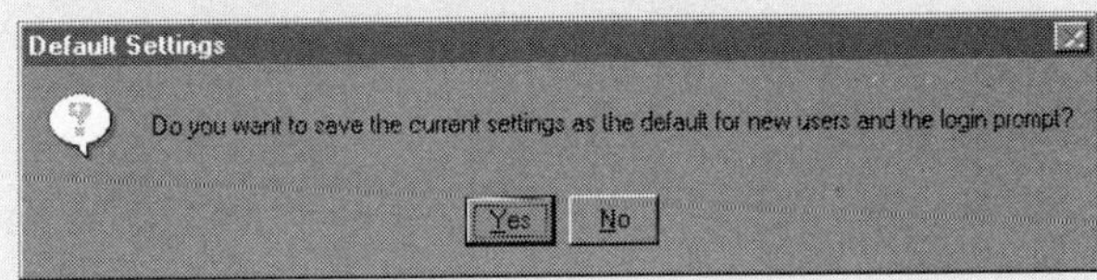

Click Yes to make the settings effective for your own user account, for all new user accounts to be added to this machine, and for the logon prompt, which normally requires you to press Ctrl-Alt-Del before you can log on.

If you click No, your new settings affect only your own user account.

Emergency Shortcuts

Each keyboard accessibility option includes an "emergency shortcut" that allows you to turn the option on or off using only the keyboard. You'll find the shortcut handy when people who need different options use the same computer. It is also especially useful when a user needs an option turned on to gain initial access to the computer. The emergency shortcut eliminates the need to open Control Panel to turn the option on, a task that might be difficult or impossible without the option activated.

Option	**Shortcut**
StickyKeys	Press either Shift key five times.
FilterKeys	Hold down right Shift for eight seconds.
ToggleKeys	Hold down Num Lock for five seconds.
MouseKeys	Press left Alt, left Shift, and Num Lock simultaneously.

If no one who uses your computer needs a particular accessibility option, consider disabling its shortcut by choosing Settings on the Accessibility property sheet and deselecting the Use Shortcut check box. That way, the option can't be turned on accidentally. If you later discover you need the option, simply reselect the Use Shortcut check box.

Keyboard Options

The Keyboard page of the Accessibility property sheet allows you to control how Windows handles keyboard input.

- StickyKeys allows you to type keystroke combinations without the need to hold down one key while you press another.
- FilterKeys can be set to ignore accidentally repeated keystrokes or brief keystrokes that are made by touching a key in error.
- ToggleKeys provides an audible notification whenever you press the Caps Lock, Num Lock, or Scroll Lock key.

StickyKeys

The StickyKeys option allows you to type key combinations, such as keyboard shortcuts, by pressing the required keys in sequence rather than simultaneously. For example, the keyboard shortcut to select all items in a window, Ctrl-A, normally requires you to hold down the Ctrl key while simultaneously pressing the A key. If you are using just one hand or a mouthstick, pressing multiple keys at the same time can present a problem. StickyKeys is the solution.

StickyKeys makes the Ctrl, Alt, and Shift keys *sticky:* when you press one of these *modifier keys*, the key remains locked down until you press and release any other key (except for Ctrl, Alt, or Shift) or a mouse button. When you press a Ctrl, Alt, or Shift key twice, the key remains locked down until you press the same key a third time.

To turn on StickyKeys, select the Use StickyKeys check box on the Keyboard tab of the Accessibility property sheet. Alternatively, you can use the StickyKeys keyboard shortcut to turn the option on or off. Simply press either Shift key five times.

The StickyKeys option has several settings you can adjust to your liking. To do so, click the Settings button to open the property sheet shown below. Then select or deselect the check boxes as your needs dictate.

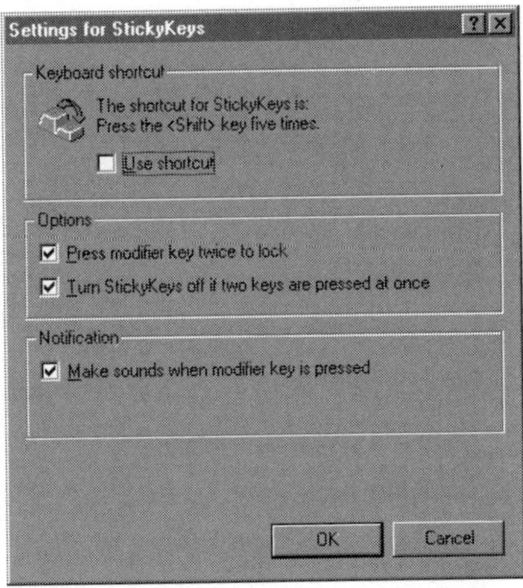

- When the Use Shortcut check box is selected, pressing the Shift key five times activates or deactivates StickyKeys. To disable this keyboard shortcut, deselect the Use Shortcut check box.
- By default, StickyKeys allows you to lock a modifier key (Ctrl, Alt, or Shift) by pressing the key twice. The modifier key remains locked until you press it a third time. As a general rule, if you need StickyKeys at all, you should leave this option enabled. You can, however, disable it by deselecting the Press Modifier Key Twice To Lock check box.
- If several people use the same computer, keep Turn StickyKeys Off If Two Keys Are Pressed At Once enabled, as it is by default. With this check box selected, users who don't require StickyKeys can turn off the feature simply by pressing a modifier key and any other key at the same time. This option is great for multiple users—the StickyKeys feature can be kept on for those who need it, and users who don't need it can use standard key combinations.
- Make Sounds When Modifier Key Is Pressed can provide useful auditory feedback each time a Ctrl, Alt, or Shift key is pressed. It's a handy reminder that StickyKeys is active. If, however, you're the only user and have no need to be reminded, deselect this check box.

TIP

One-Hand Keyboard Layouts

Windows NT includes two Dvorak keyboard layouts designed for single-handed users. There's one for people who use only their right hand, and one for those who use only their left. These layouts also work if you type with a single finger or a mouthstick. No additional equipment is required to use these layouts. *For information about installing these layouts, called "US–Dvorak for right hand" and "US–Dvorak for left hand," see "Switching Keyboard Layouts," page 392.*

FilterKeys

The FilterKeys option provides precise control over the keyboard repeat rate. It is particularly useful when involuntary hand movements cause accidental key presses. To activate this option, select the Use FilterKeys check box on the Keyboard tab of the Accessibility property sheet.

You can adjust several FilterKeys settings. To do so, click the Settings button to open the property sheet shown below.

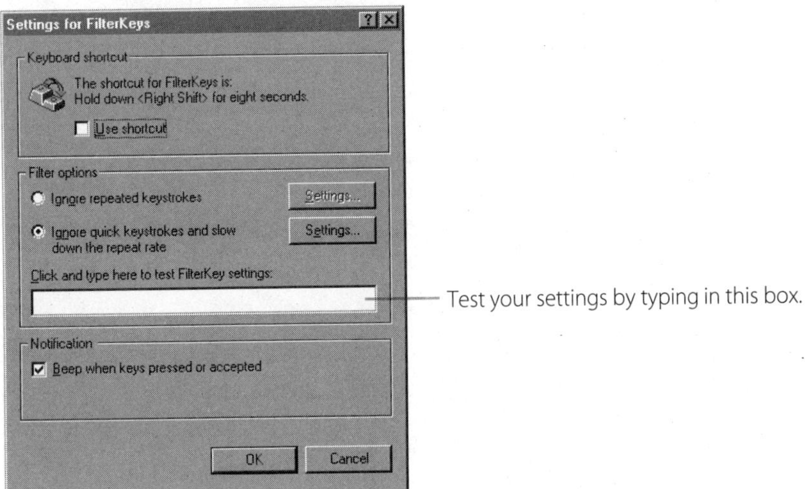

- When the Use Shortcut check box is selected, pressing and holding the right Shift key for eight seconds activates or deactivates FilterKeys. To disable this keyboard shortcut, deselect the Use Shortcut check box.
- Use the Ignore Repeated Keystrokes option button to instruct Windows to ignore all but the first keystroke when a key press is rapidly repeated. Click the Settings button to adjust and test the minimum time within which repeated keystrokes are ignored.

SEE ALSO
For more information about setting the keyboard repeat rate, see "Adjusting the Keyboard Repeat and Cursor Blink Rates," page 115.

- The Ignore Quick Keystrokes And Slow Down The Repeat Rate option causes the computer to ignore keys that are pressed only briefly. When FilterKeys is active, these settings override Control Panel's Keyboard repeat settings. Click the Settings button to adjust and test the time settings for this option. Select No Keyboard Repeat on the Advanced Settings property sheet to turn off the keyboard repeat feature altogether. With this option selected, it doesn't matter how long you hold down a key; it won't repeat under any circumstances.
- The Beep When Keys Pressed Or Accepted check box, when selected, causes the computer to beep twice for each successful keystroke. The computer beeps whenever a key is pressed, and beeps a second time when the keystroke is accepted because it's been held down the requisite time.

ToggleKeys

The ToggleKeys option causes Windows to sound a tone each time the Caps Lock, Num Lock, or Scroll Lock key is pressed. The only ToggleKeys setting you can make is to enable or disable the keyboard shortcut.

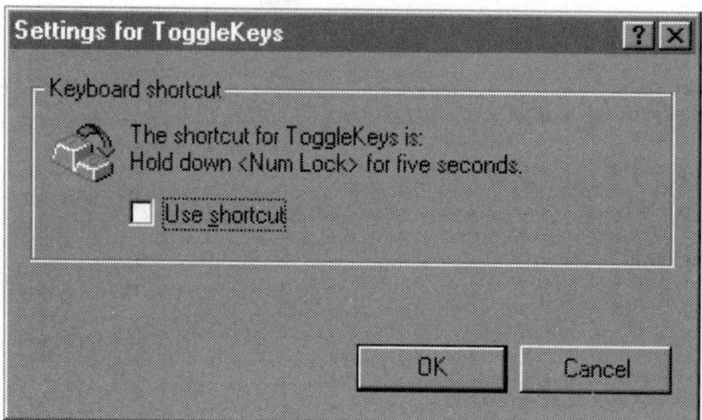

- When the Use Shortcut check box is selected, pressing and holding the Num Lock key for five seconds activates or deactivates ToggleKeys. To disable this keyboard shortcut, deselect the Use Shortcut check box.

Sound Options

The options on the Sound page of the Accessibility property sheet are useful if you are hearing-impaired or work in a noisy environment.

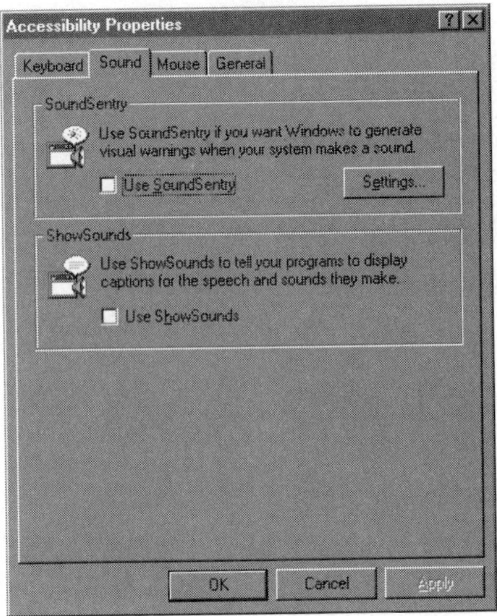

SoundSentry

The SoundSentry option causes Windows to display a visual cue whenever your computer beeps. To turn on SoundSentry, simply select the Use SoundSentry check box.

Click the Settings button to specify which part of the screen flashes when a program plays a sound.

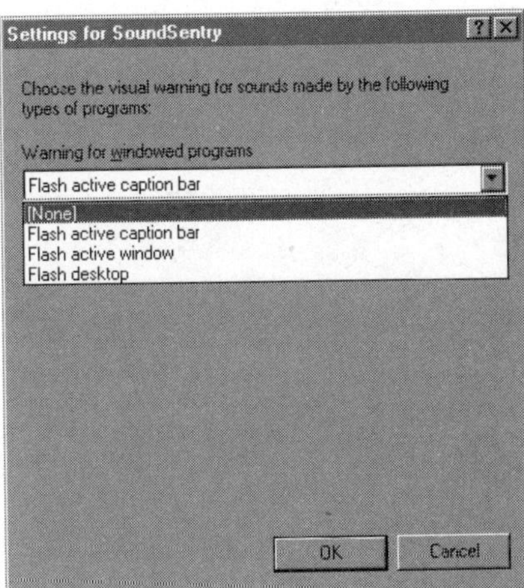

> SoundSentry visual cues occur only when your system plays a sound through its internal speaker. (Most programs that use the internal speaker are MS-DOS–based programs.) Sounds played through external speakers via a sound card do not invoke SoundSentry.

ShowSounds

ShowSounds is the Windows equivalent of closed-captioned television. In applications that use digitized speech or other audible cues, ShowSounds instructs the application to provide visible feedback, such as text captions. Not all programs have this capability. To turn on ShowSounds, simply select the Use ShowSounds check box.

Mouse Alternatives

Yes, it is possible to use Windows NT without a mouse. Although most mouse actions in Windows have a keyboard alternative, some tasks can be performed only by moving the mouse pointer, clicking, and dragging. The MouseKeys option allows you to use the numeric keypad to simulate these mouse actions.

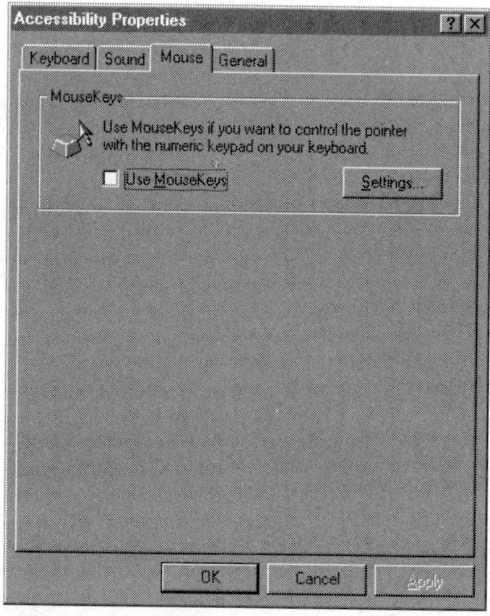

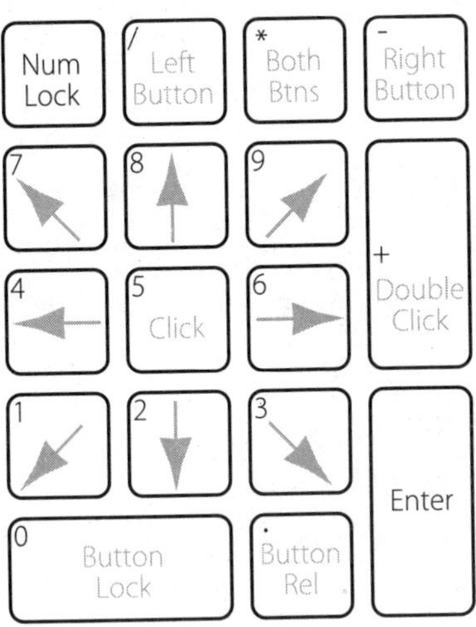

With MouseKeys, you can use the numeric keypad, shown above, to do the following:

- To move the mouse pointer, press any number key except 5 or 0. The arrows in the illustration above show the direction in which each key moves the pointer. If you hold down a directional number key, the mouse pointer begins moving slowly and then accelerates to its maximum speed.
- To select which mouse button to use for clicking and dragging, press the slash (/) key to select the left button, the minus (–) key to select the right button, or the asterisk (*) key to select both buttons. Your selection stays in effect until you select another; you don't need to select a button before each click or drag.
- To click the selected button, press the 5 key.
- To double-click the selected button, press the plus (+) key.
- To drag with the selected button, position the mouse pointer on the object and press the 0 key (Ins). Then use the directional number keys to move the mouse pointer. Press the decimal point (.) key (Del) to "release" the mouse button, which completes the drag operation.

You can adjust several MouseKeys settings. To do so, click the Settings button to open the property sheet shown below.

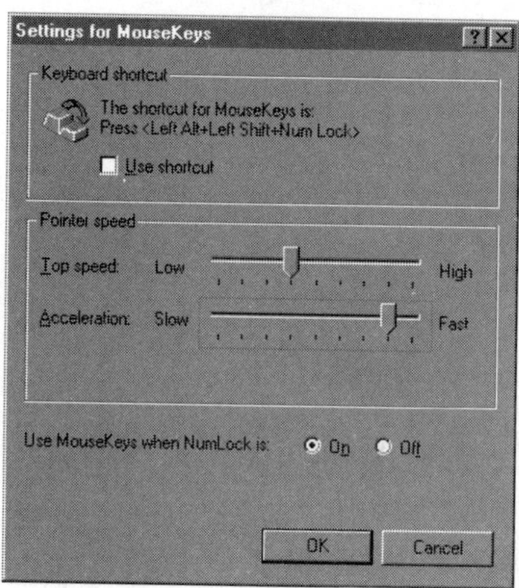

- When the Use Shortcut check box is selected, pressing the left Alt, left Shift, and Num Lock keys simultaneously, activates or deactivates MouseKeys. To disable this keyboard shortcut, deselect the Use Shortcut check box.
- Adjust the Top Speed slider to set the mouse pointer's maximum speed when you hold down a directional number key.
- Adjust the Acceleration slider to control how quickly the mouse pointer reaches its top speed when you hold down a directional number key.
- The option buttons at the bottom of the property sheet determine whether MouseKeys are active when your keyboard's Num Lock setting is on or off. If you normally use the keyboard's numeric keypad for its arrow keys, select On. If you normally use the numeric keypad as a 10-key number pad, select Off. This way, you can use the numeric keypad as you normally do. When you want to use the keypad to control the mouse pointer, press the Num Lock key to change the Num Lock setting.

General Settings

The General tab of the Accessibility property sheet lets you choose whether Windows automatically turns off accessibility features and how Windows notifies you when a feature is turned on or off.

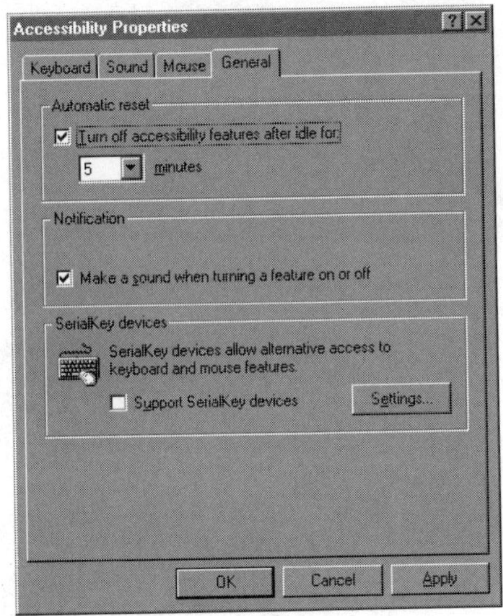

- You can instruct Windows to deactivate accessibility features that haven't been used for a specified time period, from 5 minutes through 30 minutes. Select the Turn Off Accessibility Features After Idle For check box, and then select a time in the Minutes drop-down list.
- The Notification option instructs Windows to play a sound when any accessibility feature is turned on or off.
- The SerialKey devices option lets you use an alternate input device attached to your computer's serial port.

CHAPTER 15

Windows NT to Go: Mobile Computing

If your work requires you to travel, you know that computing on the road presents a number of challenges. You need to work in a physically scaled-down environment, you need to be able to get your electronic mail via modem, and you need to be able to access information stored on a computer or server at your office. In addition, there is the headache of synchronizing files that you carry with you on your laptop with versions of the same files stored at the office.

Windows 95 has a reputation as the preferred operating system for portable computers, and it does offer some important features not included in Windows NT, including power management and Plug and Play support. However, if you're used to using Windows NT, and if your portable computer has the requisite horsepower to run Windows NT, you'll find that it makes a perfectly suitable traveling system.

The following Windows NT features can help reduce the trials and complexity of mobile computing:

- The new Briefcase utility makes it easy to synchronize your traveling files with the files on your office system. You simply pack your Briefcase when you're ready to travel and unpack it when you return.
- Dial-Up Networking (and a suitably equipped server at your office), lets you can stay current with data stored at the office. Dial-Up Networking also makes it easy to send and receive electronic mail while you're away; you simply use the same procedures you would use at the office, and Windows NT makes the connections via modem.
- Hardware profiles acknowledge the reality that a traveling system is not a single, static, system. It might be a standalone computer, a network workstation, or both, spending part of the day attached to a docking station. With plug-in PC Card adapters, accessories can come and go as your needs dictate. Windows NT lets you set up a hardware profile for each configuration you use.
- The Telephony section of Control Panel lets you set up multiple sets of dialing parameters for different calling locations—area codes, calling-card numbers, and access numbers, for example. While you're traveling, any dialing or communications application that's written for Windows NT or Windows 95 can dial appropriately from any of your locations. *For information about setting up dialing locations, see "Changing Dialing Settings," page 383.*

Synchronizing Files with Briefcase

When you travel, you might need to take copies of documents stored on your office computer or network server. On return, you'll want to recopy any of those files that you've changed back to the folders from which they came. Sometimes synchronizing mobile and home-base document versions is a simple matter, but sometimes it's not. If you copy a great many files to your traveling machine, for example, it can be a nuisance to figure out which ones you really need to copy back to the office computer and which ones you don't. The matter becomes even more complex if you have one computer for home use and one for the office. If you regularly work at both computers, you probably have parallel copies of important documents on each, and you need to be careful not to overwrite a later version of a file with an earlier version.

The Briefcase utility takes care of these details for you. When you put a copy of a file in a Briefcase, Windows keeps track of where the file came from and always knows which version of the file—the one in the Briefcase or the one outside the Briefcase—is the more current. An Update command, available from Briefcase's menu bar or context menu, automatically updates the older version with the newer.

TIP

You can also use Briefcase to synchronize document versions on your office computer and a network server.

The basic procedure for using Briefcase is as follows:

1. Open an existing or new Briefcase on your portable computer.
2. Copy into this Briefcase all documents that you need to travel with.
3. While traveling, work with your documents in the Briefcase.

TIP

Work on Documents Inside Your Briefcase

Don't move a document out of the Briefcase to work on it. If you do, Windows can no longer keep track of which version of the document is the current version. If you don't want to work on a document in its present location—for example, if it's stored in a Briefcase on a floppy disk—move the entire Briefcase.

4 On return, open the Briefcase and use either the Update All or the Update Selection command.

The details vary, however, depending on whether or not your portable computer can be connected via network to your office computer. *For details, see "Using Briefcase with a Network Connection" and "Using Briefcase with Floppy Disks," on the next page.*

TIP

Right-Drag Into Your Briefcase

If you right-drag a file into a Briefcase, the default option on the context menu is Make Sync Copy. This is the option you want. When you make a sync copy, Windows duplicates the file and at the same time records (in a hidden Briefcase file) information about the file's properties. It uses this information later to determine which version of the file is current.

When you right-drag a folder into a Briefcase, the context menu includes the Make Sync Copy command as well as a Make Sync Copy Of Type command. Make Sync Copy copies the entire folder (including all files and subfolders) into the Briefcase. Make Sync Copy Of Type lets you make sync copies of particular file types only—for example, all Microsoft Excel spreadsheets.

Creating a Briefcase

You might find an icon labeled My Briefcase on your desktop. If you do not see this icon, right-click the desktop (or within any folder window), choose New from the context menu, and choose Briefcase from the submenu that appears. Once created, a Briefcase looks and acts like an ordinary folder in most respects: it appears as an icon in its parent folder window and in Windows NT Explorer windows (albeit with a unique icon), its contents are displayed when you double-click its icon, and so on.

By default, a new Briefcase you create is given the name New Briefcase. Like other objects in Windows, you can rename a Briefcase by selecting its icon and pressing F2.

Using Briefcase with a Network Connection

You'll find it easiest to use Briefcase if you first connect your laptop to your office network. Then you can simply copy as many files as you need from your networked office computer to the Briefcase on your portable computer. When it comes time to synchronize, reconnect to the network. Then use the Update All or Update Selection command from the Briefcase on the portable computer.

Using Briefcase with Floppy Disks

If your portable and office computers cannot be connected, you must use floppy disks as intermediaries between the two machines. In this case, you need to be aware of one limitation: a Briefcase cannot span multiple disks. This doesn't mean you can take only one floppy disk's worth of files on the road. Rather, it means you might need to take along multiple Briefcase folders. Here's the procedure:

1. Put a floppy disk (preferably a freshly formatted one) into your office computer's floppy drive.
2. Open My Computer and double-click the icon for your floppy drive.
3. In the floppy drive's folder window, right-click, choose New, and then choose Briefcase.

   The first time you open a new Briefcase, a Briefcase wizard appears. Simply click Finish to dismiss the wizard. When you do this, the wizard sets up your new Briefcase, creating the hidden files that Windows will use to track the status of your files.

4 Copy files into this new Briefcase until the floppy disk is somewhat less than full. Don't fill the disk, because your files need room to grow as you work with them.

5 Insert the floppy disk into your portable computer's floppy drive and move the Briefcase to your portable's hard disk.

NOTE

You can work directly on the floppy disk if you prefer, but moving the Briefcase to the hard disk offers several advantages:

- You don't need to carry floppy disks (or a floppy disk drive, if it's an external unit) when you travel.
- Access to files is faster on a hard disk.
- A hard disk is more reliable.

6 Repeat steps 1 through 5 using as many floppy disks as you need, but give each Briefcase a unique name before moving it to your portable computer.

7 On your return, move each Briefcase back to a floppy disk, transfer the disk to your office computer, and use the Update All or Update Selection command.

Getting Status Information About Briefcase Files

In icon view, the inside of a Briefcase looks pretty much like the inside of any other folder window, except for the presence of a Briefcase menu. But if you switch to details view, Briefcase provides useful information about the provenance and status of your documents. As shown below, you can see which files have changed since you copied them into the Briefcase.

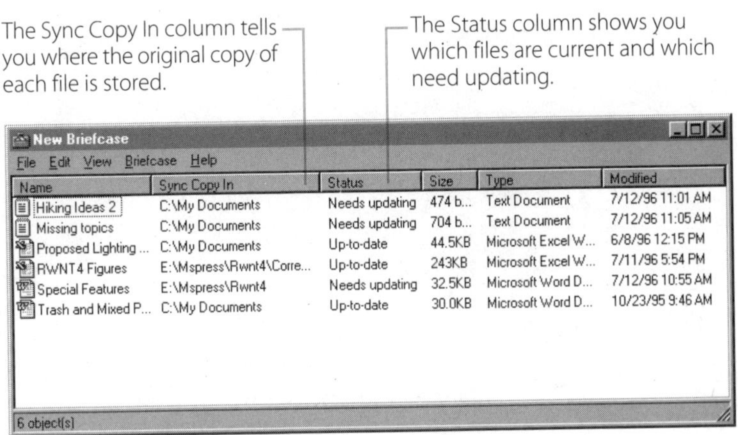

When your Briefcase is on line with the computer on which it was created (for example, when your portable is connected to your office computer network, or when the Briefcase is on a disk in the office computer's floppy drive), you can get status information about a particular file by right-clicking it and viewing the Update Status page of its property sheet. Figure 15-1 shows the Update Status page for a file that has been changed in the Briefcase.

FIGURE 15-1.
The property sheet for a Briefcase file can tell you where the file's sync copy resides and which version of the file is more current.

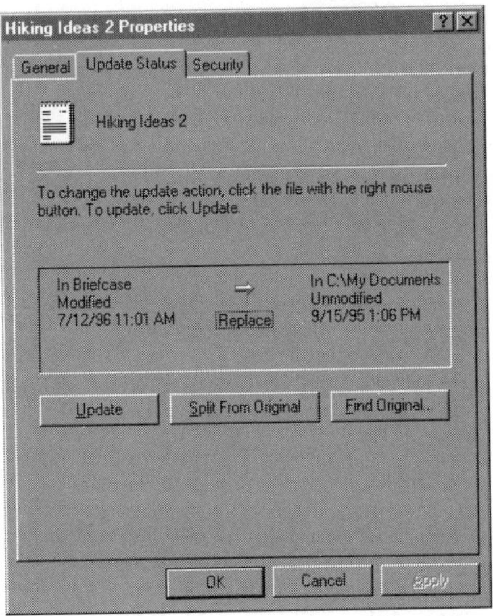

Updating Files

When you're ready to synchronize your Briefcase files with their sync copies (the original copies outside the Briefcase), you can either work with one file at a time or update the whole Briefcase at once. To update a single file, select it, and then choose Update Selection from the Briefcase menu. (You can also update a group of selected files this way. Hold down the Ctrl key while you click each file you want to update. Then choose Update Selection.)

To update the entire Briefcase, choose Update All. You'll see a dialog box similar to the one shown in Figure 15-2.

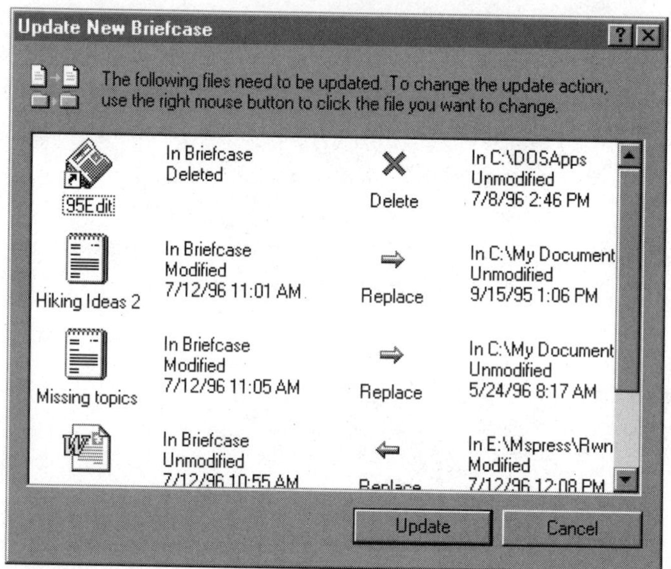

FIGURE 15-2. When you choose Update All, Windows uses left-pointing and right-pointing arrows to show which copy of each changed file is newer.

Notice that the Replace arrows in the center of the dialog box can point either direction, depending on which version of a file is most current. When you click the Update button, Windows replaces the older version of each file, wherever it resides, with the newer version.

If the update action that Briefcase proposes for an item is not the action you want, right-click its entry in the update dialog box. Then, from the context menu (shown below), choose the action you prefer.

To copy the "sync" version over the "in Briefcase" version, right-click the file's icon and choose this Replace command.

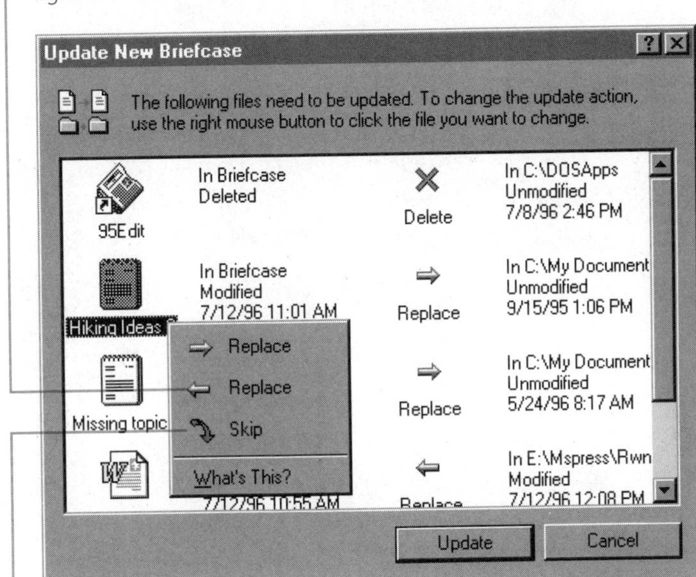

To prevent changes to either file, choose Skip.

Divorcing a Briefcase File from Its Sync Copy

If you move a file from a Briefcase to any other folder, the link between that file and its sync copy is broken. The result is an ordinary copy. You can also sever the link between a file and its sync copy without removing it from the Briefcase. To do this, select the file and choose Split From Original from the Briefcase menu. In Briefcase's Status field, your file will then be listed as an *orphan*. You can carry as many orphans as you please in your Briefcase.

Creating New Files While Traveling

While you're on the road, you'll probably create new files as well as modify existing ones. Any such files that you store in your Briefcase will also enjoy orphan status. Briefcase's Update commands will not copy these files to your desktop machine for you (because Briefcase would not know where they should go), but you can do that manually by using the same techniques you would use to copy files between any two ordinary folders.

Deleting Files from a Briefcase

When you delete a file from a Briefcase, its icon disappears from the Briefcase window, as you might expect. But the file's sync copy remains in place, and Briefcase remembers this association. When you choose Update All, information about the deleted file appears alongside the information about other files that have changed. The first entry shown in Figure 15-2 on page 412 shows how Briefcase presents information about a deleted file. At this point, you have three options:

- You can accept the default update action, which is to delete the sync copy of the file that you already deleted from the Briefcase.

WARNING

Accepting the default update action (Delete) deletes the original file in addition to the Briefcase copy you already deleted. Be sure this is what you want before you accept that choice!

- You can re-create the Briefcase copy. To do so, right-click the file's icon and choose Create.
- You can leave the sync copy in place, and let Briefcase forget about the file it once contained. To do so, right-click the file's icon and choose Don't Delete. If you choose this option, the file will no longer appear in the update dialog box.

NOTE

If you delete the sync copy instead of deleting the Briefcase copy, choosing Update Selection or Update All presents similar options. If you choose the third option, Don't Delete, the Briefcase copy becomes an orphan.

Using Dial-Up Networking

Dial-Up Networking allows you to connect to a computer at another site using your modem. The computer to which you connect is called the *remote access server*. The computer initiating the call (your computer) is called the *remote access client*, or *Dial-Up Networking client*. Altogether, this feature of Windows NT is called *remote access service*, or *RAS*. Dial-Up Networking is the name of the application that controls the process from the remote computer.

Alternative Connection Options

In addition to using a modem with a standard telephone line, remote access clients can connect to a remote access server via ISDN (a high-speed digital telephone service), X.25 (a wide-area network connection through a packet-switching network), or Point-to-Point Tunneling Protocol (PPTP), a protocol that permits secure access to corporate networks through the Internet. Because these acronym-drenched options require significant hardware and software setup effort by the administrator of a Windows NT Server system—a topic that is beyond the scope of this book—we'll leave it to that administrator to set up the hardware and software needed on your system to make the connection. Once the system is set up, however, you'll find that using a connection through the routes mentioned above is similar to using the dial-up connection described in the sections that follow.

Dial-Up Networking lets you access shared resources on the remote access server—and, because the remote access server typically acts as a gateway to additional network servers, other network resources as well. Once you've connected to the remote access server, you can:

- Browse the remote network using Network Neighborhood
- Access remote folders and files using UNC path specifications
- Map remote folders to drive letters on your own computer
- Access remote printers

SEE ALSO

For information about Network Neighborhood, using remote folders and files, and mapping folders to drive letters, see Chapter 11, "Using and Sharing Files on the Network."

In other words, all the techniques you use to work with local-area network resources function the same way with a remote, or wide-area, network.

For Dial-Up Networking to work, the computer you connect to must be configured to act as a remote access server. A Windows NT Server system acting as a remote access server can handle up to 256 remote sessions at once. A system running Windows NT Workstation or Windows 95 with Microsoft Plus! can also be set up to act as a remote access server, but it can handle only one remote client at a time. (Windows 95 alone does not include the ability to act as an RAS server, but RAS server support for Windows 95 is included in Microsoft Plus!) RAS software and hardware to handle multiple remote sessions is also available from other vendors.

If you have Windows NT 4 at both ends of the connection (that is, as client and server), you use the same remote access service on both computers. The sections that follow describe how to set up and use the Windows NT remote access service. You'll also see how to use the Windows NT remote access service to connect to a remote access server that is running an operating system other than Windows NT 4.

Setting Up the Remote Access Service

Whether you're planning to use your computer as a remote access server or as a Dial-Up Networking client, you must first install and configure the remote access service. It can be set up when Windows NT is originally installed on a computer (by default, the Setup program sets up the remote access service if it detects that the computer is a laptop), or you can set it up later.

NOTE

To install and configure the remote access service, you must be logged on as a member of the Administrators group.

1 In Control Panel, double-click the Network icon to display the Network property sheet.

TIP

A faster way to reach the Network property sheet is to right-click the Network Neighborhood icon and choose Properties.

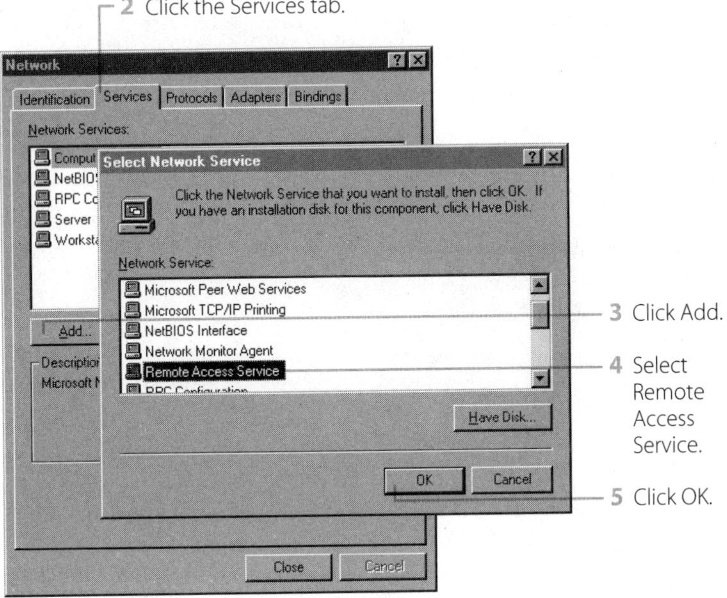

NOTE

If the Network Services list on the Network property sheet's Services page includes Remote Access Service, the remote access service is already installed. You can skip this entire procedure. If you select Remote Access Service and click Properties, you can confirm that the service is configured properly, and correct it if necessary. The dialog boxes that appear are the same as those shown here.

6 Windows NT then asks for the location of the setup files. Insert your Windows NT CD-ROM and correct the path shown, if necessary. Then click Continue.

No CD-ROM drive in your laptop? Put the Windows NT CD-ROM in a shared network drive and then connect to that drive while the laptop is connected to the network to access the files you need for setup. *For information about sharing drives and connecting to network drives, see Chapter 11, "Using and Sharing Files on the Network."*

After Windows NT copies the required files to your hard disk, the Add RAS Device dialog appears, as shown below.

SEE ALSO
For information about the modem setup wizard, see "Installing a Modem," page 713.

7 Select the port you will use for remote access. The list includes installed modems, multiport adapters, ISDN adapters, and X.25 smart cards. If the modem you want to use is not listed, click Install Modem and let the wizard set up your modem.

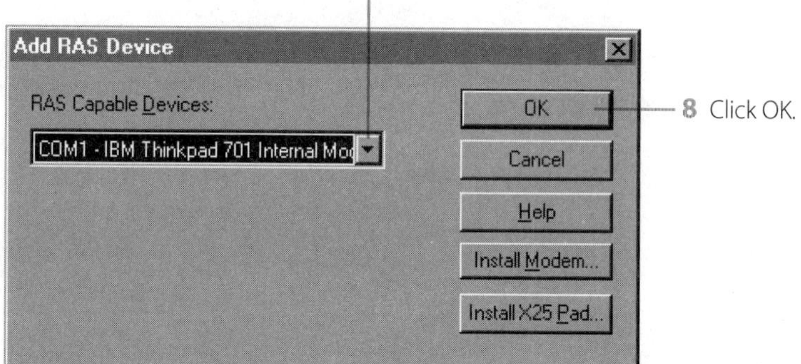

9 In the Remote Access Setup dialog box, select the port you're going to use and then click Configure.

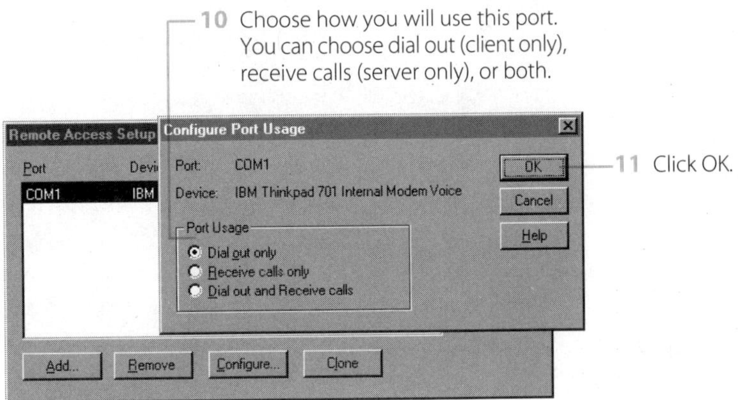

12 In the Remote Access Setup dialog box, click Network.

13 Select the protocol (or protocols) you will use for making Dial-Up Networking connections.

Network Configuration
Dial out Protocols:
NetBEUI
TCP/IP
IPX
OK
Cancel
Help

NOTE

If any ports on your system are set up to receive calls, the Network Configuration dialog box also includes server-related settings. With those settings, you can select which network protocols the remote access server will support, and for each protocol you select, you can restrict access to the server computer only or let remote clients access the entire network to which the server is attached. You can also set up TCP/IP and IPX addressing options.

Selecting a Network Protocol

Dial-Up Networking supports three network protocols: NetBEUI, TCP/IP, and IPX. You can use any or all. This means that you can use Dial-Up Networking to connect with a Microsoft (that is, Windows NT, Windows 95, Windows for Workgroups, or LAN Manager), UNIX, or Novell Netware network. You don't need to understand how a network protocol works (or even what it is!). The key to selecting a protocol for dial-up networking is that it must be the *same* protocol as the one that's used on the remote access server. If you don't know which protocol that is, ask your system administrator.

If you're setting up a server and a client on a small network, you'll find that NetBEUI is the easiest protocol to use because it doesn't require any additional configuration. TCP/IP requires each computer on the network to have an IP address, and Windows NT offers several methods for assigning IP addresses and correlating those addresses with machine names. Likewise, IPX requires assignment of an IPX address (network number) to each client, and additional services must be installed on the client and the server.

14 In the Remote Access Setup dialog box, click Continue.

15 In the Network property sheet, click Close.

You'll then need to restart your computer before you can use remote access.

Granting Dial-In Access

If you plan to use your computer as a remote access server (the computer that receives a call from a Dial-Up Networking client), you'll need to grant dial-in access to users who will connect to the server. To do that, you use User Manager, which is located in the Start menu's Administrative Tools (Common) group. Start User Manager and then follow these steps:

1 In User Manager, select the user (or users) to whom you want to grant dial-in access.

2 Open the User menu and choose Properties.

3 In the User Properties dialog box, click the Dialin button.

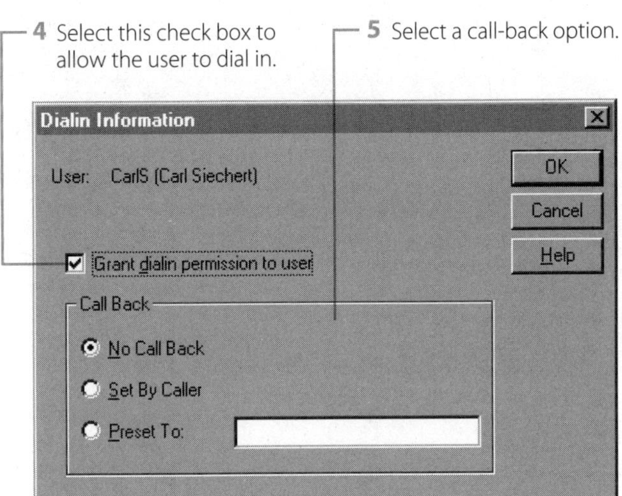

The call-back options can be used as an additional security measure as well as to determine who pays for the phone call. If you select an option other than No Call Back, when the server receives a call, it authenticates the user and then disconnects the call and dials the user's modem.

- Choose No Call Back if you want the remote user to make a connection with a single call to the server.
- Choose Set By Caller if you want the caller to be able to specify a phone number for a return call.
- Choose Preset To and specify a telephone number if you want the server to call the user at a particular number. This reduces the likelihood that an intruder who has come upon a valid username and password can access your system.

6 Click OK in the Dialin Information dialog box, and then click OK in the User Properties dialog box.

Starting the Remote Access Server Service

The Remote Access Server service must be running on the computer that you plan to use as a remote access server. When that service is running, any ports that are set to receive calls can be used only for remote access. You can't, for example, use a communications program to dial out using one of those ports. Therefore, by default, when you set up the remote access service, the Remote Access Server service is set to start manually at your command.

To start the Remote Access Server service, follow these steps:

1 Double-click the Services icon in Control Panel.

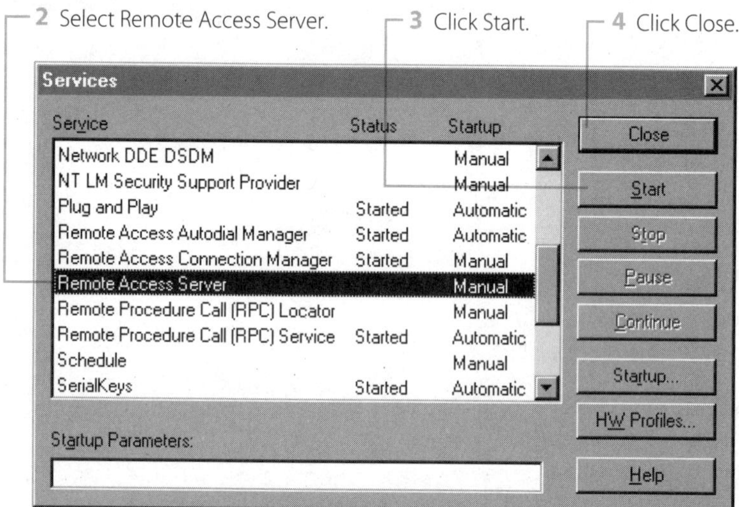

Your computer is now set to receive calls from remote users.

TIP

Start the Remote Access Server Service Automatically

If you want the Remote Access Server service to start automatically each time you run Windows NT, open the Services dialog box and select Remote Access Server. Then click Startup, select Automatic, and click OK.

Setting Up a Dial-Up Networking Phonebook Entry

If you set up Windows NT to include remote access service, you'll find an icon called Dial-Up Networking in your My Computer folder.

Before you can connect to a remote access server the first time, you need to set up a phonebook entry for the connection. You do that as follows:

1. Choose Dial-Up Networking from the Accessories section of your Start menu. Alternatively, open My Computer and double-click the Dial-Up Networking icon.
2. If you've never before set up a remote connection, step 1 displays an "empty phonebook" message. Clicking OK takes you directly to the New Phonebook Entry wizard.

   Otherwise, click the New button in the Dial-Up Networking dialog box.
3. In the wizard's first dialog box, type a descriptive name for your new phonebook entry. Then click Next to continue.
4. In the wizard's second dialog box, titled Server, select the options that are appropriate for the system you're going to connect with. Then click Next to continue.
5. In the wizard's Phone Number dialog box, select the Use Telephony Dialing Properties check box. Then supply the country, area code, and phone number required to connect to your remote access server. When you are finished, click Next to continue.

TIP

If you travel with your computer, be sure to select the Use Telephony Dialing Properties check box in the Phone Number dialog box. This way, if you dial from a different country or area code, Windows NT determines when it's appropriate to include the country code and area code, whether to use a calling card for billing, and so on. Then all you need to do is set up a dialing location when you move your computer. *For information about setting up a dialing location, see "Changing Dialing Settings," page 383.*

6 Click Finish to store the new entry in your Dial-Up Networking phonebook.

Connecting to a Remote Access Server

Once you've set up a Dial-Up Networking phonebook entry, you can access the remote server by selecting the entry in the Dial-Up Networking dialog box (shown below), and then clicking Dial. (To open the Dial-Up Networking dialog box, choose Dial-Up Networking from the Accessories section of your Start menu or open My Computer and double-click the Dial-Up Networking icon.)

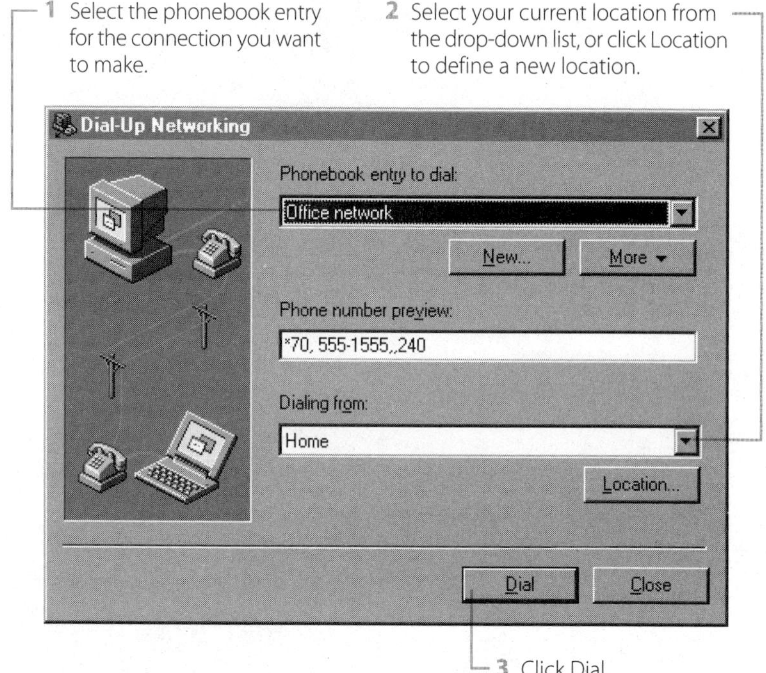

The first time you do this, you'll be asked to identify yourself by typing a username, password, and domain (or workstation name, if you're not logging on to a Windows NT Server domain) in a dialog box like the one shown below. Note that you must enter account information that's valid on the remote network—which may or may not be the same logon information you use to log on to your computer. (In addition to dialing your own company's network, for example, you might use Dial-Up Networking to connect with a client's network, or with an Internet service provider.)

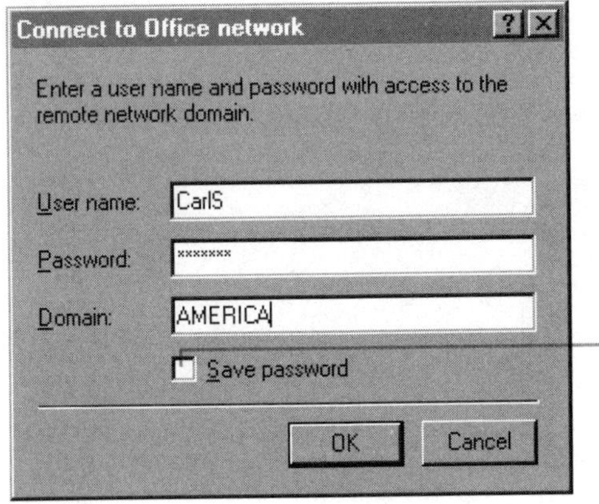

Select this check box to save yourself the trouble of retyping your password each time you connect. If you're concerned about the possibility that another user will use your computer to try to connect to your remote access account without your permission, do not select this check box.

To connect, click the OK button.

After you've connected to the remote server, and after the server has authenticated your logon information, a dialog box like the one shown on the next page appears. By default, the Dial-Up Networking dialog box closes upon successful connection to a remote server. (Thereafter, you control your call with Dial-Up Networking Monitor, which initially appears as an icon in the taskbar's notification area.)

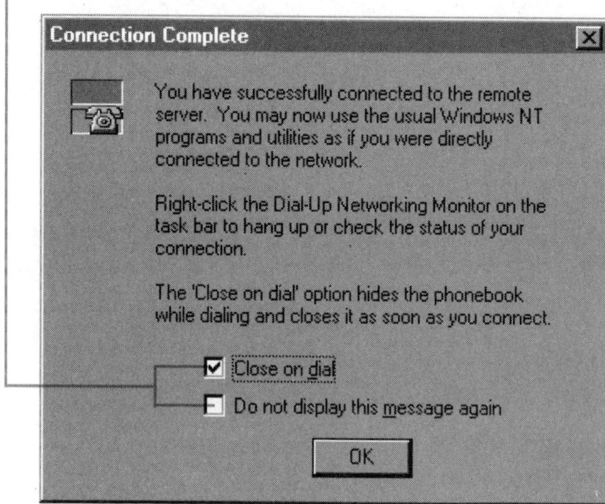

To see what resources are available while you're connected, double-click your Network Neighborhood icon. Except that it's probably not as fast, everything should work the way it does when you're connected directly to the network.

To terminate the session, right-click the Dial-Up Networking Monitor icon in the taskbar's notification area and choose Hang Up.

Using Dial-Up Networking Monitor

While you're connected to a remote server, Dial-Up Networking Monitor (not the Dial-Up Networking dialog box) lets you monitor and control your connection. It reports on the status and progress of an active connection, and you use it to terminate a connection or make a new connection.

You can use any of the following methods to open the Dial-Up Networking Monitor dialog box:

- If Dial-Up Networking Monitor's icon appears in the taskbar's notification area, double-click the icon or right-click it and choose Open Dial-Up Monitor.
- In the Dial-Up Networking dialog box, click More and then choose Monitor Status.
- Open Control Panel and double-click the Dial-Up Monitor icon.
- Click the Start button and choose Run. In the Run dialog box, type *rasmon*, the program name for Dial-Up Networking Monitor, and then click OK.

The Status page in Dial-Up Networking Monitor, shown below, shows how long you've been connected, how much data has flowed in each direction, and the number of errors.

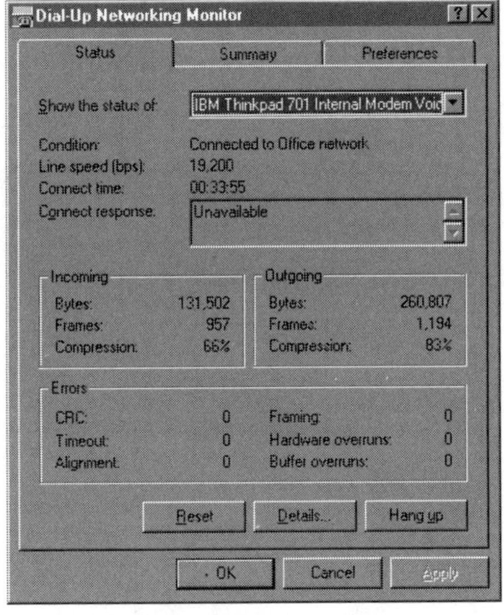

TIP

A high number of transmission errors can indicate a "noisy" telephone line. Sometimes hanging up and redialing solves the problem.

You can customize Dial-Up Networking Monitor with options on the Preferences page, shown below.

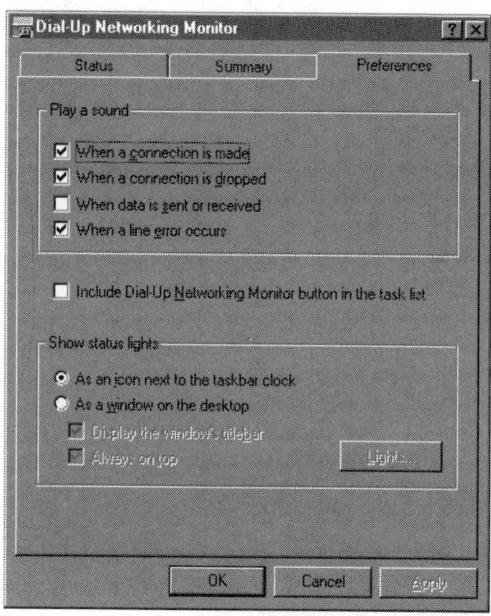

If you prefer watching flashing lights instead of Dial-Up Networking Monitor's minuscule taskbar icon, select the option button labeled "As a window on the desktop." This displays Dial-Up Networking Monitor in a small, resizable window like the one shown below.

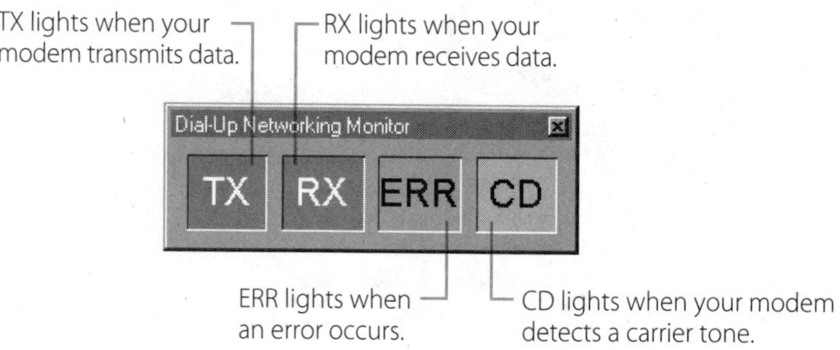

If you have more than one remote access port, the window includes a set of lights for each port, allowing you to monitor all ports simultaneously—and enjoy a cool light show!

Reconnecting to a Remote Folder or File

Dial-Up Networking includes a feature called RAS AutoDial, which maps network addresses to Dial-Up Networking phonebook entries. RAS AutoDial keeps track of every connection to a network address made over a remote access link. Whenever the network address is referenced (for example, you double-click a shortcut to a document on a remote server, or you open a folder window for a remote folder), Windows NT offers to dial the phonebook entry where that address was last found. It makes this offer through a dialog box like the one shown below:

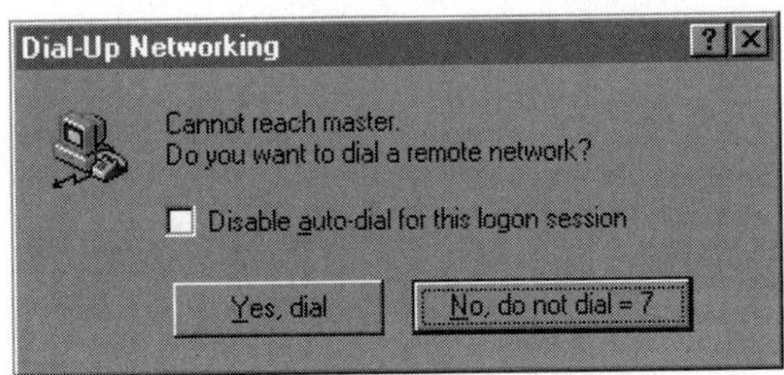

If you don't click "Yes, dial" before the "No, do not dial" button's 15-second countdown timer reaches 0, RAS AutoDial clicks the latter button for you.

RAS AutoDial will gladly dial automatically without first displaying the confirmation dialog box. If you want to enable this option, follow this steps:

1. In the Dial-Up Networking dialog box, click More.
2. Choose User Preferences.
3. Click the Appearance tab.
4. Deselect the Always Prompt Before Auto-Dialing check box.
5. Click OK.

You can also enable or disable RAS AutoDial for particular dialing locations. To do so, open the User Preferences dialog box (as described above), click the Dialing tab, and place checks by the locations where you want RAS AutoDial enabled.

TIP

To simplify reconnection to a particular remote folder or file, create a shortcut for it *while you're connected to the remote server.* Then, after you disconnect, you can reconnect by double-clicking the shortcut. Alternatively, you can map a remote folder to a drive letter on your own system. Then you can reopen that "drive" just as you would reopen an ordinary local drive. If Windows determines that the mapped drive is not part of your local-area network, it presents a dialog box asking if you want to use a dial-up connection. *For information about creating a shortcut, see "Using Shortcuts to Run Programs and Open Documents," page 73. For information about mapping a folder to a drive letter, see "Mapping a Network Folder to a Drive Letter," page 277.*

Logging On to Your Network with Dial-Up Networking

After you set up the remote access service on your computer, you'll see that a "Logon using Dial-Up Networking" check box appears in the Logon Information dialog box when you first log on to Windows NT.

If you select this check box, Windows NT makes a dial-up connection as part of the logon process, so that your network is available right away.

If you do not select the check box (because a phone line is not available, or because you don't need access to any network resources), you can still log on. If you have a domain account, specify your username, password, and domain name as if you were connected to the network. You're then logged on to Windows NT, and you can use local resources. Because you're not actually connected to the network, Windows NT uses locally cached information from the domain security database to authenticate your logon.

Modifying a Phonebook Entry

To modify a Dial-Up Networking phonebook entry, open the Dial-Up Networking dialog box, select the entry you want to change, and click More. Doing so displays a menu of commands, as shown below. Table 15-1 describes the purpose of each command.

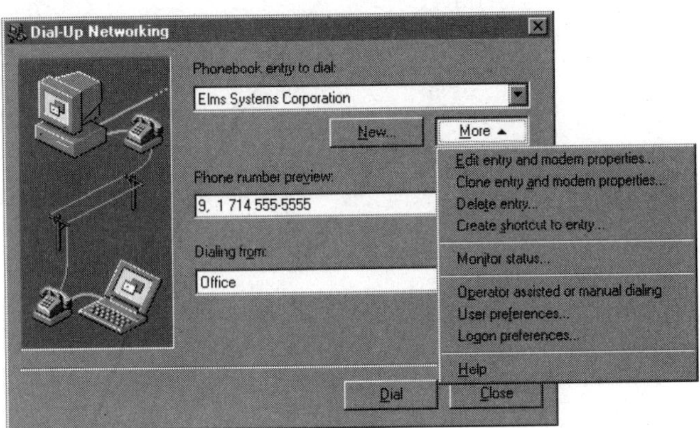

TABLE 15-1. Commands Displayed by More Button

Command	Function
Edit Entry And Modem Properties	Displays the Edit Phonebook Entry dialog box, where you can modify all manner of settings *(see details below)*
Clone Entry And Modem Properties	Duplicates the selected phonebook entry, which allows you to make a similar entry without starting from scratch
Delete Entry	Deletes the selected phonebook entry
Create Shortcut To Entry	Creates a shortcut to the selected entry on the desktop or in a folder you specify
Monitor Status	Opens Dial-Up Networking Monitor *(for details, see "Using Dial-Up Networking Monitor," page 426)*
Operator Assisted Or Manual Dialing	When this command is checked, to make a connection, you click Dial, pick up the telephone handset, and use the telephone to dial the number; hang up the handset after the modem takes over the connection

(continued)

TABLE 15-1. *continued*

Command	Function
User Preferences	Displays the User Preferences dialog box, where you can set a variety of options that determine how Dial-Up Networking operates on your system
Logon Preferences	Displays the Logon Preferences dialog box, which contains settings similar to those in the User Preferences dialog box, except that they affect Dial-Up Networking only when it's used to log on to Windows NT initially (that is, when you select "Logon using Dial-Up Networking" in the Logon Information dialog box that appears when you start Windows NT)
Help	Displays help topics about Dial-Up Networking

Choose Edit Entry And Modem Properties to view or modify the settings for the selected phonebook entry. A dialog box like the one shown below appears.

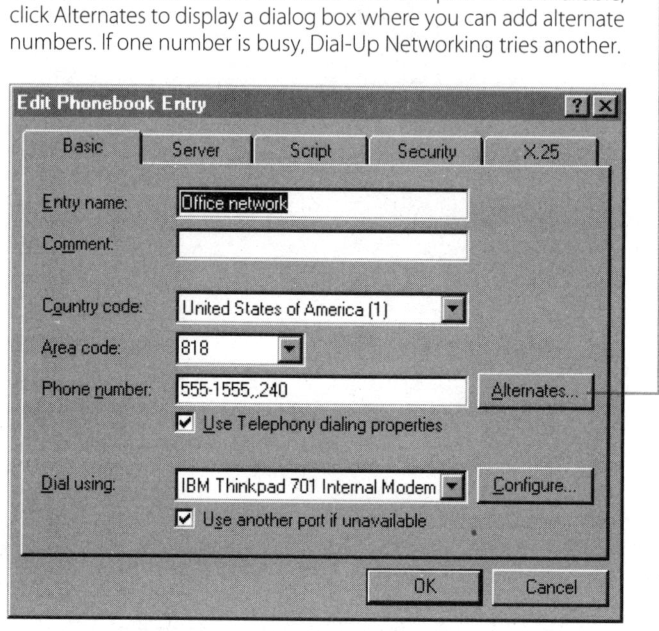

- On the Basic page (shown above), you specify a name, one or more phone numbers for the entry, and a modem to use.
- On the Server page, you provide information about the remote server, including which network protocols it uses (NetBEUI, TCP/IP, or IPX) and which remote access protocol is required. Dial-Up Networking supports three remote access protocols: PPP, SLIP, and Microsoft RAS protocol. The one you choose depends on the remote server's operating system:
    - If the remote server uses Windows NT 3.5 or later, or Windows 95 with Plus!, select PPP.
    - If the remote server uses Windows NT 3.1 or Windows for Workgroups, select Microsoft RAS.
    - If the remote server uses UNIX, select PPP or SLIP. (Check with the system administrator.)
    - If you're connecting to an Internet service provider, select PPP or SLIP. (Check with the provider.)
- The Script page lets you specify a "script" (a series of commands to log on to an account) to run when Dial-Up Networking establishes a connection. You'll need to use this option when connecting to certain Internet service providers.
- The Security page lets you set authentication and password options, which must coincide with similar settings on the remote server.
- The X.25 page lets you specify a network and other options for use with an X.25 connection.

Using Hardware Profiles

With Windows NT, you can set up a *hardware profile* for each different configuration of your computer. Each hardware profile can have a different set of devices and services enabled or disabled. If your portable computer has a certain PC Card adapter that you don't use all the time, you might want to set up a profile that enables services related to that adapter, and another that does not. One common use of hardware profiles is to have one profile for use when you're connected to the network, and another when you're away from the network.

> **NOTE**
>
> In the language of Windows NT, a *device*—more accurately called a *device driver*—is a program that enables a particular hardware device (or group of related devices) to communicate with the operating system. A *service* is a process that performs a specific system function.

If you have more than one hardware profile set up on a computer, you select which profile to use when you start the computer. After the computer's power-on self test (and the flex-boot menu, if you have more than one operating system installed), the hardware configuration menu appears. Use the arrow keys to highlight a hardware profile, and then press Enter to complete the boot process.

Creating a Hardware Profile

The first step in using hardware profiles is to duplicate an existing profile.

> **NOTE**
>
> You must be logged on as a member of the Administrators group to add a hardware profile.

To duplicate an existing profile, do this:

1 In Control Panel, double-click the System icon to display the System Properties dialog box.

TIP

Another way to reach the System Properties dialog box is to right-click the My Computer icon and choose Properties.

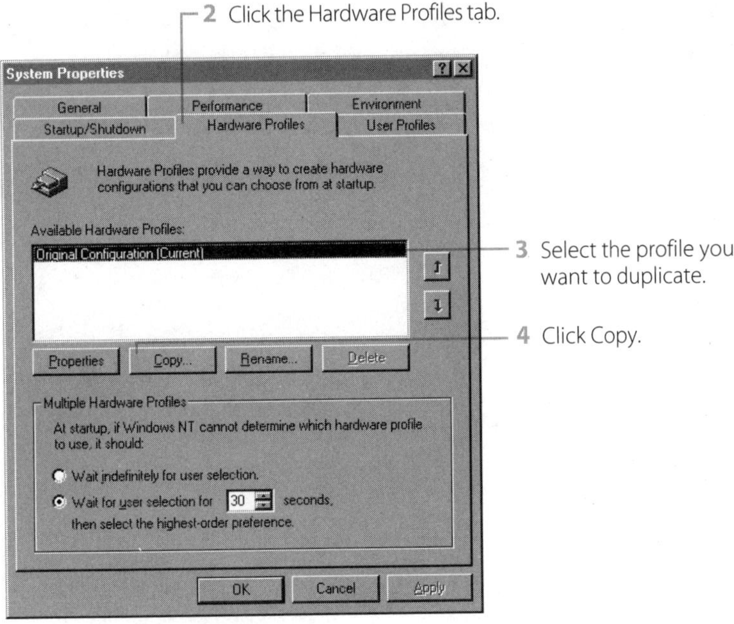

5 Give your new profile a name, and then click OK to return to the System Properties dialog box.

6 Select whether you want Windows NT to wait until you select a hardware profile when you start the system, or to automatically select one if you don't respond within a certain amount of time.

> **NOTE**
>
> If you allow Windows NT to proceed automatically, it selects the hardware profile at the top of the list. To move a profile to the top, select it and then click the up arrow button to the right of the list.

7 Click OK.

Creating a "No Network" Hardware Profile

After you duplicate a hardware profile, as described above, you have more than one hardware profile—but they're all the same. If you sometimes use your computer when it's not attached to the network, you might want to create a hardware profile specifically for that purpose. Doing so lets your system start and operate faster because it doesn't make attempts to find network resources.

To create a "no network" profile, follow these steps:

1 Open the System Properties dialog box and select the Hardware Profiles page.

2 Select the profile for which you want to disable network capability.

3 Click Properties.

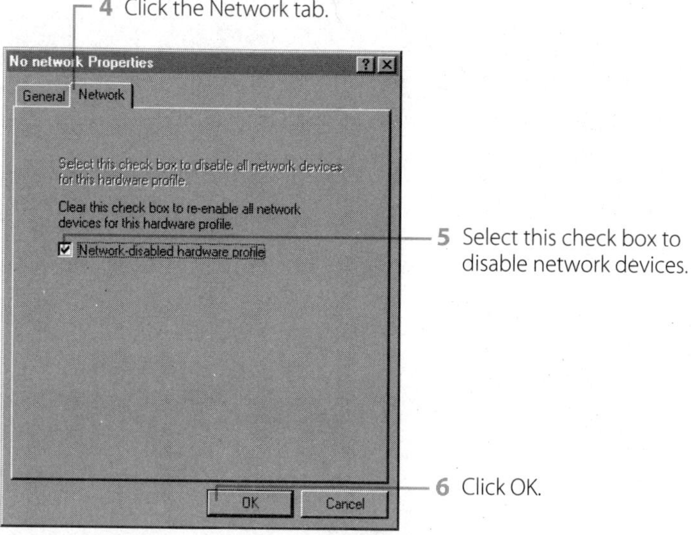

7 Click OK in the System Properties dialog box.

Your changes take effect the next time you start your system.

Customizing a Hardware Profile

In addition to the network devices and services that are controlled by the setting described in the previous section, each device and each service in Windows NT can be enabled or disabled for each hardware profile. To enable or disable particular devices or services for a profile, follow these steps:

1 In Control Panel, double-click the Devices icon or Services icon, depending on whether you want to modify settings for devices or services.

Both icons produce a dialog box similar to the one shown below.

2 Select the device or service you want to enable or disable.

3 Click HW Profiles.

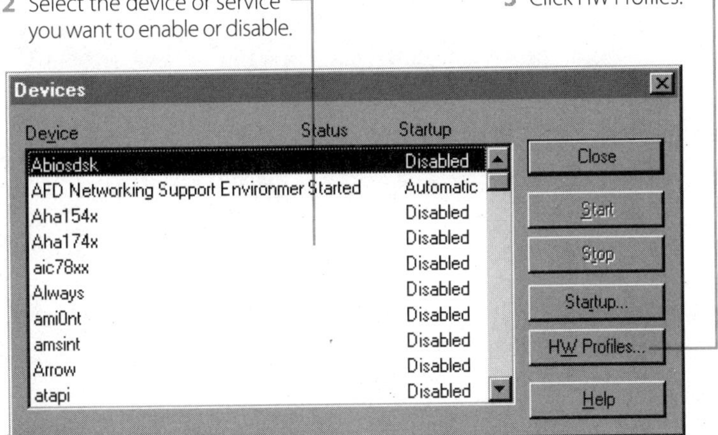

NOTE

Unfortunately, many devices and services have cryptic names that give hardly a clue to their real purpose—and Windows NT documentation doesn't include a complete list. If you're unsure about what a particular driver does, it's best to leave its settings unchanged.

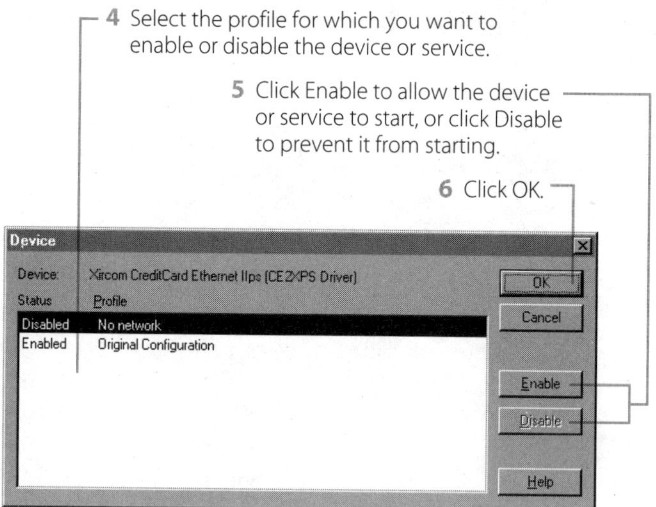

7 Repeat steps 2 through 6 for other devices or services.

8 Click Close in the Devices or Services dialog box.

Your changes take effect the next time you start your system.

CHAPTER 16

Protecting Your Data with Backup

You don't have to use computers for long to know the frustration of losing data. It happens to everyone. Although Windows NT can't prevent mistakes and accidents from occurring, Windows NT Backup, the backup program included with Windows NT, provides a form of insurance to help you deal with such misfortunes.

The built-in networking features of Windows NT make it easy to design backup strategies in which administrators (usually using third-party software) back up machines throughout the network periodically without intervention by individual users. You might still need to perform local backup tasks, however. For example, some administrators choose to back up only network drives, so any personal files you have on your local hard drive do not get backed up automatically.

With Windows NT Backup, you can back up files from your own hard drive or from network drives to a tape drive attached to your computer. You can use either a SCSI tape drive, such as a 4-mm DAT drive, or a tape drive that's attached to the floppy-disk controller, such as a QIC (quarter-inch cartridge) drive.

You can select individual files, folders, or entire volumes to back up. And you can specify whether to include all files or only those that haven't already been backed up. Because Windows NT Backup has no file-size limitation, your backup sets can span more than one tape.

Windows NT Backup also includes an easy-to-use restore command with which you can copy particular files or all files from your backup tape to your original disks (or to some other disks). When you need to restore files, you view a catalog of backup sets that includes file and folder information, so you can select the files to restore.

If You Don't Have a Tape Drive

If you don't have a tape drive connected to your computer (and your files aren't automatically backed up via the network), you can still practice safe computing. Although Windows NT Backup cannot back up to floppy disks or to another hard drive, Windows NT includes three tools that can save backup copies of your important files on floppy disks, on another hard disk, or on a removable cartridge:

- Backup.exe, a descendant of the backup program included with MS-DOS, can be run in a Command Prompt window. (Type *backup /?* at the command prompt for more information.) Its companion program, Restore.exe, restores files to their original location.
- XCopy is a command-line utility that lets you copy files to another location. (Type *xcopy /?* at the command prompt for more information.)
- Briefcase can also be used to store archival backups. *For information about Briefcase, see "Synchronizing Files with Briefcase," page 407.*

Backup Types and Strategies

Windows NT Backup supports five common backup types: normal, incremental, differential, copy, and daily.

- A *normal* backup copies all selected files to tape, regardless of when the files were last changed, and clears the archive attribute for each file to mark it as backed up.
- An *incremental* backup copies only the selected files that have changed since your most recent normal or incremental backup. It also clears the archive attribute for each file. Therefore, the first incremental backup after a normal backup copies all files that have changed since the normal backup, the second incremental backup copies only those files that have changed since the first incremental backup, and so on.
- A *differential* backup copies only the selected files that have changed since your most recent normal or incremental backup. Unlike incremental backups, however, the archive attribute is not cleared during a differential backup. Therefore, successive differential backups copy all the files that have changed since the last normal (or incremental) backup, not just the ones that have changed since the last differential backup. A typical backup strategy combines weekly normal backups with daily differential backups.
- A *copy* backup copies all selected files, like a normal backup, but it does not clear the archive attribute. Therefore, you can use it to perform a special backup (before installing new software, for example) without affecting your normal backup routine.
- A *daily* backup copies all selected files that were changed on the day the backup is done. It does not clear the archive attribute. You can use daily backups to save your day's work without affecting your normal backup routine.

Selecting a backup type involves evaluating tradeoffs between safety on the one hand, and time and media space on the other. If safety were your only concern, you could back up your entire hard drive every hour. But you wouldn't have any time to work, and you'd spend a fortune on backup tapes. If spending minimal time and money on backups were your only concern, you might back up only a few crucial files once a month. Common sense suggests there must be a happy medium.

A common strategy combines normal and differential backups as follows:

- At some regular interval, such as once a week, perform a normal backup.
- At regular intervals between normal backups—for example, at the end of each work day—perform a differential backup.

With this strategy, if the unthinkable happens and you need to restore one or more files, you need to look in only two places to find the most recent version of any file: the most recent normal backup and the most recent differential backup.

How Does Backup Know Which Files to Back Up?

Like most operating systems, Windows NT maintains an *archive attribute* for each file. Every file is either marked as needing to be archived (backed up), or it isn't marked.

Whenever a program creates or modifies a file, the operating system marks the file as needing to be archived by setting the archive attribute, which indicates that the file has changed since the last archive. When Backup sees a file with the archive attribute set, it backs up the file and, if you're performing a normal or incremental backup, clears the attribute. The next time Backup runs, the archive attribute is gone (unless you've modified the file again) and Backup knows that it doesn't need to back up the file.

You can view (and set or clear) the archive attribute for a file by viewing the file's property sheet. *For more information about file attributes, see "Setting Attributes for Folders, Files, and Shortcuts," page 153.*

SEE ALSO

For information about selecting a backup type, see "Selecting Backup Options," page 450.

Differential backups take longer than incremental backups (and require more tape), so some users prefer to use an incremental backup as their daily backup. If you follow this strategy, it's a good idea not to collect more than a half-dozen or so incremental backups between full backups. Otherwise, you might have to search through a lot of backup sets to find particular files in the event that you need to restore them from the backup tape.

TIP

Rotate Your Backups

For extra security, it's a good idea to rotate backup tapes. For example, if you do a full backup once a week and differential backups on the intervening days, you might want to keep one week's worth of backups on one tape and then use a different tape the following week. If disaster strikes twice—your original storage medium *and* your backup tape are both damaged—you'll still be able to restore files from the previous time period's backup tape. The files you restore probably won't be the most current versions, but you'll be better off than if you had to re-create everything from scratch.

If possible, store your backup tapes away from your computers. Otherwise, if you experience a fire or theft you may lose both your originals and your backups.

Deciding What Files to Back Up

Exactly what you need to back up depends on your circumstances, of course, but here's a general principle worth observing: don't make your backup routine so onerous and time-consuming that you lose the motivation to adhere to it.

In practice, what this means for many users is the following:

- Exclude from your regular normal and differential backup routine program files and DLLs that you have installed from diskettes. Instead, back these files up *before* you install the programs in the first place. Keep programs and data in separate folders so you can easily exclude programs from backups.

SEE ALSO

For information about specifying the files to back up, see "Selecting Files to Back Up," page 448.

- Exclude CD-ROM–based program files and DLLs from normal and differential backups if you have created a full backup of the entire hard disk on which those programs are installed.
- Include all data files (documents) in your normal and differential backups. These are the files that change the most and that would be most difficult to replace.
- If you don't have a regular normal and differential backup routine, at least perform ad hoc backups of the files you're currently working with. If you don't have a tape drive, use Windows NT Explorer to copy these files to another hard disk. If you don't have another hard disk, copy them to floppies. It doesn't take that long.

Backup and Windows NT Security

You can back up all the files for which your user account has read permission, whether the files are stored on your own computer or on a shared network drive. If your account is a member of the Administrators or Backup Operators group, you can bypass normal file permissions to back up files.

To restore files, you must have write permission for the folder to which you want to restore the files, or you must be logged on as a member of the Administrators or Backup Operators group.

If someone else (usually a network administrator) backs up all or part of your system and your computer is not part of a Windows NT Server domain, you'll need to give that person the appropriate rights on your computer. *(For information about granting rights to others, see "Assigning Rights to Users and Groups," page 575.)*

To work efficiently, most backup programs that are not designed specifically for Windows NT bypass the operating system and directly access the computer's hardware. Windows NT does not permit this because any program that bypasses the operating system can bypass security. Therefore, backup tools written for earlier versions of Windows will not work with Windows NT—regardless of your user account privileges.

Starting Windows NT Backup

Before you run Windows NT Backup, insert a tape cartridge in the tape drive. (Certain tape drives send a "no tape in drive" to Event Viewer's application log every few seconds if you run Backup without a tape; this can quickly fill the log with useless messages.) Then click the Start button and choose Programs, Administrative Tools (Common), Backup.

TIP

If Backup does not appear on the Administrative Tools (Common) submenu, you can get the program running by the following method: double-click My Computer, right-click the icon for any local disk drive, choose Properties, click the Tools tab, and then click Backup Now.

NOTE

If you have not already installed a driver for your tape backup device (or if the tape drive is turned off), Backup balks when you start it and informs you that no tape drive is detected. You must install the driver, using the Tape Devices applet in Control Panel. *For information about installing a tape device driver, see "Installing a Tape Drive," page 716.*

SEE ALSO

For information about installing Windows NT Backup, see "Adding or Removing Parts of Windows NT," page 696.

Figure 16-1 on the next page shows the initial Backup window, which contains two document windows. (The Tapes window is minimized.) The Drives window shows local drives and network drives that are mapped to a drive letter. Network connections that you make without mapping a drive letter do not appear in the Drives window. Therefore, to back up data from a network drive, you must first map that drive to a drive letter.

TIP

You don't need to quit Backup to make additional connections. Use Windows NT Explorer to make your connections, and then choose Refresh from Backup's Window menu to update the Drives window.

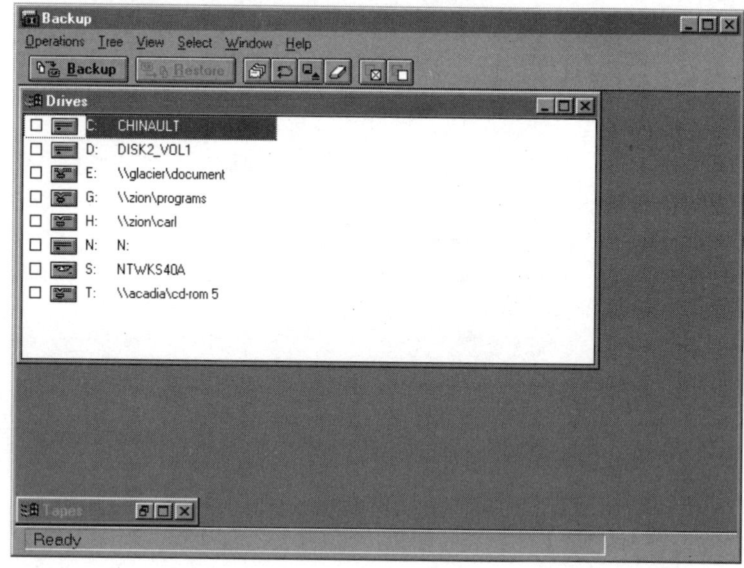

FIGURE 16-1.
This computer has three local hard drive partitions (drives C, D, and N), a CD-ROM drive (drive S), and four network connections (drives E, G, H, and T).

The Backup toolbar provides one-click access to Backup's most commonly used features. Table 16-1 explains the purpose of each tool.

TABLE 16-1. Backup Toolbar

Toolbar Icon	Description
Backup	Backs up data from disk to tape
Restore	Restores data from tape to disk
	Loads the catalog of backup sets from a tape
	Retensions the tape, which eliminates loose spots on the tape by fast forwarding to the end of the tape and then rewinding
	Rewinds the tape and (on drives that can do so) ejects the tape cartridge

(continued)

TABLE 16-1. *continued*

Toolbar Icon	Description
	Erases the tape
	Checks all selected items in the current window
	Unchecks all selected items in the current window

TIP

You can also start Backup from a Command Prompt window, which allows you to easily run repetitive backup processes, and to schedule backups. *For details, see "Backing Up from the Command Prompt," page 455.*

Formatting a Tape

Before you can back up files to a tape cartridge, you have to format the tape. This is easy but time-consuming. Proceed as follows:

1. Insert the tape in your tape drive.
2. Run Backup.
3. Choose Format Tape from the Operations menu.

The Format Tape dialog box appears with a warning to let you know that formatting a tape erases everything on the tape. If the tape doesn't contain information you want to save, click Continue to begin the formatting process. If the Continue button is not available but you hear your tape drive working, wait a moment or two. Sometimes it takes a few seconds for Backup to recognize that there's a tape ready to use. In a few moments, the Continue button in the Format Tape dialog box should become available.

 NOTE

> If your tape drive uses preformatted tapes, you don't need to format the tapes. In this case, the Format Tape command on the Operations menu is unavailable.

While you're formatting, you can make modest use of the computer to which the tape drive is attached. Because it can take Backup more than an hour to format a sizable tape, you might want to begin your formatting at the end of a work day.

Compatibility with Other Backup Programs

Windows NT Backup uses Microsoft Tape Format (MTF), the same format used by Seagate Backup Exec and some other third-party backup programs. Therefore, tapes created with Windows NT Backup can be read by those programs. You can also use Windows NT Backup to read tapes created by Seagate Backup Exec and other programs that use MTF—as long as the tapes were not created using software compression, which is not supported by Windows NT Backup.

The Backup program included with Windows 95 uses a different format, so tapes created by Windows NT Backup cannot be read by Windows 95 Backup, and vice versa.

Backing Up Files

Performing a backup with Windows NT Backup is a three-step process:

1. Select the files you want to back up.
2. Select the backup options.
3. Run the backup.

Selecting Files to Back Up

You select the files to back up by marking them in the Drives window or in one of the file-selection windows that it spawns. Begin by opening the Drives window. Then click the check box next to the drive, folder, or file that you want to back up.

Selecting Entire Drives

To select all the files on a drive, simply click the check box to the left of the drive letter and volume name in the Drives window.

Selecting Particular Folders and Files

If you want to back up certain folders or files without backing up the entire drive on which they're stored, double-click the drive's icon in the Drives window. (Alternatively, you can highlight the drive and press Enter.) This opens a file-selection window, as shown below.

Click the check box for the files or folders that you want to back up.

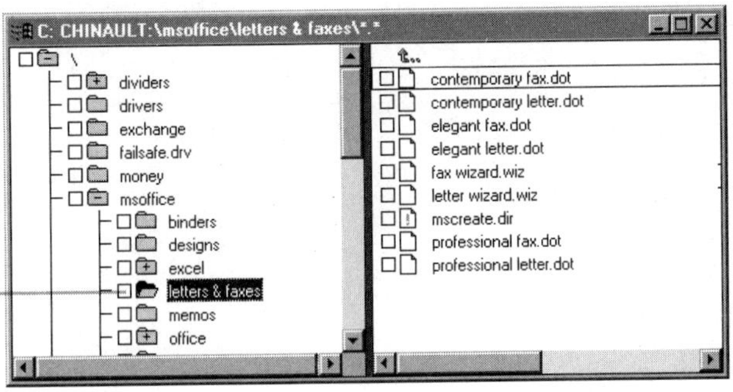

C: CHINAULT:\msoffice\letters & faxes*.*

\
dividers
drivers
exchange
failsafe.drv
money
msoffice
binders
designs
excel
letters & faxes
memos
office

contemporary fax.dot
contemporary letter.dot
elegant fax.dot
elegant letter.dot
fax wizard.wiz
letter wizard.wiz
mscreate.dir
professional fax.dot
professional letter.dot

The file-selection window has a left pane and a right pane similar to those in Windows NT Explorer. The left pane displays an outline of the folders on the drive, and the right pane displays the contents of the folder that's highlighted in the left pane. Simply click a folder in the left pane to display its contents in the right pane.

Some folder icons in the left pane include a plus sign, indicating that these folders contain other folders. Double-click one of these icons (or the folder name) to expand the outline to show the subfolders. Double-click again to collapse the outline.

TIP

You can display more information about each file with the All File Details command on the View menu. When All File Details is selected, you get a view similar to the details view in Windows NT Explorer. Otherwise, you get filenames only (similar to list view).

To select all the files in a folder (including subfolders), simply click the check box to the left of the folder name. You can do so in either the left pane or the right pane—whichever is most convenient.

Select individual files in the same manner: simply click the check box to the left of the filename.

TIP

You can highlight a group of adjacent files in the right pane by dragging over the range of filenames. (Alternatively, you can click the first filename, and then hold the Shift key while you click the last one in the group.) To select all the highlighted files for backup, click the Check button on the toolbar. You can also use this technique to select a range of drives in the Drives window.

NOTE

Selecting a drive, folder, or file does not in itself ensure that the file will be backed up. Regardless of your selections, you can back up a file only if you have permission to read the file. *(For information about permissions, see "Access Types and Permissions," page 583.)* The backup type you choose also determines whether a particular selected file will be backed up. A file that hasn't changed since the last backup won't be backed up if you choose an incremental backup, for example. *(For information about backup types, see "Backup Types and Strategies," page 441.)*

Selecting Backup Options

After you select the files you want to back up, click the Backup button on the toolbar, or choose Backup from the Operations menu. The Backup Information dialog box appears, as shown on the next page.

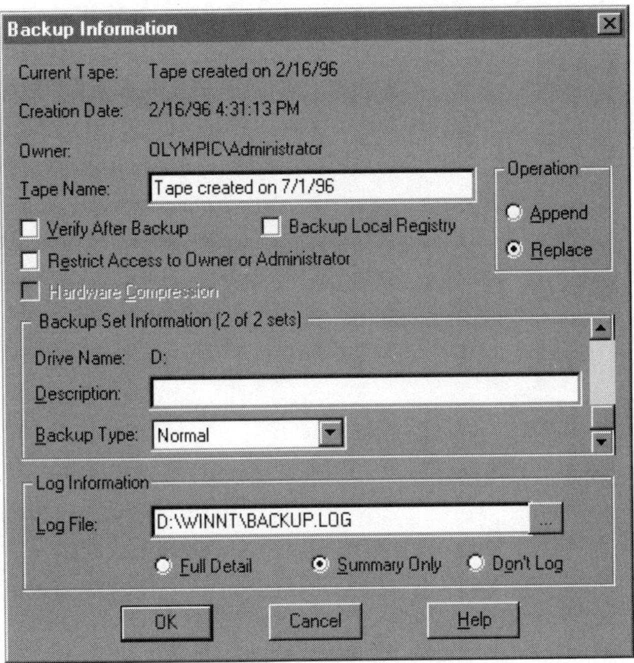

In the Backup Information dialog box, you specify the backup type and set other backup options. The chock-full dialog box provides the following information and settings:

- If the tape in the drive already contains backup data, the Current Tape and Creation Date fields show the tape's name and the date of the first backup set. The Owner field shows the owner of the first backup set on the tape.
- In the Operation group, select whether you want to append the current backup to the existing tape data, or replace the information already on the tape.
- If you choose the Replace option, you can assign a name to the tape in the Tape Name box. Backup proposes a default name of "Tape created on (today's date)."

- If you select the Verify After Backup check box, Backup confirms the backup by comparing the files on the drive and on the tape after the backup is complete.

NOTE

> If you use your computer during the backup and you change any of the files that were backed up, the verify option reports errors. Be sure to read the backup log to see if the errors merely reflect changes that have taken place while the backup was in progress.

TIP

> **Verify Your Backup**
> Although it considerably increases the time to perform a backup, you should always select the Verify After Backup box. Otherwise, you'll have no assurance that *anything* is being written to tape. Discovering that you have a defective tape drive is not something you'll want to deal with while trying to restore lost files.

- Select the Backup Local Registry check box if you want to include the Windows NT registry files in your backup set. You'll need to restore the registry as well as all other files if you ever have to rebuild your system from scratch—so it's a good idea to include it in your backups.

NOTE

> The Backup Local Registry check box is available only when the drive that contains the registry files is displayed in the Backup Set Information section of the Backup Information dialog box.

- If you select the Restrict Access To Owner Or Administrator check box, only the person who creates (and therefore owns) the tape, or a member of the Administrators or Backup Operators group, can read, write, or erase the tape with Backup. If you (as the owner) want to restore files to another computer in the same domain, you must log on with the same user account name. This prevents others from restoring files from your tapes to sneak a peek at what you have backed up. This option is available only when Replace is the selected operation.

- Select Hardware Compression if you want your tape drive to compress files as they're backed up. Doing so typically doubles the amount of information you can store on a tape. Not all tape drives support hardware compression; this option is unavailable if your drive does not support compression.
- In the Backup Set Information group box, you can view and change information about a particular backup set. Each drive that contains files to back up is stored as a separate backup set. If your current backup includes more than one backup set, a scroll bar lets you view and change the following information for each set:
    - Drive Name displays the drive letter and name.
    - You can enter a Description for each backup set. The description appears in the Tapes window when you view a tape catalog.
    - The Backup Type determines which files will be backed up.

TIP

Unlike files in a folder, backup sets on a tape can have identical names. If you do two incremental backups on Monday and want to call them both Monday Incremental, for example, that's not a problem to Windows NT Backup. If you need to restore files from a tape with identically named backup sets, you'll be able to distinguish the sets by their creation times.

- In the Log Information group box, you can choose what data, if any, will be recorded in the backup log file. Summary Only (the default) logs only major events such as erasing a tape, starting a backup, and failing to open a file. Full Detail logs everything, including the name of each file and folder that's backed up.

Running the Backup

After you have made all the settings you want in the Backup Information dialog box (whew!), you're ready to begin the actual backup process. Simply click OK. While Backup does its job, you can sit back and relax, secure in the knowledge that if the world collapses around you, you'll have your backup tape!

If you chose Replace in the Operation group and the tape is not blank, Backup pauses to ask if you really want to wipe out the existing data. If you confirm that you do, the disk light flickers, the tape whirs, and the backup starts. A backup status dialog box appears, as shown below.

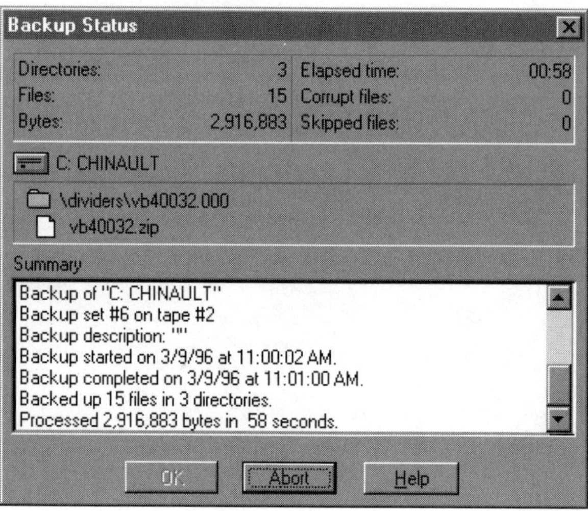

The Backup Status dialog box displays the number of directories (folders), files, and bytes that have been backed up, and the elapsed time. In addition, it displays the number of corrupt files and files that have been skipped because of read errors or, more likely, because a file is open or locked by another application. The Summary box displays the same information that is written to the backup log, and you can scroll through it to see which files caused problems.

> **TIP**
>
> While the backup is taking place, you can still work with your computer—except that, if your tape drive is connected to the floppy-disk controller, you cannot use your floppy drive while the tape drive is active.

During the backup, the OK button is inactive, but the Abort button is active in case you want to quit. If you click Abort, the current file will be completed before Backup resigns its task.

> **TIP**
>
> **Backing Up to Multiple Tapes**
>
> You can back up more files than will fit on a single tape. If you fill a tape, Backup prompts for another. Backup also can split files across tapes.
>
> After Backup finishes copying all files in your backup set, it records the location of each backed-up file on the last tape. Be sure to number your tapes! That way, if you need to restore one or more files from the set, you'll be able to find the right tape quickly and easily.

Backing Up from the Command Prompt

The graphical Windows interface makes Windows NT Backup easy to learn and use. However, after you've backed up the same drive with the same commands 30 times in 30 days, you might be ready for a shortcut. Fortunately, Windows NT Backup also works as a command-line utility. *For details on using the command prompt, see Chapter 18, "Using the Command Prompt."*

When you run Backup from the command prompt, it runs in a window. But instead of waiting for mouse and keyboard input, it performs the actions you specified on the command line. You'll see buttons pushed and status displayed as if a ghost has taken over your machine. When it's all over, Backup terminates.

Backup's program name is NTBackup.exe. To use it from the command prompt, use the following syntax:

```
NTBackup Backup [pathnames [options]]
```

"Backup" is required as the first argument. *Pathnames* takes the place of information entered in the Drives and file-selection windows. You can include entire drives or folders, but not individual files. Of course, it's not as convenient or flexible as checking the items you want in a dialog box, but you generally don't need complex backup selections. If you run out of space for pathnames on the command line, you can use multiple Backup commands.

Options takes the place of entries in the Backup Information dialog box. Most check boxes in the dialog box have a corresponding command-line option. Absence of the option is equivalent to leaving the check box unchecked. Table 16-2 shows command-line options and the corresponding dialog-box fields.

You might want to experiment with the command-line syntax before putting commands into batch programs that run automatically. When you run Backup interactively, it displays warnings and gives you a chance to change your mind if you do something dangerous. When you run it from the command prompt, Backup assumes that you know what you're doing. Be sure that you do.

TABLE 16-2. **Backup Command-Line Options**

Option	Dialog Box Field	Action
/A	Operation	The backup set is appended to the current tape. If you do not use this option, the backup set replaces all previous contents of the tape.
/V	Verify After Backup	All items are verified by comparing the disk version with the tape version.
/B	Backup Registry	The Windows NT registry files are backed up.
/R	Restrict Access to Owner or Administrator	Backup restricts access to the person who created the tape or members of the Administrators and Backup Operators groups. The option is ignored if you do not use the /A option.
/HC:ON	Hardware Compression	Backup uses the tape drive's data compression capability.
/D *text*	Description	Backup stores *text* as the description of the backup set.
/T *type*	Backup type	The *type* can be Normal, Incremental, Differential, Copy, or Daily. If you do not use the /T option, Normal is assumed.
/L *filename*	Log File	A log file named *filename* is created.
/E	Log Information	If you use this option in combination with the /L option, a simple log file with events only is created. If you do not use the /E option, the log file shows the name of each file and folder. The /E option is ignored if you do not use the /L option.

 TIP

You might think you can use the NTBackup command to restore files by specifying Restore instead of Backup as the first argument on the command line. You can't. But, as a practical matter, restoring from the command prompt doesn't make much sense. You shouldn't have to restore very often; and when you do, the operation will be different each time.

Here are some batch-program examples of Backup commands. We'll call the first example NormalC.bat:

```
@echo off
cd %temp%
%systemroot%\system32\ntbackup backup c: /d Normal
  /l n.log
```

This batch program creates a new backup set (overwriting any existing backup sets) and does a normal backup of the C drive.

We'll call this example IncrmntC.bat:

```
@echo off
cd %temp%
%systemroot%\system32\ntbackup backup c: /a /t
  incremental /d Incremental /l i.log
```

This batch program does an incremental backup of the C drive, appending the backup set to any existing backup sets.

Now let's assume that you want to do a normal backup every Friday night at 11:30 P.M., after everyone has gone home, and incremental backups Monday through Thursday at 11:30 P.M. Use the At command to call the appropriate batch program.

```
C:\>at 23:30 /every:F "normalc"
C:\>at 23:30 /every:M,T,W,Th "incrmntc"
```

For more information about batch programs, see "Using Batch Programs," page 546.

You must have appropriate security privileges to run the At command. After you set everything up, you can forget it—except you must be sure that the tape drive has a tape with enough space for the backup every weeknight.

Scheduling Automatic Backups with the At Command

The At command allows you to schedule execution of a command—such as a batch program that runs Backup—at some specified time. Before you can use the At command, you must start the Schedule service by following these steps:

1. Log on to Windows NT as a member of the Administrators group.
2. Open the Control Panel folder and double-click the Services icon.
3. Select the Schedule service.
4. If the service is not marked Automatic in the Startup column, click Startup. Select the Automatic option button.

   If you want to back up network drives that are attached to other computers, select a logon account that has appropriate privileges for those drives, such as a member of the Backup Operators group, in the This Account box. (The local System Account can back up only local drives.) Then type the password for the account you selected.
5. Click OK. Henceforth the Schedule service starts automatically whenever you start your computer.
6. Click Start to start the Schedule service, and then close the Services window.
7. Use the Start menu's Run command (or open a command prompt window) to enter a command that runs your backups at schedule intervals, like this:

```
at 23:30 /every:F "ntbackup backup
   c: /b /d Full /l backup.log"
```

This command performs a normal backup, including the registry, every Friday at 11:30 P.M., and records the results in a file named Backup.log.

You need to set up the Schedule service and any At commands you want only once. Thereafter, At-scheduled programs run automatically, regardless of what user is logged on to the computer.

For more information about the Run command, see "Running Programs and Opening Documents with the Run Command," page 71. For more information about command prompt windows and getting help about specific commands, such as the At command, see Chapter 18, "Using the Command Prompt."

Restoring Files

To restore files from a backup set, start by launching Windows NT Backup. The process for restoring files is similar to that for backing up files:

1. Select the files you want to restore.
2. Select the restore options.
3. Run the restore operation.

Selecting Files to Restore

When Backup backs up files to tape, it creates a catalog of backup sets on each tape. Each backup set contains a catalog of all the files in the backup set. (If a backup set spans more than one tape, the set catalog is on the last tape in the set.) To restore files from tape, you must first find the files you want in the backup catalogs. Follow these steps:

1. Select the tape you want to restore from and insert it in the tape drive.
2. If the Tapes window is closed, double-click the Tapes icon to open the window. Backup displays the first backup set on the tape in the Tapes window.

   Notice the question mark on the folder icon for the backup set. This indicates that the catalog of files in the set has not yet been loaded. At this point you can't tell from the display whether there is only one backup set on the tape or whether the catalog of backup sets has not been loaded.

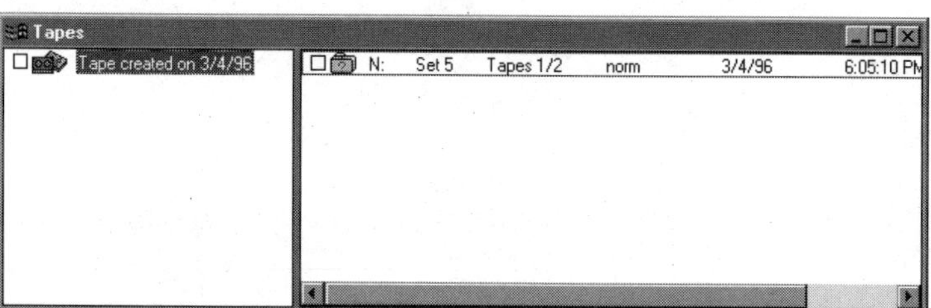

3 Load the catalog of backup sets by clicking the Catalog button on the toolbar or by double-clicking the Tape icon in the left pane of the Tapes window. The Catalog Status dialog box appears while the drive loads the catalog of backup sets. When the catalog is finished loading, all of the backup sets are displayed, each with a question mark in its folder icon because no file catalogs have been loaded.

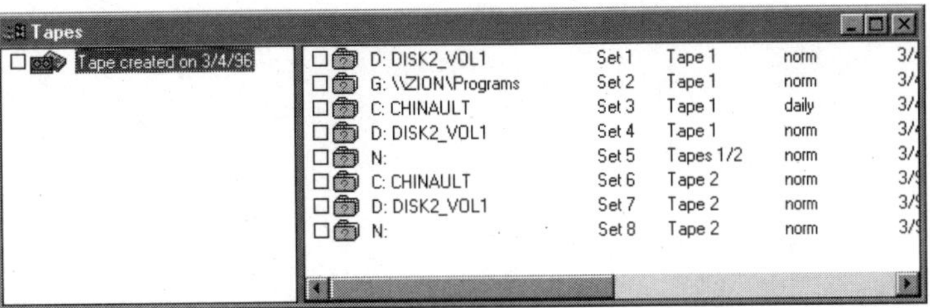

4 In the Tapes window, select the backup set you want by clicking the check box to the left of the folder icon. If you want to restore only certain files or folders, double-click the desired folder icon. In order to display the file-selection window, Backup must first load the file catalog. A status dialog box with an Abort button appears while the file catalog is read. When the file catalog is finished loading, the question mark in the folder icon changes to a plus sign and the file-selection window for the backup set appears.

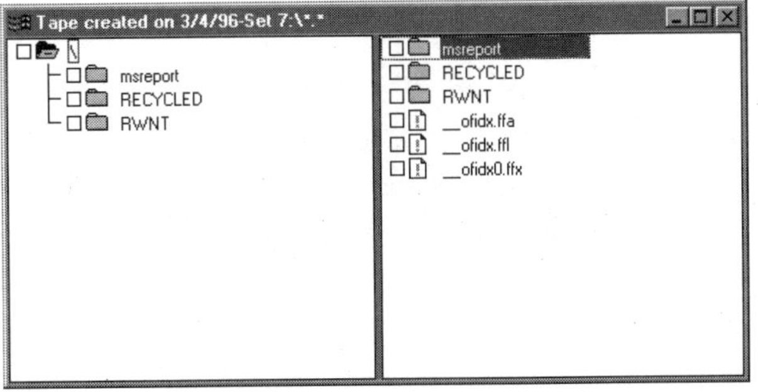

File selection works the same for restoring as for backing up.

When Disaster Strikes: Recovering Everything

Restoring a few misplaced files is a relatively simple process with Windows NT Backup—but what if your hard drive comes to a grinding halt and you lose your entire system? Take a few deep breaths, cross your fingers, and then follow these steps:

1. Reinstall Windows NT. (If you're using Windows NT Server, be sure you set it up to use the same mode you used prior to the "unfortunate incident": primary domain controller, backup domain controller, or workgroup server.)

   Unfortunately, you cannot run Windows NT Backup from a floppy disk or from another operating system, such as MS-DOS; you must install Windows NT.

2. Run Windows NT Backup. (If you get a message that no tape drive is detected, you need to install a driver for your tape backup device and restart the system. *For details, see "Installing a Tape Drive," page 716.*)

3. Use the restore operation as described in this chapter to restore all your lost files. In the Restore Information dialog box, be sure to select the Restore Local Registry check box.

4. Shut down and then restart the system.

5. Say "hallelujah!"

Selecting Restore Options

After you select the files you want to restore, click the Restore button on the toolbar, or choose Restore from the Operations menu. The Restore Information dialog box appears, as shown on the next page. (The Restore Information dialog box bears a strong resemblance to the Backup Information dialog box, so it might be familiar to you.)

Specify the destination for your restored files.

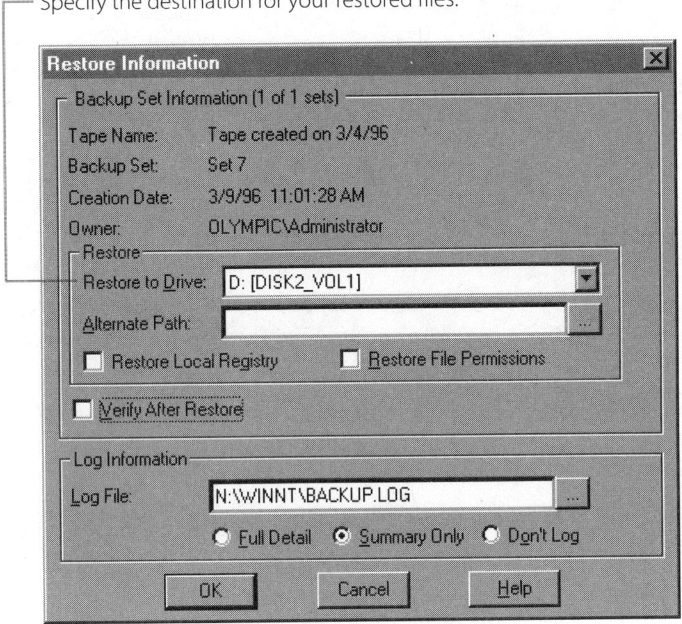

If you selected files from more than one backup set, a scroll bar in the Backup Set Information group box lets you display and set options for each set. Make the following settings:

- Select the drive you want to restore to in the Restore To Drive box. (It does not need to be the same drive from which the files were backed up.)
- If you want to restore files to a folder other than the one from which they were backed up, type the new folder's path in the Alternate Path box, or click the … button to browse for the folder you want.
- Select Restore Local Registry if you want to restore the Windows NT registry files. (After you restore the registry, you'll need to restart your computer for the restored registry to take effect.)

- Select Restore File Permissions if you want to set the file permissions the way they were when the files were backed up. If you don't select this box, files inherit the permission settings from the folder into which they're restored.
- Select Verify After Restore if you want Backup to reread the tape and compare the tape files with the disk files after restoring.

When you've made the appropriate settings for each backup set, examine the settings in the Log Information group box, and change them if you like. As with backup logs, a summary log includes entries for major events, such as starting or completing a restore operation, failing to restore a file, and so on. If you choose Full Detail, the log includes the name of every file you restore.

Running the Restore Operation

After you have made all the settings you want in the Restore Information dialog box, simply click OK to begin restoring files. The Restore Status dialog box, shown below, appears during the restore operation and displays the contents of the backup log.

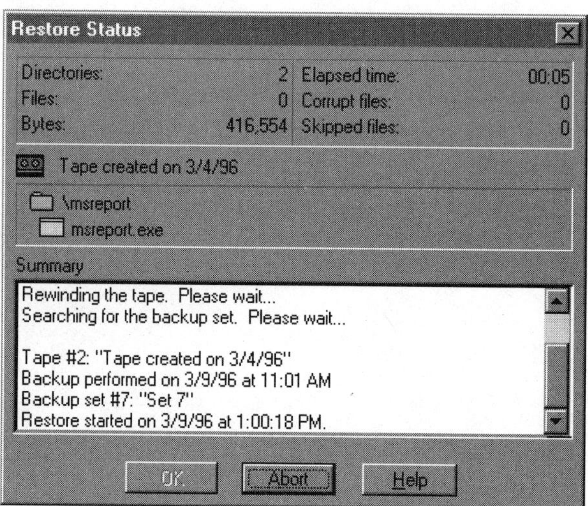

If a file to be restored has the same name as a file already in the destination folder, a message box like the one shown below appears. Choose Yes if you want to overwrite the existing file, or choose No if you want to leave the disk file in place. If you choose Yes To All, Backup overwrites the existing file, and then continues the restore operation without pausing for additional file-replace confirmation messages.

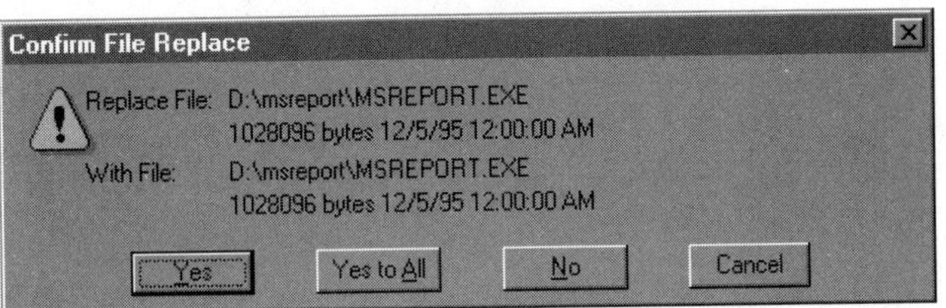

CHAPTER 17

Using Programs for Other Operating Systems

With Windows NT, you can run programs written for certain other operating systems as easily as you can run programs written specifically for Windows NT. Because it runs these programs seamlessly, you generally don't need to know a program's origin or type to run it. Specifically, you can run applications written for:

- **Windows 95.** Except for programs that can violate Windows NT security (by directly accessing the disk, for example), programs written for Windows 95 work exactly the same in Windows NT. Therefore, they are not discussed in any detail in this chapter.
- **Windows 3.x.** On the surface, programs written for Windows 3.x act much like Windows NT–based programs, but there are a few differences under the hood. Those differences are explained in this chapter.
- **MS-DOS.** You can run most MS-DOS–based programs inside windows that make them look and behave much like Windows-based programs. This chapter explains how to do that, and more, with MS-DOS–based programs.

- **OS/2.** In a tip of the hat to Microsoft's role in the development of early versions of OS/2, Windows NT runs 16-bit character-based programs written for OS/2 versions 1.x and 2.x.
- **POSIX.** Windows NT supports character-based POSIX applications, which typically are UNIX-based applications that are recompiled to the POSIX standard using Windows NT.

While running programs for these operating systems, you have all the benefits of Windows NT computing. For example, you can:

- Run multiple applications simultaneously
- Cut and paste information between applications, including applications written for different operating systems
- Take advantage of multitasking to, say, run a lengthy macro in an MS-DOS–based spreadsheet while you focus your attention on another program

Windows NT also manages resource contention for these "foreign" programs. So, for example, if you print a document from an MS-DOS–based word processor and your printer is busy, your document joins the printer queue just as though it had come from a Windows NT–based program.

In this chapter we'll survey the ins and outs of running programs written for these other operating systems under Windows NT, with particular emphasis on the two most widely used classes: programs for Windows 3.x and programs for MS-DOS.

What About Programs that Won't Work?

With a few exceptions, you can use Windows NT to run any program written for these other operating systems. The exceptions? Programs that directly address the hardware or use their own disk device drivers or graphics device drivers. Many communications programs and disk utilities fall into these categories, and those programs simply won't run in Windows NT. You'll need to ask the program's publisher if a version of the program or device driver is available for Windows NT.

Starting Programs

 **SEE ALSO**

For more information about starting programs, see Chapter 3, "Running Programs and Opening Documents."

With Windows NT, you start any program—whether it's written for Windows NT, Windows 95, Windows 3.x, MS-DOS, OS/2, or POSIX—in the same way. You can use any of these techniques:

- Choose the program from the Start menu, if it's there.
- Double-click the icon for the program in a folder or Windows NT Explorer window.
- Choose the Start menu's Run command, and then type the name of the program in the Open text box.
- Run Command Prompt and then type the name of the program at the command prompt.
- Double-click the program's icon in Program Manager or File Manager, the program launchers used in Windows 3.x and earlier versions of Windows NT.

If you start the program from either the Run dialog box or the command prompt, you might need to include the program's path as well as its name. Starting a program using either of these techniques is exactly like starting it from the command prompt in MS-DOS.

 TIP

Entering Command-Line Arguments
You can add a document name or other arguments to a command line when you start a program by combining two of the preceding methods. Drag the icon for the program from a folder or Windows NT Explorer window to the Open text box in the Run dialog box. You can then edit the command line before you click OK to launch the program.

In addition to these methods, you can, of course, create shortcuts for any of your programs and run them by double-clicking the shortcut icon. Creating a shortcut for a program written for another operating system is exactly like creating a shortcut for a Windows-based program. *For information about creating shortcuts, see "Creating a Shortcut," page 75.*

Running Windows 3.x–Based Programs

Windows NT easily runs most programs written for Windows 3.x. In general, they behave just like programs written for Windows 95 or Windows NT. But underneath, Windows 3.x–based programs, sometimes called "16-bit applications," are different from Windows NT–based programs, or "32-bit applications."

Windows 3.x is a 16-bit operating system. This means that it processes information—a number, memory address, or whatever—in 16-bit chunks. Windows NT, on the other hand, is a 32-bit operating system and processes information in 32-bit chunks. Because of this, programs for the two operating systems are written and compiled differently.

To bridge this gap, Windows NT includes a subsystem—a set of programs and routines for running other types of programs—for Windows 3.x–based applications. The environment presented to such applications by the subsystem is comparable to enhanced mode in Windows 3.x. That means applications have use of virtual memory, a feature of Windows 3.x enhanced mode that allows applications to use disk space as an extension of physical memory, much like the paging file used by Windows NT. And they can use other features common to Windows 3.x and Windows NT, such as OLE and DDE.

 TIP

Starting Your First Application Faster

Because Windows NT uses a subsystem to run 16-bit applications, starting the first Windows 3.x–based application in a Windows NT session takes a little bit longer than subsequent ones. You can save a few seconds when you're ready to run that first application by loading the subsystem when you log on. To do so, make a shortcut for the Windows 3.x subsystem, Wowexec.exe, and put it in your Startup group. The Windows 3.x subsystem remains active until you log off—even if no Windows 3.x–based applications are running.

Differences that Make a Difference

Although Windows NT allows you to run older Windows 3.x–based applications instead of requiring you to run to the software store (with credit card in hand) in search of an upgrade, there are some significant drawbacks to using these 16-bit applications under Windows NT. Among them:

- Most 16-bit applications do not support long filenames. In such applications, names of folders and files are rather cryptic, and often annoyingly similar. For example, documents called "Treating diseases of the foot" and "Treatise on nineteenth-century music" appear as treati~1.doc and treati~2.doc in the File Open dialog box displayed by Microsoft Word, version 6.0—and there's no easy way to tell which is which.

(Windows NT provides long filename information to all applications that understand them, so some 16-bit applications can use long filenames.)

- In general, 16-bit applications do not run as fast as comparable 32-bit applications because:
    - Windows NT–based applications can use multiple "threads" to perform several tasks simultaneously, whereas 16-bit applications use only a single thread, even on a multithreaded operating system such as Windows NT.
    - Calls made by a 16-bit application must be translated for the 32-bit operating system. And when the operating system returns information to the application, it must be translated into 16-bit form. This translation process, called "thunking," adds to execution time. (Fortunately, 32-bit instructions run faster than their 16-bit equivalents, partially offsetting the thunking time.)

  (Of course, poorly written 32-bit applications, or 32-bit applications that do not employ the advantages of a 32-bit operating system, are likely to be no faster than their 16-bit predecessors.)

- Some 16-bit applications use 16-bit device drivers, which are not supported in Windows NT. Applications that directly access hardware must supply a Windows NT virtual device driver and a Windows NT 32-bit device driver—or else they won't run.
- DLLs written for 16-bit applications cannot be used by 32-bit applications, and vice versa. (A DLL is a *dynamic-link library*, a collection of program-code modules that can be shared by two or more programs.) Because the setup program for most applications installs all the DLLs needed by the application, you won't

be aware of this distinction most of the time. But if, for example, you have a macro written for Word 6.0 (a 16-bit application) that accesses one or more DLLs, it won't work with Word 7.0 (a 32-bit application).

How Can You Tell?

Because Windows 3.x–based applications run effortlessly under Windows NT, it's sometimes difficult to know whether you're using a 16-bit or a 32-bit application. All applications that sport the "Designed for Windows 95" or "Designed for Windows NT" logo on their packaging are supposed to be 32-bit. A better indicator, though, is to look at the application itself. In Windows NT Explorer, right-click a *shortcut* to the program in question and choose Properties. (If there's no shortcut, create one and then follow this procedure.) Click the Shortcut tab. If the Run In Separate Memory Space check box is available (that is, it's not grayed out), then the application is a 16-bit, Windows 3.x–based application.

Compatibility with Win.ini and System.ini

SEE ALSO

For information about the registry, see "Working with the Registry," page 741.

Windows 3.x uses two text files, Win.ini and System.ini, to store configuration information for Windows itself and for applications you run. In Windows NT, this configuration information is stored in the registry, and Win.ini and System.ini are no longer required by Windows NT. Some Windows 3.x–based applications depend on the existence of those files however, and Windows NT accommodates such applications.

If you install Windows NT into the same folder where Windows 3.x is installed, the first time you run Windows NT it extracts configuration information about your Windows 3.x setup from Win.ini and System.ini and adds this information to the registry.

But you'll still find a Win.ini and a System.ini file in your Windows NT folder—whether or not you install Windows NT into the same folder as Windows 3.x, and even if you've never had Windows 3.x installed. These files are provided for the use of applications that require them for storing their configuration information.

NOTE

If you have a flex-boot system with Windows NT and Windows 3.x, changes you make in one environment will not appear when you boot into the other environment (unless you have both systems installed in the same folder). Similarly, configuration information saved by applications while running in one environment will not appear when you run the same application in the other environment.

Avoiding Crashes

When you start a Windows 3.x–based application, by default it runs in the same memory space as other Windows 3.x–based applications. This provides the most efficient use of memory, and works best for most applications. However, if one Windows 3.x–based application in a shared memory space hangs or crashes, it's likely to bring down all the others with it—and you'll lose any unsaved information in all the applications.

TIP

Virtual DOS Machines

The technical term for what we're calling "memory space" is *virtual DOS machine*, or *VDM*. When programmers mention Windows NT's "multiple VDM" capability, they're talking about the ability to run each Windows 3.x–based application in a separate memory space.

If you have an application that frequently hangs (locks up and won't accept additional commands) or crashes (causes a GPF error, for example), you should run it in a separate memory space (or update to a Windows NT version of the program!). To set up a Windows 3.x–based application to run in a separate memory space, follow these steps:

1. Right-click the Start button and choose Explore.
2. Navigate to the shortcut for the application you want to change.
3. Right-click the application's shortcut and choose Properties.

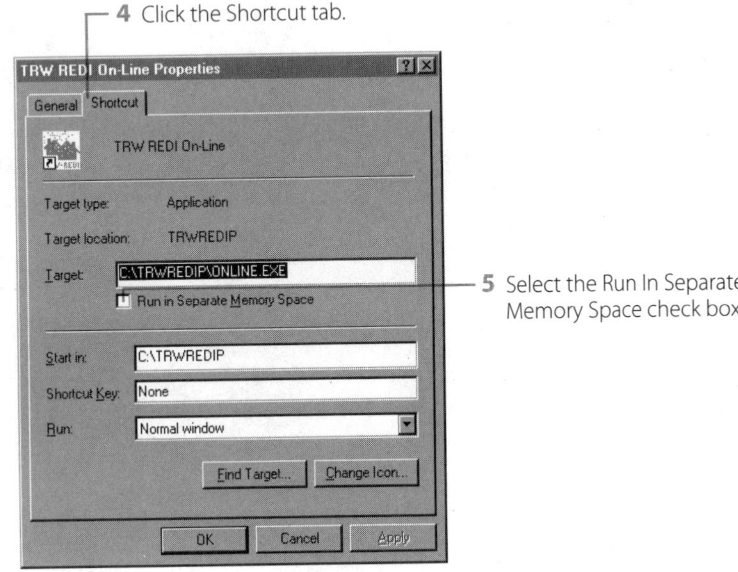

If you normally launch your Windows 3.x–based application by double-clicking a document icon in a folder or Windows NT Explorer window, you'll want to change the file type so that it opens its associated application in a separate memory space. To do so, follow these steps:

1 In a folder window or Windows NT Explorer window, open the View menu and choose Options.

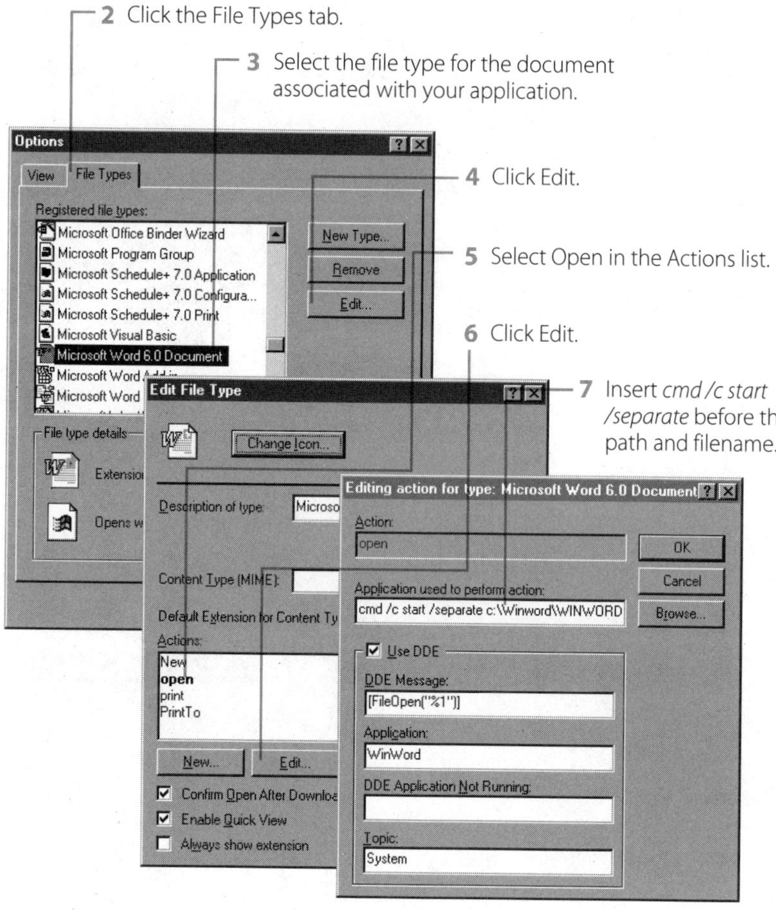

8 Click OK in each dialog box.

 TIP

Use Separate Memory Space for Demanding Programs
Use the separate memory space setting to increase the performance of Windows 3.x–based applications that make intensive use of memory due to floating-point calculations or graphics.

In addition to preventing an application from disrupting others, running Windows 3.x–based applications in separate memory spaces confers some additional benefits:

- You get true multitasking of Windows 3.x–based applications, because the scheduler in Windows NT automatically handles multitasking between different memory spaces.
- Applications in separate memory spaces are more responsive because each application has its own input queue.
- You can run multiple copies of applications that normally do not allow you to do so. You can, for example, print a long document in one window while editing another document in a second window.
- If you're lucky enough to have an SMP (symmetric multiprocessor) computer, Windows NT can allocate processes for applications in separate memory spaces among multiple processors.

Separate Memory Space for 32-Bit Applications

You might expect that a separate memory space would be beneficial for running 32-bit applications as well. Doing so is unnecessary because of the discipline that Windows NT automatically imposes on 32-bit applications. Windows NT uses *preemptive* multitasking instead of the *cooperative* multitasking of Windows 3.x, which depends on an application to hand over processing time to the next application. (Like children, some applications refuse to cooperate.) In addition, multiple input queues prevent any single 32-bit application from interrupting other applications. Windows NT also provides protected memory spaces for each 32-bit application, which prevent ill-mannered 32-bit applications from corrupting the memory space of other applications.

Running MS-DOS–Based Applications

If you were unable to run certain large MS-DOS–based programs under Windows 3.x, you may be pleasantly surprised to discover that your programs run fine under Windows NT. That's because Windows NT stores more of its own driver files in extended memory, thereby making a smaller demand on the memory range used by MS-DOS–based programs. Each of your MS-DOS sessions should be able to access considerably more memory than it could when running under earlier versions of Windows—or even under MS-DOS 6 alone. Each MS-DOS–based application runs in a separate "virtual DOS machine" comparable to a PC with 1 MB of RAM. Approximately 620 KB of conventional memory is available to applications.

A smaller footprint in conventional memory is only one of Windows NT's features that improves support for MS-DOS–based programs compared to earlier versions of Windows. Other such features include a streamlined interface for tailoring the way individual programs use memory and other resources (eliminating the need for the PIF Editor program supplied with earlier versions of Windows), the ability to run MS-DOS–based programs in scalable windows, and the ability to tailor the MS-DOS environment on a program-by-program basis.

Of PIFs and Property Sheets

If you installed Windows NT 4 as an upgrade to an earlier version of Windows or Windows NT, you may already have Program Information Files (PIFs) for some of your MS-DOS–based applications. If so, Windows NT 4 will continue to use the settings in your PIFs as you run your applications in the new environment.

NOTE

In a folder window's details view, the file type for a PIF is shown as "Shortcut to MS-DOS Program."

SEE ALSO

For information about application property sheets, see "Working with Your Programs' Property Sheets," page 492.

If you run a program for which no PIF exists, Windows NT runs the program with the settings found in a file called _Default.pif. In the majority of cases, these default settings allow the program to run effectively, so you don't need to concern yourself with property settings. If you want, however, you can adjust the program's settings by working with its property sheet. When you make any changes to the property sheet, Windows NT records your choices in a newly created PIF.

NOTE

If you examine a property sheet in Windows NT 4, you'll see that it contains all the settings that appear in PIFs for Windows 95 or Windows 3.x. Many of those settings, however, have no effect in Windows NT. Changes you make to those settings are effective only when you run the PIF under Windows 95 or Windows 3.x. The settings that Windows NT ignores are noted in this chapter, but not described. For more information about them, click the question-mark icon next to the property sheet's close icon, and then click the setting in question to see a description.

NOTE

If you start your application from a command prompt window or by using the Run command instead of double-clicking its icon (or a shortcut), the PIF settings aren't used. Instead, the application uses the command prompt window's console properties. *For information about setting console properties, see "Customizing Command Prompt Windows," page 506.*

Terminating an MS-DOS Session

The best way to end any MS-DOS–based program is to use the program's normal Quit or Exit command. Doing so ensures that the program is terminated in an orderly manner and that you're given the option to save any work created in the program.

CAUTION
You could lose work or damage open data files by using a Windows procedure to shut down an MS-DOS–based program. It's safer to use the program's normal Quit or Exit command instead.

If you're running an MS-DOS–based program in a window, however, you can also close it by clicking the Close button at the right edge of the title bar, by choosing Close from the Control menu, or by double-clicking the Control-menu icon. Normally, it's not a good idea to use any of these methods for shutting your program down, however, because Windows cannot ensure that your program is ready to be terminated.

When you use a Windows procedure to close an MS-DOS–based program, Windows NT displays a warning. You can then ignore the warning and go ahead with your program's termination (click End Task in the warning message box), or you can go back to your program and use its own shut-down procedure (click Cancel). Windows NT also requires you to close all MS-DOS–based programs before logging off or shutting down Windows NT itself.

Depending on how an option on the MS-DOS–based program's property sheet is set, the program may remain visible in a window after you shut it down. If it does, the title bar for the closed program's window will include the word *Inactive*. A program marked "Inactive" has already shut itself down, so it's perfectly safe to close its window by clicking the Close button. (The option to keep a closed program visible in an inactive window is handy at times because it allows you to see the program's final output, including any messages displayed by the program if it happens to terminate abnormally. *For information about using this option, see "Keeping a Program's Final Screen Visible at Close," page 496.*)

Full-Screen Versus Windowed Display

On an x86-based computer, you can run any character-based program for MS-DOS either in full-screen mode or in a window. (Graphics-based programs run only in full-screen mode. On RISC-based computers, all MS-DOS–based applications run only in a window.) If you run a program in full-screen mode, it looks exactly as it does when you run it under MS-DOS. If you run it in a window, it has a title bar, a Control menu, and all the other standard window paraphernalia. Figure 17-1 illustrates an MS-DOS–based program running in a window.

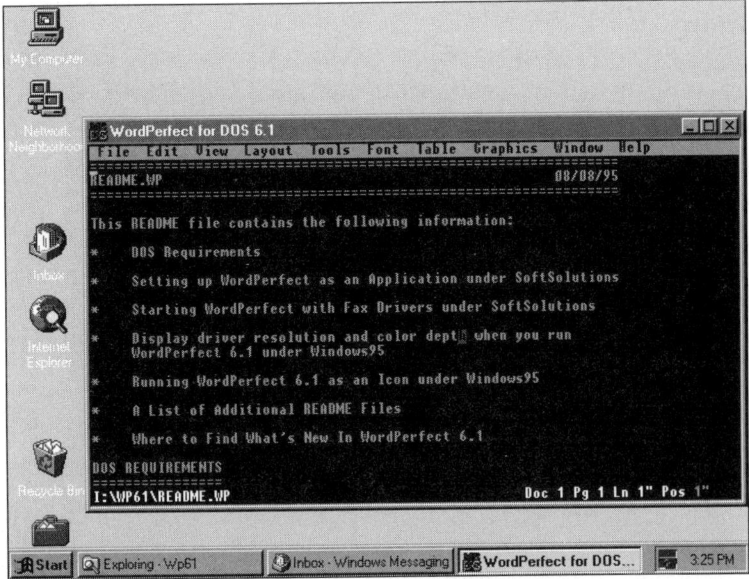

FIGURE 17-1.
In windowed display, an MS-DOS–based program has all the standard window equipment—a title bar, sizing buttons, a Control-menu icon, and so on.

Advantages of Full-Screen Display

One advantage of full-screen mode is that the program gets the maximum amount of screen real estate—the same amount of display space it would have if you were running the program in MS-DOS. If you run in a window, you can maximize the window, but the presence of the window title bar means you'll still have something less than the full screen to work with.

NOTE

"Maximizing" an MS-DOS window does not necessarily fill the screen, as it does with a resizable Windows-based application. The portion of the screen that the maximized window occupies depends on your Windows display resolution, the display mode used by the MS-DOS–based application, and the font size you select. *(For information about changing the Windows display resolution, see "Changing Display Resolution," page 95. For information about font-size options, see "Selecting a Font," page 511.)*

You might find that some programs' features work only in full-screen mode. For example, WordPerfect for DOS has a graphics display mode that provides a WYSIWYG view of your document. If you choose that view while WordPerfect is running in a window, the application is "frozen" until you switch to full-screen mode.

When using full-screen mode, you can switch to a different program by pressing Alt-Tab to invoke the task switcher, by pressing Ctrl-Esc to invoke the Start menu, or by first switching to windowed display. When you switch away from a full-screen MS-DOS–based program, a button for the program appears on the taskbar. You can switch back to the full-screen program by clicking its taskbar button.

TIP

Switching to the Desktop

If you have more than one full-screen MS-DOS session running and you want to switch from a full-screen MS-DOS session to the desktop, press Alt-Tab to invoke the task switcher. Then, while holding down the Alt key, click anywhere outside the task switcher. This takes you to the desktop.

You can also switch to the desktop by pressing Ctrl-Esc, which displays the desktop and opens the Start menu.

Advantages of Windowed Display

Windowed display confers several benefits that you don't get with full-screen display:

- You can keep several programs in view at the same time.
- You can more easily switch between programs.
- You can copy (but not cut) material from one program and paste it into another.
- You can read or modify your program's property sheet.

Switching Between Full-Screen and Windowed Display

Provided your MS-DOS–based program is not one of the few that run only in full-screen display, and provided you have not disabled the Alt-Enter shortcut key, you can switch from full-screen display to windowed display by pressing Alt-Enter. If you're running in windowed mode, you can use Alt-Enter to switch to full-screen display.

 TIP

Switching Without Alt-Enter

If you want to switch from full-screen to windowed display but you've disabled the Alt-Enter shortcut key (because it's used for another purpose by your application), press Alt-Tab or Ctrl-Esc to switch to another program. Then right-click the taskbar button for the program you switched away from. Choose Properties from the context menu, click the Options tab in the property sheet, and select the Window option button.

Mouse Options

If your MS-DOS–based program supports a mouse, and you run the program in full-screen mode, the MS-DOS–based program "owns" the mouse. That is, you can choose commands, make selections, or do anything else with the mouse that you could do if you were running the program in MS-DOS.

For more information about copying to the Clipboard, see "Copying from an MS-DOS–Based Application," page 486.

If you run the program in a window, you have a choice about mouse ownership. You can let the MS-DOS–based program own the mouse as in full-screen mode, or you can let Windows own it. If the program owns the mouse, you will need to use the Mark command on the Control menu in order to copy anything to the Clipboard. If you let Windows own it, you can use your mouse to select information and copy it to the Clipboard, exactly as in a Windows-based program. But you won't be able to use the mouse for choosing commands in the MS-DOS–based program.

Whichever mouse mode you elect to use, you can use the mouse to change the window's size or position, or to choose commands from the Control menu. In other words, the issue of who owns the mouse arises only when the mouse pointer lies within the client area of the program's window. On the borders or the title bar, Windows always retains control of the mouse.

Two settings control mouse ownership—and neither one is available through an application's property sheet (as they are in Windows 95). The QuickEdit setting determines whether the mouse performs its usual program functions (such as selecting commands) or selects text for copying to the Clipboard. The Hide Mouse Pointer command resolves a conflict that causes certain applications to display *two* mouse pointers—one for Windows and one for the application itself.

QuickEdit Mode

SEE ALSO
For more information about the Console property sheet's Options page, see "Setting Other Options," page 512.

QuickEdit mode, when selected, causes Windows to take ownership of the mouse so you can use it to easily select, copy, and paste text. Because it prevents the MS-DOS–based program from using the mouse for any other purpose, it's most useful in programs that don't use a mouse. To select QuickEdit mode:

1 Run your MS-DOS–based program.

2 Press Alt-Spacebar or click its Control-menu icon to open the Control menu, and then choose Properties.

3 Click the Options tab.

4 Select QuickEdit Mode.

5 Click OK.

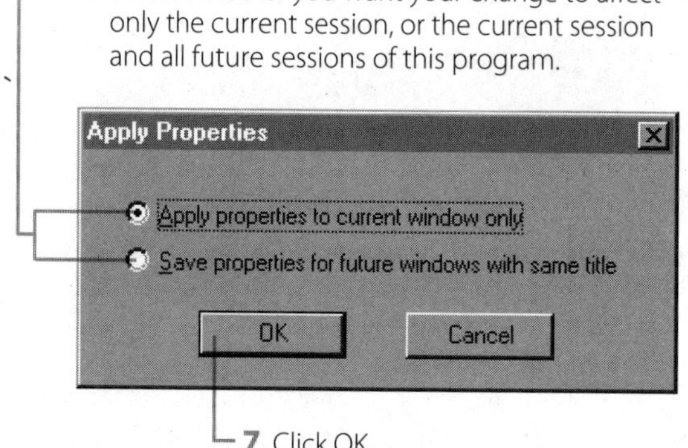

Hide Mouse Pointer Command

With most MS-DOS–based applications that support a mouse, the mouse functions the same way in both full-screen and windowed display mode. The only difference is the shape of the mouse pointer: in full-screen mode it's a rectangular block, and in a window it's an arrow.

However, some applications—WordPerfect for DOS is an example—display two mouse pointers when you run the application in a window. Moving the mouse moves the arrow-shaped Windows mouse pointer, but clicking and dragging has no effect in your application. Meanwhile, the application's block-shaped mouse pointer sits motionless, anxious but unable to help. The solution for such applications is to open the Control menu and choose Hide Mouse Pointer. When you do so, the Windows arrow pointer disappears, and the block pointer leaps around the window at your every mouse movement, enjoying its newfound freedom.

Freedom has its limits, of course, and you'll quickly find that your mouse is constrained to its application window, unable to cross the window border to select another application—or even to open the active application's Control menu. When you're ready to escape this mouse trap, do one of the following:

- Press Alt-Tab to switch to another application.
- Press Ctrl-Esc to open the Start menu.
- Press Alt-Spacebar to open your application's Control menu, and then choose Display Mouse Pointer.
- Close your application.

Using Copy and Paste

SEE ALSO
For more information about copying and pasting, see Chapter 10, "Exchanging Information: OLE and the Clipboard."

Windows NT provides basic copy-and-paste services (without OLE) for MS-DOS–based applications, just as it does for Windows-based programs. The procedures for copying and pasting are nearly the same in both kinds of applications.

Copying from an MS-DOS–Based Application

To copy a block of data from a windowed MS-DOS–based application:

1. Right-click the title bar, choose Edit from the Control menu, and then choose Mark on the submenu that appears.
2. Drag the mouse to select the data you want to copy.
3. Press Enter or right-click anywhere in the window.
4. Activate the document into which you want to paste, position the insertion point where you want the copied material to appear, and choose the Paste command.

SEE ALSO
For more information about the QuickEdit option, see "QuickEdit Mode," page 484.

If you've turned on the QuickEdit option for your MS-DOS–based application, you can omit step 1. How do you know if the QuickEdit option is on? Simply drag with the mouse and see what happens. If QuickEdit is on, the word *Select* appears in the program's title bar as soon as you start dragging. If it does not, you are not in QuickEdit mode, and you need to choose the Mark command before making your selection.

Note one important difference between selecting text in an MS-DOS–based application and selecting text in a Windows-based application: in an MS-DOS–based application, your selection is always rectangular, even if that means that lines of text are truncated on the left, the right, or both. The figure below shows an example of a text selection in an MS-DOS window. In contrast, when you select text in a Windows-based application, your selection follows the flow of your text, whether or not that produces a rectangular block.

When you select text in an MS-DOS–based application, your selection is rectangular, even if that means lines are truncated.

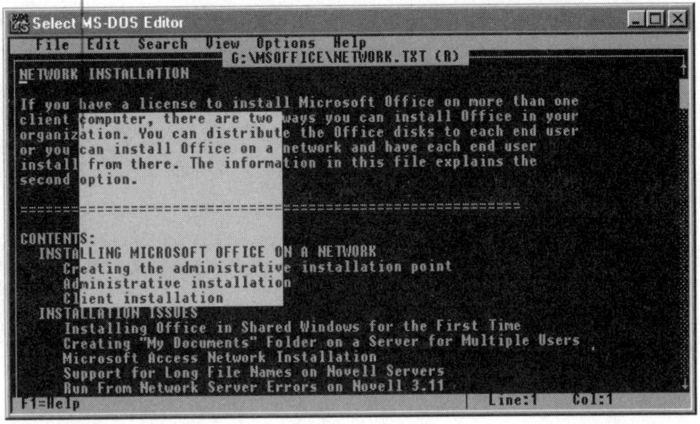

Selecting Text with the Keyboard

You can also select data in an MS-DOS–based application using the keyboard. Open the Control menu by pressing Alt-Spacebar. Press E to open the Edit submenu, followed by K to choose the Mark command. A rectangular cursor appears in the upper left corner of the application's window. This is your (unexpanded) selection. Use the Up, Down, Left, and Right arrow keys to position this cursor in one corner of the area you want to select. Then hold down the Shift key while you use arrow keys to expand the selection. When you have made your selection, press Enter to copy it to the Clipboard.

Pasting into an MS-DOS–Based Application

To paste data into an MS-DOS–based application, simply position the cursor where you want the pasted data to appear. Then open the Control menu, choose Edit, and choose Paste. If you have QuickEdit turned on, you can right-click anywhere in the window to paste at the cursor location.

Note that the Paste command in an MS-DOS–based application is always active, even if the Clipboard is empty or contains data in a format that's not appropriate for your application. If you try to paste graphics data into a text-based application, you'll get an error message when you paste. A different error message appears if the Clipboard is empty when you try to paste.

Also be aware that when you paste text into an MS-DOS–based application, Windows feeds characters to the application exactly as if you had typed them yourself at the keyboard. That is, the program itself cannot tell that the characters aren't coming directly from the keyboard. If you paste into a program that performs some kind of validation—for example, a spreadsheet that checks cell entries for correct formulation, or a program editor that verifies correct programming code—your paste may be interrupted by error messages from the application.

If you experience other kinds of problems pasting into an MS-DOS–based program, try disabling the Fast Pasting option. With this option on (as it normally is), Windows feeds character data to your program as fast as it can. Most, but not all, programs can accept this fast transfer. If yours cannot, open the Misc page of your program's property sheet and deselect the Fast Pasting check box.

Setting the MS-DOS Configuration

The files Autoexec.nt and Config.nt set the configuration used by MS-DOS–based programs. These two files serve a purpose similar to that of Autoexec.bat and Config.sys in MS-DOS, but they also have important differences:

- Autoexec.bat and Config.sys must be located in the root directory of your boot drive. Autoexec.nt and Config.nt must be located in the %SystemRoot%\System32 directory. (*%SystemRoot%* is the environment variable that specifies the location of your Windows NT folder, which is normally C:\Winnt.)

- Autoexec.bat and Config.sys are the only configuration files needed or available under MS-DOS. In Windows NT, Autoexec.nt and Config.nt are the default configuration files, but you also have the option of specifying different files with settings tailored for the application you're planning to run. In other words, you can have default Config.nt and Autoexec.nt files that are applied to all your normal MS-DOS–based programs and different versions for certain programs with special requirements.

NOTE

Don't confuse MS-DOS configuration files with command prompt initialization or logon initialization files. Autoexec.nt and Config.nt affect only MS-DOS–based programs. The command interpreter, CMD.EXE, is a Windows NT–based program and is not affected by anything in these configuration files. *For details, see "Initializing Command Prompt Sessions," page 549.*

SEE ALSO

For information about application property sheets, see "Working with Your Programs' Property Sheets," page 492.

To specify custom Config and Autoexec files to be used by a particular application, first click the Windows NT button on the Program page of the application's property sheet. This displays a dialog box like the one shown below.

Specify the path and filename of your custom configuration files if you don't want to use Autoexec.nt or Config.nt.

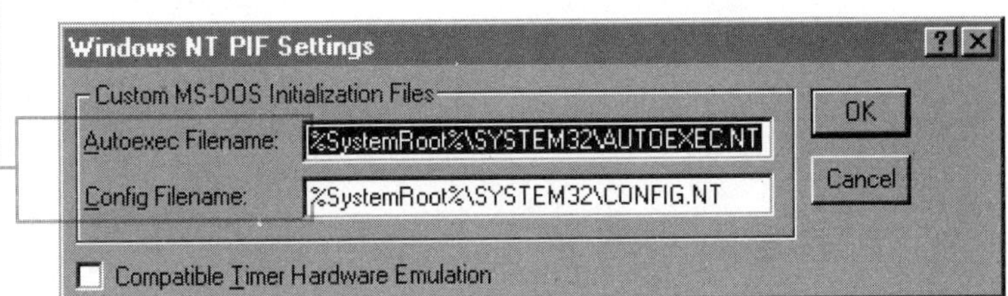

TIP

If you create custom Config and Autoexec files, base them on the default Config.nt and Autoexec.nt files. Then you'll be sure to include the basic information required to configure an MS-DOS session.

Using Config

In MS-DOS, the Config.sys file contains commands to load device drivers and set configuration parameters. In order to be compatible with all versions of MS-DOS, Windows NT does not validate commands in Config.nt. It executes the commands that it recognizes in Config.nt, and ignores anything it doesn't understand.

You probably won't need to modify Config.nt. However, if you acquire new programs for MS-DOS, you might need to make changes. If the manual for your MS-DOS–based program recommends a particular setting for Config.sys, put it in Config.nt. The setting might not be used by Windows NT, but usually it won't do any harm.

Device drivers are the exception. If your Config.sys loads a device driver with a Device= or DeviceHigh= statement, you might not be able to load the same driver in Config.nt. Table 17-1 suggests how you should handle device drivers commonly used with MS-DOS.

You can generally experiment safely with Config.nt settings. Windows NT protects the rest of the operating system from your MS-DOS–based programs, so failures won't harm the system. Naturally, you won't want to do much experimenting with valuable data in your MS-DOS–based programs, but usually the questionable device drivers you test will fail when loading—before the program even starts.

TIP

> To see output from device drivers in Config.nt and from programs in Autoexec.nt, put the EchoConfig statement at the start of Config.nt. Use the Rem statement to add comments or to comment out statements during testing. Comment out the EchoConfig statement when you finish testing.

TABLE 17-1. MS-DOS Device Drivers

Device Driver	Comments
HIMEM.SYS	Use the Windows NT version if you have programs that require it or if you use it in MS-DOS. Windows NT installs this in Config.nt by default.
ANSI.SYS	Use the Windows NT version if you have MS-DOS–based programs that require it. The Windows NT command interpreter is not an MS-DOS–based program and it does not recognize ANSI escape sequences. Therefore, you can't use them with the Prompt or Echo commands.
COUNTRY.SYS and SETVER.EXE	Use the Windows NT versions as you would the MS-DOS versions if you have MS-DOS–based programs that need them.
EMM386.EXE	Don't use it. Windows NT automatically provides equivalent functionality and more.
SMARTDRV.SYS	Don't use it. Windows NT has built-in disk caching.
RAMDRIVE.SYS	Don't use it. Windows NT doesn't support (and generally doesn't need) RAM drives.
DBLSPACE.SYS and DRVSPACE.SYS	Don't use them. Windows NT can't recognize or set up DoubleSpace or DriveSpace drives on a local hard drive, although it can use compressed drives shared from a networked MS-DOS computer.
Network drivers	Don't use them. Windows NT has built-in networking.
Drivers for hardware devices	You generally won't be able to use the MS-DOS versions. Some vendors might provide Windows NT versions of device drivers.

Using Autoexec

In your Autoexec file, you should load any programs that your MS-DOS–based programs need. The default Autoexec.nt file loads Mscdexnt.exe, Redir.exe, and Dosx.exe. These programs enable CD-ROM extensions, network services, and extended MS-DOS services needed by some MS-DOS–based programs.

NOTE

Your Autoexec.bat file, if you have one, is used by Windows NT for only one purpose: when you start your system, Windows NT scans Autoexec.bat for any environment variables set by Set or Path commands, and adds them to the system environment variables. All other statements in Autoexec.bat are ignored. *For more information, see "Initializing Environment Variables," page 538.*

TIP

Don't use the standard Autoexec.nt to start a memory-resident program. If you do, another instance of the program gets launched with each MS-DOS–based program, which wastes memory. If you must use a memory-resident program with a certain application, create a custom Autoexec file and specify that Autoexec in the application's PIF.

Working with Your Programs' Property Sheets

Each of your MS-DOS–based programs has a property sheet that spells out everything Windows NT needs to know to run your program. Windows NT records your property-sheet settings in a Program Information File, or PIF. You can use the property sheet to adjust such things as the amount of memory allocated to a program, the program's initial display mode (full-screen or windowed), the icon associated with the program, and so on.

To get to a program's property sheet, right-click its entry in a folder or Windows NT Explorer window. Then choose Properties from the context menu.

NOTE

Unlike Windows 95, when you choose Properties from a running application's Control menu, you'll see its console property sheet. Console property sheets provide a similar group of settings, but changes you make there do not get saved as part of the program's PIF. *For information about console properties, see "Customizing Command Prompt Windows," page 506.*

SEE ALSO

For more information about the General page, see "Inspecting Folder and File Properties," page 136. For information about the Security page, see Chapter 20, "NTFS Security," and Chapter 21, "Auditing."

The property sheet's General page includes information about the size of the program, its creation and most-recent-access dates, and so on. The Security page, which appears only for PIFs stored on an NTFS volume, lets you view and set permissions and monitor usage of the PIF. These are the standard pages and functions that you'll see for any file object; they don't have any special purpose in a PIF.

Options on the Program Page

The Program page of an MS-DOS–based program's property sheet includes basic information about a program, such as its name and location. The figure below shows the settings you can make in Windows NT.

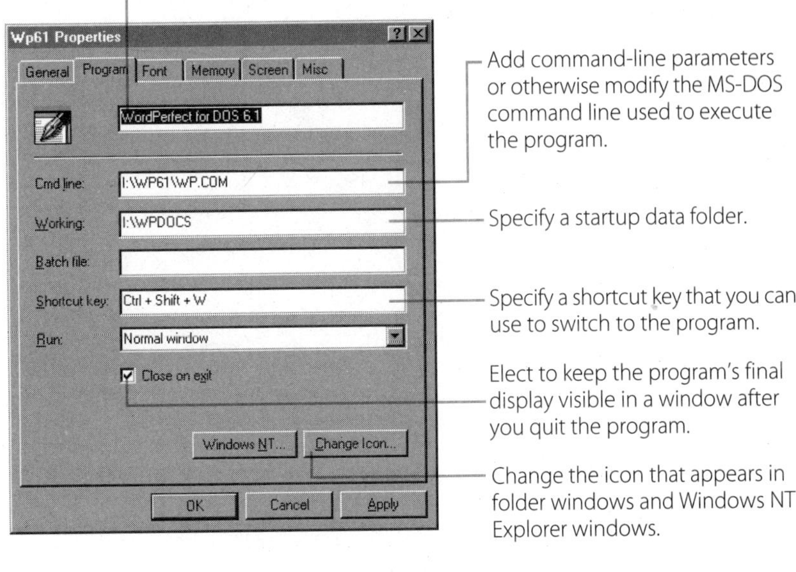

The Program page also includes a Windows NT button, which lets you select Config and Autoexec files that set up your MS-DOS configuration before the program runs. *For information about using the Windows NT button, see "Setting the MS-DOS Configuration," page 488.*

> **NOTE**
>
> The Batch File text box and the Run drop-down list have no effect in Windows NT. They appear here because Windows 95 and Windows NT use the same PIF settings, but these settings are effective only when you run the PIF under Windows 95.

Changing a Program's Title Bar Caption

To change the text that appears on a program's title bar, simply modify whatever appears in the first text box of the Program page. For example, typing *WordPerfect* in the first text box of the property sheet shown on the previous page changes the title bar from "WordPerfect for DOS 6.1" to "WordPerfect."

Adding Command-Line Parameters

The second text box in the Program page, the one marked Cmd Line, specifies the command line that MS-DOS uses to run your program. Many programs allow you to specify one or more command-line parameters following the name of your program's executable file. Depending on the program involved, parameters can be used for such things as loading a data file at the same time the executable is launched, modifying some aspect of the program's behavior, and so on. If you regularly want your MS-DOS–based program to use a particular command-line parameter, you can specify that parameter in the Cmd Line text box. Be sure to include a space character immediately after the name of the executable file, just as you would if you were entering the parameter at the MS-DOS command prompt.

 TIP

Entering Parameters When You Run a Program

If you include a question mark as a program parameter (that is, you follow the program name in the Cmd Line box with a space and a question mark), Windows pauses to ask for any command-line parameters whenever you start the program. This is useful, for example, for programs that use the name of the file you want to open as a command-line parameter.

Specifying a Startup Folder

The Working text box in the Program page lets you specify an initial data folder ("directory" in MS-DOS parlance) to be used by the MS-DOS–based program. For example, if you enter *c:\mystuff* on the Working line for the WordPerfect property sheet, WordPerfect will initially be set to read files from and save files to the folder C:\MyStuff. This line is blank by default, which means the program makes its own choice about what default data folder to use. In most programs, the default data folder is the folder in which the program's executable file is stored.

Specifying a Shortcut Key

SEE ALSO

For information about assigning a shortcut key to a Windows-based program, see "Assigning a Shortcut Key to a Shortcut," page 78.

On the Shortcut Key line, you can specify a keyboard shortcut for switching to the MS-DOS–based program. For example, if you run the MS-DOS–based version of Systat 6.0 under Windows NT, you might want to supply Systat with the shortcut Ctrl-Alt-S. Note, though, that unlike a shortcut key assigned to a Windows-based program, the shortcut you give to an MS-DOS–based program cannot be used to launch the program. It works only for switching to the program after the program is already running.

The shortcut key you assign must include the Ctrl key and/or the Alt key plus one character key (a letter, number, or symbol). If the shortcut key you assign is one that's used by a Windows-based application, it won't work in that application while the MS-DOS–

based application is running. For example, if you assign Ctrl-A to your application and run it, pressing that key combination, which normally selects all text in a document or window, switches to the MS-DOS–based application rather than selecting all text.

Keeping a Program's Final Screen Visible at Close

If an MS-DOS–based program terminates abnormally, it might be useful to keep the program's final screen output visible in a window after the program closes. That way you can read any error messages that the program may have displayed.

To exercise this option, clear the Close On Exit check box on the Program page of the property sheet.

Changing a Program's Icon

Windows assigns a default MS-DOS icon to all MS-DOS–based applications. This icon appears on your program's title bar, on its taskbar button, and in your folder and Windows NT Explorer windows. If you'd like to choose a different icon, click the Change Icon button near the bottom of the Program page. A selection of alternative icons appears in the ensuing dialog box. If none of those suit you, specify an .ICO file (or the name of a .DLL or .EXE file that contains icon resources) on the File Name line of that dialog box. Or click the Browse button and navigate to a file that contains icon resources.

Options on the Font Page

The Font page looks like it allows you to choose alternative display fonts to be used when an MS-DOS–based program is running in a window. Unfortunately, it ain't so. Selecting a font here is effective only when you run the program under Windows 95, not while you're running Windows NT.

To select a different font for use with Windows NT, visit the console property sheet instead. *For details, see "Selecting a Font," page 511.*

Options on the Memory Page

The Memory page, shown below, allows you to allocate memory to your applications in particular amounts and in various categories. Those categories are as follows:

Conventional	Memory in the 0–640 KB range
Expanded (EMS)	Physical memory above 1024 KB that is "mapped" into ranges between 640 KB and 1024 KB
Extended (XMS)	Memory above 1024 KB

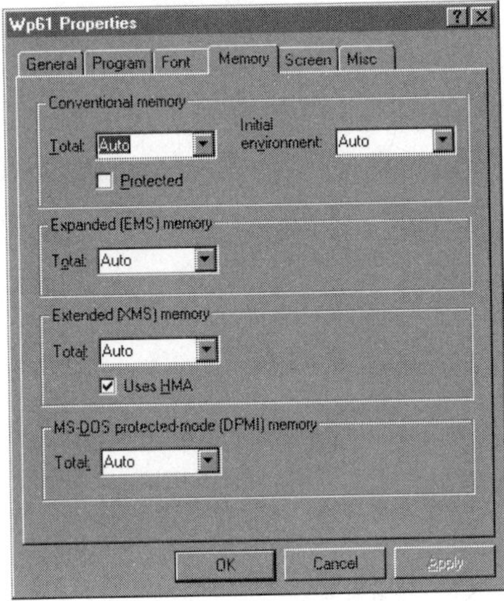

In all three cases, the default setting, Auto, should work for most programs.

For conventional memory, Auto means that Windows supplies your application with as much memory as it can. Unless you're running a particularly small-scale MS-DOS–based application and you need to conserve memory for other programs, it's unlikely you'll find a good reason not to choose Auto.

Auto also means "as much as possible" in the EMS and XMS drop-downs. In rare cases, an MS-DOS–based program may have trouble handling an unlimited amount of EMS or XMS memory. If your program is one of the exceptional few, use these drop-down lists to reduce the available EMS or XMS memory.

The Initial Environment and MS-DOS Protected-Mode (DPMI) Memory settings have no effect in Windows NT. They appear here because Windows 95 and Windows NT use the same PIF settings, but these settings are effective only when you run the PIF under Windows 95.

Options on the Screen Page

The Screen page of an MS-DOS–based program's property sheet lets you choose between full-screen and windowed display mode and override two of Windows' performance defaults. The figure below shows the settings you can make in Windows NT.

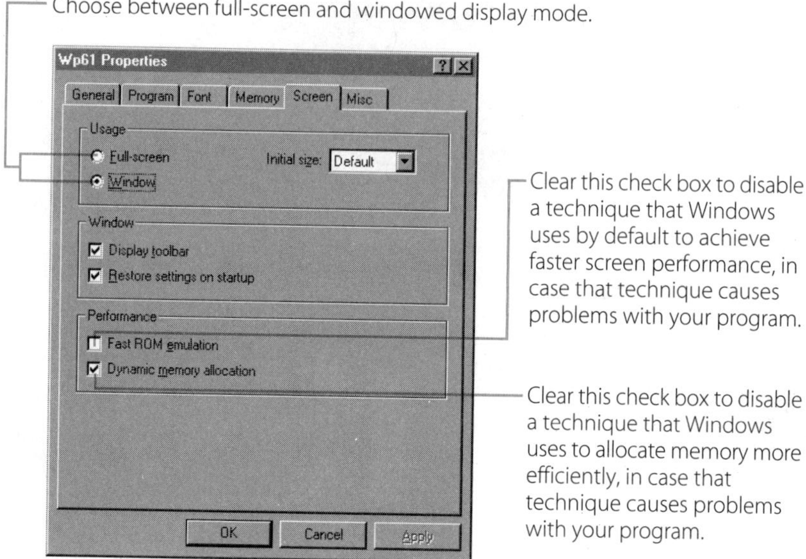

NOTE

The Initial Size, Display Toolbar, and Restore Settings On Startup settings have no effect in Windows NT. They appear here because Windows 95 and Windows NT use the same PIF settings, but these settings are effective only when you run the PIF under Windows 95.

TIP

Setting Screen Options Through Console Properties

Although some PIF property sheet settings are ignored by Windows NT, you can use console properties to make equivalent settings for your applications. To set the initial size and to set the screen size and position at startup, visit the console property sheet's Layout page. *For more information, see "Setting the Window Size and Position," page 509.*

Choosing Between Full-Screen and Windowed Display

You can switch a program between full-screen and windowed display at any time, simply by pressing Alt-Enter. Should you want to change the default display mode, you can do so by visiting the property sheet's Screen page and selecting the Full-Screen or Window option button.

Turning Off Video ROM Emulation

To achieve faster screen performance, Windows normally uses volatile memory (RAM) to emulate video routines that are stored in read-only memory (ROM). If you experience any abnormal screen behavior in an MS-DOS–based program, try turning this emulation off. Clear the Fast ROM Emulation check box on the Screen page.

Turning Off Dynamic Memory Allocation

Programs use considerably less video memory when displaying text than when displaying graphics. When an MS-DOS–based program switches from a graphics display to a text display, Windows normally takes advantage of the "memory dividend" so that more memory will be available for other programs. When an MS-DOS–based program switches back to a graphics display, Windows reallocates memory to the MS-DOS session. If you experience any problems switching from text mode to graphics mode in an MS-DOS–based program, try turning off this "dynamic memory allocation." Clear the Dynamic Memory Allocation check box on the Screen page of the property sheet.

Options on the Misc Page

Options on the Misc page of an MS-DOS–based program's property sheet, shown below, provide control over shortcut keys and other matters.

Adjust the "idle sensitivity"—the amount of time Windows will wait before reducing the resources allocated to an idle MS-DOS–based program that has the focus.

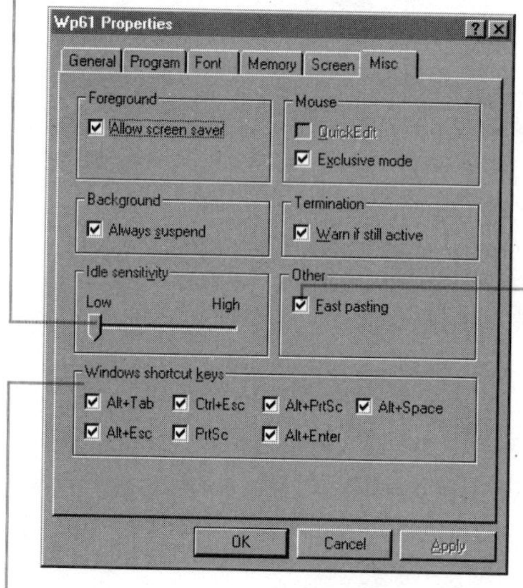

Adopt a slower pasting mode for an MS-DOS–based program that cannot accept data from the Clipboard as quickly as Windows normally supplies it.

Disable certain keystroke combinations (such as Alt-Tab) that are normally used by Windows so that those combinations can be used by an MS-DOS–based program.

NOTE

Settings in the Foreground, Mouse, Background, and Termination boxes have no effect in Windows NT. They appear here because Windows 95 and Windows NT use the same PIF settings, but these settings are effective only when you run the PIF under Windows 95.

TIP

Setting Mouse Options

You can select QuickEdit mode via the console property sheet. Exclusive mode is equivalent to selecting the Hide Mouse Pointer command. *For information about these options, see "Mouse Options," page 583.*

Adjusting the Idle Sensitivity

When an MS-DOS–based program running in the foreground sits idle—for example, while it's waiting for your next keystroke—Windows makes some of the resources it normally allocates to that program available to other running programs. The Idle Sensitivity slider on the Misc page gives you some control over how much idle time Windows tolerates before reallocating resources. If your program seems less responsive than you want it to be, move the slider to the left. If you want other programs to run more quickly while your MS-DOS–based program has the focus, move the slider to the right.

Slowing the Paste

If Windows doesn't correctly paste data from the Clipboard into an MS-DOS–based program, try clearing the Fast Pasting check box on the property sheet's Misc page. This will slow the rate at which Windows feeds Clipboard data to the program.

SEE ALSO

For more information about pasting, see "Using Copy and Paste," page 486.

Disabling Windows Shortcut Keys

Windows normally reserves certain keystroke combinations for itself, even while an MS-DOS–based program has the focus. For example, if you press Alt-Enter while working in an MS-DOS–based program, Windows assumes that keystroke combination is intended for it, rather than for the MS-DOS–based program. The reserved keystroke combinations and their normal effects are as follows:

Alt-Tab	Lets you switch to a different program
Ctrl-Esc	Displays the Start menu
Alt-Print Scrn	Copies the current window to the Clipboard as a bitmap
Alt-Spacebar	Displays the current program's Control menu
Alt-Esc	Switches the focus to another program
Print Scrn	Copies the desktop to the Clipboard as a bitmap
Alt-Enter	Switches between full-screen and windowed display

To make any of these shortcuts available to an MS-DOS–based application, clear the appropriate check box in the Windows Shortcut Keys section of the Misc page.

CHAPTER 18

Using the Command Prompt

Just as compact discs have largely displaced vinyl LP records in home music systems, the graphical user interface of Windows NT has largely displaced the command-line interface of earlier operating systems. But most stereo systems still have provisions for attaching a phonograph, and Windows NT still offers a command-line interface. Audiophiles insist to this day that LPs provide a richer sound that's truer to the original—and command-line enthusiasts prefer the power and speed of entering commands at the C> prompt. And although CDs and the Windows NT graphical interface offer greater convenience and ease of use than their predecessors, sometimes you must use the older system to achieve a goal, whether it's to hear an old Iron Butterfly album (that's not available on CD) or to compare two files with the FC command (which offers functionality available only at the command prompt).

Like Windows, Windows NT allows you to enter commands, run batch programs, and run applications by typing commands at the command prompt. If you're accustomed to performing file-management and disk-management operations at the command line, there's no need to change your ways in Windows NT. In Windows NT you can open multiple command prompts, each in its own separate session, protected from any failures that might occur in other sessions.

You can run any supported command or application at the command prompt, regardless of which operating system it was designed for—Windows NT, Windows 95, Windows 3.x, MS-DOS, OS/2 1.x, or POSIX. In addition to starting programs, you can use the command prompt to:

- Issue Windows NT commands, which include almost all commands from MS-DOS 5 plus many new commands
- Copy and paste information between applications
- Administer or use network resources
- Communicate on a TCP/IP-based network, such as the Internet
- Pipe or redirect data between subsystems

You can customize your command prompt sessions in various ways, and Windows NT includes tools such as Doskey and batch programs that make it easier to use command prompt sessions.

Starting and Ending Command Prompt Sessions

To get to the command prompt, do any of the following:

- Choose Command Prompt from the Start menu's Programs folder.
- Choose the Run command from the Start menu and type *cmd.*

- Double-click the Cmd icon in the System32 folder (a subfolder of your Windows NT folder).
- Double-click any shortcut for Cmd.exe.

Cmd.exe Versus Command.com

Cmd.exe is to Windows NT what Command.com is to MS-DOS. Both are command interpreters whose primary functions are to display the command prompt and to read, interpret, and execute what you enter at the prompt. But Cmd.exe running under Windows NT is a far more powerful command interpreter that can run programs from multiple operating systems, even though it might look and act like MS-DOS.

The default prompt in a command prompt session is the current drive and folder followed by a greater than sign, like this:

```
N:\WINNT\profiles\CarlS\Desktop>
```

TIP

Opening Additional Command Prompt Sessions

You can open as many command prompt windows as you like. With each additional window, you start another command prompt session. For example, you might want to open two command prompt windows to see two directories in side-by-side windows. To open another command prompt window, type *start* or *start cmd* at the command prompt. (These commands produce the same result. If you don't type a program name after "start," Windows NT assumes you want to start Cmd.exe.)

When the command prompt window is active, you can end a command prompt session in any of the following ways:

- Type *exit* at the command prompt.
- Click the Close button.

- Click the Control-menu icon and choose Close from the Control menu.
- Double-click the Control-menu icon.

If you are running a character-based program in the command prompt window, you should use the program's normal exit command to terminate the program before attempting to close the window and end the command prompt session. However, if you are sure the program doesn't have any unsaved files, you can safely and quickly close it using one of the last three methods listed above. A dialog box appears asking if you really want to terminate the program.

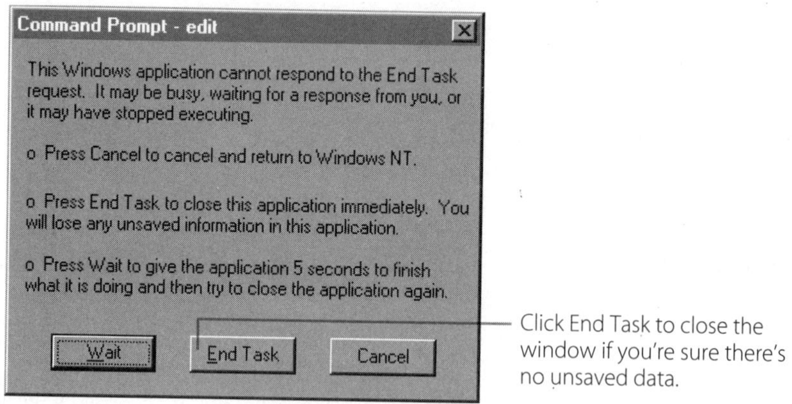

Click End Task to close the window if you're sure there's no unsaved data.

Customizing Command Prompt Windows

You can customize the appearance of a command prompt window in several ways: you can change its size, select a font, even use eye-pleasing colors. And you can save these settings independently for each shortcut that launches a command prompt session, so you can make appropriate settings for different tasks.

Consoles, Windows, and Command Prompts

A *window*, as you probably learned the first day you used Windows or Windows NT, is that rectangular area of your screen in which an application displays its information. Character-based programs (ones that are designed to use your display adapter's standard text modes, such as most MS-DOS–based programs) run in a special type of window called a *console*. Many of the standard procedures for using applications and customizing their appearance are (if you'll excuse the expression) thrown out the window when you use a console.

Command prompt sessions always run in a console.

To customize a command prompt window, you make settings on a property sheet that you can reach in any of three ways:

- Double-click the Console applet in Control Panel.
- Right-click a shortcut that opens a command prompt window, and choose Properties from the context menu.
- Click the Control-menu icon on a command prompt window and choose Properties from the Control menu.

TIP

Finding a Command Prompt Shortcut

If the command prompt shortcut that you want to change is located on the Start menu, you can navigate to it as follows:

1. Right-click the Start button and choose Explore. This opens Windows NT Explorer, with your Start Menu folder selected.
2. Expand the entries in Windows NT Explorer's left pane until the folder that contains the shortcut you're interested in is displayed.
3. Select the folder in the left pane.
4. Right-click the shortcut in the right pane to display its context menu.

Although these three methods display similar property sheets, they each have different effects, and their interaction can be confusing. This is what happens:

- The Console applet lets you view and change the *default* settings for consoles. The default settings are used by all command prompt shortcuts for which you have not made any settings using the other methods, and for all new command prompt shortcuts you create. The Console settings are also used by character-based applications for MS-DOS that do not have a PIF, and which do not store their own settings. *(For more information about MS-DOS–based applications and PIFs, see "Running MS-DOS–Based Applications," page 478.)*
- The property sheet for a shortcut lets you view and change the settings for all sessions you start with that shortcut—but it does not affect the Console-applet settings, nor does it affect sessions you start from another shortcut.
- The property sheet that appears when you choose Properties from a command prompt window's Control menu offers you a choice:

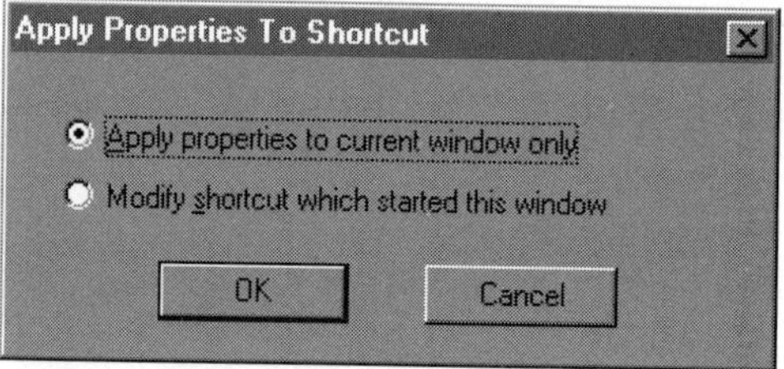

If you select "Apply properties to current window only," your changes are discarded when you close the window. If you select "Modify shortcut which started this window," your changes affect the current session and all future sessions that you start from the same shortcut. This is equivalent to changing the shortcut's property sheet directly.

Which method should you use? If you want to make default settings for all command prompt sessions (and you haven't modified your shortcuts' properties), use the Console applet because it's easy to get to. If you want to make different settings for different sessions (or if you've already modified the properties for the shortcut you want to change), use whichever property-sheet method you're most comfortable with. They're equally effective.

Setting the Window Size and Position

To change the screen position where a newly launched command prompt window appears, open the window's property sheet (using any of the methods described above) and click the Layout tab.

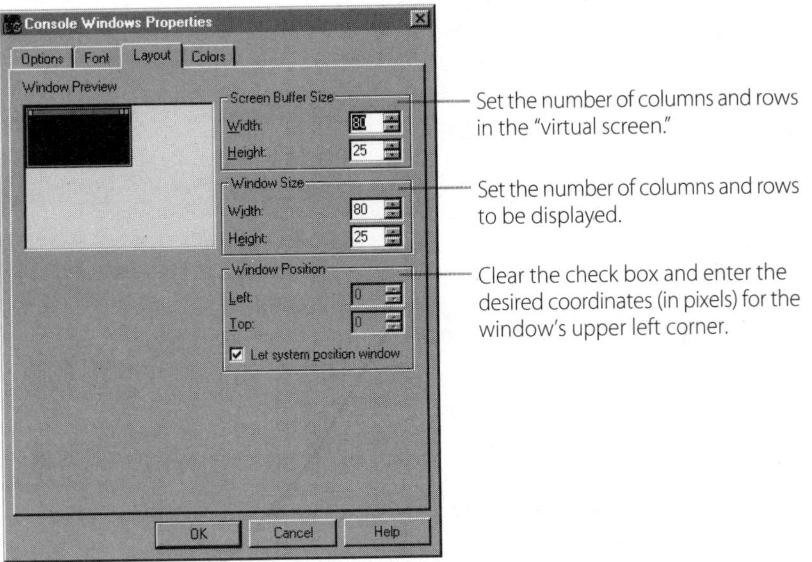

The property sheet maintains two different sizes—the screen buffer size and the window size. The width for both sizes is specified in columns (characters); the height is specified in rows (text lines).

The screen buffer settings control the size of the "virtual screen," which is the maximum extent of the screen. Standard screen sizes are

80×25, 80×43, or 80×50, but you can set your command prompt screen to any size you want. (Some programs that you launch from a command prompt session, however, might work correctly only with standard screen sizes. In such cases, Windows NT automatically adjusts the screen buffer size to the closest size that the program understands.)

The window size settings control the size of the command prompt window on your screen. In most cases, you'll want it the same size as the screen buffer. But if your screen is crowded, you can reduce the window size. If you do, scroll bars are added so you can scroll to different parts of the virtual screen. The window size settings can never be larger than the screen buffer size settings.

NOTE

Because you specify a window size as a number of columns and rows of characters, the size of those characters also affects the amount of space a console occupies on your display. *For information about changing the character size, see "Selecting a Font," below.*

TIP

Setting the Window Size and Position Visually

Rather than guessing at the settings for window size and window position, you can use this procedure:

1. Open the command prompt window.
2. Drag the window's borders to adjust its size, and drag its title bar to adjust its position.
3. Click the Control-menu icon and choose Properties from its menu.
4. Click the Layout tab, and you'll see the settings that reflect the window's current condition.
5. Click OK to apply the settings.
6. Select "Modify shortcut which started this window" and click OK to save the settings.

Selecting a Font

Unlike most Windows-based applications, applications in a command prompt window can display only one font at a time. And compared to most Windows-based applications, your choice of fonts is limited, as you'll see if you click the Font tab in the command prompt window's property sheet.

The Window Preview box shows the relative size of the console on the screen if you use the currently selected font and size.

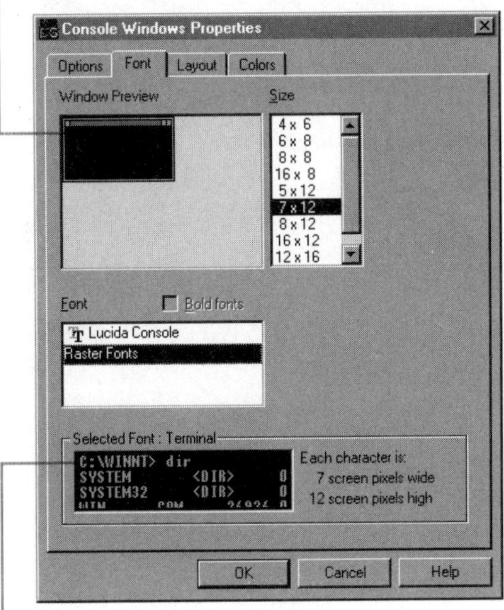

This box shows an actual-size sample of the selected font and size.

You should make a selection in the Font list first, because your choice here determines the contents of the Size list. If you select a TrueType font (such as Lucida Console in the figure above), you'll find point sizes to choose from in the Size list. *(For information about point sizes, see "Font Size," page 190.)* If you select Raster Fonts, you'll find character widths and heights (in pixels, or screen dots) in the Size list, as in the figure above.

Settings you make on the Font tab are effective only when the command prompt session runs in a window, not when it runs full-screen. *See "Full-Screen Versus Windowed Display," page 480.*

Setting Colors

You can set the color of the text and the background of the command prompt window. You can also set the color of the text and the background of pop-up windows that originate from the command prompt, such as the command history.

To set colors, click the Colors tab in the command prompt window's property sheet. The dialog box shown below appears.

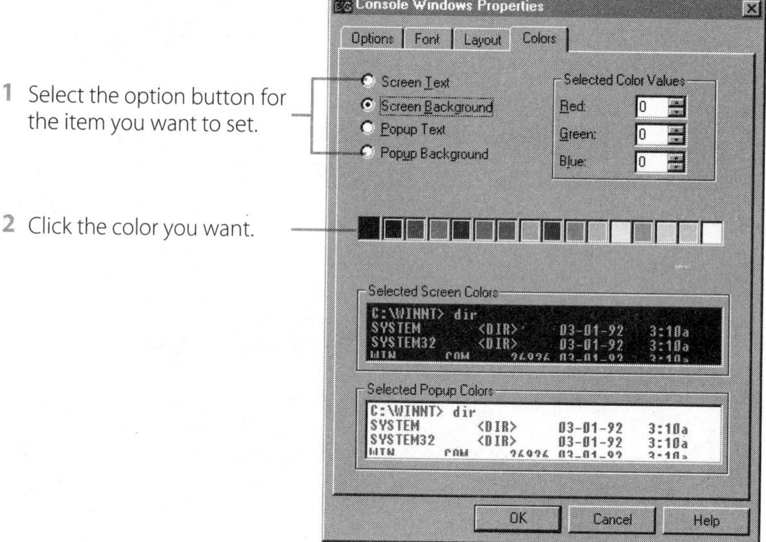

1 Select the option button for the item you want to set.

2 Click the color you want.

Setting Other Options

The Options tab in the command prompt window's property sheet, shown on the next page, offers a grab bag of options that affect how your command prompt window operates.

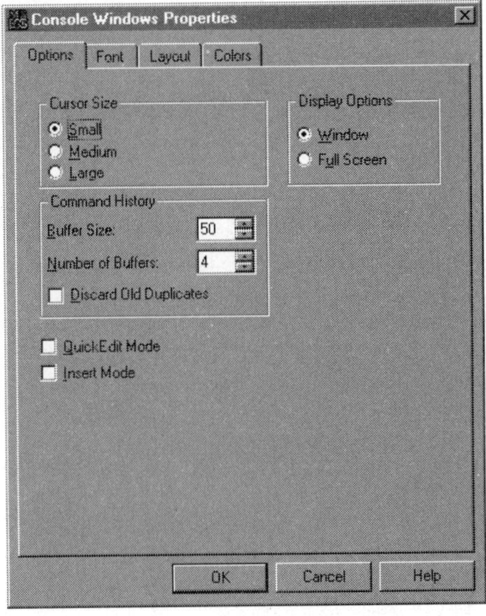

- The Cursor Size option buttons control the size of the blinking cursor in a command prompt window.
- The Display Options determine whether your command prompt session appears in a window or occupies the entire screen. (These options are not available on RISC-based computers, which always display command prompt sessions in a window.) *For more information, see "Full-Screen Versus Windowed Display," page 480.*
- The Command History options control the buffer used by Doskey.
  - Buffer Size specifies the number of commands to save in each command history.
  - Number Of Buffers specifies the number of command history buffers to use. (Certain character-based programs other than Cmd.exe use Doskey's command history. Doskey maintains a separate history for each such program that you start.)

- Selecting Discard Old Duplicates uses the history buffers more efficiently by not saving duplicate commands.

For more information about command history, see *"Using Doskey Macros," page 542.*

- QuickEdit Mode provides a fast, easy way to copy text from (and paste text into) command prompt windows with a mouse. (If you don't select QuickEdit Mode, you can use commands on the Control menu for copying and pasting text.) *For details, see* *"Using Copy and Paste," page 486.*

Starting Programs

You can start all kinds of programs at the command prompt—programs for Windows NT, Windows 95, Windows 3.x, MS-DOS, OS/2 1.x, or POSIX—so you don't need to know a program's origin or type to run it. If it's on your disk, simply type its name (and path, if needed) followed by any parameters. It should run with no questions asked.

If you're starting a character-based program, it runs in the command prompt window. When you terminate the application, the command prompt returns. But if you start a graphics-based program for Windows, it opens in its own window, leaving the command prompt window in place. Although it's in a separate window, the command prompt window is frozen, waiting for the Windows-based application to close.

You can see how this works by typing *calc* at the command prompt to start the Calculator accessory. Although you can switch back to the command prompt window, typing in it has no effect—until you close the Calculator window.

In many situations, you'll want to run applications in addition to the command prompt session, not instead of it. That way, you can continue using the command prompt to launch other programs, for example.

For these situations, Windows NT provides the Start command, which allows you to start a program in a new window without freezing the command prompt window.

Type *start* before the program name to start the program in a new window.

You can type additional commands without first closing the program you started.

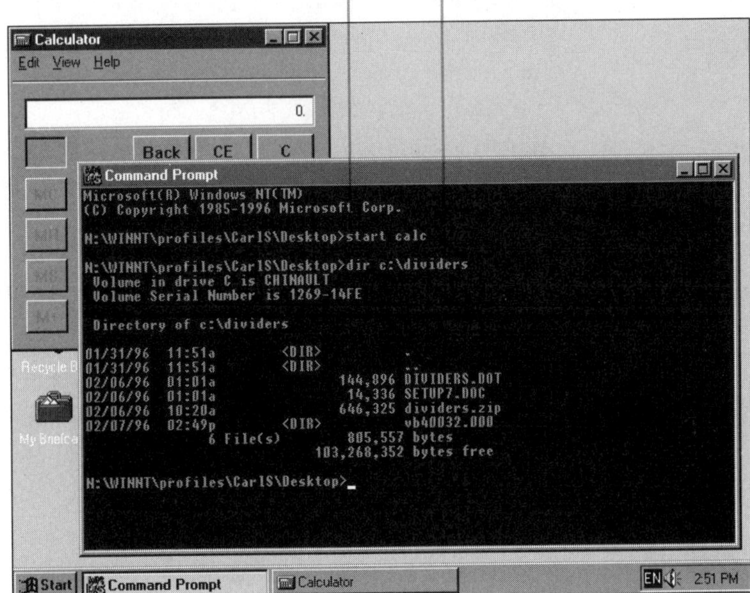

The Start command has several useful options for specifying how a started program should appear on your desktop. For Windows-based programs, you can use /min or /max to make the program open in a minimized or maximized window. For character-based programs, you can enter (in quotation marks) the title that you want to appear on the program window. For more information about the Start command, type *start /?* at the command prompt.

 NOTE

Place any parameters or switches that you use with the Start command *before* the name of the program or command you want to start. Anything after the program name is passed to the program as a command-line parameter, and is ignored by Start.

Using Commands

In most respects, entering commands or running programs at the Windows NT command prompt is the same as using the command prompt of any other operating system. MS-DOS, OS/2, UNIX—if you've used one command prompt, you've used them all. Every operating system has a command to delete files, another to display lists of files, another to copy files, and so on. The names and details may be different, but it's the same cast of characters.

The commands and features available at the Windows NT command prompt most closely resemble those of MS-DOS 5—with some important enhancements and additions.

Getting Help

The first thing you need to know about using the command prompt is how to get help. You can get help on any command-line program or internal command supplied with Windows NT in two ways. You can:

- Type the name of the command followed by */?*. For example,

```
C:\>dir /?
```

- Type *help* followed by the name of the program. For example,

```
C:\>help dir
```

For help with network-related commands, precede your help request with *net*. For example, type *net view /?* or *net help view* for information about the Net View command. (With the Net commands, "net help *command*" provides more detailed help than "net *command* /?")

Either method brings up exactly the same help screen showing the command followed by its argument syntax. Let's take the Tree command as an example:

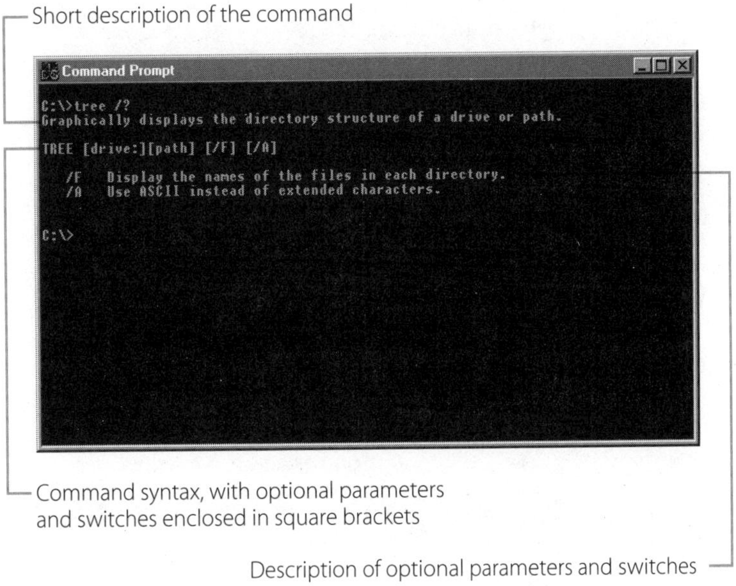

Short description of the command

```
Command Prompt
C:\>tree /?
Graphically displays the directory structure of a drive or path.

TREE [drive:][path] [/F] [/A]

   /F   Display the names of the files in each directory.
   /A   Use ASCII instead of extended characters.


C:\>
```

Command syntax, with optional parameters and switches enclosed in square brackets

Description of optional parameters and switches

If this terse form of help is not enough, you can get full details on all Windows NT commands from a Windows NT help file. To open the help file, choose Help from the Start menu, and then double-click the book icon for Windows NT Commands. Double-click this book's first topic, Windows NT Commands. Alternatively, at the command prompt type:

```
C:\>start winhlp32 ntcmds
```

You'll soon find that you don't need full help very often. After you get used to the way commands work, the simple command-line help will be enough.

You can also type *help* with no arguments to get a list of the internal commands and system utilities provided with Windows NT.

Editing the Command Line

When working at a command prompt, you often enter the same command several times, or enter several similar commands. If you make a mistake when typing a command line, you don't want to retype the whole thing—just fix the part that was wrong. Windows NT includes a feature similar to the MS-DOS Doskey utility, which recalls previous commands and lets you edit them on the current command line.

Command-line editing works the way you might expect. The Left and Right arrow keys move the cursor left and right. The Ins key toggles between insert and overwrite modes. The Del key deletes the character at the cursor, and the Backspace key deletes the character to the left of the cursor. It's no different than editing a single line in most text editors. Table 18-1 shows the editing keys and what they do.

TABLE 18-1. Command-Line Editing Keys

Key	Function
Up	Recalls the previous command in the command history
Down	Recalls the next command in the command history
PgUp	Recalls the earliest command used in this session
PgDn	Recalls the most recent command used
Left	Moves left one character
Right	Moves right one character
Ctrl-Right	Moves right one word
Ctrl-Left	Moves left one word
Home	Moves to the beginning of the line
End	Moves to the end of the line
Esc	Clears the current command
F7	Displays the command history in a scrollable pop-up box
F8	Displays commands that start with characters currently on the command line
Alt-F7	Clears the command history

 **SEE ALSO**

For more information about using Doskey, see "Using Doskey Macros," page 542.

The command-line recall feature works by keeping a history of the commands entered during the command prompt session. To display this history, press the F7 key. A window pops up that shows the commands you have recently entered. Scroll through the history with the arrow keys to select the command you want. Then press Enter to reuse the selected command, or press the Left arrow key to place the selected text on the command line without executing the command. (This lets you edit the command before executing it.)

 **TIP**

It's not necessary to display the pop-up window to use the command history. You can scroll through the history with the Up and Down arrow keys.

 **SEE ALSO**

For information about copying and pasting text in a command prompt window, see "Using Copy and Paste," page 486.

The F8 key provides a useful alternative to the Up arrow key. The Up arrow key moves you through the commands to the top of the command buffer and then stops. The F8 key does the same, except that when you get to the top of the buffer it cycles back to the bottom. Furthermore, F8 displays only commands in the buffer that begin with whatever you type before you press F8. Type *d* at the command prompt (don't press Enter) and then press F8 a few times. You'll cycle through recently entered commands that start with *d,* such Dir and Del. Now type *e* (after the *d*) and press F8 a few more times. You'll cycle through Del commands along with any others that start with *de*. You can save a lot of keystrokes with F8 if you know the first letters of the command you're looking for.

Using Wildcards

Windows NT, like MS-DOS, recognizes two wildcard characters: ? and *. The question mark represents any single character in a filename. For example, the command

```
C:\docs>dir c?t.doc
```

matches Cat.doc, Cot.doc, and Cbt.doc.

The asterisk matches any number of characters. In MS-DOS, the asterisk works only at the end of the filename or extension. Windows NT handles the asterisk much more flexibly, as the following examples show.

Let's assume that you have a folder containing three files named Ate.doc, Bate.doc, and Bat.doc. All three contain the letters *AT*—one at the beginning, one in the middle, and one at the end. Now suppose you want to find the one with AT at the beginning. Enter this command:

```
C:\docs>dir at*.doc
```

Sure enough, this command shows only Ate.doc. Now look for AT at the end:

```
C:\docs>dir *at.doc
```

Windows NT finds only Bat.doc. What will the following command do?

```
C:\docs>dir *at*.doc
```

Windows NT finds all three files because Windows NT interprets the asterisk as *zero or more* characters. Ate.doc is found because it has zero characters before AT, and Bat.doc is found because it has zero characters after AT.

TIP

Separate Search Groups with Periods

With long filenames that have multiple extensions separated by periods, the asterisk can be used to match characters within each group. For example, let's assume that your current folder contains the files A.A.A, A.B.C, C.B.A, and A.B.C.D. The command *dir *.b.** matches A.B.C, C.B.A, and A.B.C.D, but not A.A.A. Typing *dir a.b.c.** matches only A.B.C and A.B.C.D.

Using Command Symbols

Old-fashioned programs that take all of their input from a command line and then run unaided can be useful in a multitasking system because you can turn them loose to do complicated processing in the background while you continue to work with other programs in the foreground. Windows NT includes features that make command-line programs easier to run and more powerful, and that let you chain programs together so that later ones use the output of their predecessors as input.

In order to work together better, many command-line programs follow a set of conventions that control their interaction.

- By default, programs take all of their input as lines of text typed at the keyboard. But input in the same format also can be redirected from a file or any device capable of sending lines of text.
- By default, programs send all of their output to the screen as lines of text. But output in the same format also can be redirected to a file or another line-oriented device such as a printer.
- Programs are written to set a number called a return value when they terminate, to indicate the results of the program.

When programs are written according to these rules, you can use the symbols in Table 18-2 to control a program's input and output, and to connect or chain programs together.

TABLE 18-2. Command Symbols

Symbol	Purpose
<	Redirects input
>	Redirects output
>>	Appends redirected output to existing data
|	Pipes output
&	Separates multiple commands in a command line
&&	Runs the command after && only if the command before && is successful
||	Runs the command after || only if the command before || fails
^	Treats next symbol as character
(and)	Groups commands

The Redirection Symbols

As in MS-DOS and UNIX, command prompt sessions in Windows NT allow you to override the default source for input (the keyboard) or the default destination for output (the screen).

Redirecting Output

To redirect output to a file, type the command followed by a greater than sign (>) and the name of the file. For example, to send the output of the Dir command to a file instead of the screen:

```
C:\bat>dir /b *.bat > batch.lst
```

This command line creates a file called Batch.lst that contains the names of all the .BAT files in the current folder.

Using two greater than signs (>>) redirects the output and appends it to an existing file. For example:

```
C:\bat>dir /b *.cmd >> batch.lst
```

This command line appends a list of .CMD files to the previously created file containing .BAT files. (If you use >> to append to a file that doesn't exist, Windows NT creates the file.)

Redirecting Input

To redirect input from a file, type the command followed by a less than sign (<) and the name of the file. The Sort and More commands are examples of commands that can accept input from a file. The following example uses Sort to filter the file created with the Dir command above.

```
C:\bat>sort < batch.lst
```

The input file, Batch.lst, contains a list of .BAT files followed by a list of .CMD files (assuming you have some of each in the current folder). The output to the screen has the same list of files sorted alphabetically by filename.

TIP

Redirecting Input and Output

You can redirect both input and output in a command line. For example, to use Batch.lst as input to the Sort command and send its output to a file named Sorted.lst:

```
C:\bat>sort < batch.lst > sorted.lst
```

Standard Output and Standard Error

Programs can be written to send their output either to the standard output device or the standard error device. Sometimes programs are written to send different types of output to each device. You can't always tell which is which because by default both devices are the screen.

The Windows NT Type command illustrates the difference. When used with wildcards (something you can't do with the Type command in MS-DOS or Windows 95), Type sends the name of each matching file to standard error and sends the contents of the file to standard output. Because they both go to the screen, you see a nice display with each filename followed by its contents.

However, if you try to redirect output to a file like this:

```
C:\bat>type *.bat > std.out
```

the filenames still appear on your screen because standard error is still directed to the screen. Only the file contents are redirected to Std.out.

Windows NT allows you to qualify the redirection symbol by preceding it with a number. Use 1> (or simply >) for standard output and 2> for standard error. For example:

```
C:\bat>type *.bat 2> err.out
```

This time the file contents go to the screen and the names are redirected to Err.out. You can redirect both to separate files with this command line:

```
C:\bat>type *.bat 2> err.out 1> std.out
```

The Pipe Symbol

The pipe symbol (|) is used to send or *pipe* the output of one program to a second program as the second program's input. Piping is commonly used with the More utility, which displays multiple screens of output one screenful at a time. For example:

```
C:\bat>help dir | more
```

This command line uses the output of Help as the input for More. The More command filters out the first screenful of Help output, sends it to the screen as its own output, and then waits for a keypress before sending more filtered output.

The Command Combination Symbols

SEE ALSO

For information about batch programs, see "Using Batch Programs," page 546. For more information about Doskey macros, see "Using Doskey Macros," page 542.)

Unlike MS-DOS, Windows NT allows you to enter multiple commands on a single command line. Furthermore, you can make later commands depend on the results of earlier commands. This feature can be particularly useful in batch programs and Doskey macros, but you might also find it convenient at the command prompt.

To simply combine commands without regard to their results, use the & symbol, like this:

```
C:\data>copy a:file.dat & edit file.dat
```

But what if there is no File.dat on drive A? Then it can't be copied to the current drive and the Edit command will fail when it can't find the file. Your screen will be littered with error messages. Windows NT provides two command symbols for better control over situations like this.

- The && symbol causes the second command to run only if the first command succeeds.
- The || symbol causes the second command to run only if the first command fails.

Consider this modified version of the earlier example:

```
C:\data>copy a:file.dat && edit file.dat
```

With this command line, if the Copy command fails, the Edit command is ignored.

Sometimes you want the opposite effect: execute the second command only if the first fails. You can do this with the || symbol, like this:

```
C:\data>copy a:file.dat || copy b:file.dat
```

This command line tries to copy the file from drive A. If that doesn't work, it tries to copy the file from drive B.

The Escape Symbol

Some command symbols are legal characters in filenames. This leads to ambiguities. You can resolve such ambiguities by using the caret (^) as an escape to indicate that whatever follows it is a character rather than a command symbol.

Consider the following command line:

```
C:\cartoons>copy f:\cartoons\Tom&Jerry
```

This copies the file F:\Cartoons\Tom to the current folder, and then executes the Jerry command—probably not what you wanted. You might think that because there is no space before or after the & symbol, the system will know that you are referring to the filename Tom&Jerry. Not true. When a command symbol appears on the command line, whatever follows it is assumed to be a command, space or no space. Use the caret as shown below to indicate that you are referring to a filename.

```
C:\cartoons>copy f:\cartoons\Tom^&Jerry
```

TIP

Instead of using the ^ symbol, you can enclose a file specification that includes command symbols (or other troublesome characters, such as spaces) within quotation marks to achieve the same effect. For example:

```
C:\cartoons>copy "f:\cartoons\Tom&Jerry"
```

Pausing or Canceling Commands

You can pause or cancel a command that you enter at the command prompt. (Keep this in mind if you accidentally request a directory of all the files—or worse, enter a command to delete all the files—on a huge network server drive!)

To pause the output of a command, press Ctrl-S or the Pause key. To resume output, press any key.

Pausing with the Mouse

If you have QuickEdit mode enabled for your command prompt window, simply click in the window to pause command output. To resume output, right-click in the window. *For information about QuickEdit, see "Setting Other Options," page 512.*

To cancel a command, press Ctrl-C or Ctrl-Break. With either key, your command is canceled, and the command prompt returns. Be aware though, that any action (such as deleting files) that occurs before you cancel the command is done—and cannot be undone.

Using Network Commands

This section describes some of the common commands for working with a network via the command prompt. Using the command prompt for these network functions is completely optional; most operations described here can also be done through Windows NT Explorer or Control Panel. You'll find, however, that it's sometimes easier and faster to use the command prompt.

You might simply be working in a command prompt window and not want to go to the trouble of switching to another window. But a more compelling reason to learn and use network commands is that you can execute a series of network commands in a batch program, and thus automate repetitive network tasks in a way that can't be done through the graphical interface.

Using Network Names

Network resources can include printers, disks, modems, tape drives, and just about any other device connected to a computer. If a user somewhere on the network makes a device on his or her computer available to the network, that device is said to be *shared*. In order to use a shared device on someone else's computer, you must *connect* to that device.

Like files and folders, network resources are assigned names so that network users can specify the devices they want to connect to. Network names are not case-sensitive, but they must conform to the following format:

\\computer name\share name

SEE ALSO
For information about sharing resources on your computer, see "Sharing Folders with Other Users," page 281, and "To Share or Not to Share," page 229.

A network name must always start with two backslashes (\\) to distinguish it from a folder name. The backslashes are followed by the *computer name,* which is the name of the computer to which the device is attached. A single backslash separates the computer name from the *share name,* which is the name assigned to the device by the user sharing it. For example, a typical name for a shared network printer might be \\Acadia\Laserjet4. A typical name for a shared CD-ROM drive might be \\NTServer\CD-Rom.

Getting Help

The first thing to learn about using network resources from the command prompt is how to get help. You can get help on most network commands with the Net Help command. Typing this command with no arguments gives you a list of all available help topics.

To get help on a specific command, type *net help* followed by the name of the command. For example,

```
C:\>net help share
```

gives the syntax and a description of the command to share a device attached to your computer. If you just need a refresher about a command's syntax and don't want to be bothered with a description of the command's purpose, use the /? switch, like this:

```
C:\>net share /?
```

You can get more detailed help from the command reference help file, which you can open by choosing Help from the Start menu and then selecting Windows NT Commands, or by entering this command:

```
C:\>start winhlp32 ntcmds
```

TIP

Help About Error Messages

When you get an error message from a Net command, an error number is displayed along with a brief description. To get more detailed information about the error, use the number as an argument of the Net Helpmsg command. For example:

```
C:\>net helpmsg 2182
```

Connecting to Shared Resources

You can connect to a shared resource by specifying a device name and a network name as part of the Net Use command, like this:

```
C:\>net use x: \\zion\document
```

This command maps a folder called \\Zion\Document as drive X. If the command succeeds, you can use drive X exactly as you would any drive on your local computer—subject to any restrictions imposed by the owner. For example, the owner might allow anyone to read files, but allow only selected users to write, modify, or delete them.

You can connect to network printers in the same way. For example:

```
C:\>net use lpt1 \\yellowstone\laserjet4
```

After this command, anything you print to LPT1 will go to the shared printer.

NOTE

If you map a network folder to a drive letter using Windows NT Explorer, you can use that drive letter at the command prompt. Similarly, if you connect to a shared folder with the Net Use command, you can use that drive letter in your Windows-based applications. *For more information about mapping drives, see "Mapping a Network Folder to a Drive Letter," page 277.*

TIP

Accessing Network Resources Without Mapping a Drive

If a shared resource doesn't have a password, you can access it directly without first mapping it to a drive letter. Simply use the network name in place of the drive name. For example, to copy Work.bat from the \Bat folder of \\Zion\Public to your C drive, use the network name instead of a drive letter, as shown below.

```
C:\>copy \\zion\public\bat\work.bat c:
```

Connecting to Password-Protected Resources

Some operating systems, such as Windows for Workgroups and Windows 95 (using share-level access control), control access to shared resources by requiring you to enter a password for the resource. (Windows NT, by contrast, maintains a list of users and groups that are permitted to access each shared resource. Passwords are assigned to users, not shared resources.)

If you are connecting to a password-protected resource, you can append an asterisk to the Net Use command, like this:

```
C:\>net use x: \\acadia\optrarx *
```

The asterisk tells Windows NT to prompt you for the password. This way, the password is not displayed as you type it. You can type the password on the command line instead of using an asterisk, but anyone looking at your screen can see the password. In batch programs, you can use the asterisk or include the password with the batch command line, as your security needs dictate.

When you are finished using a resource, you can disconnect from it with the Net Use command's /Delete switch (usually abbreviated as /D), like this:

```
C:\>net use x: /d
```

Browsing Network Resources

The Net View command browses the network for the servers and shared resources you might be interested in. First you browse domains or workgroups to see which servers are available, and then you browse the servers to see which shared resources are available. (For purposes of this discussion, workgroups function exactly like domains. But the terms are not synonymous. *For a description of the differences between domains and workgroups, see "Domains and Workgroups," page 273.*)

A domain is a group of servers. A small network might have only one domain. In a large corporation, the network might be organized into many domains. For example, a company might put each floor, building, or branch office in a separate domain. When you log on to Windows NT, you log on to a domain—usually one recommended by your system administrator. You can browse the servers in your domain by typing *net view*, which displays a list of servers similar to the following.

```
C:\>net view
Server Name            Remark
-------------------------------------------------------------
\\ACADIA               CD server
\\BADLANDS             Chris' Pentium
\\DENALI               Tommy Boy
\\KATMAI               Fax server
\\VOYAGEURS            Stan DeGulis
\\YELLOWSTONE          Paula Kausch
The command completed successfully.
```

The following command checks to see which other domains are available for browsing.

```
C:\>net view /domain
```

To view the servers in a domain other than your own, specify the domain name, like this:

```
C:\>net view /domain:boston
```

After you've found the name of a server, you can browse its shared resources. For example, typing *net view \\acadia* might display information similar to this:

```
Shared resources at \\acadia

CD server

Share name   Type     Used as    Comment

-------------------------------------------------------------------------------
CD-ROM 1     Disk                Windows 95
CD-ROM 2     Disk                Bookshelf '95
CD-ROM 3     Disk     W:
CD-ROM 4     Disk                Corel DRAW!
CD-ROM 5     Disk     T:         Microsoft TechNet
CD-ROM 6     Disk                Microsoft drivers
OPTRARX      Disk                Drivers for Lexmark
ROOT         Disk                Root directory
The command completed successfully.
```

When you find a resource you're interested in, you can use the Dir or Tree command to examine its contents (as long as you have been granted appropriate permissions), like this:

```
C:\>tree /f \\acadia\root | more
```

Browsing through lists of computers and shared resources should raise some concerns about how you want your own computer to appear. Remember that everyone on the network can see your computer name and the shared resources you have. Be sure to keep sensitive data in folders that are not shared, or set the permissions

SEE ALSO

For information about sharing resources on your computer, see "Sharing Folders with Other Users," page 281, and "To Share or Not to Share," page 229.

appropriately. If you do want to share a resource, be sure to add comments so that browsers will know what you are offering. Comments are optional when you set up your own shares, but they can save a lot of frustration for people searching for information.

Setting Your System Clock

You can use the Net Time command to synchronize your computer's time setting with the time of a master "time server." Normally the network administrator assigns a computer to keep time for a group or company. If you are instructed to use the computer \\Timesvr, for example, you can use the following command to synchronize the time on your computer:

```
C:\>net time \\timesvr /set /y
```

The /Set switch is required to set your computer's time. Without the /Y switch, the network shows the time and asks if you want to set your computer's time to match the server's time. This switch (or its partner /N) is used frequently with network commands to specify yes (or no) in response to a prompt.

TIP

Synchronizing Your Clock Automatically

You might want to synchronize the time periodically by placing the Net Time command in a logon script or by calling it periodically with the At command. For example:

```
C:\>at 02:00 /every:f "net time \\timesvr /set /y"
```

For information about logon scripts, see "Specifying a Logon Script," page 566. For information about the At command, see "Scheduling Automatic Backups with the At Command," page 459.

Abbreviating Network Commands with Doskey

If you frequently use network commands at the command prompt, you can save some typing with Doskey. Use Notepad or another editor to create a file named Net.mac that contains the following information:

```
;= Connect to a share, reconnect if that
;= is the default
use=net use $*
;= Connect temporarily to a share, don't
;= reconnect regardless of default
uset=net use $* /persistent:no
;= Connect permanently to a share, reconnect
;= regardless of default
usep=net use $* /persistent:yes
;= Disconnect from a share
unuse=net use $1 /delete
;= View the shares on a server
vshares=net view $*
;= View the servers in a domain
vservers=net view /domain:$1
;= View the available domains
vdomains=net view /domain
;=
```

Then load the macros with this command:

```
C:\>doskey /macrofile=c:\bat\net.mac
```

You don't need to know how the macros work to start using them. *For more information about Doskey, see "Using Doskey Macros," page 542.*

Using TCP/IP Commands

TCP/IP (Transmission Control Protocol/Internet Protocol) is a widely used networking protocol. Although it was originally used primarily on UNIX systems, TCP/IP is increasingly popular even on smaller networks because it is the lingua franca of the Internet—and we all know how popular *that's* become. Your own system might have TCP/IP set up to communicate with other computers on your network, with the Internet, or both.

Because TCP/IP originated on UNIX systems with a command-line interface, commands developed for TCP/IP are still with us today in Windows NT. These commands are useful for setting up and troubleshooting TCP/IP connections as well as for communicating with servers running other operating systems, such as UNIX.

NOTE

> To use any of the TCP/IP commands, you must have the TCP/IP protocol set up on your computer. To see if you do, right-click Network Neighborhood and choose Properties. Then click the Protocols tab to see a list of installed protocols.

Getting Help

The same Windows help file that explains Windows NT's native commands and network commands also describes the TCP/IP commands. To open the help file, choose Help from the Start menu and then select Windows NT Commands from the list of titles. Alternatively, enter this command at the command prompt:

```
C:\>start winhlp32 ntcmds
```

Whichever method you choose, you'll find the TCP/IP commands listed in their own section.

If you prefer command-line help, you should be aware of a difference in UNIX-based commands. UNIX uses a hyphen to identify command-line switches instead of the slash used by MS-DOS and Windows NT. Therefore, to get help about a particular command, type the name of a command, followed by a *hyphen* and a question mark, like this:

```
C:\>ping -?
```

Communicating Over TCP/IP Networks

The repertoire of TCP/IP commands supported in Windows NT includes basic connectivity applications, such as finger, ftp, lpr, rcp, rexec, rsh, telnet, and tftp. (Believe it or not, this gobbledygook is probably familiar to UNIX veterans.) These utilities allow Windows NT users to interact with and use resources on non-Microsoft hosts, such as UNIX workstations.

TIP

Internet Explorer provides easier access to FTP (file transfer protocol) sites than using the ftp command. (Many companies use FTP sites as repositories of files that you can retrieve.) Simply enter the URL (Internet address) for the site you want to connect to in the same way you would for a World Wide Web page. *For details, see "Connecting to FTP and Gopher Sites," page 369.*

Using TCP/IP Diagnostic Tools

In addition to the connectivity applications, Windows NT includes several diagnostic tools, such as arp, hostname, ipconfig, lpq, nbtstat, netstat, ping, route, and tracert. These utilities can be used to detect and resolve TCP/IP networking problems.

For example, the ping command verifies your connection to a remote system by sending some information to that system and waiting for a reply. You can enter either an IP address (an IP address is a group of four numbers, such as 205.162.124.20, that uniquely identifies every connected device) or a host name. Successfully pinging Microsoft while connected to the Internet produces the following results:

```
C:\>ping www.microsoft.com

Pinging www.microsoft.com [198.105.232.5] with 32 bytes
  of data:

Reply from 198.105.232.5: bytes=32 time=432ms TTL=50
Reply from 198.105.232.5: bytes=32 time=350ms TTL=50
Reply from 198.105.232.5: bytes=32 time=235ms TTL=50
Reply from 198.105.232.5: bytes=32 time=215ms TTL=50
```

If you don't have a working connection, you'll get a "Request timed out" or "Bad IP address" error message instead.

Using Environment Variables

Command-prompt operating systems traditionally use environment variables as a means for programs to share information and read global settings. (Windows NT—and applications written for Windows NT—use the registry for the same purpose.)

Viewing Environment Variables

The Set command allows you to examine as well as set environment variables. To examine the current environment variables, open a command prompt window and type *set* (without any arguments). Windows NT displays a listing of all the current environment variables and their values, as the following typical example shows.

```
COMPUTERNAME=OLYMPIC
ComSpec=N:\WINNT\system32\cmd.exe
HOMEDRIVE=Z:
HOMEPATH=\profiles\carls
HOMESHARE=\\zion\users
NUMBER_OF_PROCESSORS=1
OS=Windows_NT
Os2LibPath=N:\WINNT\system32\os2\dll;
Path=N:\WINNT\system32;N:\WINNT
PATHEXT=.COM;.EXE;.BAT;.CMD
PROCESSOR_ARCHITECTURE=x86
PROCESSOR_IDENTIFIER=x86 Family 5 Model 1 Stepping 5,
  GenuineIntel
PROCESSOR_LEVEL=5
PROCESSOR_REVISION=0105
PROMPT=$P$G
SystemDrive=N:
SystemRoot=N:\WINNT
TEMP=N:\TEMP
TMP=N:\TEMP
USERDOMAIN=AMERICA
USERNAME=CarlS
USERPROFILE=N:\WINNT\profiles\CarlS
windir=N:\WINNT
```

Predefined Environment Variables

Many of the environment variables in the example above are ones that Windows NT automatically sets with information about your system. You can use these values in batch programs, Doskey macros, and command lines—and if you're a programmer, in the programs you write. The system-defined environment variables include:

- **Information about your place in the network.** COMPUTERNAME contains the name of your computer, USERDOMAIN contains the name of the domain you logged on to, and USERNAME contains your logon name.
- **Information about your computer.** PROCESSOR_ARCHITECTURE contains the type of processor (such as "x86" or "MIPS"), and PROCESSOR_IDENTIFIER, PROCESSOR_LEVEL, and PROCESSOR_REVISION provide specific information about the processor version.
- **Information about Windows NT.** SystemRoot contains the drive and folder in which Windows NT is installed (normally C:\Windows or C:\Winnt); SystemDrive contains only the drive letter.
- **Information about your programs.** When you type a program name (to start the program) without typing its path, Windows NT looks first in the current folder. If the program isn't located in the current folder, Windows NT looks in each folder listed in the Path variable.
- **Information about your home folder.** HOMEDRIVE and HOMEPATH contain the drive and path, respectively, of your home folder, which is the default folder used by File Open and Save As dialog boxes (some applications override this setting) and the startup folder for new command prompt sessions. HOMESHARE contains the network name of the shared folder that contains your home folder. *(For information about setting the home folder, see "Specifying a Home Folder," page 568.)*
- **Information about the command prompt.** PROMPT contains codes that define the appearance of the command prompt itself. (For details, type *prompt /?* at the prompt.)

Setting Environment Variables

To set an environment variable, use the Set command followed by the variable name and value. For example:

```
C:\>set FullName=Carl Siechert
```

When you use the Set command to set an environment variable, the variable is in effect in the current command prompt session and in any sessions or programs started from that session. To set environment variables that will be permanent for all command prompts and programs, use Control Panel's System applet, as explained in the following section.

You can use any case when you specify an environment variable in Windows NT. Unlike MS-DOS, which converts all environment variable names to uppercase, Windows NT remembers the case you use when you define a variable. However, you cannot define multiple variables with the same name and different case. Windows NT commands ignore the case of variable names.

Although Windows NT internally ignores the case of environment variable *names*, it retains the case of the *value* you assign to a variable. The environment variable's value is always supplied to programs in the same case you used when you assigned it.

Initializing Environment Variables

You can preset environment variables every time you log on. Every command prompt session and every program you run sees these values. You can change them within a command prompt session, or even start a specific session with different values. But for now let's talk about the starting point.

Windows NT presets some environment variables, and then lets you set additional variables. Three factors determine what your environment variables will be after you log on:

- Any variables set in your Autoexec.bat file
- System variables set by Windows NT
- User variables you set with the System applet in Control Panel

When you log on, Windows NT scans the Autoexec.bat file in the root folder of your boot drive. If you use the flex-boot feature, this is the same Autoexec.bat file used by MS-DOS. At logon, the system does not actually execute Autoexec.bat as it does when booting MS-DOS or Windows 95. It simply scans for environment variables initialized with the Set command.

To set environment variables specific to Windows NT, use the System applet. Double-click the System icon in Control Panel, and when the System property sheet appears, click the Environment tab.

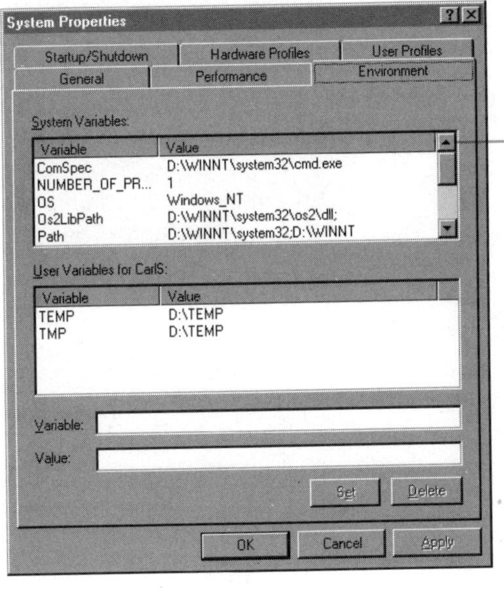

System environment variables are the same for all users who log on. To change or add a system environment variable, you must be logged on as a member of the Administrators group.

CAUTION

If you are logged on as a member of the Administrators group, you can set new user variables *and* system variables, but Windows NT provides no clear indication of which type you're adding. When you type a new variable name and value and then click Set, Windows NT adds it to the list box (system or user) in which you last clicked.

Set any variables you want in the User Variables group. To modify an existing variable, select it and then edit the Value field. To set a new variable, type its name in the Variable field and its value in the Value field. In either case, click Set when you finish. To remove an existing variable, select a variable and then click Delete.

Your new variables are initialized and remembered when you click OK to leave the System applet, but they do not affect currently running programs. If you are running a command prompt session, the session and programs run from it do not use the new settings. If you terminate the session and start a new one, your new settings will be in effect. (You can verify this with the Set command.) Similarly, if you have Windows-based programs that use environment variables, you must close and restart them before they will recognize the new settings.

Variables set in the System applet have precedence over variables with the same names in Autoexec.bat. Thus, for example, if Autoexec.bat includes the statement

```
set temp=C:\DOS\TEMP
```

but you use the System applet to add the line *temp=C:\WINNT\TEMP*, the Temp variable will have the value C:\WINNT\TEMP.

The Path variable is handled a little differently. Its final value is determined by all three sources—the System Variables section, the User Variables section, and Autoexec.bat.

By default, Windows NT includes the system root folder (normally C:\Winnt or C:\Windows, depending on whether you installed Windows NT over Windows 3.1) and its System32 subfolder in the Path variable set in the System Variables section. Then suppose you have some POSIX-based programs that you put in the C:\Binposx folder. You would set the following user-environment search path with the System applet:

Path = C:\BINPOSX

Let's assume that your MS-DOS search path is set in Autoexec.bat as

```
path c:\dos;c:\bat;
```

The effective path (which you can confirm with the Path command) is

```
C:\Winnt\system32;C:\Winnt;C:\Binposx ;c:\dos;c:\bat;
```

Using Environment Variables in Commands and Programs

To use the value of an existing environment variable, enclose it in percent signs (%). For example, the SystemRoot variable is automatically set to the drive and folder where your Windows initialization files are installed. You can change to this folder with the following command:

```
C:\>cd %systemroot%
```

Windows NT recognizes environment names within percent signs almost anywhere—on the command line, in batch programs, and in property sheets for programs and shortcuts.

Using an environment variable in the command line for this shortcut to the Paint application allows you to copy the shortcut to other systems that are configured differently—and expect it to work without modification.

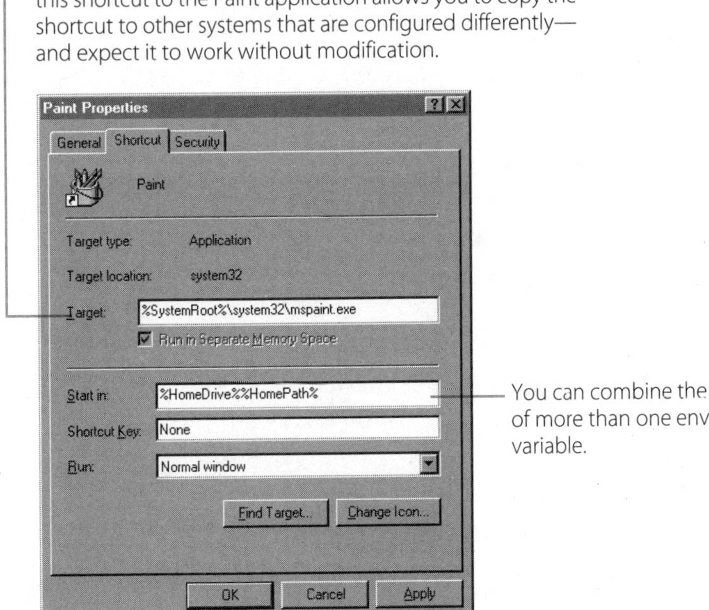

You can combine the values of more than one environment variable.

Using Doskey Macros

For information about batch programs, see "Using Batch Programs," page 546.

When you have a task to automate, Doskey macros serve as the first level of automation. A *macro* is a keystroke sequence that is passed to the command interpreter when you type the name of the macro. Macros are easy to define, take up little disk space and memory, and execute instantly. They work best for shortening long commands and assigning a name to a simple sequence of commands. At some point, you'll find that the tasks you want to automate are too complex for macros. When that happens, move up to the second level of automation—batch programs.

Doskey macros and batch programs are two similar ways to create new commands by combining existing commands and programs. In both cases, you essentially give simple names to longer commands or sequences of commands.

Defining Macros

The simplest Doskey macro is one that gives a short name to a long command. Starting the command-reference help program at the Windows NT command prompt normally requires a long command line. You can abbreviate that command by entering the following:

```
C:\>doskey h=start winhlp32 ntcmds
```

This command defines a macro named H; the content of the macro is the text that follows the equal sign. After defining this macro, you can get help on Windows NT commands at any time with the following command:

```
C:\>h
```

If you want to eliminate an existing macro (perhaps because you gave it the wrong name), simply assign the name a blank value, like this:

```
C:\>doskey h=
```

Managing Macros

Doskey macros are local to each command prompt session. If you define a macro in one session, it won't work in other sessions. If you exit the session in which you defined it, your macro is gone. You should save useful macros so that you can load them whenever and wherever you want.

The easiest way to save macros in a file is with Doskey's /Macros switch. This switch displays all active macros on the screen. However, the default action isn't very useful; normally you'll want to redirect your macros to a file. For example:

```
C:\>doskey /macros > c:\cmdinit.mac
```

After you create a file with Doskey macros from one session, you can read them into another session with the /Macrofile switch, like this:

```
C:\>doskey /macrofile=c:\cmdinit.mac
```

Of course, you don't really want to type this command line every time you start a new command prompt window, so you should put it in your initialization file. *(For information about initialization files, see "Initializing Command Prompt Sessions," page 549.)*

After you develop a library of macros, you can organize them in different files. You'll probably want one group that you load automatically in every command prompt window. Then you might want to add a few more files for different types of work. You might have a Backup.mac file that you load only when you're backing up files, or a Program.mac for programming tasks. You can create or edit macro files with any text editor (WordPad, Notepad, or Edit, for example).

NOTE

If you use WordPad to create or edit macro files, be sure you save your files as text documents.

TIP

Placing Comments in Macro Files

Windows NT doesn't have a comment character for macro files, but you can define your own. Choose a character that you would never use as a command—a semicolon is a good choice—and follow it by an equal sign so that Doskey won't complain about an illegal macro. Then add the text of your comment. (Technically, you're defining a macro named ";" with the comment text.) For example:

```
;= Set 80x50 line mode
50=mode con:lines=50

;= Set 80x25 line mode
25=mode con:lines=25

;= Set a given number of lines
Lines=mode con:lines=$1

;= Set a given number of columns
Cols=mode con:cols=$1

;=
```

The ;= at the end cleans up by clearing the macro assigned to the semicolon character.

Using Parameters in Macros

In macros, you use $1 to $9 to represent up to nine command-line parameters. (In batch programs, you use %1 to %9 for the same purpose.) For example, you might write the following macro to shorten the name of the Start command to the letter *S*.

```
C:\>doskey s=start $1
```

You wouldn't really want this macro because it accepts only one parameter. If you type *s edit /b autoexec.nt*, you start the editor, but the /H switch and the name of the file to edit are lost. You could add *$2 $3 $4* (and maybe more) to your macro, but Doskey has a better solution.

In Doskey macros, $* represents all the arguments passed, even if there are more than nine. This is one of the few areas where Doskey macros are actually more powerful than batch programs, which are limited to nine replaceable parameters.

```
C:\>doskey s=start $*
```

Using Symbols in Macros

You can use redirection, piping, and command combination symbols in macros, but you must use the escape symbol (^) before each symbol. *(For more information about these symbols, see "Using Command Symbols," page 520.)* Otherwise, the symbols are interpreted as part of the command line instead of part of the macro. For example, you might try defining a macro that saves your current macros to a file, like this:

```
C:\>doskey macsave=doskey /macros > %temp%\current.mac
```

What this command actually does is redirect the output of the macro definition line up to the redirection symbol (>) to Current.mac. But the Doskey command doesn't produce any output, so you end up with an empty file. Meanwhile, the MacSave macro has been defined to display macros to the screen instead of to a file. Here's the correct definition command:

```
C:\>doskey macsave=doskey /macros ^> %temp%\current.mac
```

You need the escape symbol only when defining a macro at the command line. Don't put it in your macro files. It won't show up when you display current macros with the /Macros switch.

Sample Macros

You might find it useful to create a group of directory-listing commands. The idea here is that each variation of the Dir command starts with *D* and has one or two modifying letters that indicate its function.

```
;= Default directory listing
D=dir $*
;= Directory listing with pause
Dp=dir /p $*
;= Directory listing of visible files sorted by
;= extension
De=dir /a-d-h-s $* /oe
;= Directory listing of visible files only
Df=dir /a-d-h-s $*
;= Wide directory listing sorted in columns
Dc=dir /d $*
;= Wide directory listing sorted in rows
Dr=dir /w $*
;= Bare directory listing of visible files only
Db=dir /b /a-d-h-s $*
;= Tree directory listing of visible files only
Dt=dir /s /a-d-h-s $*
;= Directory listing of both short and long
;= filenames
Dx=dir /x $*
;=
```

To use these macros, enter the data in your editor, save it as a macro file called Dir.mac, and load it with the Doskey /Macrofile switch. When using the macros, you can include additional options on the command line.

Using Batch Programs

A batch program (sometimes called a *batch file*) is a text file that contains a sequence of commands to be executed. You define a sequence of commands, name the sequence, and then execute the commands by entering the name at the command prompt—or by launching a shortcut that has the batch program's name as its command line.

When you execute your batch program, the command interpreter opens the file and starts reading the statements. It reads the first line, executes the command, and then goes on to the next line. On the surface, this is just the same as if you typed each line yourself at the command prompt. In addition to eliminating repetitive keystrokes, batch programs can vary their behavior based on command-line parameters you enter, the existence (or non-existence) of files you specify, and certain other conditions. Batch programs can also respond to values returned by programs and to the values of environment variables.

Creating Batch Programs

To create a batch program, use Notepad if you like a graphics-based editor, or Edit if you prefer a character-based editor. Alternatively, you can use WordPad or any other word processor that can produce unformatted files.

In Windows NT, you can name your batch programs with a .BAT or .CMD extension. The Windows NT command interpreter will attempt to execute commands from any file with either of these extensions. If you have two batch programs in the same folder with the same base name but different extensions, the .BAT file will be executed—not the .CMD file.

Using Batch Commands

A batch program can contain any command you can enter at the command prompt, including commands to start other programs, native Windows NT commands, network commands, TCP/IP commands, and Doskey macros. In addition, Windows NT supports several *batch commands*—commands that generally make sense only when executed from a batch program. For information about these commands, look for the "batch commands" section in the Windows NT Commands help file.

Sample Batch Program

This batch program quickly wipes all of the data off a floppy disk, leaving the disk bare except for a label name. It improves on the standard Format command by eliminating Format's sometimes-annoying feature of pausing three times—first to remind you to insert the disk, second to ask for the label, and third to ask if you want to format another. You can get rid of those interruptions by creating a new WipeOut command that works when you enter a command to specify the drive and the volume name, like this:

```
C:\>wipeout b datadisk
```

Our WipeOut program, shown below, works only on drives A and B, because the last thing anyone needs is a quick, efficient way to reformat a hard disk.

```
@echo off
rem Check for missing argument
if "%1"=="" goto Syntax
rem Validate drive argument
for %%d in (a A b B) do if %1==%%d goto Format
echo Invalid - specify floppy drive A or B
echo.
goto Syntax
:Format
rem Create file to supply input to Format
echo.    > %temp%\WIPEOUT.TMP
echo n >> %temp%\WIPEOUT.TMP
rem Format using file input to suppress prompts
format %1: /q /v:%2 < %temp%\WIPEOUT.TMP > NUL
rem Delete the temporary file
del %temp%\WIPEOUT.TMP
goto Done
rem Display syntax message after invalid input
:Syntax
echo SYNTAX: WipeOut {A^|B} [volume]
:Done
```

If you've created batch programs for MS-DOS, you'll be pleased to discover that Windows NT overcomes several limitations of MS-DOS batch programs with new commands and enhancements to old commands. For example, the PushD and PopD commands let you change to a directory (folder) and later change back to the original directory. Similarly, the SetLocal and EndLocal commands let you create environment variables for use only while the batch program runs, automatically restoring the original environment variables upon completion. The escape symbol and the ability to use environment variables anywhere within a batch program also increase the flexibility and power of the batch programming language.

Customizing Your Configuration

You can configure the way your command prompt sessions and non-Windows-based programs work in several ways. The tools you use to configure command prompt sessions and character-based programs include:

- Autoexec.bat and the System applet in Control Panel to set user environment variables *(See "Initializing Environment Variables," page 538.)*
- Batch programs to perform initialization *(See "Initializing Command Prompt Sessions," below, and "Specifying a Logon Script," page 566.)*
- Autoexec.nt and Config.nt to configure default behavior for MS-DOS–based programs *(See "Setting the MS-DOS Configuration," page 488.)*
- Program properties, initialization batch programs, and system configuration files to set behavior for specific MS-DOS–based programs *(See "Working with Your Programs' Property Sheets," page 492.)*

Initializing Command Prompt Sessions

You can execute a sequence of commands every time you start a command prompt session by attaching an initialization batch program to the Start-menu icon for the command prompt. For example, you might want to always load a file with your favorite Doskey macros.

Use the /K switch with Cmd.exe to attach an initialization program to command prompt sessions. The /K switch (which has no equivalent in MS-DOS) tells Windows NT to run the command that follows and then return to the command prompt.

To set up command prompt initialization, do the following:

1 Write an initialization batch program. For example, CmdInit.bat might contain the following:

```
@echo off
rem Load standard Doskey macros
doskey /macrofile=C:\CMDINIT.MAC
rem Do other initialization tasks here
```

2 Right-click the Start button and choose Explore. Navigate to the folder that contains the Command Prompt shortcut. (Unless it's been moved, the shortcut is in the Programs folder.)

3 Right-click the Command Prompt shortcut and choose Properties from the context menu.

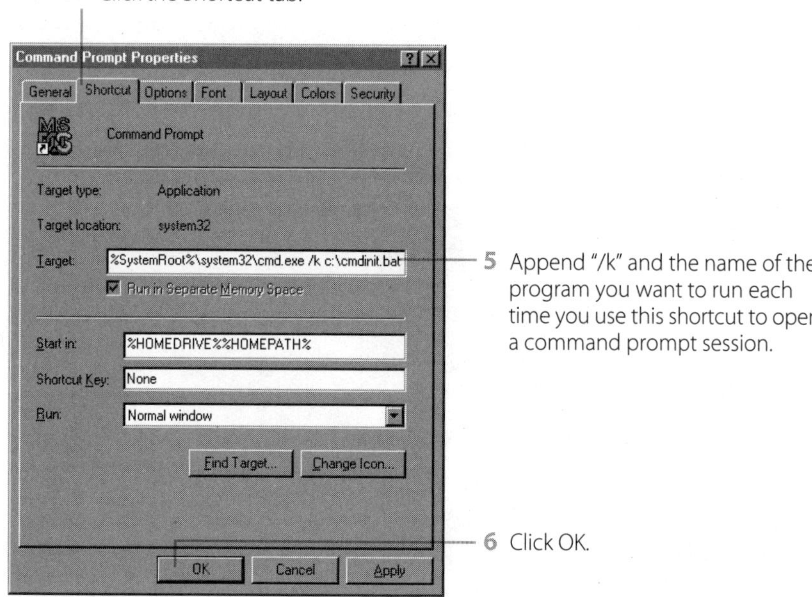

TIP

It's a good idea to choose a standard folder for all of your initialization files. Our example uses the root folder, but you can use your home folder, %SystemRoot%, System32, or a folder created for the purpose.

You can also set up a Doskey macro so that a command prompt window started from the command prompt initializes the same way. For example, you can name your macro CmdS (for Cmd Standard) and add the following line to CmdInit.mac:

```
CmdS=start cmd /k c:\cmdinit.bat
```

Different Shortcuts for Different Purposes

Perhaps you want one command prompt shortcut that loads a particular set of Doskey macros, one that starts an 80×25 window, and another that starts an 80×50 window. Create a shortcut for each variant *(for information about creating shortcuts, see "Creating a Shortcut," page 75)*, and customize it using the techniques described in this chapter. You can change the command prompt's appearance and other options *(see "Customizing Command Prompt Windows," page 506)*, and you can run a program each time you start a command prompt session with a particular shortcut, as explained in this section.

PART 4

Security and Administration

CHAPTER 19

Windows NT Security

This chapter provides an introduction to Windows NT security. We'll look at the government security standard that Windows NT was designed to meet, and describe basic security concepts, such as *permissions*, *rights*, *accounts*, and *user groups*. Then we'll take a tour of User Manager, the program that lets system administrators create and modify user accounts.

Some of the material in this chapter is of interest primarily to system administrators. To set up accounts and modify the rights associated with those accounts, for example, you need to be logged on with an administrative account. Even if you are not an administrator, however, a general understanding of security issues will enhance your ability to use Windows NT effectively. In particular, it's valuable to understand the concepts of user groups, rights, and permissions.

Windows NT's approach to security can be described as *discretionary*. That means that each securable system resource—each printer or file server, for example—has an owner, who has discretion over who can and cannot access the resource. Usually, a resource is owned by the user who created it. If you create a disk file, for example, you are that file's owner under ordinary circumstances. (System administrators, however, can take ownership of resources they do not create.)

For more information about NTFS, see Chapter 20, "NTFS Security."

To exercise full discretionary control over individual files, you must store those files on an NTFS volume. Windows NT supports the FAT file system used by MS-DOS for the sake of compatibility, but the FAT system was not designed with security in mind. To enjoy the full benefits of Windows NT security, you must use NTFS.

Security Overview

The security provided by Windows NT meets the United States Department of Defense standard known as C2. The most important requirements of this standard are as follows:

- Each user must identify himself or herself when logging on.
- The system must insulate objects assigned to processes. For example, memory used by a program must be made inaccessible to other programs, and programs must not be able to read data from deleted files.

- The owner of a resource must be able to control access to that resource.
- System administrators must be able to audit system events and restrict access to the event log.
- The system must protect itself from external tampering.

One of the ways Windows NT meets these requirements is by assigning each user a *security ID (SID)*. Your SID, a gigantic number guaranteed to be unique, follows you around wherever you go in Windows NT. When you log on, the operating system first validates your user name and password. Then it creates a *security access token*. You can think of this as the electronic equivalent of an ID badge. It includes your name and SID, plus information about any user groups to which your account belongs. (User groups are described later in this chapter). Any program you start gets a copy of your security access token.

Whenever you attempt to walk through a controlled "door" in Windows NT (for example, when you connect to a shared printer) or any time a program attempts to do that on your behalf, the operating system examines your security access token and decides whether to let you pass. If access is permitted, you notice nothing. If access is denied, you see a grayed-out menu or dialog-box control, or, in some cases, you get to hear a beep and read a noxious message.

In determining whom to pass and whom to block, Windows NT consults the resource's *access control list (ACL)*. This is simply a list showing which SIDs have which kinds of access privileges. Every resource subject to access control has an ACL.

To meet the security requirement that system administrators must be able to audit system events, Windows NT maintains a detailed event log and provides a program called Event Viewer that administrators can use to manage the log. *For more information about auditing and Event Viewer, see Chapter 21, "Auditing."*

Permissions and Rights

Windows NT distinguishes two types of access privileges: *permissions* and *rights*. A permission is the ability to access a particular object in some defined manner—for example, to write to an NTFS file or to modify a printer queue. A right is the ability to perform a particular system-wide action, such as resetting the clock.

SEE ALSO
For a list of Windows NT rights, see Table 19-2 on page 576.

The owner of a resource (or an administrator) assigns permissions to the resource via its property sheet. For example, if you are the printer owner or have administrative privileges, you can restrict someone from using a particular printer by visiting the property sheet for that printer. Administrators set rights via User Manager. For example, if you have an administrative account, you can use User Manager to grant someone the right to load a device driver.

NOTE

In this book, as in many of Windows NT's messages and dialog boxes, *privileges* serves as an informal term encompassing both permissions and rights.

User Accounts

The backbone of Windows NT security is the ability to uniquely identify each user. Windows NT assigns each user a *user account*. The user account is identified by a *username* and password, which the user enters when logging on to the system. Windows then controls, monitors, and restricts access to system resources based on the permissions and rights associated with each user account by the resource owners and the system administrator. *For information about managing user accounts, see "Using User Manager," page 563.*

In addition to such "normal" user accounts, Windows NT provides two special accounts that have predefined sets of permissions and rights associated with them: the Administrator account, and the Guest account.

Administrator Account

Every computer running Windows NT has a special account named Administrator. This account has full rights over the entire computer. It can create other user accounts and is generally responsible for managing the computer. Many system features and rights are off limits to accounts other than Administrator (or another account that belongs to the Administrators group). For example, most features in User Manager, the tool used to manage user accounts, are disabled when the user is not Administrator or a member of the Administrators group. *For more information about groups, see "User Groups," page 559, and "Using User Manager," page 563.*

Guest Account

Most Windows NT systems also include an account named Guest. This account resides at the other end of the privilege spectrum. It is designed to allow an infrequent or temporary user such as a visitor to log on to the system and use it in a very restricted manner. Choices made by the system administrator determine the level of access afforded to the Guest account. The administrator can also decide to disable the Guest account.

User Groups

User groups allow a system administrator to create classes of users sharing common privileges. For example, if everyone in the accounting department needs access to the Payables folder, the administrator can create a group called Accounting and grant the entire group access to that folder. If the administrator then adds all user accounts belonging to employees in the accounting department to the Accounting group, these users will automatically have access to the Payables folder. A user can belong to one group, more than one group, or no group at all.

Groups are a valuable administrative tool. They simplify the job of ensuring that all members with common access needs have an identical set of privileges. But even if you're not an administrator, you're likely to work with groups if you assign permissions to files that you own on an NTFS volume. *See "Attaching Security to Files," page 581.*

Permissions and rights are cumulative. That means that if a user belongs to more than one group, he or she enjoys all the privileges accorded to both groups. *For more information, see "How Conflicts Are Resolved," page 584.*

For convenience, Windows NT provides a number of predefined, standard groups: Administrators, Power Users, Users, Guests, Backup Operators, Replicator, and several special system groups. Each of these groups has various privileges associated with it by default. Administrators can use the predefined groups exactly as Windows NT provides them, or they can make adjustments as needed. Here is an overview of the predefined groups.

Administrators Group

The Administrators group, which includes the Administrator account by default, has more control over the system than any other user group. All accounts in the Administrators group automatically receive the privileges reserved for the system administrator.

Although members of the Administrators group have maximum control, it is possible for a user to create a file that an Administrators group member cannot access by normal means. The NTFS file system allows users to deny access to particular users or user groups, including the Administrators group. An administrator thus restrained can access the file only by assuming ownership of it, and that action generates an entry in the system event log. *See "Taking Ownership of a File or Folder," page 592.*

Power Users Group

The Power Users group is intended for those who need many, but not all, of the privileges of the Administrators group. Power Users cannot take ownership of files, back up or restore directories, load or unload device drivers, or manage the security and auditing logs. Unlike ordinary users, however, Power Users can share directories and create local printers.

Users Group

The Users group is a catch-all group. It provides base-level access to the system. Members of the Users group cannot share directories or create local printers (unless they also happen to be members of the Power Users or Administrators group). Except for the special Administrator and Guest accounts, all user accounts are members of the Users group by default. Usually, the great majority of users are members of the Users group and no other.

When a Windows NT computer participates in a domain, the Users group includes all members of the Domain Users global group. This means that anyone accessing your system over the network from another computer in your domain enjoys the same privileges as members of the Users group on your own system.

Guests Group

The built-in Guest account is automatically a member of the Guests group. Users who log on infrequently are also good candidates for the Guests group. Privileges granted to regular, well-known users of the system (who are usually members of the Users group) can be withheld from members of the Guests group. This limits these users' access and improves security.

Backup Operators Group

Members of the Backup Operators group have the right to back up and restore folders and files. Backup operators also have access to Windows NT Backup. *For information on backing up, see Chapter 16, "Protecting Your Data with Backup."*

Replicator Group

The Replicator group is a special group that usually contains only one member: the domain user account that uses the system's Directory Replicator service. Although other users can be part of this group, it is not customary because the group is intended strictly for automated maintenance of folders. (Directory Replicator is a Windows NT Server tool and is beyond the scope of this book.)

System Groups

Windows NT manages four special system groups for the system. These groups are not normally displayed in User Manager's group selection lists, but can appear in certain other User Manager lists. Table 19-1 lists the four system groups.

TABLE 19-1. System Groups

Group	Members
Everyone	A group containing anyone who uses the computer, including both local and remote users in the Interactive and Network groups; members can access the network, connect to the computer's shared folders, and use the computer's printers
Interactive	A subset of the Everyone group containing users who are interactive, local users
Network	A subset of the Everyone group containing users who access the computer through the network
System	The operating system itself

Local Versus Global User Groups

The predefined groups we've covered in this chapter are examples of local user groups. If you participate in a domain, you might also come across some additional global user groups. These include the predefined groups Domain Admins, Domain Guests, and Domain Users, as well as other global groups set up by your administrator. Global user groups can include users who access your computer from other parts of the domain. They can be set up only on a system running Windows NT Server.

Using User Manager

User Manager is a program that lets administrators (the built-in Administrator account plus any other members of the Administrators group) manage user accounts. If you have administrative privileges, you can use this program to do the following:

- Create, rename, disable, and delete accounts
- Change account properties
- Create and delete groups
- Add users to or remove users from groups
- Specify password and lockout policies for all users on a computer
- Assign rights to users and groups
- Specify which events should be audited

You'll find User Manager on the Administrative Tools (Common) menu, near the bottom of the Programs section of your Start menu.

NOTE

The following pages describe the User Manager offered by Windows NT Workstation. Windows NT Server includes a program called User Manager for Domains, which offers additional administrative features. User Manager for Domains is beyond the scope of this book.

Creating an Account

To add a new user to your system, choose New User from User Manager's User menu. The dialog box shown in Figure 19-1 on the next page appears.

The Username field specifies the name the new user will use to log on. This name must be unique. The password field specifies the password the user will employ for his or her first logon. The typical procedure is to supply an initial password and require the user to change it during the first logon. To set things up that way, simply select the User Must Change Password At Next Logon check box.

FIGURE 19-1.
The New User dialog box allows you to set up a new user account.

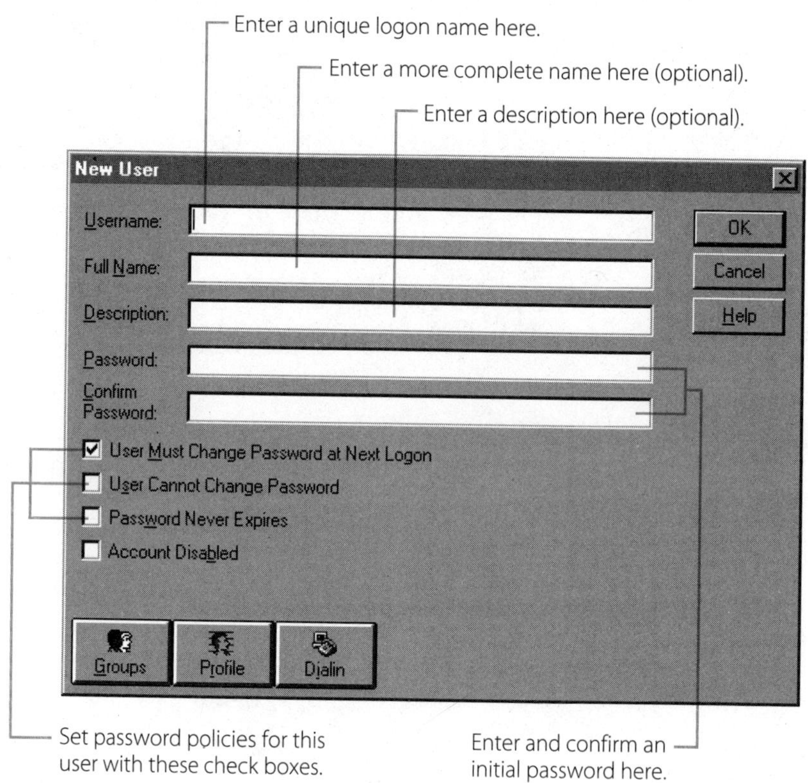

NOTE

> Passwords in Windows NT are case sensitive. To log on, a user must type uppercase (capital) and lowercase letters exactly the way they're entered in the New User dialog box.

If you select the Password Never Expires check box, that setting overrides any password age that you specify via the Account Policy dialog box. *For more information about password settings, see "Setting Password and Lockout Policies," page 572.*

Specifying Group Memberships

New users by default are assigned to the Users group. To change this affiliation or add a new user to one or more additional groups, click the Groups button at the bottom of the New User dialog box, and then fill out the following dialog box:

To add a group membership, select the group here and click Add.

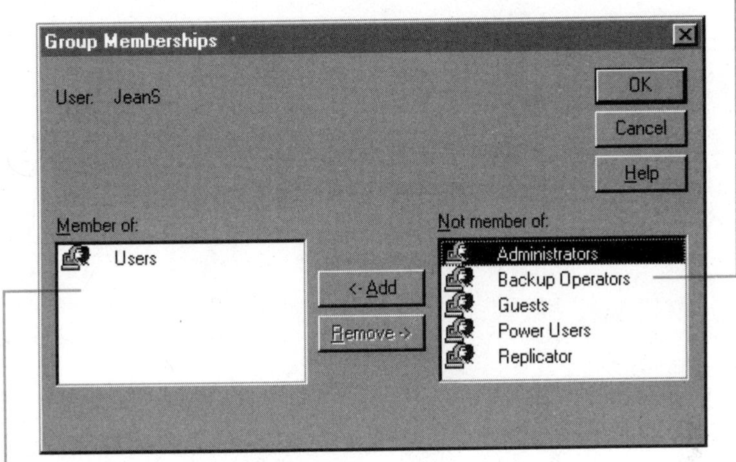

To remove a group membership, select it here and click Remove.

Creating a Roaming Profile

A *user profile* is a file used by Windows NT to re-create a user's preferred system environment when that user logs on. The profile contains the following user-preference information:

- User-definable settings for Windows NT Explorer
- The personal (top) section of the Start menu's Programs submenu
- Taskbar properties
- Network drive and printer connections
- Desktop display and sound settings, including wallpaper, screen saver, appearance, Plus! settings, and sound-file mappings
- Certain application-specific settings (many of the Windows NT accessory programs, for example, as well as some other applications written for Windows NT, record settings in the user's profile)

 SEE ALSO

For more information about the registry, see "Working with the Registry," page 743.

This information is recorded in the HKEY_CURRENT_USER section of the Windows NT registry, and copied to a system file named NTuser.dat. A separate version of NTuser.dat is maintained for each user.

Windows NT maintains a default user profile and ordinarily makes that the starting point for any new user's version of NTuser.dat. When a user logs on for the first time, Windows NT creates a new folder to store the new user's own profile, and copies the default profile into that new folder. Changes that the user makes to the default profile are then recorded in the user's copy, not in the default profile.

For domain users, administrators can create special user profiles called *roaming profiles*. A roaming profile is stored on a server (a copy is kept locally as well, for use in case the server is unavailable at logon), allowing the domain user to have the same environment settings regardless of where he or she logs on.

To create a roaming profile for a new user, click the Profile button at the bottom of User Manager's New User dialog box. (See Figure 19-1 on page 564). This takes you to the User Environment Profile dialog box shown in Figure 19-2.

The network path specification must be in the form *server**share**profilename,* where *profilename* is the name of the new user.

Specifying a Logon Script

 SEE ALSO

For more information about batch programs, see "Using Batch Programs," page 546.

A logon script is a program file that runs whenever a user logs on. Any file with extension .BAT, .CMD, or .EXE can be used as a logon script.

To employ a logon script on a user's local computer, put the script in the system32\repl\import\scripts subfolder of the Windows NT system folder (typically C:\Winnt). Then specify the name of the script in the Logon Script Name text box of the User Environment Profile dialog box, as shown in Figure 19-2.

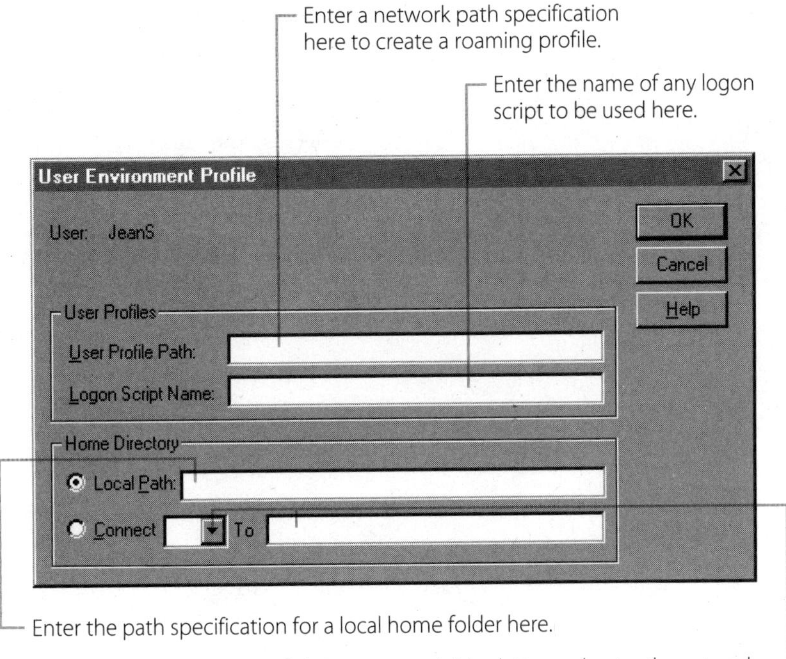

FIGURE 19-2.
The User Environment Profile dialog box lets you specify user profile and home folder settings.

TIP

Use Environment Variables in the Path

If you're not sure of the location of the Windows NT system folder, you can supply a relative path in the Logon Script Name text box by using the environment variable %systemroot%, like this:

%systemroot%\system32\repl\import\scripts*scriptname*

where *scriptname* is the filename for the logon script.

Another useful environment variable is %username%, which contains the username of the current user. By using %username% as a folder name or filename, for example, you can make the same entries in the User Environment Profile dialog box for all users. *For more information about environment variables, see "Using Environment Variables," page 536.*

Specifying a Home Folder

A user's home folder (shown in Figure 19-2 on the previous page as *home directory*) is the default folder that appears on the File Open and File Save As dialog boxes (except for applications that specify their own working folder). It is also the default folder for Command Prompt sessions. The home folder may be local or on a server, and users can share a common home folder. To specify a local home folder, enter a path specification in the Local Path text box of the User Environment Profile dialog box, as shown in Figure 19-2.

To use a folder on a network server as a home folder, select the Connect option button on the User Environment Profile dialog box, as shown in Figure 19-2. Then proceed as follows:

1. Enter an available drive letter in the box to the right of the Connect button (or click the arrow to the right of the box to select an available drive letter from a drop-down list).

2. Enter the full network (UNC) path specification for the remote folder in the To box.

Granting Dial-In Permission

A user with dial-in permission can employ Dial-Up Networking to log on to Windows NT via a modem. To grant this permission, click the Dialin button at the bottom of the New User dialog box shown in Figure 19-1 on page 564, and then fill out the following dialog box:

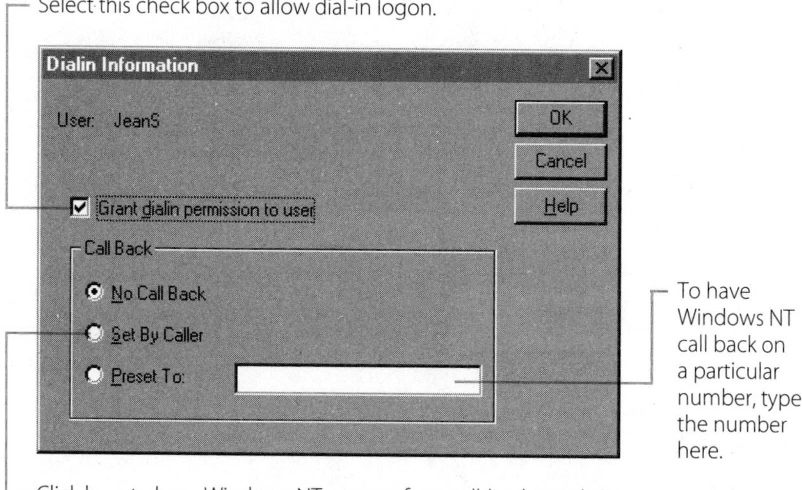

In addition to granting dial-in permission, you can set up the account so that Windows NT automatically calls the user back, thereby letting the network incur the phone charges. If the user might call from several different locations, select the Set By Caller option button. Windows NT will then prompt for a call-back number. If the user always dials in from the same location, it's preferable to use the Preset To option. That way, you get an extra measure of protection against logon by unauthorized parties.

Note that neither call-back option works if the user dials in through a switchboard.

Modifying Account Properties

To modify any property associated with an existing account (other than the account's name), select the account name in User Manager's upper window and then choose Properties from the User menu (or simply double-click the account entry in User Manager's upper window). You'll arrive at the same dialog box you used to set up the account in the first place.

Renaming, Deleting, and Disabling Accounts

To rename an account, select it in User Manager's upper window and then choose the Rename command. Note that changing the account's name means changing the username—the name the person uses to log on to Windows NT.

SEE ALSO
For information about security IDs, see "Security Overview," page 556.

To delete an account, select it in User Manager's upper window and then choose the Delete command. Windows NT displays a prompt informing you that if you delete an account and then subsequently create a new account with the same username, none of the properties, rights, or permissions of the old account will be applied automatically to the new one. Because Windows NT assigns a new security ID (SID) to the new account, you will have to set up the reinstated user from scratch.

> **NOTE**
>
> You cannot delete the Administrator and Guest accounts. If you don't want a Guest account, disable it.

If you are removing a user from your system with the expectation that that user will return after some period of time, you might find it more convenient to disable the account rather than delete it. You can then re-enable the account (with all its properties, rights, and permissions) at the appropriate time.

To disable an account, select its entry in User Manager's upper window, choose the Properties command, and then select the Account Disabled check box in the User Properties dialog box. To reinstate a disabled account, visit the same dialog box and deselect this check box.

Creating a New Local Group

To create a new local group, choose the New Local Group from the User menu and fill out the following dialog box:

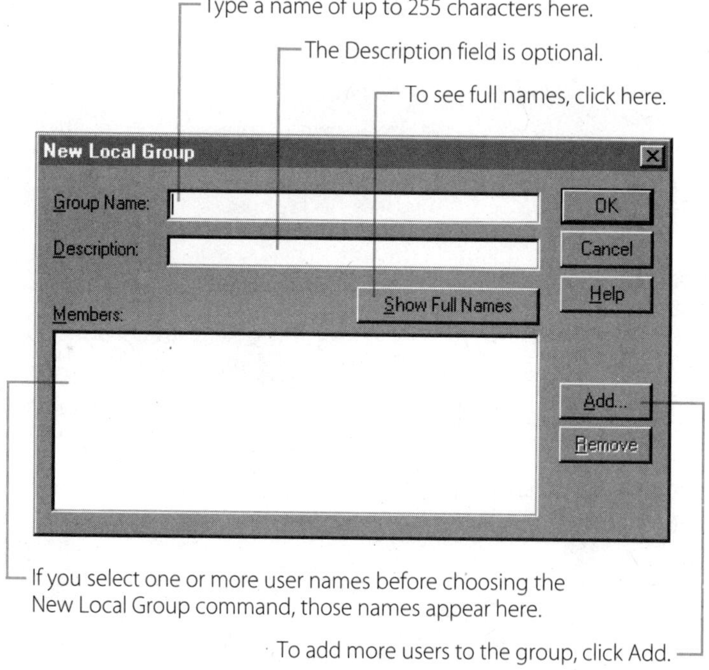

If your computer participates in a domain, your new group can include not only local users but also users and global groups from other computers in that domain and any trusted domains. Note that you cannot add a local group to another local group. To make all or some of the members of one local group members of another, copy the group instead. *See "Copying a Local Group," on the next page.*

Clicking the Add button takes you to a dialog box similar to the one shown in Figure 19-3.

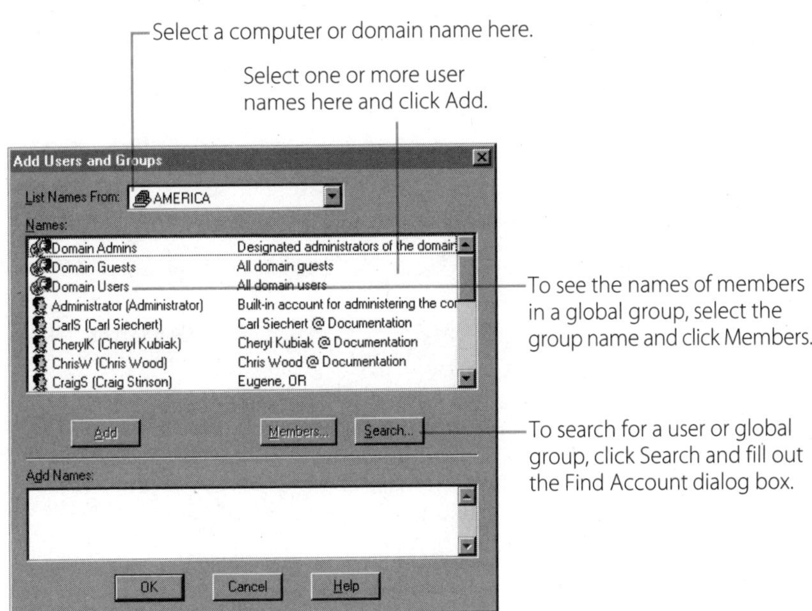

FIGURE 19-3.
This dialog box lets you add new users or groups and search for existing users or groups.

Be aware that using the Show Full Names button may be time-consuming if your computer participates in a domain that has many trusted domains.

Changing the Properties of a Local Group

To change the description or membership of a local group, select it in User Manager's lower window and choose the Properties command from the User menu. (Or double-click the group name.) In the ensuing dialog box, click Add to add members to the group. To remove one or more users, select their names and click Remove.

To change the rights of a local group, use the Policies menu's User Rights command. *See "Assigning Rights to Users and Groups," page 575.*

Copying a Local Group

The simplest way to make one group the nucleus of a larger group is to copy the first group. Select the group name, choose the User menu's Copy command (or press F8), and supply a new group name. Note that rights assigned to the source group are not duplicated in the copy process. *You must assign rights separately, as described in "Assigning Rights to Users and Groups, page 575.*

Setting Password and Lockout Policies

With the Policies menu's Account command, you can set a variety of parameters that control password and lockout behavior for all local accounts. The Account Policy dialog box looks like this:

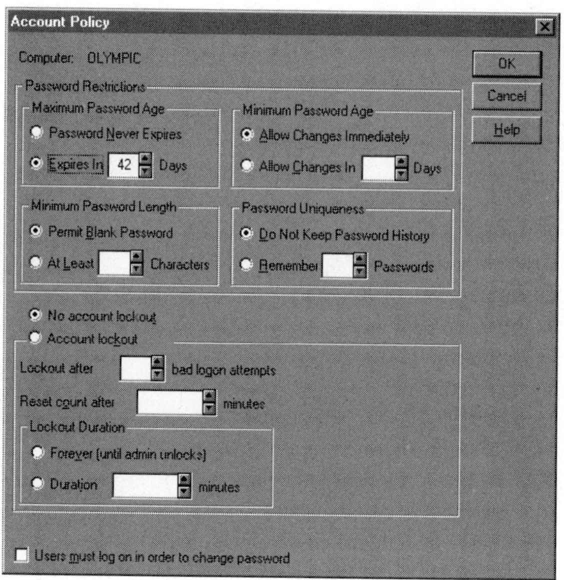

Maximum Password Age settings dictate how long a password remains valid before it expires. Select the Password Never Expires option button if you want passwords to remain valid indefinitely. Otherwise, select the Expires In option button and type a number of days between 1 and 999.

Minimum Password Age settings let a system administrator set the amount of time a password must be used before the user is allowed to change it. Select the Allow Changes Immediately option button to specify that a password can be changed at any time. Otherwise, select the Allow Changes In option button and type a number of days between 1 and 999.

Minimum Password Length settings force passwords to be longer than a certain number of characters. (Requiring longer passwords may enhance security, because longer passwords are harder to guess.) Select the Permit Blank Passwords option button to permit users to have no password at all, or select the At Least option button and type a number between 1 and 14.

Changes to the minimum password length setting do not apply to current passwords.

Password Uniqueness settings can force users to pick a password that they haven't used recently, rather than reusing an old one. When a password expires, many users avoid the hassle of remembering a new password by alternating between two passwords, thereby reusing the same passwords over and over again. This compromises security. To avoid this problem, select the Remember Passwords option and specify a number between 1 and 24. When the user changes his or her password with this option in effect, the system compares the new password to the list of remembered passwords. If there is a match, the new password is rejected and the user is not allowed to make the change.

If you use the Remember Passwords option, it's best not to allow immediate password changes. Otherwise, users can defeat the password history feature by simply creating a sequence of passwords at random.

Changing Your Logon Password

You don't have to be an administrator to change your password. If you get tired of using the same old password every day when you log on, you can trade that password in for a new one. Here's how:

1 From anywhere in Windows NT (you don't need to have any particular application running), press Ctrl-Alt-Del to display the Windows NT Security dialog box.

2 Click Change Password.

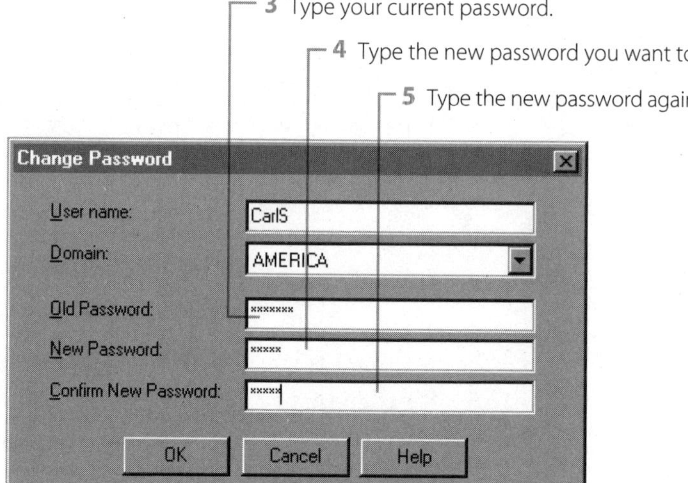

Click OK in the message box that appears, and then click Cancel or press Esc to close the Windows NT Security dialog box.

To protect your privacy, Windows displays asterisks as you type your old and new passwords. You must type your new password twice to ensure that you've typed it accurately. If the New Password and Confirm New Password lines don't match, or if your entry on the Old Password line is incorrect, Windows rejects your new password.

The lockout options, at the bottom of the Account Policy dialog box, govern Windows NT's behavior in the event that a user types the wrong password. The default setting is No Account Lockout. If you select the Account Lockout option and fill out the remainder of this part of the dialog box, Windows NT prevents a user from logging on after he or she enters a specified number of incorrect passwords within a specified time interval. Choose the number of wrong passwords to be allowed and the time interval in the Lockout After and Reset Count After fields. You can also specify how long the user is to be locked out. The default value here is 30 minutes. You can specify any duration from 1 to 99,999 minutes, or you can have the user locked out forever—or until an administrator unlocks the user, whichever comes first.

If you are an administrator, you can unlock a locked-out user by selecting the user's name in User Manager's upper window, choosing Properties from the User menu, and clearing the Account Locked Out check box.

Assigning Rights to Users and Groups

To assign or change the rights for a user or group, choose the Policies menu's User Rights command. The following dialog box appears:

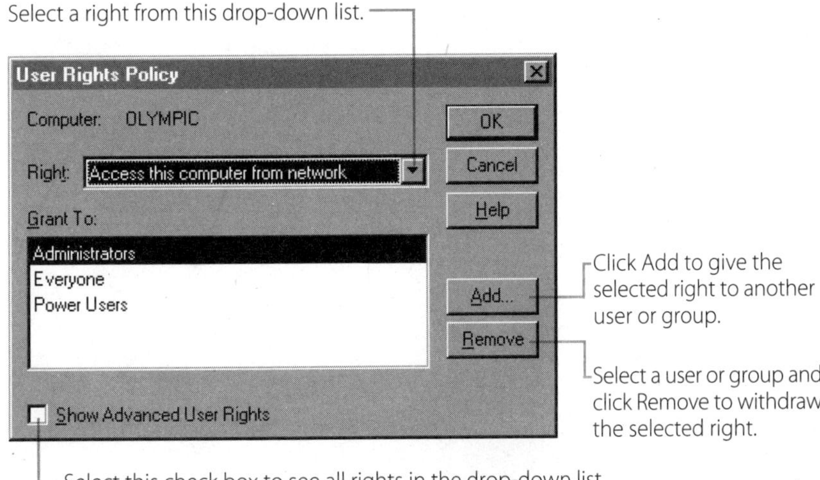

Clicking the Add button takes you to the Add Users and Groups dialog box, which displays a list of users and groups. This dialog box functions like the one of the same name shown in Figure 19-3 on page 571, except that it initially shows groups only. To add individual users to the list, click the Show Users button.

Table 19-2 lists the default rights assignments by group. Rights marked with an asterisk are "advanced" rights, which appear in the User Rights Policy dialog box only if you select the Show Advanced User Rights check box.

TABLE 19-2. Default Rights

Group	Default Rights
Administrators	Access this computer from network Back up files and directories Bypass traverse checking* Change the system time Create a pagefile* Debug programs* Force shutdown from a remote system Increase quotas* Increase scheduling priority* Load and unload device drivers Log on locally Manage auditing and security log Modify firmware environment values* Profile single process* Profile system performance* Restore files and directories Shut down the system Take ownership of files and other objects
Backup Operators	Access this computer from the network Backup files and directories Bypass traverse checking* Log on locally Restore files and directories Shut down the system
Everyone	Access this computer from the network Bypass traverse checking* Log on locally Shut down the system

*Advanced rights

(continued)

TABLE 19-2. *continued*

Group	Default Rights
Guests	Access this computer from the network Bypass traverse checking* Log on locally Shut down the system
Power Users	Access this computer from the network Bypass traverse checking* Change the system time Force shutdown from a remote system Increase scheduling priority* Log on locally Profile single process* Shut down the system
Replicator	Access this computer from the network Bypass traverse checking* Log on locally Shut down the system
Users	Access this computer from the network Bypass traverse checking* Log on locally Shut down the system
(no one)	Act as part of the operating system* Add workstations to domain* Create a token object* Create permanent shared objects* Generate security audits* Lock pages in memory* Log on as a batch job* Log on as a service* Replace a process level token*

*Advanced rights

CHAPTER 20

NTFS Security

Windows NT provides the ability to secure access to many shared resources. The most important securable shared resources are your files. You can set up your Windows NT system so that you have complete control over any user's ability to read, write, create, or modify your shared resources, regardless of which file system you use—FAT or NTFS.

 SEE ALSO

For information about controlling access to shared folders on a FAT volume, see "Sharing Folders with Other Users," page 281.

On NTFS volumes, Windows NT offers additional security options. In addition to managing security of folders you share over the network, you can also manage security of your files and folders for local users (that is, users who log on to your workstation). And you can apply security restrictions to any file or folder; on FAT volumes you can set permissions only at the folder level.

NTFS Pros and Cons

NTFS is one of two file systems supported by Windows NT 4. A file system is the structure in which files are organized, named, and stored on disk. (The other file system is called FAT—for File Allocation Table—the same file system used by MS-DOS.) In addition to the security advantages described in this chapter, NTFS offers several other advantages over the FAT system:

- NTFS stores information more efficiently on very large hard disks.
- NTFS provides faster access to files.
- NTFS provides better data recovery in the event of disk problems because NTFS maintains a transaction log of disk activities.
- NTFS supports file compression. (MS-DOS–based disk compression programs—such as DriveSpace, DoubleSpace, or Stacker—do not work with Windows NT.) *For information about compressing files, see "Using File Compression," page 727.*

So what's wrong with NTFS? There's really only one disadvantage: NTFS volumes can't be read by other operating systems, such as MS-DOS or OS/2. Therefore, if you use flex-boot on your computer to run an operating system other than Windows NT, you won't be able to access information on your NTFS volumes. (You can, however, access shared NTFS volumes over a network, even while your computer is running another operating system.)

You can convert a FAT volume to a NTFS volume. *For details, see "Converting a Volume to NTFS," page 637.*

Attaching Security to Files

For each file on a volume, the FAT file system stores the file's name, size, and last modification date and time. In addition to storing this information, NTFS also maintains an *access control list*, or *ACL*, that defines the type of access that users have to the files and folders on the system. Every file and folder stored on an NTFS volume has an ACL associated with it. *For more information about ACLs, see "Security Overview," page 556.*

NTFS file security is managed using the Security tab of a file's property sheet. To get there:

1 Right-click a file in Windows NT Explorer or in a folder window.

2 Choose Properties from the context menu.

3 Click the Security tab.

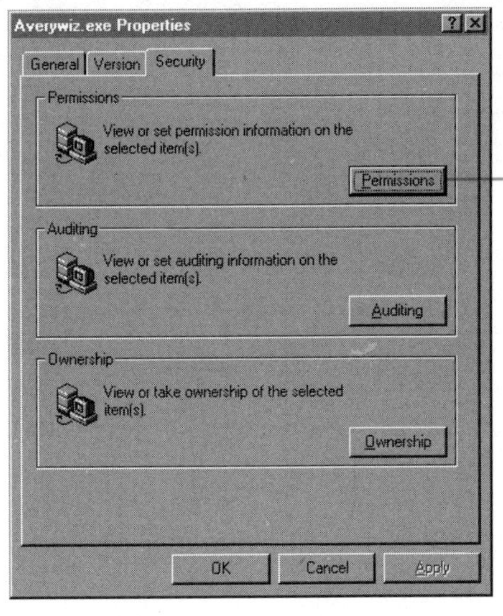

4 Click Permissions to specify who can use the file, and what they can do with it.

SEE ALSO

For information about the Auditing button, see Chapter 21, "Auditing." For information about the Ownership button, see "Taking Ownership of a File or Folder," page 592.

NOTE

If the selected file is not stored on an NTFS volume, the Security tab doesn't appear because security is implemented only for NTFS volumes.

NOTE

Clicking a button on the Security tab produces an "access denied" message if you are not the owner of the selected file and the owner has not assigned you access privileges.

When you click the Permissions button on the Security tab, a File Permissions dialog box appears, similar to the one shown in Figure 20-1.

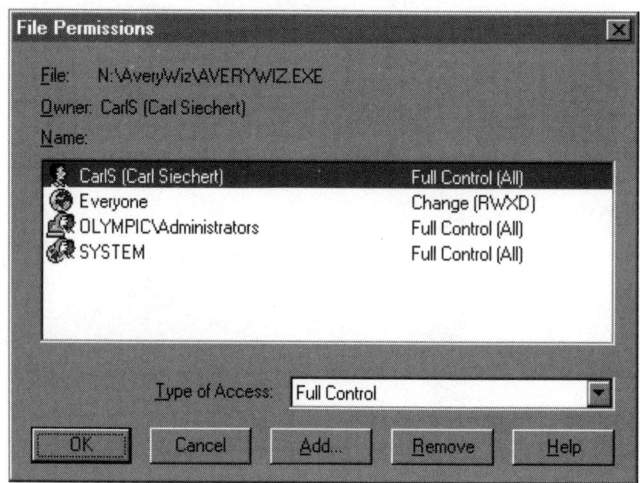

FIGURE 20-1.
The File Permissions dialog box displays the users and groups that are permitted to access a file.

NOTE

If you are not the file's owner, you might be warned that you are only allowed to view, not change, the permissions for the file. In this case, the Add and Remove buttons in the File Permissions dialog box are disabled.

You use this dialog box to view and change a user's access to a file. In this example, the dialog box shows that the selected file, Averywiz.exe in the AveryWiz folder on drive N, is owned by Carl Siechert. The Name list box shows that the file's ACL has four entries—one for the user CarlS, one for the Everyone group, one for the Administrators group, and one for a special user called SYSTEM. (SYSTEM is not really a user; it is the Windows NT operating system itself.) The right side of the Name list box displays the type of access each user or group has to the selected file. In this example, CarlS and the Administrators group have Full Control access and the Everyone group has Change access.

NOTE

> If the displayed Owner does not include a full name in parentheses, the name shown is a group name, not a username. (A file can be owned by a group or an individual user.)

Access Types and Permissions

You can think of the access types listed in the Name list box as shorthand for specific combinations of permissions. In this example, the letters *RWXD* after the Change access type indicate the specific permissions. Table 20-1 shows the individual permissions and their abbreviations.

TABLE 20-1. File Permissions

Permission	Abbreviation	Description
Read	R	Allows the user to view the contents of the file
Write	W	Allows the user to change the contents of the file
Execute	X	Allows the user to run the file—which is useful only if the file is an executable file, such as an .EXE or .BAT file
Delete	D	Allows the user to delete the file
Change permissions	P	Allows the user to modify the permissions associated with the file
Take ownership	O	Allows the user to assume ownership of the file

The Type Of Access drop-down list in the File Permissions dialog box offers four predefined access types. Table 20-2 shows the individual permissions that each access type includes.

TABLE 20-2. Predefined Access Types for Files

Type of Access	Associated Permissions
No Access	None
Read	Read and Execute (RX)
Change	Read, Write, Execute, and Delete (RWXD)
Full Control	All

For many situations, the predefined access types do not provide enough control over the access that a user or group has to a file. For example, you might want a user to be able to display a file's permissions, which requires Read, Write, or Execute permission for the file. But you might not want to give the user Change access because Change includes all of these permissions plus Delete. To accommodate such situations, you can assign permissions individually. To do this, select the username or group whose access privileges you want to modify in the Name list box, and then select Special Access from the Type Of Access drop-down list. The Special Access dialog box appears, similar to the one shown in Figure 20-2.

How Conflicts Are Resolved

Using groups provides an easy way to assign and prohibit access to files and folders for many users. However, the effects of adding and removing permissions to a group are sometimes problematic. The most obvious problem involves granting access to a group when one or more members of the group should not have a particular permission. *(For information about user-account groups, see "User Groups," page 559.)*

To give the user or group full control over the file, select the Full Control option button.

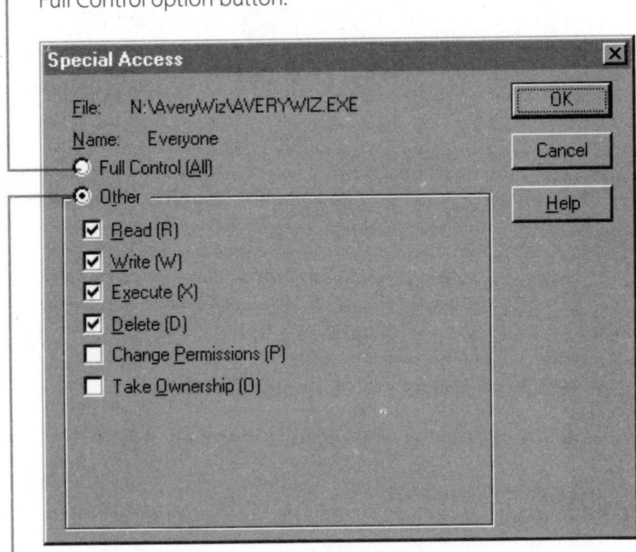

To specify individual permissions, select the Other option button and select the check boxes for the permissions you want the user or group to have.

FIGURE 20-2. Specify any combination of permissions in the Special Access dialog box.

When making security changes, it is important to understand that permissions are cumulative. Therefore, you should always review a group's membership to be sure you are not granting a permission to someone who should not have that permission. For example, let's examine a scenario involving two users: Anthony, a member of the Human Resources group, and Melinda, a member of the Accounting group. Anthony has Read permission for the January.xls file in the Payroll folder. Melinda has Change access to this file.

If Delete permission for the file is given to the Human Resources group, Anthony receives that permission because he is a member of the Human Resources group. Because permissions are cumulative, Anthony continues to have Read permission for the file, but also gains Delete permission.

The No Access access type is an exception to the cumulative rule. It overrides all other permissions, regardless of how the No Access access type or the individual permissions are assigned. If the Human Resources group, for example, is given No Access to the file, Anthony is denied access to the file—even if you explicitly give him Full Control access.

 TIP

Use Groups for Setting Permissions

Because permissions are cumulative, you must devise your security management strategy with some care. Perhaps the simplest approach is to rely on groups for all security settings, rather than making settings and modifications for individual users. Instead of approaching the problem as granting access to users for particular files, think of granting access to groups. Do this only once—and then add and remove users from the groups.

In our example, the Accounting group should have Change access to the accounting files. Because Melinda works in Accounting, she is a member of the Accounting group and has all of the same permissions as her coworkers. However, there might be another group of users with greater access to the accounting files—perhaps called Accounting Supervisors. This group has Full Control access to all accounting files. If Melinda is promoted to a management position, her new access needs can be addressed by moving her from the Accounting group to the Accounting Supervisors group. If her access is modified directly, she might not automatically receive all of the permissions she needs. Furthermore, in a large organization, explicitly managing permissions for individual users can become very tedious.

Attaching Security to Folders

 SEE ALSO

For information about setting permissions for shared folders on a FAT volume, see "Sharing Folders with Other Users," page 281.

Although the effect of setting permissions for folders is mostly the same as setting permissions for files, there are some important differences.

Most importantly, when you change the permissions for users' access to a folder, you (optionally) change the permissions for the files within the folder as well. However, permissions for the folder's

SEE ALSO
For information about setting file permissions, see "Attaching Security to Files," page 586.

subfolders and the files in the subfolders are not changed, unless you explicitly request that the changes you make to the folder's permissions be propagated to those subfolders and their files.

Because changes to a folder's permissions might change the permissions associated with a particular file, the Name list box in the Directory Permissions dialog box, shown in Figure 20-3, displays two sets of permissions in parentheses for each user and group. The first set shows the permissions for the folder; the second set shows the permissions for files in the folder.

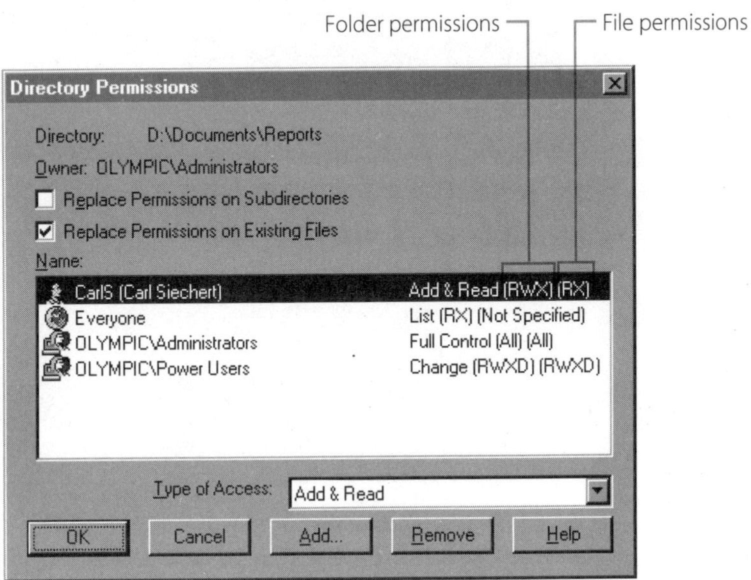

FIGURE 20-3.
The Directory Permissions dialog box displays the users and groups that are permitted to access a folder.

NOTE

> *Directory* is the traditional term for what is now called a *folder*. Although Microsoft has endeavored to use newspeak, old habits die hard, as evidenced by the appearance of "directory" throughout the folder permissions dialog boxes.

Table 20-3 on the next page shows the access types that are predefined for folders by Windows NT. A major difference between the predefined access types for folders and those for files (see Table 20-2 on page 584) is that folders can be secured against reading. If a user does not have Read permission for a folder, he or she cannot see the files within that folder. (The user might see subfolders, however, if the user has Read permission for the subfolders.) Windows NT security is very stringent in this respect. Not only can a user be denied access to files, he or she can be prevented from even knowing what files are in a folder.

TABLE 20-3. Predefined Access Types for Folders

Type of Access	Associated Folder Permissions	Associated File Permissions
No Access	None	None
List	Read and Execute (RX)	Not Specified
Read	Read and Execute (RX)	Read and Execute (RX)
Add	Write and Execute (WX)	Not Specified
Add & Read	Read, Write, and Execute (RWX)	Read and Execute (RX)
Change	Read, Write, Execute, and Delete (RWXD)	Read, Write, Execute, and Delete (RWXD)
Full Control	All	All

NOTE

When file permissions are shown as "Not Specified," that user or group cannot use files in the folder unless permissions set on the individual files permit access.

The Type Of Access drop-down list in the Directory Permissions dialog box has two options in addition to those shown in Table 20-3:

- The Special File Access option works in the same manner as the Special Access option in the File Permissions dialog box. Selecting it brings up the Special File Access dialog box, which allows you to customize the permissions assigned to the files in the selected folder.

- The Special Directory Access option brings up the Special Directory Access dialog box, which is nearly identical to the Special Access dialog box. Instead of modifying the permissions for the files in the selected folder, however, it modifies permissions for the folder itself.

As in the Special Access dialog box for files (shown in Figure 20-2 on page 585), select the Full Control option button to give the user full control over the selected folder. Or select the Other option button and select the appropriate permission check boxes to specify exactly which permissions you want to grant to the user.

Changing Permissions for a File or Folder

Although it is easiest to administer file access privileges by adding users to groups that already have certain file permissions, one or more users might need access privileges not given to any group. In this case, you need to explicitly change a user's permissions. In other situations, you might want to update the permissions for an entire group.

 **TIP**

> Before changing the access privileges of groups, you might want to first determine who is in the group. *For details, see "Adding a User or Group," page 591.*

You can alter a user's or a group's access privileges to a file or folder by doing the following:

1. Right-click the file or folder in Windows NT Explorer or in a folder window.
2. Choose Properties from the context menu.
3. Click the Security tab.
4. Click Permissions.

5 When the File Permissions (Figure 20-1 on page 582) or Directory Permissions (Figure 20-3 on page 587) dialog box appears, select the user or group (in the Name list box) whose access privileges you want to change. *(If you want to add permissions for a user or group that's not listed, see "Adding a User or Group," page 591.)*

6 Select the new access type from the Type Of Access drop-down list. Or, if you want to give the user or group a special combination of permissions, select Special Access from the Type Of Access drop-down list. This opens the Special Access dialog box, shown in Figure 20-2 on page 585, where you can select individual permissions.

7 If you've used the Special Access dialog box, click OK to return to the File Permissions or Directory Permissions dialog box.

8 If you need to make changes to the permissions for other users or groups, return to step 5.

9 If you are changing permissions for a folder, select the Replace Permissions On Existing Files check box to change the permissions for files already in the folder. Select the Replace Permissions On Subdirectories check box if you want your changes to be propogated to all of the folder's subfolders and the files in those subfolders.

10 Click OK to save the changes you've made.

TIP

Changing Permissions for Multiple Files or Folders

If you select more than one file or folder in Windows NT Explorer before clicking the Permissions button, the changes you make affect all of the selected files or folders. If the existing permissions are not the same for all the items in your selection, a message appears, advising you that the new permissions you set will be the same for the entire selection.

Adding a User or Group

If the user or group whose access privileges you want to change is not listed in the Name list in the File Permissions or Directory Permissions dialog box, follow these steps:

1 Click Add in the File Permissions or Directory Permissions dialog box to bring up the Add Users And Groups dialog box, shown below.

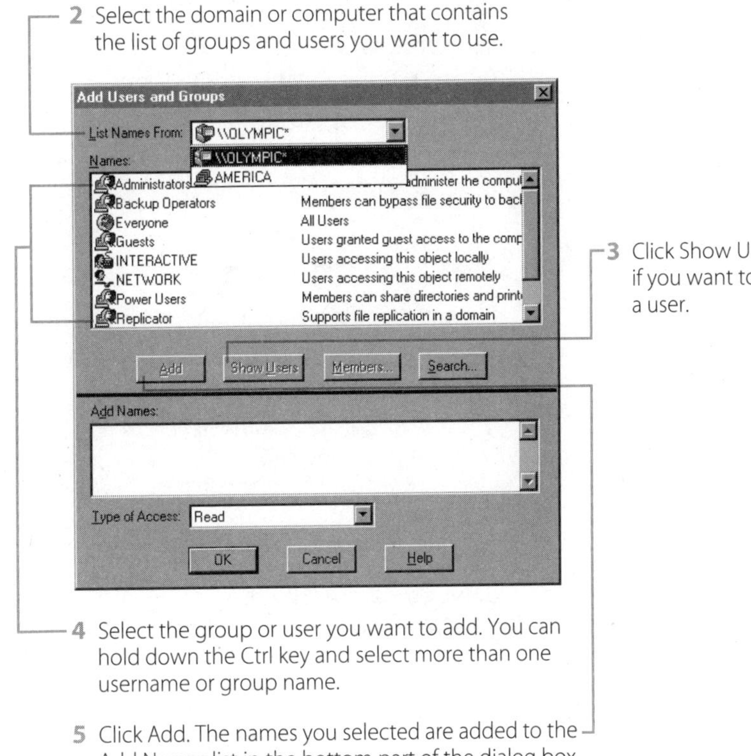

6 If you need to add more usernames or group names, return to step 4. Otherwise, click OK to close the dialog box and return to the File Permissions or Directory Permissions dialog box.

TIP

You can directly edit the Add Names list by typing in usernames and group names separated by semicolons, or by deleting usernames or group names.

If you have a large number of users or groups, you can find users or groups by clicking Search in the Add Users And Groups dialog box. This opens the Find Account dialog box, which allows you to search for users more easily.

When you want to see which users belong to a particular group, select the group in the Names list in the Add Users And Groups dialog box and click Members. This opens the Local Group Membership or Global Group Membership dialog box (depending on the type of group you selected), which allows you to select the names of users to be added, or to simply view the names of users in the group.

Removing a User or Group

If you want to remove a user or group from the File Permissions or Directory Permissions dialog box, simply select the name and then click Remove. As you would expect, this removes the name from the list and therefore denies access to the user or members of the group.

SEE ALSO

For more information about permissions a user acquires by being a member of different groups, see "How Conflicts Are Resolved," page 584.

Unless, that is, the user or members of the group are also members of another group listed in the permissions dialog box. Such users will still have access to the file or folder. If your intent is to positively deny access to certain users or group, don't remove them from the Names list. Instead, change their Type Of Access to No Access.

Taking Ownership of a File or Folder

It is sometimes necessary to take ownership of a file or a folder. For example, if a user who owns a file will no longer be responsible for its maintenance, a system administrator can take ownership of the file before granting ownership to another user, or another user can take ownership of the file directly.

In order to take ownership of a file or folder, you must have Take Ownership permission for the file or folder. To take ownership of a file or folder, follow these steps:

1. Right-click the file or folder in Windows NT Explorer or in a folder window.
2. Choose Properties from the context menu.
3. Click the Security tab.
4. Click Ownership. The Owner dialog box appears, as shown below.

5. Click Take Ownership.

Remember that a file can have only one owner. If you take ownership of a file, you take the ownership away from another user. However, it is also possible for a group to own a file. In that case, all members of the group have Creator/Owner access to the file.

TIP

> To see who owns a file, follow steps 1 through 4, above, and close the Owner dialog box without clicking Take Ownership.

Remember that the user who creates a file or folder is the owner of that file or folder (until ownership is taken by someone else). Although every member of the Administrators group has the power to take ownership of the file or folder, the owner always has the final say on who has access to the file.

A User's View of Security

We've discussed the different features that are available to system administrators and file owners for setting file permissions. But how are everyday system users affected by security?

When a user attempts to perform an operation on a secured file, Windows NT checks the file's access control list. If the ACL allows access, the user's request is granted. However, if the user does not have access privileges to the file, the request is denied. The exact error message the user gets depends on which application is running. For example, an attempt to delete a protected file in Windows NT Explorer results in a dialog box message similar to the one shown below.

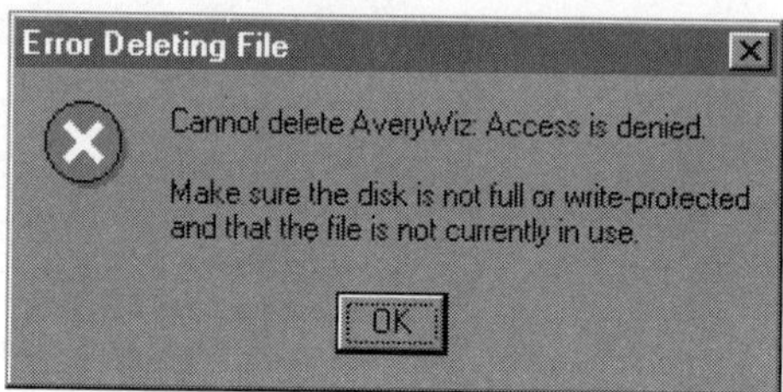

Don't be misled by the "disk is not full" and other red-herring messages. The key here is "Access is denied."

Security on New Files and Folders

So far, our discussion of security has dealt with security settings on existing files and folders. To complete your understanding of Windows NT file security, you should understand how security affects newly created files and folders.

The rule is very simple: new files and folders assume the permissions associated with the folder in which they are created. For example, if you create a file in a folder to which the Accounting department has Change access and the Human Resources department has Full Control access, the Accounting department has Change access and the Human Resources department has Full Control access to the newly created file.

Similarly, if you *copy* existing files or folders to a different folder or *move* existing files or folders to a different volume, the copies assume the permissions associated with the destination folder, because you are, in fact, creating new files or folders when you create copies or move between volumes. On the other hand, if you *move* existing files or folders to a different folder on the same volume, the files or folders keep their existing permissions; they do not inherit permissions from their new home.

NOTE

When you resave an existing document in many MS-DOS–based and Windows 3.x–based applications, the application actually saves to a temporary file, deletes the original file, and then renames the temporary file. With such applications, any unique permissions you have applied to the document are lost. The new copy of the document takes on the permissions of its containing folder.

CHAPTER 21

Auditing

Monitoring, or *auditing*, system usage is often a helpful tool in the administration of system security. For example, repeated attempts to log on with an improper password might be an indication that unauthorized users are trying to gain access to the system. Or, repeated failures at accessing a folder or file might indicate that some software was incorrectly installed or that security for the file was improperly set up.

To this end, Windows NT provides the ability to audit security events by recording attempts at accessing system resources. In this chapter, we examine the various auditing tools at the disposal of a system administrator or resource owner. We examine their purpose and use, and explain what information they supply when used properly.

About Auditing

When a user attempts to access a system resource, Windows NT checks the resource's access control list to determine whether the user should be allowed access. This is the essence of Windows NT security.

If auditing is enabled, you can also request that Windows NT audit access to a given resource. *(See "Enabling Auditing," page 600.)* Windows NT will then record (in a file called a log) any attempts to access a given resource. You might want to request that Windows NT record all failed print jobs on a given printer, for example, or record all failed file-read requests for a certain folder.

Windows NT records this information in the security log, one of the three system-wide logs that Windows NT manages. Windows NT also manages a system log, which records events generated by components of the operating system, such as display or network drivers, and an application log, which records events generated by applications. For example, Windows NT Backup generates events when you erase a tape, restore files, and so on.

Event Viewer

Before we examine how to audit events, let's first take a look at Event Viewer—the application that allows you to examine the events that have been recorded. To start Event Viewer, click the Start button and choose Programs, Administrative Tools (Common), Event Viewer.

You can use Event Viewer to examine any of the three logs—system, security, or application—by choosing the appropriate command from Event Viewer's Log menu, shown below.

The currently selected log is indicated by a check mark next to its name on the Log menu.

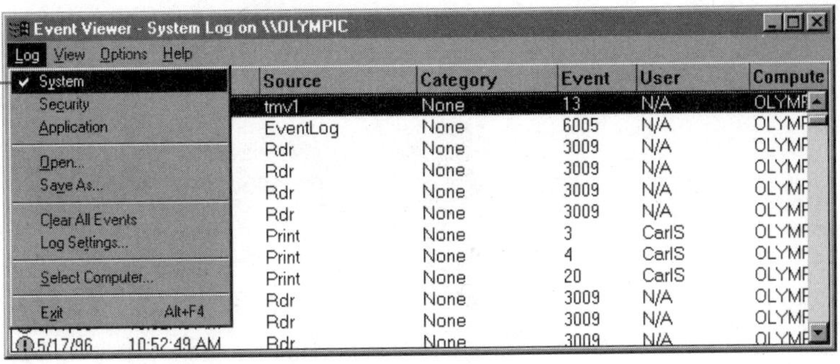

NOTE

You must be logged on as a member of the Administrators group to view Event Viewer's security log. (A system administrator can grant security-log access to other groups and user accounts by assigning the "manage auditing and security log" right. *For details, see "Assigning Rights to Users and Groups," page 575.*)

SEE ALSO

For more information about Event Viewer and other logs, see "Monitoring System Activities with Event Viewer," page 650.

Because this chapter deals with security, we'll concentrate on the security log. If you select the security log by choosing the Security command from the Log menu, you'll see a window similar to the one shown here:

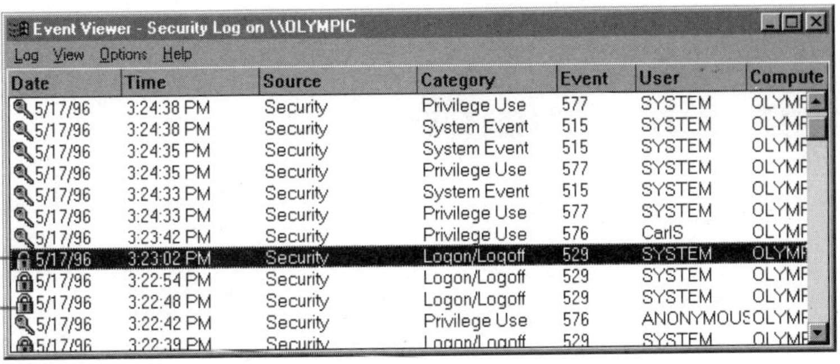

An unauthorized user has apparently been attempting to gain access to the system. These unsuccessful logon events, identified with a lock icon, happened within a few seconds of each other.

SEE ALSO

For information about the icons in Event Viewer, see "Viewing a Log," page 651.

If you want more information about an item in the log, double-click the item, or select it and choose the Detail command from Event Viewer's View menu. The Event Detail dialog box appears, similar to the one shown below.

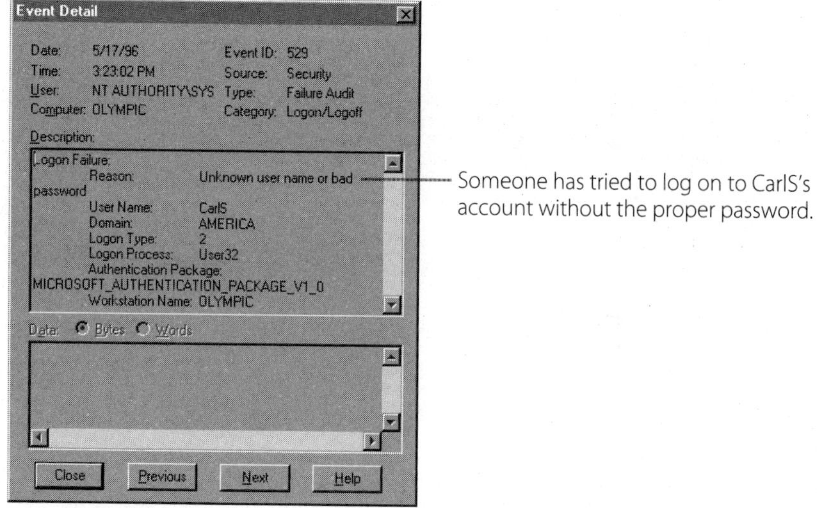

By carefully examining all unsuccessful logon events, you might be able to find a pattern in the attempts to gain access to the system. You can then take measures to tighten up security, such as warning users to change their passwords, and monitoring the security log more closely.

Enabling Auditing

No events are written to the security log until you enable auditing, which you do via the User Manager application. Even if you set up auditing for files, folders, or printers, as explained later in this chapter, those events aren't recorded unless you also enable auditing in User Manager.

TIP

Avoid Auditing If You Don't Need It

Like IRS audits, security audits can be time consuming. (OK, security audits aren't *that* bad.) When you enable auditing, the system must write an event record to the security log for each audit check the system performs. Because this can severely degrade system performance, audit only the events that are important to you.

NOTE

You must be logged on as a member of the Administrators group to enable auditing. (And unlike most rights, the right to enable auditing can't be given to other users or groups.)

To enable auditing, follow these steps:

1 Start User Manager by clicking the Start button and choosing Programs, Administrative Tools (Common), User Manager.

2 Open the Policies menu and choose Audit. The Audit Policy dialog box appears.

3 Click Audit These Events.

4 If you want to audit access to files, folders, or printers, select the File And Object Access check boxes.

SEE ALSO

For information about the other check boxes in the Audit Policy dialog box, see "Auditing Other User Activities," page 608.

5 Click OK and then close User Manager.

Auditing File and Folder Access

If you have the proper privileges, you can set up auditing of certain files or folders on your system. Windows NT can audit a variety of events, and can audit different events for different users.

NOTE

You must be logged on as a member of the Administrators group (or your logon account must have the "manage auditing and security log" right) to audit files and folders.

TIP

Avoid Auditing Too Many Successful Events

Although auditing is a useful technique for monitoring access to your system, you should be careful when auditing busy folders or files—and be particularly careful about auditing successful accesses. Each time a user successfully completes an operation on the file or folder, Windows NT writes a record to the security log to reflect the access. This slows down your system and adds many events of little value to the log, thereby making it more difficult to find real security breaches.

To set up auditing for files and folders, do the following:

1. Use User Manager to enable auditing. Be sure to select the File And Object Access events in the Audit Policy dialog box. *(For details, see "Enabling Auditing," page 600.)*
2. Select the files or folders you want to audit. *(For details, see "Displaying Audit Settings for Files and Folders," below.)*
3. Select the users and groups whose access to the selected files or folders you want to audit. *(For details, see "Specifying Users, Groups, and Events to Audit," page 604.)*

Displaying Audit Settings for Files and Folders

Use the Security tab on the property sheet for a file or folder to display its audit settings. Follow these steps:

1. Right-click a file or folder in Windows NT Explorer or in a folder window.
2. Choose Properties from the context menu.
3. Click the Security tab.

> **NOTE**
>
> If the selected file or folder is not stored on an NTFS volume, the Security tab doesn't appear because auditing and other security features are implemented only for NTFS volumes.

4. Click the Auditing button.

   The File Auditing (or Directory Auditing) dialog box appears, similar to the one shown below.

Select a name to see which events are audited for that user or group. The settings can be different for each user or group.

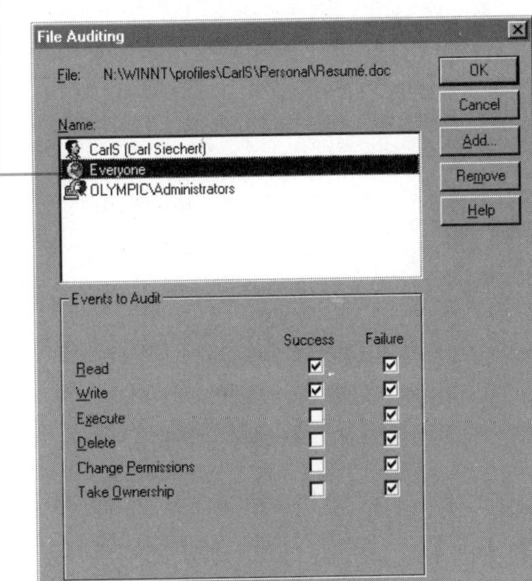

If an event's Success check box is selected, Windows NT generates a security log record containing (among other things) the time and date of each successful attempt at the event by the specified user or group for the specified file or folder. Similarly, if an event's Failure check box is selected, Windows NT generates a security log record each time the specified user or group unsuccessfully attempts the event for the specified file or folder.

TIP

Changing Audit Settings for Multiple Files or Folders

If you select more than one file or folder in Windows NT Explorer before you click the Auditing button, the changes you make affect all of the selected files or folders. If the existing audit settings are not the same for all the items in your selection, a message appears, asking if you want the same audit settings for the entire selection.

Specifying Users, Groups, and Events to Audit

While the File Auditing or Directory Auditing dialog box is displayed, you can specify the users and groups whose access to the selected files or folders you want to audit. And for each user or group, you can specify which types of access should generate entries in the security log. You can specify different auditing events for each user and group.

To audit file or folder access by a user or a group, take these steps:

1. Display the File Auditing or Directory Auditing dialog box for the files or folders you want to audit. *(For details, see the previous section, "Displaying Audit Settings for Files and Folders.")*

2 Select Replace Auditing On Subdirectories to have your audit settings replace the current settings (if any) for all subfolders of the selected folder. (Directory Auditing dialog box only)

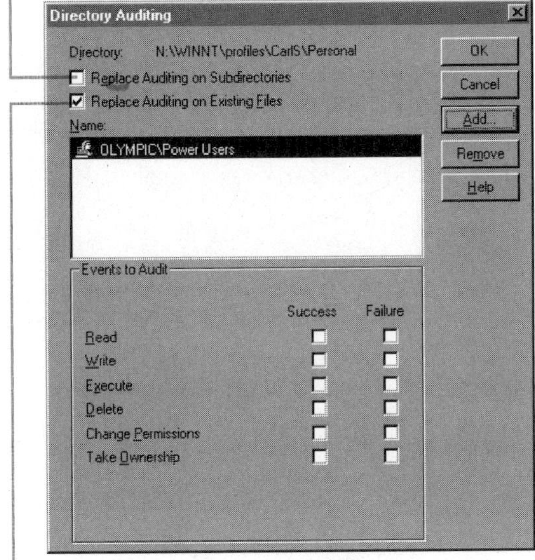

3 Select Replace Auditing On Existing Files to have your audit settings replace the current settings (if any) for all files in the folder. Clear the check box to have your settings apply to the folder, but not to its files. (Directory Auditing dialog box only)

4 If the username or group whose access you want to audit does not appear in the Name box, click Add to bring up the Add Users And Groups dialog box. *For details about using the Add Users And Groups dialog box, see "Adding a User or Group," page 591.*

5 Select the username or group whose access to the file or folder you want to audit, and then select the appropriate check boxes in the Events To Audit group box.

6 Click OK when you have made all the changes you want.

Auditing Access to Printers

Windows NT can audit several printer events, and can audit different events for different users. All of the printer security features are managed through the Printers folder.

NOTE

You must be logged on as a member of the Administrators group (or your logon account must have the "manage auditing and security log" right) to audit printers.

To set up printer auditing, follow these steps:

1. Use User Manager to enable auditing. Be sure to select the File And Object Access events in the Audit Policy dialog box. *(For details, see "Enabling Auditing," page 600.)*
2. Open the Printers folder by clicking the Start button and choosing Settings, Printers.
3. Right-click the icon for the printer you want to audit, and then choose Properties.
4. Click the Security tab.
5. Click the Auditing button. The Printer Auditing dialog box appears, as shown below.

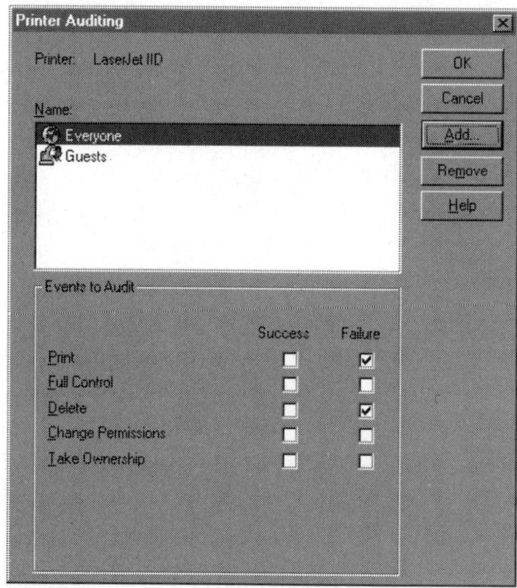

6 If the username or group whose access you want to audit does not appear in the Name box, click Add to bring up the Add Users And Groups dialog box. *For details about using the Add Users And Groups dialog box, see "Adding a User or Group," page 591.*

7 Select the username or group whose access to the printer you want to audit, and then select the appropriate check boxes in the Events To Audit group box.

8 Click OK when you have made all the changes you want.

> **TIP**
>
> It is often useful to audit unsuccessful print jobs and deletions from the print queue, because these events might indicate a problem with the printer or difficulty in using the printer.

When Windows NT logs a printer event such as successful printing or deletion from the print queue, the event record is written to the system log. Security events, such as attempts to access a printer for which an account does not have access rights, result in an event record being written to the security log. A successful print job generates a record in the system log that is similar to the one shown here in the Event Viewer's Event Detail dialog box.

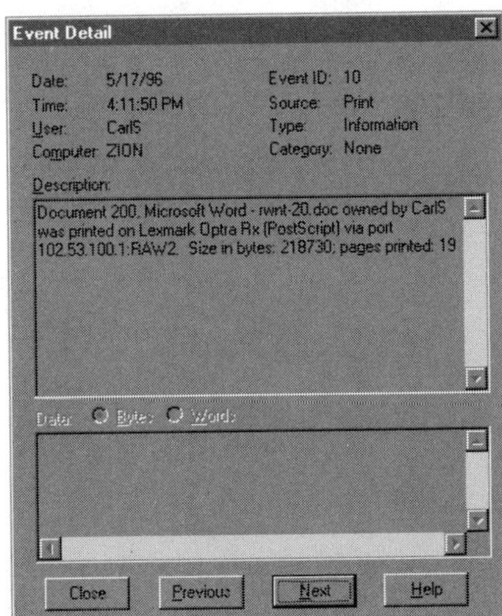

Auditing Other User Activities

In addition to auditing access to files and printers, Windows NT also can audit other activities, such as logon and logoff events, and requests to shut down or restart the system. Some of these events are recorded in the system log and others are recorded in the security log.

You must be logged on as a member of the Administrators group to change Audit Policy settings.

To set up auditing for these other events, follow these steps:

1 Start User Manager by clicking the Start button and choosing Programs, Administrative Tools (Common), User Manager.

2 Open the Policies menu and choose Audit. The Audit Policy dialog box appears.

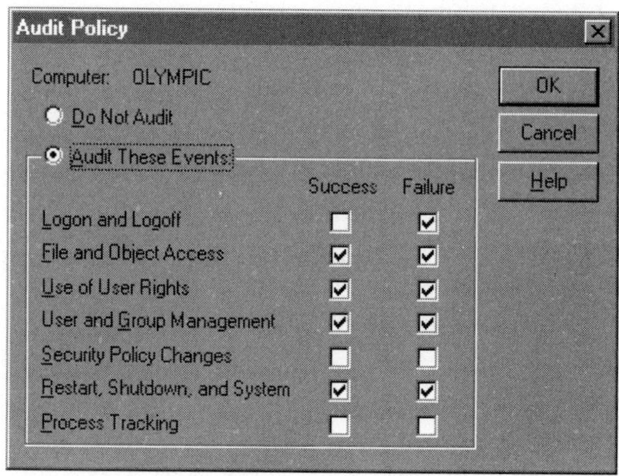

3 Select the events you want to audit. Table 21-1 describes these events.

4 Click OK and then close User Manager.

SEE ALSO

For information about user rights, see "Permissions and Rights," page 558. For information about user accounts and groups, see "Using User Manager," page 563.

TABLE 21-1. Audit Events

Event Type	Description
Logon and Logoff	Occurs when a user logs on or logs off a workstation, or connects via a network
File and Object Access	Occurs when a user accesses a file or printer that is set for auditing, as described in this chapter
Use of User Rights	Occurs when a user exercises a user right (other than logon, logoff, and network access rights, which trigger other types of events)
User and Group Management	Occurs when a user account or group is created, changed, or deleted; when a user account is renamed, enabled, or disabled; or when a password is set or changed
Security Policy Changes	Occurs when a user changes audit policies (that is, makes changes in the Audit Policy dialog box) or user rights policies
Restart, Shutdown, and System	Occurs when a user restarts or shuts down the computer, or when an event occurs that affects the security log
Process Tracking	Arcane events such as program activation, handle duplication, indirect object access, and process exit; generally not useful for everyday security concerns

PART 5

Maintaining Your System

CHAPTER 22

Managing Disks

Way back when the dust settled, and you finally knew in your bones what all those pieces of your computer were meant to do, one fact was obvious: without disks, you had no way to save, recall, or archive your work. Disks, especially hard disks, are as essential to computer use as books and other print documents are to a paper-based world.

This chapter has little to do with saving data, but has everything to do with giving that data a congenial and well-designed home. It is about Disk Administrator, a tool that allows you to manage the space on your hard disks.

Using Disk Administrator

Disk Administrator is a powerful aid in configuring and managing space on a hard disk, but it is not a tool you use frequently. You use Disk Administrator to:

- Check disk size or the assigned letters of volumes or CD-ROM drives. *(For more information, see "Starting Disk Administrator," below.)*
- Set up a new hard disk or partition. *(For more information, see "Managing Disk Partitions," page 624.)*
- Assign a different drive letter to an existing volume or CD-ROM drive. *(For more information, see "Assigning a Drive Letter," page 632.)*
- Consolidate separate regions of free space into a single volume set. *(For more information, see "Working with Volume Sets," page 638.)*
- Maximize disk performance by spreading data across two or more disks in a stripe set. *(For more information, see "Working with Stripe Sets," page 641.)*

A Safer Fdisk

If you're familiar with MS-DOS, you might recognize Disk Administrator as something of a super, graphical Fdisk. Even if you've never used Fdisk, however, you will most likely still recognize Disk Administrator as a tool for managing the spaces, known as *partitions*, on the hard disks attached to your system.

Working with the storage space on a hard disk is a tricky proposition because it can easily damage or destroy disk contents, as many people know from procedures such as formatting, unformatting, and directory and file recovery. From this standpoint, one of the best aspects of Disk Administrator—other than ease of use—is its "awareness" of potentially harmful activities.

Whenever you use Disk Administrator to alter a hard disk in such a way that information can be lost, Disk Administrator makes no changes to your system until you quit (or explicitly ask it to make the changes), and even then it makes the changes only after requesting confirmation. Furthermore, Disk Administrator refuses to remove the active partition or any logical drive or volume containing NT system files, thus protecting the files you need to start and run Windows NT from inadvertent deletion.

Unlike Fdisk, which can immediately and irrevocably remove your startup partition and make your hard disk inaccessible, Disk Administrator adopts a kinder, gentler approach to hard-disk management.

TIP

Back Up Your Disk Configuration

Save your old disk configuration on a floppy disk before making changes in Disk Administrator. This allows you to restore an earlier disk configuration if you change your mind. *(For information, see "Saving and Restoring Disk Configurations," page 644.)*

Starting Disk Administrator

To start Disk Administrator, click the Start button and then choose Programs, Administrative Tools (Common), Disk Administrator.

NOTE

You must be logged on as a member of the Administrators group to use Disk Administrator.

The first time you start Disk Administrator, the dialog box shown on the next page appears. (This dialog box also appears the first time you run Disk Administrator after you add a new disk to your computer.) Click OK to continue to Disk Administrator's main window.

SEE ALSO

For information about ways to change the look of the screen, see "Customizing the Display," page 618.

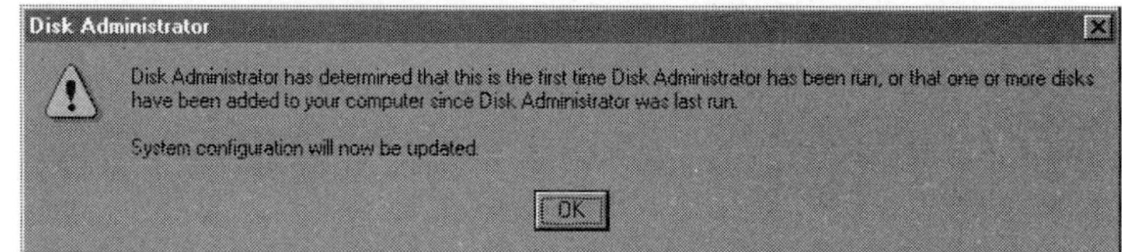

NOTE

On some computers, the first time you run Disk Administrator you'll be interrupted by one additional message, stating "no signature found." Disk Administrator relies on a 4-byte "signature" in the master boot record of each disk to identify the disk, and it can write the signature if one doesn't already exist. This area of the disk is not used by most other operating systems, so it should be safe to click Yes to accept Disk Administrator's offer to write a signature. But before you do, be sure you have a current backup of the data on your disk.

Disk Administrator then presents a fuss-free window that shows the hard disks and CD-ROM drives attached to your system. The window does not show hard disks to which your computer is connected over the network.

Each disk is represented by a *disk bar* on which each partition and logical drive is shown as a labeled segment.

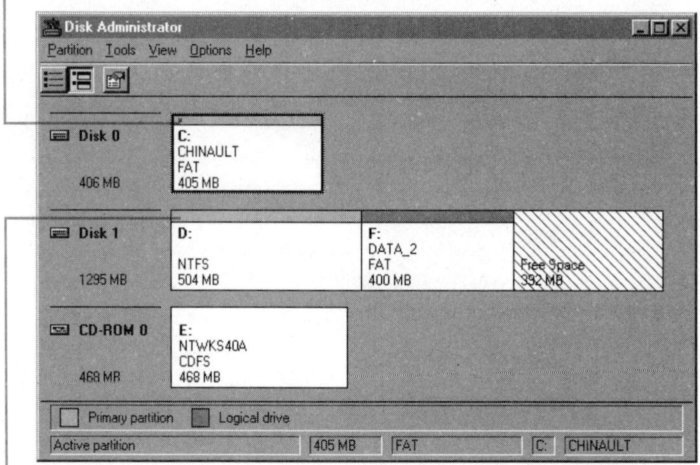

Disk Administrator shows the relative sizes of the disks (although the shortest disk bar is never less than 25 percent of the longest disk bar), and the relative sizes of the partitions and logical drives on each disk.

When you first start Disk Administrator, no partition is selected. To select a partition or logical drive, click it. The selected partition or logical drive then appears with a bold border, and information about the selected item appears in Disk Administrator's status bar, as shown on the previous page. To select additional partitions or logical drives, hold down Ctrl and click each one. You can select partitions or logical drives with the keyboard too: use the Up and Down arrow

How Can a Disk Drive Be Logical?

If you don't know much about disk drives and you always assumed that logic was the domain of Greek philosophers and Sherlock Holmes, you might be puzzled by references to logical drives on a hard disk. Well, logic in this sense doesn't have a whole lot to do with syllogisms or deductive reasoning. When applied to a disk drive, the word *logical* is in a sense the opposite of *physical*. Specifically, a logical drive is a portion of a physical hard disk that you set aside, format, assign a drive letter, and treat as if it were a separate disk of however many megabytes you decide to set aside.

The term *disk* (or *hard disk*) refers to the physical hard disk drive installed in your computer. Your computer's first hard disk drive is identified in Disk Administrator as Disk 0. If you have additional hard drives installed, they're identified as Disk 1, Disk 2, and so on.

Each disk can be divided into one or more *partitions*.

One type of partition, an *extended partition*, can be further divided into one or more *logical drives*.

When a partition or logical drive is formatted for a particular file system (FAT or NTFS) and assigned a drive letter, it's called a *volume*.

Thus, a system with a single hard disk may appear in Windows NT Explorer to have several local hard disks—er, *volumes*—identified as C, D, E, and so on.

And if that's not confusing enough, partitions from more than one disk can be combined and formatted as a single drive identified by a single drive letter. Such an arrangement is called a *volume set*.

Similarly, a *stripe set* combines partitions from more than one disk into a single volume.

Each of these terms—partition, extended partition, logical drive, volume, volume set, and stripe set—is described in greater detail later in this chapter. By necessity, these terms sometimes crop up before they're fully described in this chapter and in Disk Administrator itself, and providing this brief definition before then seems, well, logical.

keys to move the selection frame to the desired disk, use the Left and Right arrow keys to move to the partition or logical drive you want, and then press Enter. To select additional items, hold down Ctrl each time you press Enter.

Customizing the Display

Most users find the default Disk Administrator window functional, easy to read, and informative in the way it shows relative disk sizes. If relativity is not your style, however, or if you want to choose your own colors, use the Options menu:

- The Colors And Patterns command lets you choose from an assortment of colors and patterns to customize the disk bars.

Select a partition or logical drive type, and then select a color and pattern for its display.

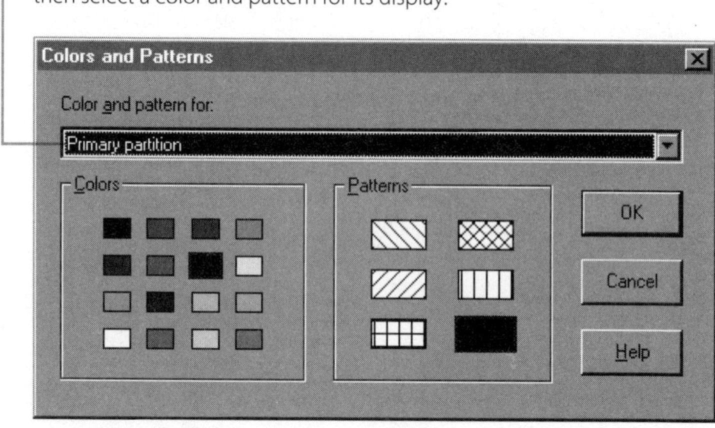

- The Disk Display command lets you choose disk bars that are relative to the sizes of the actual disks, or equal disk bars for all disks.
- The Region Display command provides similar options for the display of partitions and logical drives within a disk bar. Your choice in the Region Display dialog box (shown on the next page) determines whether partitions and logical drives occupy equal-sized pieces of the disk bar, or pieces proportional to their size on the hard disk.

Click Reset All to restore decision-making for all disks to Disk Administrator.

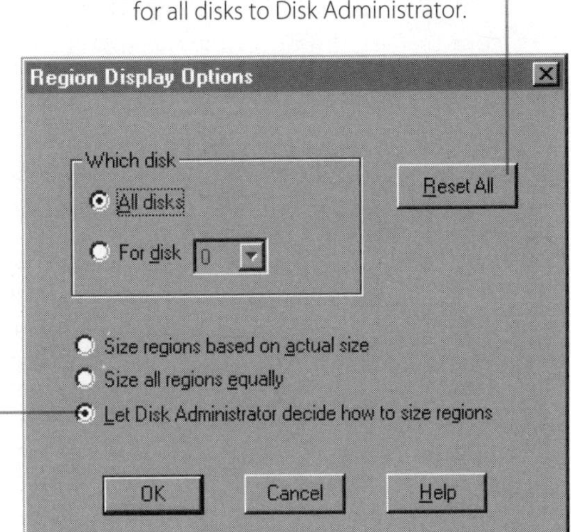

Disk Administrator determines the "best fit"—proportional or equal—based on the number of regions on a disk and the overall size of the disk bar.

- The Tool Bar, Status Bar, and Legend commands display or hide their namesake screen elements. (The legend identifies the type of partition associated with each color or pattern.)
- The Customize Toolbar command lets you add or remove tools, or change their order.

To add a button, select it and then click Add.

To delete a button, select it and then click Remove.

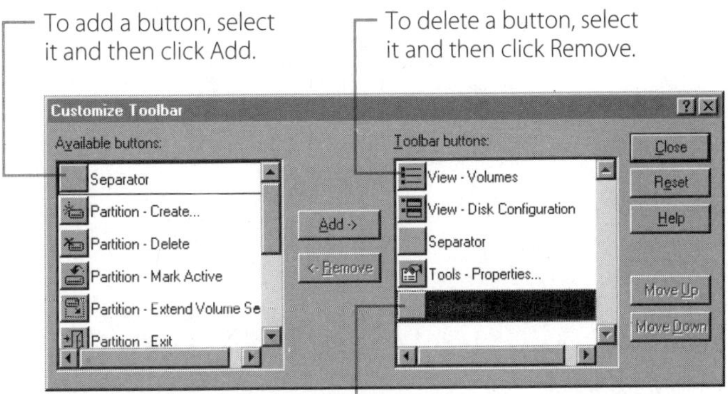

To change the order, select a button and then click Move Up (to move left on the toolbar) or Move Down (to move right).

Quitting Disk Administrator

You quit Disk Administrator in much the same way that you quit any other Windows NT program. You can do any of the following:

- Click the Close button.
- Choose Exit from the Partition menu.
- Double-click the Control-menu icon.
- Choose Close from the Control menu.
- Press Alt+F4.

If you made any changes to the configuration of any hard disks, Disk Administrator asks if you want to make the changes permanent with the message, "Changes have been made to your disk configuration. Do you want to save the changes?"

WARNING

Be sure of your changes before you choose Yes. When Disk Administrator saves your changes, all the information on your disks will be irretrievably lost—unless you previously saved your old disk configuration on a floppy disk. *See "Saving and Restoring Disk Configurations," page 644.*

SEE ALSO

For information about creating and using an Emergency Repair Disk, see "Using Repair Disk Utility," page 737.

If you choose Yes, Disk Administrator updates its internal description of your hard disk and then suggests that you create a new Emergency Repair Disk. (It's good advice. Take it.) In some cases (an on-screen message advises you), you must restart the system for your changes to take effect.

If you choose No, Disk Administrator closes without saving the changes you made—leaving your disks in the same condition as when you started.

Understanding Disk Partitions

To any operating system, including Windows NT, a partition is a portion of a hard disk that is treated as a data-saving world unto itself. A section of the disk with its own starting and ending track numbers, a partition is essentially a drive within a drive. With Windows NT, you can have up to four partitions per hard disk. The illustration below shows how partitions are related to the disk as a whole and to the volumes you refer to in retrieving and saving files. For ease of reference, the hard disk in the illustration is shown as it would be represented by Disk Administrator—that is, as if it had been "unwound" and stretched out linearly.

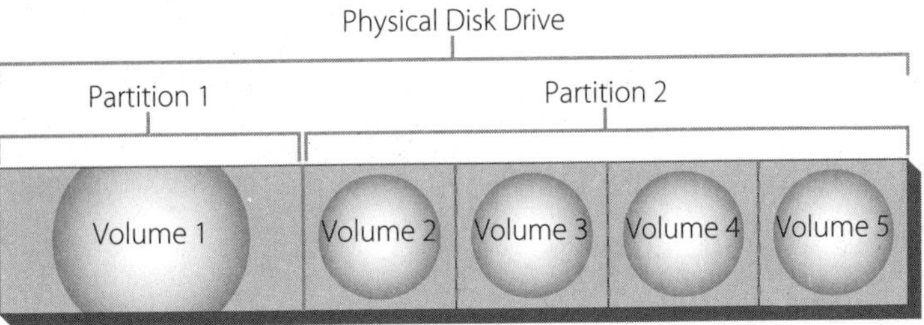

TIP

Reasons for Partitioning Disks

You might want to partition a disk for any of several reasons, such as:

- You need the security features of NTFS, but sometimes you must use MS-DOS to run old applications.
- You find it easier to organize, manage, and back up your files by putting certain types of files on different volumes.

For example, suppose you have a 1620-MB hard disk. You can, if you choose, dedicate the entire hard disk to Windows NT. In that case, the physical disk and the volume are identical. You might, however, decide to break that 1620 MB into smaller chunks: 200 MB for a flex-boot MS-DOS/Windows NT startup drive, plus 920 MB for NTFS, and another 500 MB for files and programs that rely on the FAT file system. In this case, because you want each portion of the drive to be independent of the others, you would format each chunk separately and assign each its own drive letter: C for the startup volume, probably D for the NTFS volume, and E for the FAT volume. Each of these resulting segments would then be a volume that is separate from, but coexists with, the others on your 1620-MB physical disk.

A partition by any name is always a distinct, physical portion of a hard disk. But when you look at partitions more closely, especially at what they hold and what they do, you find subtler shades of meaning attached to them. Depending on the function it performs, a partition can be *primary* or *extended*, and it can be an *active*, *system*, or *boot* partition.

Primary and Extended Partitions

A primary partition is the one used by your operating system. With Windows 95 or MS-DOS, the primary partition usually holds all of the operating system. With Windows NT, the primary partition can hold the system's startup files only, or both the startup files and the files needed to give the operating system its functionality. If your computer is set up as a flex-boot system, the primary partition contains the other operating system and part or all of Windows NT.

You can create four primary partitions, or three primary and one extended partition per hard disk. You cannot subdivide a primary partition into multiple logical drives as you can an extended partition.

An extended partition can occupy whatever space remains after you create your primary partition or partitions. You cannot boot from an extended partition, and you can have only one per hard disk, but you can divide the space in it into as many logical drives as you want, of whatever size you want.

Each drive in an extended partition can be formatted separately for NTFS or the FAT file system, and is treated as a physically separate disk drive. During installation, you can set up Windows NT to start from the primary partition but run from a logical drive in an extended partition.

This hard disk is divided into a 504-MB primary partition and a 792-MB extended partition that is further divided into two logical drives, F (formatted for the FAT file system) and J (formatted for NTFS).

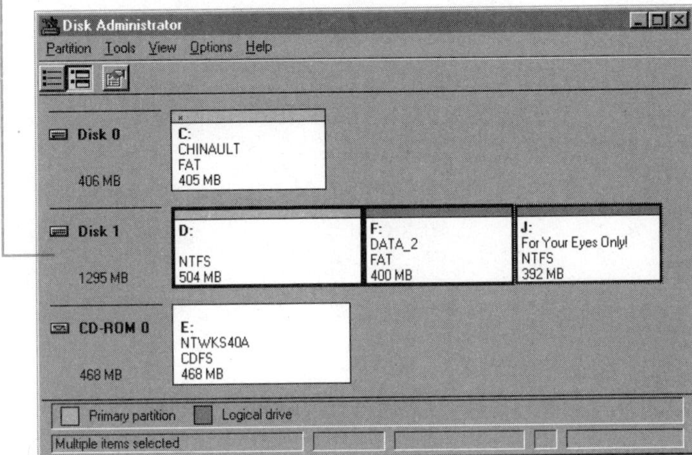

System, Active, and Boot Partitions

Whereas primary and extended partitions refer to physical portions of a disk, system partition, active partition, and boot partition refer to functionality.

The system partition contains the files needed to load Windows NT and enable the operating system to use your hardware. It must always be a primary partition, and on x86-based computers, it must be marked "active" (a term you might remember from the MS-DOS Fdisk program).

The active partition is the partition from which the computer starts up. It too must be a primary partition. If you use Windows NT exclusively, the active partition is the same as the system partition. If you use Windows NT and Windows 95 or MS-DOS, the active partition must contain the startup files for both operating systems. If you use Windows NT and OS/2, each operating system occupies its own system partition. Therefore, in order to run OS/2, you must use Disk Administrator to mark the OS/2 partition as active, and then reboot. *(For details, see "Marking the Active Partition," page 630.)*

The active partition concept applies only to x86-based computers. RISC-based computers are handled by special configuration programs. With these computers, the system partition does not have to be marked active in order for the machine to boot.

The boot partition, which sounds like it ought to be the one you boot from, is actually the partition that contains the Windows NT system and support files. If you run Windows NT from a single partition (either FAT or NTFS), the boot partition is, indeed, the same as the system partition. If you start the system from a FAT partition but install Windows NT in a different (NTFS) partition, the FAT partition is the system partition and the NTFS partition is the boot partition.

Managing Disk Partitions

Creating or deleting a partition represents a significant step in the configuration or reconfiguration of a hard disk. Creating a new partition turns disk space into virgin territory ready for definition as one or more logical drives, each of which you must format before using. Deleting an existing partition essentially means wiping out everything stored in it. In a sense, partitioning all or part of a new hard disk is like creating storage where there was just the possibility of storage before.

 TIP

When You Should Delete a Partition: Rarely

Because partitioning is such a sweeping act, usually the only time you need to create new partitions is when you set up a hard disk for the first time or when you plan to rebuild and reformat a used hard disk. The only time you should consider deleting a partition is when you want to reorganize a disk and are certain that all important programs and data have been backed up to another medium. Deleting a partition means starting over.

If your entire hard disk has already been assigned to either a primary or an extended partition, you cannot create a new partition without first deleting an old one. There are some limits to this capability, however, because Disk Administrator does not allow you to delete either the primary partition on the startup hard disk (always called disk 0) or an extended partition if it contains the Windows NT system files. If you have a flex-boot system, you can do this kind of partitioning by booting with a Windows 95 startup disk, or with MS-DOS, and using the Fdisk utility. Be forewarned, however, that deleting the primary partition makes your entire hard disk unusable until you repartition and reformat the drive, and reinstall your system software—not a task to be taken lightly.

Creating a Primary Partition

To create a new partition, you need free—that is, unformatted—space on your hard disk. This space can belong to a portion of a new hard disk that you have not assigned to either a primary or an extended partition, or it can be space you make available by deleting an existing partition.

To create a new primary partition (one that cannot be divided into multiple logical drives), do the following:

1 In the Disk Administrator window, select the disk space you want to include in the partition.

2 Choose Create from the Partition menu. (Disk Administrator will warn you that the partition might not be accessible from Windows 95 or MS-DOS if the partition's starting or ending cylinder value is too high.)

3 Choose the partition size by clicking the up or down arrow or typing, and then click OK.

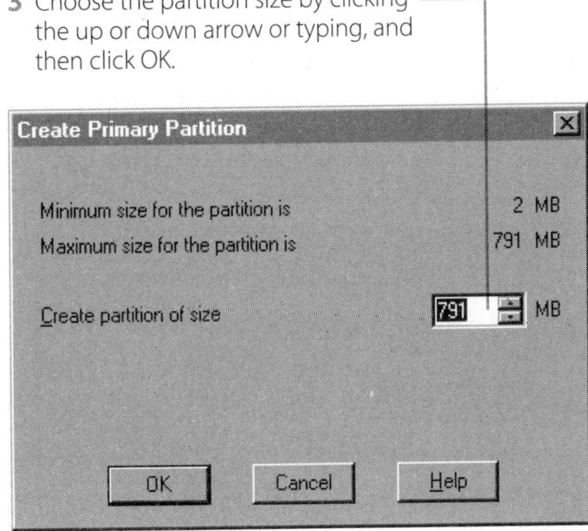

Disk Administrator creates the new partition and assigns it the next available drive letter. You can assign a different drive letter with the Assign Drive Letter command on the Tools menu. *For more information, see "Assigning a Drive Letter," page 632.*

Before you can use the new partition, you must format it for a particular file system. *For details, see "Formatting a New Partition or Logical Drive," page 628.*

NOTE

> If the free space you selected is already part of an existing extended partition, the Create command produces an almost identical dialog box for creating a new logical drive. This dialog box appears because you cannot create a new partition within an existing partition.

Creating an Extended Partition

If your hard disk contains no more than three primary partitions, you can create an extended partition in the remaining space. The main benefit of an extended partition is its ability to support more than one logical drive in a single (large) portion of the disk. Using an extended partition, you can define different-sized logical drives and assign each the drive letter and type of file system you want it to use.

To create an extended partition, do the following:

1. In the Disk Administrator window, select the free space you want to assign to the partition.
2. Choose Create Extended from the Partition menu.
3. Type or choose the partition size you want in the dialog box that appears.

After you create an extended partition, you must define one or more logical drives within it and format each separately, as explained in the following sections.

Creating a Logical Drive

A logical drive is a part of an extended partition that you "wall off" and format so that you can use it as if it were a truly separate disk drive. Creating a logical drive is very similar to creating a new partition. It is, in fact, the second step in preparing an extended partition for use. To create a new logical drive, you must begin with some free space in an extended partition. To create the drive, do the following:

1. In the Disk Administrator window, select the free space you want to assign to the drive.

2. Choose Create from the Partition menu. (Yes, the same command you use in creating a new primary partition. If the space has not been partitioned, Windows NT assumes that you want to create a primary partition; if the space has been partitioned, Windows NT assumes that you want to create a logical drive.)

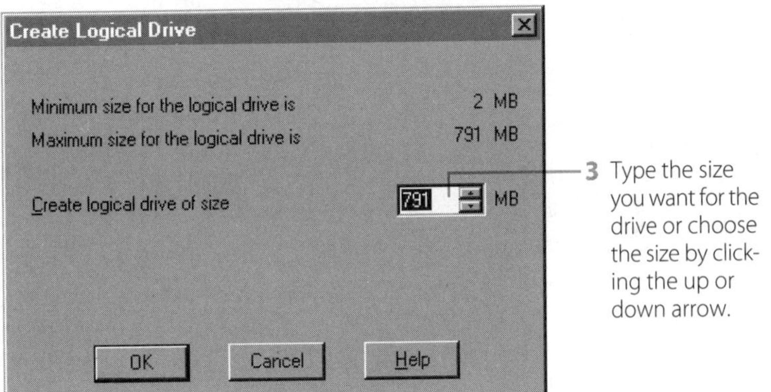

3 Type the size you want for the drive or choose the size by clicking the up or down arrow.

4. Click OK, and the new drive appears in the disk bar with the next available drive letter assigned by Windows NT. You can assign a different drive letter with the Assign Drive Letter command on the Tools menu. *For more information, see "Assigning a Drive Letter," page 632.*

5. Format the new drive as explained in the following section.

Formatting a New Partition or Logical Drive

SEE ALSO

For information about reformatting an existing partition or logical drive, see "Formatting an Existing Volume," page 631.

Before you can use a new primary partition or a logical drive within an extended partition, you must format it and, if you want, give it a volume label—a descriptive name, such as DATA FILES—that gives you and others an idea of the types of information stored on it.

To format a new partition or a logical drive in an extended partition, do the following:

1. In the Disk Administrator window, select the newly created partition or logical drive.
2. Open the Partition menu and choose Commit Changes Now.
3. Disk Administrator asks you to confirm your intentions. Click Yes.
4. Open the Tools menu and choose Format.

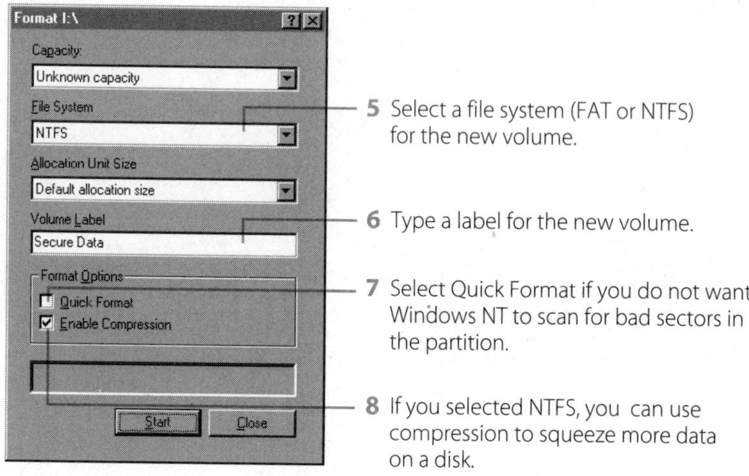

9. Click Start to begin formatting.

Deleting a Partition or Logical Drive

The most important thing to know about deleting a partition or logical drive is this: *All information in the partition or drive will be irrevoca-*

SEE ALSO

For information about backing up files, see Chapter 16, "Protecting Your Data with Backup."

bly lost. So be sure that you've backed up all needed programs and data files before deleting. Although the partition or drive won't actually be deleted until you quit Disk Administrator and confirm your intention (or choose Commit Changes Now from the Partition menu), knowing what you're about to do and why will avoid jolts to your nervous system.

On an x86-based system, Windows NT will not allow you to delete the following:

- The active partition on your startup hard disk
- The partition containing your Windows NT system files (if, for example, you place them on a logical drive in an extended partition)
- An extended partition that contains logical drives (you must delete the drives first, and then delete the partition)

WARNING

If you're using a RISC-based computer, take care when deleting partitions. Unlike x86-based computers, your system does not require you to set an active (system) partition. Thus, it is possible for you to delete the partition that contains your Windows NT startup files. If you mistakenly begin to delete this important partition, quit Disk Administrator and choose No when it asks if you want to save your changes.

To delete a partition or a logical drive in an extended partition, do the following:

1. Verify that all needed files have been backed up.
2. Select the partition or logical drive you want to delete. (If the partition you want to delete is an extended partition, you must first delete any existing logical drives within it.)
3. Choose Delete from the Partition menu and confirm your intention when the Confirm dialog box appears.

Disk Administrator then changes the on-screen representation to show free space in the area formerly occupied by the partition.

TIP

Changing File Systems

Don't delete a partition or logical drive if all you want to do is change its file system. If you want to change from FAT to NTFS, you can use the Convert command in a command prompt window. This command converts the volume without destroying its contents. *(For details, see "Converting a Volume to NTFS," page 637.)*

If you want to change from NTFS to FAT, you must reformat the volume, which destroys all its data—but there's still no need to delete and re-create the partition or logical drive. Simply select the volume, and then choose Format from the Tools menu. *(For details, see "Formatting an Existing Volume," page 631.)*

Marking the Active Partition

The active partition on a hard disk is the one from which an x86-based computer boots. On these machines, one primary partition—the one containing the files needed for startup—must be marked active for the computer to start itself and an operating system. The active partition must always be on the first hard disk attached to the system (Disk 0).

If you're familiar with MS-DOS and the Fdisk program, you already know that Fdisk includes an option for setting the active partition. With Windows NT, you use Disk Administrator to do the job. Disk Administrator indicates the current active partition with a small asterisk in the color bar above the partition. If you use Windows NT exclusively, or if you use Windows NT and Windows 95 or MS-DOS, you do not have to change the active partition. In fact, Disk Administrator won't let you. The Mark Active command is grayed out and inactive. However, if you use another operating system, such as OS/2, you must mark its system partition as active and reboot in order to use the alternate operating system.

To mark the active partition and start a different operating system, do the following:

1 In the Disk Administrator window, select the partition you want to mark active.

2 Choose Mark Active from the Partition menu.

3 Reboot the computer.

Working with Volumes

A *volume* in Windows NT is any space on a hard disk that is formatted for use by a particular file system. A volume is equivalent to a formatted partition or logical drive. If you have a flex-boot Windows NT/MS-DOS system, for example, your drive C, which is formatted for the FAT file system, represents one volume. If your Windows NT files (other than the startup files) are stored on drive D, that drive represents another volume.

Formatting an Existing Volume

You might want to format an existing volume for one of these reasons:

- To change the volume's format from NTFS to FAT
- To delete all the information in the volume so you can reuse it

WARNING

> Formatting a volume destroys all its files, so be sure this is what you want. If you want to change the format from FAT to NTFS, use the Convert command. *For details, see "Converting a Volume to NTFS," page 637.*

To format an existing volume, do the following:

1 Select the volume you want to format.

2 Open the Tools menu and choose Format.

3 In the Format dialog box, select a file system and type a label for the reformatted volume. Select Quick Format if you do not want Windows NT to scan for bad sectors.

4 Click Start to begin formatting.

Assigning or Changing a Volume Label

If you choose not to assign a volume label during formatting, or if you later decide to change a volume label to a more descriptive one, you can do so by using the Properties command on Disk Administrator's Tools menu.

The volume label on a FAT volume can be up to 11 characters long and can include spaces. Whether you type uppercase or lowercase letters, the volume label is stored in uppercase letters only. (Some applications, including Windows NT Explorer, display volume labels with an initial capital and the rest of the name in lowercase.) A FAT volume label cannot include the following characters:

* ? / \ | . , ; : + = [ ] < > "

Only one restriction applies when you assign a volume label for an NTFS volume: the maximum length is 32 characters. You can use any symbols you want, and uppercase and lowercase letters are retained (and displayed) exactly as you type them.

Assigning a Drive Letter

Windows NT normally takes charge of drive assignments, parceling out the letters during startup according to a few simple rules:

1. It assigns the letter closest to the start of the alphabet to the first primary partition on each of your hard disks, beginning with C for the primary partition on your startup hard disk, D for the first primary partition on the second hard disk (if any), and so on. (A and B are reserved for floppy drives.)
2. It then assigns the next available letters, in order, to the logical drives on your hard disks, one after the other, beginning with the first hard disk (Disk 0), then the second, third, and so on.
3. Windows NT assigns drive letters to the remaining primary partitions, if any, on your hard disks.
4. After drive letters have been assigned to all hard disk partitions, Windows NT assigns letters to CD-ROM drives and removable-cartridge drives.

The result, although it can look disjointed on a system with two or more hard disks, is understandable, as you can see from this illustration:

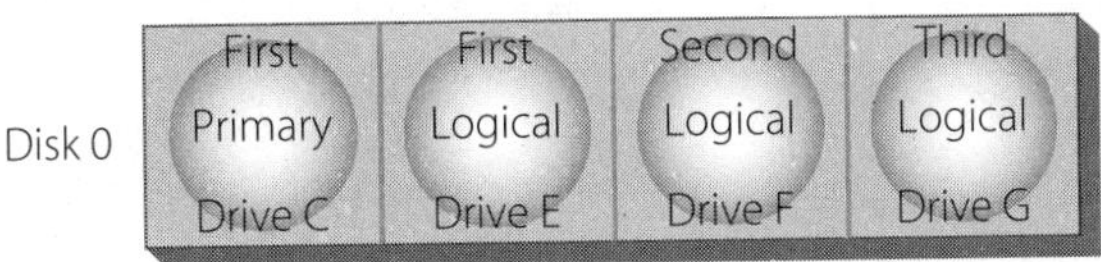

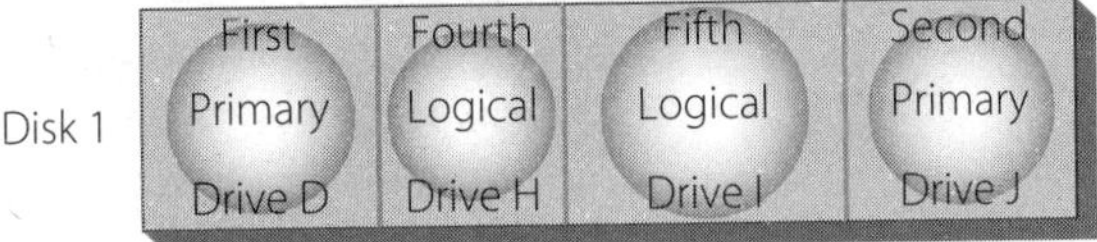

As you add new hard disks or other mass-storage devices such as removable-cartridge drives and CD-ROM drives to your system, you might find that a system-assigned drive letter interferes with a mapped network drive. For example, some companies have traditionally mapped drive E to a shared network drive. This made sense in a time when few systems had more than one local hard drive, CD-ROM drives hadn't been invented, and it was important to use letters near the beginning of the alphabet for network mappings to conserve a few precious bytes of memory in a system with only 640 KB of RAM.

Many applications remember the drive letter of the files they use, so you cannot arbitrarily change the letter of a drive that contains a program's files (or, in some cases, document files created by the program) without "breaking" the program or its documents.

The solution in such a case is to continue using your existing drive mappings for access to existing drives—and assign new drive letters to the new volumes you create with Disk Administrator.

You can use Disk Administrator to permanently assign particular drive letters to specific volumes and mass-storage devices. This is called *static assignment*. It means that later on, if you add another volume, for example, Windows NT will assume that the statically assigned drive letter is unavailable for use.

To assign a letter to a particular volume or mass-storage device, do the following:

1. In the Disk Administrator window, select the volume or mass-storage device whose drive letter you want to change.
2. Open the Tools menu and choose Assign Drive Letter.

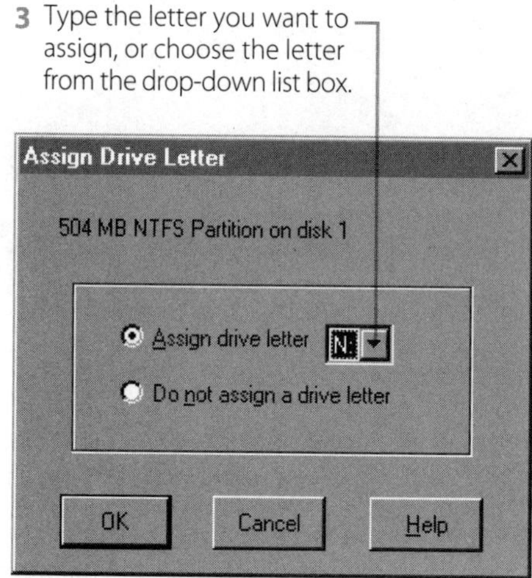

Choosing the second option, "Do not assign a drive letter," deletes the letter assigned to a volume or drive. Although it might sound like an intriguing way to access more than 24 drives, it merely allows you to *have* more than 24, but you cannot access drives without a letter. If you have that many volumes or drives, a better solution is to combine them in a volume set or stripe set. *For details, see "Working with Volume Sets," page 638, and "Working with Stripe Sets," page 641.*

Displaying Volume Property Sheets

The property sheet for a volume provides a few morsels of information about a volume, such as the amount of used and unused space. It also gives you quick access to other disk-management functions, as shown on the next page.

SEE ALSO

For information about buttons on the Tools page, see "Finding and Repairing Disk Errors," page 739, and Chapter 16, "Protecting Your Data with Backup." For information about the Sharing page, see "Sharing Folders with Other Users," page 281. For information about the Security page, see Chapter 20, "NTFS Security," and Chapter 21, "Auditing." For information about compression, see "Using File Compression," page 727.

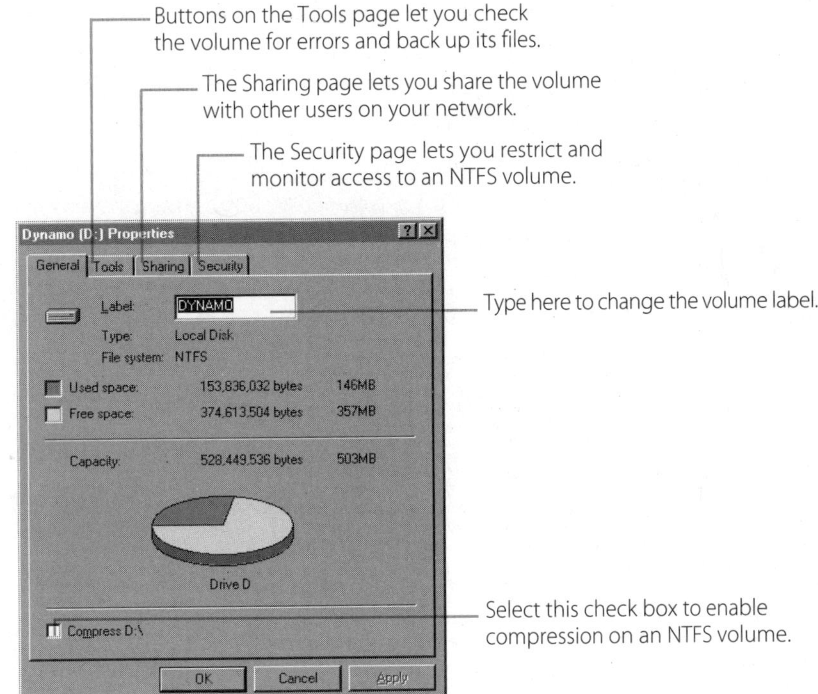

To display the property sheet for a volume, select the volume and then do one of the following:

- Open the Tools menu and choose Properties.
- Click the Properties tool.
- Right-click the volume and choose Properties from the context menu.
- Press Alt-Enter.

Using Volumes View

In Disk Administrator's standard Disk Configuration view, the disk bars show the physical relationship of the disks, partitions, and volumes. In addition, the type of partition, drive letter, volume label, file system, and volume size are displayed within the disk bars.

Disk Administrator's Volumes view, shown below, offers an entirely different view of your volumes. This tabular view provides information about all of your volumes and logical drives—but does not include information about unused space on a disk, which can be viewed only in Disk Configuration view. Volumes view has one other shortcoming vis-à-vis Disk Configuration view: you cannot see which disk a volume resides on.

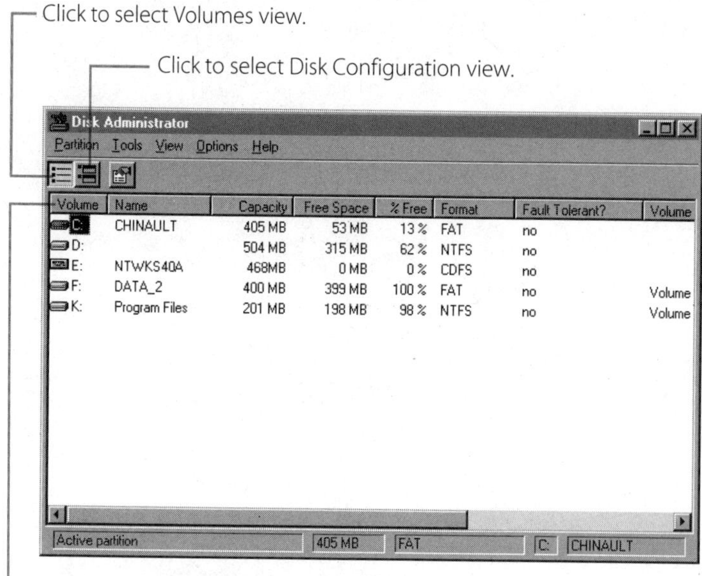

Click any column heading to sort the list of volumes by the content of that column.

In Volumes view, nearly all the partition management functions—formatting, assigning a volume label or drive letter, setting the active partition, deleting a partition, and viewing a volume's properties—are available just as they are in Disk Configuration view. But because a disk's unused space is not displayed, you cannot create partitions or logical drives.

To select Volumes view, do one of the following:

- Open the View menu and choose Volumes.

- Click its tool on the tool bar.
- Press Ctrl-V.

To return to Disk Configuration view, do one of the following:

- Open the View menu and choose Disk Configuration.
- Click its tool on the tool bar.
- Press Ctrl-D.

Converting a Volume to NTFS

SEE ALSO

For more information about FAT versus NTFS, see "NTFS Pros and Cons," page 580.

The FAT file system, which is used by computers that run Windows 95 and MS-DOS, has the advantage of being compatible with those operating systems as well as Windows NT. But NTFS, the file system favored by Windows NT, offers greater security and speed, among other advantages. For these reasons, you might want to convert a volume that you use only with Windows NT to NTFS. The Convert command lets you do just that, and unlike formatting, it does so without destroying the files on the volume.

To convert a volume to NTFS, follow these steps:

SEE ALSO

For more information about command prompt sessions, see Chapter 18, "Using the Command Prompt."

1. Click the Start button and choose Programs, Command Prompt to open a command prompt window.
2. At the command prompt, type this command line:

```
convert d: /fs:ntfs
```

   Replace *d* with the letter of the drive you want to convert. The drive you specify can't be the current drive.

NOTE

> If Windows NT can't lock all users off the drive—for example, if a running program is using a file on the drive or if the drive is being shared over the network—the conversion is delayed until the next time you shut down and restart your computer.

Working with Volume Sets

Because Windows NT can work with multiple disks and partitions, a volume can sometimes be a collection of up to 32 discontinuous, different-sized spaces on up to 32 disks, all treated as if they were a single large volume with the same drive letter, as shown below. Such a collection of disk spaces is called a *volume set.*

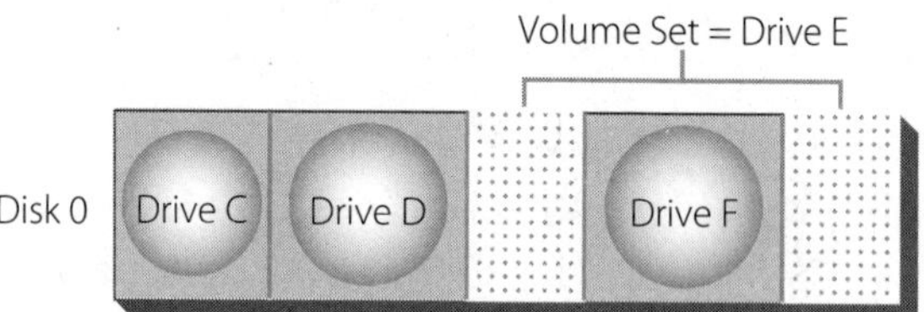

Or a volume set can span more than one disk, like this:

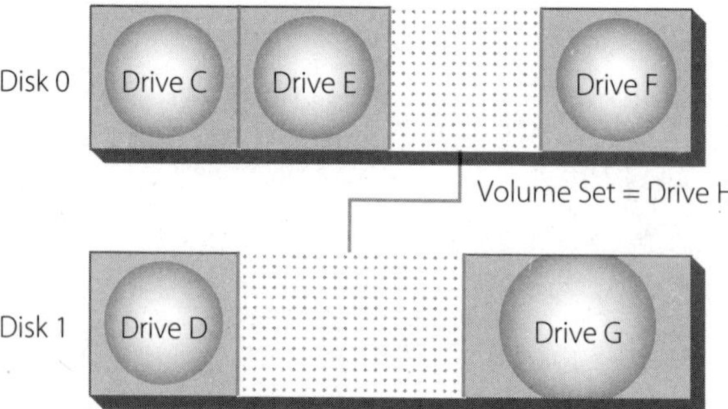

Such unions provide two obvious advantages:

- You combine several smaller areas into one large logical area without having to repartition the disk.
- You cut down on the number of drive letters in use, because a single drive letter refers to more than one storage segment on one or more disks.

Volume sets can have one additional but less obvious benefit. If you create a volume set that spans more than one disk, you might find that system performance improves. This is because disk reads and writes, which are normally slow in relation to other activities, are more efficient when spread across two or more disks.

Creating a Volume Set

CAUTION

If you have a flex-boot system, volume sets you create in Windows NT are not available when you use the other operating system (including Windows 95 and MS-DOS)—even if the volume set is formatted for the FAT file system.

To create a volume set with Disk Administrator, you must begin with two or more areas of free space on one or more disks. These spaces can be pre-existing, or you can create them during the current session by deleting existing partitions or logical drives. After the spaces you need are free, do the following:

1. In the Disk Administrator window, select the areas you want to combine into the volume set. (You select multiple disk regions by clicking one and then holding down Ctrl while you click the others.)

2. Choose Create Volume Set from the Partition menu. The Create Volume Set dialog box appears.

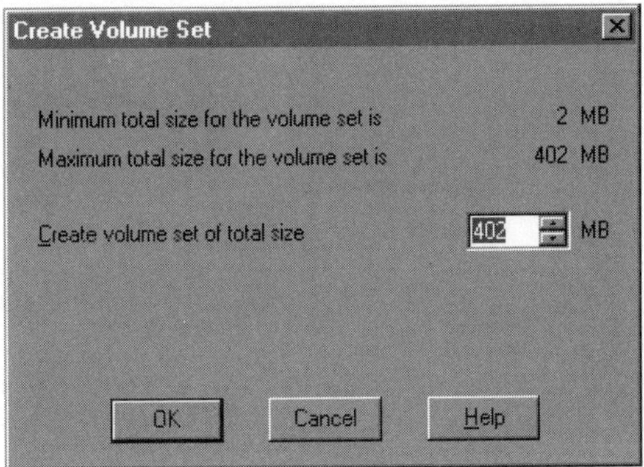

Specify the size of the volume set you want and click OK. If you create a volume set that is smaller than the total free space in the selected areas, Disk Administrator divides the free space proportionally so that each piece of the volume set represents approximately the same percentage of the original free space in each selected area.

When the Disk Administrator window reappears, the volume set is displayed in the disk bar, with the same identifying color or pattern and the same drive letter at the top of each area in the volume set. If you click one portion of the volume set, you'll notice that Disk Administrator selects every area in the volume set.

Before you can use a volume set, you must format it, just like any other partition or logical drive. *For details, see "Formatting a New Partition or Logical Drive," page 628.*

Extending a Volume Set

Although you cannot shrink a volume set, you can extend a volume set by adding one or more additional areas of free space. The only requirement is that the volume set must be formatted for NTFS.

To extend a volume set, do the following:

1. In the Disk Administrator window, select both the volume set and the free space you want to add to it.
2. Choose Extend Volume Set from the Partition menu. The Extend Volume Set dialog box appears.

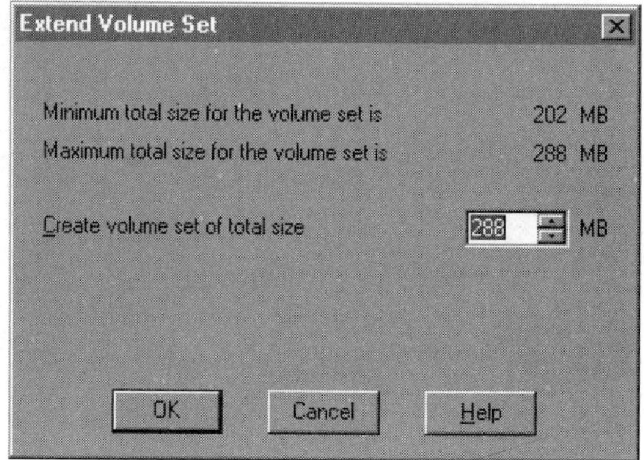

Specify the new total size of the volume set. If you specify less than the total amount of free space, Disk Administrator distributes the space assigned to the volume set as described in the previous section, "Creating a Volume Set."

Deleting a Volume Set

Deleting a volume set is equivalent to deleting a partition or a logical drive in that all information stored in the volume set is lost. To delete a volume set, back up all the information you want to keep, and then:

1 In the Disk Administrator window, select the volume set you want to delete.

2 Choose Delete from the Partition menu.

Just as when you delete a partition, Disk Administrator cautions you that all data will be lost and asks you to confirm your intention. If you continue, the deleted drive appears as free space on the disk bar. When you quit Disk Administrator, you'll be asked if you want to make the changes permanent. If you do, Disk Administrator saves the changes and restarts the computer.

Working with Stripe Sets

Striping is a data storage technique that layers information evenly across two or more disks, using a volume called a *stripe set*. Windows NT Workstation supports striping that layers data in equal blocks across 2 through 32 disks. Stripe sets improve system performance by making disk access more efficient. However, unlike striping with parity and mirroring, which are available with Windows NT Server, striping does not provide data protection.

CAUTION

If you have a flex-boot system, stripe sets you create in Windows NT are not available when you use the other operating system (including Windows 95 and MS-DOS)—even if the stripe set is formatted for the FAT file system.

Fault-Tolerant Disk Storage with Windows NT Server

Windows NT Server, the enhanced form of Windows NT designed for use on large network servers that are managed by professional network administrators, supports two additional data storage techniques that allow the server to recover from disk failure or data loss: striping with parity and disk mirroring. Striping with parity protects data with parity information that can be used to recover the data if part of a "stripe" is lost when a disk fails. Mirroring, as its name implies, protects data by duplicating it on two disks so that if one of the disks fails, data can still be recovered from the "mirror image" on the other disk.

Stripe Sets Versus Volume Sets

You can visualize a stripe set as something like the following—although in real life, of course, the disks containing the set are unlikely to be as symmetrically organized as the ones shown here:

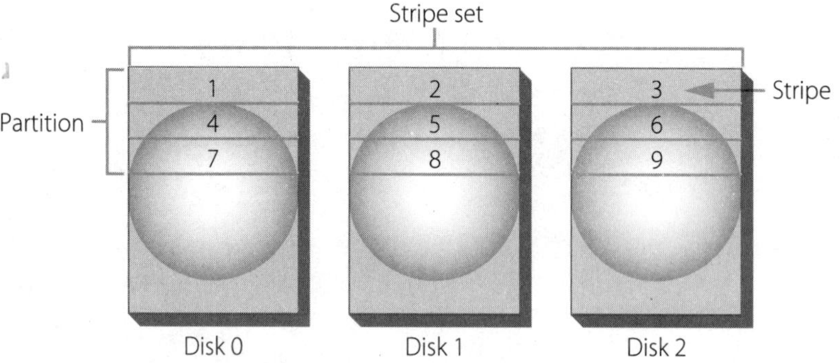

After such a stripe set is created, information is layered across the disks in the numeric order shown.

Stripe sets differ from volume sets in two important respects:

- A stripe set can be created only on a system with two or more disks; a volume set can be created on a single disk.
- A stripe set, because it layers data evenly across disks, contains partitions that are approximately equal in size. A volume set can include partitions of different sizes.

Stripe sets and volume sets are alike, however, in four significant respects:

- Both are referenced by a single drive letter.
- Both lose all data if one of the disks fails.
- Both are selected and deleted as entire units, even though the storage areas they cover are physically separated on the same disk or on different disks.

- Both are invisible to Windows 95 and MS-DOS because they handle disk storage in a way that Windows 95 and MS-DOS cannot recognize.

Creating a Stripe Set

To create a stripe set, you need areas of free space on 2 through 32 disks that you want to combine. The process is simple:

1. In the Disk Administrator window, select the areas you want to combine.
2. Choose Create Stripe Set from the Partition menu. Specify the size of the stripe set you want in the Create Stripe Set dialog box that appears, and click OK.

When Windows NT creates the stripe set, it divides the areas of free space you selected into equal-sized partitions on each of the disks you specified.

Deleting a Stripe Set

As is the case with partitions, volume sets, and logical drives, deleting a stripe set means losing all information stored in it, so back up all data you want to keep before proceeding. Otherwise, deleting a stripe set is easy:

1. In the Disk Administrator window, select the stripe set you want to delete.
2. Choose Delete from the Partition menu.

Because such a deletion affects data and the organization of your hard disks, Windows NT asks for confirmation before carrying out the command. Remember, too, that the deletion isn't permanent until you quit Disk Administrator. If you have second thoughts, quit Disk Administrator and click No when asked if you want to record the change.

Saving and Restoring Disk Configurations

Disk Administrator, with its built-in conservatism, always requests confirmation before making any permanent changes to your disk configuration. You can, however, choose to save the current configuration or restore an earlier (saved) configuration. If you want, you can also search for the configuration used by a different installation of Windows NT and overwrite the current configuration with that of the other installation.

WARNING

> When you restore or replace one configuration with another, be aware that data loss can occur if you change the definition of drives, volume sets, or stripe sets. Even though Disk Administrator asks for confirmation before making potentially destructive changes to a disk, be sure you know what you're doing, and always involve your system administrator in any such activity.

When Disk Administrator saves or alters the current disk configuration, it affects the following:

- Drive letters
- Volume sets
- Stripe sets

Saving, restoring, and searching for a disk configuration are all handled by the Configuration command on the Partition menu. When you choose this command, a submenu appears with three commands:

SEE ALSO

For information about creating and using an Emergency Repair Disk, see "Using Repair Disk Utility," page 737.

- Save saves the current configuration on a floppy disk in a file named System. Choosing this command causes Disk Administrator to display a dialog box asking you to place a formatted disk in drive A. You can save the configuration either on an Emergency Repair Disk, or you can use a different disk.

- Restore restores an earlier, saved configuration. Choosing Restore produces two dialog boxes. First comes a warning and a request for confirmation telling you that drive letters and other configuration information might be lost. If you click OK to confirm, a second dialog box asks you to insert the disk containing the saved configuration in drive A.

- Search causes Disk Administrator to search for other Windows NT installations on your computer. Choosing this command and confirming your intention when asked causes Disk Administrator to begin searching. If other installations are found, a list of those installations is displayed. Select the one you want and click OK to replace the current configuration with the installation you selected.

CHAPTER 23

Monitoring Your System

Whether you're in charge of a single workstation or an entire network, it's always possible that the imps of electronics will suddenly start gobbling memory, blocking communication lines, causing gridlock on a hard disk, or producing pandemonium on the data bus. At those times, you might wish you could dive into the system to take an up-close and personal look at what's going on. Well, you can't; but with Windows NT, you can check on what the computer system is doing. You can then put aside a lot of guesswork and base corrective actions on fact.

Before you go any further, you should know that much of this chapter is not necessarily for everyone. Four Windows NT programs are covered here:

- Event Viewer
- Server
- Task Manager
- Performance Monitor

These are specialized tools that you don't need in order to use Windows NT. You can run applications and access shared folders, files, and printers without ever using Performance Monitor, for example. After reading this chapter, you'll probably be intrigued enough to experiment once or twice with these tools, but normally you won't have to pay much attention to them.

Why not? First, because Windows NT has the ability to fine-tune itself to some degree without your intervention. Second, because system monitoring falls largely into the realm of network administration, the job of the all-powerful person who determines how computers on the network are accessed, by whom, and with what levels of permission. For people with such job descriptions, system monitoring tools can help keep the whole show running smoothly.

Still, the ability to monitor the system is a significant feature of Windows NT. So even if you are not a network administrator, you'll find this chapter useful if you want to monitor or fine-tune your own system.

What Do You Monitor?

System monitoring is one of those subjects you can look at from several perspectives, seeing different pieces of the whole from each. Basically, however, system monitoring boils down to looking at the system from three related, but still separate, points of view:

- First, there's the issue of "What's going on in there?" For this, Windows NT provides Event Viewer. Event Viewer lets you monitor a whole slew of happenings, known collectively as *events*, that are stored continually in a set of files called *event logs*. Events can range from innocuous and expected occurrences, such as logon/logoff activities and print jobs, to serious and unexpected errors, such as driver problems or a disk on which storage space is becoming scarce. With Event Viewer, you can record and monitor significant incidents related to the computer, its security, and its applications.

- Second, there's the issue of how a computer is being used as a server. Is it being accessed too often at particular times of day? Are too many users attempting to open the same file at the same time? Can the computer handle the demands made on it as both a print server and a file server? To check on a computer's use as a server, you use the Server applet in Control Panel. With thc Server applet, you can find out who is using the server, which resources are being used, and even how much time has passed since a particular person used a particular resource.

- Third, there's the issue of how the computer itself is performing. Here, you are concerned not so much with *what* is happening (that is, with events), as you are with *how well* the computer is making things happen. If you're a programmer, for example, you might be interested in how quickly and effectively your program is running under Windows NT. This area of monitoring focuses on matters such as processor time, memory use, disk access, cache effectiveness, and the behavior of threads and processes.

  When you need to know how well your computer is functioning, turn to Task Manager, which provides information about a few key indicators of performance and system usage. For more a more comprehensive look, use Performance Monitor, which allows you to view, chart, record, and analyze system efficiency. Performance Monitor also lets you monitor another Windows NT computer on your network.

Monitoring System Activities with Event Viewer

To Windows NT, an event is any occurrence that is potentially noteworthy—to you, to other users, to the operating system, or to an application. Event Viewer is the operating system's means of telling you about these events. It functions as a combination report card and status report by storing lists of events in log files that you can review, archive, or transfer to a database or spreadsheet for analysis.

Windows NT recognizes three broad categories of events: system events, security events, and application events. Each of these event types are recorded in separate log files.

System events are generated by Windows NT itself and by installed components, such as services and devices. They are recorded in a file called the *system log*. Windows NT classifies system events according to their severity as either errors, warnings, or information events, as follows:

- *Errors* are system events that represent possible loss of data or functionality. Examples of errors include events related to network contention or a malfunctioning network card, and loss of functionality caused by a device or service that doesn't load at startup.
- *Warnings* are system events that represent less significant or less immediate problems than errors. Examples of warning events include a nearly full disk, a timeout by the network redirector, and data errors on a backup tape.
- *Information events* are all other system events that Windows NT logs. Examples of information events include someone using a printer connected to your computer, or the successful loading of a database program.

Security events are generated by Windows NT when an activity you choose to audit succeeds (a *success audit*) or fails (a *failure audit*). Security events are recorded in a file called the *security log*. They

SEE ALSO
For more information about security events, see Chapter 21, "Auditing."

include file-related events, such as attempts to access files or change permissions (NTFS volumes only), and other security-related events, such as logon/logoff events and changes to security policies.

Application events are generated by applications and are recorded in a file called the *application log*. The application developer determines which events to monitor, and how those events will be recorded in the application log. Windows NT Backup, for example, records an application event whenever you erase a tape or run a backup.

The importance of a Windows NT log depends on your situation. If you work in a security-conscious environment, or one in which users freely access resources on each other's machines, you'll find the event logs useful in helping you keep track of who, what, when, and where. If you don't care about such details, the security log will probably be of little interest to you, but the system log can still be helpful in diagnosing performance problems and hardware errors, and the application log can give you insight into how certain applications are working. Although applications must be designed to record their "thoughts" in the application log, those that do provide an obvious benefit—to you, your technical support person, and even the developer—by profiling their behavior in the log.

If your computer is set up to share files or a printer with other users, checking the system log for print jobs and the security log for logon/logoff access will give you a feel for how and when your computer's resources are being used. Although the information might simply make you feel more in control of your system, you might also find patterns that help you determine better ways to manage it.

Viewing a Log

You can easily see what a log looks like even if you never before thought of monitoring your system. To view a log, open Event Viewer by clicking its icon, which you'll find in the Start menu's Administrative Tools (Common) group. If you're running Event Viewer for the first time, the system log appears, as shown on the next page. To view a different log, choose its name from the Log menu.

Event Viewer - System Log on \\YOSEMITE

Log View Options Help

Date	Time	Source	Category	Event	User	Computer
6/21/96	11:17:18 AM	NETLOGON	None	5715	N/A	YOSEM
6/19/96	5:18:13 PM	Rdr	None	3012	N/A	YOSEM
6/19/96	5:16:18 PM	Rdr	None	3012	N/A	YOSEM
6/19/96	3:49:38 PM	NETLOGON	None	5715	N/A	YOSEM
6/19/96	3:47:08 PM	Print	None	8	CarlS	YOSEM
6/19/96	3:46:49 PM	Print	None	6	CarlS	YOSEM
6/19/96	3:46:31 PM	Atdisk	None	9	N/A	YOSEM
6/19/96	3:46:13 PM	Atdisk	None	9	N/A	YOSEM
6/19/96	3:46:13 PM	Atdisk	None	9	N/A	YOSEM
6/19/96	3:34:52 PM	NETLOGON	None	5717	N/A	YOSEM
6/19/96	3:34:42 PM	BROWSER	None	8015	N/A	YOSEM
6/19/96	3:34:42 PM	BROWSER	None	8015	N/A	YOSEM
6/19/96	3:34:38 PM	NETLOGON	None	5717	N/A	YOSEM

NOTE

To view audit events, you must be logged on as a member of the Administrators group.

In addition to the date, time, and computer name, the display includes the following items:

- The icon at the far left of each line identifies the event type. You might see any of the following icons in an event log:

  Indicates an error event, such as a loss of data or functionality

  Indicates a warning event, such as a nearly full disk

  Indicates an information event, such as someone using a printer attached to your computer

  Indicates a success audit event, such as someone successfully logging on to the system

  Indicates a failure audit event, such as an unsuccessful attempt to log on to the system

- The Source column shows the name of the application software or system component that logged the event. In the illustration, for example, Print refers to the printer manager and Atdisk refers to the system component that manages certain disk controllers.
- The Category column tells you how the event is classified by the source. Although all you see is None in the illustration above, categories can be descriptive. The security log, for example, shows categories such as Logon/Logoff and Object Access (for file and folder access).
- The Event column shows the number used to identify each particular type of event. This number is associated with a text description that appears when you view an event's details.
- The User column identifies the user account involved in generating the event. Many events, particularly system events, are not generated by a particular user, so these events show N/A in the User column.

TIP

Sorting Entries in Event Viewer

Event Viewer's sorting options are few: you can sort by date, in descending or ascending order. To select a sort order, open the View menu and choose Newest First or Oldest First.

Examining Event Details

To get a closer look at an event in the Event Viewer window, select the event you want to see. Then use one of these methods to open the Event Detail window:

- Double-click the event.
- Press Enter.
- Open the View menu and choose Detail.

All methods lead to a window similar to the one shown below.

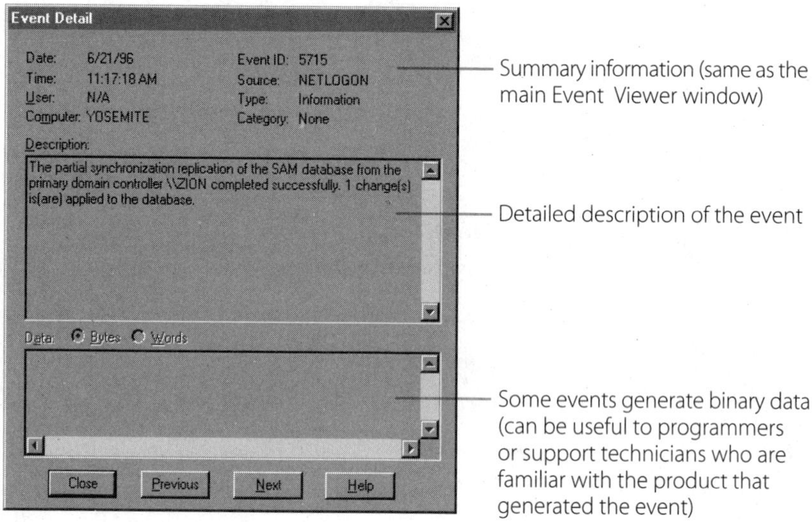

Summary information (same as the main Event Viewer window)

Detailed description of the event

Some events generate binary data (can be useful to programmers or support technicians who are familiar with the product that generated the event)

If you want to view details for other events, you can do so without first returning to the main window: click Previous or Next to display the event above or below the currently displayed event. When you're done viewing event details, click Close to return to Event Viewer's main window.

Filtering Events

As you can see from even a cursory look at your system log, events can pile up quickly, obscuring those of a particular type (such as print jobs) or those that occurred at a particular date and time (such as repeated, failed logon attempts). You can use Event Viewer to pinpoint clusters of events, or those that occur cyclically, by filtering the log to display only the events that interest you. To do this:

1. In the Event Viewer window, choose the log you want to filter—system, security, or application—from the Log menu.
2. Choose Filter Events from the View menu. The Filter dialog box appears.

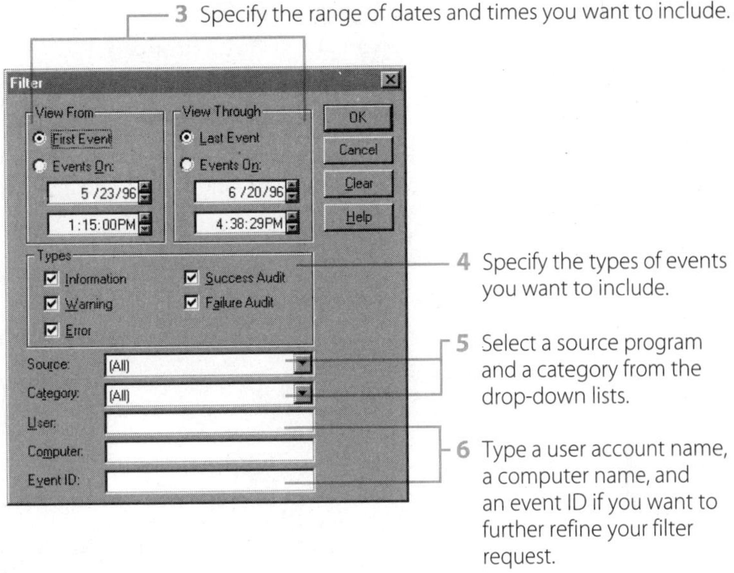

7 When you have set up the filter as you want it, click OK.

In a few seconds, a list of events matching your specifications appears on screen. The following illustration, for example, shows the results of filtering a system log to include only print activity by CarlS between 8 A.M. and 6 P.M. on June 18, 1996.

The title bar lets you know that a filter is in effect.

Event Viewer - System Log on \\YOSEMITE (Filtered)

Log View Options Help

Date	Time	Source	Category	Event	User	Compute
6/18/96	2:32:31 PM	Print	None	2	CarlS	YOSEMIT
6/18/96	2:29:46 PM	Print	None	4	CarlS	YOSEMIT
6/18/96	1:49:09 PM	Print	None	3	CarlS	YOSEMIT
6/18/96	1:48:12 PM	Print	None	4	CarlS	YOSEMIT

To restore all the events to your Event Viewer window, open the View menu and choose All Events.

Searching for an Event

The Find command on Event Viewer's View menu provides another way to search a log. Although less useful than filtering by dates and times, Find is exactly what you need when you want to find a single needle in an event haystack. When you choose Find, a dialog box similar to the one shown below appears.

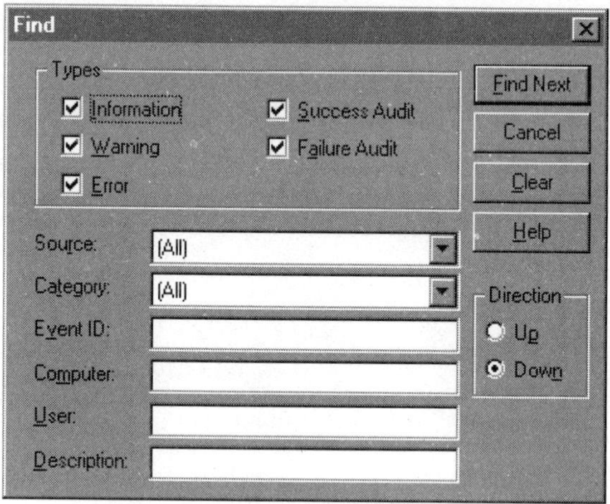

Much of this dialog box is similar to the Filter dialog box, but some elements are different:

- The Description box allows you to type a portion of the text description you see when you view the event details. If you specify text here, you can zero in on exactly the event or events you seek. However, the Find command does not search for binary data; you cannot type a set of hexadecimal numbers and expect Find to show you the event that produced those numbers in the Detail dialog box.

- The Direction option buttons let you specify the direction of the search. Select Down to search through the event log from the current position to the end, or select Up to search from the current position back to the beginning. When Find reaches the end of the log, it asks if you want to continue searching from the other end.
- The Find Next button is the Find command's version of OK, meaning "go and do it." The first time you use Find, you might assume that the dialog box will remain on screen so that you can click Find Next again if the Find command locates the wrong event among several similar or identical events. Not so. The dialog box disappears when you click Find Next, but you can repeat the search from the keyboard. Press F3 to repeat the search until you find the event you want.

Managing Logs

If one of the logs becomes filled to capacity and its settings don't permit removal of the oldest events, a message appears telling you that the log is full. If this happens, you can restore peace and serenity by saving the log (if you want to preserve its contents) and then choosing the Clear All Events command from Event Viewer's Log menu. Alternatively, you can reduce the minimum amount of time that events must be saved before they are overwritten. These options are described in the following sections.

Saving a Log

You can save the events recorded in your logs for historical purposes, for comparison over time, or to document or analyze system use. To save a log file:

1. Choose the Save As command from Event Viewer's Log menu.
2. In the Save As Type list box, select the format in which to save the log. You can save a log in one of three formats:
   - Select Event Log Files if you want to be able to reopen the log in Event Viewer.

- Select Text Files if you want to use the data in a word processor document.
- Select Comma Delim. Text if you want to use the data in a spreadsheet or database.

3 Click Save.

NOTE

When you save a log, all events are included, even if the current display is filtered.

If you choose one of the text formats, events are listed in the currently displayed sort order (newest first or oldest first). The text formats produce the smallest files, but that's because the files do not include the events' binary data, which can be seen only with Event Viewer's Details view.

Viewing a Saved Log

If you save a log as an Event Log File, you can open it in Event Viewer, where it looks just like any current event log. (Lest there be any confusion, Event Viewer's title bar includes the name of the file rather than the name of a current log.) To open a saved Event Log File, choose Open from Event Viewer's Log menu.

The two text formats produce files that can be used in another application, such as a word processor, spreadsheet, or database. You can use that application's features to filter, sort, and format the event log in a form that suits your purposes. For example, you could use Microsoft Excel to open a system log saved in comma-delimited text format, delete the columns you don't need, apply a little formatting, and sort the events by source and then by event ID.

Clearing a Log

Event Viewer doesn't allow you to erase individual events from a log. (That would make it too easy for nefarious users to cover their tracks.) But you can erase all events from a log. To clear a log:

1 In the Event Viewer window, display the log you want to clear by choosing it from the Log menu.

2 Choose the Clear All Events command from the Log menu.

CAUTION

When you clear a log, its events are irretrievably erased from the current log. You cannot restore events to a current log, even if you save the log before clearing it.

You can clear a log whether or not you save it first. Like any good application, however, Event Viewer is cautious and protective of your data. It always assumes that you really, really want the information and so it will not clear a log without first prompting, "Do you want to save this event log before clearing it?" This message appears even if you saved the log a few seconds before.

Modifying Log Settings

By default, the system, security, and application logs each hold 512 KB of information. If the log becomes full, another default tells Windows NT to begin overwriting the oldest information, but only if it is at least seven days old. (If the log becomes full before seven days have passed, new events are not recorded.) To adjust either or both of these default settings:

1 Choose the Log Settings command on Event Viewer's Log menu.

2 Select the log whose settings you want to change.

3 Specify the new size of the log.

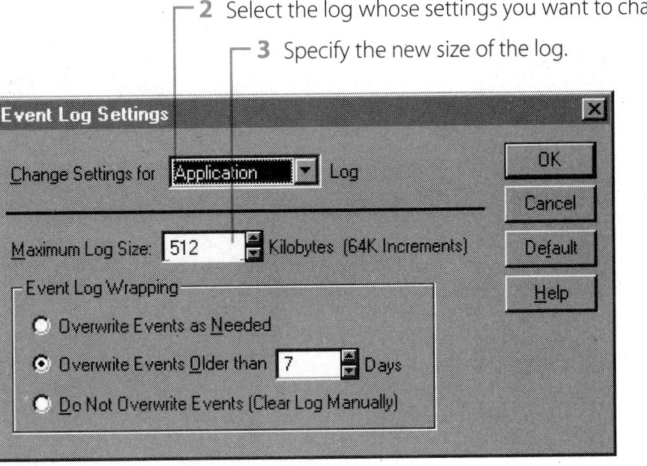

4 In the Event Log Wrapping group box, choose the option you want to use when the log reaches its maximum size.

NOTE

If you specify a size smaller than the current size of the log, you must clear the log before the new size takes effect. This extra step prevents you from destroying existing records by inadvertently making the log too small to hold all of the currently recorded events.

- If you select Overwrite Events As Needed, all events are recorded, but old events might be discarded before you have a chance to review them.
- The second option ensures that events are not deleted until a certain time (you can specify 1 through 365 days) has elapsed. This is a good choice if you archive logs on a regular schedule. If the log reaches its maximum size before the specified time has passed, however, the system stops recording events until you clear the log or the requisite time has passed so that old events can be overwritten.
- The last option, which requires you to clear the log manually, means that when the log is full, the system stops recording events until you clear the log.

NOTE

If the system stops recording events because the log is full, a warning message appears on-screen.

TIP

Restoring the Default Settings
Choose Log Settings from the Log menu, select a log, and then click Default to restore the default settings: a 512-KB log file that overwrites events older than seven days when the file is full.

Monitoring Other Computers

If you're responsible for monitoring system, security, and application-related events on computers other than your own, you can do so without leaving your chair. To do so, use the Select Computer command on Event Viewer's Log menu, which produces the dialog box shown below.

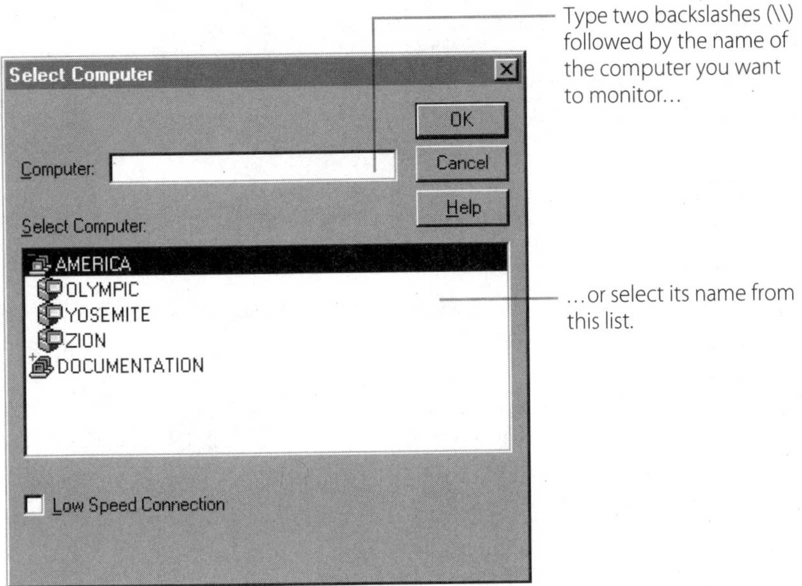

You can monitor computers running Windows NT Workstation, Windows NT Server, or LAN Manager 2.x. Other operating systems, including Windows 95, Windows 3.x, and OS/2, do not maintain logs that Event Viewer can monitor.

Monitoring System Use with Server

For information about sharing files and folders, see "Sharing Folders with Other Users," page 281.

SEE ALSO

For information about sharing printers, see "To Share or Not to Share," 229.

If you regularly share files and other resources with other users, Server provides you with some interesting and useful information about your computer. Although you share files, folders, and printers by using property sheets for those objects, you monitor and control user access to your shared resources with Server.

You can use Server to check on:

- Who is connected to your computer
- Which resources have been made available for sharing
- Which resources are in use, and by whom
- Which folders can be replicated on your computer
- Who receives administrative alerts—notices of problems related to security, resource availability, and access

Server is a Control Panel applet. To start Server, click the Start menu, select Settings, and then click Control Panel. After Control Panel opens, double-click the Server icon. A small window appears, as shown below.

Number of users connected to your computer

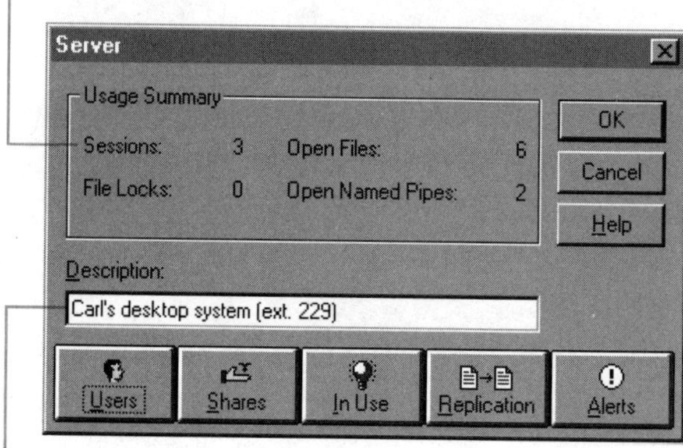

Optional comment that identifies your computer in Network Neighborhood

Monitoring Users

With Server, you can see who is currently using which resources on your computer, as well as how long the person has been logged on and how much time has passed since the user last initiated an action.

To view this information, click Users in the Server window to display this dialog box:

Select the name of a user to display the resources that person is using.

For each open resource, Server displays the number of times the resource has been opened, and the amount of time the resource has been open.

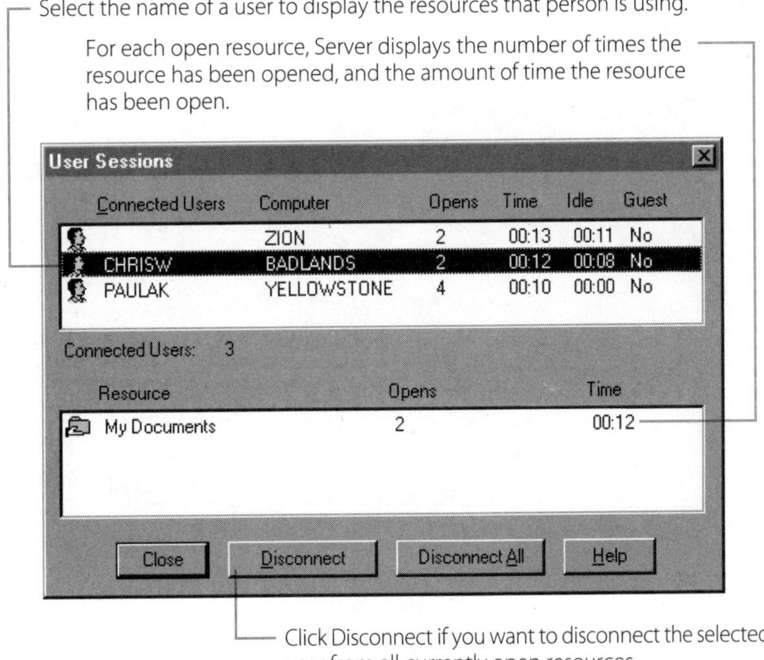

Click Disconnect if you want to disconnect the selected user from all currently open resources.

Monitoring Shared Resources

Server's Shares button shows essentially the same information as the Users button, but from a different perspective. When you click the Shares button, you see a dialog box like the example on the next page.

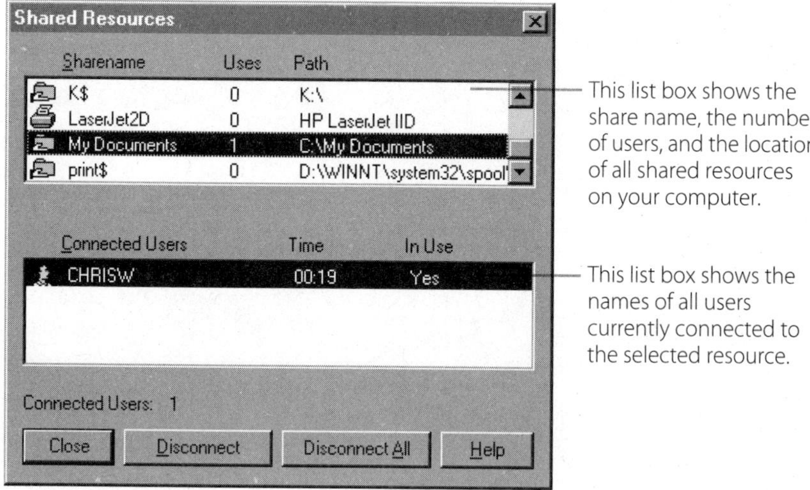

As in the User Sessions dialog box, you can use the Disconnect and Disconnect All buttons to kick users off the computer, either individually or as a group. Heed the warning messages that appear when you do that, however, because disconnecting a user could cause that person to lose data.

Controlling Resource Use

When you want to see exactly who is doing what and where, you use Server's In Use button. Clicking it produces the following dialog box.

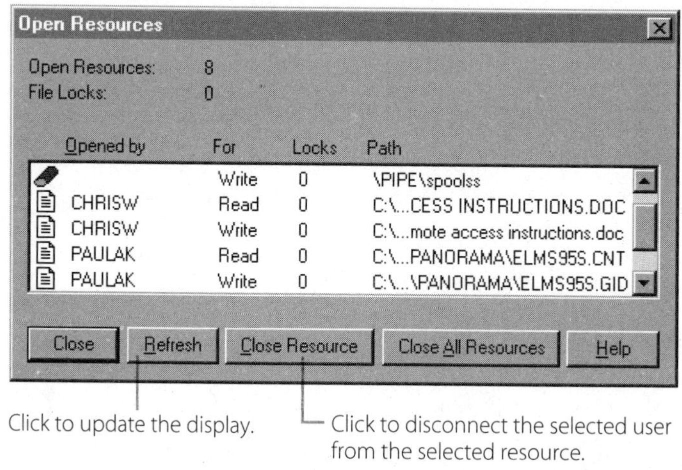

This dialog box lists each open resource (at the file level, rather than the share level displayed in the User Sessions and Shared Resources dialog boxes), the name of the connected user, the type of permission held by the user, the number of locks on the resource, and the path to the resource.

Making Your Intentions Clear

If you work on a single-user system, you might give little thought to rebooting the computer or turning it off at will. When your computer participates in a network, however, these simple acts require a little more reflection on your part. When you share files or other resources on your computer, you are responsible not only for letting people use the resources, but also for ensuring that they do not lose data.

To avoid both data loss and the specter of irate colleagues whom you've unceremoniously bumped off the computer, make a habit of notifying everyone connected to your computer before you shut down, close resources, or disconnect users. (Note that this does not include logging off. You can safely log off your machine without affecting connected users.)

To warn others of an impending shutdown:

1. Click the Start button and choose Run.
2. Use the following form of the Net Send command:

```
net send /users message
```

This sends a message to all users connected to your machine. Replace *message* with whatever message you want to send. For example:

```
net send /users Shutdown in 10 minutes; get ready.
```

Note: The Windows NT Messenger service must be running for a computer to receive messages and alerts sent out over the network. To check on or start the Messenger service, use Control Panel's Services applet. If you are administering a shared computer, be sure that your users know about this service. If you are using resources on a shared computer, check your own system to be sure that the Messenger service is turned on.

Replicating Folders

Although this feature is not directly connected to monitoring server use, Server also provides support for the replication of folders. A folder and its files can reside and be modified on a server (always a Windows NT Server machine) but they can be duplicated on Windows NT workstations. When folders are replicated, any changes to the "master" copy are transferred to all workstations on which duplicates reside. Replication is thus a means of centralizing file and folder management, yet ensuring that accurate copies exist wherever they are needed. Folder replication can be enabled only on a server running Windows NT Server (the export machine). If you are running Windows NT Workstation, you can import replicated folders, but you cannot make them available for export.

Sending Alerts

Windows NT supports a type of warning message called an administrative alert. These alerts are generated by Windows NT under circumstances that can affect the use of a server or its resources—circumstances related to security, user access, and user sessions, as well as physical events such as printer problems.

With Server, you can control which computers and users are sent administrative alerts. To do this, click the Alerts button in the Server dialog box. When you do, a dialog box similar to the one shown below opens.

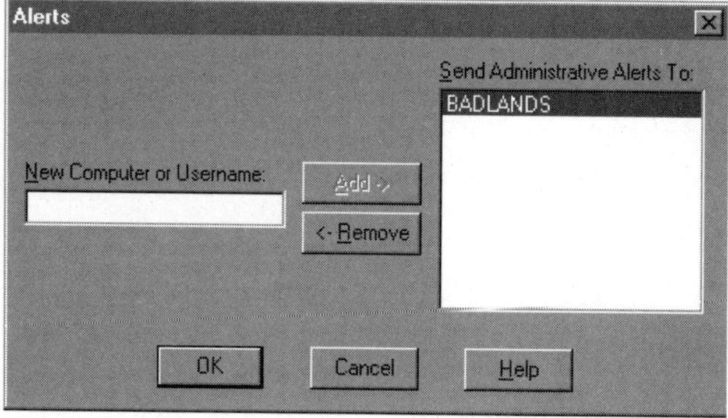

- To add a computer or a user to the alert list, type either the computer name (for example, \\YOSEMITE) or the username (for example, CraigS) in the New Computer Or Username text box and click the Add button.
- To remove a computer or a user, select the computer name or username in the Send Administrative Alerts To list box and click the Remove button.

NOTE

In order for your computer to send alerts, both the Alert and Messenger services must be running. In order for a computer to receive alerts, the Messenger service must be running on it. To check on or start either of these services, use Control Panel's Services applet. If the service's status does not show "Started," highlight the service you want and click the Start button to start the service. To start the service automatically at system startup, click the Startup button and select Automatic.

Monitoring Performance with Task Manager

Task Manager provides an easy way to monitor a few key indicators of your system's performance. In particular, Task Manager focuses on these three indicators:

- CPU (processor) usage
- Virtual memory usage
- Processes (roughly equivalent to programs)

SEE ALSO

For information about Performance Monitor, see "Monitoring System Efficiency with Performance Monitor," page 671.

Although it can be a useful tool, Task Manager provides information about only a handful of indicators. And, except for a graph that shows the last few minutes' activity, Task Manager does not track these indicators over time, so you can't use it for identifying chronic or sporadic conditions; it only shows what is happening here and now. When Task Manager doesn't provide the information you need, however, you can turn to a more sophisticated tool for monitoring and tracking performance: Performance Monitor.

Starting Task Manager

Unlike most applications included with Windows NT, Task Manager does not have a shortcut on the Start menu. To start Task Manager, do one of the following:

- Right-click an unoccupied area of the taskbar and choose Task Manager from the context menu.
- Press Ctrl-Alt-Del and then click the Task Manager button. (When you press Ctrl-Alt-Del, all your windows disappear, and only the Windows NT Security dialog box is visible. Don't fret. As soon as you click Task Manager, your windows reappear along with the newly opened Task Manager window.)

The first time you start Task Manager, the Applications page is selected, as shown below.

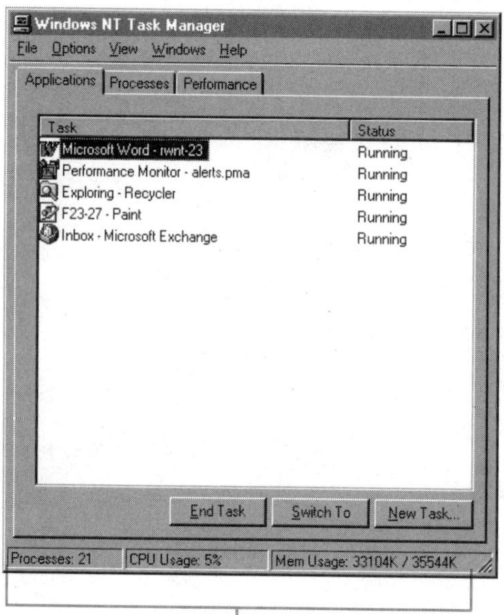

The status bar displays the number of processes, CPU usage, and virtual memory usage.

The main part of the window displays the names of all applications you've started, along with their status. You can select an application and then switch to it or end it by clicking the appropriate button.

Understanding the Processes Page

The Processes page, shown below, lists all the currently running processes. Click the Processes tab to display this page.

A *process* is an executable program (such as Windows NT Explorer or Microsoft Word), a service (a function controlled by Control Panel's Services applet, such as Event Log or Messenger), or a subsystem (such as the one for Windows 3.x applications).

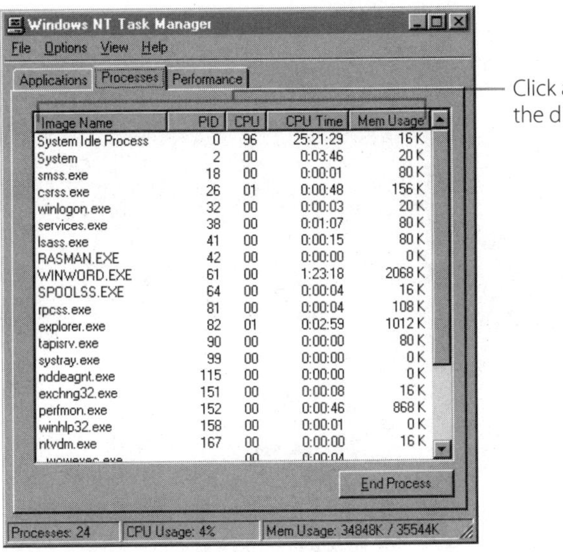

Click a column title to sort the display by that column.

You can use this page to see which processes are running, and which ones are dominating processor and virtual memory usage.

By default, the Processes page displays for each process:

- Image Name: The process name
- PID: The process ID, a number that uniquely identifies a process while it runs

- CPU: The percentage of elapsed time that the process used the processor (CPU) to execute instructions
- CPU Time: The elapsed time (in seconds) that the process has been running
- Mem Usage: The number of kilobytes of virtual memory used by the process

Other process-related columns are also available for display. To make your selections, choose Select Columns from the View menu while the Processes page is displayed.

Understanding the Performance Page

Click the Performance tab and you'll find lots of charts and numbers that tell you how your system is doing, as the example below shows.

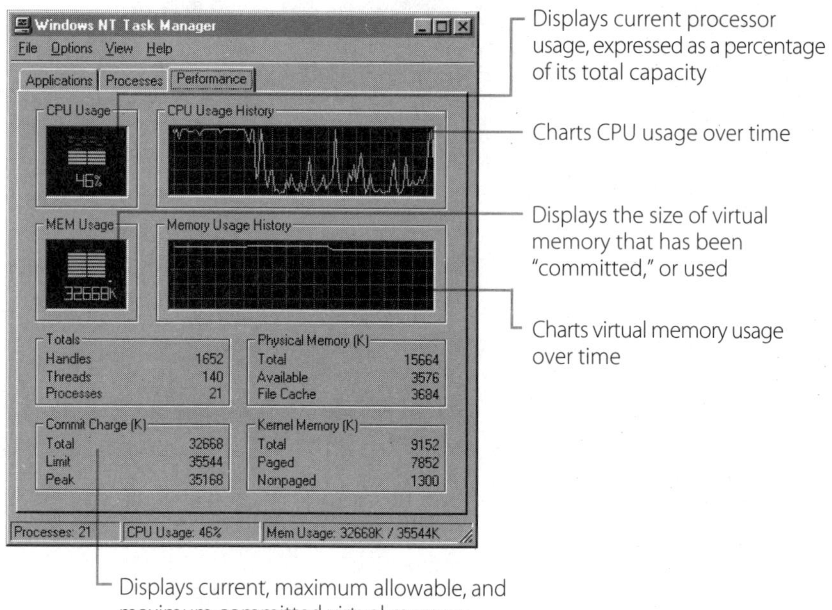

Task Manager displays an icon in the taskbar's notification area. This icon is a miniature representation of the CPU Usage box, so you can monitor processor usage at a glance—even when Task Manager is minimized.

 **TIP**

Avoiding Taskbar Clutter

Choose Hide When Minimized from Task Manager's Options menu. Then when you minimize Task Manager, it doesn't display a button on the taskbar. You can restore Task Manager by double-clicking its notification-area icon.

Monitoring System Efficiency with Performance Monitor

As its name implies, Performance Monitor helps you see how efficiently a computer is working. Performance Monitor is a diagnostic tool that can help you:

- Establish baseline performance values for any network computer running Windows NT.
- Save and compare performance values taken at different times so you can see whether, and in what way, a computer's response degrades as new or increased demands are made on it.

When you use Performance Monitor, you specify one or more activities that you want to track. What exactly can Performance Monitor track? Everything from relatively mundane but critical activities, such as processor time and disk access, to far more exotic beasts, such as the number of nonpaging read bytes per second handled by the network redirector, or the number of times per second Windows NT switches from one program thread (portion of an application) to another.

Simple or exotic, the activities you choose to observe can be displayed by Performance Monitor in any of several ways, the most interesting being a "live" chart that resembles the output of a electrocardiograph or, perhaps, a lie detector. Here, for example, is a chart showing processor time and disk activity:

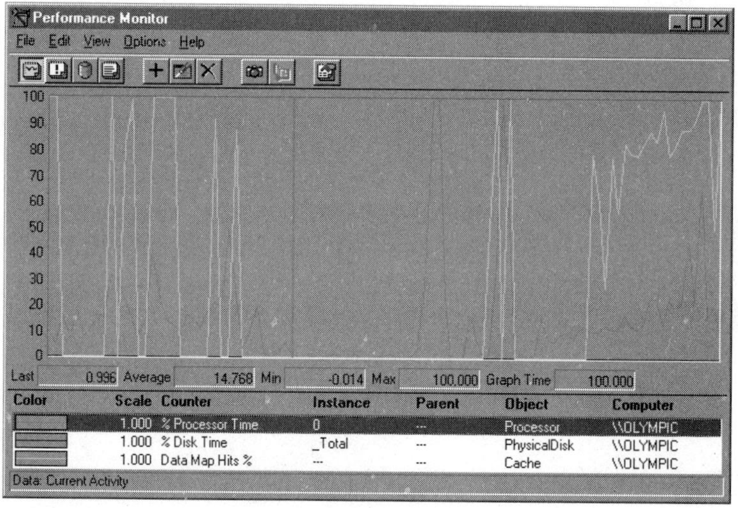

TIP

This book introduces the main features of Performance Monitor. To really put Performance Monitor through its paces, especially in monitoring network performance, you need a deeper understanding than this book can provide. A good source for more information is *Concepts and Planning*, a book included with Windows NT Server.

Objects and Counters

To understand how Performance Monitor keeps track of what's happening in the system, you must know what objects and counters are. Like the dials and gauges in a car, objects and counters are ways of tagging and keeping track of all the activity that goes on "under the hood."

In Windows NT, an object is any portion of a computer's resources that can be assigned characteristics and manipulated as a single identifiable element. Windows NT "sees" a computer system, its programs, and its data files as a collection of manageable objects, each of a certain type with its own characteristics or attributes. Typical objects on most computers include the processor, memory, the paging file, and physical and logical disks. The complete list of objects varies from one system to another, depending on what hardware is installed, what network protocols are used, and so on.

What are counters? They are recorders that track various types of information about the objects they are assigned to. The processor, for example, is an object to Windows NT. With Performance Monitor, you can view the information gathered by a number of counters specific to the processor object. Each of these counters is descriptively named for you, and you can choose among them. There are, for instance, counters named % Processor Time, % User Time, and % Privileged Time. Each monitors a different phase of processor activity.

Some objects have several *instances*. A computer with multiple processors, for example, has an instance of the Processor object for each processor. Similarly, a computer with more than one hard disk has an instance of the PhysicalDisk object for each one. Objects with multiple instances include separate counters for each instance, as well as a counter for the total of all instances.

Alternative Views

Performance Monitor provides four views: chart, report, log, and alert. You can select the view you want by choosing its name from the View menu or by clicking its toolbar icon.

- Chart view provides the most colorful and easily interpreted data.
- Report view provides a neat, columnar alternative that displays values as numbers rather than up-and-down lines on a graph.
- Log view, in contrast to both charting and reporting, takes the long view, recording object behavior for as long as you want, whenever you want, and enabling you to save that data for later review and analysis.
- Alert view, the most specialized, acts like a system smoke detector by notifying you every time the behavior of a monitored counter goes above or below a value you specify.

Starting Performance Monitor

Before you use Performance Monitor to monitor disk activity, you must do a little preparatory work. This involves starting the disk performance counters, which are turned off by default. You only have to do this once, but until you start these counters, you cannot use Performance Monitor to track physical and logical disk activity. (All other counters are always available.) To start the disk performance counters:

1. Log on as a member of the Administrators group.
2. Start a command prompt window and type:

   ```
   diskperf -y \\computername
   ```

   replacing *computername* with the name of the machine you want to monitor.
3. Restart the computer you specified.

TIP

Disabling Disk Performance Counters

When you are through monitoring disk performance, use the Diskperf command to turn off the disk performance counters, because they slightly increase disk access time, especially on computers with a slow processor. To do so, follow the steps above, replacing the *-y* with *-n*.

Whether or not you start the disk performance counters, you can open and work with Performance Monitor without logging on as a member of the Administrators group. Click the Start menu, select Programs, Administrative Tools (Common), and then click Performance Monitor.

Using Chart View

When you start Performance Monitor, the first thing you see is a singularly unimpressive blank window, as shown below. This is Performance Monitor's charting window. You can also look at performance data from other points of view, but charting is the default, so it's a good place to get started.

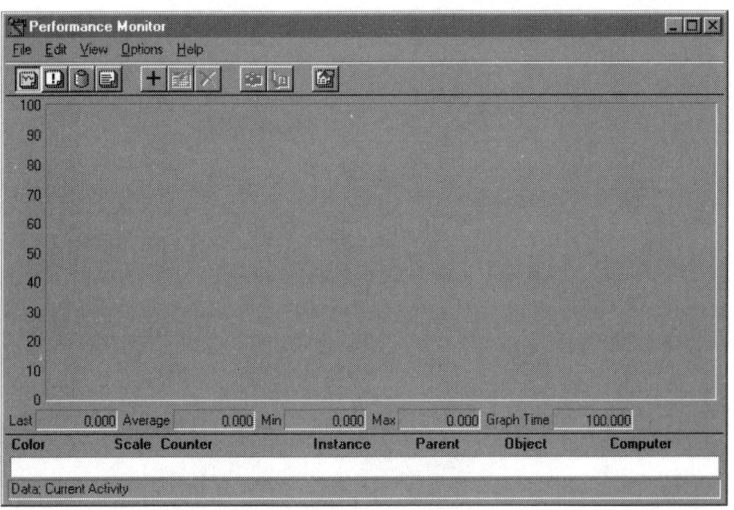

The window is blank at first because Performance Monitor needs you to tell it what objects to chart.

SEE ALSO

This chapter explains *how to use* Performance Monitor. For suggestions on *what to monitor* to improve your system's performance, see "Identifying Performance Bottlenecks," page 731.

Choosing Counters to Chart

Performance Monitor is capable of tracking a large number of counters. Some are quite exotic; others, which you'll see here, are easier to understand. To choose one or more counters to chart:

1 Open the Edit menu and choose Add To Chart. The following dialog box appears.

2 Type the name of the computer you want to monitor, or click the ... button to select from a list.

3 Click the arrow to display a list of available objects, as shown in Step 4.

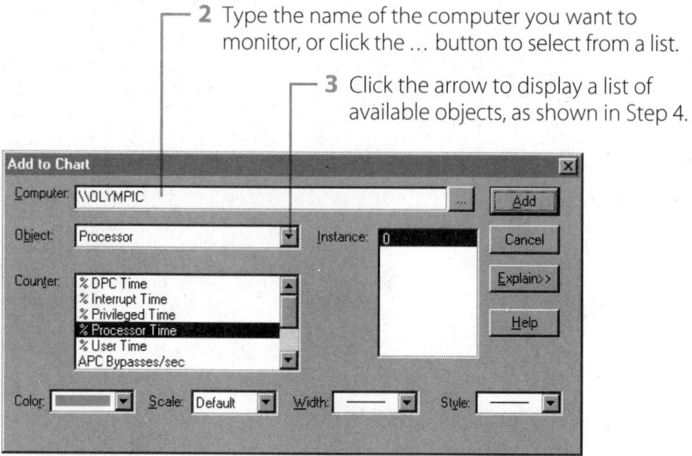

4 Select an object to monitor. Doing so changes the content of the Counter and Instance boxes, as shown in Steps 5 and 6.

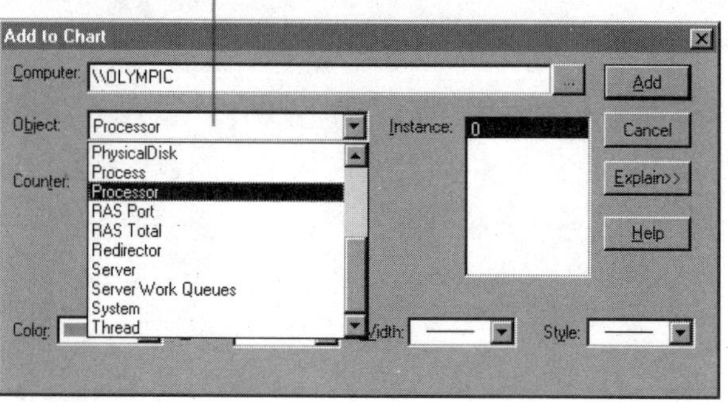

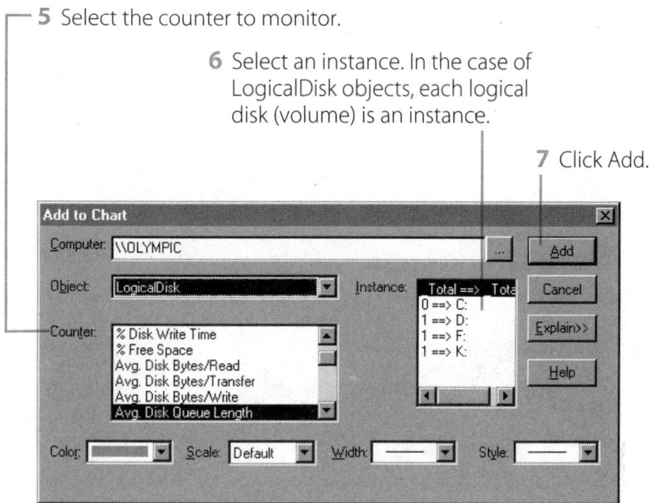

TIP

If you don't understand what a particular counter is or what it shows, select it and click the Explain button. A definition appears at the bottom of the dialog box.

8 Repeat steps 2 through 7 to add additional counters to the chart.

9 When you're through adding counters, click Done. (The Cancel button changes to Done after you add a counter.) The dialog box closes and a chart plotting the counters you chose begins to appear.

TIP

Deleting Counters from the Display

To delete a single counter, select its name in the legend near the bottom of the window, and then press the Del key. To wipe the slate and delete all the counters, choose New Chart from the File menu.

A Closer Look at the Chart Window

The chart window provides an eyeful of information in a colorful, crowded display. The following illustration identifies the various parts of the standard display (other than the chart itself), which are described below.

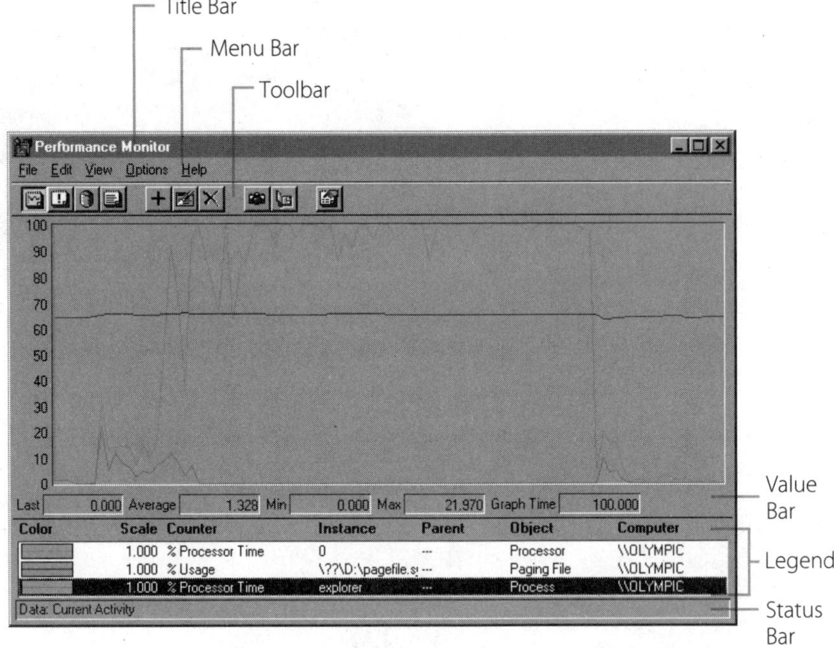

- The *title bar* and *menu bar* are familiar window elements, but in Perfomance Monitor they have a unique feature: you can hide them. To do so, choose Menu And Title from the Options menu. To restore them in the absence of a menu, double-click the window or use the command's keyboard shortcut, Ctrl-M.
- The *toolbar* buttons are described in Table 23-1. To hide the toolbar, choose Toolbar from the Options menu. Use the same command to restore the toolbar.

TABLE 23-1. Performance Monitor Toolbar

Toolbar Icon	Description
	Displays the chart view
	Displays the alert view
	Displays the log view
	Displays the report view
	Adds a counter to the current view
	Modifies the appearance of the selected counter
	Deletes the selected counter from the current view
	Updates the counter data
	Places a comment (bookmark) in a log file
	Displays the options dialog box for the current view

- The boxes in the *value bar* display, from left to right, the last, average, minimum, and maximum values currently displayed in the chart for the object selected in the legend. The Graph Time box shows the interval, in hundredths of seconds, between updates to the chart. To hide the value bar, or change the update interval, choose Chart from the Options menu. *For details, see the following section, "Customizing the Chart Display."*
- The *legend* displays the names of the counters you chose to chart, along with the color, line style, and line weight (thickness) Performance Monitor uses for each.

- The *status bar* displays a description of each menu command as you highlight it. The status bar can provide useful information about the current display, but if you find nothing useful about it, hide the status bar by choosing Status Bar from the Options menu.

If minimalism is your style, your chart window can quickly be simplified to include only the chart, like this:

Customizing the Chart Display

In addition to customizing your display by hiding display elements you don't need, you can customize the appearance of the chart itself. You can do any of the following:

- Change the color, width, and pattern (style) of any counter-tracking line. To adjust any of these items, double-click the counter's name in the legend area to display the dialog box shown below. Select a color, width, and style, and then click OK.

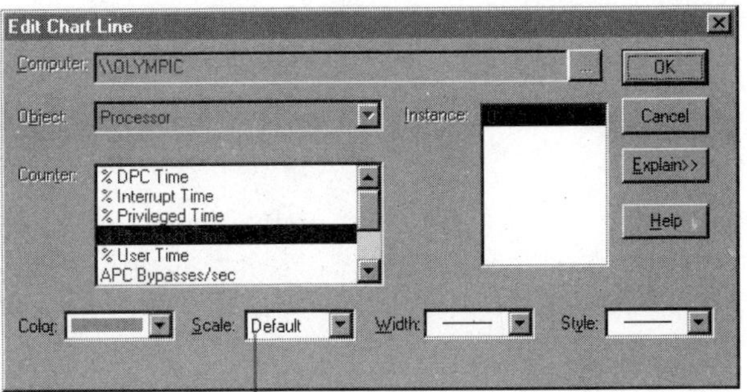

You can change the relationship of the chart line to the (unscaled) values to the left of the chart, thus moving the chart line up or down in the graph.

TIP

Emphasizing a Particular Line

Use a heavier line for the most important counter to emphasize it. Line width can be more effective than line style (dotted, dashed, and so on) for emphasis. (You can use styles only with the thinnest line.)

- Display grid lines and labels, switch from a line graph to a histogram (bar chart), and adjust the vertical maximum value and the update interval. To make any of these changes, choose Chart from the Options menu. The dialog box shown below appears.

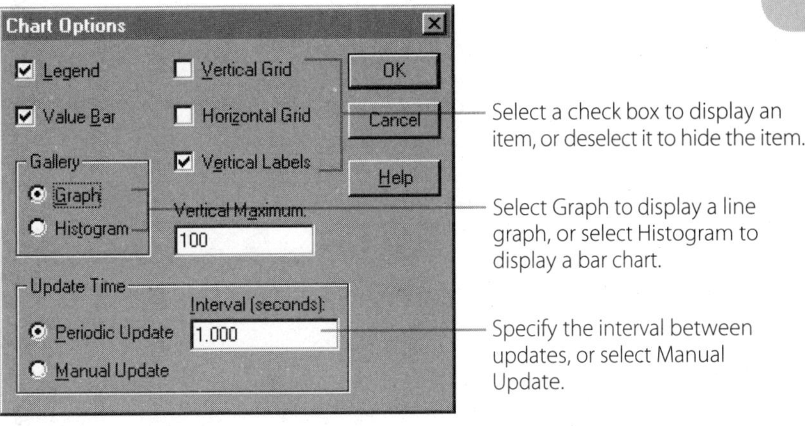

Select a check box to display an item, or deselect it to hide the item.

Select Graph to display a line graph, or select Histogram to display a bar chart.

Specify the interval between updates, or select Manual Update.

NOTE

If you select Manual Update, the chart remains static until you press Ctrl-U, choose Update Now from the Options menu, or click the Update tool.

- Turn on chart highlighting so that the line representing the selected counter is displayed in white. This option has no menu command; you turn it on and off by pressing Ctrl-H or the Backspace key.

Exporting Charts

When you chart performance, you might assume that Performance Monitor records the data somewhere so you can review the information later. It doesn't. (Performance Monitor can record the data in a log file. *For details, see "Using Log View," page 684.*) A chart lives very much in the present.

Does this focus on the present mean that you cannot save charted information? Not at all. You can export chart data to a text file for use in a word processor, spreadsheet, or database.

TIP

When you export a chart to a file, you export its data as text, with values separated either by commas or by tabs. Exporting a chart does not mean that you send a picture of it to another program. But you can import the text file into a program that's capable of graphing, such as Microsoft Excel, and re-create the chart in a format that suits your needs.

To export a chart:

1. Watch the chart. When the data you want to export is displayed, choose Export Chart from the File menu.
2. When the Export As dialog box appears, assign a filename and select a file type: Export CSV Files for a comma-separated format, or Export TSV Files for a tab-separated format.
3. Click Save.

TIP

Printing a Chart

Another way to preserve chart contents is to take a snapshot of the screen whenever something significant occurs. Use the standard Windows technique for capturing and printing a screen, as follows:

1. Press Alt-PrtSc to copy an image of the active window to the Clipboard.
2. Clipboard contents are temporary, so as soon as you've captured the image you want, minimize Performance Monitor and start Paint. (You'll find Paint's shortcut in the Accessories folder.)
3. When Paint opens, choose Paste from the Edit menu to turn the image into a Paintbrush document.
4. Use the commands on Paint's File menu to Save or Print the image.

Using Report View

A Performance Monitor report is basically a chart in text form, like this:

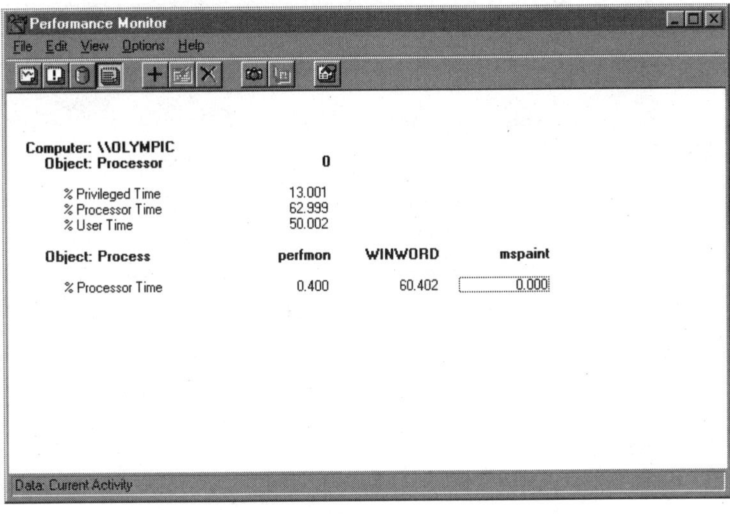

Although you can't see it happening in the illustration, the report displays constantly changing values for the objects and counters you choose to monitor. Creating a report is almost the same as creating a chart:

1 In the Performance Monitor window, choose Report from the View menu.

2 Choose Add To Report from the Edit menu.

3 Choose the objects and counters you want to monitor, click Add, and then click Done.

Exporting Reports

You can export a report to a comma-separated or a tab-separated text file with the Export command in the same way you export a chart. *(For details, see "Exporting Charts," page 682.)*

Unlike a chart, however, an exported report contains only a single set of values—those displayed at the time the report is exported. To save multiple sets of values, export the data as a chart, or log the data as described below and view it later in report view.

Using Log View

Logging is the way to create a historical performance record for a computer or network you are monitoring. By logging activity over time, for example, you can establish a baseline for the system and determine when and where performance bottlenecks occur. Or you can monitor system performance before and after a significant change, such as a hardware upgrade or a reassignment of files, folders, or users to other machines in an attempt to ease the load on a busy server.

When you log object behavior, Performance Monitor stores the information you request in a file. The file contains the data collected for each object counter, at the intervals you request and for the length of time you keep the log active. After you create a log, you can later retrieve it and—this is important—replay the information it contains in any view you choose: chart, alert, log, or report. You can even focus on the specific segment of time that interests you.

Extensions and Then Some

In addition to log data, Performance Monitor can save window and workspace settings, and can export the data in the current window to a text file for use with a word processor or a spreadsheet. To distinguish between different views and export types, Performance Monitor uses a number of filename extensions. When you first start using Performance Monitor logs, these extensions can be confusing because the File Open command lists files with one extension, the File Export command lists files with another extension, and the Options Log command lists files with yet a third extension. None of these are required or enforced; they are simply conventions that can help you organize your work. To help you get your bearings, the following list gathers all of these extensions into one place for easy reference:

- .LOG files contain the data you collect.
- .PMC files store the settings (but not the data) you use to create a chart.
- .PML files store the settings you use to create a log. These settings list the objects and counters you monitor, not the data gathered for them in a .LOG file.
- .PMR files store the settings (but not the data) you use to create a report.
- .PMA files store the settings you use to create alerts.
- .PMW files store the settings for your entire workspace, which comprises the settings for all Performance Monitor views.
- .CSV and .TSV files contain the data from the current view exported as a text file in comma-separated (.CSV) or tab-separated (.TSV) format.

Performance logs, like event logs, can grow quickly and can take up a surprising amount of disk space. The moral of the story: plan ahead. Give some thought to which objects are most appropriate to the task, and consider experimenting with charting or reporting before logging, so you can decide on a time interval that gives you a sufficient but not overwhelming amount of data for analysis.

Starting and Stopping a Log

To start a log, you begin by choosing Log from the View menu. When you do this, a new Performance Monitor window opens:

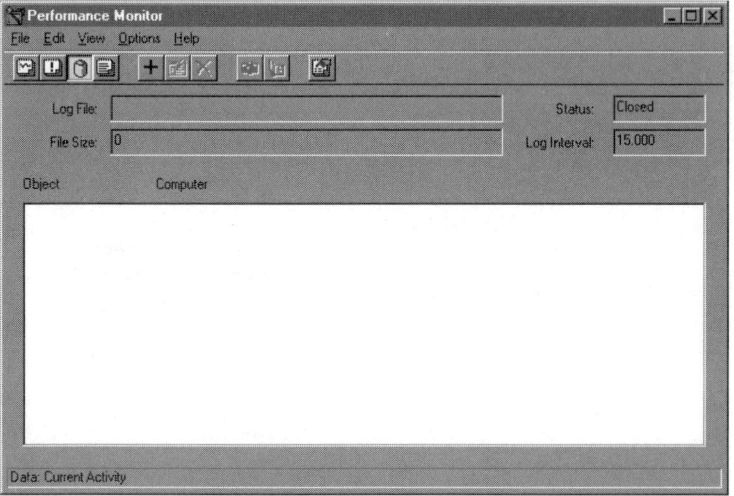

Just as when you choose chart view, the window appears empty. The status bar tells you that the log is expecting to monitor current activity, but the Status text box at the top of the window tells you that the log is closed. You must open the log and add some objects to it:

1 In the Performance Monitor window, choose Add To Log from the Edit menu. A simple dialog box appears.

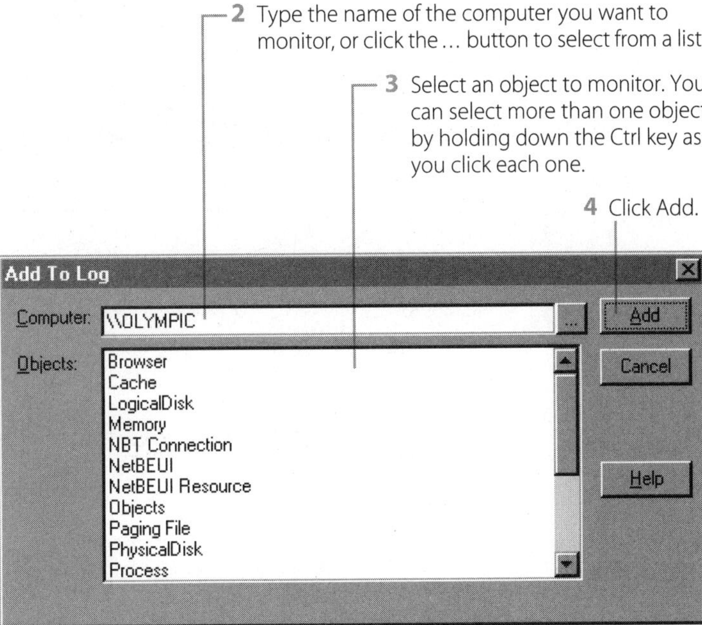

NOTE

The Add To Log dialog box does not include a list of counters like those in the Add To Chart dialog box. There's a reason for this: when you add an object to the log, you don't add individual counters for that object; you add every single one. In this respect, creating a log is like marrying into a large family: pick one, and you get 'em all.

5 Repeat steps 2 through 4 to add additional objects to the log.

6 When you're through adding objects, click Done. (The Cancel button changes to Done after you add an object.) The dialog box closes.

7 After you've told Performance Monitor what to log, you can start the process. Choose Log from the Options menu. The Log Options dialog box appears, as shown below.

8 Specify a name for your log file. Be sure to include the .LOG extension; Performance Monitor does not include it automatically.

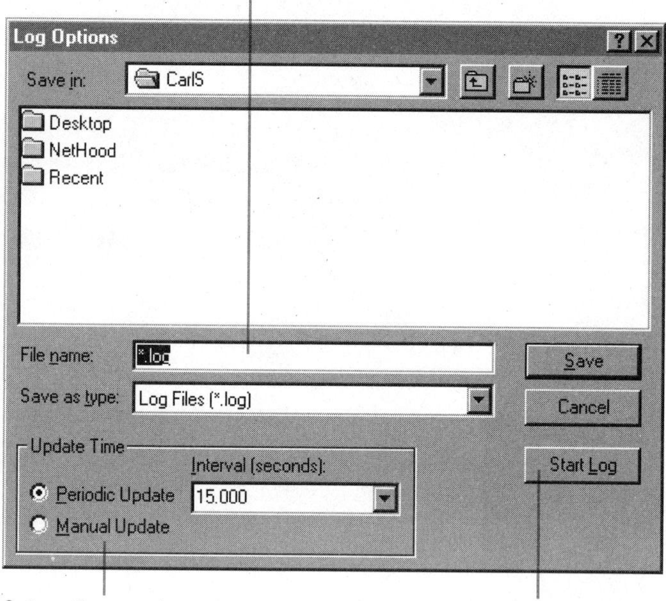

9 Specify an update interval.

10 Click Start Log.

Adding Bookmarks

While a log is recording, you can mark significant occurrences with "bookmarks," which allow you to quickly find those occurrences when you review the logged data. To do so, choose Bookmark from the Options menu.

After you start the log, the Log Options dialog box closes, and you're left with a rather unexciting Performance Monitor display, similar to the one shown here:

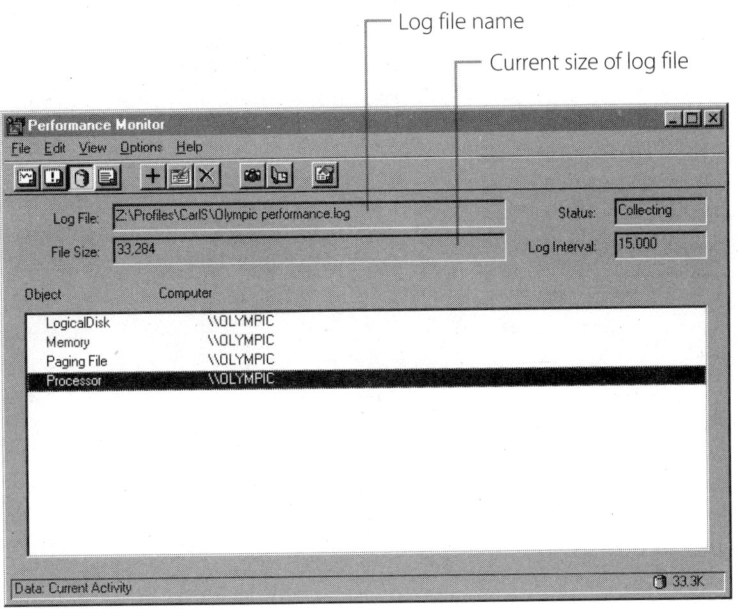

When you want to stop recording data, choose Log from the Options menu again and click the Stop Log button.

That's it. Now, how do you take a look at what you've got?

Viewing a Log

Opening and viewing a recorded log is not the most intuitive procedure in the world for two main reasons: you don't use the File Open command as you might expect, and the mere act of opening a log doesn't display its contents. This is how you go about viewing a log:

1 In the Performance Monitor window, choose Data From from the Options menu. This dialog box appears:

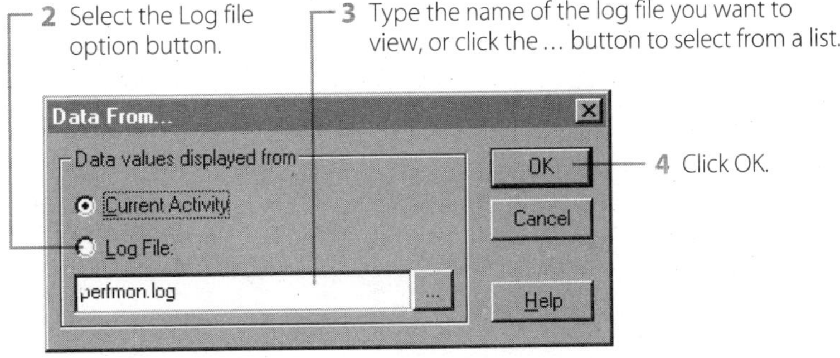

At this point, the Performance Monitor window remains stubbornly blank, but the status bar at the bottom displays a message such as "Data: important.log," telling you that any data you choose to view will be taken from the log file you selected rather than current activity.

5 Choose the view you want from the View menu. Once you've recorded a log, you can view it in the chart, report, or alert view.

6 Choose the Time Window command from the Edit menu. The dialog box that appears, shown below, lets you display logged data for a specified time period.

To indicate starting and stopping times, drag either end of the bar. (The light portion represents the period to be displayed; the dark color uncovered by the light bar represents the period that won't be displayed.

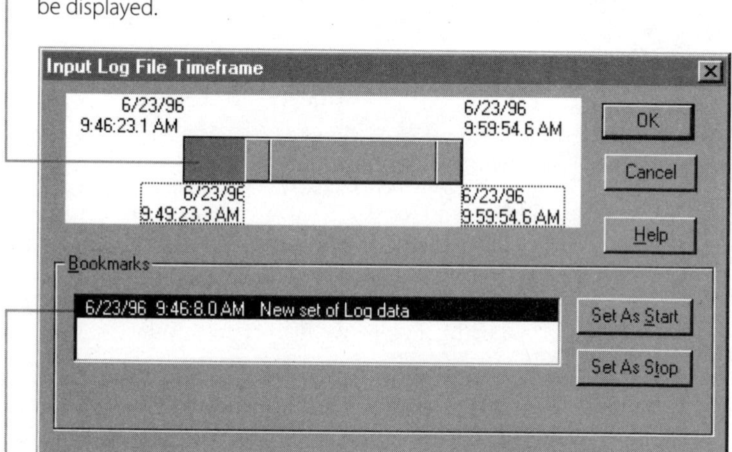

To set the beginning or ending time to the time a bookmark was added to the log, select the bookmark and click Set As Start or Set As Stop.

7 Click OK in the Input Log File Timeframe dialog box.

8 To display the data from the log, choose Add To from the Edit menu. The standard Add To dialog box appears, but when you view a log, the Object list contains only the names of the objects recorded in the log. For example, if you logged only processor, memory, cache, and physical disk activity, these are the only objects you see listed.

Choose the object for which you want to view log data and click Add. Next, choose the counters and, if appropriate, the instances that interest you. Do the same for every object and counter you want to view, and click Done when you finish. There's your log.

Using Alert View

Alerts are designed to help you determine when and where a noteworthy event has occurred. In Performance Monitor, you can use alerts to check the behavior of a specific counter at periodic intervals, and to determine whether its performance is above or below a certain value. For example, if your system doesn't seem to be working efficiently, you can use Performance Monitor alerts to find out when, say, memory pages/sec exceed 20 or physical disk activity exceeds 75 percent for sustained periods, or free disk space is running short.

As you work with Performance Monitor, you are notified whenever an alert occurs. If you are working in alert view, you see a report-like display that gives you the details—including time, date, alert value, and other essentials—of every instance for which Performance Monitor finds that the counter value is beyond the value you specified. If you are working in a different view, a status bar indicator notifies you whenever an alert is registered, as shown below.

The color of the circle, which matches the color in the legend shown in alert view, identifies the type of alert.

Data: Current Activity 4

The number indicates the number of alerts since you've checked the alert view.

To set up alerts, do the following:

1 In the Performance Monitor window, choose Alert from the View menu.

2 Choose Add To Alert from the Edit menu.

3 Select the object, counter, and instance that interests you.

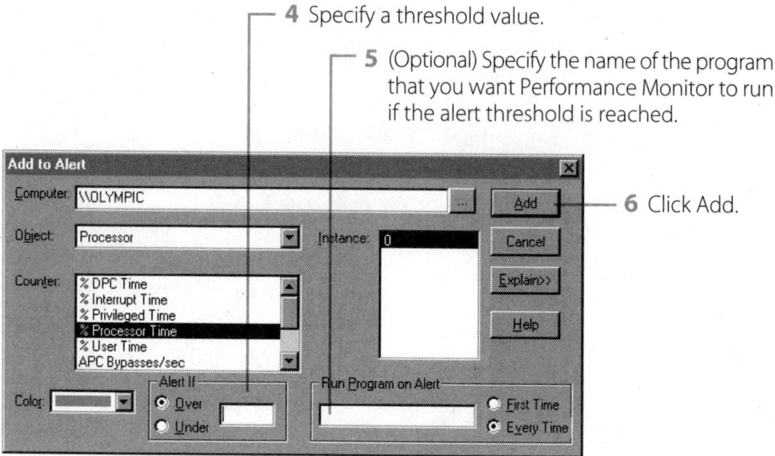

7 Repeat steps 3 through 6 to add additional alerts.

8 When you're through adding alerts, click Done. (The Cancel button changes to Done after you add an object.)

If you want Performance Monitor to switch to alert view or send a message to another workstation whenever an alert occurs, choose Alert from the Options menu to display the dialog box shown below, where you can set these and other options.

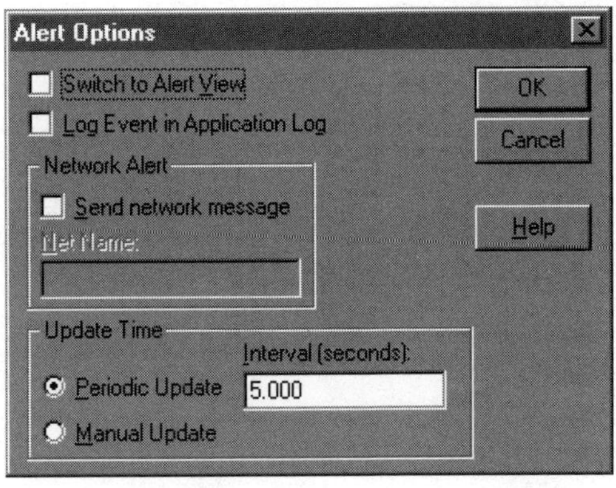

As with charts and reports, you can export alerts to a comma-separated or a tab-separated file for use in a spreadsheet, database, or other application. *For details, see "Exporting Charts," page 682.*

Reusing View Settings and Workspace Settings

If you're establishing a baseline for measuring system performance, or if you need to check system use regularly at particular times of day, you'll want to save and reuse your Performance Monitor settings. You can save the settings for a single view, or for several views you've opened to monitor the behavior of the same or different objects. When you save settings, you not only save a record of the selected objects and counters, you also save the view's display options. You do not, however, save the data in the window.

TIP

Saving Settings Versus Exporting Data

Remember the difference between saving settings (the monitoring environment, so to speak) and saving data (your Performance Monitor logs). Forget this distinction and you might find yourself confused about whether to use the Open command on the File menu or the Data From command on the Options menu, as well as wondering why the Open command does not display the log you saved so carefully the last time you used Performance Monitor.

Use the following File-menu commands to save and reuse Performance Monitor settings:

- To save the settings of the current view, choose Save (Chart, Report, Alert, or Log) Settings. If you have not already saved the current settings, Performance Monitor asks you to assign a filename for the settings.
- To save workspace settings, choose Save Workspace. If you have not already saved the current settings, Performance Monitor asks you to assign a filename for the settings. The workspace settings include the window size and position as well as settings for all four views.
- To open a view or a workspace with previously saved settings, choose Open.

TIP

To open settings for a single view, choose the view you want before you choose Open from the File menu. By default, the File Open dialog box displays the names of files with the extension appropriate for the view you're in—.PMC for charts, .PMR for reports, and so on.

CHAPTER 24

Installing and Uninstalling Software and Hardware

Windows NT 4 has taken major strides toward making it easy for users to change components of their systems. The new Add/Remove Programs item in Control Panel, for example, simplifies the task of bringing new applications on board or helping old ones disembark. And thanks to some new setup wizards, many of the potential frustrations and bewilderments associated with hardware changes have been eliminated.

In this chapter, we'll survey the tools and wizards that Windows supplies to help you keep your system current as your hardware and software needs change.

Adding or Removing Parts of Windows NT

Windows NT includes both essential and optional components. Among the latter are such things as screen savers, wallpaper images, accessory programs, and games. When your system was first set up, chances are the person doing the setup installed many, but not all, of the optional components. As time passes you might find you need certain items that aren't currently installed. Alternatively, you might discover that some of the Windows accessories are merely taking up space on your hard disks without serving any useful purpose. In either case, it's easy to make the appropriate adjustments.

To add or remove an optional component of Windows NT, start as follows:

1. Choose Settings from the Start menu.
2. Choose Control Panel.
3. Double-click the Add/Remove Programs icon.
4. Click the Windows NT Setup tab.

These steps bring you to the Windows NT Setup page of the Add/Remove Programs dialog box, shown in Figure 24-1.

In this dialog box, optional components of Windows are listed by category. On the system depicted in Figure 24-1, 9 of 14 accessory programs are currently installed, and those 9 consume a total of 7.1 megabytes of hard-disk space.

Categories with all components installed are marked with a check in a white check box. Categories in which some, but not all, components are installed are marked with a check in a gray check box. Figure 24-1 shows a system on which all components in the Accessibility and Microsoft Exchange categories, but only some components in the Accessories, Communications, and Games categories, are currently installed.

FIGURE 24-1.
To add or remove components of Windows, click the Windows NT Setup tab in the Add/Remove Programs dialog box.

To add or remove a component, first select the component's category, and then click the Details button. This reveals a list of the items that make up the selected category, as shown in Figure 24-2.

FIGURE 24-2.
To find out what's in a category, select it and click the Details button.

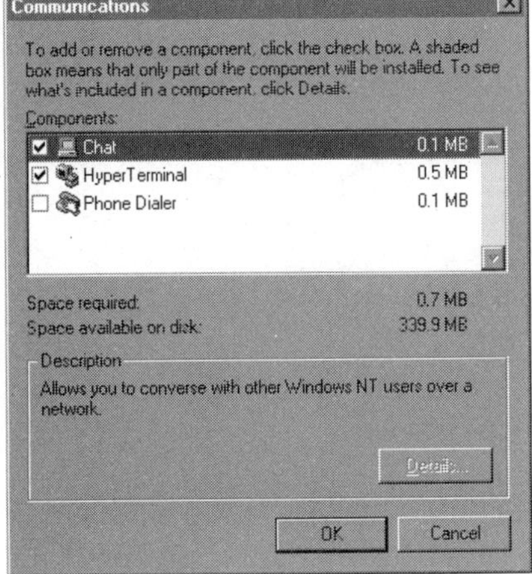

Here again, installed items are flagged with check marks. The system shown in Figure 24-2, for example, currently has two of the three communications items installed. The Phone Dialer program is not installed.

To install a component, click its check box to put a check mark in it. To remove a component, click its check box to remove the check mark.

NOTE

In most Windows dialog boxes, clicking the text next to a check box has the same effect as clicking the check box itself. This is not the case in the Add/Remove Programs dialog box. Here selecting the text simply gives you an opportunity to read a description of the selected item. To change the state of the check box, you have to click the check box itself.

When you finish marking and unmarking the check boxes, click OK twice—once to return to the property sheet shown in Figure 24-1 on the previous page, and a second time to close the property sheet. If you're installing an item, Windows might prompt you to insert the Windows NT CD-ROM. (If you installed Windows NT initially from a network server, Windows looks on that server for the components it needs; be sure the network is available.) If the location of the Windows NT files has changed since Windows NT was originally set up—to a different CD-ROM drive or to a different server, for example—type the new location when prompted, or click Browse.

NOTE

The Windows NT CD-ROM includes files for all supported computers. The files you need are located in the folder that identifies your computer's processor type: \I386 for Intel 486 or Pentium, \Ppc for Power PC, \Alpha for Digital Alpha AXP, or \Mips for MIPS R4000.

Installing Applications

To install an application from a floppy disk or a CD-ROM, follow these steps:

1. Choose Settings from the Start menu.
2. Choose Control Panel.
3. Double-click the Add/Remove Programs icon.
4. Insert the first disk in a floppy-disk drive or the CD-ROM in a CD-ROM drive.
5. Click the Install button.
6. Click the Next button.

NOTE

You can use this procedure for both Windows-based and MS-DOS–based programs.

Most applications include a program called Setup or Install. This program takes care of getting the application copied to your hard disk, updating the Windows registry, creating a new Start-menu item, and so on. When you click the Install button in Control Panel's Add/Remove Programs dialog box, the install wizard scans each of your floppy-disk drives in turn, followed by any local CD-ROM drives, until it finds a program called Setup or Install. As soon as it locates such a program, the wizard presents a screen similar to the one shown in Figure 24-3 on the next page. If the name of the installation program shown on the command line of this screen is correct, simply click the Finish button. In the unlikely event that the wizard has proposed the wrong installation program, you can click Browse instead of Finish, and then find the correct program from the ensuing dialog box.

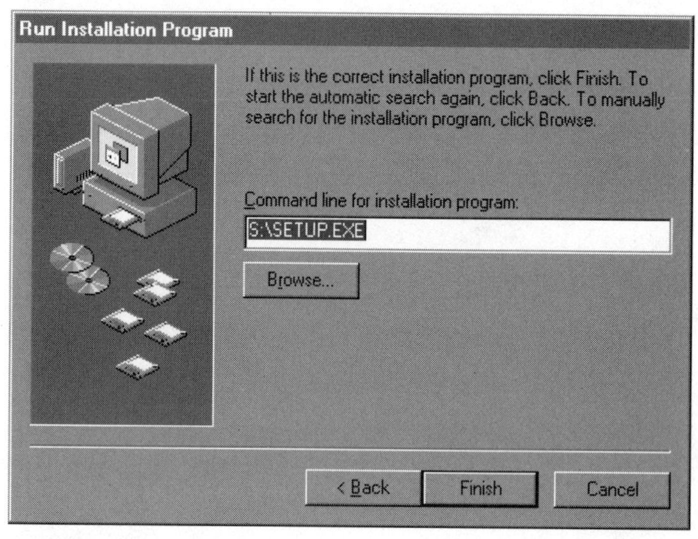

FIGURE 24-3.
The Install wizard automatically finds a program named Setup or Install and then asks you to confirm that it has found the correct installation program.

When you click Finish, Windows runs the installation program. At that point, the new application's installation program will probably ask you some questions about where you want the program installed, what optional components you want to install, and so on. If you're installing from floppy disks, you'll also be prompted to change disks from time to time.

Personal and Common Groups

Most setup programs install one or more icons for the program on your Start menu. But if more than one user has an account on your computer, a program's icons might appear to come and go, leading you to believe that the program wasn't installed correctly. The reason for this potential confusion is that Windows NT provides two groups of Start menu items—a common group and a personal group. Folders and icons in the common group are available to all comers; folders and icons in your personal group appear only when you log on.

You can control which of these groups program folders and icons end up in. By default, program folders and icons are added to the Start menu's common group if you install the application while logged on as a member of the Administrators group. If you are logged on with a non-administrative account, program folders and icons are added to your Start menu's personal group.

(continued)

NOTE

You don't *have* to use the install wizard to set up a new application. Any technique that runs your program's Setup or Install program will get the job done. The install wizard merely provides a simple, consistent method for installing applications that doesn't require any typing or searching through folders.

Personal and Common Groups ***continued***

You can move or copy items from a personal group to the common group or vice versa if you know where to look (and you have the appropriate permissions). The Profiles subfolder of the Winnt folder contains a folder named All Users and additional folders named for each user with an account on your system. Within each of these folders, you'll find a Start Menu\Programs subfolder. This subfolder in the All Users folder stores the common group items; the Start Menu\Programs subfolder in each user's folder stores the items in that user's personal group, as shown below.

Folders and icons in the common group are in Profiles\All Users\Start Menu\Programs.

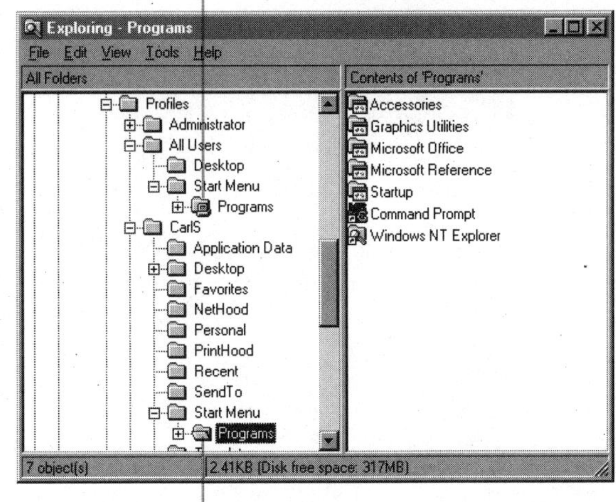

Folders and icons in the personal group for the user CarlS are in Profiles\CarlS\Start Menu\Programs

(continued)

Personal and Common Groups *continued*

If your Profiles folder is stored on an NTFS volume, you should *copy* items between groups rather than moving them. (If you want to move items, copy them first and then delete the originals.) Doing so ensures that the items inherit the permissions of the destination folder. If you move the items, they retain their original permissions, which might prevent their use by the intended users. *For information about moving or copying folder items, see "Moving or Copying Folders, Files, and Shortcuts," page 141.*

Uninstalling Applications

If you've ever tried to remove a Windows-based application from your system "by hand," you probably know that the task is anything but trivial. Getting rid of an unneeded program by simply deleting files is complex for the following reasons:

- Many Windows-based applications use .DLL files in addition to .EXE files. DLLs, *dynamic-link libraries*, are components that can be shared by two or more applications. Such components might or might not be stored in the same folder as the application's .EXE files. Even if you know exactly which DLLs a program uses, deleting them might damage another application that relies on some of the same DLLs.
- Most Windows-based applications create entries in the registry, the database in which Windows records all vital information concerning your hardware and software. Even if you safely delete all executable components of your Windows-based application, the registry would no longer accurately describe your system if you don't also correctly modify the registry. (And working directly with the registry can be confusing, if not downright risky.)
- Some Windows-based applications (in particular, many older ones) either create their own "private" configuration (.INI) files or create entries in a Windows configuration file called Win.ini.

Private .INI files might or might not be stored in the same folder as the rest of an application's files. Completely eradicating a Windows-based application means getting rid of its .INI files (or its entries in Win.ini) as well as removing all of its other components.

For all of these reasons, but particularly because of the possibility of inadvertently deleting a DLL needed by some other application, it's best not to try removing Windows-based programs by simply going into a folder and deep-sixing its files. Instead, try the following steps (in order):

1 Check to see if the Add/Remove Programs tool knows how to uninstall the program for you.

When you install most newer programs, the program's setup routine also installs an "uninstall" routine and informs Windows NT of its existence via the registry. The Add/Remove Programs tool then adds the program to the list of programs that it knows how to uninstall. (See Figure 24-4.) If the program you want to remove is on this list, you can remove it by selecting it and clicking the Add/Remove button.

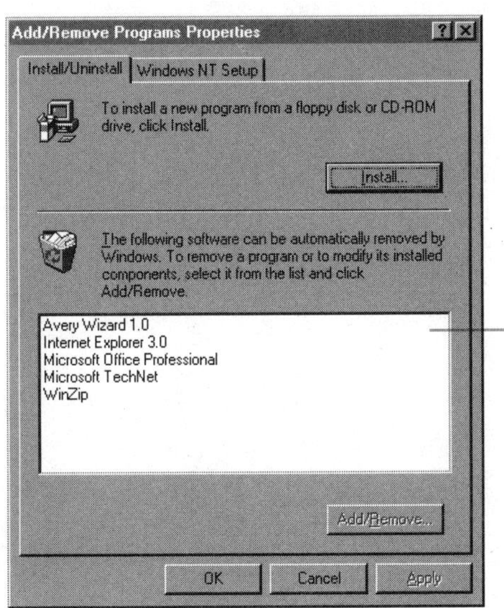

FIGURE 24-4. Newer programs can often be uninstalled automatically.

TIP

Uninstalling Part of a Program
The uninstall routine for many larger applications also lets you add or remove individual components if you don't want to remove the application altogether. To find out what options are available, select the application and then click Add/Remove. Even if the only available option is to uninstall the program completely, the uninstall program will warn you before any files are deleted or changed—and give you an opportunity to back out without proceeding.

2 If Control Panel's Add/Remove Programs tool doesn't show your program in its list, check to see if there's an uninstall application in the folder where your program itself is stored.

It's possible your program has an uninstall utility, but the Add/Remove Programs tool doesn't know about it. Look for something labeled "Remove" or "Uninstall." With most Microsoft applications, the Setup program also serves to uninstall the application. If you don't find an obvious uninstall utility, check your program's documentation to see if it provides any useful information.

3 If you're still not sure how to remove the program, give the program vendor's tech-support service a call. Ask them exactly what files you should and should not delete.

TIP

Back Up Beforehand
Before you delete or move a Windows-based application, it's a good idea to back up any parts of your system that might be affected. At a minimum, this includes the folder in which the program is currently stored and all its subfolders, your Windows NT folder (on most systems, that's C:\Winnt) and its subfolders, and the local registry. You can use the Windows NT Backup program for this purpose. *For information about Windows NT Backup, see Chapter 16, "Protecting Your Data with Backup."*

Moving Applications

The task of moving a Windows-based application from one disk or folder to another, like that of deleting an application, is seldom simple. The Windows-based program you want to move might rely on dynamic-link libraries (DLLs), which might or might not be stored in the same folder with the rest of the program's executables. And it might use a configuration (.INI) file in which (among other things) its current disk and folder are recorded. Simply packing up all the files in an application's folder and shipping them off to some other folder might work for the most rudimentary Windows-based applications, but more often than not you'll find the program will not run properly (or at all) in its new home.

If you must relocate a Windows-based application, the safest way to do it is to delete the program first, using whatever removal services are provided either by Windows NT or your application. After you've deleted it, reinstall it in the appropriate folder.

Installing New Hardware

Removing or relocating applications may be a pain sometimes, but it's a walk in the park compared to the travails that can attend the installation of new hardware. Traditionally, the act of adding a new peripheral or device has been an exercise in frustration for many personal computer users, as well as a heavy expense for corporate support departments.

Hardware devices typically compete for a limited number of input-output (I/O) addresses, memory addresses, interrupt request (IRQ) lines, and direct memory access (DMA) channels. In order for your system to work properly, all of its pieces have to dance together without stepping on each other's toes. For example, if your new sound card wants the same interrupt request line as your existing network adapter, something's got to give (in this case, the new sound card). Resolving a conflict of this kind often entails some combination of the following: determining which resource is in contention, finding a nonconflicting alternative setting for one of the devices, making a physical adjustment to the hardware (moving a jumper, for example), and modifying some aspect of the software that uses the device.

To alleviate these difficulties, Windows NT includes setup wizards for some devices and a simple interface for installing others. Windows NT 4, alas, does not support Plug and Play devices, nor does it offer a single Add New Hardware wizard that assists in setting up any type of device. You'll find these features in Windows 95—and probably in the next version of Windows NT.

TIP

Use a Windows 95 System Resource Report

Setting up a device in Windows 95 on a flex-boot system does not set up the device for use with Windows NT. However, its advanced hardware configuration features can provide some useful information. For example, you might find it helpful to see how devices are configured in Windows 95, and then apply that information in Windows NT. If Windows 95 is one of your flex-boot options, restart your computer and run Windows 95. Then double-click the System icon in the Windows 95 Control Panel, click the Device Manager tab, and click Print.

The tool you use to install a new device depends on the type of device. Table 24-1 points you in the right direction.

Some general guidelines and procedures apply to most hardware:

- Before you install a device, check the Windows NT Hardware Compatibility List (HCL) to be sure the device is supported by Windows NT. Don't assume that any device on the market is supported; many are not. Although device support in Windows NT 4 is substantially improved over earlier versions of Windows NT, it still does not support the wide variety of devices supported by Windows 95.

TABLE 24-1. Tools for Installing New Hardware

Device Type	Control Panel Tool	For More Information
Display Adapter	Display	See "Installing a Display Adapter," page 710
Keyboard	Keyboard	See "Installing a Key-board," page 711
Modem	Modems	See "Installing a Modem," page 713
Mouse	Mouse	See "Installing a Mouse," page 712
Network Adapter	Network	See "Installing a Network Adapter," page 712
PC Card Adapter	PC Card (PCMCIA)	See "Installing PC Card Adapters," page 716
Printer	Printers	See "Adding a Printer," page 222
SCSI Adapter	SCSI Adapters	See "Installing a SCSI Adapter," page 715
Sound Card	Multimedia	See "Installing a Sound Card," page 714
Tape Drive	Tape Devices	See "Installing a Tape Drive," page 716
Uninterruptible Power Supply	UPS	See "Installing an Uninterruptible Power Supply," page 717
Other	Multimedia	See "Installing a Sound Card," page 714

SEE ALSO
For information about accessing files on the Internet, see Chapter 13, "Surfing with Internet Explorer."

A copy of the HCL is included with Windows NT, and you can obtain a current version on the World Wide Web or from Microsoft's FTP server, using the following URLs:

http://www.microsoft.com/ntserver/hcl/hclintro.htm

ftp://microsoft.com/bussys/winnt/winnt/winnt_docs/hcl

- Before you use Windows NT to install and configure a driver, install the hardware device itself.
- You must be logged on as a member of the Administrators group to install or remove any hardware device. (Even without such credentials, however, you can examine the property sheets for your devices.)
- Most install procedures present a list of devices for which Windows NT provides a driver. If Windows NT does not provide a driver for a device you're installing, you'll need a driver from another source, such as the device manufacturer. To install such a driver, click the Have Disk button that appears in the dialog box that lists the drivers provided with Windows NT.
- If a driver for the device you select is not already installed on your hard disk, Windows prompts you to insert the Windows NT CD-ROM. If the location of the Windows NT files has changed since Windows NT was originally set up, type the new location when prompted, or click Browse.

NOTE

> The Windows NT CD-ROM includes files for all supported computers. The files you need are located in the folder that identifies your computer's processor type: \I386 for Intel 486 or Pentium, \Ppc for Power PC, \Alpha for Digital Alpha AXP, or \Mips for MIPS R4000.

- Certain devices require drivers that can be loaded only when the system starts. When you install such a device, Windows NT presents a dialog box similar to the one shown below.

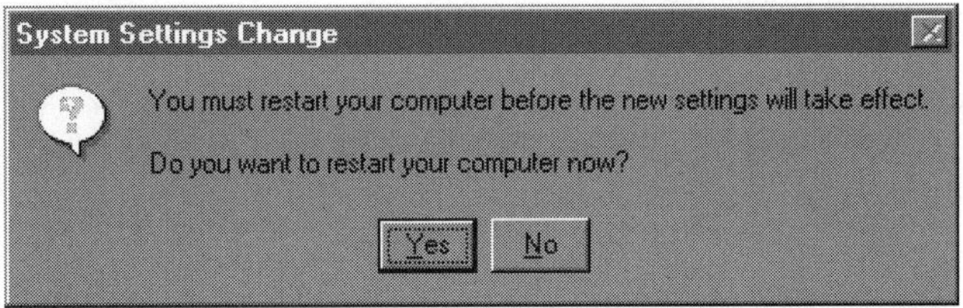

You can click Don't Restart Now and go on about your business, or if you're anxious to test the new device, click Restart Now. Either way, your changes take effect the next time you start Windows NT.

- Device drivers, in addition to being installed, must be *started* before they can be used by Windows NT. *For information about starting device drivers, see "Starting and Stopping Device Drivers," page 718.*

When Changes Go Awry

If you make a change to your configuration settings that causes problems when you restart, press Spacebar when the following message appears (briefly) during startup:

Press spacebar NOW to invoke the Hardware Profile/Last Known Good menu

Pressing Spacebar causes Windows NT to ignore the most recent configuration you specified and return to the most recent *workable* configuration. (When the system and all services start with no errors, and you successfully log on, Windows NT saves the hardware configuration as the "Last Known Good" configuration.) You can use this method to restore your system to a condition that is known to work, and then try reinstalling the hardware with different settings.

Installing a Display Adapter

To install a new display adapter, follow these steps:

1 Double-click the Display icon in Control Panel.

You can also get to the Display property sheet by right-clicking the desktop and choosing Properties.

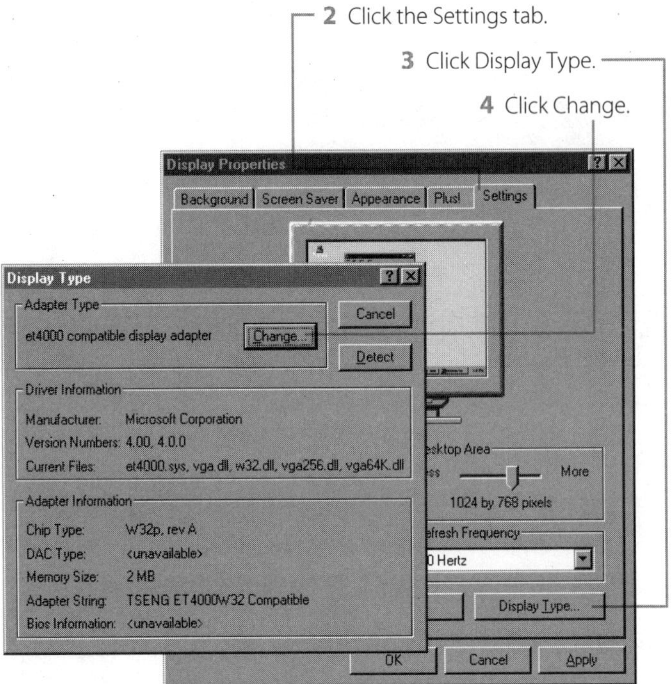

5 Select the manufacturer and model of your display adapter in the dialog box that appears, and then click OK.

6 Follow the on-screen instructions.

NOTE

If you are unsure of the display adapter's make and model, click Detect in the Display Type dialog box. This copies all display drivers to your hard disk and then, after you restart the computer, determines which one is best for your system.

Installing a Keyboard

To install a new keyboard, follow these steps:

1 Double-click the Keyboard icon in Control Panel.

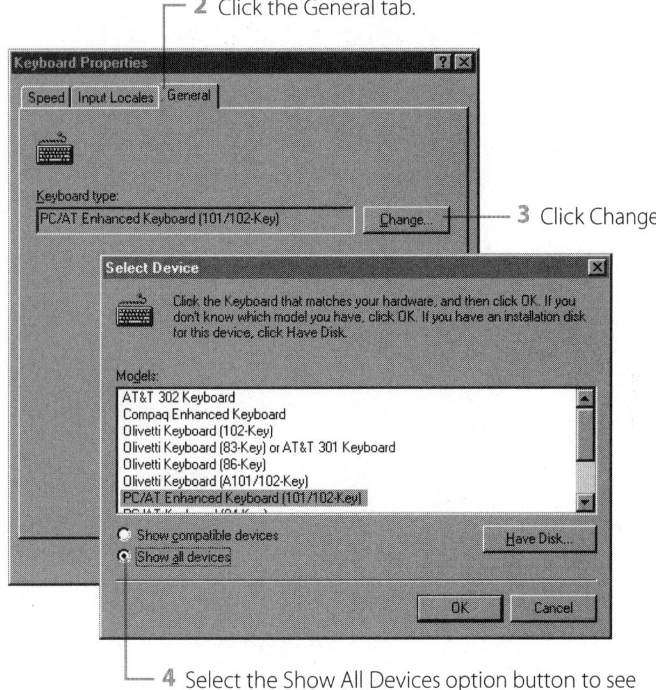

2 Click the General tab.

3 Click Change.

4 Select the Show All Devices option button to see the complete keyboard make-and-model list.

5 Select your keyboard and click OK.

6 Follow the on-screen instructions.

Installing a Mouse

To install a new mouse, follow these steps:

1. Double-click the Mouse icon in Control Panel.
2. Click the General tab in the Mouse property sheet.
3. Click the Change button.
4. Select the Show All Devices option button to see the complete mouse make-and-model list.
5. Select your mouse and click OK.
6. Follow the on-screen instructions.

Installing a Network Adapter

To install a new network adapter (sometimes called a *network interface card*, or *NIC*), follow these steps:

1. Double-click the Network icon in Control Panel.

You can also get to the Network property sheet by right-clicking the Network Neighborhood icon and choosing Properties.

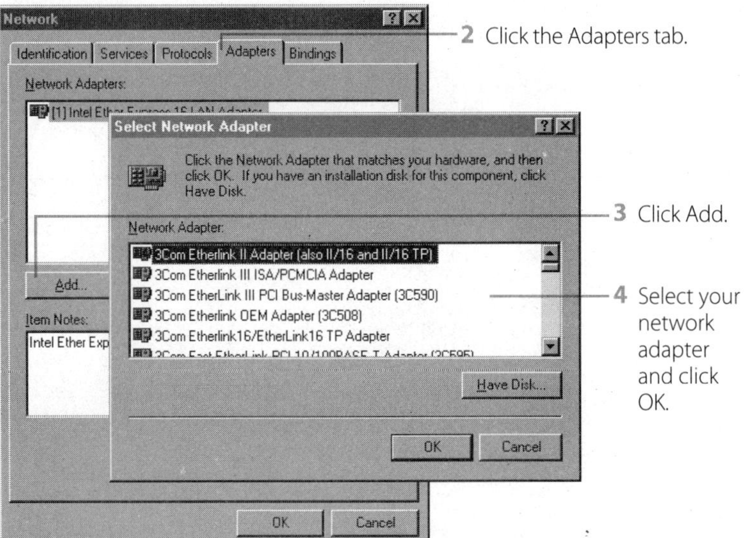

Installing a Modem

To install a new modem, follow these steps:

1 Double-click the Modems icon in Control Panel.

2 Click the Add button in the Modems property sheet.

The Install New Modem wizard appears.

3 Click the Next button, and the wizard begins checking your system's COM ports in an attempt to find a modem, as shown below.

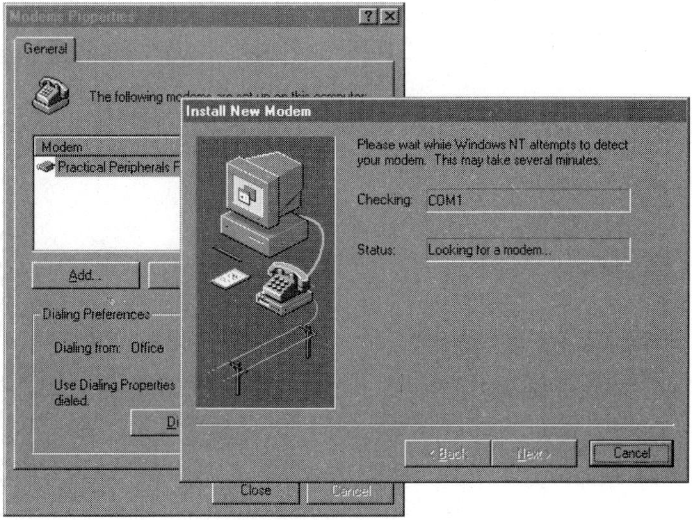

4 Follow the on-screen instructions.

If the wizard is unable to detect and identify your modem, it presents a list of modem manufacturers and models from which you can select.

Installing a Sound Card

To install a new sound card, follow these steps:

1 Double-click the Multimedia icon in Control Panel.

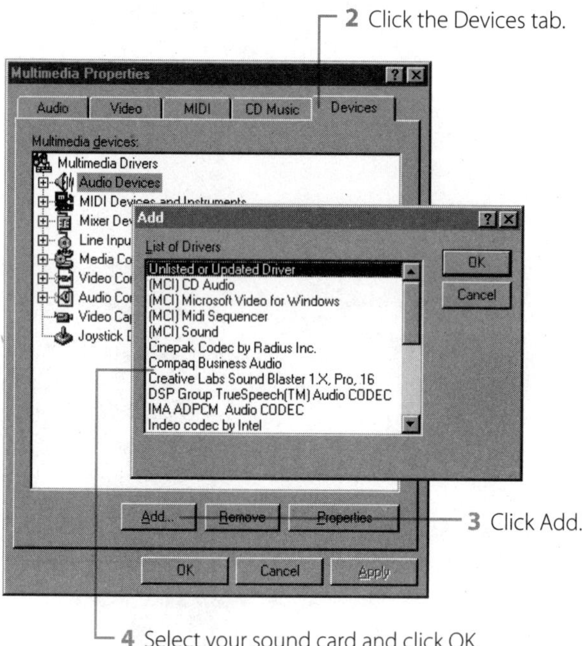

NOTE

Unlike most of the hardware-installation dialog boxes, the Add dialog box produced by the Multimedia property sheet does not include a Have Disk button. If you want to install a driver for a device that's not listed (and you have a Windows NT 4 driver for the device), select Unlisted Or Updated Driver, and then click OK.

5 Follow the on-screen instructions.

TIP

If the device you want to add is not listed and you don't have a driver supplied by the manufacturer, look in the Drvlib\Audio folder on the Windows NT CD-ROM.

The Multimedia dialog box is also used to install drivers for other types of devices. This includes not only the device types listed on the Devices tab—such as MIDI devices and joysticks—but *any* type of device for which you have a Windows NT 4 driver, and for which there is no "standard" place for installing a driver. Follow the steps for installing a sound card, and select Unlisted Or Updated Driver in the Add dialog box.

Installing a SCSI Adapter

A SCSI (small computer system interface) adapter provides an interface that connects certain hard drives, CD-ROM drives, tape drives, scanners, and other devices to your computer. To install a SCSI adapter, follow these steps:

1 Double-click the SCSI Adapters icon in Control Panel.

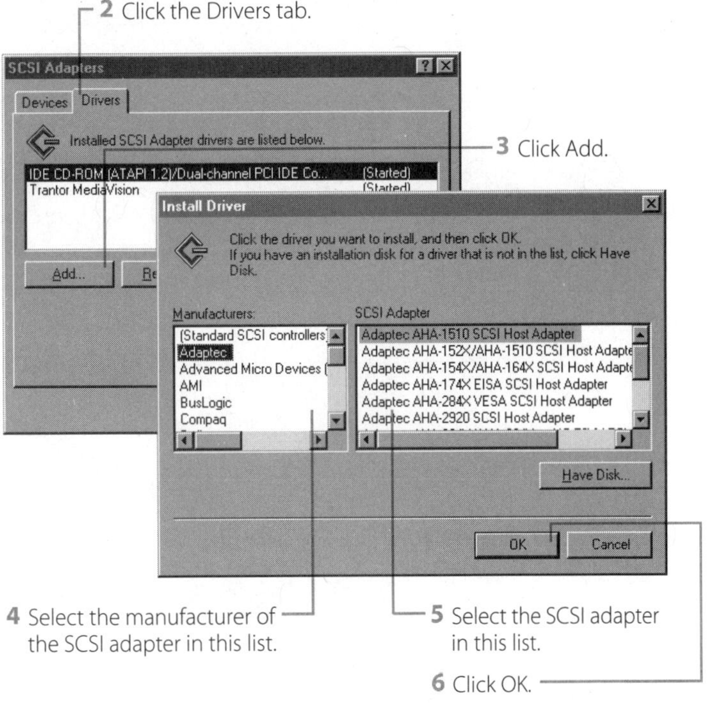

7 Follow the on-screen instructions.

Installing a Tape Drive

To install a new tape drive, follow these steps:

1 Double-click the Tape Devices icon in Control Panel.

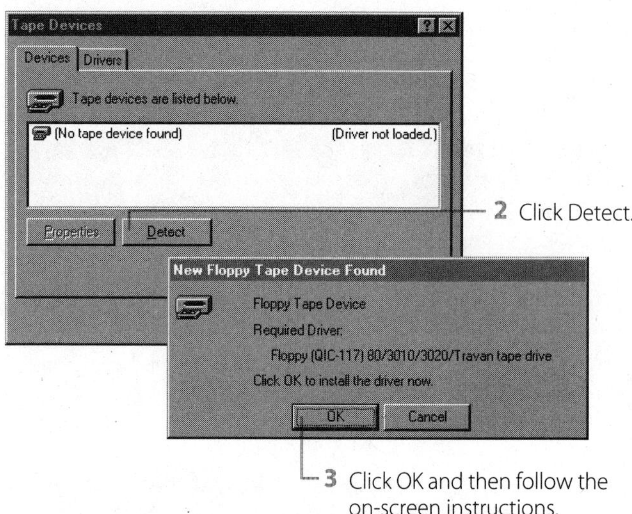

2 Click Detect.

3 Click OK and then follow the on-screen instructions.

Installing PC Card Adapters

PC card adapters are credit card–sized adapters for a variety of functions that are most often used in portable computers. (Unlike a certain musician who changed his name from a simple word to an unpronounceable symbol, the computer industry went the other way: *PC card* is the new name for an unpronounceable acronym, *PCMCIA*.)

To install a PC card adapter, follow these steps:

1 Double-click the PC Card (PCMCIA) icon in Control Panel.

NOTE

In many cases, a message appears if you double-click the PC Card (PCMCIA) icon and no driver has been installed for a card that's inserted in a PC card slot. If that happens, simply click OK and follow the on-screen instructions to install the driver.

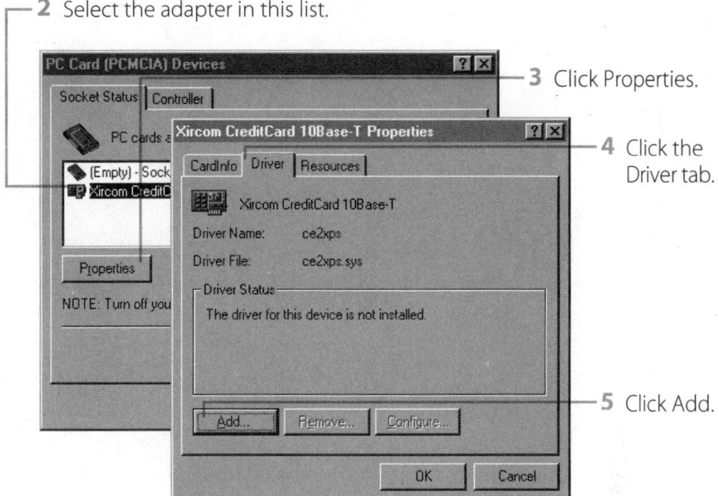

6 Follow the on-screen instructions.

Installing an Uninterruptible Power Supply

An uninterruptible power supply (UPS) is a battery-powered device that keeps the computer running during a power outage—or lets the computer shut down gracefully. When power problems occur, the UPS supplies battery power to the computer. It also notifies Windows NT of the problem via a serial cable connection.

To configure a UPS, double-click the UPS icon in Control Panel. In the dialog box that appears, shown on the next page, set the options that are appropriate for your UPS.

To enable UPS notification signals, select this check box and select the COM port that the UPS is connected to.

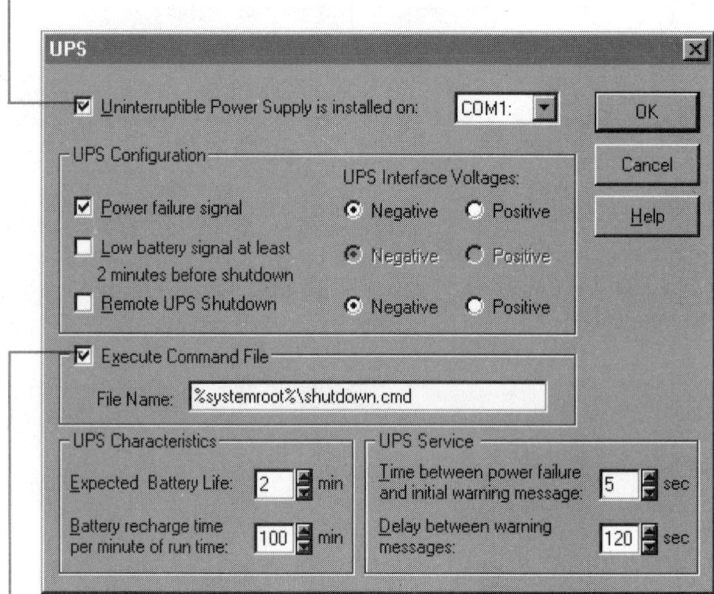

You can automatically run a program (such as one to disconnect users) as the last gasp before the power shuts down: select this check box and specify the name of the program file.

Starting and Stopping Device Drivers

In order to run properly, each hardware device you use in Windows NT requires one or more *device drivers*. The drivers need to be installed, as described earlier in this chapter, and they also need to be *started* before you can use the device. In most cases, device drivers start automatically when you restart the computer.

The Devices applet in Control Panel determines how and when device drivers start. To see what options are available, follow these steps:

1 In Control Panel, double-click the Devices icon.

2 Select the device for which you want to set startup options.

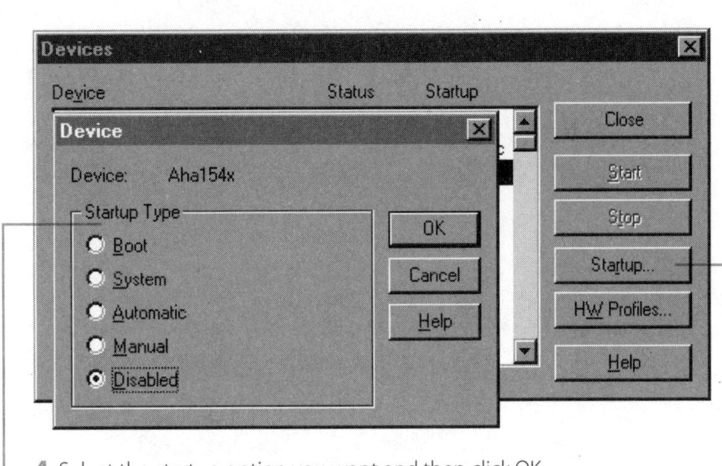

- Devices marked Boot, System, or Automatic start every time the system starts. Boot devices start first, then System devices, and then Automatic devices.
- Devices marked Manual start only if you select the device in the Devices dialog box and click Start, or when another device or program starts them.
- Devices marked Disabled cannot be started by a user; they can be started only by the system.

5 Repeat steps 2 through 4 for other devices.

6 Click Close in the Devices dialog box.

Your changes take effect the next time you start your system.

TIP

Determining Which Driver a Device Uses

Because the names that appear in the Devices list are often rather cryptic, it's sometimes difficult to figure out which device driver controls a particular device. You can often find the driver name by looking at the property sheet for the device in question. Double-click the Control Panel icon that you use to install or configure a device type. *(See Table 24-1 on page 707.)* Select the device, and then click the Properties button. In most cases, this displays a tabbed dialog box that includes on one of its pages the name of the driver(s) used by the device.

Uninstalling Hardware

After permanently removing a device from your system, you should let Windows NT know the device is gone. If you don't, errors (recorded in the system log) might occur as services and devices fail to start. And, more importantly, Windows NT will not be able to reassign the resources formerly used by the device.

SEE ALSO

For information about the system log, see "Monitoring System Activities with Event Viewer," page 650.

To inform Windows that a device is no longer present, follow these steps:

1. Open the same Control Panel applet that you used to install the device.
2. Select the name of the item you removed.
3. Click the Remove button.

CHAPTER 25

Optimizing and Troubleshooting

If you've upgraded from Windows 3.x to Windows NT, you've already taken the most important step toward enhancing the efficiency of your system and the performance of your Windows-based applications. Windows NT includes major architectural changes designed to give you a faster-running and more robust operating environment.

Windows NT users, therefore, should have less need to tinker with their systems in order to achieve optimum performance with Windows NT 4. Barring device conflicts, inadequate memory, or a full hard disk, you should be able to set up Windows NT 4 and run it—without losing sleep over inscrutable lines in your System.ini file or wondering whether you've chosen the right size and type of swap file. Nevertheless, there are some things you should know about how to keep Windows NT 4 and your applications humming along in good cheer.

Managing Virtual Memory

Like earlier versions of Windows, Windows NT uses your hard disk as an extension of internal memory, moving data to a paging file on disk when memory becomes full and restoring it from disk to memory as needed. This use of the hard disk is known as *virtual memory*. The benefit of this arrangement is that you can run more programs at one time than your system's physical memory would allow.

Within a size range that you can specify, Windows NT 4 adjusts the paging file's size in accordance with system demand.

 TIP

Delete Files You No Longer Need

If you have files on your hard disk that you no longer need, they're taking up space that Windows NT could use for virtual memory. Before you adjust virtual memory settings, delete unnecessary files so that you can reserve additional hard disk space as virtual memory.

Adjusting Virtual Memory Settings

By default, Windows NT creates the paging file on the hard disk that contains your Windows NT system files. If you have another hard disk that's faster or has more available space, you might achieve some performance gain by setting up a paging file on that disk. You can set up a paging file on any or all of your local hard disk volumes.

 **NOTE**

> You must be logged on as a member of the Administrators group to change virtual memory settings.

To view or modify virtual memory settings, follow these steps:

1. Right-click the My Computer icon and choose Properties from the context menu. (Or double-click the System icon in Control Panel.)
2. Click the Performance tab of the System property sheet.
3. In the Virtual Memory box, click the Change button.

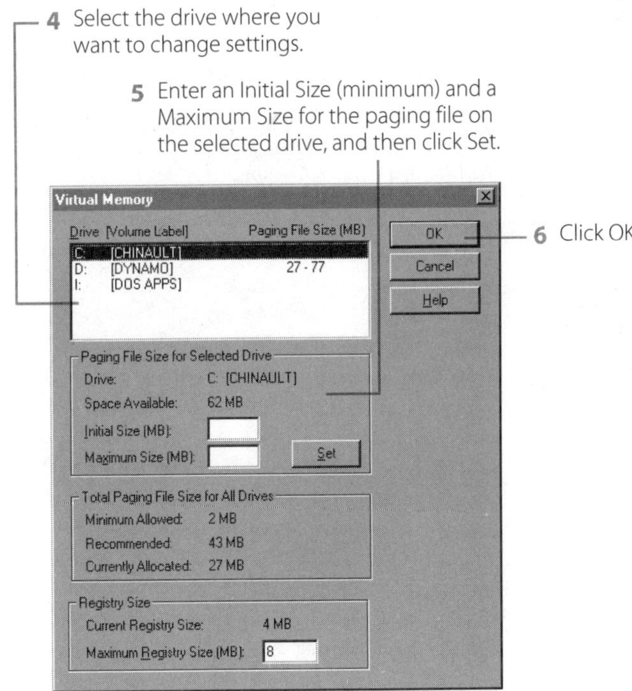

TIP

Determining the Best Values

A good starting point for the Initial Size setting is the amount of your computer's physical memory plus 12 MB—or the Recommended value under Total Paging File Size For All Drives. (This initial size can be spread across several drives if necessary.)

7 In the System property sheet, click Close.

8 If you made changes to the settings, click Yes to restart your computer.

If you can afford to tie up the disk space, you'll get the best performance by specifying a large initial size, as well as a large maximum size. The reason is that a file of the initial size is automatically created and available when Windows NT runs. If that's not large enough, Windows NT expands the paging file up to the maximum size you specify—but doing so is slow because it takes time to allocate the space, and increasing the paging file will likely cause increased disk fragmentation

TIP

Need More Space with Flex-Boot?

The paging file on each drive is called Pagefile.sys, and it's located in the drive's top-level (root) folder. You can't delete Pagefile.sys while Windows NT is running, but if you use flex-boot to run a different operating system, you can safely delete the Windows NT paging files when you use the other operating system. Windows NT will create a new paging file automatically the next time you start Windows NT.

Maximizing Available Hard Disk Space

Because Windows NT uses your hard disk for virtual memory, and because many Windows-based applications write temporary files to disk while you work, you must sometimes make a conscious effort to maintain enough available hard disk space. Although the capacity of current hard drives was unimaginable just a few years ago, it seems that current software—Windows NT included—quickly consumes whatever hard disk space you throw at it—and then wants some more.

To free up disk space, you can take the following measures:

- Empty the Recycle Bin. To do so, right-click the Recycle Bin icon and choose Empty Recycle Bin.
- Reduce the maximum size of your Recycle Bin. *For details, see "Setting Your Recycle Bin's Capacity," page 151.*
- Back up unneeded files to tape or copy them to a floppy disk and remove them from your hard disk. *For more information, see Chapter 16, "Protecting Your Data with Backup."*
- Find and remove temporary files. *See "Finding and Removing Temporary Files," below.*
- Delete applications or Windows NT components that you no longer need. *For details, see "Uninstalling Applications," page 702, and "Adding or Removing Parts of Windows NT," page 696.*
- Use compression on NTFS volumes. *For details, see "Using File Compression," page 727.*

Finding and Removing Temporary Files

For more information, see Chapter 7, "Using the Find Command."

Many applications create temporary files while performing certain operations. If all goes according to plan, the application removes the temporary files when they're no longer needed. But if a program closes unexpectedly (a nice way of saying "crashes"), temporary files remain on your hard disk. You can use the Find command to quickly find and, if you choose, delete temporary files. Follow these steps:

1. Close all programs to be sure no temporary files are currently in use.
2. Open the Start menu and choose Find.

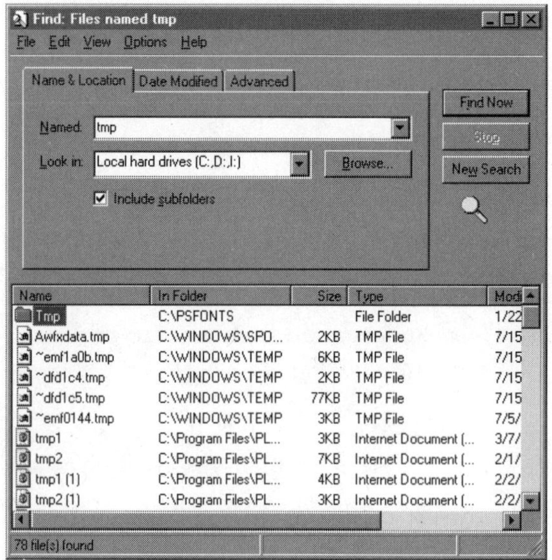

3 In the Named box, type *tmp*, *temp*, or ~, characters that are commonly included in the names of temporary files.

Other Candidates for Deletion

Some programs use other filename extensions to identify backup versions of documents before you make changes. If you no longer need the older versions, you can safely delete these files, which often have one of these filename extensions:

.bak .bk? .old .syd .000 .001

4 In the Look In box, select Local Hard Drives.

5 Click Find Now.

6 When the results appear, select the files that are no longer needed, and then press the Del key.

 **NOTE**

Do not delete any folders named Temp or Tmp; delete only the files they contain. Many programs require these folders in order to run properly.

 **TIP**

Do Some "Spring Cleaning"
You can also use the Find command to ferret out files larger than a certain size and/or older than a certain date. With this technique, you might find files you no longer need—and be able to quickly increase your available disk space.

Using File Compression

If your hard disk is formatted as an NTFS volume, you can use compression to increase the effective capacity of the volume. You can compress individual files, or you can compress an entire folder or volume and all the files it contains.

How much extra room you get depends on what kind of data your files hold. Windows NT achieves its compression by identifying patterns in your data. Files that are highly structured—for example, a bitmap graphics file, in which certain pixel patterns appear over and over—can be compressed more than files whose contents are relatively random. Executable files and DLLs are usually less compressible than documents. In the typical case in which both executables and documents are involved, you can expect the effective size of your disk to nearly double.

What about performance? Your computer's processor has to do extra work when reading or saving compressed files. On the other hand, your system has to spend less time interacting with your hard disk because the files occupy fewer clusters. Because the hard disk is a relatively slow component of your system, you may experience no performance penalty at all when using compression. And if your uncompressed disk doesn't have room for an adequate paging file, you'll undoubtedly get better performance by using compression.

DriveSpace and DoubleSpace

Windows NT can't use drives compressed with DriveSpace, DoubleSpace, or other compression utilities for Windows 95 or MS-DOS. Sorry, but there's no way around it. If you need access to certain files from Windows NT and another operating system, you must store those files on an uncompressed FAT volume, the only storage method that's compatible with Windows NT, Windows 95, Windows 3.x, MS-DOS, and OS/2.

Compressing a File

To compress one or more files, follow these steps:

1. Select the file(s) in a folder window or a Windows NT Explorer window.
2. Right-click (or open the File menu) and choose Properties.
3. Near the bottom of the property sheet's General page, select the Compressed check box.
4. Click OK.

You cannot compress Pagefile.sys, the paging file used for virtual memory by Windows NT.

Compressing a Folder or Volume

The steps for compressing a folder or volume are nearly identical to those for compressing a single file:

1. Select the folder or volume in a folder window or a Windows NT Explorer window.
2. Right-click (or open the File menu) and choose Properties.

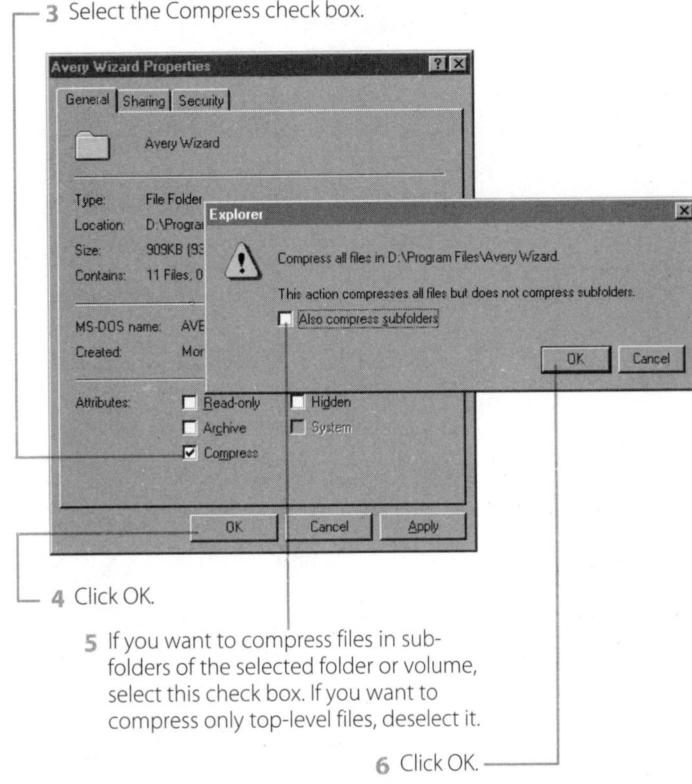

Compressing Floppy Disks

Because compression is available only for NTFS volumes, and because FAT is the only format available for floppy disks, you can't use Windows NT file compression to increase the capacity of floppy disks. If you're trying to save a file that won't fit on a single disk, your best bet is to use a file compression utility that uses the .ZIP format made popular by PKWARE, Inc. A number of vendors sell utility programs that "zip" and "unzip" files.

Identifying and Working with Compressed Files

Compressed files look and act like ordinary files. Windows NT compresses files "on the fly" (that is, without requiring any special action by you). When you read a file from a compressed disk, the file is automatically expanded. The net result is that, while you continue to work with your files the way you always have, your disk has much more room than it had before.

You can identify a compressed file by viewing its property sheet. As shown in the illustration below, the property sheet includes two indications of file compression.

The property sheet shows the compressed size as well as the normal (uncompressed) size.

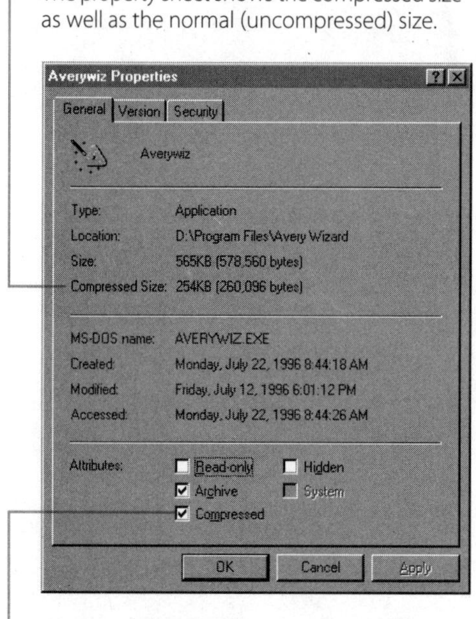

A check here identifies a compressed file.

Windows NT has another, more apparent, way to identify compressed files, but to use it you must first do the following:

1. In a folder window or Windows NT Explorer, open the View menu and choose Options.

2 On the View page, select the check box labeled "Display compressed files and folders with alternate color."

3 Click OK.

After you select this option, the names of compressed files and folders appear in blue.

 TIP

Because compressed files are shown in blue, if you want to differentiate them from uncompressed files you can't use blue as your Window Text color in the Appearance page of the Display property sheet. *For information about the Appearance page, see "Changing Colors, Fonts, and Text Sizes," page 97.*

When you create a new file or copy an existing file into a compressed folder, the new file is compressed automatically. Similarly, if you move a file from another volume into a compressed folder, it will be compressed automatically. However, when you move a file between folders on the same NTFS volume, it retains its compress attribute. That is, a compressed file remains compressed and an uncompressed file remains uncompressed.

Identifying Performance Bottlenecks

 SEE ALSO

For information about using Performance Monitor, see "Monitoring System Efficiency with Performance Monitor," page 671.

A bottleneck, in short, occurs when demand for a particular resource (such as memory, hard disks, or processor time) exceeds supply, causing the system to slow down. Performance Monitor is a valuable tool that helps to identify performance bottlenecks.

Unfortunately, because of the wide variety of systems and components, and because different computers serve different needs, there's no single optimum way to configure all systems. Entire books have been written on optimizing system performance (and this isn't one of them). We can, however, offer some suggestions on where to begin your search for performance bottlenecks using Performance Monitor.

- Monitor the % Usage and Usage Peak counters in the Paging File object. If % Usage approaches 100 percent or if Usage Peak is close to the maximum paging file size, consider increasing the initial size of your paging file. *See "Adjusting Virtual Memory Settings," page 722.*
- To see if you have enough memory, monitor Avg. Disk Sec/Transfer counter in the Physical Disk object and Pages/Sec counter in the Memory object. If the product of these counters exceeds 0.1, too many swaps to the paging file are occurring, and you should consider adding memory to your system.
- Monitor the % Processor Time counter in the Processor object. If it continually exceeds 85 percent, you would do well to upgrade your processor.

Preparing for Problems

It's natural to think "it will never happen to me." The longer you use computers, the more likely it is that you've already been cured of that notion. But for those who haven't, here's an additional nudge to take a few simple precautions so that you can more easily dig yourself out of the hole that inevitably lies ahead.

First, of course, get in the habit of backing up your hard disk frequently and regularly. Then use two tools included with Windows NT—Windows NT Diagnostics and Repair Disk Utility—to take a snapshot of your system when it is working well. Armed with a current backup, a Windows NT Diagnostics report, and an Emergency Repair Disk, you should be up and running in short order.

May you never need to use them!

Optimizing Disk Performance with a Defragmenter

When you store files on a freshly formatted disk, Windows writes each file's data in a set of adjacent disk clusters. On a FAT volume, one file might use clusters 3 through 24, for example, the next 25 through 31, a third 32 through 34, and so on. As soon as you begin deleting files, however, this neat pattern is likely to be broken.

For example, if you delete the file that occupies clusters 25 through 31, and then create a new file 20 clusters in length, Windows stores the new file's first 7 clusters in 25 through 31 and the remaining 13 somewhere else. This new file, in other words, would be *fragmented*; it would occupy at least two non-contiguous blocks of clusters. As you add and delete more files, the odds are good that more and more of your files would be fragmented.

(The process of allocating disk space to files on NTFS volumes is different, but fragmentation occurs on NTFS volumes as well as FAT volumes.)

Fragmentation does not affect data integrity, but it does reduce the efficiency of your hard disk. Fragmented files take longer to read and write than contiguous ones.

You can eliminate disk fragmentation and enhance Windows' performance with regular use of a disk defragmenter. Such programs rearrange files, storing each file in a block of contiguous sectors.

With the Defragment Now button on the Tools page of a disk's property sheet, Windows NT provides the means to run a defragmenter. Alas, no such utility is included with Windows NT, and you'll see that the Defragment Now button is grayed out until you install a defragmenter. Defragmenters for Windows NT are available from several vendors. (Defragmenters written for Windows 95 or MS-DOS do not work with Windows NT.)

You can defragment a disk without a defragmenter, but it's not a pleasant task: you must back up all the files to tape, format the volume, and then restore the files from tape. *For information about backing up and restoring files, see Chapter 16, "Protecting Your Data with Backup." For information about formatting, see "Formatting Disks," page 159.*

Using Windows NT Diagnostics

Windows NT Diagnostics does not, as its name implies, perform in-depth testing of your system. It does, however, present a wealth of information about your system. That information can be useful in resolving resource conflicts or device compatibility issues, for example.

You'll find an icon for Windows NT Diagnostics in the Start menu's Administrative Tools (Common) group. When you click it, you'll see a multitabbed window similar to the one shown below.

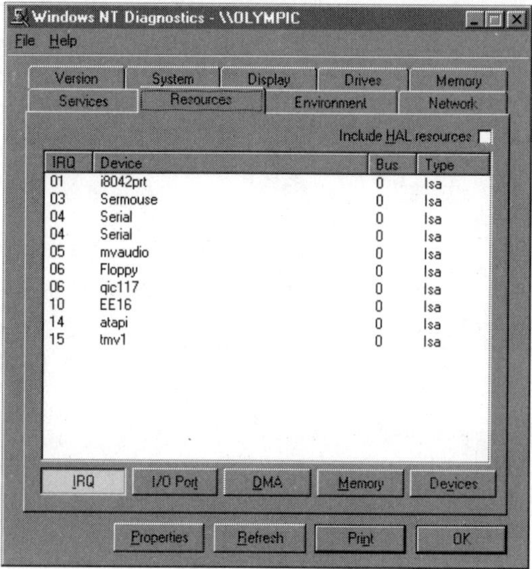

The pages in Windows NT Diagnostics present the following information:

- The Version page shows the version number of Windows NT, including any service packs or upgrades. It also shows your registration number, which you might need if you call product support services.

- The System page identifies the type of processor(s) in your system and provides information about the BIOS.
- The Display page identifies your display adapter and the drivers it uses.
- The Drives page lists all your local drives (floppy drives, hard drives, CD-ROM drives, and removable cartridge drives) and mapped network drives. You can arrange the drives by type or by drive letter.
- The Memory page displays information about your computer's physical memory and virtual memory
- The Services page lists all installed services and devices, and shows their current status.
- The Resources page shows information about IRQ (interrupt request) lines, I/O ports, DMA (direct memory access) channels, memory used by devices, and devices in use.
- The Environment page lists system environment variables and user environment variables for the current user.
- The Network Page displays logon status, information about transport protocols, and network performance statistics.

If you aren't overwhelmed by the information displayed on the pages, you can get even more information about a particular object by selecting it and clicking the Properties button at the bottom of the Windows NT Diagnostics window.

Most of this information is available elsewhere in Windows NT. But the value of the Windows NT Diagnostics program is that it assembles all the information into one neat place—and allows you to save it for future reference. To save the information, click the Print button (or choose Print Report from the File menu). A dialog box like the one shown on the next page appears.

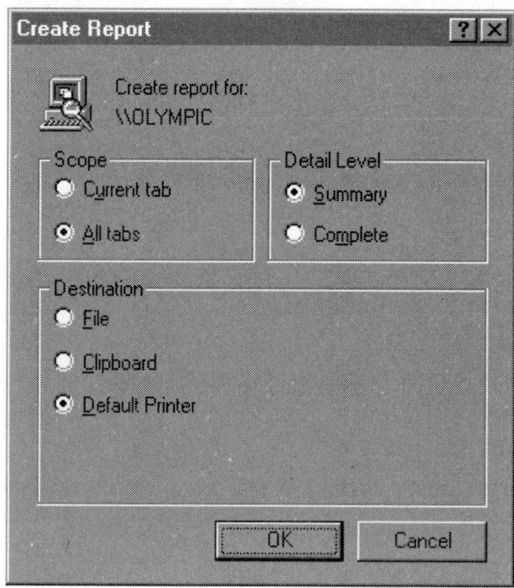

For purposes of repairing a system, the best settings for a report are:

- All Tabs
- Summary
- Default Printer

These settings ensure that you have sufficient information—and that it's on paper in case the system won't start.

You don't need to understand all the information presented by Windows NT Diagnostics; most of it you'll never need. But having all the information available ensures that you'll have the nugget you *do* need when the chips are down.

Using Repair Disk Utility

Repair Disk Utility creates an Emergency Repair Disk (sometimes called an ERD), which includes system settings that you can use to reconstruct your system should it become necessary. It includes registry files, information about your hard disk partitions, and devices you have installed.

TIP

Keep Two ERDs

Create an Emergency Repair Disk now. Create a new one whenever you make significant changes to your hardware or software setup. Keep your two most recent ERDs—the current one and the one made before your most recent changes.

Creating an Emergency Repair Disk

To create an Emergency Repair Disk, follow these steps:

1. Click the Start button and choose Run.
2. In the Run dialog box, type *rdisk* and click OK.

The Repair Disk Utility appears, as shown below.

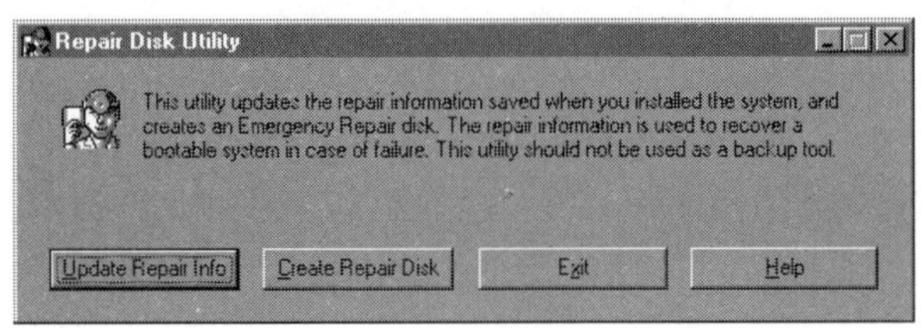

3. Click Update Repair Info.

CAUTION

If you click Create Repair Disk, Repair Disk Utility copies the repair information that's currently stored on your hard disk—which might not be current. Click Update Repair Info first to update that information and *then* create an ERD.

CAUTION

Repair Disk formats the floppy disk before saving the configuration files; all data currently on the floppy disk will be lost.

A series of message boxes appears, as shown below.

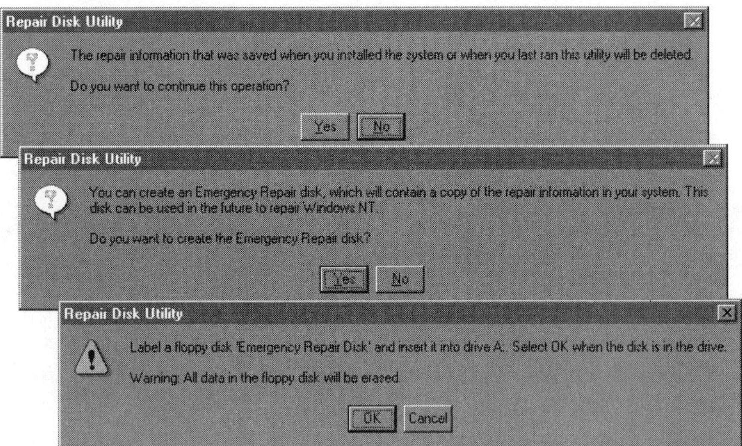

4 Insert a high-density floppy disk in drive A, and then click Yes or OK in each message box as it appears.

Using an Emergency Repair Disk

If your system files become damaged or your computer won't start, the ERD can provide the backup you need.

CAUTION

Because the Emergency Repair Disk contains information about a specific computer, it should be used only with the system on which it was created.

If your Winnt directory is on a FAT volume, and you can boot your computer with another operating system (such as MS-DOS or Windows 95), you can copy the files from the Emergency Repair Disk to your \Winnt\System32\Config folder. (You can't do this while Windows NT is running because it protects the files that are already on the hard disk.)

For the most catastrophic failures, you'll need your original Windows NT 4 CD-ROM and the three Setup floppy disks to reinstall Windows NT. With your computer turned off, insert the first Setup disk, and then turn on your computer. When the "Welcome to Setup" screen appears, press R. As the message on that screen explains, pressing R causes Setup to repair a damaged Windows NT installation. Setup will check each Windows NT file on your hard disk, and replace those that are corrupt. Setup then uses the information from your Emergency Repair Disk to restore the registry and security database.

Finding and Repairing Disk Errors

Windows NT includes a disk-checking utility that can be used with any hard disk or floppy disk. The Check Disk program finds and (optionally) fixes errors involving the organization of files and other data structures, including:

- Problems with the file allocation table (FAT)
- Problems involving long filenames
- Lost clusters
- Cross-linked files
- Problems involving the directory structure

(The *file allocation table* is a data structure that keeps track of the physical location and file ownership of each cluster on a disk formatted as a FAT volume. A *cluster*, also known as an *allocation unit*, is the smallest group of sectors that the operating system can allocate to a file. A *lost cluster* is one that's not used by any file but that the FAT hasn't marked as available for new data. A *cross-linked file* is a file containing clusters that have been erroneously allocated to more than one file.)

Check Disk can also be used to find physical disk errors (bad sectors). The program doesn't physically repair your media, but it moves data away from any bad sectors it finds.

You must be logged on as a member of the Administrators group to run Check Disk.

To run Check Disk:

1 In My Computer or Windows NT Explorer, right-click the icon for the volume you want to check and choose Properties.

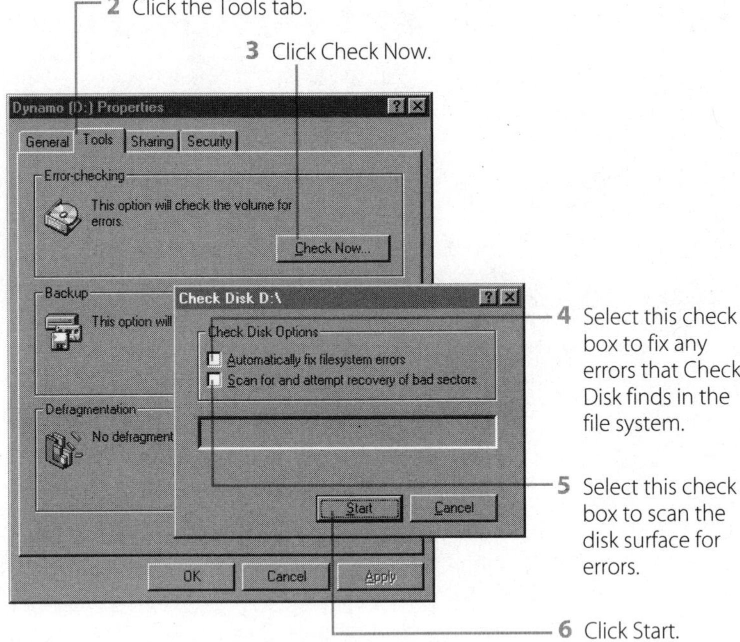

If you select the Automatically Fix Filesystem Errors check box, all files must be closed for Check Disk to run. If the disk is currently in use, a message asks if you want to reschedule Check Disk for the next time you restart your system. If you choose Yes, Check Disk runs the next time you start Windows NT.

If you choose Yes to run Check Disk the next time you start Windows NT, you won't be able to log on until Check Disk finishes its checking—a process that can take several minutes.

When Check Disk finds an error, it displays a dialog box that explains the error and, in some cases, offers choices about correcting the problem.

Testing the physical integrity of every disk cluster takes time, particularly with large disks. While Check Disk is testing, you can continue to work, but you may find your system rather sluggish.

Working with the Registry

The registry is a centralized database of information about your computer, the operating system, and your applications. It is stored as a group of files in the System32\Config and the Profiles*username* subfolders of your Windows NT folder (C:\Winnt in most cases).

You rarely need to concern yourself with the registry because applications and the operating system update it for you automatically. (Actually, applications cannot write directly to the registry files; they send a request to the operating system, which maintains exclusive control over the registry.) For example, if you select a new toolbar arrangement in Microsoft Word or a new color scheme for your Windows NT desktop, that information gets stored in the registry.

At some point, however, you might find it necessary to poke around in the registry—whether it's to implement a cool tip you read in a magazine, or to uninstall a program that didn't furnish a working uninstall routine. Windows NT provides a tool called Registry Editor for such exploring. You can learn a lot about the inner workings of Windows NT and your system—perhaps more than you wanted to know—by exploring the registry.

WARNING

Despite the aura of mystery surrounding the registry, it's perfectly safe to *look* in the registry with Registry Editor. However, be sure you know what you're doing before you make any deletions, additions, or other changes. Changes you make are immediately made in the registry, and there is no "undo" function in Registry Editor. You can render your system unusable if you make a mistake. (But that's what backups and Emergency Repair Disks are for, right?)

To start Registry Editor:

1 Click the Start button and choose Run.

2 In the Run dialog box, type *regedt32* and click OK.

Your system also has a Registry Editor program called Regedit.exe, which provides a subset of the features available in Regedt32.exe and presents the registry as a single hierarchy. You can use whichever version you prefer.

Practice Safe Exploring

If you want to dip your toes into the registry, but you're not sure what lies under the surface, choose Read Only Mode from Registry Editor's Options menu. You'll be able to safely explore the registry with no possibility of causing problems. In this mode, Registry Editor won't let you make additions, deletions, or changes to the registry.

The registry uses a hierarchical structure to store its data. Registry Editor, shown in Figure 25-1, displays the hierarchy in windows similar to those of Windows NT Explorer or Windows Messaging.

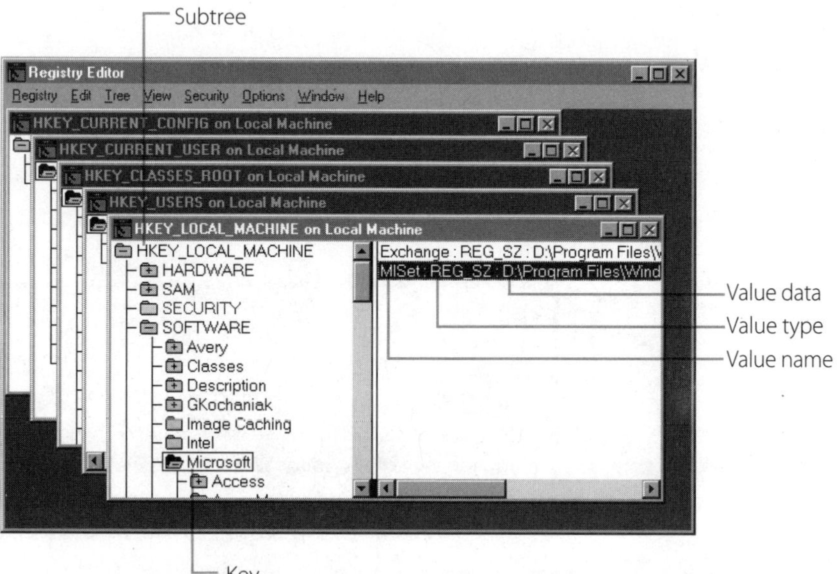

FIGURE 25-1.
The Regedt32 version of Registry Editor presents each subtree in a separate window.

Each window in Registry Editor contains one of the *subtrees* that are at the top of the registry hierarchy. These subtrees are described below:

- HKEY_LOCAL_MACHINE stores information about your computer, including a list of hardware devices installed, their device drivers, driver settings, and hardware profiles.
- HKEY_USERS stores user profile information about users and their preferences, including desktop settings, network connections, and application preferences.
- HKEY_CLASSES_ROOT contains file-association data (that is, which program to run with each document type) and information about OLE.
- HKEY_CURRENT_USER shows user profile information about the user who is currently logged on. (It's actually a pointer to the current user's key in HKEY_USERS.)
- HKEY_CURRENT_CONFIG shows information about the active hardware configuration. (It's actually a pointer to the current configuration's key in HKEY_LOCAL_MACHINE.)

Below the subtrees in the registry hierarchy are *keys*, which are shown with folder icons in the left pane of the Registry Editor windows.

The "files" these folders contain are called *values*. Values always appear in the window's right pane. Each value has a name and contains data. Data can be one of several types. REG_SZ, for example, is the data type code for text strings.

Like filenames with a full path specification in Windows NT, values can be uniquely identified by listing the hierarchy leading to the value, separating each element with a backslash. For example, the highlighted value in Figure 25-1 is:

\HKEY_LOCAL_MACHINE\Software\Microsoft\MlSet

To change a value's data, simply double-click the value, and an edit dialog box appears. To add a value, select the key that will contain the value, and then choose Add Value from the Edit menu. To add a key, select the parent key of your new key, and then choose Add Key from the Edit menu.

Once you're comfortable working with Registry Editor, you're likely to find occasions to use it. Many computer magazines offer tips on tweaking your system that can be implemented only by "hacking the registry" with Registry Editor.

Resources for More Information

Unfortunately, no single manual or book contains all the information you need to optimize your system and solve problems when they arise. If such a tome existed, it's likely that no one could lift it, let alone find the information they need. But you can probably find the assistance you need in one of the following:

- If you have Internet access, Microsoft has a searchable Web site at http://www.microsoft.com. There you can find knowledge-base articles, free utility programs and software updates, and lots more.
- Web search pages, such as Yahoo!, Lycos, and Alta Vista, provide links to dozens of other Windows NT–related sites.
- On-line user-to-user help (and there are plenty of knowledgeable users willing to help) is available in the Microsoft support newsgroups on the Internet (point your news reader to msnews.microsoft.com), as well as in forums on CompuServe and America OnLine.

- The Windows NT Help system—yes, the same one that includes many short topics that include only the obvious information you figured out on your own—includes an interactive tool for solving many problems. To use one of these troubleshooters, open the Start menu and choose Help. Click the Contents tab and then double-click the Troubleshooting book. Double-click one its topics to display a troubleshooter like the one shown below, and then click the buttons to (hopefully) find your way to the solution.

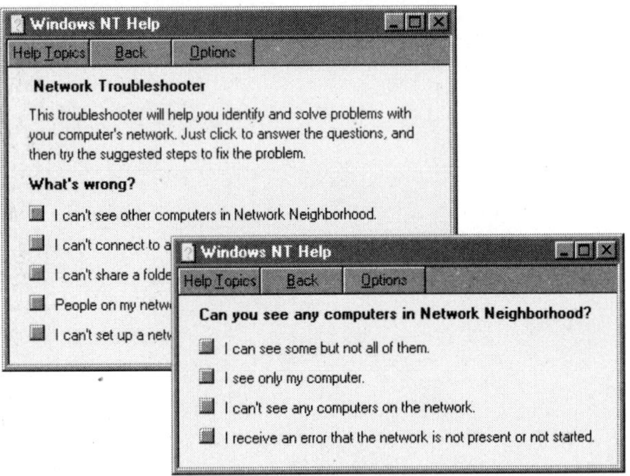

- The *Microsoft Windows NT Resource Kit*, published by Microsoft Press, approaches the bulk of that unliftable tome mentioned above, and it's chock full of technical details.

TIP

Keeping up with the Latest

If you're serious about getting maximum performance from Windows NT, it's a good idea to read one or two of the Windows NT–specific magazines regularly. There you'll find plenty of reviews of the latest, hottest hardware, as well as new tips for squeezing more power out of what you already have.

Index

D

N

Q

R

T

X

Z

Colophon

The manuscript for this book was prepared using Microsoft Word 7.0 for Windows and submitted to Microsoft Press in electronic form. Pages were composed by ArtSource, Inc., using Adobe PageMaker 6.01 for Windows, with text type in Garamond and display type in Myriad Black. Composed pages were delivered to the printer as electronic prepress files.

Cover Graphic Designer

Greg Erickson
Robin Hjellen

Interior Graphic Designer

designlab
www.dzynlab.com
dzynlab@aol.com

Interior Graphic Artist

Paula J. Kausch

Composition and Layout

ArtSource, Inc.

Windows NT Explorer

You can use Windows NT Explorer to navigate through the folders and files on your computer. Change the view to see a list of items or to see each item as an icon.

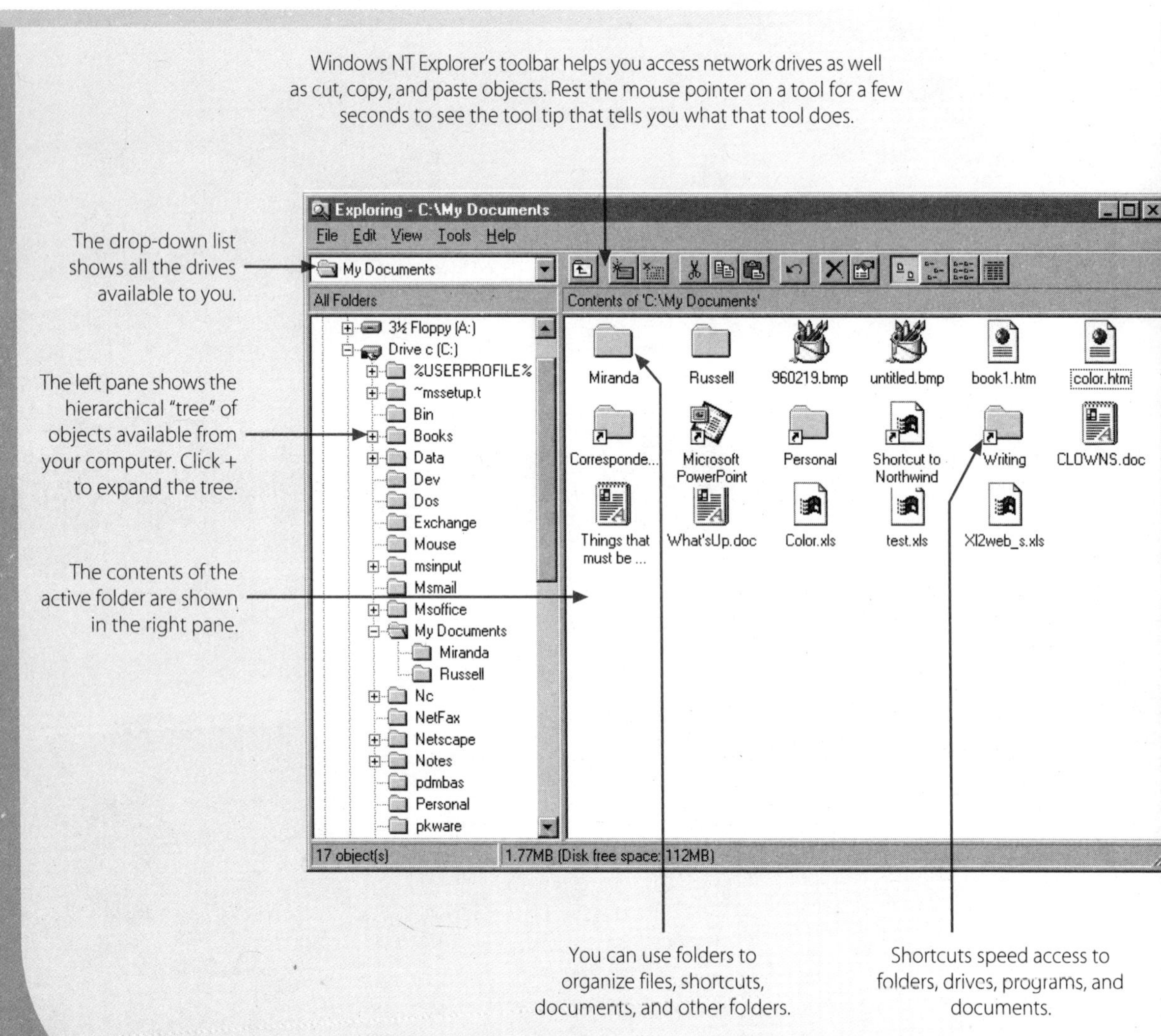

Running Windows NT quick reference card

Common Toolbar Tools

These tools are ones you are likely to see in many different windows and applications in Windows NT. For a reminder of a tool's purpose, rest your mouse pointer on any tool to display a "tool tip."

Creates a new document

Opens an existing document

Saves a document on disk

Prints a document

Displays a preview of the printed page

Deletes the selection and moves it to the Clipboard

Copies the selection and moves it to the Clipboard

Pastes information from the Clipboard

Deletes the selected object

Reverses your last action

Moves to the parent folder of the current folder

Assigns a drive letter to a network drive

Disconnects from a network drive

Displays a property sheet for the selected object

Displays help information about the next object you click

Mouse Power

With Windows NT 4, the second button on the mouse finally has a purpose! And dragging is no longer a, uh, drag. Here are some examples of mighty mousing—be sure to try these techniques on other objects too.

To Do This	Right-Click
Arrange the icons on your desktop Paste an object or a shortcut onto the desktop Undo the last action taken on the desktop Create a new document, folder, or shortcut Change how your desktop looks by changing the display properties	A blank area of the **desktop**
Change the arrangement of windows on your screen Undo the last change in the window arrangement Change the taskbar properties	A blank area of the **taskbar**
Change the items on the Start menu Find an item on the Start menu	The **Start button**
Arrange the icons in a folder Paste files, folders, or shortcuts into a folder Undo the last action in a window Create a new document, folder, or shortcut View or change the properties of a drive or folder	A blank area in a **folder** window or in Windows NT Explorer's **right pane**
Open, print, or view a file's contents Send a file to any destination on your Send To menu Cut or copy a file Create a shortcut to a file Delete or rename a file View or change the properties of a file	A **file** icon or name in a folder window or in Windows NT Explorer's **right pane**

Mouse Power *(continued)*

To Do This	Right-Click
Explore or open a folder Find a file in a folder Share a folder with other users on a network Send a folder to any destination on your Send To menu Cut or copy a folder and its contents Paste files, folders, or shortcuts into a folder Create a shortcut to a folder Delete or rename a folder View or change the properties of a folder	A **folder** icon or name in a folder window or in Windows NT Explorer
Explore or open a drive Find a file on a drive Share a drive Format a drive Paste a file or folder onto a drive Create a shortcut to a drive View or change the properties of a drive	A **drive** icon or name in a folder window or in Windows NT Explorer
Format text Cut or copy text	**Selected text** in a document
Display the Control menu	A window's **title bar**
See an object menu of commands related to an object	**Any icon or object**

Drag	To	Action
A program icon	The Start button	Adds the program to the Start menu
A program icon	The desktop or another folder	Creates a shortcut to the program
A document or shortcut	Another folder on the same drive	Moves the document or shortcut
A document or shortcut	A folder on a different drive	Copies the document or shortcut
Any file while holding Shift and Ctrl	The desktop or a folder	Creates a shortcut to the file
Any file while holding Shift	The desktop or another folder	Moves the file
Any file while holding Ctrl	The desktop or a folder	Copies the file
A file on your hard drive	Recycle Bin	Moves the file to the Recycle Bin
A file on a floppy disk or network drive	Recycle Bin	Deletes the file

Installing New Software and Hardware

To Install	Do This
Fonts	Drag font files to the Fonts folder (accessible from Control Panel)
Printers	From the Start menu, choose Settings and then Printers. Then double-click the Add Printer icon
Programs	From the Start menu, choose Settings and then Control Panel. Double-click the Add/Remove Programs icon, and then click the Install/Uninstall tab
Windows Components	From the Start menu, choose Settings and then Control Panel. Double-click the Add/Remove Programs icon, and then click the Windows Setup tab
Modems	From the Start menu, choose Settings and then Control Panel. Double-click the Modems icon, and then click the Add button

Register Today!

Return this
Running Microsoft® Windows NT® Workstation
version 4
registration card for a Microsoft Press® catalog

U.S. and Canada addresses only. Fill in information below and mail postage-free. Please mail only the bottom half of this page.

1-57231-226-2A ***RUNNING WINDOWS NT WORKSTATION*** ***Owner Registration Card***

NAME

INSTITUTION OR COMPANY NAME

ADDRESS

CITY STATE ZIP

NO POSTAGE
NECESSARY
IF MAILED
IN THE
UNITED STATES

BUSINESS REPLY MAIL
FIRST-CLASS MAIL PERMIT NO. 108 REDMOND, WA

POSTAGE WILL BE PAID BY ADDRESSEE

MICROSOFT PRESS REGISTRATION
RUNNING WINDOWS NT WORKSTATION
PO BOX 3019
BOTHELL WA 98041-9946